David in the Desert

Beihefte zur Zeitschrift für die alttestamentliche Wissenschaft

Edited by
John Barton, Reinhard G. Kratz, Nathan MacDonald,
Sara Milstein and Markus Witte

Volume 514

David in the Desert

Tradition and Redaction in the
"History of David's Rise"

Edited by
Hannes Bezzel and Reinhard G. Kratz

DE GRUYTER

G

ISBN 978-3-11-060406-1
e-ISBN (PDF) 978-3-11-060616-4
e-ISBN (EPUB) 978-3-11-060527-3
ISSN 0934-2575

Library of Congress Control Number: 2020949796

Bibliografische Information der Deutschen Nationalbibliothek
The Deutsche Nationalbibliothek lists this publication in the Deutsche Nationalbibliografie;
detailed bibliografic data are available on the Internet at http://dnb.dnb.de.

© 2021 Walter de Gruyter GmbH, Berlin/Boston
Typesetting: Meta Systems Publishing & Printservices GmbH, Wustermark
Printing and binding: CPI books GmbH, Leck

www.degruyter.com

MIX
Papier aus verantwor-
tungsvollen Quellen
FSC
www.fsc.org   FSC® C083411

Preface

From 2nd till 5th September 2018, the symposium "David in the Desert" was held at the Friedrich-Schiller-Universität Jena. Under this catchy but rather enigmatic title – and under the less catchy but more explanatory subtitle "International Symposium on the Interrelation of Tradition and Redaction in the 'History of David's Rise' and its Impact on a Reconstruction of the History of the 'Early Monarchic Period' in Israel" – a group of esteemed colleagues and good friends followed our call and made it possible for us to realise a project which had its origins in some coffee break discussions at the Colloquium Biblicum Lovaniense in 2014.

We look gratefully back on those days of intense scholarly discussion in a collegial and amicable atmosphere – and we look hopefully forward to the days when it will be possible to meet again not only digitally but in real life. The numerous cross-references between the articles of this volume bear witness to the constructive and stimulating discussions of the Jena conference – and at the same time they illustrate how important it is for scholarly exchange to know and to meet each other not only in writing or digitally but also physically.

Our gratitude goes to the publishers of de Gruyter, especially Dr. Eva Frantz, Alice Meroz, and Sabina Dabrowski for their patience, and the editors of the series BZAW for accepting our manuscript, to Dr. Sarah Köhler for the perfect preparation and coordination of the Jena symposium, to Simon Büchner and Dr. André Zempelburg for their editorial work with this book, and to Martina-Britta Boltres and Julius Sperling for preparing the indices.

The meeting in Jena, and hence this publication, would not have been possible without the generous funding by the Fritz Thyssen Foundation. תודה רבה.

Erfurt / Göttingen, September 2020   Hannes Bezzel / Reinhard G. Kratz

https://doi.org/10.1515/9783110606164-201

Contents

Hannes Bezzel and Reinhard G. Kratz
Introduction

As in many fields of Old Testament / Hebrew Bible studies, well-known theories about the origin of the Biblical traditions about king David have been questioned in the course of the last two or three decades.

On the one hand, this concerns the historical reconstruction of the socio-political situation in the Levant during the early Iron Age in general and of David's reign in particular. Concepts of a strongly centralised "empire" as it is depicted in 2 Sam 8 which were a basic part of the historical narrative of ancient Israel until not so long ago, have been abandoned, questioned or heavily modified because of the archaeological findings.[1] Instead, attention has been given to smaller structures, and the paradigm has shifted from the terms of "empire" to those of "chiefdom" or "clan".[2] With this, some biblical passages have gained weight for the rewriting of the narrative of the "historical David" while others lost their former importance. Especially the later king's beginnings as they are depicted in 1 Sam 16–2 Sam 5 have been put into focus anew. Accordingly, the "historical David" has been described in terms of an "outlaw",[3] a "condottiere"[4] or a Hapiru leader.[5]

On the other hand, the familiar redaction-critical hypothesis of an ancient literary source covering the first part of the David story, as it was put classically by Leonhard Rost with his "History of David's Rise"[6] has been doubted, too. In 2000, Marsha C. White and Reinhard G. Kratz independently argued that these chapters first and foremost served the purpose of connecting traditions about Saul and David respectively which used to be independent of each other before.[7]

Taken together, these two hypotheses, the historical and the redaction-critical, which, of course, both have not been unchallenged, raise several questions:

---

1 Cf., for example, the discussion between FINKELSTEIN 2010: 3–28 and MAZAR 2007: 117–40; Mazar 2010: 29–58.
2 Cf. the development in textbooks for German students from DIETRICH 1997: 148–201 to BERLEJUNG ³2009: 59–192, 101–3; KRATZ ²2017: 17–20.
3 Cf., for example, DIETIRCH 2010: 57*.
4 DALLMEYER / DIETRICH 2002: 109–10.
5 Cf. MCKENZIE 2002: 126–7; FINKELSTEIN / SILBERMAN 2006: 39–42; FINKELSTEIN 2013: 134–5.
6 Cf. ROST 1926: 132–3.
7 Cf. WHITE 2000: 281–2; KRATZ 2000: 182–6.

https://doi.org/10.1515/9783110606164-001

- If the "History of David's Rise" is correctly identified as a secondary literary bridge which was created in order to bring together the characters of and traditions about Saul and David, what does this interpretation mean for the reconstruction of the history of the time in question, viz., the early Iron Age?
- More concretely, the question is whether, and if so, where, there is ancient material preserved between 1 Sam 16–2 Sam 5, and which pieces of the passage in question are to be seen as younger, redactional additions. In short, this is nothing else but the old literary-critical task of separating tradition and redaction – but it has to be asked anew under the recent premises.
- Generally speaking, the methodological problem is affected of how the historical interpretation of archaeological findings and the redaction-critical analysis of the Biblical texts can or should not interact with each other: Which part can the Biblical text and its reconstructed literary history play in the reconstruction of the history of Israel – and in which way can the archaeological findings and their interpretation support or criticise the diachronic analysis of the text? As clear as both approaches are necessarily connected with each other, as clear is the danger of circular argumentation in both cases.

The papers read at the symposium which have been collected in this book, deal with these questions from a redaction-critical as well as from an archaeological point of view. Some colleagues do so by means of drawing broader pictures while others present focused case studies on certain episodes. Taken together, the articles address nearly every chapter between 1 Sam 16 and 2 Sam 1 in detail,[8] and offer several hypotheses for the literary historical reconstruction of the "History of David's Rise" and its historical backgrounds.

PETER PORZIG starts by addressing the topic from a point of view which one might call early reception history. He asks for the image of "*David in the Judean Desert*", viz. in the (so-called "non-biblical") Dead Sea Scrolls. Not surprisingly, the two dominating aspects here are "David the musician" and "David the warrior". PORZIG draws a direct line from the former in 11Q5 XXVII,2–11 to 1 Sam 16:14–23, which he identifies as the youngest version of the story about how David got to Saul's court, and from the latter in 1QM XI,1–5a to late additions highlighting holy war ideology in 1 Sam 17.

OMER SERGI provides an overview over the recent archaeological interpretation of the settlement history in the Early Iron Age, especially around Jerusalem

---

[8] According to the title of the conference, the episodes in 2 Sam 24 and the Saul stories in 1 Sam 28; 31 did not receive special attention in this context.

and on the Benjamin Plateau. He concludes that the latter must have been under Jerusalemite domination, and therefore argues against the theory that the
traditions about Saul would been of (Northern) Israelite origin. Instead, he regards Jerusalemite scribes as the circles in which traditions both about Saul the
Benjaminite and David the Ephratite were handed down. Both kings shared the
collective identity Israelite which in the stories about them originally would not
yet refer to the polity in the North but to a clan identity. The historical background of the stories between 1 Sam 9 and 2 Sam 5 were to be seen in the
9th century BCE, displaying a geo-political situation before Hazael's campaign
around 840.

In this dating he meets with SARA KIPFER. KIPFER, however, puts the focus
on the "Land of the Philistines" in the Southern coastal plain and the Negev.
From a literary-critical look at 1 Sam 27 she turns to a "landscape critical analysis" (66) of the area before returning to the text. Its basic layer in 1 Sam
27:2,3a,5–12 is understood as a very old tradition which Kipfer interprets historically as reflecting the situation of the 11th and 10th century with a "power vacuum" (93) in the Negev. The two papers by Sergi and Kipfer illustrate that David's
relations with the Philistines in general and with Achish of Gath in particular
belonged to the dominating themes of the discussion during the conference.

MAHRI LEONARD-FLECKMAN also deals with 1 Sam 27 and the area which is
described in this chapter. However, she is more interested in the "social landscape" (103) of the Shephelah and what it means to "cross over" (עבר) the
"boundaries" or "territory" (גבול) in this context. She points out that thinking
in categories of defined borders between an Israelite and a Philistine territory,
as it can be seen for example in 1 Sam 27:1, would not mirror the spatial conceptions of the Early Iron Age. Therefore, she tentatively questions the nearly unanimous dating of 1 Sam 27 to an early literary stage. Nevertheless ancient – oral –
traditions might be preserved in the written story.

WALTER DIETRICH, then, gives a source-critical summary of more than three
decades of his analytical work with the books of Samuel. He advocates a model
which one might call in terms of Pentateuchal research a *Fragmentenhypothese*.
Two larger narrative cycles, one dealing with the "Rise and Decline of the Saulides" (133), the other collecting stories "about David the freebooter" (137) as
well as several smaller independent tales were combined by the "Court Narrator" (129) in the late 8th or early 7th century to the narrative of the Books of
Samuel. As such, it was later made part of a Deuteronomistic History.

Contrary to Dietrich, GRAEME AULD reconstructs the literary history of 1 Sam
with its tales about Samuel, Saul, and David as an interpretative process in
order to provide answers to questions which arise to the careful reader of the
source material. This latter has to be seen in the "Book of Two Houses" (BoTH),

to be found in the synoptic materials of Sam–Kgs and Chr. One highlighted aspect of this reworking of the source material in Sam–Kgs is the elaboration of the two parallel triangular relations between Saul–his sons–David on the one side and Solomon–Jeroboam–Rehoboam on the other.

If one wants to stick with the terminology known from the history of Pentateuch research, HANNES BEZZEL thinks more in terms of an *Ergänzungshypothese*. He detects the oldest connection between the literary corpora about Saul and David in a narrative which tells the story about the succession in the reign over Israel without the well-known conflict between the two protagonists. Based on an analysis of 1 Sam 18, he finds this story in 1 Sam 14:52; 17*; 18:2,5aβ.b,20,22,26a,27b,28b,(30?); (22:2?); 23:1abα,2abα,5a; 27:2*,3a,5,6; 29:1,11b; 31:1–13*; 2 Sam 1:1aα.bα,2aα².β,3,4,11,12a.bα¹β; 2:1.2aα.3a^{LXX}.4a (without עַל־בֵּית יהוה); 5:6.

RONNIE GOLDSTEIN illustrates in his article, how text-criticism and redaction-criticism are connected with each other. By suggesting a new solution for an old text-critical *crux* in 1 Sam 19:22, he detects a small-scale redactional bracket between 19:22 and 20:41. By means of this redactional technique, both stories were situated at the same location and thus brought into dialogue. To the careful reader, the sharp contrast between Saul and Jonathan in their relation to David is highlighted: The father chases David while the son makes a covenant with him.

JEREMY HUTTON is again interested in the bigger lines. With respect to the literary history of the Books of Samuel, he argues for a kind of *Urkundenhypothese*. Two independent coherent sources, an HDR₁ and an HDR₂, were combined by a redactor in the forming process of the later book. 1 Sam 21:2–10* and 22:6–23*, which often are seen as either a coherent literary unit or determined in terms of *Fortschreibung*, he now – and different to his 2009 monograph – regards as stemming from two different independent sources. That the *"Quellenmodell"* (200) should be preferred over the *Fragmenten-* or *Ergänzungshypothese*, would be corroborated by the "objective testimony" (204) of 1 Sam 17–18 with their long version (MT) and short version (LXX^B). With the question how the textual situation in 1 Sam 17–18 should be interpreted and which consequences might be drawn for the redaction-critical analysis, HUTTON addresses another point which was intensely debated during the Jena conference.

Two contributions are dedicated to Achish, king of Gath, in particular. GEORG HENTSCHEL and CARL EHRLICH both enquire into the stories in 1 Sam 21:11–26 and 27:1–28:2; 29:1–11 with a side-glance at 1 Kgs 2:39–40 and against the background of the extra-biblical references, especially from Ekron. Though taking rather different approaches to the matter, both reach similar conclusions. According to HENTSCHEL neither the tale about David's first flight to Gath nor the second one – in their final shape – should be understood to be older than the 7th century. EHRLICH highlights the compositional function of both episodes as providing a frame around the entire "David in the Desert" cycle. With the mentioning of "Ikausu" or "Ikayuš" in a list dated to the reign of Esarhaddon and the famous Ekron inscription in mind, he argues in favour of dating the composition of the "History of David's Rise" between 722 and 587, most likely to the reign of Josiah. Both Hentschel and Ehrlich stick to the biblical episodes in their massoretic[9] final shape and abstain from reconstructing the *Vorstufen* of the text. Likewise, both concede that it would be quite likely that in these stories older memory especially concerning the importance of Gath would have been preserved.

REINHARD MÜLLER focuses on 1 Sam 23, David's sojourn in Keïla. Re-evaluating the analysis made by Timo Veijola in 1984,[10] he finds a basic layer in 1 Sam 23:1abα,2abα,5a*(without וָאַנְשׁוֹ), and 13a*(without כְּאַרְבַּע מֵאוֹת אִישׁ), held in annalistic style. The result of the literary-critical analysis is quite similar to BEZZEL'S – its interpretation, however, is different. While MÜLLER reads this basic stratum with the paradigm of David as a *ḥapiru* leader in mind, BEZZEL is more reluctant in applying the *ḥapiru* phenomenon of the 2nd millennium to Iron Age texts and realities.

NATAN EVRON closely investigates one of the so-called doublets in Samuel: the stories about the Ziphites' report to Saul in 1 Sam 23:19–24a; 26:1. Overarching theories about the composition of the books of Samuel notwithstanding, in this special case, EVRON regards the duplication not as the result of a combination of separate sources but of *Fortschreibung*. A (slightly shorter) version of 1 Sam 23:19–24 originally had its direct continuation with 26:1 and the following story in this chapter. EVRON strengthens his argumentation by comparing the story with Ancient Near Eastern documents about intelligence activity, thus providing a good interpretation for the difficult to translate phrase אֶל נָכוֹן in 23:23; 26:4.

By comparing the "History of David's Rise" with extra-biblical Ancient Near Eastern royal inscriptions and hero tales, CYNTHIA EDENBURG emphasises two important observations: 1) Extra-biblically, there is – until now – no equivalent for the genre of a longer 3rd person narrative as it is presented in the book of Samuel or between 1 Sam 16 and 2 Sam 5. 2) The wilderness motif is not common to ANE stories about heroes who are forced to go into exile. Taken together with the analysis of the notions about David's several escapes in 1 Sam 19–27, she draws the conclusion that originally the son of Jesse's departure from Saul's

---

9 Critique of the Massorete's vocalisation of אָכִישׁ notwithstanding, cf. EHRLICH: 241.
10 Cf. VEIJOLA 1990.

court in 1 Sam 19 may have followed directly with the former's arrival at Gath in 1 Sam 27. Successively, the sojourn in the wilderness accrued to the text, first with 1 Sam 23:14,19; 26:2–25, then with 1 Sam 21:11b–16; 23:19–25:44. Concerning the dating of an early version of this HDR, she meets with HENTSCHEL and EHR-LICH in the 7th century – but not on the same textual basis.

ALEXANDER A. FISCHER also regards the flight-rescue-pattern as an editorial device. However, he is more confident than EDENBURG when it comes to identi-fying formerly independent core-pieces. In 1 Sam 26, he extracts a hero tale in 1 Sam 26:3aα.bα,5aαb,6aα₁(lacuna),12abα(until יְדֹוד),13a,14aα₁,16aβγ(without עַל־מְשִׁיחַ יהוה),16b, to be dated to the days of the Judahite middle monarchy. This basic layer was edited by two redactional layers. The first one integrated the story into the narrative of David on the run from Saul – thereby establishing the parallel with ch. 24, whereas the second one consists of successively added theological commentaries. Thus, in the case of 1 Sam 24 and 26, the question of the origin of the doublets in 1 Sam is answered by FISCHER in redaction-critical terms: Two different and independent traditions would have made parallels by a redactor who aligned them with each other.

From this short summary of the contributions to "David in the Desert" it becomes clear what the main topics of our discussion at Jena and beyond have been. The exact attribution of quarter verses to precisely dated redactional sta-ges left aside, the remaining differences in opinion all in all refer to four points, some of which still resemble the opening questions:

–   To what extent can we or must we extrapolate from the political situation as it is mirrored in the texts to the dating of the respective texts' basic – literary – layer? In concrete terms: If especially the role of Gath in 1 Sam points to a situation prior to the 2nd half of the 9th century, does this imply that the respective *texts* have to be dated to a time close – and if, how close? – to a time before Hazael's conquest? Or do we have to deal here with a case of come down historic memory, as in the case of Hazor and Josh 11:10?

–   On which level can the textual differences, especially between MT and LXX[B] be utilised for the formation of hypotheses of the literary history of the books of Samuel? Do the differences, especially between the so-called long version and the short version in 1 Sam 17–18 mirror relatively late expan-sions – or shortenings – of an otherwise complete Samuel scroll? Or do they point to ancient independent traditions or literary sources?

–   Finally, what is the best model for describing the literary history of the books of Samuel? By analogy with Pentateuchal research, the 19th century models *Dokumentenhypothese*, *Fragmentenhypothese*, and *Ergänzungshy-pothese* have been used. In fact, every scholar represented in this volume operates with a combination of all three – the matter of dispute being only which model provides the best explanation for which textual phenomena.

– This becomes acute when it comes to identifying independent sources or traditions: What criteria must be met in order to define a story as literary independent? Which standards on coherence should we demand of our reconstructions – and to what degree is it acceptable to work with the assumption of fragments?

It is highly questionable whether all these questions or even some of them will ever be answered to everybody's satisfaction. However, the articles collected in this volume in their entirety want to stimulate further reflection on these issues – with regard to the stories about "David in the Desert" and beyond.

Bibliography

Berlejung, Angelika. ³2009. Geschichte und Religionsgeschichte des antiken Israel. Pages 59–92, 101–103 in: *Grundinformation Altes Testament*. Edited by Jan Christian Gertz et al. UTB 2745. Göttingen: Vandenhoeck & Ruprecht.

Dallmeyer, Hans Jürgen, and Walter Dietrich. 2002. *David – ein Königsweg: Psychoanalytisch-theologischer Dialog über einen biblischen Entwicklungsroman*. Göttingen: Vandenhoeck & Ruprecht.

Dietrich, Walter. 1997. *Die frühe Königszeit in Israel: 10. Jahrhundert v. Chr.* BE 3. Stuttgart: Kohlhammer.

Dietrich, Walter. 2010. *Samuel: Teilband 1. 1Sam 1–12*. BK 8/1, Neukirchen-Vluyn: Neukirchener.

Finkelstein, Israel, and Neil Asher Silberman. 2006. *David und Salomo: Archäologen entschlüsseln einen Mythos*. München: C. H. Beck.

Finkelstein, Israel. 2010. A Great United Monarchy? Archaeological and Historical Perspectives. Pages 3–28 in: *One God – One Cult – One Nation: Archaeological and Biblical Perspectives*. Edited by Reinhard G. Kratz and Hermann Spieckermann. BZAW 405. Berlin/New York: de Gruyter 2010.

Finkelstein, Israel. 2013. Geographical and Historical Realities Behind the Earliest Layer in the David Story. *SJOT* 27: 131–50.

Kratz, Reinhard G. 2000. *Die Komposition der erzählenden Bücher des Alten Testaments: Grundwissen der Bibelkritik*. UTB 2157. Göttingen: Vandenhoeck & Ruprecht.

Kratz, Reinhard G. ²2017. *Historisches und biblisches Israel: Drei Überblicke zum Alten Testament*, Tübingen: Mohr Siebeck.

Mazar, Amihai. 2007. The Search for David and Solomon: An Archaeological Perspective. Pages 117–140 in: *The Quest for the Historical Israel: Debating Archaeology and the History of Early Israel*. Edited by Israel Finkelstein and Amihai Mazar. Atlanta: Society for Biblical Literature 2007, 117–140.

Mazar, Amihai. 2010. Archaeology and the Biblical Narrative: The Case of the United Monarchy. Pages 29–58 in: *One God – One Cult – One Nation: Archaeological and*

Biblical Perspectives. Edited by Reinhard G. Kratz and Hermann Spieckermann. BZAW 405. Berlin/New York: de Gruyter 2010.

McKenzie, Steven L. 2002. *König David: Eine Biographie*, Berlin/New York: de Gruyter.

Rost, Leonhard. 1926. *Die Überlieferung von der Thronnachfolge Davids*. BWANT 42. Stuttgart: Kohlhammer.

Veijola, Timo. 1990. David in Keïla: Tradition und Interpretation in 1Sam 23,1–13* [1984]. Pages 5–42 in: *David: Gesammelte Studien zu den Davidüberlieferungen des Alten Testaments*. Schriften der Finnischen Exegetischen Gesellschaft 52. Helsinki: Finnische Exegetische Gesellschaft / Göttingen: Vandenhoeck & Ruprecht.

White, Marsha C. 2000. The History of Saul's Rise: Saulide State Propaganda in 1 Samuel 1–14. Pages 271–92 in *"A Wise and Discerning Mind": Essays in Honor of Burke O. Long*. Edited by Saul M. Olyan and Robert C. Culley. BJSt 325. Providence (RI): Brown University Press.

Peter Porzig
David in the Judean Desert

Beobachtungen an ausgewählten Qumrantexten

Dass sich hin und wieder Forscher in Jena treffen, ist eine Binsenweisheit. Dass
darunter nicht selten Bibelwissenschaftler und dezidiert auch Alttestamentler
sind, ist hingegen das Verdienst der Fachvertreter vor Ort. Denselben ist dafür
zu danken, dass man ihren Einladungen gern und stets mit besonderer Freude
folgt, nicht zuletzt, wenn man sich aus Göttingen dorthin aufmacht.[1] – Der Titel
dieses Aufsatzes lautet „David in the Judean Desert", was man nicht von ungefähr abkürzen könnte zu „DJD", also dem Namen der offiziellen Editionsreihe
der Handschriften vom Toten Meer, der „Discoveries in the Judean Desert". Er
soll das Thema des Symposiums mit ebendiesen Handschriften in Beziehung
setzen. Im Folgenden wird deshalb nicht ein umfassendes, gar vollständiges
Bild Davids in den Qumranschriften[2] gezeichnet werden – das haben andere
bereits besser gemacht als der Verfasser es jemals könnte; zu erwähnen sind
etwa Craig E. Evans[3] oder Peter W. Flint[4] –, sondern es sollen einige kleine
Beobachtungen beigesteuert werden, die diesen oder jenen Aspekt der „Wüste",

---

1 Dafür sei den Organisatoren, Hannes BEZZEL und Reinhard Gregor KRATZ, sowie dem anderen Lehrstuhlinhaber, Uwe BECKER, an dieser Stelle herzlich gedankt.
2 Wenn im Folgenden von Qumran die Rede ist, so sind damit im allgemeinen die Schriftrol-
lenhöhlen 1Q–11Q gemeint; die Siedlung nur, wenn darauf hingewiesen wird. Die „Handschriften vom Toten Meer" sind die dort und an einigen wenigen anderen Orten gefundenen antiken
Manuskripten, die sich als Handschriften späterhin biblischer Werke, Apokryphen und Pseudepigraphen sowie als genuine Schriften einer Gemeinschaft darstellen, die in den als „Ge-
meinschaftsregel" (1QS u. 4QS) und „Damaskusschrift" (die mittelalterliche Handschrift CD,
von der in Höhle 4 parallele Handschriften gefunden wurden) greifbar sind. Insofern die Verbindung von Siedlungsresten und Schriftrollen in neuerer Zeit mit guten Gründen in Frage
gestellt wird, ist überall dort, wo im Folgenden von „Qumrangemeinschaft" o.ä. die Rede ist,
die Gruppe gemeint, die für die Sammlung und Verbringung der Handschriften in die Höhlen
verantwortlich zeichnet. Damit ist über ihr mögliches (geographisches) Zentrum, über ihre
Struktur (etwa die Frage, ob es sich um eine einzige Gemeinschaft oder um mehrere „Satelli-
tengruppen" handelt) sowie über ihr Verhältnis zu anderen Gruppierungen des zeitgenössischen Judentums noch nichts gesagt. Insbesondere die vermeintliche Abgrenzung zu einem
„Mainstream"-Judentum erscheint dem Autor des Beitrags in hohem Maße problematisch.
3 EVANS 1997.
4 FLINT 2000; FLINT 2005.

Anmerkung: Vorgetragen in Jena am 2. September 2018. Die allgemeine Form des einführen-
den Vortrags wird hier weitgehend beibehalten.

https://doi.org/10.1515/9783110606164-002

in der David sich laut Symposiumstitel befindet, von der kargen Mergelterrasse[5] am nordwestlichen Toten Meer aus erhellen oder bereichern könnten. Dabei wird vor allem der Musikant Beachtung finden, als den man David ja auch aus der Hebräischen Bibel kennt.[6] Ob man sich in die folgenden Auslassungen genauso versenken kann wie in ein auf der Harfe vorgetragenes Saitenspiel,[7] ist freilich schwer vorherzusagen und, wenn man ehrlich ist, wohl auch eher unwahrscheinlich.

1 David in den Texten aus Qumran

Eigentlich sollte man bei einem Mann vom Kaliber Davids, dem prominentesten unter den Königen Israels erwarten, dass die Erzählungen aus seiner Jugend,[8] von seinem nicht nur militärischen Aufstieg,[9] seinem legendär gewordenen Königtum[10] und den Ereignissen um seine Thronfolge[11] ein beliebtes Thema in späteren Schriften darstellen.[12] Umso mehr sollte das für die Handschriften einer Gruppe gelten, die doch – ganz gleich wie man sich ihre positiven Figuren der nahen Heilszeit vorstellen mag –,[13] wie ja in Ansätzen bereits die Hebräische Bibel, einen königlichen Messias aus dem Haus Davids erwartete.[14] Schon deswegen also sollte die Figur oder doch das Ideal des davidischen Königtums eine prominente Rolle in den Handschriften aus Qumran gespielt haben.

Ein Blick in die Konkordanz unter dem Lemma „David" ergibt denn auch recht veritable 29 Belegstellen,[15] wohlgemerkt: für die so genannten „nichtbiblischen" Texte aus Qumran.[16]

Eine kurze Übersicht (ohne Anspruch auf Vollständigkeit):
CD   = *Damaskusschrift = CD V,2.5 (Davids Entlastung mithilfe der Lade)*; VII,16 (Zit. Am 9,11 u. *Auslegung*),

---

5 Zur Lage vgl. Xeravits / Porzig 2015: 1–6.
6 Vgl. etwa 1Sam 16,14–23 (s. u. S. 22).
7 Damit sei an das Harfenspiel Anne Bezzels zwischen den Vorträgen des Symposiums erinnert.
8 Ab 1Sam 16,13.
9 Je nach Abgrenzung zwischen 1Sam 16 und 2Sam 5(*).
10 Etwa 2Sam 6–8(*).
11 Auch hier je nach Abgrenzung 2Sam 6–1Kön 2(*).
12 Man denke etwa an die Chronikbücher.
13 Dazu einschlägig Xeravits 2003.
14 Beispielhaft seien Jes 11 und Jer 23, davon abhängig Ez 34, vgl. Ez 37,24 f., genannt.
15 Verwendet wurde Accordance, Version 12, OakTree Software, Inc., 2016.
16 Die Bezeichnung ist natürlich anachronistisch und aus anderen Gründen problematisch, wird aber hier aus praktischen Gründen beibehalten. Vgl. Xeravits / Porzig 2015: 7 f.

1QM	=	*Kriegsregel = 1Q33 = 1Q(Særæ̱k ha-) Milḥāmāh = 1QM XI,2 (im Gebetskontext, zusammen mit Goliat),*
4Q161	=	*4QJesaja-Pescherᵃ = 4QpIsaᵃ f8–10,17 (Auslegung von Jes 11,1–5),*
4Q174	=	*4QMidrasch zur Eschatologieᵃ = 4QMidrEschᵃ f1+2i,7.11–13 (Zit. der Natansweissagung 2Sam 7,10 f.13 f. u. von Am 9,11; Auslegungen),*
4Q177	=	*4QMidrEschᵇ f5+6,7; f12+13i,2 (zit. Ps 11,1–3; Einleitung zu Zit. Ps 6,2–3),*
4Q252	=	*4QGenesiskommentar A = 4QCommGen A V,2. 4 (Zit. Jer 33,17 & Auslegung),*
4Q285	=	*4QBuch des Krieges = 4QSep̱ ær ha-Milḥāmāh f7,3 (Auslegung von Jes 10,34–11,1),*
4Q397	=	*4QEinige Werke der Toraᵈ = 4QMiqṣāt Maʿᵃśêh ha-Tôrāhᵈ = 4QMMTᵈ f14–21,10 („Kanonformel"[?]),*
4Q398	=	*4QpapMMTᵉ f11–13,1; f14–17ii,1 (Geschichtsrückblick im C-Teil: „Erinnert euch an David")*
4Q457b	=	*4QEschatologischer Hymnus = 4QEschatological Hymn II, 2 („David freute sich, dass er brachte ...")*,
4Q479	=	*4QNachkommen Davids = 4QText Mentioning Descendants of David f1,4 f. (sehr fragmentarisch),*
4Q504	=	*4QWorte der Himmelskörperᵃ = 4QDiḇrê ha-Mᵉʾôrôtᵃ = 4QDibHamᵃ f1+2Riv,6 (Bundesschluss mit David),*
4Q522	=	*4QProphezeiung Josuas = 4QProphecy of Joshua f22–26,1.4 (par. Psalm 122),*
6Q9	=	*6QApokryphon zu Samuel / Könige = 6Qpap apocrSam-Kgs f22i,4 (unklar),*
11Q5	=	*11QPsalmenrolleᵃ = 11Q Psᵃ XXVII,2; XXVIII,3.13 (David's Compositions u. Ps 154 = 2. Syrischer Psalm),*
11Q11	=	*11QApokryphe Psalmen = 11QapocrPs V,4 (David-Widmung des vorletzten nicht-kanonischen Psalms),*
11Q13	=	*11QMelchisedek- / Malkî-Ṣædæq-Midrasch = 11QMelch II,10 (Psalmen als „Lieder Davids" in Zit.-Einleitung Ps 82,1),*
11Q14	=	*11QSep̱ ær ha-Milḥāmāh f1i,7 (Auslegung von Jes 10,34–11,1, s. o. 4Q285).*

In später biblischen Büchern, aber nicht im MT: 1 Sam 21,1 (Klärung: Und *David* machte sich auf), 2 Sam 3,23 (Klärung: „*David*" statt „der König"); 19,10 (Klärung: „der König *David*" statt „der König"), Jes 38,6 (Und aus der Hand des Königs von Assur werde ich dich und diese Stadt *um meiner und um meines Knechtes Davids willen* [*lᵉmaʿᵃnî û-lᵉmaʿan Dāwîd ʿaḇdî*] retten, und ich werde diese Stadt beschützen), Ps 33,1 (*zusätzliche kurze Überschrift*); 99,1; 104,1; 123,1 (*zusätzliche Widmungen*). Komplizierter liegen die Dinge einzig bei 2Sam 24,16.20 (4QSamᵃ = 4Q51 f164+165,1–9); vgl. dazu die einschlägige Literatur zu 4QSamᵃ.

Dennoch ist dieses Ergebnis, bei Lichte besehen, recht mager: Die meisten der Belege sind nämlich – mehr oder minder – einfach wörtliche *Zitate* aus der Hebräischen Bibel, anhand derer man demnach bedauerlicherweise kaum etwas über David erfährt, was man nicht schon vorher gewusst hätte. Enthusiasmierend ist das zunächst kaum. Peter Flint nennt für die Hebräische Bibel folgende Kategorien: Als „important theological symbol"[17] und „paradigmatic

---

17 FLINT 2000: 178.

figure"[18] sei David „(a) Israel's greatest king and founder of Israel's foremost dynasty with whom God made a covenant; (b) the man after God's own heart who accomplished much despite his flaws; (c) the Psalmist par excellence; and (d) the inspiration for [...] messianic hopes".[19] Diese positiven Züge verstärken sich im Lauf der Überlieferung, wie unschwer bereits am Verhältnis des Davidbilds der Chronik zu dem der Samuel- und Königebücher zu erkennen ist.[20] Anschließend gruppiert Flint den Qumranbefund entsprechend um die vier Schwerpunkte: „(1) David as Psalmist, (2) David as Righteous Example, (3) David as a Wisdom or Prophetic Figure, and (4) David in Eschatological and Messianic Traditions."[21] Schon an der Einteilung bemerkt man: „The references to David in the Qumran scrolls build on themes in the Hebrew Bible".[22]

Aber immerhin: Wenn hier heute „David in the Judean Desert" im Zentrum stehen soll, kommt der Verfasser damit nicht nur der Bitte der Veranstalter des Symposions nach, sondern nicht zuletzt einer Aufforderung, die der bisweilen so genannte „Lehr(er)brief"[23] aus Qumran an seinem Schluss enthält. 4QMMT, *Miqṣat Ma'aśæh ha-Tôrāh*, endet im dritten und letzten (meist „C" genannten) Abschnitt[24] mit den folgenden Worten:

> „[23]... *Gedenke der Könige Israe*[*ls*], und *bedenke* ihre Taten!
> Wer immer von ihnen [24][die To]ra [...] fürchtete, wurde aus Nöten gerettet. Sie waren die, welche die Tora su[chte]n (und) [25]deren Sünden [verge]ben wurden.
> *Gedenke* [ ] *Davids*, der ein Mann frommer (*scil.* Taten) war! [ ]
> Auch [26]er wurde aus großen Nöten ge[ret]tet, und ihm wurde verziehen.
> [Und] auch haben wir an dich geschrieben [27]von den Werken der Tora, die wir für dich – von dem wir ge[se]hen haben, [28]dass bei Dir Klugheit und Wissen der Tora sind – [27]und für dein Volk für gut erachtet haben. [28]*Bedenke* dies alles und ersuche ihn (*scil.* Gott) um das, was dein Planen leite, [29]böses Sinnen und ruchlosen Plan jedoch von dir entferne, [30]auf dass du dich freust am Ende der Zeit, wenn Du herausfindest, was wahr ist von unseren Worten.
> [31]Es wird dir nämlich zur Gerechtigkeit gerechnet werden, wenn du das Rechte und das Gute vor ihm tust – dir selbst zugute [32]und (*scil.* auch) Israel."[25] (4QMMT C 23–32)

„Gedenke Davids", der „ein Mann frommer Taten" war (*'îš ḥasdîm*): Bereits diese Bezeichnung deutet eines der Themen an, das im Davidbild der Qumrantexte

---

18 Ebd.
19 Ebd.
20 Das ist oft gesehen worden, hier vgl. neben FISCHER 2009, vor allem DIETRICH / HERKOMMER (eds.) 2003, und POMYKALA 2003.
21 FLINT 2000; vgl. ebd. 178 f.
22 FLINT 2000, 180.
23 Zum Text vgl. DJD 10.
24 Zu den Problemen eines solchen „Composite Texts" vgl. KRATZ 2006.
25 Zum Text vgl. QIMRON / STRUGNELL 1994.

im Vordergrund steht. Die „frommen Taten" (Z. 23) sind, wie der Abschnitt in
seinem parallelen Aufbau zeigt, nichts anderes als das Fürchten und Suchen –
mit anderen Worten: das Halten – der Tora.[26] Hält man sich an die darin enthal-
tenen Gebote, wird einem sogar mancher Fehltritt vergeben,[27] und jeder Leser
oder jede Leserin von 4QMMT wissen natürlich, dass auch David selbst so man-
ches auf dem Kerbholz hatte. Wer sich stattdessen der Auslegung des Schreibens entsprechend verhält – auch der Adressat, möglicherweise angesehene
Kreise in Jerusalem,[28] der darf sich sogar in eine Reihe mit ʾAbrā(hā)m und
Pînᵉḥās stellen, denen ihr Tun zuerst zur Gerechtigkeit gerechnet wurde (Z. 31;
vgl. ḥāšaḇ lô (lᵉ-)ṣᵉdāqāh Gen 15,6 und Ps 106,31). Das ist durchaus als Wink
mit dem Zaunpfahl gemeint, und zwar dahingehend, dass man sich der Ausle-
gungspraxis der Qumrangemeinschaft anschließen sollte. Aber welche „Taten"
mussten David wohl verziehen werden?

Darüber gibt eine Passage der vermutlich in der Qumrangemeinschaft entstandenen und jedenfalls überlieferten Damaskusschrift Auskunft. In Höhle 4
in mehreren Exemplaren und in einer mittelalterlichen Handschrift aus der Kai-
roer Gᵉnîzāh erhalten,[29] liest man über David:

1 ‏... ועל הנשיא כתוב
2 ‏לא ירבה לו נשים ודויד לא קרא בספר התורה החתום אשר
3 ‏היה בארון כי לא נפתח בישראל מיום מות אלעזר
4 ‏ויהושע ויושוע והזקנים אשר עבדו את העשתרת ויטמון
5 ‏נגלה עד עמוד צדוק ויעלו מעשי דויד מלבד דם אוריה
6 ‏ויעזבם לו אל ...

„¹... Und über den Fürsten (ha-nāśîʾ) steht geschrieben: ²Er soll sich nicht viele Weiber[30]
halten (Dtn 17,17).
Aber Dāwîd hatte nicht im versiegelten Buch der Tora gelesen, das ³in der Lade war; denn
es war nicht geöffnet worden in Israel seit dem Tage, da ʾÆlʿāzār starb ⁴und Jᵉhôšuᵃʿ {und
Jôšᵘᵃʿ}[31] und die Ältesten, da man den ʿAštārôt diente. Und es war verborgen ⁵und wurde
nicht enthüllt bis zum Auftreten Ṣādôqs. Und die Werke Dāwîds wurden aufgehoben (?) –
mit Ausnahme des Blutes des ʾÛrîjāh, ⁶und Gott erließ sie ihm. ..." (CD V,1b–6a)

Wahrscheinlich handelt es sich bei der Passage um einen literarischen Zusatz,
der den Zusammenhang der Ausführungen über die „drei Netze Belials" (šᵉlô-
šæt mᵉṣûdôt Bᵉlîjaʿal), einer Auslegung von Jes 24,17, ein wenig unschön stört.[32]

---

26 Gemeint ist natürlich: in der Auslegung, die das Werk 4QMMT vertritt.
27 Vgl. die Passage in der Damaskusschrift (s. u.).
28 Einführend Xeravits / Porzig 2015: 164–71.
29 A. a. O. 154–63.
30 Die Übersetzung folgt der von Ed. Lohse (²1971: 75; mit kleinen Änderungen).
31 Dittographie.
32 Vgl. dazu ausführlich Porzig 2009: 267–69.

Darin hieß es direkt vor unserer Passage von gewissen „Mauerbauern" (*bônê ha-ḥajiṣ*),[33] sie seien in zweien dieser Netze gefangen, nämlich der „Unzucht" (o. „Hurerei": *zānût*)[34] und wohl auch der „Verunreinigung des Tempels" (*ṭᵉmeʾ ha-miqdāš*), wie es CD IV,20 ankündigt. Anhand der Beispiele „Arche Noah" – „je zwei und zwei sind sie in die Arche gegangen" – und „König" / „Fürst" (nach Dtn 17) wird deutlich, dass strikte Monogamie gefordert ist. Das findet seine sachliche Fortsetzung eigentlich in der Beschreibung der Verunreinigung des Tempels in Zeile 6b: „und auch verunreinigen sie das Heiligtum" (*wᵉ-gam mᵉṭammᵉʾîm hem ʾet ha-miqdāš*).[35] Die längliche David-Passage fällt aus dem Rahmen und bläht den Abschnitt unnötig auf. Offenbar zielt sie auf eine Entlastung Davids: Auch er war den Frauen gegenüber ja nicht immer abgeneigt! „What to do?" möchte man da mit Craig A. Evans[36] ausrufen. Zugleich soll so natürlich verhindert werden, dass man sich David etwa auch in dieser Sache zum Vorbild nehme. Alles Sonstige liegt – auch mit der Einschränkung durch die Bluttat an Uria (2Sam 11) deutlich im Fahrwasser von 1Kön 15,5: *raq sbi-dᵉḇar Ûrîjāh ha-Ḥittî* – gänzlich im Bereich des Normalen und Erwartbaren der späteren, davidfreundlichen deuteronomistischen und chronistischen Tradition. Dass die Glosse in 1Kön 15,5 in der ursprünglichen Septuaginta noch fehlt, sei hier nur angemerkt. Die Tatsache mag für einen überaus jungen Zusatz sprechen, an den die Qumranschriften ihrerseits anknüpfen.[37]

So mag man also, abgesehen von dem besagten Schönheitsfehler mit Uria, das Urteil über David ganz im Sinne der Chronik[38] oder des Lehrschreibens 4QMMT zu einem „Mann der frommen (bzw. treuen) Taten", oder kurz zu einem „guter Mensch" zusammenfassen.[39] Oft genug folgt auf diese Bemerkung das, was Clemens Brentano einst in seinem Lustspiel „Ponce de Leon"[40] formuliert hat, und was seither vielfach zitiert worden ist: „Guter Mensch, schlechter Musikant." Als Nachweis diene mir hier kein geringerer als Julius Wellhausen, der

---

33 In Anspielung auf Ez 13,10.

34 Vgl. etwa Ez 16 u. 43,7 f.

35 Vgl. Ez 5,11; 22,26(!); 23,38 und vor allem wieder 43,7 f.: „Und das Haus Israel wird meinen heiligen Namen nicht mehr unrein machen (*loʾ jᵉṭammᵉʾû ʿôd*) – weder sie noch ihre Könige – durch ihre Hurerei (*bi-znûtām)*".

36 EVANS 1997: 186.

37 Zu dieser Aussage vgl. insb. den ebenso betitelten Aufsatz von Thilo RUDNIG 2010, „Außer in der Sache mit Uria, dem Hethiter".

38 Vgl. etwa 2Chr 6,42.

39 Der heutzutage erschreckenderweise anzutreffende *abusus* der Wendung in Form des als Schimpfwort verstandenen „Gutmenschen" liegt dabei in mehrfacher Hinsicht mehr als fern.

40 Die Aussage des Sevillaners Valerio „Diese schlechten Musikanten und guten Leute" steht wohl im Hintergrund der Wendung (BRENTANO 1982: V,2, in: ID., Werke 12, 588).

in einem Brief an Abraham Kuenen aus dem Dezember 1876 genau dies zur Charakterisierung des Grafen Baudissin getan hat.[41]

Anders als bei Baudissin würde man David allerdings mehr als unrecht tun, wollte man ihn als „schlechten Musikanten" hinstellen. Vielleicht wusste das niemand besser als die Verfasser der in Qumran gefundenen Psalmenrolle,[42] die in etwa der Mitte des 1 Jh.s unserer Zeit kopiert wurde. Über die aus der Hebräischen Bibel bekannten Psalmen hinaus findet sich darin, neben den aus 2Sam 23 bekannten „letzten Worten" Davids in Kolumne XXVII,[43] eine Aufzählung der musikalischen oder doch wenigstens musikalischeren Werke des israelitischen Königs.[44] „David's Compositions", was auch im Englischen neben der Bedeutung von „Werken" bzw. „dessen, was David verfasst hat", nicht zuletzt die Bedeutung trägt, die der wörtlichen deutschen Übersetzung „Davids Kompositionen" entspricht. Angesichts dieses Verzeichnisses möchte man umso lauter „Guter Mensch, guter Musiker!" ausrufen.

„David's Compositions" (11Q5 = 11QPs^a XXVII,2–11)

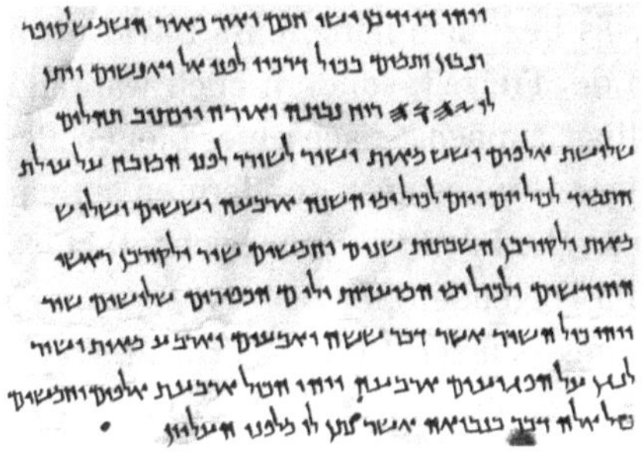

2[45] (vacat) ויהי דויד בן ישי חכם ואור כאור השמש וסופר
3 (vacat) ונבון ותמים בכול דרכיו לפני אל ואנשים ויתן
4 (vacat) לו יהוה רוח נבונה ואורה ויכתוב תהלים
5 שלושת אלפים ושש מאות ושיר לשורר לפני המזבח על עולת
6 התמיד לכול יום ויום לכול ימי השנה ארבעה וששים ושלוש
7 מאות ולקורבן השבתות שנים וחמשים שיר ולקורבן ראשי
8 החדשים ולכול ימי המועדות ולים הכפורים שלושים שיר
9 ויהי כול השיר אשר דבר ששה וא{ר}בעים וארבע מאות ושיר
10 לנגן על הפגועים ארבעה ויהי הכול ארבעת אלפים וחמשים
11 כול אלה דבר בנבואה אשר נתן לו מלפני העליון

Abb. 1

„²Und *Dāwîd bæn Jišaj* war weise und erleuchtet wie das Leuchten der Sonne, ^und ein Schreiber, ³sowohl einsichtig als auch vollkommen auf all seinen Wegen vor Gott und Menschen. ⁴JHWH hatte ihm nämlich einen einsichtigen und erleuchteten Geist gegeben. Und er schrieb Psalmen: ⁵dreitausendsechshundert, und Lieder zum Vortrag vor dem Altar anlässlich des stetigen, ⁶tagtäglich (darzubringenden) Opfers, für jeden Tag des Jah-

---

41 Das Zitat WELLHAUSENS an KUENEN: WELLHAUSEN 2013 36 (Nr. 37; 28. 12. 1876).

42 11Q5 = 11QPs^a; dazu neben den einschlägigen Editionen grundlegend die Arbeit von Eva JAIN 2014: 168–77, 241–85; außerdem SANDERS 1965; SANDERS 1967.

43 S. dazu gleich. Zur Funktion dieses und des folgenden Stückes und der Sonderüberlieferungen vor allem JAIN 2014: 241–85.

44 Kol. XXVII, 2–11. S. dazu im Folgenden.

45 Die Einrückung der ersten Zeilen erklärt sich am ehesten aus fehlerhaftem Material (Beschaffenheit des Leders, vgl. SANDERS 1965: 14, 93; KLEER 1996: 290). Anders DAHMEN 2003: 252.

res: dreihundertvierundsechzig, [7]und für die Darbringung an den Sabbaten: zweiundfünf-
zig Lieder, und für die [8]Darbringung an den Monatsersten, für jeden Tag der Festzeiten
sowie für den Versöhnungstag: dreißig Lieder. [9]Die Zahl aller Lieder, die er von sich gab,
betrug vierhundertsechsundvie{r}zig, und Lieder [10]zum Musizieren für solche, die von
etwas befallen waren: vier. – Die Gesamtzahl belief sich auf viertausendfünfzig.
[11]All diese gab er in Form einer Prophezeiung von sich, die ihm von vor dem Höchsten
her gegeben war."[46] (11Q5 = 11QPs[a] XXVII,2–11)

Da wundert sich nicht nur der Laie, sondern auch der musikalische Fachmann
dürfte staunen: 4 050 Kompositionen! Darunter die runde Zahl von 3600 Psalmen, 364 Tages-, 52 Wochen-, und 30 Monats- und Feiertagsliedern. Das entspricht zusammen schließlich nicht weniger als ungefähr sechseinhalb Köchel-
verzeichnissen der Werke des – *nota bene!* – Berufsmusikers Wolfgang
Amadeus Mozart.[47] Im Falle Davids bräuchte man freilich, z. B. bei täglicher
Komposition eines Liedes oder Psalms, gut elf Jahre, und bei einem angenommenen frühen Einstieg in die Nebentätigkeit des Komponierens zur späteren
Haupttätigkeit im militärischen und politischen Bereich blieben noch immer
ungefähr ein bis zwei Lieder pro Woche. Es liegt also nahe, dass David nach
Ansicht des Textes ebenfalls nicht nur in der Freizeit, sondern auch während
seiner Arbeitszeit komponiert hat. Das klingt zunächst nach einer bloßen Behauptung, ist andererseits aber kein völliges Hirngespinst, sondern entspricht
tatsächlich dem Bild Davids, das die Hebräische Bibel von ihm zeichnet. Ja, es
lässt sich sogar nachgerade beweisen (s. im Folgenden).

Schauen wir genauer auf das Verzeichnis. Zunächst (Z. 2–4) wird David[48]
in den höchsten Tönen gelobt: Er sei weise (genauso, wie es 2Sam 14,20 Joab
in den Mund gelegt hatte),[49] ja, sogar „erleuchtet wie das Leuchten der Son-

---

46 Wörtlich „durch Prophetie". Davor ist wohl *nittan* (d. h. *Nifʿal*) zu vokalisieren. Bei aller
inhaltlichen Klarheit bleibt die Formulierung ein wenig ungewöhnlich. – Für das Folgende sei
auch auf die konzise Analyse von Böhm 2017: 16–21, verwiesen.
47 Vgl. von Köchel [8]1983 / 1999. Nicht zuletzt vergleiche man das Genre der Kantaten zu den
einzelnen Sonntagen des Kirchenjahres.
48 Von Wacholder stammt der Vorschlag, „Sohn des Jesse" quasi als eschatologisch-messia-
nischen Titel aufzufassen (1988: 71) – was aber nicht nötig ist, da ein gewisser „eschatological
flavor" (a. a. O., 34 Anm. 48) ohnehin bereits mit der Erwähnung Davids einhergeht – Das beginnt freilich schon in 2Sam 7, den Chronikbüchern und den späteren Psalmensammlungen
selbst. In Qumran zeigt es sich dann ausgeprägt (vgl. ebd.). Das bedeutet aber kaum, dass hier
quasi eine Trennung vorgenommen werden kann, wie es Wacholder andeutet: Der „„second
David' will compose a fantastic number of psalms and hymns to be employed in the eschatological cultus" (a. a. O., 71 f.). Dagegen spricht schon die Formulierung im Erzähltempus.
49 „Mein Herr aber ist weise (*ḥākām*), wie die Weisheit des Boten Gottes, dass er alles weiß,
was auf Erden geschieht (*lā-daʿat ʾæt-kål-ʾašær bā-ʾāræṣ*)." (2Sam 14,20), vgl. vor allem auch
die „letzten Worte" 2Sam 23,2 und die in Qumran gern ausgelegte Weissagung Jes 11; hier V. 2.

ne" – das erinnert an 2Sam 23,4,[50] wo der gerechte Regent, David, mit der „Sonne des Morgens" verglichen wird. Nicht von ungefähr sind ja seine „letzten Worte" (2Sam 23,1–7) ebenfalls in der Psalmenrolle enthalten (Kol. XXVI–XXVII)![51] Doch weiter: David war auch ein „Schreiber" (2Sam 11,14; vgl. 24,10 u. ö.,[52] außerdem war immerhin sein Onkel *Jᵉhônātān* ein Schreiber: *sôper hû'*, 1Chr 27,32). Schließlich ist er *nābôn*, was auch so etwas wie „kundig" oder „gewandt" heißen kann, wie 1Sam 16,18, wo David als „redegewandt" *(nᵉbôn dābār)* bezeichnet wird. Davids Leben war „vollkommen" (√*tmm*) vor Gott und Menschen (so auch 2Sam 22,24 f. par. Ps 118,24 f.). Der Grund für all dies liegt natürlich im von JHWH gegebenen einsichtigen und erleuchteten Geist (vgl. 1Sam 16,1–13 u. ö.).

Das nun folgende Verzeichnis (Z. *4fin.5*–10) hat weniger direkte Parallelen. Es beginnt mit der runden Zahl von 3600 Psalmen. Letztlich ist sie kaum zu erklären. Bisherige Versuche gehen zumeist davon aus, dass dahinter die in der Chronik genannten 24 Priesterabteilungen (*maḥlᵉqôt*, gemäß 1Chr 23,6–24) stehen.[53]

Gemeinhin zählt man dazu: *Jᵉḥî'el, Zetām, Jô'el, Šᵉlômôt* (o. *Šᵉlômît*), *Ḥᵃzî'el, Ḥārān, Jaḥat, Zînā'* (o. *Zîzā'*), *Jᵉ'ûš, Bᵉrî'āh, 'Ahᵃron, Mošæh, Šelômît, Jᵉrîjāhû, 'Amarjāh, Jaḥᵃzî'el, Jᵉqam'ām, Mîkāh, Jiššîjāh, 'Æl'āzār, Qîs, Maḥlî, 'Edær* und *Jᵉremôt*. Für jede dieser Abteilungen wäre dann jeweils ein kompletter Psalter (à 150 Psalmen) verfasst worden, zusammen wären das die besagten 3600.[54] In 2Chr 29,25–30 liest man noch mehr Details. Dort stellt Hiskia die Leviten im Tempel auf, *bi-mᵉṣiltajim bi-nᵉbālîm û-bᵉ-kinnorôt* („mit Zithern, mit Harfen und mit Leiern") „nach dem Befehl Davids und Gads, des Sehers des Königs, und

---

50 Vgl. V. 3 f.: „Wer gerecht über die Menschen herrscht, wer gottesfürchtig herrscht, [4]der ist wie das Licht des Morgens (*kᵉ-'ôr boqær*), wenn die Sonne aufstrahlt *(jizraḥ-šāmæš)*."
51 Jedenfalls deren letzter Vers 7 in XXVII,1. Man darf wohl davon ausgehen, dass der Inhalt der Verse 2Sam 23,1–6 sich am Ende von Kol. XXVI befunden hat. Die Deutung der gesamten „Compositions" als „commentary upon 2 Samuel 23:1–7", wie sie WACHOLDER (1988: 41) annimmt, trifft „formally" (ebd.) zwar durchaus zu, vermag aber den Bezugsrahmen des Textes nur unzureichend zu erklären. Mit BÖHM (2017: 16–21, vgl. KLEER 1996: 296, 302) ist von einer Fortschreibung für den Kontext in der Psalmenrolle auszugehen und nicht, wie DAHMEN (2003: 257) vermutet, von einer älteren und dann überarbeiteten Komposition. Zur Komposition vgl. wiederum JAIN 2014.
52 Wenn SANDERS hier „literate" statt des wörtlicheren „scribe" übersetzt (1965: 92; vgl. SANDERS 1967: 137), ist das in der Sache kaum ein Unterschied, war doch der Schreiber nicht weniger schriftgelehrt als der Schriftkundige gebildet.
53 Vgl. SARNA 1979.
54 Hinzu kommt die aparte Beobachtung, dass sich im Rahmen der Gematria für *Dw(j)d* in *plene*-Schreibung (*kᵉtîb māle'*) der Wert 24 ergibt (4 + 6 + 10 + 4) und 24 × 150 = 3600. Für die defektive *Schreibung (kᵉtîb ḥāser)* ergibt sich die Zahl 14 (4 + 6 + 4). Doch vgl. WACHOLDER 1988: 38 f.).

des Propheten Nathan, denn der Befehl war durch den Herrn, durch seine Propheten" ergangen; sie spielen „mit den Instrumenten Davids" (*bi-ḵᵉlê Dāwîd*, V. 26), „unter Begleitung der Instrumente Davids (*'al-jᵉdê ḵᵉlê Dāwîd*, o., mit LXX, nur *'æl* oder *'al*: zu den Instrumenten Davids), des Königs von Israel" (V. 27), anschließend sollen die Leviten nicht nur „mit den Worten Davids *(bᵉ-dibrê Dāwîd)* und des Sehers Asaf" singen, sondern auch „mit Freude" (*'ad-lᵉ-śimḥah*; V. 30).

Das würde allerdings bedeuten, dass zu diesem Zeitpunkt die Zahl der Psalmen bereits auf 150 festgelegt war. Doch war sie das überhaupt? So sicher man sich zunächst zu sein scheint: Die Septuaginta hätte man bekanntlich gegen sich, ja, selbst den masoretischen Text! Kein Geringerer als der Masoret und Schreiber (der Handschrift MS Heb B. N° 19.ₐ), also des *Codex Leningradensis / Petropolitanus*, *Šᵉmû'el bæn Ja'ᵃqoḇ*, gibt in seinen Anmerkungen am Ende der *Ketûḇîm* höchstpersönlich die Zahl der Psalmen mit 149 (*me'āh wᵉ-'arbā'îm wᵉ-tiš'āh*) an.[55]

Die danach genannten „364 Lieder" setzen einen Sonnen- (bzw. lunisolaren) Kalender voraus und nicht den geläufigen Mondkalender mit 354 Tagen, wie man schon immer gesehen hat.[56] Ob das als Indiz für eine qumranische Verfasserschaft ausreicht, darf bezweifelt werden. Ein Hindernis war es hingegen kaum, denn dieser aus 1. Henoch und Jubiläen bekannte Kalender war auch der Gemeinschaft von Qumran ein Anliegen. Die 52 Wochenlieder bereiten wenig Probleme. 364 plus 52 sind schon einmal 416, hinzu kommen die Festtage inklusive des höchsten darunter, des Versöhnungstages, wie es in Zeile 8 verlautet, 30 an der Zahl. Auch hier kann man viel rechnen und hat viel gerechnet. Eine einleuchtendere Erklärung als die von William Brownlee[57] aus dem Jahre 1958 hat jedoch aus meiner Sicht bisher niemand finden können: Legt man der Zählung den Festkalender von Lev 23 zugrunde, erhält man als Summe von 12 Monatsersten, 8 Tagen *Pæsaḥ* plus *Maṣṣôt*, 8 Tagen *Sukkôt* und je einem für *Šāḇu'ôt* und *Jôm ha-Kippurîm* in der Summe genau 30.

---

55 So fol. 463r, Kol. 3, Z. 21. – Für die 150 spricht sich insb. SKEHAN aus (1967/8: 278), doch vgl. auch die Kritik von CHYUTIN (1994: 367–70). Wiewohl die Psalmenrolle Anzeichen für einen liturgischen Gebrauch aufweist (so bes. GOSHEN-GOTTSTEIN 1966), bleibt letztlich doch „everything that has been said concerning the purpose of the *Psalms Scroll* [...] essentially conjecture." (NITZAN 1994: 17). Dass nichtsdestotrotz der Psalter schon eine im Wesentlichen abgeschlossene Komposition war (SKEHAN 1973, u. ö.), könnte auch unabhängig davon zutreffend sein. Zur Debatte um die Kanonizität vgl. die Arbeiten von WILSON 1985a, und WILSON 1985b: insb. 63–92.
56 Vgl. The Dead Sea Psalms Scroll, 134. Vgl. zur Bedeutung FLINT, David's Solar Psalter. The Structure and Provenance of 11QPsᵃ, in: FLINT 1997: 172–201.
57 BROWNLEE 1964/66: 570.

James VanderKam hat in einem klugen Aufsatz nachzuweisen versucht, dass *alle* Zahlen, die in „David's Compositions" genannt sind, sich auf kalendarische Gegebenheiten beziehen.[58] Das gelte, neben der kaum anders zu deutenden 446, die der Text ja gesondert zusammenfasst, auch für die Zahl 3600. Das ist als Alternative in jedem Fall erwägenswert: In 1Hen 75,1–3 sind für den zugrundeliegenden Kalender vier interkalendarische Tage genannt,[59] obwohl auch dieser Kalender sich mit 364 Tagen begnügt. Dort wären 3600 Tage genau 10 mal 360 Tage = 10 Jahre, und auch die verbleibende Zahl 4 (die Anzahl der Lieder für die „Besessenen") entspräche genau dieser Anzahl von Interkalationstagen. Sollte er damit Recht haben – was keinesfalls ausgeschlossen werden soll –, wären die Beobachtungen im Folgenden natürlich noch weniger als das Gedankenspiel, das sie ohnehin nur darstellen wollen. Nur: Leider weiß man bei VanderKam weder, was sich hinter der Dauer von ominösen zehn Jahren eigentlich verbergen sollte, noch ist irgendwie erklärlich, warum in 11QPsᵃ direkt im Anschluss – ausgerechnet – die *364* als Summe der Tage eines Jahres erwähnt wird, zu denen dann ja die besagten 4 Lieder eigentlich nicht mehr recht passen, denn ein 364 + 4 = 368-Tage-Jahr hat m. E. nun beim besten Willen keiner der in Jubiläenbuch, 1. Henoch, der Hebräischen Bibel oder Qumran belegten Kalender zu bieten. So wird man für die erste der Zahlen nicht viel mehr sagen können, als dass es eine „runde" Zahl ist, deren Zweck vielleicht auch darin liegen könnte, den Nachfolger Salomo, nach 1Kön 5,12 Dichter von (immerhin auch) 3000 Sprüchen und 1005 Liedern, zu übertreffen. Auch die Tatsache, dass die kleinste der Zahlen auf „Besessene"[60] verweist, will sich nicht recht der Erklärung durch Interkalation oder dergleichen fügen. Doch woher stammt die Zahl dann?

Gehen wir also dieser kleinsten Anzahl unter den Liedern einmal nach, die durch die Wendung *lᵉ-naggen ʿal ha-pᵉgûʾîm*, „zum Musizieren für solche, die von etwas ‚befallen' (o. ‚geschlagen', o. ‚besessen') waren", näher bestimmt ist. Die Wurzeln √ngn und √pgʿ sind dabei beide auf ihre je eigene Weise interessant. Zuerst zu *niggen*, bis auf eine Ausnahme – die „Saitenschläger" in Ps 68,26 (im *Qal*) – ausschließlich im *Pîʿel* belegt, das in etwa „musizieren" bedeuten

58 VANDERKAM 1999; leicht abgewandelt WACHOLDER 1988; ähnlich CHYUTIN 1994.

59 ዐለ ፡ ይትዌሰኩ, 4 ʾǝlla yǝtǝwessaku, „vier, die dazugezählt werden" (1Hen 75,1).

60 Eine Übersetzung mit „prayer" (TALMON 1966: 215f. Anm. 11) oder „meeting" und daraus folgend „Interkalationstag", an dem nämlich zwei Jahresviertel à 90 Tage aufeinander „treffen", scheint mir etwas gekünstelt (so CHYUTIN 1994: 370, u. a.). Die 90 stellt CHYUTIN insgesamt ins Zentrum: 90 × 45 sind 4050, also die Anzahl der Kompositionen Davids, 45 × 89 hingegen die (Salomo in 1Kön 5 zugesprochenen) 4005 Werke (demnach also keinesfalls perfekt). Doch ist die Lesung von 11QPsᵃ „as a calendar" (ebd., 369) wirklich wahrscheinlich, und sei es für eine Redaktionsstufe? Vgl. auch CHYUTIN 1993.

dürfte. Die einschlägigen Lexika erfassen das natürlich genauer, nach HALAT etwa ist √ngn Pi. so etwas wie „zupfen", „die Saiten anschlagen" oder „in die Saiten greifen",[61] vornehmer noch: „ein Saiteninstrument spielen". Dementsprechend war die nᵉgînāh ein Stück „Saitenmusik" oder auch das dafür benötigte Instrument: so oder so taucht es in mancher Psalmenüberschrift auf;[62] im Sirachbuch[63] als nᵉginôt šîr, was ebenfalls Saiteninstrumente zum Begleiten eines Liedes bezeichnen dürften. Weitere gebräuchliche Saiteninstrumente sind der næḇæl,[64] gern mit „Harfe" übersetzt, und *last not least* der Kinnor (kinnôr),[65] der zumeist als „Leier" oder „Zither" in den Übersetzungen auftaucht, traditionell aber ebenso gut als „Harfe" gedeutet, wenn man dabei auch eher den genannten næḇæl assoziiert. Das Belegspektrum in der Hebräischen Bibel ist vielsagend: √ngn pi. kommt dort 1Sam 16,16–18.23; 18,10 u. 19,9; 2Kön 3,15; Jes 23,16 u. 38,20; Ez 33,32 sowie in Ps 33,3 vor. Für das Thema „David" sind davon natürlich vor allem die Belege interessant, in denen er selbst die Saite schlägt, und das sind immerhin vier der neun Belege: 1Sam 16,16.23; 18,10 und 19,9. In all diesen Versen ist daran gedacht, wie David sein Instrument in die Hand (bᵉ-jādô) nimmt und darauf musiziert, in allen geht es um das Verhältnis zu König Saul:[66] Zunächst die Diener Sauls über David, den Sohn Isais: „Und wenn der böse Gottesgeist auf dir ist, wird er (*scil.* David) *in die Saiten greifen*, und das wird dir gut tun" (16,16),[67] „wenn der Gottesgeist auf Saul war, nahm David die Leier und *griff in die Saiten*" (16,23), „am folgenden Tag durchdrang ein böser Gottesgeist Saul ... während David wie jeden Tag *in die Saiten griff*" (18,10), „der Geist JWHWs lag als böser Geist auf Saul, als er in seinem Haus

---

61 Umgangssprachlich kommt einem unwillkürlich das (aufs Niederdeutsche zurückgehende?) mit dem österreichischen „Schrammeln" verwandte „Schremmeln" in den Sinn, wie man es zur spontanen Liedbegleitung auf der Gitarre macht.
62 Dabei besonders interessant natürlich die Davidspsalmen: Ps 4,1; 6,1 (*mizmôr lᵉ-Dāwid*); 54,1, 55,1 (*maśkîl lᵉ-Dāwid*); 61,1 (einfaches *lᵉ-Dāwid*); vgl. auch Ps 69,13.
63 Sir 47,16; vgl. Ms B 16*verso*, 16).
64 1Sam 10,5; 2Sam 6,5; 1Kön 10,12; Jes 5,12; 14,11; Am 5,23; 6,5; Ps 33,2; 57,9; 71,22; 81,3; 92,4; 108,3; 144,9; 150,3; Neh 12,27; 1Chr 13,8; 15,16.20.28; 16,5; 25,1.6; 2Chr 5,12; 9,11; 20,28; 29,25.
65 Gen 4,21; 31,27; 1Sam 10,5; *16,16.23*; 2Sam 6,5; 1Kön 10,12; Jes 5,12; 16,11; 23,16; 24,8; 30,32; Ez 26,13; Ps 33,2; 43,4; 49,5; 57,9; 71,22; 81,3; 92,4; 98,5; 108,3; 137,2; 147,7; 149,3; 150,3; Hi 21,12; 30,31; Neh 12,27; 1Chr 13,8; 15,16.21.28; 16,5; 25,1.3.6; 2Chr 5,12; 9,11; 20,28; 29,25.
66 Zur Person Sauls vgl. neben der eingehenden Studie Bezzels (2015) nicht zuletzt die lesenswerte Biographie von Hentschel in der Reihe der „Biblischen Gestalten" (Hentschel 2003), in die direkt und indirekt manche Erkenntnisse aus seiner Kommentierung der Samuelbücher (vgl. Hentschel 1994a; Hentschel 1994b) eingegangen sind.
67 Man beachte: Der Geist, laut V. 13 „von jenem Tag an" auf David liegend, ist Saul laut V. 14 entzogen – möglicherweise ein jüngeres Überlieferungsstratum (vgl. dazu Müller 2018: 283 mit Anm. 97).

saß und seinen Speer in der Hand hielt – während David *in die Saiten griff*" (19,9). Das sind vielleicht nicht zufällig genau vier Erwähnungen![68] Man denke an die „vier" noch ungeklärten Lieder aus dem Verzeichnis der Psalmenrolle, *David's Compositions*. Und jedes Mal ist vom Saitenspiel dann die Rede, wenn Saul vom bösen Geist geschlagen oder besessen ist, beziehungsweise, in der Sprache der Psalmenrolle ausgedrückt: wenn Saul zu den *peḡûʿîm* gehört, also zu den „(von einem Geist) Besessenen"!

pāḡaʿ bedeutet biblisch zunächst so etwas wie „treffen" oder „begegnen",[69] nicht selten sind das beschriebene Treffen oder die Begegnung allerdings der eher unschönen Art: im schlimmsten Fall heißt es: „über jemanden herfallen, um ihn zu töten" (so die Priesterschaft von *Nôb* in 1Sam 22,17 f.; *Qal*), im *Hip̄ʿîl*: „jemand von etwas verletzen lassen". Saul beauftragt seine Diener und *Dôǰeg*, die Priester zu *Nob* zu töten (1Sam 22[70]), David wiederum einen der eigenen Männer, den namenlosen amalekitischen Boten zu töten (2Sam 1). Salomo schließlich beauftragt *Benājāhû ḫæn-Jehôǰādāʿ*, *Jôʾāb* zu töten (1Kön 2). Wenn man so will, umschreibt die Wurzel √pgʿ dabei geradezu das, was man heute einen „Auftragsmord" nennen würde. Das zugehörige Nomen *pæḡaʿ* ist so etwas wie „Geschick" oder „Zufall" – was einem eben „begegnet", mit *rāʿ* verbunden durchaus auch „Missgeschick", vgl. arab. *faǧaʾa* „überfallen, plötzlich kommen".

Es ist ein oft zu beobachtendes Phänomen der Aufnahme der Schriften der nachmaligen Hebräischen Bibel in den Schriften in Qumran, dass diese dort ansetzen, wo jene enden, d. h. sie sich in das Gefälle der innerbiblischen Auslegung stellen bzw. sich an späte und späteste Fortschreibungen anhängen.[71] Könnte das, einmal umgekehrt – nämlich vom Qumrantext aus – gefragt, vielleicht auch hier der Fall sein? Zwar ist nicht erwiesen und vermutlich auch nicht zu erweisen, dass es sich bei der Psalmenrolle um einen Text handelt, der in der Gemeinschaft von Qumran verfasst oder fortgeschrieben wurde,[72] aber nichtsdestotrotz gibt es Hinweise, dass die Komposition den später zum Bestandteil des masoretischen Texts gewordenen Konsonantentexts voraussetzt, mit Blick auf verschiedene Aspekte ergänzt und die Reihenfolge der Psalmen

---

68 Die Beziehung zu den Samuelbüchern hatte auch Cooper 1983: 127 f., gesehen, die Zahl 4 ist aber keinesfalls *conjecture*, um auf 450 zu kommen.

69 Vgl. die einschlägigen Lexika.

70 Zu dieser Passage vgl. vor allem Hentschel 2010: 188–90.

71 Dazu vergleiche nicht zuletzt die Veröffentlichungen von R. G. Kratz.

72 Doch vgl. das oben zum Kalender Gesagte sowie Goshen-Gottstein 1966. Prosateile wie „David's Compositions" innerhalb der Sammlung mögen auf Kanonizität oder liturgischen Gebrauch hinweisen oder gerade nicht hinweisen, für oder gegen eine Hypothese einer Herkunft aus der Qumrangemeinschaft („sectarian text") ist damit ohnehin nichts gewonnen.

sekundär umstellt.[73] Knüpft also dieser Qumrantext mit seiner Betonung des auch für die Beruhigung der Besessenen tätigen Komponisten und Musikers David, möglicherweise ebenfalls an spätere Texte an? Freilich: Eine Antwort auf diese Frage können nur die Bücher Samuelis selbst geben.

2 „David als Musikant" in den Samuelbüchern

Saul dürfte nach dem eben Gesagten durchaus außer Gefecht gesetzt gewesen sein, als bzw. wenn ihn der böse Geist überfiel und David ihm spielte (in 1Sam 16,14–23; 18,10 und 19,9). Die vier Stellen finden sich also in einer Erzählung darüber, wie David an den Hof Sauls kommt. Die entsprechende Fassung der Geschichte ist bekanntlich eine von dreien, die jede „in besonderer Weise David auf den Schauplatz bringen, nämlich 1) 15 $_{35}$[b]–16 $_{13}$, die Salbung Davids im Kreise seiner Brüder, 2) 16 $_{14-23}$, die Berufung Davids an Sauls Hof, wie er durch sein Saitenspiel den bösen Geist von Saul verscheuchen soll, endlich 3) Cap. 17, David und Goliath. Die beiden letzteren Stücke bringen zugleich David an den Hof Sauls".[74] „Die beiden Darstellungen schließen sich unbedingt und in allen Punkten aus; daß sie neben einander Aufnahme fanden, erklärt sich wohl nur aus der volksthümlichen Schönheit und Beliebtheit der zweiten und dem geschichtlichen Ansehen, das die erste genoß."[75] Entweder durch Salbung, durch Erfolge als Krieger oder eben als Zitherspieler, der den König besänftigen konnte, wenn dieser von einem bösen Geist getroffen war, sei David an den Hof gekommen. Das Urteil Buddes hört man schon deutlich im Wortlaut seiner Aufzählung, dass nämlich von den genannten der Bericht von 1Sam 16,14–23 „an sich und wegen des ferneren Verlaufs entschieden den Vorzug"[76] hat. Er erscheint am wenigsten ableitbar von allen und ist denn auch den meisten Auslegern der David-Saul-Überlieferung als die älteste erschienen. Aktuell verweise

---

73 Das dürfte wohl doch die wahrscheinlichere Antwort auf die Frage sein, wie sich die andere Reihenfolge in 11Q5 erklären lässt (JAIN 2014: 254 u. *passim*, zur Stabilität ebd., 237–41, gegen DAHMEN 2003). Zwar ist die „kanonische" Form des Textes ganz allgemein in der Entstehungszeit der Qumranhandschriften noch nicht erreicht, doch lassen sich die angenommenen Umstellungen besser in diese Richtung erklären als umgekehrt, wie JAIN in ihrer Studie eindrücklich gezeigt hat.
74 BUDDE 1902: 113. Erst von hier geriet Goliat dann auch in 1Sam 11 (V. 2b), vgl. MÜLLER 2018: 265. Die dazwischenliegenden Kapitel 1Sam 13–14 sind eine spätere Komposition, vgl. BEZZEL 2016: insb. 465 f.; anders freilich HUTTON 2009: 362 f.
75 BUDDE 1890: 211.
76 A. a. O., 214.

ich hier statt einer langen Liste auf Julius Wellhausen,[77] genauso gut wären hier Reinhard Kratz (jedenfalls bis 2000), Jeremy Hutton[78]oder Karl Budde[79] zu nennen. In diese Reihe gehört auch Walter Dietrich, der in seinem ausführlichen Biblischen Kommentar die erste Fassung der Geschichte in 1Sam 16,1–13 seinem „Höfischen Erzähler" zugeschrieben hat. Angesichts der Doppelung durch den folgenden Abschnitt 14–23 stellt Dietrich die berechtigte Frage: „Warum sollte ein und derselbe Erzähler zwei, in ihren Konturen scharf voneinander unterschiedene Geschichten erfinden, um die Figur Davids auf die Erzählbühne zu führen?" Ein Grund findet sich natürlich kaum. Dietrichs Schlussfolgerung: „So ist von vornherein zu vermuten, dass eine Erzählung von David als Musiktherapeuten dem höfischen Erzähler vorgegeben war und er sie an die von ihm selbst verfasste von der Salbung angefügt hat. Ist es so, dann ist mit Spuren einer Bearbeitung von seiner Hand zu rechnen."[80]

Diese Beantwortung der Frage schüttet bedauerlicherweise, man verzeihe die Formulierung, das Kind mit dem Bade aus. Sie setzt nämlich zweierlei bereits voraus: dass, erstens, beide Abschnitte der „Höfische[] Erzähler" geformt hat, und dass, zweitens, diesem eine alte Erzählung, eine Quelle, vorgelegen hat. Indes sollte m. E. zunächst doch auch die andere Antwort auf die rhetorische Frage im Spiel bleiben, nämlich die, dass die Verse 14–23 von einem *späteren* Verfasser herrühren – sei es als Fortsetzung zu 16,1–13, sei es als auch *literarisch* erste oder als zweite Variante der Geschichte, wie David zu Saul kam. Ist, in eine Frage gegossen, das Motiv des „die Laute schlagenden Pagen" wirklich literarisches „Urgestein"[81] und damit zugleich „Urquell" der späteren Überlieferung von David als musikalisch begabtem Psalmendichter? Das müsste natürlich zunächst gezeigt werden. In seinem Buch über „Die frühe Königszeit" hatte Dietrich, worauf er selbst verweist, lediglich die beiden Halbverse 18b und 19b als spätere Zusätze vom Übrigen abgetrennt und war sich auch der Zuordnung zu einer alten Quelle (noch) nicht so sicher: Die Geschichte in 1Sam 16,14–23 hängt „zusammen mit dem Motiv von der Krankheit Sauls – Davids musikalische Darbietungen schaffen Saul Erleichterung – und könnte mit ihm zusammen erzählerische Invention prodavidischer Erzähler sein."[82] Erheblich komplizierter und diffiziler stellt sich die ausgefeilte – und auf ihre Weise durchaus plausible – Literarkritik im späteren Kommentar dar: Nach ihr wurde „eine rela-

---

77 Ebd.
78 Hutton 2009: 365.
79 Budde 1890: 114.
80 Dietrich 2015: 253.
81 Seybold 2003: 148.
82 Dietrich 1997: 181.

tiv knappe Grunderzählung" einer „relativ breite[n] redaktionelle[n] Bearbeitung" unterzogen. Der Text sei hier in Dietrichs Übersetzung wiedergegeben:[83]

> [14]*Und der Geist Jhwhs war von Saul gewichen,* **und [Saul] erschreckte immer wieder ein schlimmer [Gottes-] Geist** *von Jhwh her.* [15]*Und die Untergebenen Sauls sagten zu ihm: Sieh doch, ein schlimmer Gottesgeist erschreckt dich ständig.* [16]*Es gebe doch unser Herr den Untergebenen vor ihm Befehl, und sie suchen einen Mann, der sich aufs Musizieren mit der Leier versteht. Und es wird dann sein, wenn ein schlimmer Geist über dich kommt – und dann musiziert er mit seiner Hand, und dir wird wohl sein.* [17]**Und Saul sagte zu seinen Untergebenen: „Seht doch für mich nach einem Mann, der gut musiziert, und bringt ihn zu mir!"** [18]**Und einer von den jungen Leuten antwortete und sprach: „Siehe, ich habe [David,] einen Sohn Isais, des Betlehemiters, gesehen, der versteht zu musizieren.** *Und er ist ein starker Kämpfer und ein Kriegsmann und von verständiger Rede und ein Mann von [gutem] Aussehen – und* JHWH *ist mit ihm."* [19]**Und Saul sandte Boten zu Isai und ließ ihm sagen: „Sende zu mir David, deinen Sohn,** *der beim Kleinvieh ist!"* [20]**Und Isai** *nahm ein Homer Brot und einen Schlauch Wein und ein Ziegenböckchen und* **schickte** *dies durch* **seinen Sohn David zu Saul.** [21]**Und David kam zu Saul und stand ihm zu Diensten.** *Und er liebte ihn sehr,* ·*und er wurde ihm ein Waffenträger.* [22]*Und Saul sandte zu Isai und ließ ihm sagen: „David möge mir doch zu Diensten sein; denn er hat in meinen Augen Gunst gefunden."* [23]**Und es war immer, wenn der Gottesgeist zu Saul kam, und dann nahm David die Leier und musizierte mit seiner Hand, und dann konnte Saul aufatmen und ihm wurde wohl, und der schlimme Geist wich von ihm.**

Als mehr als einmal ausgewiesener und redlicher Exeget legt Dietrich zunächst die *Kriterien* seiner Literarkritik offen. „Es ist eine Grunderkenntnis der Redaktions- bzw. Kompositionskritik, dass Passagen innerhalb selbstständiger Überlieferungen, die auf einen weiteren Kontext verweisen, sehr oft redaktioneller Natur sind."[84] Entsprechend findet Dietrich in der präsentierten Fassung ja auch „gerade die … Brücken von 16,14–23 zu den umgebenden Erzählungen" verdächtig, „vom Höfischen Erzähler eingesetzt worden zu sein."[85] Für zwei andere Verse (15 f.) kann er auf sprachliche Anlehnungen an ebendiesen Erzähler verweisen, während der Rest eher Vermutung bleibt, bleiben muss. Die erhaltene schriftliche Quelle wird dann noch um „hypothetische Ergänzungen" bereichert: Da ist zum einen der Name der ersten Hauptfigur, die vom Höfischen Erzähler in Vers 14b getilgt worden sein muss, da er selbst ihn ja bereits in V. 14a genannt hat; sodann der Name der zweiten Hauptfigur, nämlich Davids, ausgerechnet bei seiner ersten Erwähnung, und zuletzt der „Geist", der Saul nach der Grundschicht erschreckt, zum „Gottesgeist" – konsistent mit dem

---

83 Vgl. den Abschnitt im Kommentar; es sind die **Quelle** des „Höfischen Erzählers" im Druck **fett**, die *Zufügungen* desselben *kursiv* gesetzt.
84 DIETRICH 2015: 253.
85 Ebd.

Ende der Erzählung V. 23, wo daneben allerdings auch ein „schlimmer Geist" nicht explizit göttlicher Natur auftritt.

Nun ist dem Kriterium Dietrichs, „dass Passagen [...], die auf einen weiteren Kontext verweisen" „innerhalb selbständiger Überlieferungen" oft sekundär sind, vollauf zuzustimmen. Jede Literarkritik muss sich auf der Suche nach Vorlagen und Quellen diesem Problem stellen. Jedoch sei die Frage erlaubt, woher in diesem Falle die Sicherheit kommt, dass es sich bei dem Stück 1Sam 16,14–23 auch wirklich um eine „selbständige Überlieferung", ja, eine ältere Quelle handelt! Denn *ohne* dass die Voraussetzung sich auch aus anderen Gründen nahelegt (etwa sprachliche oder literarische), läuft der Exeget Gefahr, sogleich in einem logischen Zirkel gefangen zu sein: So könnte er leicht in so gut wie jedem, egal wie eng im Kontext verzahnten Stück eine Quelle finden. Spricht er dem Text alle auf den Kontext verweisenden, „unselbständigen" Elemente ab (und zwar weil sie nicht selbständig sind!) – der Sache nach wäre das eine Spielart der Tendenzkritik –, so bleibt am Ende natürlich auch eine „selbständige Quelle" übrig, die sich zuvörderst dadurch auszeichnet, keine Verbindungen zum größeren Kontext aufzuweisen. Aber gerade das war doch zuerst zu zeigen! Um nicht missverstanden zu werden: Es ist durchaus nicht unmöglich, dass es sich im vorliegenden Fall um solch eine Quelle handelt, wie Dietrich behauptet, und auch, dass in 16,14–23 eine ältere oder die älteste Fassung der Geschichte vorliegt, wie David zu Saul kommt. In *dieser Form* ist das aber m. E. schwerlich nachweisbar, zudem *literarische* Kriterien in der Analyse eine lediglich untergeordnete Rolle spielen. Stutzig macht darüber hinaus die bereits genannte Beobachtung, „schon dieser Urfassung der Geschichte wohn[e] eine prodavidische Tendenz inne", auch wenn David „nichts als ein Musikus"[86] sei. Dass solch „prodavidische Tendenzen" oftmals in späten Texten begegnen, wie nicht zuletzt der Chronik, sei hier nur angemerkt. Doch auch für den Erzählzusammenhang wäre es misslich, wenn David darin wirklich „*nichts* als ein Musikus"[87] wäre, „ein des Waffenhandwerks unkundiger Fant",[88] wie Wellhausen sagt (dagegen spräche das in V. 18 freilich Gestrichene). Für die gesamte weitere Überlieferung, abgesehen einmal von den beiden schlaglichtartigen Szenen in 18,10 und 19,9,[89] spielt es überhaupt keine Rolle, wieder mit Wellhausen gesprochen, „wie aber dieser Mann den Hof bezauberte"[90] dank seiner musikalischen Fähig-

---

86 Beide Zitate: Dietrich 2015: 255.
87 Ebd. (Hervorhebung P.P.).
88 Wellhausen 2001: 261.
89 Bereits daraus folgt, dass diese Speerszenen, wie Sara Kipfer wohl richtig urteilt, eher „jüngeren Datums" sein dürften (Kipfer 2015: 63).
90 Wellhausen [10]2004: 54.

keiten. Überdies ist von den beiden parallel gestalteten Stellen 1Sam 18,10 f. und 19,9 f., die erzählerisch eine klare Dublette bilden, mit Sicherheit nur eine ursprünglich. Zweimal der Speer, zweimal das Zitherspiel Davids, zweimal kommt das Opfer davon. Schon Wellhausen hielt 19,9 f. für ursprünglich und 18,10 f. für die redaktionelle Verdopplung, was angesichts des textkritischen Befundes durchaus wahrscheinlich ist. Die Septuaginta enthielt nämlich verschiedene Verse in Kap. 18 noch nicht, darunter auch V. 10 f. Demnach ist Doppelung redaktionell zu erklären. Sicher ist, dass beide Szenen mit 1Sam 16,14–23 zusammenhängen und ihre relative chronologische Einordnung somit vom dort Erzählten abhängt. Kurzum: Vor die Wahl „Dietrich 1997" (in der Biblischen Enzyklopädie) oder „Dietrich 2012" (im Biblischen Kommentar) gestellt, würde die Entscheidung des Verfassers eher zugunsten von „Dietrich 1997" ausfallen, wo, wie erwähnt, der Abschnitt bis auf zwei kleine Zusätze einheitlich bleibt. Vielleicht ist aber auch der Position Heinrichs, der im Hintergrund den dritten Kanonteil vermutet,[91] der also David nicht nur als Kriegsheld und gerechten König, sondern auch als Musikant und Dichter der Psalmen ansieht, noch ein wenig abzugewinnen. Freilich: Ob es sich tatsächlich um den „Kanonteil" im engeren Sinne (und insofern noch anachronistischer als der Begriff des „Kanons" selbst) handelt oder doch eher um ein eher zur Chronik passendes Davidbild,[92] und auch, ob in dem gesamten Stück nur ein einziger Vers zu einem älteren Textbestand gehört, ist mir durchaus fraglich, letzteres sogar mehr als fraglich.[93] Der späte David hingegen, bei dem ja auch Texte der Psalmen im Zusammenhang verwendet werden, könnte hingegen tatsächlich bereits im Hintergrund stehen.

Nun wird man natürlich mit Recht nach der positiven Seite der Medaille fragen – wenn nicht 1Sam 16,14–23, was dann? Auch wenn in diesem Zusammenhang eine Festlegung nicht zwingend notwendig ist, sei auf den Aufsatz des mittlerweile im Ruhestand befindlichen schwedischen Bischofs und früheren Göttinger Alttestamentlers Erik Aurelius hingewiesen, den Doktorvater des Hauptorganisators dieses Symposiums. In der Festschrift für Rudolf Smend von 2002 hat er im Anschluss an Hugo Gressmann (und andere) für den ursprünglichsten Kandidaten der Geschichten, wie David an Sauls Hof kam, gute und überzeugende Gründe für die Priorität einer Grundschicht von 1Sam 17,1–18,5*, David und Goliat, vor 1Sam 16,14–23 gegeben: 1) Auf 1Sam 14,52 („Und solange Saul lebte, tobte der Krieg gegen die Philister. Und wenn immer Saul einen

---

91 HEINRICH 2009: 112–30; außerdem 95–111; Textpräparation ebd., 380 f.
92 Dies scheint zur Erklärung des Textes ausreichend zu sein.
93 HEINRICH 2009: 130: 1Sam 16,21abβ, vgl. 1Sam 14,52. Hier ist die Reduktionsmethode denn doch auf die Spitze getrieben.

Krieger sah, einen tüchtigen Mann, holte er ihn zu sich.") folgt 1Sam 16,14 nicht recht flüssig, auch nicht dann, wenn man die erste oder zweite Vershälfte einer anderen Hand zuweist. Aurelius: „Wenn [die älteste Einführung Davids] aber, wie es der Konsens will, in 16,14–23 vorliegen soll, dann ist der Scharniervers 14,52 gerade als solcher recht merkwürdig formuliert. Er hätte eher lauten müssen: ‚Und Saul wurde von einem bösen Geist geplagt, solange er lebte, und wenn Saul irgendeinen höflichen und saitenspielenden Mann sah, zog er ihn an sich.'" (65 f.). Wie ungezwungen dagegen 17,1: „Und die Philister sammelten ihre Heere zum Kampf ...‟! 2) 1Sam 17,12 ist die „einzig ordentliche Einführung Davids" (66), zumindest ist sie voraussetzungsloser als die vorangehenden.[94] 3) Hat man David und Saul literarisch verbunden (und geht nicht sogleich davon aus, eine Verbindung sei der Überlieferung historisch vorgegeben),[95] so liegt es näher, den Bereich der Philisterkriege zu wählen als den des Saitenspielers. In jedem Fall ist für die weitere Geschichte dieser Aspekt *notwendig* – und findet sich denn ja auch als Motiv in 1Sam 16,14–23. 4) 1Sam 16,14–23 lassen sich vorzüglich als Fortschreibung von V. 1–13 verstehen,[96] und 5) die Wortwahl des Abschnitts weist auf eine vergleichsweise späte Entstehungszeit ($b\bar{a}\,{}^{\varsigma}at$ pi.[97] neben $r\hat{u}^a\dot{h}$). Nicht zuletzt aber sind sehr wahrscheinlich in 1Sam 17 die Verbindungen zur vorangehenden Erzählung (Verse 12 und 15) nachgetragen. Unnachahmlich sagt Erik Aurelius: „Die Harmonisierungen mit Kap. 16 in 17,12 und 17,15 sind so eindeutig sekundär, daß sie geradezu unwiderlegbar das beweisen, was sie verhüllen sollen: daß Kap. 17 ursprünglich nichts von Kap. 16 voraussetzt, sondern David zum ersten Mal einführen will. Entweder hat Kap. 17 einmal für sich existiert, oder aber es ist im jetzigen Zusammenhang älter als Kap. 16.‟[98]

---

94 Das ist von den meisten Auslegern übersehen worden, bzw. muss die Einführung dann in die Vorgeschichte des Textes verlegt werden, was natürlich schon methodisch misslich ist.

95 Auch die historische Wahrscheinlichkeit spräche im vorliegenden Fall wohl eher für diese Möglichkeit. Welche andere Möglichkeit hätte jemand, eine Karriere am Königshof zu machen, wenn nicht die des militärischen Erfolgs? Nur indem der aufsteigende Krieger am Hof zufrieden ist, wird er dem Herrscher nicht gefährlich werden. Doch geht es den Erzählungen nicht um historische Plausibilität, sondern vielmehr, mit einer Wendung Uwe BECKERS gesagt, letztlich um theologisch produktive Rede „vom israelitischen Menschen und seinem Glaubensgrund" (BECKER ²2006: 95).

96 Das hat AURELIUS (2002: 66) gezeigt: in diesen Versen wird gezeigt, was die Geistübergabe an David für Saul bedeutete, und ein Grund für die Feindschaft zwischen Saul und David gegeben; bereits erwogen von KRATZ 2000: 183 f.

97 1Sam 16,14 f.; 2Sam 22,5 par. Ps 18,5; Jes 21,4; Hi 3,5; 7,14; 9,34; 13,11.21; 15,24; 18,11; 33,7, außerdem im *Nif̔al* Est 7,6; Dan 8,17; 1Chr 21,30. (Vgl. sonst nur noch $b^e{}^{\varsigma}\bar{a}t\bar{a}h$ Jer 8,15 par. 14,19.) Das Sprachargument ist freilich nur im Zusammenspiel mit den anderen genannten Hinweisen zulässig.

98 AURELIUS 2002: 61.

Das liegt nicht nur im Bereich des Möglichen, sondern Aurelius ist vollauf zuzustimmen. Auch wenn Kratz sich in der „Komposition" schlussendlich gegen 1Sam 17 und für die Mehrheit der Ausleger entscheidet, sei dennoch seine Beobachtung erwähnt: „In 17,1 ff ist David noch ein Knabe, wird als kriegstüchtiger Held entdeckt und kommt so an Sauls Hof. [... D]as paßt gut zu 14,52, und die Erzählung hat einen schönen Erzählanfang in 17,1 ff bzw. 17,12, wo David regelrecht eingeführt wird, und zwar so, als kennten ihn Saul und der Leser noch nicht."[99] Später, erstmals in der englischen Übersetzung der „Komposition" von 2005 angedeutet, hat sich Kratz denn auch zu dieser „alternative ... which is well worth considering"[100] bekehrt.

3 Die Kriege Davids und die Kriege JHWHs

Mit 1Sam 17 ist man freilich, wenn auch indirekt und vermutlich ohne es recht zu bemerken, bereits wieder im Bereich der Qumrantexte, und das heißt nicht zuletzt auch: ist der Verfasser in vertrauteren Gefilden angelangt. Zu den spätesten Ergänzungen in diesem Kapitel 1Sam 17 gehören bekanntlich die Verse, die das Geschehen zu einem JHWH-Krieg machen (u. a. V. 41–46.47), ja sich im „Zusatz im Zusatz" (Erik Aurelius) sogar bis zu einem „JHWHs ist der Krieg!" steigern können, ähnlich höchstens noch in 2Chr 20,15 formuliert „Nicht euer ist der Krieg, sondern Gottes!" Wer wollte bei einem solch spektakulären Gotteskrieg nicht an die Qumrangemeinschaft und ihre „Kriegsregel" 1QM denken. In Form einer gewaltigen Kriegsliturgie erzählt sie vom endzeitlichen Kampf gegen die Feinde Gottes, schließlich sogar zu einem Kampf der „Söhne des Lichts" gegen die „Söhne der Finsternis" in kosmischen Dimensionen stilisiert.[101]

1 כיא אם לכה המלחמה ובכוח ידכה רוטשו פגריהם לאין קובר ואת גולית הגתי איש גבור חיל
2 הסגרתהׄ ביד דויד עבדכה כיא בטח בשמכה הגדול ולוא בחרב וחנית כיא לכה המלחמה ואת
3 פלשתיים הכנ[י]עׄ פעמים רבות בשם קודשכה וגם ביד מלכינו הושעתנו פעמים רבות
4 בעבור רחמיכה ולוא כמעשינו אשר הרעונו ועלילות פשעינו לכה המלחמה ומאתכׄה הגבורה
5 ולוׄא לנו ... ...

„[1]Sondern *dein ist der Krieg!* Und durch die Kraft deiner Hand wurden ihre (scil. der Gegner) Leichname zerschmettert, so dass es kein Begraben (mehr) gab. *Gôljat*, den Gatiter,

---

99 KRATZ 2000: 184.
100 WELLHAUSEN 1963: 213 Anm. 36.
101 Diese Begrifflichkeiten dürften sich späterer redaktioneller Bearbeitung, wahrscheinlich in der Qumrangemeinschaft, verdanken; vgl. schon die Hinweise bei VON DER OSTEN-SACKEN 1961: 41–50 (vgl. ebd. 28–40).

den wehrhaften Kriegsmann, ²liefertest du aus in die Hand *Dāwîds*, deines Knechts; denn er vertraute auf deinen großen Namen und nicht auf Schwert noch Speer.
Ja, dein ist der Krieg! Und die ³Philister demü[tig]te er viele Male durch deinen heiligen Namen. Und auch durch unsere Könige hast du uns viele Male errettet, ⁴um deines Erbarmens willen, und nicht gemäß unseren Taten, wo wir böse waren, und unseren frevelhaften Werken.
Dein ist der Krieg, – und von dir her [kommt] die Stärke, – ⁵und nicht unser." (1QM XI,1–5a)

So schließt sich hier der Kreis: Wie eingangs in 4QMMT steht David wiederum als Vorbild im Zentrum der Aufmerksamkeit. Jene Könige Israels, die trotz ihrer Übertretungen (und denen der Mitglieder der Gemeinschaft) mit JHWHs Hilfe das Volk erretten konnten, sind diesem König also keineswegs nur zeitlich nachgeordnet. Im gerade zitierten priesterlichen Gebet während des Endkampfes dieser Welt steht das hymnische Lob Davids an zentraler Stelle, und auch damit knüpfen die Schriften aus Qumran wieder genau dort an, wo die spätesten Passagen der (fast vorliegenden) Hebräischen Bibel enden: am Ideal des – fast! – fehlerfreien Königs, des tapferen Kriegshelden – und letztlich wohl auch des Musikers David, des Verfassers und Sängers all der genannten Psalmen und Lieder. Man mag den Satz wagen, dass für *dieses* Bild ganz gleichgültig ist, ob David „zithert" oder „leiert". Mit anderen Worten: „Wir werden nie erfahren, ob David zur Leier gesungen oder zumindest gesummt hat", wie Dietrich zutreffend in seinem Kommentar anmerkt: Dieser, wenn man so sagen darf, „Negativanzeige" bleibt eigentlich nur hinzuzufügen: Ob die Zahl der Lieder Davids 4050 betrug, oder weniger, oder auch mehr – all das werden wir kaum je erfahren. Aber auch wenn es uns nicht mehr möglich ist, sichere Antworten zu geben, so kann man aus den *Fragen*, die sowohl die späterhin biblischen Texte als auch die Qumranschriften uns gleichsam *aus* der Wüste Judas heraus stellen, viel – nicht nur – über David – und ich füge wieder hinzu: nicht nur, aber vielleicht auch – über David *in* der Wüste lernen. Nicht zuletzt den Forschern, die sich je und je hier in Jena treffen und in Zukunft treffen werden, seien vielfältige und zahlreiche Einsichten und Erkenntnisse, sei ein gemeinsames Lernen gewünscht.

Illustrations

Abbildung 1: 11Q5 col. XXVII (detail), plate 974 (PAM 43.791; available at the Leon Levy Dead Sea Scrolls Digital Library, https://www.deadseascrolls.org.il/explore-the-archive/image/B-285202 [08.10. 2020]). Courtesy of The Leon Levy Dead Sea Scrolls Digital Library; Israel Antiquities Authority, Photo: Najib Anton Albina.

Bibliography

Auld, A. Graeme and Erik Eynikel, eds. 2010. *For and against David: Story and History in the Books of Samuel*. BETL 232. Leuven et al.: Peeters.

Aurelius, Erik. 2002. Wie David ursprünglich zu Saul kam (1 Sam 17). Pages 44–68 in *Vergegenwärtigung des Alten Testaments: Beiträge zur biblischen Hermeneutik: Festschrift für Rudolf Smend zum 70. Geburtstag*. Edited by Christoph Bultmann et al. Göttingen: Vandenhoeck & Ruprecht.

Becker, Uwe. ²2006. Das Exodus-Credo. Historischer Haftpunkt und Geschichte einer alttestamentlichen Glaubensformel. Pages 81–100 in *Das Alte Testament – ein Geschichtsbuch?! Geschichtsschreibung oder Geschichtsüberlieferung im antiken Israel*. ABIG 17. Edited by Uwe Becker and Jürgen van Oorschot. Leipzig: Evangelische Verlagsanstalt.

Beckwith, Roger T. 1982/84. The Courses of the Levites and the Eccentric Psalms Scrolls from Qumran. *RevQ* 11:499–521.

Bezzel, Hannes. 2015. *Saul: Israels König in Tradition, Redaktion und früher Rezeption*. FAT 97. Tübingen: Mohr Siebeck.

Bezzel, Hannes. 2016. Saul und die Philister: Redaktionskritische Überlegungen zu I Sam 13–14. Pages 459–68 in *The Books of Samuel: Stories – History – Reception History*. BETL 284. Edited by Walter Dietrich. Leuven: Peeters.

Böhm, Christiane. 2017. *Die Rezeption der Psalmen in den Qumranschriften, bei Philo von Alexandrien und im Corpus Paulinum*. WUNT II/437. Tübingen: Mohr Siebeck.

Brentano, Clemens. 1982. Ponce de Leon. Ein Lustspiel. Pages 345–636 in *Dramen I: Prosa zu den Dramen*. Edited by Hartwig Schultz. Vol. 12 of *Clemens Brentano: Sämtliche Werke und Briefe*. Edited by Jürgen Behrens et al. Stuttgart et al.: Kohlhammer.

Brownlee, William H. 1964/66. The Significance of 'David's Compositions.' *RevQ* 5/20:569–74.

Budde, Karl. 1890. *Die Bücher Richter und Samuel, ihre Quellen und ihr Aufbau*. Gießen: Ricker.

Budde, Karl. 1902. *Die Bücher Samuel*. KHC 8. Freiburg i. B.: Mohr.

Chyutin, Michael. 1993. מלחמת לוחות־השנה בתקופת בית שני: ועריכת מזמורי תהילים על־פי לוח־השנה [*Milḥæmæt lûḥôt ha-šānāh bi-tᵉqûfat Bayit Šēnî: Wā-ᶜᵃrîḳat mizmôrê Tᵉhîllîm ᶜal-pî lûᵃḥ-ha-šānāh. = The War of the Calendars in the Period of the Second Temple and the Redaction of the Psalms According to the Calendar*.] Tel Aviv: Modan.

Chyutin, Michael. 1994. The Redaction of the Qumranic and the Traditional Book of Psalms as Calendar. *RevQ* 63:367–95.

Cooper, Alan M. 1983. The Life and Times of King David According to the Book of Psalms. Pages 117–31 in *The Poet and the Historian: Essays in Literary and Historical Biblical Criticism*. Edited by Richard Elliott Friedman. HSS 26. Chico, CA: Scholars Press.

Dahmen, Ulrich. 2003. Psalmen-Psalter-Rezeption im Frühjudentum: Rekonstruktion, Textbestand, Struktur und Pragmatik der Psalmenrolle 11QPsᵃ aus Qumran. *Studies on the Texts of the Desert of Judah* 49. Leiden / Boston: Brill.

Dietrich, Walter. 1997. *Die frühe Königszeit in Israel: 10. Jahrhundert v. Chr.* Biblische Enzyklopädie 3. Stuttgart *et al.*: Kohlhammer.

Dietrich, Walter. 2015. *Samuel (1Sam 13–26)*. BKAT 8/2. Neukirchen-Vluyn: Neukirchener Theologie.

Dietrich, Walter, and Hubert Herkommer, eds. 2003. *König David – Biblische Schlüsselfigur und europäische Leitgestalt*. Freiburg, CH / Stuttgart: Universitäts-Verlag / Kohlhammer.

Evans, Craig A. 1997. David in the Dead Sea Scrolls. Pages 182–97 in *The Scrolls and the Scriptures: Qumran Fifty Years After*. Edited by Stanley E. Porter and Craig A. Evans. SJSP 26. Sheffield: Academic Press.

Fischer, Alexander A. 2009. „David (AT)." *Das Wissenschaftliche Bibellexikon im Internet* (www.wibilex.de). (https://www.bibelwissenschaft.de/de/stichwort/16233/, April 2019).

Flint, Peter W. 1997. *The Dead Sea Psalms Scrolls and the Book of Psalms*. Leiden: Brill.

Flint, Peter W. 2000. David. Pages 178–80 in *Encyclopedia of the Dead Sea Scrolls*. Edited by Lawrence H. Schiffman and James C. VanderKam. Vol. 1 of *Encyclopedia of the Dead Sea Scrolls*. Edited by Lawrence H. Schiffman and James C. VanderKam. 2 Vols. Oxford: Oxford University Press.

Flint, Peter W. 2005. The Prophet David at Qumran. Pages 158–67 in *Biblical Interpretation at Qumran*. Edited by Mathias Henze. Grand Rapids: Eerdmans.

Goshen-Gottstein, Moshe H. 1966. The Psalms Scroll (11QPsª): A Problem of Canon and Text. *Textus* 5:22–33.

Heinrich, André. 2009. *David und Klio: Historiographische Elemente in der Aufstiegsgeschichte Davids und im Alten Testament*. BZAW 401. Berlin: De Gruyter.

Hentschel, Georg. 1994a. *1. Samuel*. NEB 33.Würzburg: Echter-Verlag.

Hentschel, Georg. 1994b. *2. Samuel*. Volume 34 of *Neue Echter-Bibel*. Ed. by Josef G. Plöger et al., Würzburg: Echter-Verlag.

Hentschel, Georg. 2003. *Saul: Schuld, Reue und Tragik eines Gesalbten*. Biblische Gestalten 7. Leipzig: Evangelische Verlagsanstalt.

Hentschel, Georg. 2010. Die Verantwortung für den Mord an den Priestern von Nob. Pages 185–99 in *For and against David: Story and History in the Books of Samuel*. Edited by A. Graeme Auld and Erik Eynikel. BETL 232. Leuven: Peeters.

Hutton, Jeremy. 2009. *The Transjordanian Palimpsest: The Overwritten Texts of Personal Exile and Transformation in the Deuteronomistic History*. BZAW 396. Berlin: de Gruyter.

Jain, Eva. 2014. *Psalmen oder Psalter? Materielle Rekonstruktion und inhaltliche Untersuchung der Psalmenhandschriften aus der Wüste Juda*. STDJ 109. Leiden: Brill.

Kipfer, Sara. 2015. *Der bedrohte David: Eine exegetische und rezeptionsgeschichtliche Studie zu 1Sam 16–1Kön 2*. SBR 3. Berlin: de Gruyter.

Kleer, Martin. 1996. *Der liebliche Sänger der Psalmen Israels: Untersuchungen zu David als Dichter und Beter der Psalmen*. BBB 108. Göttingen: Vandenhoeck & Ruprecht.

Ritter von Köchel, Ludwig. ⁸1983 (reprint 1999). *Chronologisch-thematisches Verzeichnis sämtlicher Tonwerke Wolfgang Amadé Mozarts nebst Angabe der verlorengegangenen, angefangenen, von fremder Hand bearbeiteten, zweifelhaften und unterschobenen Kompositionen*. Edited by Franz Giegling. Wiesbaden: Breitkopf und Härtel.

Kratz, Reinhard G. 2000. *Die Komposition der erzählenden Bücher des Alten Testaments: Grundwissen der Bibelkritik*. Göttingen: Vandenhoeck & Ruprecht.

Kratz, Reinhard G. 2005. *The Composition of the Narrative Books of the Old Testament*. Transl. by John Bowden. Translation of Reinhard G. Kratz „Komposition." London / New York, NY: T&T Clark International.

Kratz, Reinhard G. 2006. Mose und die Propheten. Zur Interpretation von 4QMMT C. Pages 151–76 in *From 4QMMT to Resurrection: Mélanges qumraniens en hommage à Émile Puech*. Edited by F. García Martínez et al. STDJ 61. Leiden: Brill.

Kugel, James L. 1990. David the Prophet. Pages 45–55 in *Poetry and Prophecy: The Beginnings of a Literary Tradition*. Edited by James L. Kugel. Ithaca: Cornell University Press.

Lohse, Eduard. ²1971. *Die Texte aus Qumran: Hebräisch und Deutsch. Mit masoretischer Punktation, Übersetzung, Einführung und Anmerkungen.* Darmstadt: Wissenschaftliche Buchgesellschaft.

Mays, James L. 1986. The David of the Psalms. *Interpretation* 40:143–55.

Müller, Reinhard. 2004. *Königtum und Gottesherrschaft: Untersuchungen zur alttestamentlichen Monarchiekritik.* FAT II/3. Tübingen: Mohr Siebeck.

Müller, Reinhard. 2018. Saul, the Charismatic King: Concepts of Political Leadership in 1 Sam 11. Pages 262–87 in *Debating Authority: Concepts of Leadership in the Pentateuch and the Former Prophets.* Edited by Katharina Pyschny and Sarah Schulz. BZAW 507. Berlin / New York: de Gruyter.

Nitzan, Bilha. 1994. *Qumran Prayer and Religious Poetry.* STDJ 12. Translation by Jonathan Chipman. Leiden: Brill.

von der Osten-Sacken, Peter. 1961. *Gott und Belial: Traditionsgeschichtliche Untersuchungen zum Dualismus in den Texten aus Qumran.* StUNT 6. Göttingen: Vandenhoeck & Ruprecht.

Pomykala, Kenneth E. 2003. Images of David in Early Judaism. Pages 33–46 in *Of Scribes and Sages, Vol. 1: Early Jewish Interpretation and Transmission of Scripture.* Edited by Craig A. Evans. London: T&T Clark International.

Porzig, Peter. 2009. The Ark of the Covenant in the Non-Biblical Texts from Qumran. Pages 203–18 in *The Dynamics of Language and Exegesis at Qumran.* FAT II/35. Tübingen: Mohr Siebeck.

Porzig, Peter, with Géza G. Xeravits. 2015. *Einführung in die Qumranliteratur: Die Handschriften vom Toten Meer.* De Gruyter Studium. Berlin / Boston, MA: de Gruyter.

Qimron, Elisha, and John Strugnell. 1994. *Qumran Cave 4. V: Miqṣat Maʿaśe ha-Torah. DJD 10.* Oxford: Clarendon Press.

Ramantswana, Hulisana. 2011. David of the Psalters. MT Psalter, LXX Psalter and 11QPsª Psalter. *OTE* 24:431–63.

Rendtorff, Rolf. 2005. The Psalms of David: David in the Psalms. Pages 53–64 in *The Book of Psalms: Composition and Reception.* Edited by Peter W. Flint and Patrick D. Miller. VT.S 99.Edited by Christl M. Maier. Leiden: Brill.

Rudnig, Thilo A. 2010. 'Außer in der Sache mit Uria, dem Hethiter' (I Reg 15,5). Jahwes und Davids Gerechtigkeit in II Sam 10–12. Pages 273–92 in *For and against David: Story and History in the Books of Samuel.* Edited by A. Graeme Auld and Erik Eynikel. BETL 232. Leuven: Peeters.

Sanders, James A. 1963. Ps 151 in 11QPss. *ZAW* 76:73–85.

Sanders, James A. 1964. Two Noncanonical Psalms in 11QPsª. *ZAW* 76:57–75.

Sanders, James A. 1965. *The Psalms Scroll of Qumran Cave 11 (11QPsª). DJD 4.* Oxford: Clarendon.

Sanders, James A. 1966. Variorum in the Psalms Scrolls (11QPsª). *HTR* 59:83–94.

Sanders, James A. 1967. *The Dead Sea Psalms Scroll.* Ithaca: Cornell University Press.

Sanders, James A. 1967/8. Cave 11 Surprises and the Question of Canon. *McCormick Quarterly* 21:284–98. Reprint 1969: Pages 101–16 in *New Directions in Biblical Archaeology.* Edited by Daniel N. Freedman and Jonas C. Greenfield. Garden City: Doubleday.

Sanders, James A. 1973. The Dead Sea Scrolls – A Quarter Century Study. *BA* 36:110–48.

Sarna, Nahum M. 1979. The Psalm Superscriptions and the Guilds. Pages 281–300 in *Studies in Jewish Religious and Intellectual History.* Edited by Siegfried Stein and Raphael Loewe. London: The University of Alabama Press.

Seybold, Klaus. 2003. David als Psalmensänger in der Bibel. Entstehung einer Symbolfigur. Pages 145–63 in *König David – biblische Schlüsselfigur und europäische Leitgestalt.* Edited by Walter Dietrich and Hubert Herkommer. Freiburg, CH / Stuttgart: Universitätsverlag / Kohlhammer.

Skehan, Patrick W. 1957. The Qumran Manuscripts and Textual Criticism. Pages 148–58 in *Volume du Congrès Strasbourg 1956.* SVT 4. Edited by the Organisation Internationale pour l'Étude de l'Ancien Testament. Leiden: Brill.

Skehan, Patrick W. 1967/8. The Scrolls and the Old Testament. *McCormick Quarterly* 21:273–83.

Skehan, Patrick W. 1973. A Liturgical Complex in 11QPs[a]. *CBQ* 35:195–205.

Skehan, Patrick W. 1986. The Qumran Psalms Scroll (11QPs[a]) and the Canonical Psalter. *JSOT* 35:85–94.

Talmon, Shemaryahu. 1966. Hebrew Apocryphal Psalms from Qumrân. *Tarbiz* 35:214–34.

Talmon, Shemaryahu. 1966. Pisqah Be'emṣa' Pasuq and 11QPs[a]. *Textus* 5:11–21.

VanderKam, James C. 1999. Studies on 'David's Compositions.' *Eretz Israel* 26:212–20.

Wacholder, Ben Zion. 1988. David's Eschatological Psalter: 11QPsalms[a]. *HUCA* 59:23–72.

Wellhausen, Julius. 1963. *Die Composition des Hexateuchs und der historischen Bücher des Alten Testaments.* Reprint. Berlin: de Gruyter (= Berlin: Reimer, 1899).

Wellhausen, Julius. 2001. *Prolegomena zur Geschichte Israels.* Reprint. Berlin: de Gruyter, (= Berlin: Reimer, [6]1905).

Wellhausen, Julius. [10]2004. *Israelitische und jüdische Geschichte.* De Gruyter Studienbuch. Berlin: de Gruyter, (= Berlin: Reimer, [7]1914).

Wellhausen, Julius. 2013. *Briefe.* Edited by Rudolf Smend. Tübingen: Mohr Siebeck.

Wilson, Gerald H. 1985a. Qumran Psalms Scroll Reconsidered: Analysis of the Debate. *CBQ* 47:624–42.

Wilson, Gerald H. 1985b. *The Editing of the Hebrew Psalter.* SBLDS 76. Chico: Scholars Press.

Xeravits, Géza G. 2003. *King, Priest, Prophet: Positive Eschatological Protagonists of the Qumran Library.* STDJ 47. Leiden: Brill.

Xeravits, Géza G., with Peter Porzig. 2015. *Einführung in die Qumranliteratur: Die Handschriften vom Toten Meer.* De Gruyter Studium. Berlin / Boston, MA: de Gruyter.

Omer Sergi
Saul, David und die Entstehung der Monarchie in Israel

Neubewertung des historischen und literarischen Kontexts von 1Sam 9–2Sam 5

1 Einführung

Die Überlieferungen über die Entstehung der israelitischen Monarchie, die in 1Sam 9–2Sam 5 verankert sind, berichten von Saul, dem ersten König der Israeliten, der es nicht vermochte, eine Monarchie mit dynastischer Erbfolge aufzubauen. Sein Rivale David, der genau darin Erfolg hatte, folgte auf ihn: David errichtete eine lange während Dynastie und übte seine Herrschaft über Israeliten und Judäer aus. Trotz der Tatsache, dass die Handlung in 1Sam 9–2Sam 5 durch eine ziemlich kohärente Erzählung gekennzeichnet ist – zumindest in ihrem Thema und ihrer Handlung –, versehen mit vielen Verknüpfungen, die die verschiedenen darin eingebetteten Berichte miteinander verbinden,[1] wird in der gegenwärtigen Forschung oft davon ausgegangen, dass diese Traditionen aus zwei unterschiedlichen Quellen stammten, welche jeweils unterschiedlichen Ursprungs seien: Nordisraelitische Traditionen über Saul (in der Regel in 1Sam 9–14 aufgeführt), die über Aufstieg und Fall des ersten israelitischen Königs berichten; und eine aus Juda stammende Sammlung von Geschichten über Davids Aufstieg, die David als legitimen Nachfolger Sauls darstellt (1Sam 16–2Sam 5). Man geht davon aus, dass die nordisraelitischen Überlieferungen über Saul erst nach dem Fall Samarias (720 v.d.Z.) nach Juda kamen und die Komposition der Geschichten über Davids Aufstieg anregten und dementsprechend auf das 7. Jh. v.d.Z. zu datieren sind. Es wird ferner angenommen, dass die Geschichten über Davids Aufstieg die erste literarische Verbindung zwischen Saul, dem Israeliten, und David, dem Judäer, schaffen,

---

1 DIETRICH / NAUMANN 2000: 276–318.

Anmerkung: Hierbei handelt es sich um die überarbeitete und aktualisierte Fassung des nachfolgend zitierten Artikels: Sergi, Omer, Erzählung, Geschichten und Geschichte in den biblischen Überlieferungen von der Entstehung der israelitischen Monarchie (1 Sam 9–2 Sam 5), in: Fischer / Claassens (eds.), Prophetie (Die Bibel und die Frauen. Eine exegetisch-kulturgeschichtliche Enzyklopädie), Stuttgart 2019: 19–43. Ich danke Dr. André Zempelburg, Jena, für die Übersetzung ins Deutsche.

https://doi.org/10.1515/9783110606164-003

und zwar um Juda als politischen und kulturellen Nachfolger des ehemaligen Königreichs Israel zu präsentieren.[2] Oder, anders ausgedrückt, es wird die These vertreten, dass die Erzählungen über Davids Aufstieg zwei ehemals unabhängige literarische Protagonisten – den ersten König Israels, Saul, sowie den ersten König von Juda, David – miteinander verbinden, nämlich um das Haus Davids, d. h. Juda, als legitimen Nachfolger des Hauses Sauls, d. h. Israel, zu präsentieren.

Im Zentrum dieser Hypothese steht die Annahme, dass die Erzählungen über Davids Aufstieg in 1Sam 16–2Sam 5 tatsächlich so etwas wie Allegorien auf die Geschichte Israels und Judas sind. Diese Annahme ist jedoch das Ergebnis einer historischen und nicht einer literarischen Beobachtung: Historisch gesehen ist es ziemlich klar, dass die Königreiche Israel und Juda unter der Herrschaft des Jerusalemer Hauses Davids niemals zu einer politischen Einheit vereinigt wurden.[3] Es wird daher angenommen, dass jede Darstellung des ersten Königs von Juda als Erben des ersten Königs von Israel nur ein judäisches „Wunschdenken" und keine genaue politische Realität widerspiegeln könnte. Das Hauptproblem bei dieser Annahme ist jedoch die Tatsache, dass sowohl die frühen Überlieferungen über Saul als auch die Erzählungen über Davids Aufstieg gut in die sozialen und politischen Gegebenheiten im südlichen Kanaan der frühen Eisenzeit eingebettet sind – deshalb gibt es keinen guten Grund dafür, sie quasi-allegorisch zu lesen. Vielmehr sollten wir zumindest versuchen sie als das zu lesen, was sie sind, nämlich ein Versuch, den Aufstieg der israelitischen Monarchie darzustellen.

Die folgende Studie zielt darauf ab, genau das zu tun, und zwar die biblischen Überlieferungen, die in 1Sam 9–2Sam 5 eingebaut sind, im Lichte ihrer historischen Kontexte (d. h. der gesellschaftspolitischen Realität) zu lesen, die sie widerspiegeln, und letztlich ihre Herkunft sowie ihre historische Bedeutung zu erörtern. Zu diesem Zweck beginne ich mit einem kurzen Überblick über die archäologischen und historischen Daten, die die Entstehung Israels und Judas als südlevantinische Flächenstaaten erhellen.

---

2 Bspw. DIETRICH / MÜNGER 2003: 39–54; KRATZ 2005: 181–82; FINKELSTEIN 2006: 171–88; DERS. 2011: 348–67; DIETRICH 2007: 247–48, 304–8; KAISER 2010: 520–45 (hier 524–26); WRIGHT 2014: 39–50, 141–46; BEZZEL 2015: 228–34; s. NAʾAMAN 2009: 211–24, 335–49, welcher diese Auffassung bereits in Frage gestellt hat.

3 Bspw. FINKELSTEIN 2010: 3–28. Zur Entstehung des Staates Juda, s.: SERGI 2013: 226–46; DERS. 2017: 1–23, und im Folgenden.

2 Die Entstehung Israels und Judas im zentralkanaanäischen Hügelland: Archäologische und historische Perspektiven

Während der EZ I (Ende des 12. bis Anfang des 10. Jh. v.d.Z.)[4] erfuhr das zentralkanaanäische Hochland eine Phase umfangreicher Sesshaftwerdung, als lokale, mobile, auf dem Land ansässige Gruppen von der Subsistenzwirtschaft, die hauptsächlich auf Tierhaltung beruhte, zu einer agrar-ländlichen Lebensweise übergingen. Dementsprechend waren die Siedler in der EZ I im Hügelland die einheimische pastoral-nomadische Bevölkerung der Berge von Samaria und Judäa. Und wenn dem so ist, kannten sie nicht nur die Gebiete gut, in denen sie sich niederließen, sondern sie waren auch ein wesentlicher Bestandteil der sozialen Struktur des Hochlands.[5] Die meisten der neu gegründeten Siedlungen ballten sich in den Bergen von Samaria zwischen dem Jesreelebene und Schilo.[6]

Das hügelige Gelände südlich von Schilo bis nach Bethel (ca. 20 km südlich von Schilo) war während der EZ I nur spärlich besiedelt, und noch weniger in der EZ IIA. Die nächste Ansammlung von Siedlungen verdichtete sich auf dem Benjamin-Plateau zwischen dem nördlich gelegenen Bethel und dem südlich gelegenen Jerusalem.[7] Bemerkenswert ist die Tatsache, dass die Ausdehnung der Siedlungen in der hügeligen Umgebung Sichems und Schilos eine klare räumliche Kontinuität zwischen den Hügeln Samarias im Norden und Süden aufweist, während südlich von Schilo oder südlich von Jerusalem eine solche klare Kontinuität nicht besteht. Dadurch bleibt die südliche Ansammlung von Siedlungen auf dem Benjamin-Plateau eher isoliert.

Das wichtigste politische und wirtschaftliche Zentrum auf den Hügeln von Samaria während des gesamten zweiten Jahrtausends v.d.Z. war Sichem (Tell Balâṭah), was sowohl aus Textquellen (ägyptische Verfluchungstexte, El-Amarna-Archiv) als auch aus archäologischen Überresten hervorgeht. Seit der MBZ II–III und bis zur EZ I (mit einer kurzen Pause in der SBZ I) war Sichem

---

4 Zum gegenwärtigen Stand der Forschung zur absoluten Chronologie der frühen EZ, beruhend auf einer Vielzahl von C14-Datierungen, vgl. LEE / BRONK RAMSEY / MAZAR 2013: 731–40. TOFFOLO / ARIE / MARTIN / BOARETTO / FINKELSTEIN 2014: 221–44.
5 Vgl. dazu z. B. FINKELSTEIN 1988; DERS. 1995: 349–65; DERS. 1996: 198–212; ROSEN 1993: 362–67, und zu Transjordanien, VAN DER STEEN 2004; PORTER 2013.
6 FINKELSTEIN 1995: 349–65; ZERTAL 2004; DERS. 2008; ZERTAL / MIRKAM 2016; GADOT 2017: 103–14.
7 FINKELSTEIN 1988: 188–92, 198–99, 201–2; FINKELSTEIN / LEDERMAN, 1997: 949–51; SERGI 2017: 5–12.

eine gut befestigte Hochlandfestung mit Heiligtümern, die auf ihrem Gipfel errichtet wurden.[8] Sichem zeigt eine klare und organische Kontinuität im Über-
gang von der SBZ zu EZ I auf.[9] Am Ende dieser Periode, nämlich im frühen
10. Jh. v.d.Z., wurde es jedoch vollkommen zerstört.[10] Während des größten Teils
der EZ IIA (10.–9. Jh. v.d.Z.) war Sichem nur spärlich besiedelt,[11] und in dieser
Zeit verlagerte sich die politische und wirtschaftliche Bedeutung zunächst nach
Tell el-Far'ah im Norden, welches mit dem biblischen Tirza identifiziert wird,[12]
und später nach Samaria.

Ende des 10. oder Anfang des 9. Jh. v.d.Z. entwickelte sich Tirza rasch von
einer eher armen Siedlung (Stratum VIIa) zu einem reichen städtischen Zentrum
mit sozialer Hierarchie, kultischen Handlungen sowie Fernhandel (Stratum
VIIb). Sie wurde kurz darauf, wahrscheinlich noch in der ersten Hälfte des 9. Jh.
v.d.Z., vollständig zerstört und während des 9. Jh. v.d.Z. aufgegeben.[13] Im frühen
9. Jh., nach Tirzas Zerstörung, verlagerten sich die Machtverhältnisse zurück in
das Kernland Samarias, wo auf einem ehemaligen landwirtschaftlichen Anwesen, welches keine städtebauliche oder monumentalbauliche Tradition aufwies,
ein aufwendiger Palastkomplex erbaut wurde.[14] Es manifestiert sich hier die
Anhäufung von Reichtum und folglich auch von politischer Macht in den Händen einer neu entstandenen Elite – der Dynastie der Omriden –, mit der allein
der Palast auf dem Hügel Samarias in Verbindung gebracht werden kann (1Kön
16,24).[15] Nimmt man an, dass das reiche landwirtschaftliche Anwesen vor der
Errichtung des Palastes der Omriden in Samaria das Anwesen der Familie gewe-

---

8 Campbell 2002; Finkelstein 2006: 349–56.

9 Campbell 2002: 210–33; Finkelstein 2006: 352.

10 Die Ausgräber datierten die Zerstörung auf das 12. Jh. v.d.Z. (Campbell 2002: 230–33), aber
in der publizierten kleinen Sammlung der EZ I befinden sich auch Gefäße, die gegen das Ende
der EZ I zu datieren sind (vgl. Finkelstein 2006: 352).

11 Das veröffentlichte Material (Campbell 2002: 235–70) lässt keinen Schluss darüber zu,
wann genau in der Eisenzeit Sichem wieder florierte – ob in der späten EZ IIA oder später in
der frühen EZ IIB. In beiden Fällen scheint es, dass Sichem während des größten Teils des
10. Jh. und wahrscheinlich bis ins 9. Jh. hinein kein Hauptakteur in der Region war.

12 Albright 1931: 241–51.

13 Zur aktuellen Bewertung der stratigraphischen und chronologischen Aufeinanderfolge in
Tell el-Far'ah, vgl. Kleiman 2018: 85–104.

14 Zur aktuellen Diskussion über die Stratigraphie der Palastanlage in Samaria, vgl. Sergi /
Gadot 2017: 103–11, hier 105–6, mit weiterer Literatur.

15 Vgl. z. B. Finkelstein 2000: 114–38; ders. 2013: 85–94; Niemann 2006: 821–42; ders. 2007:
184–207.

sen sei,[16] dann spiegelt es den Reichtum wider, den die Omriden bereits ansammelten, bevor sie an die Macht kamen.[17]

Im frühen 9. Jh. v.d.Z. erweiterten die Omriden ihre politische Vormachtstellung von ihrem Sitz im Kernland Samarias aus auf weite Gebiete, in denen verschiedene soziale Gruppen lebten – dies geht ebenso aus biblischen wie außerbiblischen Quellen hervor.[18] Die Ausweitung der politischen Hegemonie der Omriden war in der Landschaft durch die Errichtung von königlichen Bauten am westlichen (Megiddo VA–IVB) und östlichen (Jesreel) Rand der Jesreelebene gekennzeichnet. Im Hulah-Tal (Hazor X–IX) wurde eine neue befestigte Stadt auf den Ruinen der ehemaligen königlichen Hauptstadt errichtet, die im zweiten Jahrtausend v.d.Z. eine der stärksten Stadtstaaten Kanaans gewesen war. Alle diese Gebäude bekundeten die Macht und den Reichtum der Dynastie des Hochlands und dienten als Schauplatz für die Integration lokaler Eliten in das Netz der neu begründeten omridischen Hegemonie.[19] Die Omriden dehnten ihre Herrschaft auch auf die trockeneren und weniger bewohnbaren Gebiete des moabitischen Flachlands aus, indem sie Patronatsbeziehungen zu lokalen Führern pastoralnomadischer Gruppen aufbauten (vgl. 2Kön 3,4) und Festungen an den wesentlichen Handelsrouten errichteten, welche die Region durchquerten.[20]

Die dramatischen Veränderungen im Machtgefüge, welche die EZ I–IIA in den Bergen Samarias (von Sichem nach Tirza und nach Samaria) charakterisieren, wirkten sich kaum oder gar nicht auf die politische Entwicklung im Süden um Jerusalem aus. Jerusalem war bereits im zweiten Jahrtausend v.d.Z. der Sitz der einheimischen herrschenden Elite gewesen.[21] Und doch tritt monumentale Architektur in der Davidsstadt – zum ersten Mal seit der mittleren Bronzezeit – erst in der frühen Eisenzeit auf, und zwar mit der Errichtung der „stepped stone structure" an den Osthängen der Davidsstadt (the eastern ridge of Jerusalem). Man ist sich nahezu einig, dass das Fundament für dieses Bauwerk nicht vor Mitte bis Ende der EZ I gelegt wurde, und zwar, genauer, im späten 11. oder Anfang des 10. Jh. v.d.Z.[22] Als Hochlandfestung und als Sitz der örtlichen herr-

---

16 Zu den archäologischen Überresten des landwirtschaftlichen Anwesens, das dem Bau des Palastes in Samaria (Building Period 0) vorausgeht, vgl. STAGER 1990: 93–107; FRANKLIN 2004: 189–202, hier 190–94.

17 Vgl. SERGI / GADOT 2017: 109.

18 Vgl. NIEMANN 2006: 821–42; NA'AMAN 2007: 399–418; FINKELSTEIN 2011: 227–42; FINKELSTEIN 2013: 83–112.

19 Vgl. NIEMANN 2006: 821–42; SERGI / GADOT 2017: 108–10.

20 Vgl. FINKELSTEIN / LIPSCHITS 2010: 29–42.

21 Vgl. NA'AMAN 1992: 257–91.

22 Ein collared rim jar, der in situ auf dem Boden einer Struktur gefunden wurde, die unmittelbar unter der Steinterrasse der Steinstufenkonstruktion vergraben wurde, sowie Tonscherben, die aus den Steinterrassen selbst geborgen wurden, datieren seinen Bau in die späte EZ

schenden Elite wird dieses Bauwerk durch die Steinstufenkonstruktion, die in der ländlichen Umgebung Jerusalems heraussticht, gekennzeichnet. Es hat daher den Anschein, dass im Jerusalem des späten 11. oder im frühen 10. Jh. v.d.Z. eine zentralisierte politische Herrschaft mit einer sich entwickelnden, hierarchisch aufgebauten sozialen Struktur begründet wurde. Um diesen sozialen Wandel zu erklären, muss der Blick von Jerusalem auf die Umgebung verlagert werden.

In der Zeit zwischen dem 14. und dem 12. Jh. v.d.Z. herrschte Jerusalem über ein eher karges Land, das hauptsächlich von pastoralen Nomaden bewohnt wurde, während es im Süden einige ortsgebundene Siedlungen gab.[23] Das 11. Jh. v.d.Z. ist durch eine gewaltige Sesshaftwerdung gekennzeichnet: Zum ersten Mal seit der Mittelbronzezeit wurden Siedlungen nördlich von Jerusalem auf dem Benjaminplateau gegründet – im Süden hingegen stieg ihre Zahl nicht wesentlich an.[24] Wenn folglich die stepped stone structure die Errichtung politischer Macht widerspiegelt, dann sollte sie hauptsächlich dazu dienen, den Siedlern nördlich von Jerusalem politische Autorität aufzuzwingen. Diese waren die einzigen Einwohner, die die Könige Jerusalems mit den erforderlichen (personellen und finanziellen) Ressourcen versorgen sowie politisch motivieren konnten, um jene zu errichten.

Es wurde bereits dargelegt, dass die Ansammlung von Siedlungen nördlich von Jerusalem in der EZ I–IIA eher isoliert waren, während die Regionen nördlich von Bethel und südlich von Jerusalem weniger dicht besiedelt waren. Das am südlichen Ende dieser Ansammlung gelegene Jerusalem war seit dem zweiten Jahrtausend der Sitz lokaler Herrscher, und im späten 11. oder frühen 10. Jh. v.d.Z. unterschied sich Jerusalem von den ländlichen Siedlungen in seiner Umgebung durch die „stepped stone structure". Angesichts des Fehlens einer territorialen Verbindung und angesichts des langjährigen politischen Status Jerusalems ist es daher schwer zu glauben, dass Sichem seine politi-

---

I oder in die sehr frühe EZ IIA, vgl. STEINER 2001: 24–8, Abb. 4.3–4.6, 29–36, Abb. 4.16; CAHILL 2003: 13–80, insb. 46–51; MAZAR 2006: 255–72; DERS. 2010: 29–58, bzgl. Jerusalem ebd., 34–49. In seinem jüngsten Beitrag zur Frage ignoriert Finkelstein völlig den collared rim jar und die erwähnten Scherben aus den Terrassen, vgl. FINKELSTEIN 2018: 190–95. Zur letzten und auf den neuesten Stand gebrachten Erörterung der Steinstufenkonstruktion, ihrer Erbauung und Datierung, vgl. SERGI 2017: 2–5.

23 Bzgl. der Region nördlich von Jerusalem vgl. FINKELSTEIN 1993: 110–31, hier 116–23. Bzgl. der Region südlich von Jerusalem vgl. die Zusammenfassung in SERGI 2017: 5–8, mit weiterer Literatur.

24 Zur aktuellen Diskussion der archäologischen Zeugnisse aus Benjamin in der EZ I–IIA, beruhend auf sowohl Ausgrabungen als auch Surveys, vgl. SERGI 2017: 8–12, mit weiterer Literatur.

sche Vormachtstellung über ländliche Siedlungen, die sich etwa 30 bis 40 km südlich befinden, hätte aufbauen können (wie dies von Finkelstein vorgeschlagen wurde),[25] insbesondere da Jerusalems politischer Status mit der Errichtung der stepped stone structure bekräftigt wurde. Darüberhinaus gab es in der frühen EZ IIA und nach der Zerstörung von Schilo und Sichem kein urbanes Zentrum im zentralkanaanäischen Hügelland nördlich von Jerusalem. Als mit Tirza und Samaria (und erst in der späten EZ IIA) neue städtische Zentren entstanden, geschah dies, wie oben dargelegt, im Kontext der Ereignisse im Norden, in Nordsamaria und in der Jesreel- und Beth Schean-Ebene. Von daher sollte eigentlich wenig Zweifel daran bestehen, dass die Siedlungen in Benjamin weit eher mit dem aufstrebenden Zentrum in ihrer Nachbarschaft in Beziehung standen – nämlich Jerusalem – als mit den Städten im Norden.

Es sollte daher der Schluss gezogen werden, dass das Benjaminplateau zu Beginn des 10. Jh. v.d.Z. politisch mit Jerusalem verbunden war, dessen politische Vorherrschaft sich wahrscheinlich zwischen Bethlehem / Beth-Zur im Süden und Bethel im Norden ausdehnte. Die Errichtung der stepped stone structure kennzeichnet daher das frühe Entstehen einer von Jerusalem aus regierten staatlichen Struktur, und Benjamin war offensichtlich von Anfang an Teil dieses Gemeinwesens. Während der gesamten EZ IIA wuchs die Macht und Stärke Jerusalems stetig an,[26] was sich in der Anhäufung von wirtschaftlichem Wohlstand und folglich politischem Einfluss in den Händen seiner herrschenden Dynastie widerspiegelt – des Hauses David. Erst nach dem Fall der Dynastie der Omriden in der zweiten Hälfte des 9. Jh. v.d.Z. konnten die Könige der davidischen Dynastie ihre Hegemonie von den judäischen Hügeln bis in die judäischen Niederungen im Westen und in die Täler Beerschebas und Arads im Süden ausdehnen.[27] Zu beachten ist außerdem der Unterschied zwischen den politischen Entwicklungen in den Hügeln von Samaria und denen in der Region Jerusalem-Benjamin: Während sich die Machtverhältnisse im Norden verschoben, kulminierend in territorialer Ausweitung und in der Bildung eines von den Omriden regierten politischen Gemeinwesens – nämlich des Königreiches Israel –, erlebte der Süden einen eher organischen Prozess von Machtzentralisierung in den Händen der herrschenden Elite Jerusalems, der wiederum zur Bildung des vom Haus David regierten territorial-politischen Staates führte – des Königreiches Juda. Während dieser Zeit war das Hochland zwischen Bethel (und später Mizpa) im Süden und Schilo (und sogar Sichem) im Norden frei von jeglichem poli-

---

25 Vgl. Finkelstein 2006: 171–88; ders. 2011: 348–67.
26 Vgl. Uziel / Szanton 2015: 233–50; ders. 2017: 429–39; Uziel / Gadot 2017: 123–40.
27 Vgl. u. a. Maier / Hitchcock / Horwitz 2013: 1–38, hier 26–38; Sergi 2013: 226–46; Lehmann / Niemann 2014: 77–94.

tischen Zentrum,[28] und daher ist es schwer vorstellbar, dass die politischen Entwicklungen im Norden irgendeinen Einfluss auf die Machtzentralisation im Süden hatten. Es ist daher offensichtlich, dass sich Israel und Juda während des gesamten 10. und 9. Jh. v.d.Z. zwar parallel, aber getrennt voneinander entwickelten. Die politische Entwicklung Israels war geprägt von Kämpfen und sich verändernden politischen Allianzen, während diejenige Judas von einer Machtzentralisierung durch Davididen in Jerusalem bestimmt wurde. Vor diesem Hintergrund soll nun das Buch Samuel in Bezug auf die Entstehung der frühen israelitischen Monarchie untersucht werden.

3 Die frühen Überlieferungen über Saul in 1Sam 9–14; 31

Die frühesten Überlieferungen über Saul werden üblicherweise im Großteil des Materials identifiziert, das in 1Sam 9,1–10,16; 11; 13–14; 31 eingebunden ist. Viele der Modelle, die für die Entstehung und das literarische Wachstum dieses Materials vorgeschlagen worden sind, basieren auf der Annahme eines langen Prozesses des Schreibens und Redigierens, was die Rekonstruktion mehrerer hypothetischer redaktioneller oder kompositioneller Stufen beinhaltet.[29] Das eigentliche Problem ist, dass all diese mehrstufigen Rekonstruktionen hochgradig spekulativ sind und deshalb in der Wissenschaft kaum Einigkeit über das Ausmaß und das literarische Wachstum der Überlieferungen über Saul besteht.[30] Andererseits ist die Bedeutung derartiger Modelle darin zu sehen, dass sie alle mit hoher Sicherheit aufzeigen, dass das in 1Sam 9–14 eingebettete Material auf frühen und vordeuteronomistischen Überlieferungen basiert. Da es aber unmöglich zu sein scheint, es Wort für Wort zu rekonstruieren, mag es zweckmäßiger sein, die Übereinstimmungspunkte hinsichtlich seines Inhalts zu untersuchen.

So besteht in der Forschung nahezu Einigkeit darüber, dass der Anfang der Erzählung über Saul in 1Sam 9,1–10,16 zu finden ist, konkret in der sagenhaften Geschichte über den jungen Benjaminiter – Sohn aus der reichen patriarchali-

---

28 Silo, welches während der EZ I eine Hochlandfestung war, wahrscheinlich das regionale Zentrum des südlichen Samaria, wurde in der Mitte des 11. Jh. v.d.Z. zerstört (FINKELSTEIN 1993: 371–93).

29 Viele dieser Arbeiten werde im gesamten Artikel erwähnt. Unter der umfangreichen Literatur zu diesem Thema seien folgende neueren Studien zu beachten: KRATZ 2005: 171–74; DIETRICH 2007: 268–91; KAISER 2010: 520–45; DERS. 2011: 1–14; BEZZEL 2015.

30 Vgl. NAʾAMAN 1990: 638–58, hier 640–45; NIHAN 2006: 88–118, hier 92–95.

schen ländlichen Elite –, welcher nach Eseln seines Vaters sucht. Auf seinem Weg trifft er den Mann Gottes, der ihm sagt, dass er eine große Tat vollbringen werde.[31] Spätestens seit Wellhausen[32] gilt als anerkannt, dass diese Erzählung in 1Sam 11,1–15 – mit Ausnahme von 1Sam 10,17–27 als einer sekundären, exilischen oder sogar postexilischen Erweiterung – fortgesetzt wird, in der die Worte des Mannes Gottes verwirklicht werden:[33] Saul führt einen erfolgreichen Feldzug nach Jabesch-Gilead und befreit die Jabeschiter von der Unterwerfung der Ammoniter.[34] Ein Streitpunkt ist, ob der erfolgreiche Kampf gegen die Ammoniter zu Sauls Krönung im Gilgal in 1Sam 11,15 führt[35] oder ob die Bemerkung von der Krönung erst später in die ursprüngliche Erzählung aufgenommen wurde.[36] Ich optiere für Ersteres und zwar nicht nur, weil es den perfekten Abschluss der Heldengeschichte des jungen Benjaminiten bildet, sondern auch, weil Sauls Königtum bereits in der Geschichte seiner Begegnung mit dem Mann Gottes vorweggenommen wird: Wie u. a. Edelman belegt, wurden Esel als königliche Tiere angesehen (vgl. 1Kön 1,33.39). Sauls Suche nach ihnen impliziert daher bereits seine Suche nach dem Königtum.[37]

Sauls Krönung in Gilgal versetzt ihn in den geografisch-politischen Ausgangspunkt der Erzählungen seiner Kriege gegen die Philister in 1Sam 13–14. Diese Erzählungen setzen Sauls Königtum voraus und sollten als direkte Fortsetzung von 1Sam 11,1–15 angesehen werden.[38] Sie bilden eine Sammlung von Anekdoten und Heldengeschichten, die zusammengewoben wurden, weil sie

---

31 Die Rekonstruktion des ursprünglichen Kerns und literarischen Wachstums der in 1Sam 9,1–10,16 dargelegten Erzählung beruhen größtenteils auf der Arbeit von Schmidt 1970: 58–102. Vgl. z. B. auch Stolz 1981: 62–70; Campbell 2003: 106–8; Dietrich 2008: 288–400; Bezzel 2015: 149–79. Als Beispiel für andere Rekonstruktionen, unter der Annahme einer einheitlichen Erzählung mit nur geringfügigen redaktionellen Eingriffen, vgl. McCarter 1980: 166–88; Na'aman 1990: 638–58; Auld 2011: 98–111.
32 Vgl. Wellhausen 1889: 240–43.
33 Vgl. Schmidt 1970: 79–80; McCarter 1980: 26–27, 184–88, 194–96, 205–7; Stolz 1981: 19–20, 73–77; Na'aman 1990: 644; Campbell 2002: 88–89, 115–16, 128–29; Kratz 2005: 171–72; Kaiser 2010: 533–38; Bezzel 2015: 151–79, 196–204.
34 Einige Forscher argumentieren jedoch dafür, dass sich die ursprüngliche Fortsetzung von 1Sam 9,1–10,16 in der Erzählung über die Kriege Sauls und Jonathans gegen die Philister in 1Sam 13–14 befunden habe (vgl. z. B. Stoebe 1973: 64–66; Dietrich 2007: 268–69; Auld 2011: 126). In der Tat nimmt die Erzählung von Sauls Begegnung mit dem Mann Gottes die Kriege mit den Philistern vorweg (1Sam 10,5a). 1Sam 13–14 setzt aber bereits das Königtum Sauls voraus – seine Inthronisation beruht allein auf seinem Sieg über die Ammoniter (1Sam 11,15, und s. u.).
35 Vgl. z. B. Schmidt 1970: 79–80; Na'aman 1990: 642–43; Kaiser 2010: 538–40.
36 Vgl. Bezzel 2015: 196–97, 200–1.
37 Vgl. Edelman 1990: 207–20, hier 208–14; dies. 2011: 161–83.
38 Na'aman 1990: 645–49.

das Thema ‚Krieg mit den Philistern' teilen,[39] aber es besteht größtenteils Einigkeit darüber, dass sie zur frühen Schicht der Überlieferungen über Saul gehören.[40]

Schließlich kommen Saul und seine Söhne im Kampf mit den Philistern auf dem Berg Gilboa zu Tode. Laut dem Bericht in 1Sam 31,1–13 heften anschließend die siegreichen Philister die Leichen von Saul und seinen Söhnen an die Mauern von Bet-Schean, doch durch eine kühne Tat bergen die Jabeschiten die Körper, bringen sie nach Jabesch-Gilead, verbrennten sie, begraben die Gebeine und trauern sieben Tage. Die Frage ist natürlich, ob der Bericht über Sauls Tod in Gilboa Teil der frühen saulischen Überlieferung war. In der Tat haben einige Forscher dies ausgeschlossen und dafür argumentiert, dass der Großteil der frühen Überlieferung über Saul allein in 1Sam 1–14 eingebaut vorliegt – das Ende sei wahrscheinlich in 1Sam 14,46–52 zu finden.[41] Der Krieg mit den Philistern als Grundthema in 1Sam 13–14, ist jedoch auch das Grundthema von 1Sam 31. In beiden Erzählungen wird David nicht erwähnt, stattdessen konzentrieren sich beide Stücke auf Saul und dessen Söhne. Darüber hinaus bringt 1Sam 31 die frühen Überlieferungen über Saul zu ihrem vollkommenen literarischen Abschluss: Saul besteigt den Thron, indem er das Volk von Jabesch-Gilead rettet, und als er stirbt, revanchieren sie sich, indem sie seinen Leichnam retteten.[42] Demzufolge gibt es keinen Grund anzunehmen, dass sich der Bericht über den Tod und die Beisetzung von Saul und seinen Söhnen in 1Sam 31,1–13 irgendwie von den Erzählungen über Sauls und Jonathans Kriege gegen die Philister in 1Sam 13–14 unterschieden habe.[43] Mit der hier erzählten Geschichte von Aufstieg und Fall eines heldenhaften Königs, liegt also die Sammlung einer frühen Erzählung vor, die sich eingebettet in 1Sam 9–14; 31 findet.[44]

---

39 Vgl. STOEBE 1973: 63–64, 240–62; MCCARTER 1980: 26–27; STOLZ 1981: 82–83. Hinsichtlich anderer Rekonstruktionen des literarischen Wachstums dieser Erzählungen vgl. JOBLING 1976: 367–76; STOLZ 1981: 87–96; KAISER 2011: 1–6; CAMPBELL 2003:134–50; BEZZEL 2015: 208–28. Für den Ansatz, die Erzählungen in 1Sam 13–14 als eher einheitliches literarisches Werk zu lesen, vgl. MCCARTER 1980: 224–52; NA'AMA 1990: 645–47. Es gibt allerdings einen Konsens in der Forschung, dass die Verwerfung Sauls in 1Sam 13,7b–15 und die Erzählung über den Altar in 1Sam 14,32–35 sekundäre Erweiterungen sind, so z. B. WELLHAUSEN 1889: 240–46; MCCARTER 1980: 230; STOLZ 1981: 82; CAMPBELL 2003: 110–15; AULD 2011: 115–16; KAISER 2011: 1–6, 9–11; BEZZEL 2015: 214.
40 Vgl. STOEBE 1973: 64–66; MCCARTER 1980: 26–27; NA'AMAN 1990: 645–47; WHITE 2000: 271–92; DIES. 2006: 119–38; KRATZ 2005: 171–74; DIETRICH 2007: 268–69; AULD 2011: 126.
41 Vgl. WHITE 2000: 271–92; KRATZ 2005: 171–74; vgl. BEZZEL 2015: 115–48.
42 Vgl. WRIGHT 2014: 67.
43 VGL. BEZZEL 2015: 229–34, s. u., insb. n. 71.
44 Vgl. EDELMAN 1990: 207–20; DIES. 2011: 161–83.

Es wird in der Regel als selbstverständlich angenommen, dass die oben skizzierten frühen Überlieferungen über Saul nordisraelitischen Ursprungs seien und dass sie wohl kaum vor dem Fall Samarias nach Juda hätten gelangen können.[45] Doch diese Überlieferungen spiegeln schwerlich die geografische oder politische Realität des Königreichs Israel wider. Vielmehr beschränkt sich ihre geografische Ausdehnung auf das Gebiet nördlich von Jerusalem im Gebiet Benjamins sowie auf den südlichsten Teil des Hügellandes Ephraims mit nur einem Ausflug nach Gilead. Das gesamte Hügelland nördlich von Bethel, welches das Herz des Königreichs Israel war, fehlt komplett. Eine nordisraelitische Perspektive wird in diesen Erzählungen nicht einmal angedeutet. Weder werden die bedeutenden politischen Zentren Israels (Sichem, Tirza und Samaria) erwähnt, noch der Kultort in Bethel, die israelitisch-königlichen Städte in den nördlichen Tälern oder die israelitischen Kultzentren in Gilead, insbesondere Penuel.[46] Darüber hinaus gibt es nicht einmal einen Hinweis auf die Geschichte Israels, seine Politik gegenüber Königreichen in der nördlichen Levante, seine angespannten Beziehungen zu Aram-Damaskus oder seine ständigen (und erfolgreichen) Bemühungen, nach Norden zu expandieren.

Sauls militärischer Ausflug nach Gilead wird oft als Ausdruck des territorialen und politischen Interesses der Israeliten an diesem Gebiet angesehen.[47] Tatsächlich gab es während des 9. und 8. Jh. v.d.Z. Zeiträume, in denen Israel mit zumindest einigen Teilen des Gilead Zusammenschlüsse gebildet hatte.[48] Soweit dies heute beurteilt werden kann, konzentrierte sich das Interesse der Israeliten an Gilead hauptsächlich auf die Furt am Jabbok, welche sich auf dem Weg von Transjordanien nach Sichem befand (vgl. 1Kön 12,25). Diese Region und die dort gelegenen Städte – Penuel, Mahanaim und Sukkot – spielen eine herausragende Rolle in der oft als israelitisch angesehenen Literatur: Die Begründung dieser Stätten wird gemäß dem vorpriesterlichen Jakob-Zyklus, welcher wiederum von vielen für den Ursprungsmythos des nordisraelitischen Königreichs gehalten wird,[49] dem namensgebenden Vorfahren Israels zugeschrieben. Außerdem sind diese auch wichtig in der Erzählung von der Verfol-

---

45 S.o., n. 2, und vgl. Schmidt 1970: 79–80; Grønbæk 1971: 267–69.
46 Mahanaim wird als Hauptstadt von Sauls Erben Ischbaal erwähnt (2Sam 3,8), doch gehört dies nicht in die sogenannten frühen Überlieferungen über Saul, sondern vielmehr zum Teil dazu, was als eine judäische Komposition angenommen wird, vgl. Naʾaman 2009: 346–48.
47 Vgl. Dieterich / Münger 2003: 41–46; Finkelstein 2006: 178–80; ders. 2011: 353–55; Wright 2014: 66–74.
48 Zur Diskussion der politischen Zugehörigkeit Gileads im 9. und 8. Jh. v.d.Z., vgl. Sergi 2016: 333–54, hier 333–37.
49 Vgl. Blum 1984: 175–86; de Pury 2006: 51–72; Hutton 2006: 161–78; Blum 2012: 181–211; Finkelstein / Römer 2014: 317–38; Sergi 2016: 333–54.

gung der Midianiter durch Gideon (Ri 8,4–21), welche als Teil einer israelitischen Sammlung von Heldengeschichten betrachtet wird.[50] Keine dieser in der israelitischen Literatur so bedeutenden Stätten findet in den frühen Überlieferungen über Saul Erwähnung. Tatsächlich zieht Saul in Jabesch-Gilead[51] in den Krieg, ein Toponym, auf das hauptsächlich in den Erzählungen über Saul Bezug genommen wird (1Sam 11,1.3.5.9–11; 31,13; 2Sam 2,4–5; 21,12 – vgl. 1Chr 10,12).[52] Hingegen wird Jabesch-Gilead nirgendwo als zu Israel gehörend erwähnt,[53] auch nicht in der Auflistung der Städte der nördlichen Stämme. Hinzu kommt, dass die Einäscherung, wie richtig bemerkt wird, keine israelitische Praxis ist – indem sie den Männern von Jabesch-Gilead zugeschrieben wird (1Sam 31,12), beabsichtigte der Verfasser wahrscheinlich, sie als Nicht-Israeliten zu kennzeichnen.[54] All dies zeugt davon, dass die Rolle des Gebiets Gilead und ihrer Bewohner in den frühen Überlieferungen über Saul nicht unbedingt den israelitischen Standpunkt widerspiegelt.

Wenn man sich das aus den frühen Überlieferungen über Saul ergebende geopolitische Bild ansieht, scheint dieses eher einen Jerusalemer Standpunkt widerzuspiegeln: Der Einflussbereich Sauls erstreckt sich hauptsächlich über Benjamin und über das südliche Hügelland Ephraims; Regionen, die gemäß der Erzählung (1Sam 13,20; 14,31) von den Philistern, welche selbst Bewohner der judäischen Schefela waren, durchzogen wurden. Die Philister werden als Krieger dargestellt, welche die bäuerliche Gesellschaft in der Region Benjamins überfallen und plündern, außerdem gelten sie als die stärkere, aggressive Partei in dem Konflikt (1Sam 13,5–6.17–18; 14). Die Israeliten hingegen werden als Landbevölkerung dargestellt, welche im Hügelland und seinen Ausläufern lebt und sich gegen die Aggressivität dieser verteidigen muss. Diese Charakteristika ziehen die Grenze zwischen den eher städtischen Gesellschaften im südwestlichen Kanaan und den ländlichen in der Region Benjamin–Jerusalem vor der EZ IIB – und wohl noch vor dem Fall Gats im letzten Drittel des 9. Jh. v.d.Z.

Der begrenzte geografische Bereich dieser Erzählungen sagt einiges aus: 1Sam 13–14 enthalten eine detaillierte topografische Beschreibung eines kleinen Gebiets nördlich von Jerusalem. Offensichtlich kannten die Verfasser von 1Sam

---

50 Vgl. GROSS 2009: 367–89, 473–74, mit weiterer Literatur. Zur Diskussion des Ortes des Durchlasses des Jabbok in Ri 8,4–21, vgl. SERGI 2016: 346–49.
51 Identifiziert mit Tell el-Maqlūb, vgl. NOTH 1953: 28–41; GASS 2005: 504–9, mit früherer Literatur.
52 Jabesch-Gilead wird ebenfalls in der Erzählung von der Schandtat in Gibea erwähnt (Ri 21), die in die späte nachexilische Zeit datiert wird (vgl. GROSS 2009: 821–22, mit vorhergehender Literatur).
53 *Pace* AULD 2015: 121, der sie als „Israelite city" bezeichnet.
54 Vgl. WRIGHT 2014: 66–68. Zur Diskussion um diesen Erzählzug vgl. BEZZEL 2015:108–10.

13–14 das Gebiet Benjamins gut, während die niederen Gebiete Kanaans – die nördlichen Täler oder die westlich von Juda gelegene Schefela – ihnen weniger bekannt waren, was auch das sonderbare Aufkommen der Philister im Jesreelebene nahelegt (1Sam 31,1.10). Während sich das archäologische Phänomen der Philister in der EZ I größtenteils auf den Südwesten Kanaans beschränkte,[55] behielt das Jesreelebene in dieser Zeit, bevor es unter israelitische Herrschaft geriet, seine frühere, spätbronzezeitlich geprägte, stadtstaaliche sowie palastwirtschaftliche soziale und politische Struktur.[56] Für die Annahme, dass die Städte im Jesreeltal, wie auch immer geartet, mit den Philistern in Verbindung standen – dies wurde von Dietrich und Münger vorgeschlagen –, gibt es keinen plausiblen Grund.[57] Finkelsteins Vorschlag, nämlich dass die Erinnerung an die Philister im Jesreeltal, insbesondere in Bet-Schean, die ägyptische Herrschaft während der späten Bronzezeit widerspiegelt,[58] ist ähnlich unwahrscheinlich. Soweit dies beurteilt werden kann, wurde das vorisraelitische Jesreelebene im historischen Gedächtnis der Israeliten als kanaanäisch (vgl. Ri 4–5) und nicht als philistäisch oder gar ägyptisch begriffen; offensichtlich war der Autor der Erzählung über Saul mit der tatsächlichen politischen oder sozialen Zusammensetzung des vorisraelitischen Jesreeltals nicht gut vertraut. Und die Philister müssen als Erzfeind des Königreichs Juda begriffen werden – dies geht deutlich aus ihrer wichtigen Rolle hervor, die sie in den Erzählungen über die frühe davidische Monarchie spielen.[59] Tatsächlich war das westlich gelegene Gat während der gesamten Gründungsphase der judäischen Monarchie das mächtigste staatliche Gebilde.[60] Nur ein Erzähler aus Jerusalem, entfernt vom Jesreelebene ansässig, würde annehmen, dass Saul im Jesreelebene auf dieselben Feinde, sprich auf die Philister, traf, denen er auch im Gebiet Benjamins begegnet war.

Aus archäologischer Sicht waren die Bewohner des Gebietes Benjamin bereits im 10. Jh. v.d.Z. mit der politischen Hegemonie der Jerusalemer verbunden. Wenn folglich die Erinnerung an einen Helden Benjamins irgendwo aufbewahrt und aufgezeichnet worden wäre, dann am ehesten in einer Jerusalemer Schreiberschule. Dies ist auch die beste Erklärung für das völlige Fehlen jeglicher Spur israelitischer Geographie, Politik oder Anliegen innerhalb dieser frühen Überlieferungen, die vielmehr die politische Wirklichkeit, Probleme und Interessen Judas widerspiegeln. Folglich stellt sich die Frage, ob die Erinnerung an

---

55 Vgl. z. B. MAEIR / HITCHCOCK / HORWITZ 2013: 1–38.
56 Vgl. FINKELSTEIN 2013: 27–36.
57 Vgl. DIETRICH / MÜNGER 2003: 48.
58 Vgl. FINKELSTEIN 2006: 182–83.
59 Vgl. SERGI 2015: 56–77, hier 64–75.
60 Vgl. SERGI 2013: 226–46; LEHMANN / NIEMANN 2014: 77–94.

einen israelitischen König in Jerusalem hätte bewahrt werden können. Um dies zu beantworten, werde ich zuerst die Erzählungen über Davids Aufstieg in ihrem historischen und literarischen Kontext diskutieren.

4 Der historische sowie literarische Kontext der Erzählungen über Davids Aufstieg (1Sam 16–2Sam 5)

Die Erzählungen über Davids Aufstieg in 1Sam 16–2Sam 5 beinhalten viele verschiedene Erzählstränge, die von einem vordeuteronomistischen Schreiber recht lose zusammengesetzt wurden. Diese Erzählungen berichten von Davids Dienst am Hofe Sauls (1Sam 16,14–23; 17–19); von Davids Flucht vor Saul (1Sam 20–26); von seinem darauffolgenden Dienst für den König von Gat (1Sam 27–2Sam 1) und zwar bis zum Tode Sauls (1Sam 31–2Sam 1) sowie von Davids Krönung – zunächst wird er der König Judas (2Sam 2,1–4), dann Israels (2Sam 5,1–3). Natürlich ist das Ausmaß und das literarische Wachstum dieser Komposition umstritten. Für den Zweck dieser Studie genügt es jedoch zu betonen, dass die Komposition trotz ihres mosaikartigen Charakters mit einem bestimmten Anstrich versehen ist, nämlich dem einer vereinigenden königlichen, pro-davidischen Ideologie, was darauf hindeutet, dass ihre Verfasser keine bloßen Kompilatoren waren.[61]

Wie oben bereits dargelegt, wird gemäß einer gängigen Auffassung in der zeitgenössischen Wissenschaft die Erzählung in 1Sam 16–2Sam 5 als die früheste literarische Verbindung zwischen dem Judäer David und dem Israeliten Saul betrachtet, welche erst nach dem Fall Samarias hätte entstehen können.[62] Diese

---

61 Zur weiteren Diskussion und bzgl. verschiedener Rekonstruktionen der Quellen und Redaktionen innerhalb dieses Zusammenhangs, vgl. z. B. WEISER 1966: 325–54; GRØNBÆK 1971; STOLZ 1981: 17–18; KRATZ 2005: 177–81. VEIJOLA (1975) wies die Zusammensetzung der Geschichte von Davids Aufstieg den deuteronomistischen Schriftgelehrten zu (vgl. VAN SETERS 2009), jedoch erreichte diese Ansicht keinen breiten wissenschaftlichen Konsens (vgl. DIETRICH 2007: 245–46). Eine kritische Übersicht über frühere Forschungsergebnisse findet sich bei DIETRICH 2007: 240–55.
62 Um klare und unterschiedliche Erzählungen innerhalb von 1Sam 16–2Sam 5 zu scheiden, sind einige Forscher so weit mit ihrer Annahme gegangen, Saul und David als ursprünglich in keiner Beziehung zueinanderstehende literarische Figuren zu begreifen (vgl. z.B. WRIGHT 2014: 31–79). Diese Versuche basieren nicht auf soliden literarischen Kriterien, so dass selbst Anhänger der Hypothese, dass die Überlieferungen über Saul nördlichen Ursprungs sind, noch immer der Meinung sind, dass es unmöglich sei, nördliche von südlichen Traditionen inner-

Folgerung basiert ausschließlich auf einer allegorischen Lesart dieser Erzählungen unter der Annahme, dass die intellektuelle judäische Elite das frühere Königreich Israel zu beerben wünschte. Es ist jedoch kaum glaubhaft, dass man sich mit Israel als Modell für eine erfolgreiche Monarchie identifizieren wollte – kurz nach deren totaler Zerstörung durch die Assyrer. Das oft derselben judäischen Elite (im 7. Jh. v.d.Z.) zugeschriebene Buch der Könige verurteilt hingegen Israel explizit – es spiegelt damit die Perspektive jener Elite auf Israel in spätmonarchischer Zeit wahrscheinlich weit besser wider.

Darüber hinaus kann diese Annahme kaum durch den Text selbst gestützt werden, welcher, wie Nadav Na'aman demonstriert,[63] ebenso wie die frühen Überlieferungen über Saul die geopolitische Organisation des südlichen Kanaans in der frühen Eisenzeit widerspiegelt: Die geografische Reichweite der Erzählungen über Davids Aufstieg beschränkt sich auf das südkanaanäische Hügelland und seine Ausläufer – die Philister kontrollieren hingegen die westliche Schefela. Dementsprechend ist David in seinem Vorgehen als Anführer einer Bande von Kriegern im judäischen Hügelland und seinen Ausläufern ziemlich eigenmächtig (1Sam 23–26; 2Sam 5), und doch steht er im Dienst des Königs von Gat, wann immer er das west- und südwärts gelegene Terrain durchkreuzt (vgl. 1Sam 27; 29–30). Das gezeichnete geopolitische Bild wird durch die Bedeutung Gats in diesen Erzählungen weiter unterstrichen (1Sam 17,4.23.52; 21,11.13; 27,2–4.11). Als Gat während des 10. und 9. Jh. v.d.Z. zur deutlich größten und wohlhabendsten Stadt im Süden Kanaans avancierte, erreichte es damit auch den Zenit seiner Macht. Nachdem Gat allerdings im letzten Drittel des 9. Jh. v.d.Z. vollständig zerstört wurde, erlangte es seine frühere Macht nie mehr zurück.[64] Folglich stimmen die Erzählungen in 1Sam 16–2Sam 5 – wie auch die in 1Sam 9–14 – mit der sozialen sowie politischen Wirklichkeit im südlichen Kanaan des 10. und 9. Jh. v.d.Z. – vor der Expansion der Judäer in die Schefela – überein. Dies wird faktisch auch dadurch belegt, dass all diese Überlieferungen Lachisch, immerhin die wichtigste in der Schefela gelegene königliche Stadt Judas in der zweiten Hälfte des 9. Jh. v.d.Z., nicht einmal erwähnen.[65] Wird all dies berücksichtigt, so sollten die Erzählungen von Davids Aufstieg nicht viel später als in das frühe 8. Jh. v.d.Z. datiert werden – dies bedeutet allerdings auch, dass diese einige Zeit vor dem Fall Samarias verfasst wurden. Aufgrund der Vertrautheit mit den geopolitischen Gegebenheit im Süden Kanaans, die

---

halb von 1Sam 16–2Sam 5 zu unterscheiden (vgl. Kratz 2005: 182; Dietrich 2007: 298–99; Kaiser 2011: 6–9).

63 Vgl. Na'aman 1996: 170–86; ders. 2002: 200–24.

64 Vgl. Maeir 2012: 26–49.

65 Vgl. Sergi 2013: 226–46; Na'aman 2013: 247–76; Lehmann / Niemann 2014: 77–94.

sich sowohl in den frühen Überlieferungen über Saul als auch in den Erzählungen über Davids Aufstieg erkennen lässt, muss mit gewisser Wahrscheinlichkeit von einer judäischen, genauer noch von einer Jerusalemer, nicht aber von einer israelitischen Perspektive ausgegangen werden. Insofern dem so ist, so scheint es zumindest, müssen beide Erzählungen zeitlich – spätestens im frühen 8. Jh. v.d.Z. – wie räumlich nahe beieinander abgefasst worden sein.[66]

Diese Schlussfolgerung kann unter literarischen Gesichtspunkten weiter gestützt werden. In der Forschung besteht eine überwiegende Einigkeit darin, dass die Erzählungen über Davids Aufstieg die frühen Überlieferungen über Saul voraussetzen.[67] Da sie jedoch davon ausgehen, dass das Material in 1Sam 9–14 zeitlich 1Sam 16–2Sam 5 vorausgeht, wird die Möglichkeit, dass die frühen Überlieferungen über Saul den Aufstieg Davids vorwegnehmen, oft übersehen. Der Umstand, dass die Erzählung Saul im Vergleich zu der negativeren Darstellung in 1Sam 16–2Sam 5 in einem positiven Licht darstellt und dass David darin keine Rolle spielt, hebe nochmals deutlich den nicht-judäischen Ursprung der Überlieferungen über Saul hervor. Dass David jedoch keine Rolle in den Erzählungen über Sauls frühen Werdegang spielt, ist offensichtlich, da nämlich die Erzählungen über David ausdrücklich Sauls Königtum anerkennen und sogar darzulegen bestrebt sind, dass jener dessen legitimer Thronfolger war. Die Behauptung, dass Saul in 1Sam 9–14; 31 in einem völlig positiven Licht dargestellt wird, scheint dazu viel zu allgemein zu sein und kaum die Nuancen der Erzählung zu erfassen.

Von Anfang an – und bereits in der legendarischen Erzählung seiner Berufung (1Sam 9,1–10,16) – wird der Charakter Saul keineswegs als besonders heldenhaft oder des Königtums würdig beschrieben. Das wohl wichtigste Charakteristikum, mit dem Saul in die Erzählung eingeführt wird, bezieht sich auf seine Erscheinung, denn er wird als große Person beschrieben (1Sam 9,2). Davon abgesehen wird gesagt, dass er „gut" war, aber keine dieser Eigenschaften (groß, gut) ist für das Königtum in besonderem Maße notwendig. Die gesamte Erzählung wird durch die Handlungen von Sauls Vater (1Sam 9,3) und Sauls Diener (1Sam 9,5–10) bestimmt – Saul selbst bleibt (beinahe) völlig untätig: Er ist der erste, welcher die Suche nach seines Vaters Eseln aufgibt und gleichzeitig Verzweiflung ausdrückt (1Sam 9,5); er bleibt zögernd, sogar als sein Diener mit neuen Lösungskonzepten für seine Probleme aufwartet (1Sam 9,6–8).[68] Zwar ist

---

66 Vgl. Na'aman 1996; 2002; Ders. *im Druck.*

67 Vgl. Stoebe 1973: 63–64; Grønbæk 1971: 262–64; Edelman 1990: 214–20; White 2000: 271–84; Dietrich 2007: 244–45.

68 Zu beachten sei auch die Formulierung in V. 8 („Und der Knecht antwortete Saul *noch einmal*"), d. h., dass der Knecht Saul ermutigen musste seine Aufgabe zu erfüllen (die Esel zu finden) und seinem Schicksal zu begegnen (Königtum).

diese Darstellung Sauls tatsächlich nicht negativ, spricht sogar eher für ihn, doch insbesondere angesichts der heroisierten Darstellung der Jugend Davids (1Sam 16–19) wird ihm kein Charakteristikum zugeschrieben, das als Vorbereitung auf seine zukünftige Funktion als Anführer zu begreifen ist.

Es braucht daher nicht zu verwundern, dass die Erzählung in Sauls Tod gipfelt (1Sam 31,1–13), die, wie bereits die Erzählung seines Aufstiegs, seine Unfähigkeit zu führen hervorhebt. Gemäß der Erzählung beging Saul nicht im Angesicht seiner Niederlage auf dem Schlachtfeld oder angesichts des Todes seiner Söhne Selbstmord, sondern weil er in Folge der Jagd auf ihn durch die philistäischen Bogenschützen „in Panik geriet" (1Sam 31,3–4). Dies ist nicht als Darstellung eines heldenhaften Todes zu verstehen, zumal Bogenschützen naturgemäß nicht in Berührungsnähe zu ihren Feinden geraten, folglich eine gewisse Distanz zu Saul haben mussten, der entweder entkommen, sich verstecken oder aber sich seinen Feinden hätte stellen können. Da außerdem Sauls Diener seinem direkten Befehl ihn zu töten widersprach, muss sogar der Selbstmord als ihm aufgezwungen erachtet werden. Und diese kurze Episode bietet ein vortreffliches Ende der Erzählung von Saul: Sauls Schicksal – von seinem Aufstieg bis zu seinem Fall – lag in der Hand eines Dieners. Eher als um die Darstellung eines heldenhaften Königs handelt es sich hier um die Beschreibung eines guten Mannes, dem nicht die Eigenschaften zu eigen waren, die einen guten König ausmachen.

Tatsächlich kann dargelegt werden, dass das gesamte Motiv von Sauls Kriegen gegen die Philister (1Sam 13–14; 31) den Aufstieg Davids vorwegnimmt. Bezzel hat insbesondere die vielen literarischen Verbindungen dargelegt, welche 1Sam 13–14 mit 1Sam 31 zu einer Einheit verbinden, um wiederum die Bühne für Davids Aufstieg in 1Sam 16–2Sam 5 vorzubereiten.[69] Schließlich endet das Motiv der Kriege Sauls mit den Philistern mit dem vollständigen Untergang des Hauses Sauls (1Sam 31,1–13 hebt den Tod Sauls und *aller* seiner Söhne hervor), was David in die Lage versetzt, das Königtum rechtmäßig zu beanspruchen (2Sam 5,1–3 – insbesondere V. 2).[70] Darüber hinaus spielen die Philister, die ihren Auftritt erstmals in den Überlieferungen über Saul haben, eine herausragende Rolle in den Erzählungen von Davids Aufstieg und erfüllen beide Male einen ganz bestimmten literarischen Zweck – sei es, dass sie das Ende des saulidischen Hauses herbeiführen oder David als einen heldenhaften Befreier darstellen (2Sam 5,17–25; 8,1):[71] Die Philister bringen die Erzählung in Richtung des

---

69 Bezzel (2015: 233) datiert diese Verbindung in das ausgehende achte oder frühe siebte Jahrhundert, hat diese Ansicht aber mittlerweile vorsichtig revidiert, vgl. Ders., 2019: 243–46.
70 Vgl. Grønbæk 1971: 262.
71 Vgl. Sergi 2015: 64–75.

unvermeidlichen Königtum Davids voran. In diesem Sinne sind die Philister das „Objekt", anhand dessen Sauls Inkompetenz im Gegensatz zu Davids Erfolg hervorgehoben wird.

In Anbetracht all dessen und obwohl es keinen Zweifel daran gibt, dass die Überlieferungen in 1Sam 9–14; 31 Saul in einem recht günstigen Licht erscheinen lassen, stellen sie ihn dennoch „nur" als einen guten Menschen dar, der (beinahe zufällig) König wurde, obwohl ihm gerade diejenigen Eigenschaften fehlten, die einen erfolgreichen Führer ausmachen. Folglich führt die Erzählung zu seinem unvermeidlich tragischen Ende, welches wiederum den Aufstieg Davids, des weitaus erfahreneren Anführers, ermöglicht. Es ist daher nicht unplausibel anzunehmen, dass die literarischen Verbindungen zwischen den frühen Überlieferungen über Saul und den Erzählungen über Davids Aufstieg nicht einseitig sind, da die ersteren die Bühne für letztere klar vorwegnehmen und sogar vorbereiten. Angesichts der Tatsache, dass sowohl die Erzählungen über Saul als auch die über David die gesellschaftspolitischen Gegebenheiten des südlichen Kanaans in der EZ IIA widerspiegeln, sollte es kaum Zweifel daran geben, dass sie das literarische Produkt einer Jerusalemer Schreiberschule sind und die Absicht verfolgen, die Ursprünge der davidischen Monarchie darzustellen. Die sich dabei zu stellende Frage lautet: Warum ersann man David, den Begründer Judas, in diesen Überlieferungen als Nachfolger des ersten Königs von Israel? Die Antwort auf diese Frage liegt im Wesen der israelitischen Identität begründet, die seitens der Erzähler der Saul- und David-Erzählung vorausgesetzt wird.

5 Israel als Verwandtschaftsidentität in den Überlieferungen über die Entstehung der israelitischen Monarchie

Die Erzählungen über Sauls Kriege mit den Philistern in 1Sam 13–14 setzen sein Königtum über Israel voraus oder erinnern zumindest an ihn als Israels militärischen Führer und Befreier (vgl. 1Sam 11,15; 14,47). Der Begriff „Israel" findet in 1Sam 13–14 vierzehnmal Erwähnung. In den meisten Fällen handelt es sich eindeutig um eine Personengruppe. Somit ist „Israel" in 1Sam 13–14 u. a. die Bezeichnung für eine Gruppe, die sich durch verwandtschaftliche Zugehörigkeit begründet, und nicht für ein räumlich definiertes Staatswesen. Der Text identifiziert die Israeliten als einen clanartigen / stammesgesellschaftlichen Verbund, der auf dem Benjaminplateau und im südlichen Hügelland Ephraims siedelt (1Sam 13,4–6.20; 14,22–24), zwischen Gibea im Süden – oder sogar Bethlehem (vgl. 1Sam 17,2) – und Bethel im Norden. Er spiegelt auch das komplexe Wesen Israels als verwandtschaftliche Gruppe wider, welche aus verschiedenen Clans – wie beispielsweise den Benjaminiten – besteht, die unter einer umfassenderen Verwandtschaftsidentität zusammengeführt sind. Als Benjaminiter (1Sam 9,1) galt Saul auch als Israelit, und so erzählen die frühen Überlieferungen über Saul die Geschichte vom Aufstieg und Fall eines Benjaminiten, der auftrat, um seine Verwandten, die Israeliten, zu regieren. Oder anders ausgedrückt, stellt die Erzählung Saul nie als den König von Israel dar – gemeint ist hier das nördliche Königreich, welches von den Omriden weit im Norden im Gebiet von Sichem und Samaria begründet wurde. Sie erzählt vielmehr, wie Saul dazu kam, seine israelitischen Verwandten zu regieren, die auf dem Benjaminplateau lebten.

Dies erfordert eine klare Unterscheidung zwischen *Israel als politischer Identität*, nämlich der seit der Zeit der omridischen Herrschaft und danach mit diesem Namen bezeichneten, räumlich definierten Staatform und *Israel als sozialer Identität*, einer sich auf Verwandtschaft gründenden Gruppe. Schon lange bevor der Name „Israel" als Bezeichnung für das Nordkönigreich diente, wurde er gebraucht, um eine auf Verwandtschaft beruhende Gruppe (in der Merenptah-Stele, Ende des 13. Jh. v.d.Z.) zu bezeichnen,[72] wie es übrigens auch bei den anderen drei Vorkommen außerhalb der hebräischen Bibel der Fall ist: in der Mescha-Inschrift, auf dem Kurkh-Monolithen und in der Dan-Inschrift (alle aus der Mitte der zweiten Hälfte des 9. Jh. v.d.Z.). Auf dem assyrischen Kurkh-Monolith (852 v.d.Z.) betrifft die Zuschreibung Ahab, der folglich als „Israelit" (KUR.syrʾalāya) und nicht als König Israels – wie im Falle Omris und Jorams auf der zeitgenössischen Mescha-Stele bzw. Dan-Inschrift – bezeichnet wird. Da der Begriff „Israel", zumindest anfangs, eine verwandtschaftliche Zugehörigkeit bezeichnende Bedeutung hatte, stellt sich folgende Frage: Wie wurde eben diese Bezeichnung, die eine auf Verwandtschaft beruhende Gruppenzugehörigkeit ausdrückt, später auf eine politische Einheit übertragen? Diese Frage wird allein durch den Umstand hervorgehoben, dass „Israel" nicht der einzige Name des Nordreichs war, sondern (von den Assyrern) auch als „das Haus Omri" bezeichnet wurde. Dass nahezu alle historischen Belege für den Begriff „Israel" in die Herrschaftszeit der Omriden gehören, gibt Anlass dazu, an der These zu zweifeln, welche besagt, dass „Israel" einzig oder hauptsächlich eine politische Identität bezeichnete, sprich der Name eines räumlich umrissenen Staatswesens war und nichts darüber hinaus.

Innerhalb altorientalischer Gesellschaften bildete verwandtschaftliche Zugehörigkeit im Kern die vorherrschende gesellschaftliche „Ideologie".[73] Man

---

72 Vgl. die Zusammenfassung in Hasel 1994: 170–204.
73 Vgl. Porter 2012: 12–37.

entwarf Verwandtschaftsbeziehungen, um die Zugehörigkeit zu einer Gruppe zu legitimieren,[74] und sie wurden verwendet um Zeit und Raum zu verlängern sowie die Vorstellung einer gemeinsamen Identität mit unbekannten anderen zu ermöglichen.[75] Verwandtschaftsbeziehungen scheinen in der Lage zu sein ihre für sie unerlässliche Intaktheit über lange Zeiträume und selbst unter unterschiedlichen politischen Gebilden zu behaupten. So konnte zum Beispiel die herrschende Elite in Ebla oder Mari ihre auf Verwandtschaft bezogene „tribale Identität" auch dann noch behaupten, als sie in einem wohlhabenden Stadtzentrum wohnte.[76] Auf ganz ähnliche Weise und geografisch den Erzählungen über Saul und David deutlich näher, stellt die gleichnamige Inschrift Mescha als „König von Moab" sowie als „Diboniter" vor. Bereits Knauf stellte fest, dass Mescha sich nicht als Moabiter identifizierte, sprich sich nicht mit dem territorialen Gemeinwesen identifizierte, welches er begründete und regierte, sondern als Diboniter[77] – wahrscheinlich handelt es sich hierbei um seine verwandtschaftsbezogene Identität, die soziale Gruppe, mit der er verbunden war.[78] Es gibt daher keinen wirklichen Gegensatz zwischen sozialer und politischer Identität, da beide gängige Identitäten darstellen. Das bedeutet, dass Israel in erster Linie eine verwandtschaftsbezogene Identität darstellte, selbst wenn der Name „Israel" dem von den Omriden regierten Gemeinwesen gegeben wurde.[79] Da außerbiblische Quellen aus der Eisenzeit Israel ausschließlich mit den Omriden identifizieren, kann darüber hinaus die Ansicht vertreten werden, dass die Omriden einer Verwandtschaftsgruppe namens „Israel" angehörten, welche schließlich dem von ihr regierten Gemeinwesen seinen Namen gab. Dies bedeutet jedoch nicht, dass alle Israeliten innerhalb der Grenzen des Gemeinwesens der Omriden lebten. Offensichtlich identifizieren zumindest die frühen Überlieferungen über Saul die Israeliten auch im Gebiete Benjamins, sprich deutlich südlich von Samaria, dem eigentlichen Kernland der Omriden.

Auch die Erzählungen über Davids Aufstieg und insbesondere die Erzählungen über Davids Dienst an Sauls Hof sind durch eine vergleichbare Darstellung Israels als sich durch Verwandtschaft auszeichnende Gruppe im Gebiet Jerusalems und Benjamins gekennzeichnet (1Sam 18–19; vgl. 2Sam 5,1–2). Dass

74 Vgl. VAN DER STEEN 2004: 126–32, mit weiterer Literatur.
75 Vgl. PORTER 2012: 57–58, 326; Porter 2013: 56–57.
76 Vgl. FLEMING 2009: 227–40; PORTER 2009: 201–25; DERS. 2012: 240.
77 Vgl. KNAUF 1992: 47–54.
78 Vgl. VAN DER STEEN / SMELIK 2007: 139–62.
79 Hinsichtlich neuerer Studien, welche das Wesen Israels als auf Verwandtschaft beruhende Identität innerhalb ihres historischen und literarischen Kontextes betonen, vgl. FLEMING 2012; WEINGART 2014: insb. 171–286, 340–60.

diese Erzählungen ein frühmonarchisches Szenario abbilden, in der die Errichtung politischer Hegemonie durch Heirat und personenbezogene Bündnisse erfolgte (vgl. 1Sam 17,58; 18,2.17), hat Willi-Plein gezeigt.[80] Gemäß ihrer Ansicht berichten die Erzählungen davon, wie ein Königum über eine Gruppe von Menschen „Israel" errichtet wird.[81] Das bedeutet, dass die Erzählung von Davids Aufstieg, wie auch die Überlieferungen über Saul, von dessen Aufstieg als König der Israeliten berichtet. Und eben aus diesem Grund wird David als Nachfolger Sauls präsentiert: es handelt sich nicht um eine Allegorie auf hypothetische Wünsche des spätmonarchischen Juda, sondern schlicht darum, dass beide, Saul und David, bestrebt waren, die Vorherrschaft über dieselbe Gruppe von Menschen – die im Jerusalemer und benjamenitischen Hochland ansässigen Israeliten – zu gewinnen.

Das Haus Davids mit seinem königlichen Sitz in Jerusalem, war selbstverständlich die herrschende Dynastie Judas. Dies bedeutet jedoch nicht, dass Davids Verwandtschaftsidentität judäisch war – (gleichermaßen wie Mescha, der König von Moab, Diboniter und nicht Moabiter war). In den Erzählungen über Davids Aufstieg zum Königtum wird er an keiner Stelle als Judäer identifiziert. In 1Sam 17,12 heißt es im Gegenteil sogar, dass seine Familie einem efratitischen, sprich israelitischen, Clan entstammte. Der Clan ließ sich wohl in Bethlehem nieder.[82] Hinzu kommt, dass David in den Erzählungen über seinen Aufstieg mindestens dreimal ausdrücklich als Israelit identifiziert wird (1Sam 18,18; 27,12; 2Sam 5,1). Besonders interessant hiervon sind Davids Worte an Saul in 1Sam 18:18: „Wer bin ich? Und wer ist meines Vaters Sippe in Israel, dass ich der Schwiegersohn des Königs würde?" Hier wird deutlich die Zugehörigkeit zu einem Israel ausgedrückt, das aus mehreren Sippen besteht, von denen Davids Familie eine ist.

Dass zumindest einige der Einwohner des Gebietes von und um Jerusalem Israeliten waren, stimmt mit dem Bild, welches die frühen Überlieferungen über Saul zeichnen, überein. Ebenso wie die frühen Überlieferungen über Saul, legen auch die Erzählungen über Davids Aufstieg von der komplexen Beschaffenheit Israels als auf Verwandtschaft beruhender Gruppe Zeugnis ab, die aus verschiedenen Clans besteht – Saul der Benjaminiter und David der Efratiter. Die Annahme einer israelitischen Herkunft Davids könnte auch erklären, warum seine Krönung über das Volk Juda (2Sam 2,1–4) nicht als selbstverständlich angesehen wird: David konsultiert vor seinem Schreiten nach Hebron nicht allein JHWH – eine Maßnahme, die er ansonsten allein vor Schlachten ergreift (vgl.

---

80 Vgl. Willi-Plein 2004: 148–53, 156–59.
81 Vgl. Willi-Plein 2004: 161–68.
82 Zu den efratitischen Siedlungen, vgl. Na'aman 2014: 516–29.

1Sam 23,2.4; 30,8; 2Sam 5,19.23–24) –, sondern er „besticht" vor seiner Ankunft die Führer Judas, indem er ihnen etwas von der aus den Kämpfen gegen die Amalekiter erlangten Beute schickt (1Sam 30:26). Demgegenüber scheint Davids Krönung über Israel (2Sam 5,1–3) um einiges folgerichtiger zu sein, denn die Israeliten selbst erklären ihn zu ihrem König: Er ist ihr Verwandter ("dein Gebein und dein Fleisch sind wir" - עצמך ובשרך אנחנו) und er stand zuvor im Dienste des Hofes Sauls, sprich im Dienste des vormaligen israelitischen Königs (2Sam 5,1–2).

Es darf gefolgert werden, dass sowohl Saul als auch David gemäß den frühen Überlieferungen über Saul sowie gemäß den Erzählungen über Davids Aufstieg einem auf Verwandtschaft beruhenden Verbund namens „Israel" angehörten, der selbst aus mehreren nördlich wie südlich gelegenen Clans bestand – benjaminitischen im Norden, efratitischen im Süden. Abgesehen von den israelitischen Clans wurde diese Region auch von judäischen und jebusitischen Clans bewohnt (z. B. 2Sam 2,1–4; 5,6).[83] Wie in den Ausführungen zum archäologischen Befund gezeigt, fielen alle diese Clans schließlich unter die politische Vorherrschaft des fortan in Jerusalem ansässigen Hauses Davids.

6 Zusammenfassung: Die biblischen Überlieferungen über die Entstehung der israelitischen Monarchie (1Sam 9–2Sam 5) aus historischer Perspektive

Die Erzählungen in 1Sam 9–2Sam 5 über die Entstehung der israelitischen Monarchie schildern den Versuch zweier lokaler Führer, eine dynastische Monarchie über einen Verbund von Menschen aufzubauen, die von den Autoren der Texte als Israeliten identifiziert wurden. Israel ist in diesen Traditionen eine Bezeichnung für einen auf Verwandtschaft beruhenden Verbund und bezeichnet daher eine soziale und keine politische Identität. Diese soziale Identität wird einem bestimmten Verbund von Menschen zugeschrieben, nämlich denjenigen Clans, welche im Gebiet Jerusalem und Benjamin leben. In 1Sam 9–2Sam 5 bezieht sich „Israel" als Name nicht auf das territorial definierte Königreich, welches seit der Zeit omridischer Herrschaft sowie darüber hinaus unter diesem Namen bekannt ist. Da die Erzählungen in die soziale und politische Wirklich-

---

83 Vgl. NAʾAMAN 2015: 481–97.

keit des früheisenzeitlichen Südkanaans, insbesondere im Kerngebiet Judas, gut eingebettet sind, spiegeln sie ferner nichts von der Entstehung oder der geopolitischen Beschaffenheit des Nordreichs wider. Somit sollten die Erzählungen in 1Sam 16–2Sam 5 über den Aufstieg Davids nicht als Allegorie eines vermuteten spätmonarchisch-judäischen Wunsches, das nördliche Königreich Israel zu beerben, gelesen werden. Vielmehr sollten sie als das gelesen werden, was sie sind, nämlich eine Erzählung über den Aufstieg der israelitischen Monarchie.

Daher ist es wichtig daran zu erinnern, dass diese Überlieferungen das literarische Produkt einer intellektuellen Elite sind, welches zeitlich der Errichtung des auf Jerusalem ausgerichteten, räumlich definierten Königreiches nachgeordnet, sprich in die zweite Hälfte des 9. Jh. v.d.Z. datiert werden sollte. Demzufolge stammt das Konzept von Israel als einer auf Verwandtschaft beruhender, im Norden sowie Süden Jerusalems ansässigen Gruppe der Arbeit von Schriftgelehrten in Diensten des in Jerusalem ansässigen Herrschaftsgeschlechts. Dieses wiederum war ständig darum bemüht, ein zentralistisch regiertes, politisch sowie sozial einheitliches Gebilde zu errichten. Nichtsdestoweniger stimmen diese Überlieferungen gut mit der oben erfolgten archäologischen Darstellung überein, gemäß derer sich Jerusalem während der EZ IIA zum bedeutendsten politischen Zentrum unter den eher vereinzelten Clustern ländlicher Siedlungen zwischen Jerusalem und Bethel entwickelte. Bei dieser Sachlage war es das Jerusalemer Herrschergeschlecht – die Davididen –, welches Israel als ihre Verwandtschaftszugehörigkeit behauptete, und infolgedessen wurde die innere Trägergruppe, auf der sie ihre Herrschaft begründeten, als israelitisch angesehen.

Was kann nun über die Historizität der Überlieferungen von der Errichtung der Monarchie Israels im Buch Samuel gesagt werden? Es lässt sich kaum bezweifeln, dass diese Überlieferungen zeitlich deutlich nach den darin dargestellten Ereignissen verfasst wurden – möglicherweise müssen sie sogar größtenteils in den Bereich der Legendenbildung eingeordnet werden. Da nun aber diese Überlieferungen der frühen Eisenzeit gut in die politische und soziale Realität Südkanaans eingebettet sind, bewahren sie zumindest in ihrem Wesen, wenn auch nicht im Detail, eine verlässliche Erinnerung an die Errichtung des judäischen Königreiches. Die Protagonisten Saul und David werden gleichermaßen als einer neu gebildeten herrschenden Elite zugehörig konterfeit, welche auf der Basis von landwirtschaftlichem Reichtum, militärischem Können und familiären Bindungen unter ihren eigenen als „Israeliten" bezeichneten Verwandten an die Macht gelangten. Eine solche Schilderung korreliert gut mit der Weise, wie wir die soziale Entwicklung verstehen, die zur Staatsbildung in der

Levante während der Eisenzeit geführt hat.[84] In dieser Hinsicht bewahren die frühen Überlieferungen über Saul und David die Erinnerung an einen Kampf um die Macht in der frühen Königszeit: Die Jerusalemer Monarchie mit Erbfolge muss als das Ergebnis eines Kampfes zwischen zwei vorherrschenden israelitischen Familien begriffen werden, die bestrebt waren, ihre politische Vormachtstellung über ihre eigenen im Norden und Süden von Jerusalem ansässigen israelitischen Verwandten zu errichten.

Bibliography

Albright, William F. 1931. The Site of Tirzah and the Topography of Western Manasseh. *JPOS* 11:241–51.

Auld, Graeme. 2011. *I & II Samuel: A Commentary*. OTL. Lousville: Westminster John Knox.

Bezzel, Hannes. 2015. *Saul: Israels König in Tradition, Redaktion und früher Rezeption*. FAT 97. Tübingen: Mohr Siebeck.

Bezzel, Hannes. 2019. Saul ben Kish – Relevant for which Identity? *WdO* 49:236–51.

Blum, Erhard. 1984. *Die Komposition der Vätergeschichte*. WMANT 57. Neukirchen-Vluyn: Neukirchener.

Blum, Erhard. 2012. The Jacob Tradition. Pages 181–211 in *The Book of Genesis: Composition, Reception and Interpretation*. Edited by C. A. Evans, J. N. Lohr and D. L. Petersen. Leiden and Boston: Brill.

Bryce, Trevor R. 2012. *The World of the Neo-Hittite Kingdoms: A Political and Military History*. Oxford: Oxford University Press.

Bunnens, Guy. 2000. *Syria in the Iron Age Problems and Definitions*. Pages 3–19 in *Essays on Syria in the Iron Age*. Edited by G. Bunnens. Ancient Near Eastern Studies Supplement 7. Louvain: Peeters.

Cahill, Jane. 2003. *Jerusalem at the Time of the United Monarchy: The Archaeological Evidence*. Pages 13–80 in *Jerusalem in Bible and Archaeology – The First Temple Period*. Edited by A. G. Vaughn and A. E. Killbrew. Atlanta: SBL Publications.

Campbell, Anthony F. 2003. *1 Samuel*. FOTL 8. Grand Rapids: Eerdmans.

Campbell, Edward F. 2002. *Shechem III: The Stratigraphy and Architecture of Shechem/Tell Balâṭah, Vol. I: Text*. ASOR 6; Boston: American School of Oriental Research.

de Pury, Albert. 2006. *The Jacob Story and the Beginning of the Formation of the Pentateuch*. Pages 51–72 in *A Farewell to the Yahwist? The Composition of the Pentateuch in Recent European Interpretation*. Edited by T. B. Dozeman and K. Schmid. SBL Symposium Series 34. Atlanta: SBL.

Dietrich, Walter. 2007. *The Early Monarchy in Israel: The Tenth Century BCE*. Biblical Encyclopedia 3. Atlanta: SBL.

Dietrich, Walter. 2008. *Samuel VIII/1,5*. BKAT. Neukirchen-Vluyn: Neukirchener.

---

84 Vgl. z. B. SCHWARTZ 1989: 275–91; BUNNENS 2000: 3–19; MAZZONI 2000: 31–59; BRYCE 2012: 163–65, 202–4; SADER 2014: 11–36.

Dietrich, Walter and Stefan Münger. 2003. *Die Herrschaft Sauls und der Norden Israels.* Pages 39–54 in *Saxa Loquentur: Studien zu Archäologie Palästinas/Israels, Festschrift für Volkmar Fritz zum 65. Geburtstag.* Edited by C. G. den Hertog, U. Hübner and S. Münger. AOAT 302. Münster: Ugarit Verlag.

Dietrich, Walter and Thomas Naumann. 2000. *The David–Saul Narrative.* Pages 276–318 in *Reconsidering Israel and Judah – Recent Studies on the Deuteronomistic History.* Edited by G. N. Knoppers and J. G McConville. Winona Lake: Eisenbrauns.

Edelman, Diane. 1990. *The Deuteronomist's Story of King Saul: Narrative Art or Editorial Product?.* Pages 207–20 in *Pentateuchal and Deuteronomistic Studies: Papers read at the XIIIth IOSOT Congress Leuven 1989.* Edited by C. Brekelmans and J. Lust. Leuven: Peeters.

Edelman, Diane. 2011. *Saul Ben Kish, King of Israel, as a 'Young Hero'?.* Pages 161–83 in *Le jeune héros: Recherche sur la formation et la diffusion d'un theme littéraire au Proch-Orient ancien.* Edited by J. M. Durand, T. Römer and M. Langlois. OBO 250. Fribourg and Göttingen: Vandenhoeck & Ruprecht.

Finkelstein, Israel. 1988. *The Archaeology of the Israelite Settlement.* Jerusalem: Israel Exploration Society.

Finkelstein, Israel. 1993. *The Sociopolitical Organization of the Central Hill Country in the Second Millennium B.C.E.* Pages 110–31 in *Biblical Archaeology Today, 1990. Proceedings of the Second International Congress on Biblical Archaeology. Supplement. Pre-Congress Symposium: Population, Production and Power, Jerusalem, June 1990.* Edited by A. Biran and J. Aviram. Jerusalem: Israel Exploration Society.

Finkelstein, Israel. 1993. *The History and Archaeology of Shiloh from the Middle Bronze Age II to Iron Age II.* Pages 371–93 in *Shiloh: The Archaeology of a Biblical Site.* Edited by I. Finkelstein. Monographs Series 10. Tel Aviv: Institute of Archaeology.

Finkelstein, Israel. 1995. *The Great Transformation: The 'Conquest' of the Highlands Frontiers and the Rise of the Territorial States.* Pages 349–65 in *The Archaeology of Society in the Holy Land.* Edited by T. Levy. London: Leicester University Press.

Finkelstein, Israel. 1996. Ethnicity and the Origin of the Iron I Settlers in the Highlands of Canaan: Can the Real Israelites Stand Up?. *Biblical Archaeologist* 59:198–212.

Finkelstein, Israel. 2000. Omride Architecture. *ZDPV* 116:114–38.

Finkelstein, Israel. 2006. The Last Labayu: King Saul and the Expansion of the First North Israelite Entity. Pages 171–88 in *Essays on Ancient Israel in Its Near Eastern Context: A Tribute to Nadav Na'aman.* Edited by Y. Amit, E. Ben Zvi, I. Finkelstein and O. Lipschits. Winona Lake: Eisenbrauns.

Finkelstein, Israel. 2006. *Shechem in the Late Bronze and the Iron I.* Pages 349–56 in *Timelines: Studies in Honor of Manfred Bietak, Vol. II.* Edited by E. Czerny, I. Hein, H. Hunger, D. Melman and A. Schwab. OLA 149. Leuven: Peeters.

Finkelstein, Israel. 2010. *A Great United Monarchy? Archaeological and Historical Perspectives.* Pages 3–28 in *One God – One Cult – One Nation.* Edited by R. G. Kratz and H. Spieckermann. BZAW 405. Berlin: de Gruyter.

Finkelstein, Israel. 2011. *Saul, Benjamin and the Emergence of Biblical Israel: An Alternative View. ZAW* 123:348–67.

Finkelstein, Israel. 2011. *Stages in the Territorial Expansion of the Northern Kingdom. VT* 61:227–42.

Finkelstein, Israel. 2013. *The Forgotten Kingdom: The Archaeology and History of Northern Israel.* ANEM 5. Atlanta: SBL.

Finkelstein, Israel. 2018. Jerusalem and the Benjamin Plateau in the Early Phases of the Iron Age: A Different Scenario. *ZDPV* 134:190–95.

Finkelstein, Israel and Zvi Lederman. 1997. *Highlands of Many Cultures: The Southern Samaria Survey, The Sites*. Monograph Series 14. Tel Aviv: Institute of Archaeology.

Finkelstein, Israel and Oded Lipschits. 2010. Omride Architecture in Moab: Jahatz and Atharot. *ZDPV* 126:29–42.

Finkelstein, Israel and Thomas Römer. 2014. Comments on the Historical Background of the Jacob Narrative in Genesis. *ZAW* 126:317–38.

Fleming, Daniel. 2009. *Kinship of City and Tribe Conjoined: Zimri-Lim at Mari*. Pages 227–40 in *Nomads, Tribes and the States in the Ancient Near East: Cross-disciplinary Perspectives*. Edited by J. Szuchman. Oriental Institute Seminar 5. Chicago: University of Chicago.

Fleming, Daniel. 2012. *The Legacy of Israel in Judah's Bible: History, Politics and the Reinscribing of Tradition*. Cambridge: University Press.

Franklin, Norma. 2004. Samaria: From the Bedrock to the Omride Palace. *Levant* 36:189–202.

Gadot, Yuval. 2017. *The Iron I in the Samaria Highlands: A Nomad Settlement Wave or Urban Expansion?*. Pages 103–14 in *Rethinking Israel: Studies in the History and Archaeology of Ancient Israel in Honor of Israel Finkelstein*. Edited by O. Lipschits, Y. Gadot and M. J. Adams. Winona Lake: Eisenbrauns.

Gadot, Yuval and Joe Uziel. 2017. The Monumentality of Iron Age Jerusalem prior to the 8th Century BCE. *Tel Aviv* 44:123–40.

Gaß, Erasmus. 2005. *Die Ortsnamen des Richterbuchs in historischer und redaktioneller Perspektive*. ADPV 35. Wiesbaden: Harrassowitz.

Grønbæk, Hans J. 1971. *Die Geschichte vom Aufstieg Davids (1 Sam. 15–2 Sam. 5): Tradition und Komposition*. Acta Theologica Danica X. Copenhagen: Prostant Apud Munksgaard.

Groß, Walter. 2009. *Richter*. HThKAT. Freiburg: Herder.

Hasel, Michael G. 1994. *Domination and Resistance: Egyptian Military Activity in the Southern Levant, ca. 1300–1185 B.C.* Probleme der Ägyptologie 11. Leiden and Boston: Brill.

Hutton, Jeremy M. 2006. Mahanaim, Penuel, and Transhumance Routes, Observations on Genesis 32–33 and Judges 8. *JNES* 65:161–78.

Jobling, David. 1976. Saul's Fall and Jonathan's Rise: Tradition and Redaction in 1 Sam 14:1–46. *JBL* 95:367–76.

Kaiser, Otto. 2010. Der historische und biblische König Saul (Teil I). *ZAW* 122:520–45.

Kaiser, Otto. 2011. Der historische und biblische König Saul (Teil II). *ZAW* 123:1–14.

Kleiman, Assaf. 2018. Comments on the Archaeology and History of Tell el-Farʿah north (Biblical Tirzah) in the Iron IIA. *Semitica* 60:85–104.

Knauf, Ernst A. 1992. *The Cultural Impact of Secondary State Formation: The Cases of Edomites and Moabites*. Pages 47–54 in *Early Edom and Moab: The Beginning of Iron Age in Southern Jordan*. Edited by P. Bienkowski. Sheffield Archaeological Monographs 7. Sheffield: Equinox.

Kratz, Reinhard G. 2005. *The Composition of the Narrative Books of the Old Testament*. London: T&T Clark.

Lee, Sharen, Christoph Bronk Ramsey and Amihai Mazar. 2013. Iron Age Chronology in Israel: Results from Modeling with a Trapezoidal Bayesian Framework. *Radiocarbon* 55:731–40.

Lehmann, Gunnar and Hermann Michael Niemann. 2014. When Did the Shephelah Became Judahite?. *Tel Aviv* 41:77–94.

Maeir, Aren M. 2012. *The Tell eṣ-Ṣafi/Gath Archaeological Project 1996–2010: Introduction, Overview and Synopsis of Results*. Pages 1–88 in *Tell eṣ-Ṣafi/Gath I: The 1996–2005 Seasons, Part 1, Text*. Edited by A. M. Maeir. Ägypten und Altes Testament 69. Wiesbaden: Harrassowitz.

Maeir, Aren, M., Louise Hitchcock and Liora K. Horwitz. 2013. On the Constitution and Transformation of Philistine Identity. *OJA* 32:1–38.

Mazar, Amihai. 2006. *Jerusalem in the 10th Century B.C.E: The Glass Half Full*. Pages 255–72 in *Essays on Ancient Israel in Its Near Eastern Context: A Tribute to Nadav Na'aman*. Edited by Y. Amit, E. Ben Zvi, I. Finkelstein and O. Lipschits. Winona Lake: Eisenbrauns.

Mazar, Amihai. 2010. *Archaeology and the Biblical Narrative: The Case of the United Monarchy*. Pages 29–58 in *One God – One Cult – One Nation*. Edited by R. G. Kratz and H. Spieckermann. BZAW 405. Berlin: de Gruyter.

Mazzoni, Stefania. 2000. *Syria and the Periodization of the Iron Age: A Cross-Cultural Perspective*. Pages 31–59 in *Essays on Syria in the Iron Age*. Edited by G. Bunnens. Ancient Near Eastern Studies Supplement 7. Louvain: Peeters.

McCarter, P. Kyle. 1980. *I Samuel: A New Translation with Introduction, Notes and Commentary*. AB 8. New Haven and London: Doubleday.

McKenzie, Steven L. 2006. *Saul in the Deuteronomistic History*. Pages 59–70 in *Saul in Story and Tradition*. Edited by C. S. Ehrlich and M. C. White. FAT 47. Tübingen: Mohr Siebeck.

Na'aman, Nadav. 1990. The pre-Deuteronomistic Story of King Saul and its Historical Significance. *CBQ* 54:638–58.

Na'aman, Nadav. 1992. Canaanite Jerusalem and Its Central Hill Country Neighbors in the Second Millennium B.C.E. *UF* 24:257–91.

Na'aman, Nadav. 1996. *Sources and Composition in the History of David*. Pages 170–86 in *The Origins of the Ancient Israelite States*. Edited by V. Fritz and P. R. Davies. Sheffield: Academic Press.

Na'aman, Nadav. 2002. In Search of Reality behind the Account of David's Wars with Israel's Neighbours. *IEJ* 52:200–24.

Na'aman, Nadav. 2007. *The Northern Kingdom in the Late 10th–9th Centuries BCE*. Pages 399–418 in *Understanding the History of Ancient Israel*. Edited by H. G. M. Williamson. Proceedings of the British Academy 143. Oxford: University Press.

Na'aman, Nadav. 2009. Saul, Benjamin and the Emergence of Biblical Israel. *ZAW* 121:211–24, 335–49.

Na'aman, Nadav. 2013. The Kingdom of Judah in the 9th century BCE: Text Analysis versus Archaeological Research. *Tel Aviv* 40:247–76.

Na'aman, Nadav. 2014. The Settlements of the Ephratites in Bethlehem and the Location of Rachel's Tomb. *RB* 121:516–29.

Na'aman, Nadav. 2015. Jebusites and Jabeshites in the Saul and David Story Cycle. *Biblica* 95:481–97.

Na'aman, Nadav. *The Scope of the pre-Deuteronomistic Saul-David Story Cycle*. In *From Nomadism to Monarchy: 30 Years Update*. Edited by I. Koch, O. Sergi and O. Lipschits. Tübingen: Mohr Siebeck, forthcoming.

Niemann, Hermann Michael. 2006. *Core Israel in the Highlands and Its Periphery: Megiddo, the Jezreel Valley and the Galilee in the 11th–8th century BCE*. Pages 821–42 in *Megiddo IV: The 1998–2002 Seasons*. Edited by I. Finkelstein, D. Ussishkin and B. Halpern. Monograph Series 24. Tel Aviv: Institute of Archaeology.

Niemann, Hermann Michael. 2007. *Royal Samaria – Capital or Residence? Or: The Foundation of the City of Samaria by Sargon II*. Pages 184–207 in *Ahab Agonistes: The Rise and Fall of the Omri Dynasty*. Edited by L. L. Grabbe; LHB/OTS 421. London: T&T Clark.

Nihan, Christophe. 2006. *Saul among the Prophets (1 Sam. 10:10–12 and 19:18–24): The Reworking of Saul's Figure in the Context of the Debate on Charismatic Prophecy in the Persian Era*. Pages 88–118 in *Saul in Story and Tradition*. Edited by C. S. Ehrlich and M. C. White. FAT 47. Tübingen: Mohr Siebeck.

Noth, Martin. 1953. Jabes-Gilead. *ZDPV* 69:28–41.

Porter, Ann. 2009. *Beyond Dimorphism: Ideologies and Materialities of Kinship as Time-Space Distanciation*. Pages 201–25 in *Nomads, Tribes and the States in the Ancient Near East: Cross-disciplinary Perspectives*. Edited by J. Szuchman. Oriental Institute Seminar 5. Chicago: University of Chicago.

Porter, Ann. 2012. *Mobile Pastoralism and the Formation of Near Eastern Civilization: Weaving Together Society*. Cambridge: University Press.

Porter, Benjamin. 2013. *Complex Communities: The Archaeology of Early Iron Age Central Transjordan*. Tucson: The University of Arizona Press.

Rosen, Baruch. 1993. *Economy and Subsistence*. Pages 362–67 in *Shiloh: The Archaeology of a Biblical Site*. Edited by I. Finkelstein. Monographs Series 10. Tel Aviv: Institute of Archaeology.

Sader, Helen. 2014. *History*. Pages 11–36 in *The Aramaeans in Ancient Syria*. Edited by H. Niehr. HdO 106. Leiden: Brill.

Schmidt, Ludwig. 1970. *Menschlicher Erfolg und Jahwes Initiative: Studien zu Tradition, Interpretation und Historie in Überlieferungen von Gideon, Saul und David*. WMANT 38. Neukirchen-Vluyn: Neukirchener.

Schwartz, Glenn M. 1989. *The Origins of the Aramaeans in Syria and Northern Mesopotamia: Research Problems and Potential Strategies*. Pages 275–91 in *To The Euphrates and Beyond: Archaeological Studies in Honor of Maurits N. van Loon*. Edited by O. M. C. Haex, H. H. Curvers and P. M. M. G. Akkermans. Rotterdam: CRC Press.

Sergi, Omer. 2013. Judah's Expansion in Historical Context. *Tel Aviv* 40:226–46.

Sergi, Omer. 2015. State Formation, Religion and Collective Identity in the Southern Levant. *HeBAI* 4:56–77.

Sergi, Omer. 2016. *The Gilead between Aram and Israel: Political Borders, Cultural Interaction and the Question of Jacob and the Israelite Identity*. Pages 333–54 in *In Search of Aram and Israel, Politics, Culture and the Question of Identity*. Edited by O. Sergi, M. Oeming and I. De-Hulster. ORA 20. Tübingen: Mohr Siebeck.

Sergi, Omer. 2017. The Emergence of Judah as a Political Entity between Jerusalem and Benjamin. *ZDPV* 133:1–23.

Sergi, Omer and Yuval Gadot. 2017. Omride Palatial Architecture as Symbol in Action: Between State Formation, Obliteration and Heritage. *JNES* 76:103–11.

Stager, Lawrence, E. 1990. Shemer's Estate. *BASOR* 277/278:93–107.

Steiner, Margret, L. 2001. *Excavations by Kathleen M. Kenyon in Jerusalem 1961–1967, Vol. III: The Settlement in the Bronze and Iron Ages*. Copenhagen International Series 9. London: Sheffield Academic Press.

Stoebe, Hans J. 1973. *Das Erste Buch Samuelis*. KAT VIII 2. Gütersloh: Gütersloher Verlagshaus.

Stolz, Fritz. 1981. *Das erste und zweite Buch Samuel*. ZBKAT 9. Zürich: Theologischer Verlag.

Toffolo, Michael B., Eran Arie, Mario A. S. Martin, Elisabetta Boaretto and Israel Finkelstein. 2014. Absolute Chronology of Megiddo, Israel in the Late Bronze and Iron Ages: High Resolution Radiocarbon Dating. *Radiocarbon* 56:221–44.

Uziel, Joe and Nahshon Szanton. 2015. "Recent Excavations Near the Gihon Spring and Their Reflection on the Character of Iron II Jerusalem." *Tel Aviv* 42:233–50.

Uziel, Joe and Nahshon Szanton. 2017. *New Evidence of Jerusalem's Urban Development in the 9th Century BCE*. Pages 429–39 in *Rethinking Israel: Studies in the History and Archaeology of Ancient Israel in Honor of Israel Finkelstein*. Edited by O. Lipschits, Y. Gadot and M. J. Adams. Winona Lake: Eisenbrauns.

Van Seters, John. 2009. *The Biblical Saga of King David*. Winona Lake: Eisenbrauns.

van der Steen, Eveline J. 2004. *Tribes and People in Transition: The Central East Jordan Valley in the Late Bronze Age and Early Iron Ages, A Study of the Sources*. Leuven and Paris: Peeters.

van der Steen, Eveline J. and Klaas A. D. Smelik. 2007. King Mesha and the Tribe of Dibon. *JSOT* 32:139–62.

Veijola, Timo. 1975. *Die ewige Dynastie: David und die Entstehung seiner Dynastie nach der deuteronomistischen Darstellung*. Helsinki: Suomalainen Tiedeakatemia.

Weingart, Kristin. 2014. *Stämmevolk – Staatvolk – Gottesvolk? Studien zur Verwendung des Israels-Namens im Alten Testament*. FAT II/68. Tübingen: Mohr Siebeck.

Weiser, Arthur. 1966. Die Legitimation des Königs Davids: zur Eigenart und Entstehung der sogen. Geschichte von Davids Aufstieg. *VT* 16:325–54.

Wellhausen, Julius. 1889. *Die Composition des Hexateuchs und der historischen Bücher des Alten Testament*. Berlin: de Gruyter.

White, Marsha C. 2000. *The History of Saul's Rise: Saulide State Propaganda in 1 Samuel 1– 14*. Pages 271–92 in *"A Wise and Discerning Mind": Essays in Honor of Burke O. Long*. Edited by S. M. Olyan and R. C. Culley. BJS 325. Providence: Brown University.

White, Marsha C. 2006. *Saul and Jonathan in 1 Samuel 1 and 14*. Pages 119–38 in *Saul in Story and Tradition*. Edited by C. S. Ehrlich and M. C. White. FAT 47. Tübingen: Mohr Siebeck.

Willi-Plein, Ina. 2004. *1 Sam. 18–19 und die Davidshausgeschichte*. Pages 138–71 in *David und Saul im Widerstreit – Diachronie und Synchronie im Wettstreit, Beiträge zur Auslegung des ersten Samuelbuches*. Edited by W. Dietrich. OBO 206. Fribourg: Academic Press.

Wright, Jacob, L. 2014. *David, King of Israel and Caleb in Biblical Memory*. Cambridge: Cambridge University Press.

Zertal, Adam. 2004. *The Manasseh Hill Country Survey, Vol. 1: The Shechem Syncline*. CHANE 21.1. Leiden and Boston: Brill.

Zertal, Adam. 2008. *The Manasseh Hill Country Survey, Vol. 2: The Eastern Valleys and the Fringe of the Desert*. CHANE 21.2. Leiden and Boston: Brill.

Zertal, Adam and Niv Mirkam. 2016. *The Manasseh Hill Country Survey, Vol. 3: From Nahal 'Iron to Nahal Shechem*. CHANE 21.3. Leiden and Boston: Brill.

Sara Kipfer

The Land "from Telam on the way to Shur and on to the land of Egypt" (1 Sam 27)

Some Remarks on a Disputed Territory

Historiography is basically concerned with time and space.[1] Since the formation of the so called *Annales school*, developed by French historians in the early 20th century, it became clear that focusing on time and single events in history is too biased. A multidimensional historiography needs to take into account the geographic space and its different time structures (see e.g. the *temps géographique* for the reconstruction of the *histoire de la longue durée*).[2] While the *spatial turn* or *topographical / topological turn* has long been claimed in cultural studies,[3] it has not been given enough attention in biblical studies so far.[4]

---

1 See KOSELLECK 2018: 25, "At the latest with Kant and Herder, it came to be a basic principle of historians that they are concerned with space and time, meaning thereby historical space and historical time, understood within the horizon of their own historicization." And he explicates: "categorically speaking, space is just as much a condition of possible history as time. But 'space' too has a history. Space is both something that should be metahistorically presupposed for every possible history and something that is historicizable, because it changes socially, economically, and politically." (27). For the problematic relationship between history and geography see DÖRING / THIELMANN ²2009: 19–24 and EBELING 2010: 121–33. For hermeneutical questions see also FLECKMAN in this volume.
2 BRAUDEL ⁶1990 and BRAUDEL 2012: 241–76.
3 The term "spatial turn" was first claimed by Edward W. Soja in his book "Postmodern Geographies. The Relation of Space in Critical Social Theory," London / New York, 1989. See DÖRING / THIELMANN ²2009: 7–8, GÜNZEL ²2009: 219–37 and GÜNZEL 2010.
4 FINKELSTEIN / SILBERMAN ²2007: 33, pointed to the importance of geographical information: "Detailed descriptions of environment and settlement patterns are perhaps the most important evidence for dating the Bible's historical texts. The sheer weight of geographical information and long lists of place-names interwoven in its stories testify to a familiarity with the ancient landscape Judah and Israel. The many biblical geographical descriptions that today appear to us as tedious lists of obscure villages and natural features interrupting the flow of the narrative were once essential components of its tales. They were intended for particular audiences who would recognize the names of the various places mentioned and evoke admiration for the achievements of the various biblical characters in a physical setting that they knew well." For more references see HUTTON 2009: 31–35.

Note: I am grateful to Christopher Ryan Jones (Johannes Gutenberg University Mainz) for improving my English and to Jeremy M. Hutton (University of Wisconsin-Madison) for his comments on this paper. Mistakes are mine alone.

https://doi.org/10.1515/9783110606164-004

1 Sam 27 is a prime example for a *landscape critical*[5] analysis. Many commentaries add a map to describe the geographical reality of 1 Sam 27.[6] But the maps mostly deal with reconstructions of the human geography, oriented toward localizations of tells and ethnic borders. None of them are interested in the precipitation isohyets, altitude graphs, the watershed, or climate zones (desert, semiarid and arid zones), and most of them even lack the watercourses. However, to better understand the environmental background of this story and its supposed historical reality it is important to gather information from topography, agronomy, hydrology, climatology, archaeology, settlement history, etc., and to address questions such as: where does the agricultural land end and where does the desert begin?[7] Is the setting of the text located in the "desert" as it is defined by geographers? Or is the term נֶגֶב used as a southern toponym,[8] with מִדְבָּר referring to a semi-arid zone and pasture?[9] And last but not least, what is the geopolitical setting of 1 Sam 27?

In recent research, it has become increasingly obvious that texts representing David as a mercenary or even vassal[10] of the Philistines contain very old traditions and information which only fit in the 10th or early 9th century.[11] For example, Israel Finkelstein has stated that the stories about David and his band reflect the nature of 'Apiru activity on the boundary between Hebron's hill country and the southern Shephela. Read against "the background of archaeological research, the geographical information embedded in the early David story in 1 Samuel depicts pre-Deuteromonistic reality that can be dated to the 10th and / or early 9th centuries BCE – in any event, before ca. 840 BCE."[12] And similarly,

---

5 For methodological issues see e.g. GOLDFARB 2012: 6–23 and HUTTON 2009: 31–43.

6 See e.g. MCCARTER 1980: 410, CARTLEDGE 2001: 309, DIETRICH 2017: 6.

7 FINKELSTEIN 1985: 51 claimed: "Before dealing with specific periods and problems in the history of the region, the quantitative aspect of the different subsistence patterns along the sedentary-nomadic continuum must be discussed."

8 For the meaning of the term "negeb" see RAINEY 1984: 88. He concludes: "The region that concerns us, therefore, is that known to modern geographers as the Beer Sheva Valley on the east and the Negev Coastal Plain of Ḥevel Ha Besor on the west."

9 See also נְאוֹת מִדְבָּר Jer 9:9; 23:10; Joel 1:19–20; 2:22; Ps 68:13. See KIPFER (in press).

10 See EHRLICH 1996: 24, "In return for their protection, David entered into a vassal relationship with Achish, king of Gath, and received the fiefdom of Ziklag in the northwestern Negeb, at the southeastern border of Philistine settlement." See also NIEMANN 2002: 83, "Das mögen die Philister gern gesehen haben, betrachteten sie doch David als Vasallen, der machtpolitisch nüchtern die Seiten zum Stärkeren zu wechseln pflegte." See also DIETRICH 2012: 93–95.

11 See e.g. HALPERN 2001: 287–88, "In effect, this is David's first historical, as distinct from literary, appearance. It is certain that he served Achish, because even the B source, which concedes the fact, is at pains to explain it away."

12 FINKELSTEIN 2013: 149. See also KNAUF 2007, "Diese Texte gehören zum Grundbestand der David-Überlieferung und sind spätestens im 9. Jh. entstanden."

albeit with different arguments, Walter Dietrich comes to the conclusion that the "rather dry account in the verses 2, 3a, 6, 7 may be old; the later, David-friendly tradition would never have implicated its hero in such escapades".[13]

I will begin with a text critical analysis focusing on the historical (time- and space-related) information as well as a literary critical reconstruction of 1 Sam 27. Further, I will analyze the landscape, agriculture, water resources, climate, and settlement history of the territory described in the text, namely the "surroundings" (שְׂדֵה פְּלִשְׁתִּים) of the Philistine territory (אֶרֶץ פְּלִשְׁתִּים 1 Sam 27:1). Finally, I will consider the geopolitical background of this area in the 11th and 10th century. I will again rely on the textual evidence in 1 Sam 27 and combine it with the data from geographical descriptions, topographic lists, toponymy etc. It is important to stress the interdependence between inductive and deductive methods used here. The combination of both methods with the manifold approaches seem to be most promising, but also carries the risk of circular argumentation. By starting with the textual reference, I give priority to "historiography" and the reconstructed literary history (deductive); only then do I analyze more generally its temporal and spatial setting. Finally, I reanalyze the text (inductive) in light of the collected geopolitical information.

1 David and the Philistines – A Historical Critical Analysis of 1 Sam 27

As it has long been noted, v. 1 and 4 are later additions combining the David and Saul story in a very stereotyped way.[14]

---

13 DIETRICH 2012: 89. See also DIETRICH 2017: 14–15, "Diese Nachrichten dürften literarisch alt und historisch zuverlässig sein." CAQUOT / DE ROBERT 1994, 325, concludes: "Que le futur roi d'Israël ait pu passer à l'enemie en devenant pour un temps vassal des Philistins, c'est un fait que nos historiens n'aurainet pu inventer, et qui est donc asssuré." Similarly STOLZ 1981: 168, "Der vorübergehende Aufenthalt Davids bei Achis von Gath ist historisch ganz sicher."
14 RENDTORFF 1971: 435, "Darin kann eine Bestätigung unsere Überlegungen über die Entstehung dieser kurzen Mitteilungen gesehen werden: Sie sind niedergeschrieben worden, um den Darstellungszusammenhang zu vervollständigen, der durch die überlieferten ausführlichen Erzählungen gegeben war; in diesem Fall bedurften die Erzählungen über Davids Aufenthalt bei den Philistern einer Einleitung, die erklärte, wie er zu den Philistern und speziell nach Ziklag kam." For the translation and text critical remarks, see also AULD 2011: 314–17.

V. 1 And David said in his heart,
    "Now I shall perish one day by the hand of Saul;
    There is no good for me but to [surely][15] escape to the land of the Philistines.
    And Saul will despair of seeking me further in all the territory of Israel,
    and I shall escape from his hand."
V. 4 And it was reported to Saul
    that David fled to Gath
    and he did not continue further seeking him.

Not only *Leitwörter*,[16] but also repetitions of phrases (so called *"Überlieferungs-elemente"*[17]) strengthen the connection between 1 Sam 27:1,4 and 1 Sam 19–26.

יַד (hand of Saul)[18]	1 Sam 18:10,17; 19:9; 22:6; 23:7,12,14, 17,20; 24:16	1 Sam 27:1 twice "perish by the hand of Saul" or "get away from his hand"
מלט, Niphal	1 Sam 19:10,12,17,18; 20:29; 22:1,20; 23:13 (Piel 1 Sam 19:11)	1 Sam 27:1 twice or even three times (*figura etymologica*)
בקשׁ, Piel[19]	1 Sam 19:2,10; 20:1; 22:23_bis; 23:10,14, 15,25; 26:2,20 (see 1 Sam 24:10; 25: 26,29)	1 Sam 27:1.4
וַיֻּגַּד לְשָׁאוּל נגד Hophal	1 Sam 19:19; 23:7	1 Sam 27:4
ברח	1 Sam 19:12,18; 20:1; 21:11; 22:17 (Abjatar as subject 22:20; 23:6)	1 Sam 27:4

The above-mentioned references do not go beyond 1 Sam 27:4. At this point, the story of David fleeing from Saul ends.[20] It is however arguable as to where the

---

15 LXX (ἐὰν μὴ σωθῶ), Peshitta and Vulgata do not translate the *figura etymologica*. See WIRTH 2016: 114 Anm. 9. Due to considerations of space one can assume that 4QSamᵃ (frgs 42 b–c) does not support this reading however. See DRIESBACH 2016: 94.
16 KIPFER 2015: 65–71. See also EDENBURG in this volume.
17 THIEL 2005: 44, "In solchen Kompositionen treffen wir also auf Kleinstüberlieferungen, Mitteilungen, die der Redaktor der Aufstiegsgeschichte bei seinen Stoffsammlungen erhielt. Hier zeigt sich viel stärker die gestaltende Hand des Redaktors: Er hat nicht nur die erhaltenen Mitteilungen disponiert und in den Gesamtverlauf seiner Geschichte einbezogen, sondern sie auch durch deutende Hinweise, die er verfaßte zuallererst miteinander und mit dem größeren Ganzen in Verbindung gesetzt. Auf diese Weise wird eine kontinuierliche Darstellung erreicht."
18 See KIPFER 2015: 59–60.
19 See KLEIN 2005: 181–82.
20 See STOEBE 1973: 475, "Ebenso schließt Kap. 27 diesen Komplex als Ganzes ab."

new story of David and the Philistines begins. One possibility would be v. 2. Achish is first mentioned in 2 Sam 21:11 but once again introduced in 2 Sam 27:2.[21]

> V. 2 And David arose,
>> and crossed over,[22] he and six[23] hundred men who were with him,
>> to Achish, son of Maoch,[24] king of Gath.

The introduction formula used here can be found throughout the Books of Samuel: וַיָּקָם דָּוִד is always followed by different verbs of movement.

וַיָּקָם דָּוִד   + הלך = 1 Sam 18:27 (see also 2 Sam 11:2)

   + ברח = 1 Sam 22:11

   + יצא = 1 Sam 23:13; 24:9

   + ירד = 1 Sam 25:1

   + בוא = 1 Sam 26:5

   + עבר = 1 Sam 27:2 (see also 2 Sam 17:22)

   + x   = 1 Sam 24:5; 2Sam 12:20; 2Sam 24,11

In 1 Sam 18:27 and in 1 Sam 23:27 it is said that David arose together with his men.

1 Sam 18:27   וַיָּקָם דָּוִד וַיֵּלֶךְ הוּא וַאֲנָשָׁיו וַיַּךְ בַּפְּלִשְׁתִּים מָאתַיִם אִישׁ

1 Sam 23:13   וַיָּקָם דָּוִד וַאֲנָשָׁיו כְּשֵׁשׁ־מֵאוֹת אִישׁ וַיֵּצְאוּ מִקְּעִלָה

In v. 3 it is said that David settled with Achish together not only with his men but also with his wives.

---

21 1 Sam 14:21 contains some similar information about Hebrews serving Philistines as mercenaries. This fact could strengthen the hypotheses, that the story of David and Saul was combined only later. At this point it was not common to serve as mercenary anymore and David's joining of the Philistines needed to be justified by the threat of Saul.

22 וַיַּעֲבֹר הוּא is missing in LXX. See McCARTER 1980: 412, "MT, LXX^AL. LXX^B unaccountably omits this, but it seems indispensable." The verb עבר is used in 2 Sam 17:22, when David crossed the Jordan (see also 1 Sam 30:10 crossing the Naḥal Besôr).

23 According to the LXX (καὶ οἱ τετρακόσιοι ἄνδρες μετ' αὐτοῦ) and presumably also 4QSam ͣ, frg 42 c only 400 men come with him. ULRICH 2010: 287, reconstructs: וּ[אַ]רְבַּע. See 1 Sam 23:13; 25:13; 27:2; 30:9–10; see also Judg 18:11,16–17; 1 Sam 13:15; 14:2; 2 Sam 15:18 etc.

24 LXX^B reads υἱὸν Αμμαχ, LXX^L Αχειμααν. The name "Achish" is a non-Semitic name. See NAVEH 1998: 35–37 and GITIN 1997: 11. A king with the name "Achish" is also known from 1 Kgs 2:39 ("Achish son of Maacah of Gath"). For an overview see also EDENBURG 2011: 34–38, TSUMURA 2007: 609–10 et al.

V. 3 And David settled with Achish in Gath,
    he and his men, each man and his house,
    and David and his two wives, Ahinoam the Jezreelite and Abigail, wife of Nabal the Carmelite.

Again, an *"Überlieferungselement"*, which occurs frequently elsewhere in the Books of Samuel, stands at the beginning of the verse.

וַיֵּשֶׁב דָּוִד   1 Sam 23:14,18
                 1 Sam 27:3
                 2 Sam 1:1; 5:9; 6:20; 12:31

David's wives, Ahinoam the Jezreelite and Abigail the Carmelite, have been mentioned in 1 Sam 25:42–43 and they reappear in 1 Sam 30:5, 2 Sam 2:2 and 3:2–3. It is not necessary to think of a developed stratum of the book connecting 1 Sam 25–30 and 2 Sam 1–4[25] since in all cases the information about David's wives seems to be dispensable. At no point is the information essential to the narrative. These verses might comprise a kind of "short note" which were later added to the David story.

According v. 5, David is powerful enough to negotiate with Achish and to determine that he wants to have his own fiefdom. David contrasts in direct speech the towns of the countryside (עָרֵי הַשָּׂדֶה) from the royal city (עִיר הַמַּמְלָכָה)[26] – obviously referring to Gath (*Tell eṣ-Ṣāfi*) as a large fortified city.[27] The expression עָרֵי הַשָּׂדֶה is contradictory since עִיר usually refers to a fortified city while שָׂדֶה simply means the open field.[28] Achish immediately fulfills David's wish in v. 6. He gives Ziklag to David as fiefdom, located somewhere in the surrounding area, namely the שְׂדֵה פְלִשְׁתִּים (v. 7).[29] Similar procedures are known from the Amarna letters (14th century): the 'Apiru not only served as

---

25 See AULD 2011: 315, "The evidence is accumulating that 1 Sam 25–30 and 2 Sam 1–4 represent a connected and developed stratum of the book."

26 See similarly 1 Sam 6:18 מֵעִיר מִבְצָר וְעַד כֹּפֶר הַפְּרָזִי. See also Josh 15:47.

27 See 1 Sam 5:8; 6:17; 7:14; 17:4,23,52; 21:11,13; 27:2–4,11; 2 Sam 1:20; 15:18; 21:20,22; 1 Kgs 2:39–41; 2 Kgs 12:18 etc. The identification of Gath with Tell eṣ-Ṣāfi should not be discussed here. See e.g. MAEIR 2012: 5–6.

28 בְּנֹתֶיהָ as allied cities or villages are mentioned in Num 21:25,32; Josh 15:45; 17:11,16; Judg 1:27; 11:26; Jer 49:2; Ezek 16:46,48,53,55 etc. See MACHINIST 2000: 58.

29 See NIESIOŁOWSKI-SPANÒ 2016: 112, "The reason why Achish is so generous to David can be seen in the next verses, depicting David's raids (1 Sam 27:8–12; 30:1–31). David is then a local warlord who makes raids in order to maintain his kin's political control over the lands of Judah and the Negev."

mercenaries fighting for a foreign king,[30] but they were also rewarded with a fiefdom.[31]

> V. 5 And David said to Achish:
> "If I have in fact found favor in your eyes,[32]
> let there be given me a place in one of the towns of the countryside,
> and let me settle there.
> And why should your servant dwell in a royal city with you?"
> V. 6 And Achish gave him Ziklag on that day.
> Therefore Ziklag belonged to the kings of Judah till this day.
> V. 7 And the number of the days
> that David settled in Philistine countryside
> were one year and four months.[33]

With the "etiology"[34] in v. 6b the story is interrupted. Its meaning is contradictory since David was not king over Judah when he received Ziklag from Achish.[35] Similarly the retrospection in v. 7 also gives some additional information about David's stay with the Philistines.[36] The story continues with the narrative form (*waw consecutivum* imperfect) in v. 8 describing David's raids and cruel bloodsheds. V. 9abα seems to be a repetition summarizing David's deeds (*waw consecutivum* perfect). In v. 8bβ, David returns to Achish. When Achish asks him, he lies and pretends to plunder the Negeb of Judah. Obviously, David did not fight against the enemies of Achish. He looted to the west instead of going east. The episode ends[37] saying that Achish was confident in David and believed that he would be his servant forever[38] (v. 12).

---

30 See Amarna Letter EA 76:17–29 (VAT 324); 132:19–21 (BM 29801); 195:24–32; 246:5–10. See also NAʾAMAN 2010a: 87–97.

31 See Amarna Letter EA 287:31 (VAT 1644); 289:21–24 (VAT 1645). See ZWICKEL 2015: 62, "Ḫabiru-Gruppen verdingen sich aber auch im Dienste anderer Könige und kämpfen auf deren Seite. Von diesen werden sie mit der Belehnung von Land belohnt."

32 LXX reads εἰ δὴ εὕρηκεν ὁ δοῦλός σου χάριν ἐν ὀφθαλμοῖς σου. DIETRICH 2017, 9, "G lässt David höflicher sein: ‚Wenn doch dein Knecht Gnade gefunden hat': möglicherweise eine Angleichung an die zweite Vershälfte."

33 LXX reads here just "four months" τέσσαρας μῆνας.

34 See CAQUOT / DE ROBERT 1994: 327, STOLZ 1981: 168 et al.

35 STOLZ 1981: 169 explains, "Für den Erzähler bedeutet die Zuweisung Ziklags an David die Einverleibung dieser Stadt in den judäischen Machtbereich; er erzählt also vom Standpunkt der späteren davidischen Herrschaft aus." See also TSUMURA 2007: 612.

36 See STOLZ 1981: 169, "Mit einer Zeitangabe beschließt der Erzähler seine summarischen Einleitungsbemerkungen."

37 In 1 Sam 28:1 a new narrative begins with וַיְהִי בַּיָּמִים הָהֵם. DIETRICH 2017: 12–13, however sees the end of the story in 1 Sam 28:2.

38 AULD 2011: 318, "The closing verse includes some striking adaptation of language drawn from Nathan's oracle and David's response in 2 Sam 7:3–29 [...]." TSUMURA 2007: 614 rather

It only becomes clear in 1 Sam 27:8–12 that his relationship with Achish, king of Gath was not marked by integrity and loyalty but by tactical cheating. 1 Sam 27 thus combines two aspects, David's cooperation with the Philistines on one hand (1 Sam 27:2,3a,5–7) and his dissociation from them (1 Sam 27:8–12) on the other.

To conclude, the information concerning time and space in 1 Sam 27 are peculiar. The word יוֹם / יָמִים appears seven times (1 Sam 27:1,6_{bis},7_{bis},10,11).[39] In addition, time adverbs are frequent (עַתָּה 1 Sam 27:1; עוֹד 1 Sam 27:1,4). The note that David lived one year and four months in Gath (וְאַרְבָּעָה חֳדָשִׁים 1 Sam 27:7) adds a technical and "historiographical" mark to the text. This is also true for the many details of location. In v. 1 the "territory" (גְּבוּל) of Israel[40] is contrasted to the "land" (אֶרֶץ) of the Philistines.[41] It is striking that in 1 Sam 27:1 the גְּבוּל יִשְׂרָאֵל is mentioned and not Judah. This is in distinction to the kings of Judah in v. 6. The אֶרֶץ פְּלִשְׁתִּים in 1 Sam 27 is only referred to in v. 1, while otherwise the expression בִּשְׂדֵה פְלִשְׁתִּים (v. 7 and 11) can be found. In the following I will analyze the geographical region which could stand behind the expression שְׂדֵה פְלִשְׁתִּים (1 Sam 27:7,11) and which is only mentioned one more time in 1 Sam 6:1 – namely the fields and surroundings of the Philistine territory.[42]

2 The Philistine Territory (אֶרֶץ פְּלִשְׁתִּים 1 Sam 27:1) and its Surroundings (שְׂדֵה פְּלִשְׁתִּים) – Some Remarks on Landscape, Agriculture, Water Resources, Climate and Settlement History

The אֶרֶץ פְּלִשְׁתִּים mentioned in v. 1 is a relatively distinct geographic territory. The expression אֶרֶץ פְּלִשְׁתִּים appears 14 times in the Hebrew Bible, including four times in the Books of Samuel (Gen 21:32,34; Exod 13:17; 1 Sam 27:1; 29:11;

---

sees parallels to the concepts of "eternal slaves" in KTU 1.14 III 23 as well as Deut 15:17 and Job 40:28.

39 See DIETRICH 2017: 12–13.

40 See FLECKMAN in this volume.

41 AULD 2011: 315, "It is not easy to decide whether he intents deliberate contrast in geographical terminology."

42 NIEMANN 2002: 71 speaks of the Shefela as "Hinterland". Here attention is given to the southern parts using the more general term "surroundings". See also Judg 1:18 using the term גְּבוּל. For more information see ALT 1968: 409–35.

30:16; 31:9; 1 Kgs 5:1; 2Kgs 8:2–3; 1 Chr 10:9; 2 Chr 9:26; Jer 25:20; Zeph 2:5).[43] The territory is bordered in the north by the Yarkon river (*Nahr el-ʿAuǧā*), in the east by the Judean Hills, in the south by the Nahal Beśor (*Wādī Ġazze*), and in the west by the Mediterranean Sea. This geographical framework includes the so-called Philistine pentapolis,[44] an alliance of politically and economically independent Philistine cities including Gaza, Ashkelon, Ashdod, Ekron (*Ḥirbet el-Muqannaʿ / Tēl Miqne*), and Gath (*Tell eṣ-Ṣāfī*)[45] (see Josh 13:3; Judg 3:3 חֲמֵשֶׁת סַרְנֵי פְּלִשְׁתִּים; see also 1 Sam 6:17).[46]

The border between this southernmost territory of the Philistines and Egypt is marked by the so-called brook of Egypt (נַחַל מִצְרַיִם).[47] The identification of this stream is debated, however. *Wādi el-ʿAriš*[48] and Nahal Beśor (*Wādī Ġazze*)[49] have both been suggested as the localization of the "brook of Egypt."[50] Since Gaza was regarded as the southern limit in some texts (Gen 10:19; 1 Kgs 5:4),

---

43 In some texts also the term פְּלֶשֶׁת is used (Exod 15:14; Isa 14:29,31; Joel 4:4; Ps 60:10; 83:3; 87:4; Sir 50:26). See NOORT 1994: 16; MACHINIST 2000: 57.

44 See also NOORT 2003: 1285, "Die Ph. sind jedoch eher geographisch als ethnisch zu deuten und als Philistokanaanäer zu charakterisieren. Daß sich bei den Ph. aber verstärkt ägäisch/ zypriotische Tradition findet, ist wahrscheinlich." See also NOORT 1996: 403–28. For the problematic of the characterization of an ethnic group with archaeological material see HERZOG / BAR-YOSEF 2002: [162]–[163].

45 See e.g. EHRLICH 1996: 3–4. NIEMANN 2002: 79, "Die Beobachtung zur Entwicklung (nicht nur) der Größenverhältnisse Aschdods, Ekrons und Gats in der Eisenzeit ergeben, daß sie nicht gleichzeitig stärker bzw. schwächer wurden oder stagnierten, sondern untereinander in Konkurrenz um die wirtschaftliche (und politische) Hegemonie in Philistäa standen." MAEIR 2007: 29–42.

46 See EHRLICH in this volume.

47 נַחַל מִצְרַיִם Josh 15:4,47; 1 Kgs 8:65 par. 1 Chr 7:8 as southern border of Israel; see also 2 Kgs 24:7; Isa 27:7; נַחֲלָה מִצְרַיִם Num 34:5.

48 EHRLICH 1996: 3, "The region of Philistia is bordered in the north by the Yarkon or Sorek rivers (depending on the period), in the south by the Wadi el-Arish (the 'Brook of Egypt'), on the east by the Judean Hills or Judah, and on the west by the Mediterranean Sea." See also NOORT 1994: 16, "Das eigentliche Philistäa wurde im Süden vom *Wādi el-ʿAriš* (Der Bach Ägyptens) begrenzt, der zugleich die Grenze zu Ägypten bildete."

49 NIEMANN / LEHMANN 2010: 218, "Das Nahal Beśor (Wādī Ġazze) bildete in der Bronze- und Eisenzeit die geographisch-klimatische Grenze des Gebietes sesshafter Bauern nach Süden. Zugleich gilt in dieser Zeit das Wadi politisch als ,Bach Ägyptens', d. h. als Grenze zu Ägypten. Erst mit der Fixierung der Grenze zwischen der 5. (Abar Nahara) und der 6. Persischen Satrapie (Ägypten) südlich von Raphia ging die Rolle der Grenze zu Ägypten auf das Wadi el-Arisch über. Damit wird für die Eisenzeit die Bedeutung und Rolle des Nahal Beśor und der hier betrachteten Orte an diesem Wadi deutlich unterstrichen."

50 According to NAʾAMAN 2005a: 238–64 the Brook of Egypt should be identified with the Nahal Beśor and only in the time of the Second Temple was it considered to be *Wādi el-ʿArīsh*. See also KEEL / KÜCHLER 1982: 101–2.

Naḥal Beśor, which lies only slightly south of Gaza, fits well into this geographical context.[51] The Egyptian influence in this region in the 12th century BCE is well attested through hieratic inscription and scarabs,[52] but the territory south of Naḥal Beśor never directly belonged to Egypt and should be seen as a "buffer zone."[53]

The so called "Southern plain" or "Pleshet coastal plain" / "Plain of Philistia" is alluvial deposit and belongs to the most important agricultural regions in Palestine.[54] The Coastal Plain at the north edge of the Negeb has a width of ~40 km and narrows northward. The Sharon and Carmel coastal plains are only ~20 and ~4 km wide respectively.[55] It is therefore also one of the largest agricultural areas.

It can be assumed that the שְׂדֵה פְלִשְׁתִּים, the hinterland of the Philistine territory, is the southernmost territory of this important agricultural area.[56] Here loess soil, "frequently covered with a thin layer of sand, is found in the inner part of the region. This configuration is conductive to agriculture: the upper sand facilitates ready absorption of the rainwater and minimum loss through evaporation, and the impermeable loess below enables most plant roots to reach the water. Due to this absorbent sand cover, the subsoil is often richer in water than might be expected from the annual precipitation average."[57] Further, the region has a heavy dewfall and the total number of dew nights in the year reaches 200–250 in the Coastal Plain.[58]

The average rainfall decreases as one moves inland from the Mediterranean Sea, roughly from west to east, as well as from north to south towards the arid Negeb. The average rainfall around the Naḥal Beśor is about 300 mm, which is

---

51 See NAʼAMAN 2005a: 247–49.
52 Hieratic inscriptions were found at *Tell eš-Šerīʻa* / *Tēl Seraʻ*, Lachish / *Tell ed-Duwēr*, Gath / *Tell eṣ-Ṣāfī, Tell el-Fārʻa* (South), *Deir el-Balaḥ*, Ashkelon, *Tell Abū Hurēre* and Beth Shean. See ZWICKEL 2012: 596.
53 See NAʼAMAN 1986: 238–39, "Sinai was a buffer zone between two countries and two civilizations, and the definition of a border posed a special problem for scribes on both sides."
54 NIEMANN / LEHMANN 2010: 216, "In der sogenannten Philister-Ebene findet sich ein Alluvialgebiet, das zu den wichtigsten Acker- bzw. Getreidegebieten der Küstenebene bzw. Palästinas zählt." For more information see REIFENBERG / WHITTLES ²1947, RAVIKOVITCH ²1970: II/3, ORNI / EFRAT ⁴1980: 15, 45–46, KARMON ²1994: 13–15, 190–91, 255–58, GAZIT 2008: 75–55, SINGER 2007.
55 See HAREL / AMIT / PORAT / ENZEL 2017: 433.
56 See FAUST 2018: 195–204 and his analyses of the settlement in the "periphery of Philistia".
57 ORNI / EFRAT ⁴1980: 46. See also RAINEY 1984: 92, "On the other hand, the impermeability of the loess surface makes possible the collection of rain water in shallow ponds or cisterns such as are still used by the Beduin in the area."
58 MANÉ ²1970: IV/1. See also ORNI / EFRAT ⁴1980: 46.

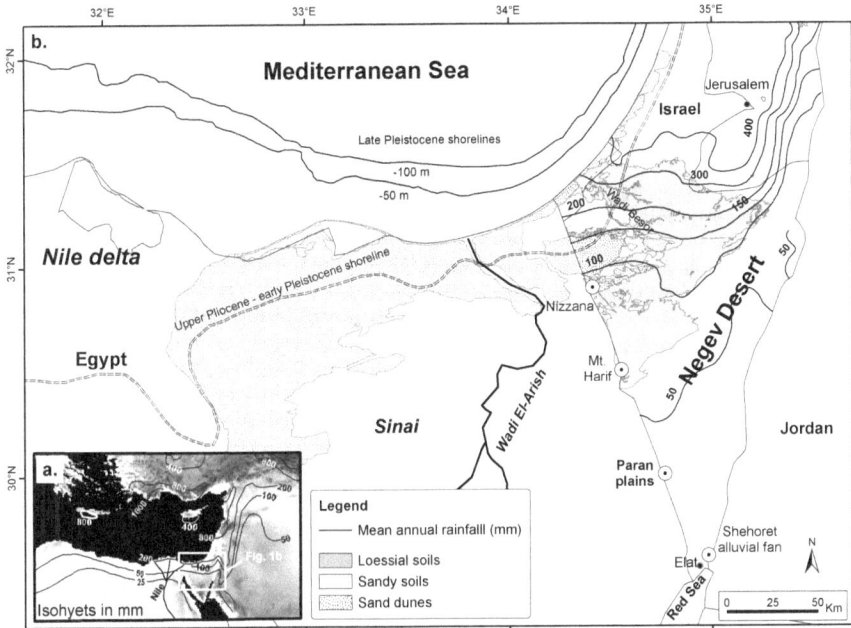

Map 1: *a.* Location map showing the digital elevation model of the eastern Mediterranean region and the mean annual rainfall isohyets (for 1961–1990 in mm; Israel Meteorological Service, 1990) *b.* Map of Israel and its surroundings showing the distribution of sand dunes and loessial and sandy soils in the Negev Desert. © AMIT / SIMHAI / AYALON / ENZEL / MATMON / ONN / PORAT /McDONALD 2011.

still enough for grain. The Naḥal Beśor, which is only referred to three times in the Hebrew Bible (1 Sam 30:9,10,21), brings water from the Negeb mountain.[59] Because of the winter floods its riverbed is 100–150 m wide.[60] It is one of the most important permanent streams in the region.[61]

To sum up, what we have here is not at all desert but an important agricultural area at the transition to the semiarid and arid region of the northern Negeb. It marks a border zone between rain-fed agriculture and pastoralism, permanent and temporary settlements (transhumanism). Furthermore, it lies between Egypt and the Levant at the crossing of the *via maris* (north-south route) and the trade route from the Mediterranean Sea to the Sinai peninsula

59 The catchment area of the Naḥal Beśor is by far the largest with 3,390 km² (compared e.g. to Naḥal Yarkon 1,752; Naḥal Qishon 1,089; Naḥal Lachish 1,006; Naḥal Shiqma 758; Naḥal Soreq 705).
60 ORNI / EFRAT ⁴1980: 46.
61 See KADMON / PICARD ²1970: V/2 B.

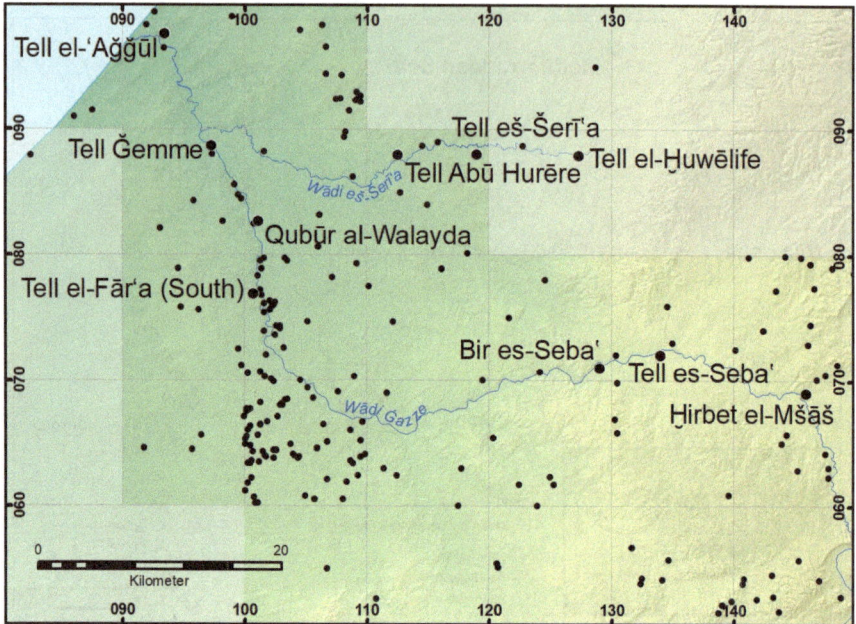

Map 2: The Southern Surroundings of the Philistine Territory © Zwickel / Kowalski.

(west-east route). It is thus a region sensitive to climatic, economic, political, demographic, and other changes.[62]

In this area, many tells dating from the Late Bronze Age II to the Early Iron Age I and IIA are located.[63] Ziklag was one of them, although its precise localization is still under debate. According to 1 Sam 27 it must be located far enough from Gath (*Tell eṣ-Ṣāfi*) so that it was possible for David to act independently.[64] At the same time it must be somewhere close to Judah, otherwise the etiology in v. 6b, saying that Ziklag belonged "to the kings of Judah to this day,"

---

62 See Niemann / Lehmann 2010: 230.

63 Oren 1982: 156–57, "Its strategic and economic importance is attested by a large number of ancient mounds in this small area, e.g. Tell el-Ajjul, Tell Jemmeh, Tell el-Farah, Tell Abu Hureireh, Tell esh-Sharia, Tell Nagila, Tell Hesi, Tell Halif, and a score of smaller Bronze and Iron Age sites."

64 Ehrlich 2002: 66, "Die Logik der biblischen Erzählung erfordert eine Lage möglichst weit entfernt von Ziklag, wo immer auch diese Stadt lag. Denn wie hätte David sonst ohne das Wissen seines philistäischen Lehnsherren Achisch gegen dessen Interessen handeln können? Die Geschichte in 1 Sam 27 setzt eine erhebliche Distanz zwischen Gat und Ziklag voraus." According to 1 Sam 30:1 David and his men came back to Ziklag after 3 days. But this information has nothing to do with the distance between Gath and Ziklag.

would not make much sense (1 Sam 27:6b לָכֵן הָיְתָה צִקְלַג לְמַלְכֵי יְהוּדָה עַד הַיּוֹם
הַזֶּה).[65] Ziklag (צִקְלַג) is mentioned 15 times in the Hebrew Bible (Josh 15:31; 19:5;
1 Sam 27:6; 30:1,14,26; 2 Sam 1:1; 4:10; Neh 11:28; 1 Chr 4:30; 2 Chr 12:1,21).
Possible identifications are *Tell el-Ḥuwēlife*,[66] *Tell eš-Šerīʿa*,[67] *Ḥirbet el-Mšāš* (*Tēl
Māśôś*)[68] and *Tell es-Sebaʿ* (*Horma?*).[69] A final localization of Ziklag is not possible according to the current state of knowledge. Volkmar Fritz stated in 1990:
"Nun hängen im Negeb alle Lokalisierungen wie in einem Mobile zusammen,
mit einem neu platzierten Namen geraten andere Teile in Bewegung."[70] Instead
of focusing on a localization of mounds I will concentrate on the region around
the Naḥal Beśor (*Wādi Ġazze*) and its tributary, the Naḥal Gerar (*Wadi eš-Šeriʿa*),
analyzing its settlement history in the 11th and 10th century BCE. I will investigate the "surroundings" (שְׂדֵה פְּלִשְׁתִּים) of Gath, or to be more precise, the hinterland of Gaza,[71] as an area of diverse cultural influence and changing political
powers.[72]

Tell el-Ḥuwēlife and *Tell eš-Šeriʿa* lie in close proximity to one another and
are located along the Naḥal Gerar (*Wadi eš-Šeriʿa*).[73] Situated between coastal,
mountain, and desert region guarding agricultural lands and water recourses,
these settlements were important landmarks with strategic and economic importance. *Tell el-Ḥuwēlife* (*Tēl Ḥālīf 1273.0879*) is situated on the southwestern
flank of the Judean Hills. It has a strategic position commanding the route from
Egypt and the seacoast into the Judean Hills toward Hebron and Jerusalem.[74]

---

65 The phrase "to this day" is often taken as deuteronomistic. See e.g. FINKELSTEIN 2002: 136,
"The main point of the story seem to be the assertion that 'Ziklag has belonged to the kings of
Judah to this day' (1Sam. 27.6) – a typical formula of the Deuteronomistic Historian [...]." As
TSUMURA 2007: 17–18 and others showed, the formula should not automatically be taken as
deuteronomistic. OREN 1982: 156 speaks about a "unique statement" and CAQUOT / DE ROBERT
1994: 327 consider it as "certificate d'authenticité". See also DIETRICH 2017: 22.
66 ALT 1968: 430–35.
67 See BLAKELY 2007: 21–26.
68 See CRÜSEMANN 1973: 218–24.
69 See GESENIUS [18]2013: 1135, DIETRICH 2017: 17–18. See also FRITZ 1990: 78–85 as well as
KOTTER / OREN 1992: 1090–93 and VETTE 2010.
70 FRITZ 1990: 84.
71 SHAVIT 2008: 151, "The city of Gaza, the largest and most prominent in this area, covered
an estimated area of ca. 10 ha, and had a population of ca. 2,000 inhabitants."
72 I try to omit the term "ethnicity", since ethnicity "in most cases, is ideology imposed by
political powers to dominate and control subordinate groups" – as HERZOG / BAR-YOSEF 2002:
[169] stressed. Ethnic groups are not "stable and permanent entities but an emerging and continuously changing reality" (HERZOG / BAR-YOSEF 2002: [168]).
73 SEGER 1984: 48.
74 SEGER 1984: 48–49, SEGER 1993: 553–59, JACOBS / SEGER 2017. See also HARDIN 2010.

The large tell covers 1,2 ha and was continuously settled from the Late Bronze Age I until the Iron Age II. However, direct evidence of Philistine influence is limited to just a small collection of late eleventh century degenerate-style Philistine potsherds.[75] Between the 10th and the 9th century "a dramatic architectural change" occurred,[76] including a massive refortification of the site with a modified casemate-wall system (Stratum VI).[77]

Tell eš-Šeri'a (*Tēl Šera'* 119.088) lies at the northern bank of Naḥal Gerar (*Wadi eš-Šeri'a*), 17 km east of *Tell el-Ḥuwēlife* (*Tēl Ḥālīf*). The tell is 1,5 ha large and has several perennial springs.[78] After a conflagration in the mid-twelfth century (Stratum IX)[79] it was resettled in the Iron Age (Stratum VIII–IV). From Philistine Iron Age I (Stratum VIII) to Israelite Iron II (Stratum VII) there is no destruction or gap in occupation; instead, a continuity in culture was apparent in the ceramic assemblage.[80] Silos demonstrate the importance of barley cultivation[81] and the material culture shows a close connection to the Philistines.[82] This intensive building activity ended in the early 9th century.[83]

Tell Abū Hurēre (*Tēl Hārōr* 11257.08795) lies 7 km east of *Tell eš-Šeri'a* (*Tēl Šera'*).[84] It is the largest tell at the northern bank of the Naḥal Gerar (*Wadi eš-*

75 Keel / Küchler 1982: 935–39.

76 Seger 1984: 49.

77 Seger 1993: 557–58.

78 Niemann / Lehmann 2010: 223, "Der Tell umfasst 1,5 ha, erhebt sich 14 m über die Umgebung und umfasst 8–10 m Schutt. Er ist mit verschiedenen ganzjährigen Quellen ausgestattet. Ein Stadttor lag vielleicht auf der Westseite. Schon in der Bronzezeit haben hier Silos Tradition." See Keel / Küchler 1982: 939–43.

79 Niemann / Lehmann 2010: 223, "Str. IX besaß eine massive Residenz eines lokalen Herrschers (oder ägyptischen Funktionärs, building 906) mit Zedernbalken und hieratischen Schriftfunden auf einer Gruppe von Schalen und Ostraka, die möglicherweise in die Zeit Ramses III. zu datieren sind." Oren 1993b: 1335, "The Canaanite settlement was probably destroyed by the Sea Peoples or by an incursion of nomads (Amalekites?) from the Negev." See also Oren 1997a: 1.

80 Oren 1982: 163, Oren 1993b: 1331. See also Oren 1974.

81 For data about barely production in the Negev Highlands see Finkelstein 1985: 55–56.

82 Niemann / Lehmann 2010: 223–24, "Die Eisenzeit wird nach einer Siedlungsunterbrechung durch Str. VIII–IV vertreten. Str. VIII weist für die Eisenzeit I drei Phasen mit Installationen und Silos auf, Philisterkeramik und Aschdod-Ware. Die Keramik in Str. VII ähnelt der von Str. VIII. Str. VII (10. Jh. bis frühes 9. Jh.?) ist die entwickeltste Eisenzeitsiedlung in 4 Phasen. Das Ende des Str. VII ist unklar."

83 Oren 1982: 161, "The latest phase in the early 9th century B.C.E. came to an abrupt end, apparently as a result of an earthquake followed by fire."

84 An identification with Gerar (גְּרָר Gen 10:19; 20:1–2; 26:1,6,17,20,26; 1 Chr 4:39; 2 Chr 14:12–13) is possible but debatable. Keel / Küchler 1982: 135, Oren 1993a; 580.

Šeriʿa).[85] The lower tell is about 1,6 ha large. The accurate size of the Early Iron Age site cannot be determined[86] but richly decorated Philistine pottery (both monochrome and bichrome, 12th–11th century BCE) as well as stone-lined grain silos document its continuing importance.[87] The site was given up in the Iron Age II period (around 1000 BCE) and only resettled in the 8th century.[88]

1,2 km upstream of the confluence of the Gerar and the Beśor stream (0963.0898) on the southern bank of Naḥal Beśor lies *Tell Ǧemme* (0973.0887).[89] The 4,92 hectare large site was continuously settled from the Middle Bronze IIB until the Persian period.[90] Similarly to *Tell Abū Hurēre* (*Tēl Ḥārōr*) (and probably also *Tell el-Ḥuwēlife* / *Tēl Ḥālīf*), Iron Age I is well represented with clear Philistine connections, while the 10th and 9th centuries are rather meagerly represented with a local pottery which led to the suggestion to assume a cultural microcosm here.[91]

After another approximately 12 km the Beśor stream flows into the Mediterranean Sea. Only 2,5 km away from the coast at the northern bank of Naḥal Beśor, *Tell el-ʿAǧǧūl* (0934.0976) is located some 6 km southwest of Gaza.[92] It was an important Tell in the Late Bronze Age (300 × 500 m) but lost its importance in the Iron Age.[93]

Tell el-Fārʿa (South) (1007.0769), covering 3 hectares, is one of the most important fortified sites in the Negeb at the southern bank of the Naḥal Beśor.[94]

---

85 Niemann / Lehmann 2010: 225, "Tel Haror bildet mit 14 ha (Unterstadt) und 1,8 ha (Akropolis) den größten Tell im Westnegev am Nordufer des Nahal Gerar."

86 Niemann / Lehmann 2010: 225, "Der Ort besaß die größte Bedeutung in der Hyksos-Periode (MBZ II), der ägyptisch bestimmten Spätbronzezeit und der Eisenzeit IB, die vermutlich die Philister prägten. Schon dies zeigt, dass wir uns in einer Übergangsregion befinden, in der die prägenden Mächte je nach politischem Kontext wechseln."

87 Oren 1997b: 475.

88 Oren 1993a: 580–84.

89 Niemann / Lehmann 2010: 229–30, "Tell Jemmeh liegt auf der Südseite des Nahal Beśor, möglicherweise eine Schwestersiedlung von Tell el-ʿAjjul, das 10 km weiter das Nahal Beśor abwärts gelegen ist. Tell Jemmeh liegt 10 km südlich von Gaza. Der 4,92 ha große, sehr stark erodierte Tell war bis zum 2. Jh. v. Chr. besiedelt mit auch noch späteren Siedlungsspuren." See also Keel / Küchler 1982: 115–22.

90 It can possibly be identified with Yurza (ירזה) / Arza, which was cited on the lists of Pharaoh Thutmose III in Karnak, as well as in Amarna letters (EA 314–316). It reoccurs in the Shoshenq list from the 10th century (Nr 133). See Aḥituv 1984: 203–4, van Beek 1992: 677, van Beek 1993: 667, Naʾaman 2005a: 243–45.

91 See van Beek 1992: 677, van Beek 1993: 669–70. See also van Beek 1997: 213–15.

92 See Tufnell / Kempinski 1993: 49, Dessel 1997: 38–40.

93 See Fischer / Sadeq 2008: 1565–66. Niemann / Lehmann 2010: 223 claim "Eisenzeitliches datierbares Material fand sich nicht." See also Keel / Küchler 1982: 96–101.

94 See Fischer 2016, Liwak 1992: 1163–65. See also Aḥituv 1984: 171–73.

It is located approximately 24 km south of Gaza.[95] It was again a very important city in the Late Bronze Age, and lasted until the Iron Age I period. It was abandoned from the middle of the ninth to the seventh century.[96]

What is most important here is that we have close to *Tell el-Fār'a* (South) six small (0,2–1 ha) Iron Age II settlements. The ceramic assemblages were homogeneous throughout this period, and indicate that these settlements existed only a very short time. It has been suggested that these are the biblical חֲצֵרִים (small farms).[97] One of them has been excavated during recent years. *Qubūr al-Walayda* (1011.0827) lies between *Tell Ǧemme* and *Tell el-Fār'a* (South) at the northern bank of Naḥal Beśor. It was established in the 12th century as part of the Egyptian administration system and later dominated by its northern or southern neighbor town *Tell Ǧemme* or *Tell el-Fār'a* (South) and used as an affiliated site (*Tochterort*).[98] In the late 10th or early 9th century it was given up.[99]

The economic, cultural, and political situation can be summarized as following: Most striking is the absence of Egyptian influence from Ramesses III (1186–1156/5 BCE)[100] or Ramesses IV (1156/5–1150 BCE) at the very latest[101] until the Palestinian campaign of Shoshenq I (925 BCE).[102] Israel Finkelstein speaks

95 See GOPHNA 1993: 441.

96 See GOPHNA 1993: 442, LEHMANN / GOLDING-MEIR / NEUMEIER-POTASHNIK / NIEMANN 2018: 142–43.

97 GOPHNA 1993: 444. WEINSTEIN 1997: 305, concludes "The Philistines apparently settled at Tell el-Far'ah while the town was still under Egyptian control and remained there after the Egyptians withdrew from southern Palestine in about the third quarter of the twelfth century BCE. The evidence for human activity at the site during the first millennium BCE is scattered. There appears to have been limited occupation during the tenth-early ninth centuries BCE [...]."

98 NIEMANN / LEHMANN 2010: 240.

99 NIEMANN / LEHMANN 2010: 232, "Qubur al-Walaydah entstand im 12. Jh. v. Chr. [...] als Verstärkung des ägyptischen Administrationssystems in Südwestpalästina zwischen Tell el-Far'a (Süd) und Tell Jemmeh, wurde dann nach kurzer Pause übernommen von Philistern in einer landwirtschaftlichen Dorf-Siedlung. Im (späten) 10. Jh. oder frühen 9. Jh. kam es zu einem Abbruch der Besiedlung."

100 See SIMONS 1937: 164–75. See KITCHEN ²2015: 244–45.

101 For an overview see FINKELSTEIN 2000: 161–65.

102 See SIMONS 1937: 178–86, KITCHEN ²2015: 432–47, DEVER 2018: 50*–58*. AHARONI ³1974: 288, summarizes "The list of towns in the Negeb, the second group, is the largest segment of Shishak's list. It includes 85 name plates, but since there are at least 14 compound names requiring two plates each, we are left with about 70 place names. This list is of special importance as being the only detailed roster of towns in the Negeb among all our sources, both biblical and Egyptian. In spite of the fact that only a small percentage of these towns have been identified to date, it is certain that not only they but the others are located in the Negeb because the term 'Negeb' itself comprises one element in several of the compound names."

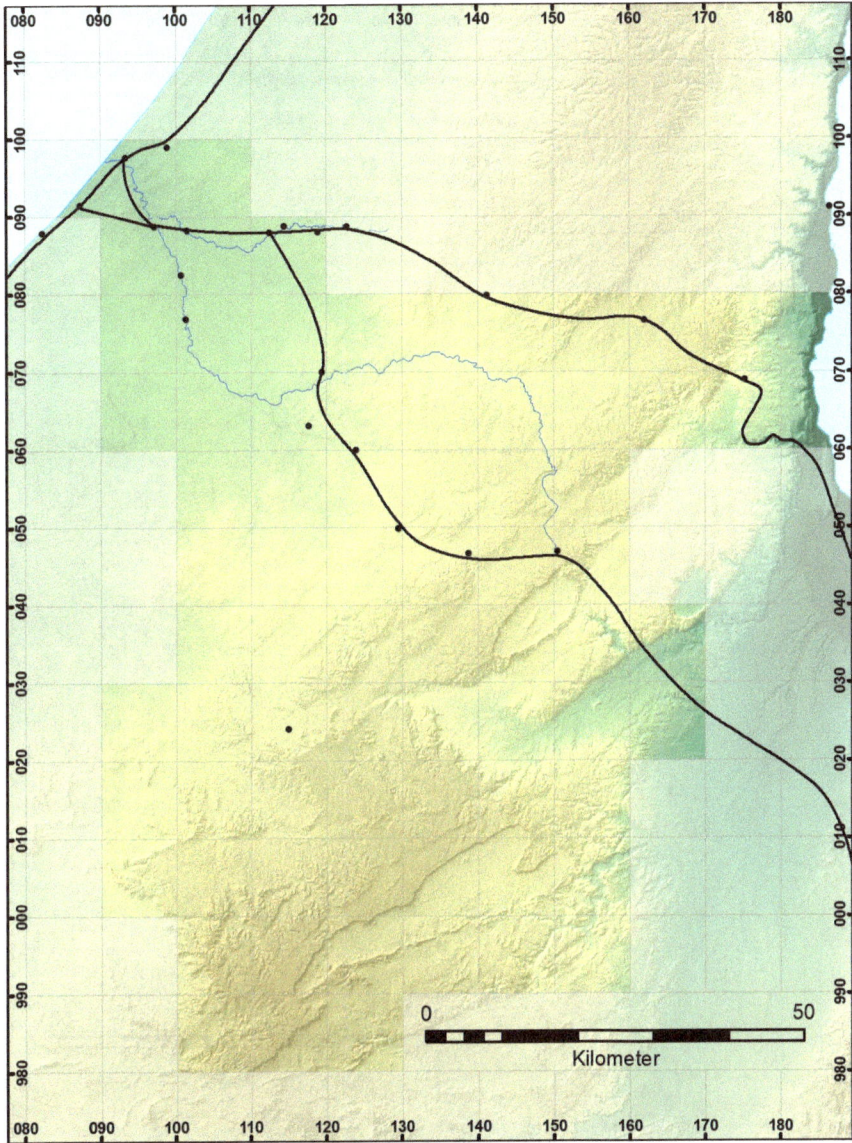

Map 3: Late Bronze Age © Zwickel / Kowalski.

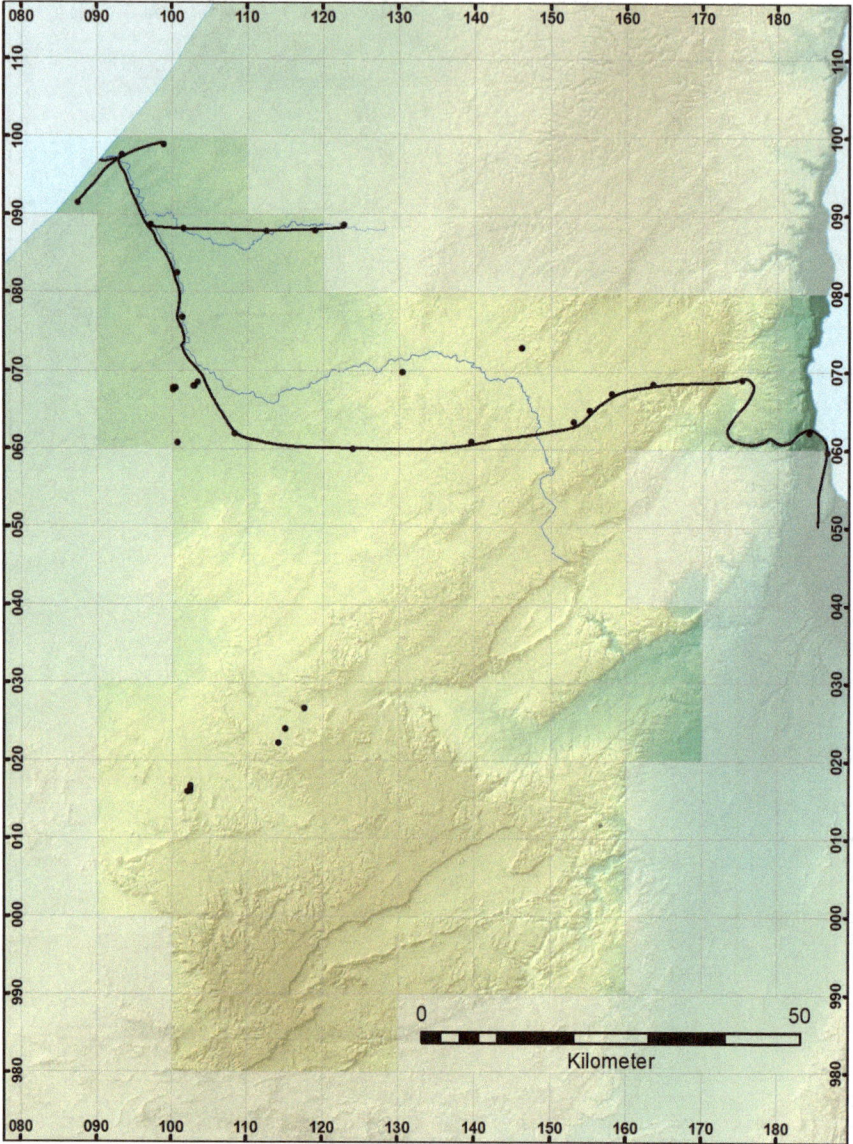

Map 4: Iron Age I © ZWICKEL / KOWALSKI.

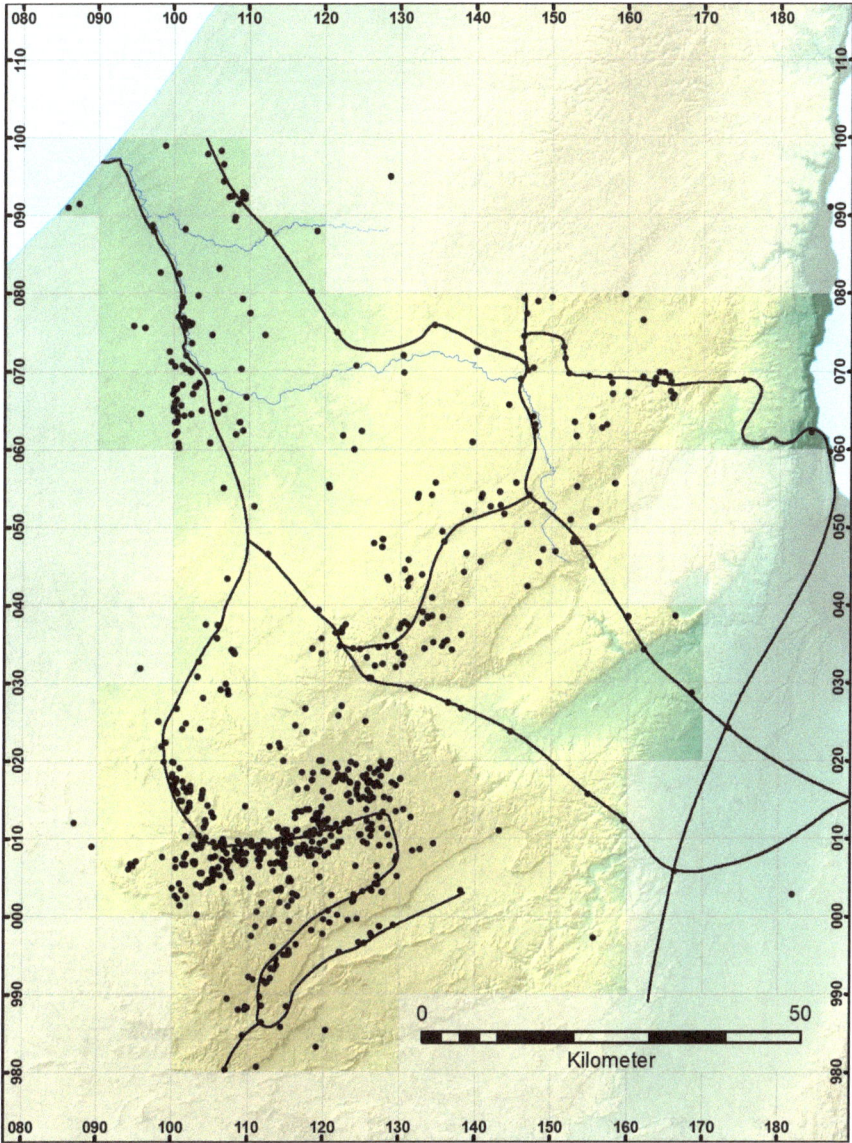

Map 5: Iron Age IB / IIA © ZWICKEL / KOWALSKI.

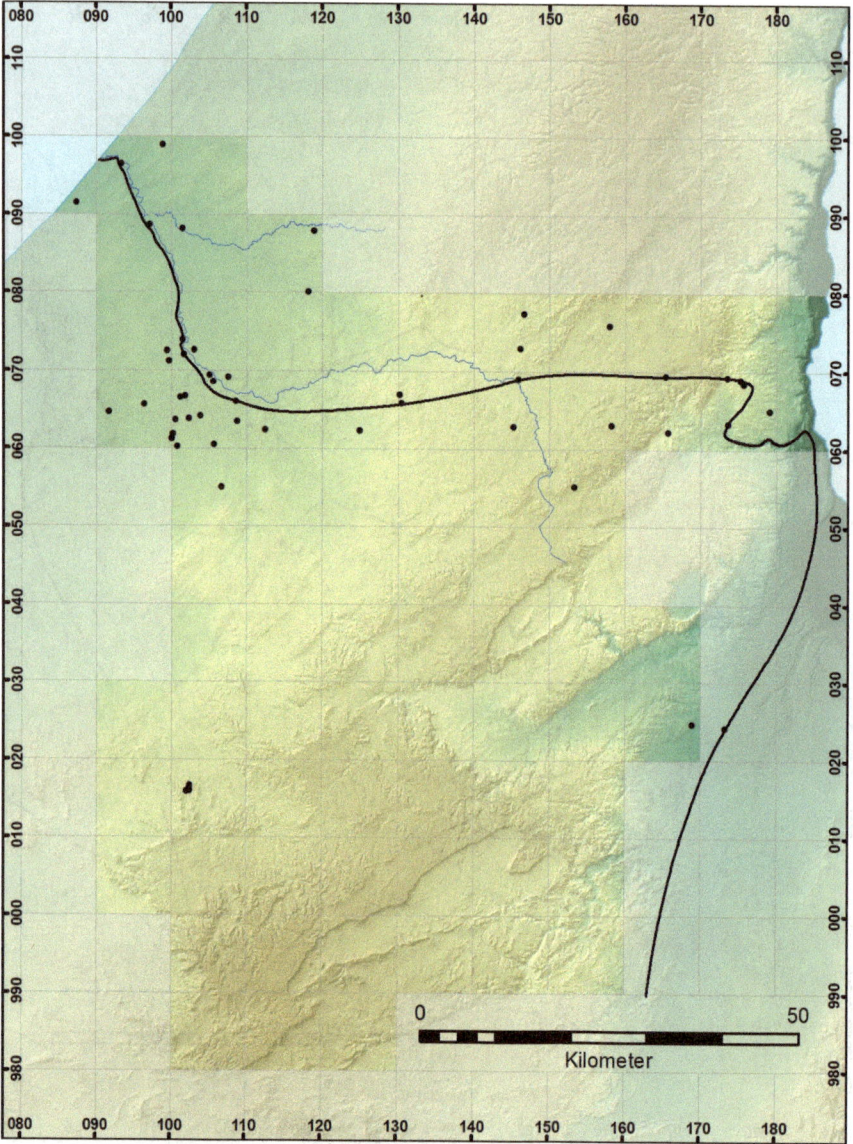

Map 6: Iron Age II © ZWICKEL / KOWALSKI.

of a "hegemony of desert groups" from around 1050 BCE until Shoshenq I campaign and continuing until 840 BCE under Egyptian influence.[103] This is a time period of more than 200 years during which Egyptian power was absent from the region, bringing about a situation of swiftly changing political influences.[104] *Tell el-'Aǧǧūl*, located on the coast and situated on the *via maris*, is a good example of an important Late Bronze Age city given up when Egypt lost its power, causing the Philistine influence to increase at the end of the 12th century.[105] There are some sites where the change from Egyptian to Philistine power in the 12th century is well attested (e.g. *Tell Ǧemme*).[106] Sites, such as *Tell eš-Šeri'a (Tēl Šera')* and *Tell el-Fār'a* (South), may have been independent regional centers and prove cultural independence.[107] They do not provide the typical Philistine settlement pattern with urban centers featuring almost no surrounding settlements but were encompassed by small villages and homesteads.[108]

Last but not least, the Iron Age IIA was a period of huge activity in this region. A closer look at the settlement history demonstrates this impressively.

During the Late Bronze Age several large tells stood alongside the roads running from north to south (*via maris*) and east to west (see Map 3).

When the Egyptians lost influence in this region the *via maris* lost its importance. Only a few large settlements stood alongside a road from the coast to the Dead Sea during the Iron Age I period (see Map 4).

Some decades later in the 11th and 10th century, after the complete collapse of Egyptian administration, were a huge number of cities and small settlements

---

103 See FINKELSTEIN 2014: 92.

104 See the evaluation based on historical texts, archaeological data, scarabs, and inscriptions in ZWICKEL 2012: 596. Similarly MÜNGER 2018: 48 concludes, "During the Late Bronze Age and again after the 8th century BCE, strong cultural contacts existed between Egypt and the Southern Levant. The time in between was significantly less intense, apart from a short and not very lasting intermezzo – with a minimal cultural impact – towards the end of the 10th century BCE."

105 NIEMANN / LEHMANN 2010: 231, "In der Eisenzeit IA war der Ort ein wichtiger administrativer Stützpunkt der Ägypter mit einem sog. ,Residenzgebäude' und einer begrenzten Expansion in das Umland. In der Eisenzeit IB gab es hier eine philistäische Siedlung. Seit der späten Eisenzeit IB nach Abzug der Ägypter fand eine philistäische Expansion in Südwestpalästina statt. Eine Siedlungsexpansion begann, die u. a. Tel Masos, Tel Esdar, Naḥal Yattir u. a. Orte umfasste. Qubur al-Walaydah war vermutlich einer der Orte dieses expandierenden Systems."

106 KEEL / KÜCHLER 1982: 117, "Die Ablösung durch die Philister* im 12. Jh.a. machte sich durch die typische Keramik bemerkbar [...]."

107 NIEMANN / LEHMANN 2010: 231, "Als wichtigste regionale Zentren kommen wohl Tel Sera' und Tell el-Far'a (Süd) in Frage."

108 FINKELSTEIN 2000: 166–74, SHAVIT 2008: 160. See also JERICKE 1997: 147–251 and ZWICKEL 2011: 150–52.

founded.[109] 36 large (at least 2,5 ha) sites are known in the Beśor region from Iron Age IB; only eight sites are situated on Bronze Age tells.[110] This change in the area's settlement pattern, consisting primarily of enclosed settlements and small farmsteads in the Negev, cannot be overlooked (see Map 5).[111]

At the end of the Iron Age IIA, maybe in connection with the Campaign of Shoshenq I (925 BCE), these settlements suddenly disappear again, so that only a couple of cities remain following a connecting road between west and east (see Map 6).

The process of sedentarization may be seen as a consequence of those changes, but the cause remains unexplained.[112] The settlements testify to the existence of trading routes which presumably operated in connection with the copper production in Feynan and Timna.[113] The camel as a mount only gained importance during this time and became an important means of transportation. It is noteworthy to point out that camels are mentioned in 1 Sam 27:9.[114] New trade routes and agricultural improvements, etc., allowed different groups to expand into the south. I will now turn again to 1 Sam 27, analyzing the geopolitical situation described in the text and trying to correlate it with the historical and archaeological information available for that region.

3 Geshurite, Amalekite, Jerachmelelite, Kenite and co. – Some Remarks on the Geopolitical Situation

David has the power of the Philistine ruler Achish on his side. From the moment when Achish gave him Ziklag as a land-grant, he was free to act more independ-

---

109 See also Na'aman 1992: 71–93 on the prosperity of the Negev Highlands. For a general overview over the Negev Highlands see also Finkelstein 1985: 52–64, Finkelstein 1984: 189–209, Cohen 1980: 7–31.

110 Gazit 2008: 77. See also Shavit 2008: 151–53.

111 Ethnic attributions are highly problematic though. For a research overview see e.g. Herzog / Bar-Yosef 2002: [166]-[168].

112 Finkelstein 1984: 189–209.

113 See Ben-Yosef / Shaar / Tauxe / Ron 2012: 64–65. The main period of copper smelting in the southern Arabah was during the 10th century BCE and it ceased at the end of the 9th century. A scarab bearing the throne name Shoshenq I (946/45–925/24 BCE) was found on the surface of Khirbat Hamra Ifdan, where Iron Age IIA smelting activities took place. See Münger / Levy 2014: Fig. 11.6.

114 Staubli 1991: 184–201. See also Finkelstein 1988: 246–47, Na'aman 1992: 86–88, Ben-Yosef / Shaar / Tauxe / Ron 2012: 65.

ently. He "exercised control over the southern frontier zone and, through periodic raids and punitive expeditions, kept in check the nomadic tribes in the neighboring Negev and Sinai deserts as far as the border of Egypt".[115]

But who was David attacking? Obviously, the Philistines and the Judeans did not have the same enemy. David pretended to attack Judah and / or Judean allies but attacked allies of the Philistines instead. What can we say about the different groups? In the text (1 Sam 27:8 and 10) we find two lists containing three tribes each. Originally, the first list may have consisted only of the name of two groups.[116]

> V. 8 And David went up and his men,
> and they made a raid against the Geshurites[117] [and the Girzite/Gizrite][118] and the Amalekite.
> For they were settling the land
> that is from Telam[119] as you come to Shur and toward the land of Egypt.

In 1 Sam 27:8 it is said that David and his men attacked the Geshurites. The Geshurites (גְּשׁוּרִי)[120] are mentioned in Josh 13:2 as living along the coast toward Egypt and adjacent to the Philistine territory:
Josh 13:2–3

זֹאת הָאָרֶץ הַנִּשְׁאָרֶת כָּל־גְּלִילוֹת הַפְּלִשְׁתִּים וְכָל־הַגְּשׁוּרִי׃
מִן־הַשִּׁיחוֹר אֲשֶׁר עַל־פְּנֵי מִצְרַיִם וְעַד גְּבוּל עֶקְרוֹן צָפוֹנָה לַכְּנַעֲנִי תֵּחָשֵׁב חֲמֵשֶׁת סַרְנֵי
פְלִשְׁתִּים הָעַזָּתִי וְהָאַשְׁדּוֹדִי הָאֶשְׁקְלוֹנִי הַגִּתִּי וְהָעֶקְרוֹנִי וְהָעַוִּים׃
This is the land that remains: all the regions of the Philistines, and all those of the Geshurites (Γεσιρι) from the Shihor,[121] which is east of Egypt, northward to the territory of Ekron, it is reckoned as Canaanite; there are five rulers of the Philistines, those of Gaza, Ashdod, Ashkelon, Gath, and Ekron, and those of the Avvim.

---

115 Oren 1982:156.
116 "The Girzite / Gizrite" is presumably a later addition. Dietrich 2017: 22 argues, "Das Grundelement dieses Abschnitts [1 Sam 27:8–12] bildet die Aufzählung von zweimal drei Stämmen: solche gegen die David Razzien durchführt (8), und solchen von denen er vorgab es zu tun (10)."
117 LXX reads ἐπὶ πάντα = כל אשר אל instead.
118 LXX reads Γεσιρι / LXX^O Γεσερι; Ketiv גִּרְזִי or Qere גִּזְרִי.
119 See below.
120 Gesenius ¹⁸2013: 232. Niesiołowski-Spanò 2016: 61, "Yet, in several passages Geshur is located clearly in the south."
121 Josh 13:3; Isa 23:3; Jer 2:18; 1 Chr 13:5; see also Josh 19:26. The Shihor (Š-Ḥr; שִׁיחוֹר) is not only described as a border river in the Hebrew Bible, but also in Egyptian texts. See Bietak 1984: 624, "Für die Lokalisierung des Sch. kommt daher am ehesten der langgestreckte namenlose See unmittelbar nördlich des *Isthmus von Qantara in Betracht. Er ist das augenscheinlichste Grenzgewässer." See also Na'aman 2005b: 265–70 and Wüst 1975: 32–38.

In the LXX the *gentilicium* Girzite / Gizrite is missing from 1 Sam 27:8. The LXX reads ἐπὶ πάντα (אֶל כֹּל אֲשֶׁר). However, the Gesiri (Γεσιρι) or Geseri (Γεσερι LXX⁰) are mentioned in the LXX instead of the Girsite or Gisrite, and this is usually how the Geshurites were translated (see Josh 13:2,11,13 et al.). It is therefore consequent that the Geshurites were only mentioned once in the LXX and that the second Gentilicium הַגִּזְרִי / גִּזְרִי is missing.[122]

Concerning the Amalekites (עֲמָלֵקִי),[123] much more information is provided. However, also in this case historical and geographical information is rare. What can be said with certainty is that the Amalekites were a nomadic tribe (proto-Bedouin) with camels, who lived somewhere in the Negeb.[124] They undertook dangerous raids and presumably also controlled the long distance trade.

Maybe they can be connected to the small settlements in the central Negeb from the Iron Age I–II period.[125] Another possibility would be to localize them in the northwest Negeb in the region towards Egypt.[126]

According to 1 Sam 27:8b the Geshurites and Amalekites where located precisely in the no-man's-land towards Egypt. They were described as the inhabitants of the land "on the way to Shur and on to the land of Egypt." Again, there are some textual difficulties to consider: MT reads מֵעוֹלָם, which does not fit very well in the context and has therefore often be changed to מִטֵּלָם.[127] The LXX is simply reading: ἀπὸ Γελαμψουρ τετειχισμένων καὶ ἕως γῆς Αἰγύπτου.[128]

---

122 The Gentilicium גִּרְזִי Qere is unkown and presumably has been changed in גִּזְרִי Ketiv (Gezerites) later. See DIETRICH 2017: 9. But Gezer is geographically much too far away to make sense in this context. Although this may be the *lectio facilior* it is best to follow the LXX – as McCARTER 1980: 413 suggested – in this case and to omit the Girsites. See also NIESIOŁOWSKI-SPANÒ 2016: 60.

123 GESENIUS ¹⁸2013: 983.

124 STAUBLI 1991: 184–201. See TIMM 1998, 386: "Die Überlieferungen des AT zu Auseinandersetzungen mit den A. sind für David am vertrauenswürdigsten [...]." See also LIPIŃSKI 2018: 25, "Ces récits semblent néanmoins renvoyer aux habitants des enclos du Négeb qui paraissait avoir existé jusqu'à une période tardive du Xe siècle. C'est ce qui pourrait expliquer l'attribution de leur assujettissement à David."

125 For the discussion see JERICKE 1997: 111–15 and FINKELSTEIN 1984: 189–209. ZWICKEL 2015: 73 concludes "Ein Blick auf die Siedlungsgeschichte im südlichen Negeb zeigt, daß sich früheisen-zeitliche Siedlungen vor allem nördlich des *Wādi es-Saba'* sowie entlang dieses Wadis (vor allem *Bīr es-Seba'*, *Tell es-Seba'*, *Ḫirbet el-Mšaš* und *Tel Esdar*) erstreckten. Da die amalekitischen Gebiete südlich des Besor (*Wādi es-Saba'*) lagen, wird man sie am ehesten mit den in dieser Zeit errichteten Bauten östlich und nordöstlich von Kadesch Barnea identifizieren können."

126 JERICKE 1997: 252–53.

127 See e.g. DIETRICH 2017: 10, McCARTER 1980: 413.

128 LXX reads Γελαμψουρ, LXX⁰ Γελαμσουρ and LXXᴸ Γες(σ)ουρ. In some cases (LXXᴹᴺ and some minunscles) also Τελαμψουρ can be found. See BARTHÉLEMY 1982: 215.

The transmitted Γελαμψουρ or Τελαμψουρ in the LXX may be explained as a contraction between מֵעוֹלָם and שׁוּר.[129] However, from some other texts a place called "Telam" is known. In 1 Sam 15:4, a place called טְלָאִים or טְלָאם is mentioned were Saul numbered the people and Josh 15:25 refers to a place called טֶלֶם located somewhere in the south of Judah listed together with Sif.[130] Although we do not have any textual evidence,[131] the frequently proposed solution reading "Telam" should therefore be preferred.[132]

Shur is mentioned five time (Gen 16:7; 20:1; 25:18; 1 Sam 15:7; 27:8) as toponym[133] and in one case as a landscape name (אֶל־מִדְבַּר־שׁוּר Exod 15:22).[134] The spring on the way to Shur (עַל־הָעַיִן בְּדֶרֶךְ שׁוּר), mentioned in Gen 16:7, is located even more precisely between Kadesh and Bered (בֵּין־קָדֵשׁ וּבֵין בָּרֶד Gen 16:14). According Gen 20:1, Abraham settled between Kadesh and Schur (אַרְצָה הַנֶּגֶב וַיֵּשֶׁב בֵּין־קָדֵשׁ וּבֵין שׁוּר וַיָּגָר בִּגְרָר) and the territory of the Ismaelites is described as "from Havilah to Shur, which is opposite Egypt" (מֵחֲוִילָה עַד־שׁוּר אֲשֶׁר עַל־פְּנֵי מִצְרַיִם Gen 25:18).[135]

1 Sam 15:6-7

וַיֹּאמֶר שָׁאוּל אֶל־הַקֵּינִי לְכוּ סֻּרוּ רְדוּ מִתּוֹךְ עֲמָלֵקִי פֶּן־אֹסִפְךָ עִמּוֹ וְאַתָּה עָשִׂיתָה חֶסֶד עִם־כָּל־בְּנֵי יִשְׂרָאֵל בַּעֲלוֹתָם מִמִּצְרָיִם וַיָּסַר קֵינִי מִתּוֹךְ עֲמָלֵק:
וַיַּךְ שָׁאוּל אֶת־עֲמָלֵק מֵחֲוִילָה בּוֹאֲךָ שׁוּר אֲשֶׁר עַל־פְּנֵי מִצְרָיִם:

Saul said to the Kenites, "Go! Leave! Withdraw from among the Amalekites, or I will destroy you with them; for you showed kindness to all the people of Israel when they came up out of Egypt." So the Kenites withdrew from the Amalekites.

So Saul defeated the Amalekites, from Havilah on the way to Shur, which is opposite of Egypt.

We can conclude that David attacked allies of the Philistines but pretended to attack Judah and / or Judean allies and that both parties shared the region

---

129 See STOEBE 1973: 474, MCCARTER 1980: 413, BARTHÉLEMY 1982: 215.

130 GESENIUS [18]2013: 424. See also NAʾAMAN 2005b: 272.

131 See MCCARTER 1980: 413, "There is no sure evidence for reading *mṭlm*, which must be listed as conjectural." See MCCARTER 1980: 261.

132 NAʾAMAN 2005b: 272.

133 NAʾAMAN 2005b: 275, concludes "Summing up, 'Shur' is a place name, marking in two biblical passages the western limits of the wanderings of the Ishmaelites and Amalekites. From the stories of David at Ziklag, we know that Shur marked the border for the nomads then dwelling in the south and, therefore should be sought in the western Negeb. Abraham's itinerary indicates that Shur lay on the main road from Kadesh-barnea to Gerar (Tel Haror), and, according to the story of Hagar, 'the way of Shur' crossed the desert on its way from Kadesh, going in the direction of Naḥal Besorat the southern edge of the settled area. The best candidate would be Tell el-Farʿah, the southernmost of the big mound laying along Naḥal Besor [...]." See also RAINEY 1984: 96.

134 GESENIUS [18]2013: 1337.

135 See KNAUF 1985: 63-64.

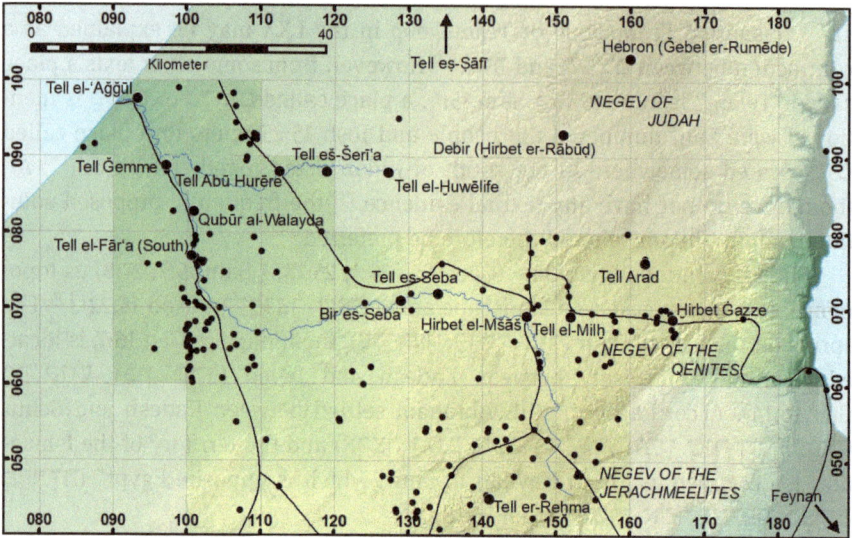

Map 7: Geopolitical Map © ZWICKEL / KOWALSKI.

described above as border zone. He mentions to Achish in v. 10b three regions in the Negeb (עַל־נֶגֶב יְהוּדָה וְעַל־נֶגֶב הַיַּרְחְמְאֵלִי וְאֶל־נֶגֶב הַקֵּינִי).[136] The term נֶגֶב in this case describes a region outside the settlement border where nomads and bedouins were active.

> V. 9 And David would strike the land,
>   and he would not keep man or woman alive,
>   and he would take flock and herd and donkeys and camels and clothing.
>   And he returned and came to Achish.
> V. 10 And Achish said to David:
>   "Against[137] whom have you raided today?"
>   And David said:
>   "Against the south of Judah and against the south of the Jerachmeelite[138] and against the south of the Qen[iz]ite.[139]"

---

136 GALIL 2001: 41, comes to a different conclusion: "In both texts (1 Sam. 27:10; 30:14), the Negeb of Judah (or 'of Judah') is the general term, while the Negeb of Caleb and the Negeb of the Jerahmeelites are the specific details." However, he agrees that the term "served concurrently as an administrative and ethnographic term" (42).

137 LXX reads ἐπὶ τίνα, 4QSamª frgs 43 reads עַל מ. DRIESBACH 2016: 314: "MT is most likely an error, although the mechanics are unclear, perhaps stemming from a confusion of אל and על" (84).

138 LXXᴮ reads Ιεσμεγα, LXXᴬ Ισραμηλει, LXXᴸ Αερων, 4QSamª frgs 43 ירדח[מ]אֵל.

139 LXXᴮᴸ reads Κενεζι. See also 1 Sam 30:29, where MT reads קֵינִי, LXXᴮᴸ Κενεζι and Q also support this name; cf. 4QSamª frgs 47 הקנזי. DRIESBACH 2016: 241. See Gen 15:19; Num 32:12; Josh 14:6,14.

V. 11 Neither man nor woman would David keep alive to bring to Gath,
saying:
> "Lest they report against us, saying:
> 'Thus David acted.'"

And this was his justice all the days,
that he settled in Philistine countryside.
V. 12 And Achish was confident in David, saying,
> "He has become utterly obnoxious among his people, among Israel;
> and he will be my servant forever."

The first named locale, the "south of Judah" (נֶגֶב יְהוּדָה 1 Sam 27:10; 2 Sam 24:7; see 2 Chr 28:18), describes the hinterland of Judah.[140] In the 10th century BCE *Hebron* (*Ğebel er-Rumēde*) and *Debir* (*Ḫirbet er-Rābūḍ*) 10 km southwest of Hebron were border towns.[141]

The Kenites (נֶגֶב הַקֵּינִי Gen 15:19; Num 24:21; 1 Sam 15:6; 27:10; 30:29; 1 Chr 2:55) lived in the northeast Negeb.[142] This territory can be located at the eastern border of the Arad-Beersheba basin. At the headwater of Naḥal B'ēr Ševaʻ (*Wādī l-Qēnī*) the "fortress" Kina (*Ḥorbat ʻŪzā / Ḫirbet Ġazze* 16570.06876; see Josh 15:22) from the 7th century was excavated.[143] The semi-desert arid region lacks water sources and the average annual rainfall of 200 mm is barely enough to support a low-yielding agriculture and was primarily used for sheep and goat herding.[144]

Southwest of the Kenites the Negeb of the Jerachmeelites (נֶגֶב הַיְרַחְמְאֵלִי 1 Sam 27:10; 2 Chr 2:9,23–27,33,42; Jer 34:29) can be located.[145] Its identification is given by the mountain Har Jeroham[146] as well as the settlement or fountain

---

140 HERZOG / BAR-YOSEF 2002: [170] stressed that an "exceptionally large number of social groups" were mentioned in this region. Beside the tribes of Judah and Simeon, groups such as the "clans of Yerahmeelites who settled the south part, the Kenites in the east, the Calebites and the Kenizzites flanking the valley in the north, and the Cherethites (related to the Philistines) in the west" (HERZOG / BAR-YOSEF 2002: [171]) are mentioned.

141 FINKELSTEIN 2013: 149 describes three territorial units: "an early north Israelite polity that ruled as far south as the area of Bethlehem-Hebron, with a possible extension to the northeast Shephelah; the kingdom of Gath, which ruled over much of the Shephelah as far south as the boundary of the Beer-sheba Valley; and the desert formation of Tel Masos in the Beer-sheba Valley and further to the south." If my localization is correct, then the so-called "desert formation" would have been allied tribes of Judah.

142 See KNAUF 2007. RAINEY 1984: 100 concludes: "In summary, the 'Negeb of the Kenite' (1 Sam. 27:10) should be sought in the eastern basin area including the valley around Arad [...]."

143 Please note that Map 7 is anachronistic at this point!

144 BEIT-ARIEH 2007: 1.

145 See RAINEY 1984: 100.

146 See FINKELSTEIN 1985: 91–92.

name *Tell er-Reḥma* (*Tēl Reḥme*) or *Bī'r er-Reḥmā* (*B'ēr Y rōḥām*) respectively (141.045). Jeroḥam is also mentioned twice in the Shoshenq list.[147] In the 10th century a settlement pattern consisting primarily of open encampments and small homesteads appears. The region around the mountain and spring in the region southeast of Beersheba is therefore to be identified as the Negeb of the Jerachmelites.[148]

1 Sam 30:27–30 contains a list of places and regions where David sent part of the spoils which he took from the Amalekites. The list may be younger than the 10th century,[149] but what becomes evident here as well are the alliances. The Amalekites were the enemies which have to be defeated, while the Jerach-meelites and Kenites belonged to allied tribes. 1 Sam 30:29, where anonymous towns of the Jerachmeelites and the Kenites are mentioned, is therefore of special interest.[150] This means that these groups lived in fortified cities and were no longer nomads or semi-nomads.[151]

4 Conclusion

1 Sam 27:2,3a,5–12 belong to the oldest part of the David story and was combined with the Saul narrative only in later times (1 Sam 27:1,4 and 3b). Whether

---

147 SIMONS 1937: 112 and 139. See also KEEL / KÜCHLER 1982: 336–37, NAʾAMAN 1992: 82–83; AḤITUV 1984: 202.

148 See GALIL 2001: 38–40.

149 ZWICKEL 2015: 73, "Diese Ortsnamensliste ist eine spätere Zufügung und kann nicht als Beleg für ein Groß-Juda zur Zeit Davids herangezogen werden [...]." JERICKE 1997: 327, "Der Grundbestand [v. 28b–30] von 1Sam 30,27–31, der in die Zeit Davids datiert werden kann, will zum Ausdruck bringen, daß David den Keniter und Jerachmeeliter und ebenso Simeon (Eter und Aschan, Jos 19,7), also alle östlich und südöstlich von Ziklag siedelnden Gruppen mit Beuteanteilen bedachte. Die vermutlich in der späten Königszeit vorgenommene Ergänzung fügt am Anfang der Liste Städte Judas nach Jos 15 und als Abschluß die Königsstadt Hebron hinzu." For more details see NAʾAMAN 2010b: 175–87, FINKELSTEIN 2013: 142–44.

150 1 Sam 30:29 וְלַאֲשֶׁר בְּרָכָל וְלַאֲשֶׁר בְּעָרֵי הַיְרַחְמְאֵלִי וְלַאֲשֶׁר בְּעָרֵי הַקֵּינִי: "in Racal, in the towns of the Jerachmeelites, in the towns of the Kenites". Instead of רָכָל LXX reads Καρμήλῳ, that is, Carmel. This place can be located at *Ḫirbet el-Kirmel* (1627.0823) just 12 km south-south-east of Hebron. It is also mentioned in Josh 15:55 and 1 Sam 25:2 and should be preferred here. For more information see DEVER 1975: 18*–19*.

151 The description of the counterattack by the Amelekites in 1 Sam 30:14

אֲנַחְנוּ פָּשַׁטְנוּ נֶגֶב הַכְּרֵתִי וְעַל־אֲשֶׁר לִיהוּדָה וְעַל־נֶגֶב כָּלֵב וְאֶת־צִקְלַג שָׂרַפְנוּ בָאֵשׁ:

We had made a raid on the Negeb of the Cherethites and on that which belongs to Judah and on the Negeb of Caleb; and we burned Ziklag down.

JERICKE 1997: 326 suggests that originally only the Negeb Kaleb was mentioned.

the dialogues (v. 5aβb,10) and monologues (v. 11bα,12b) were part of those very old traditions from the beginning cannot be answered here.[152] However, the text makes it obvious that it is concerned with a territory under changing political influences.[153]

To conclude, the Naḥal Beśor region – as I have demonstrated – was not desert but a fertile region with good agricultural conditions. Silos, grinding stones and sickle blades found at the excavated sites "indicate that the population practiced dry farming."[154] As a border zone between rain-fed agriculture and pastoralism, permanent and temporary settlements (transhumance), between Egypt and the Levant, at the crossing of the *via maris* (the north-south route) and the trade route from the Mediterranean Sea to the Sinai peninsula (the west-east route) this region was especially sensitive to shifts of power.[155] The analysis of settlement history shows that a huge change between the Iron Age IB and the Iron Age IIA, roughly between the 11th and 10th centuries can be observed, and this fits very well with the geopolitical situation described in 1 Sam 27. The power of the Philistine was concentrated on the coastal plain, in the Philistine pentapolis and its surroundings.[156] After the Egyptians' loss of power, different conflicting parties – including proto-Bedouins such as the Amalekites – destabilized the region. This power vacuum left open space for new tribes and groups to emerge. The significant number of archeological finds can lead to the assumption that some of the Bronze Age city states were only given up in this time and that a new sedentarization process started with tribes such as the Jerachmeelites and

---

152 For DIETRICH 2017: 16, this is one of the main reasons to ascribe large parts (1 Sam 27:1,3b,4,5,[8],9–12) to the Narrative History of the Early Monarchy, which he dates to the late 8th century.

153 RAINEY 1984: 98 assumes, "In fact, the appointment of David as a vassal stationed at Ziklag may have been intended to fill the power vacuum in the western Negeb because there was no longer an entity such as the Gerar city-state in that area."

154 FINKELSTEIN 1985: 62.

155 See FINKELSTEIN 1985: 157, "Throughout history then, the fate of the arid zones of the southern Levant was decided according to the changing balance between three forces: global powers, such as Egypt, Assyria, the Neo-Babylonians and Rome; local authorities, such as the Philistine city-states and the entities of the southern hill country – Iron II Judah and the later Hasmonean state; and the economic and political power of the desert people."

156 ZWICKEL 2015: 73, "Offenbar von Ziklag aus unternahm David mit einigen seiner Leute Streifzüge in benachbarte Gebiete, um dort zu plündern (1 Sam 27,8–10; vgl. auch 1 Sam 30,7–24). Damit änderte sich die Stellung Davids erheblich! War er zuerst auf Seiten der Judäer und versuchte, deren Herden vor Streifscharen zu schützen, so führte er nun selbst derartige Raubzüge durch. Andererseits zeigt 1 Sam 30,1, daß auch Ziklag Opfer der Raubzüge der Amalekiter sein konnte. Der südliche Negeb scheint in jener Zeit sehr stark umstritten gewesen zu sein; exakte Grenzverläufe und abgesteckte Gebiete gab es noch nicht."

Kenites. This was a perfect situation in which a bandit chief like David could take advantage of the power vacuum and gain ascendancy over a disputed territory, and it is precisely this situation that is reflected in the story in 1 Sam 27.

Illustrations

Map 1: *a*. Location map showing the digital elevation model of the eastern Mediterranean region and the mean annual rainfall isohyets (for 1961–1990 in mm; Israel Meteorological Service, 1990). *b*. Map of Israel and its surroundings showing the distribution of sand dunes and loessial and sandy soils in the Negev Desert © AMIT / SIMHAI / AYALON / ENZEL / MATMON / ONN / PORAT / MCDONALD 2011, fig. 2a and b.
Map 2: The Southern Surroundings of the Philistine Territory © Wolfgang ZWICKEL / Krister KOWALSKI.
Map 3: The Negev in Late Bronze Age © Wolfgang ZWICKEL / Krister KOWALSKI.
Map 4: The Negev in Iron Age I © Wolfgang ZWICKEL / Krister KOWALSKI.
Map 5: The Negev in Iron Age IB / IIA © Wolfgang ZWICKEL / Krister KOWALSKI.
Map 6: The Negev Iron Age II © Wolfgang ZWICKEL / Krister KOWALSKI.
Map 7: The Negev: Geopolitical Map © Wolfgang ZWICKEL / Krister KOWALSKI.

Bibliography

Aharoni, Yôḥānān. 1974. *The Land of the Bible. A Historical Geography*. Translated form the Hebrew by A. F. Rainey. London: Burns & Oates.
Aḥituv, Shmuel. 1984. *Canaanite Toponyms in Ancient Egyptian Documents*. Jerusalem / Leiden: Magnes Press / Brill.
Amit, Rikva, and Ori Simhai, Avner Ayalon, Yehouda Enzel, Ari Matmon, Crouvi Onn, Naomi Porat, Eric McDonald. 2011. Transition From Arid to Hyper-arid Environment in the Southern Levant Deserts as Recorded by Early Pleistocene Cummulic Aridisols. *Quarternary Science Reviews* 30:313–323.
Alt, Albrecht. 1968. Saruhen, Ziklag, Horma, Gerar. Pages 409–35 in *Kleine Schriften zur Geschichte des Volkes Israel*. Vol. 3. Edited by Martin Noth. München: C. H. Beck'sche Verlagsbuchhandlung, first published in 1935: *JPOS* 15:294–341.
Auld, A. Graeme. 2011. *1 & 2 Samuel: A Commentary*. The Old Testament Library. Louisville, KY: Westminster John Knox Press.
Barthélemy, Dominique. 1982. *Critique textuelle de l'Ancien Testament. Rapport final du Comité pour l'analyse textuelle de l'Ancien Testament hébreu institué par l'lliance Biblique Universelle*. OBO 50. Fribourg / Göttingen: Universitätsverlag Freiburg / Vandenhoeck & Ruprecht.
Beit-Arieh, Itzhaq. 2007. *Horbat 'uza and Horvat Radum. Two Fortresses in the Biblical Negev*. Monograph Series of the Institute of Archaeology of Tel Aviv University 25. Tel Aviv: Emery and Claire Yass Publications in Archaeology.
Ben-Yosef, Erez, and Ron Shaar, Lisa Tauze, Hagai Ron. 2012. A New Chronological Framework for Iron Age Copper Production in Timna (Israel). BASOR 367:31–71.

Bietak, Manfred. 1984. "Schi-Hor." Pages 623–26 in Vol. 5 of *Lexikon der Ägyptologie*. Edited by W. Helck and W. Westendorf. Wiesbaden: Harrassowitz, 1975–1992.

Blakely, Jeffrey A. 2007. The Location of Medieval/Pre-Modern and Biblical Ziklag. *PEQ* 139:21–26.

Blakely, Jeffrey A. / Hardin, James W. 2018. Coming to Recoginze that Sedentary Agriculture, or Farming, Was Rarely Practiced in the Hesi Region. Pages 229–63 in: *Archaeology and History of Eighth-Century Judah*. Edited by Zev I. Farber and Jacob L. Wright. ANEM 23. Atlanta: SBL Press.

Braudel, Fernand. ⁶1990. *The Mediterranean and the Mediterranean World in the Age of Philip II*. New York: Harper & Row.

Braudel, Fernand. 2012. History and the Social Science. La *Longue Durée*. A new Translation by Immanuel Wallerstein of 'Histoire et Sciences sociales: La longue durée, *Annales E.S.C.* (1958), 13 (4): 725–753.' Pages 241–76 in *The Longue Durée and World-Systems Analysis*. Edited by Richard E. Lee. New York: State University of New York Press.

Caquot, André and Philippe de Robert. 1994. *Les livres de Samuel*. CAT 6. Genève: Labor et Fides.

Cartledge, Tony W. 2001. *1 & 2 Samuel*. Smyth & Helwys Bible Commentary 7. Macon, GA: Smyth & Helwys Publishing.

Cohen, Rudolf. 1980. The Iron Age Fortresses in the Central Negeb. Pages 7–31 in *Drei Studien zur Archäologie und Topographie Altisraels*. Beihefte zum Tübinger Atlas des Vorderen Orients Reihe B. Geisteswissenschaften 44. Edited by Rudolph Cohn and Götz Schmitt. Wiesbaden: Dr. Ludwig Reichert.

Crüsemann, Frank. 1973. Überlegungen zur Identifikation der Hirbet el-Mšāš (Tēl Māśôś). *ZDPV* 89:211–24.

Dessel, J.P. 1997. "Ajjul, Tell el-." Pages 38–40 in Vol. 1 of *The Oxford Encyclopedia of Archaeology in the Near East*. Edited by Eric M. Meyers. Oxford: Oxford University Press.

Dever, William G. 1975. A Middle Bronze I Cemetary at Khirbet el-Kirmil. *Eretz-Israel* 12:18*–33*.

Dever, William G. 2018. Shoshenq and Solomon: Chronological Considerations. *Eretz-Israel* 33:50*–55*.

Dietrich, Walter. 2012. David and the Philistines: Literature and History. Pages 79–98 in *The Ancient Near East in the 12th–10th centuries BCE. Culture and History. Proceedings of the International Conference held at the University of Haifa, 2–5 May, 2010*. Edited by Gershon Galil, Ayelet Gilboa, Aren M. Maeir, and Dan'el Kahn. AOAT 392. Münster: Ugarit-Verlag.

Dietrich, Walter. 2015. *Samuel*. BKAT VIII/2. Neukirchen-Vluyn: Neukirchener Verlag.

Dietrich, Walter. 2017. *Samuel*. BKAT VIII/3. Neukirchen-Vluyn: Neukirchener Verlag.

Döring, Jörg, and Tristan Thielmann. ²2009. Einleitung: Was Lesen Wir Im Raume? Der *Spatial Turn* und das geheime Wissen der Geographen. Pages 7–45 in *Spatial Turn. Das Raumparadigma in den Kultur- und Sozialwissenschaften*. Edited by Jörg Döring and Tristan Thielmann. Bielefeld: Transcript-Verlag.

Driesbach, Jason K. 2016. *4QSamuel and the Text of Samuel*. VT.S 171. Leiden: Brill.

Edenburg, Cynthia. 2011. Notes on the Origin of the Biblical Tradition Regarding Achish King of Gath. *VT* 61:34–38.

Ebeling, Knut. 2010. Historischer Raum: Archiv und Erinnerungsort. Pages 121–33 in *Raum. Ein Interdisziplinäres Handbuch*. Edited by Stephan Günzel. Stuttgart / Weimar: J. B. Metzler'sche Verlagsbuchhandlung / Carl Ernst Poeschel Verlag GmbH.

Ehrlich, Carl S. 1996. *The Philistines in Transition: A History from ca. 1000–730 BCE.* Leiden: E. J. Brill.

Ehrlich, Carl S. 2002. Die Suche nach Gat und die neuen Ausgrabungen auf Tell eş-Şāfī. Pages 56–69 in *Kein Land für sich allein. Studien zum Kulturkontakt in Kanaan, Israel/ Palästina und Ebirnâri für Manfred Weippert zum 65. Geburtstag.* Edited by Ulrich Hübner and Ernst A. Knauf. OBO 186. Freiburg / Göttingen: Universitätsverlag Freiburg / Vandenhoeck & Ruprecht.

Faust, Avraham. 2018. The Land of the Philistines? Reexamining the Settlement in the Periphery of Philistia. *Eretz-Israel* 33:195–204.

Finkelstein, Israel. 1984. The Iron Age "Fortresses" of the Negev Highland: Sedentarization of the Nomads. *Tel Aviv* 11:189–209.

Finkelstein, Israel. 1988. Arabian Trade and Socio-Political Conditions in the Negev in the Twelfth–Eleventh Centuries B.C.E. *JNES* 47:241–52.

Finkelstein, Israel. 1995. *Living on the Fringe: The Archaeology and the History of the Negev Sinai and Neighbouring Regions in the Bronze and Iron Ages.* Sheffield: Sheffield Academic Press.

Finkelstein, Israel. 2000. The Philistine Settlements: When, Where, and How Many? Pages 159–80 in *The Sea Peoples and Their World: A Reassessment.* Edited by Eliezer D. Oren. Philadelphia: University of Pennsylvania.

Finkelstein, Israel. 2002. The Philistines in the Bible: A Late-Monarchic Perspective. *JSOT* 27:131–67.

Finkelstein, Israel. 2013. Geographical and Historical Realities Behind the Earliest Layer in the David Story. *SJOT* 27:131–50.

Finkelstein, Israel. 2014. The Southern Steppe of the Levant ca. 1050–750 BCE: A Framework for the Territorial History. *PEQ* 146:89–104.

Finkelstein, Israel and Neil A. Silberman. [2]2007. *David and Solomon: In Search of the Bible's Sacred Kings and the Roots of the Western Tradition.* New York: Free Press.

Fischer, Erika. 2016. "Tell el-Fār'a Süd." In *Das Wissenschaftliche Bibellexikon.* Edited by Stefan Alkier, Michaela Bauks and Klaus Koenen. Online: http:// www.bibelwissenschaft.de/stichwort/73825/.

Fischer, Peter M., and Moain Sadeq. 2008. "'Ajjul, Tell El." Pages 1565–66 in Vol. 5 of *The New Encyclopedia of Archaeological Excavations of the Holy Land.* Edited by Ephraim Stern, Hillel Geva, Alan Paris, and Joseph Aviram. Jerusalem / Washington, DC: Israel Exploration Society / Biblical Archeology Society, 1993–2008.

Fritz, Volkmar. 1990. Der Beitrag der Archäologie zur Historischen Topographie Palästinas am Beispiel Ziklags. *ZDPV* 106:78–85.

Galil, Gershon. 2001. The Jerahmeelites and the Negeb of Judah. *JANES* 28:33–42.

Gazit, Dan. 2008. Permanent and Temporary Settlement in the South of the Lower Besor Region: Two Case Studies. Pages 75–85 in *Bene Israel. Studies in the Archaeology of Israel and the Levant During the Bronze and Iron Ages Offered in Honour of Israel Finkelstein.* Edited by Alexander Fantalkin and Assaf Yasur-Landau. Leiden: Brill.

Gesenius, Wilhelm. [18]2013. *Hebräisches und Aramäisches Handwörterbuch über das Alte Testament.* Berlin: Springer Verlag.

Gitin, Seymour. 1997. A Royal Dedicatory Inscription from Ekron. *IEJ* 47:1–16.

Gitin, Seymour. 1998. Philistia in Transition: The Tenth Century BCE and Beyond. Pages 162–83 in *Mediterranean Peoples in Transition: Thirteenth to Early Tenth Centuries BCE. In Honor of Professor Trude Dothan.* Edited by Seymour Gitin, Amihai Mazar, and Ephraim Stern. Jerusalem: Israel Exploration Society.

Goldfarb, Jorge D. 2012. On Landscape Criticism and Literary Criticism. *Landscapes. The Journal of the International Centre for Landscape and Language* 5:6–23. Online http://ro.ecu.edu.au/landscapes/vol5/iss1/15.

Goldschmidt, M. J. and S. Schmorak. ²1970. "Catchment Areas." No. V/1 in *Atlas of Israel. Cartogrphy, Physical Geography, Human and Economic Geography, History*. Edited by David H. K. Amiran, et al. Jerusalem: Survey of Israel, Ministry of Labour.

Gophna, R. 1993. "Far'ah, Tell el- (South)." Pages 441–44 in Vol. 2 of *The New Encyclopedia of Archaeological Excavation in the Holy Land*. Edited by Ephraim Stern, Ayelet Lewinson-Gilboa, Joseph Aviram. Jerusalem / Washington, DC: Israel Exploration Society / Biblical Archeology Society, 1993–2008.

Günzel, Stephan. ²2009. Spatial Turn – Topographical Turn – Topological Turn. Pages 219–37 in *Spatial Turn. Das Raumparadigma in den Kultur- und Sozialwissenschaften*. Edited by Jörg Döring and Tristin Thielmann. Bielefeld: transcript-Verlag.

Günzel, Stephan. 2010. *Raum. Ein Interdisziplinäres Handbuch*. Stuttgart / Weimar: J. B. Metzler'sche Verlagsbuchhandlung / Carl Ernst Poeschel Verlag.

Halpern, Baruch. 2001. *David's Secret Demons: Messiah, Murderer, Traitor, King: The Bible in Its World*. Grand Rapids: William B. Eerdmans Publishing.

Hardin, James W. 2010. *Household and the Use of Domestic Space at Iron II Tell Halif: An Archaeology of Destruction, Reports of the Lahav Research Project Excavations at Tell Halif, Israel*. Vol. 2. Winona Lake, IN: Eisenbrauns.

Harel, Maayan, and Rivka Amit, Naomi Porat, Yehouda Enzel. 2017. Evolution of the Southeastern Mediterranean Coastal Plain. Pages 433–45 in *Quaternary of the Levant: Environments, Climate Change, and Humans*. Edited by Yhouda Enzel and Ofer Bar-Yosef. Cambridge: Cambridge University Press.

Herzog, Zeev, and Ofer Bar-Yosef. 2002. Different Views on Ethnicity in the Archaeology of the Negev. Pages [151]–[181] in Aharon Kempinski Memorial Volume. *Studies in Archaeology and Related Disciplines*. Beer-Sheva XV. Edited by Eliezer D. Oren and Shmuel Aḥituv. Beer-Sheva: Ben-Gurion University of the Negev Press.

Holladay, John S. and Stanley Klassen. 2014. From Bandit to King: David's Time in the Negev and the Transformation of a Tribal Entity into a Nation State. Pages 31–46 in *Unearthing the Wilderness. Studies on the History and Archaeology of the Negev and Edom in the Iron Age*. Edited by Juan Manuel Tebes. Ancient Near Eastern Studies Supplement 45. Paris, Walpole, MA: Peeters.

Hutton, Jeremy M. 2009. *The Transjordanian Palimpsest: The Overwritten Texts of Personal Exile and Transformation in the Deuteronomisitic History*. BZAW 396. Berlin: de Gruyter.

Jacobs, Paul F. and Joe D. Seger. 2017. *Lehav VI: Excavations in Field I at Tell Halif 1976–1999, The Early Bronze III to Late Arabic Strata*. Reports of the Lehav Research Project Excavations at Tell Halif Israel. Vol. 6. Winona Lake, IN: Eisenbrauns.

Jericke, Detlef. 1997. *Die Landnahme im Negev: Protoisraelitische Gruppen im Süden Palästinas*. ADPV 20. Wiesbaden: Harrassowitz.

Karmon, Yehuda. ²1994. *Israel: Eine geographische Landeskunde*. Wissenschaftliche Länderkunden 22. Darmstadt: Wissenschaftliche Buchgesellschaft.

Keel, Othmar, and Max Küchler. 1982. *Orte und Landschaften der Bibel: Ein Handbuch und Studienreiseführer zum Heiligen Land*. Band 2: Der Süden. Göttingen: Brenzigier / Vandenhoeck & Ruprecht.

Kipfer, Sara. 2015. *Der bedrohte David. Eine exegetische und rezeptionsgeschichtliche Studie zu 1Sam 16 – 1Kön 2*. SBR 3. Berlin: de Gruyter.

Kipfer, Sara. In press. "Kulturland und Wüste." in *Handbuch Alttestamentliche Anthropologie*. Edited by Jan Dietrich, Alexandra Grund, Bernd Janowski, and Ute Neumann-Gorsolke. Tübingen: Mohr Siebeck.

Kitchen, Kenneth A. ²2015 *The Third Intermediate Period in Egypt: 1100–650 B.C.* Oxford: Aris & Phillips.

Klein, Johannes. 2005. Davids Flucht zu den Philistern (1 Sam. XXI 11 ff.; XXVII–XXIX). *VT* 60:176–84.

Knauf, Ernst Axel. 1985. *Ismael. Untersuchungen zur Geschichte Palästinas und Nordarabiens im 1. Jahrtausend v. Chr*, Wiesbaden: Harrassowitz.

Knauf, Ernst Axel. 2007. "Keniter." In *Das Wissenschaftliche Bibellexikon*. Edited by Stefan Alkier, Michaela Bauks and Klaus Koenen. Online: https://www.bibelwissenschaft.de/stichwort/23400/.

Koselleck, Reinhart. 2018. *Sediment of Time: On Possible Histories*. Translated and edited by Sean Franzel and Stefan-Ludwig Hoffmann. Standford: Standford University Press.

Kotter, Wade R., and Eliezer D. Oren. 1992. "Ziklag." Pages 1090–93 in Vol. 6 of *The Anchor Bible Dictionary*. Edited by Noel David Freedman et al. New York: Doubleday.

Lehmann, Gunnar, and Revital Golding-Meir, Bat-Ami Neumeier-Potishnik, Hermann M. Niemann. 2018. Excavations at Tell *el-Fārʿah* (South): 1998–2002. *ZDPV* 134:109–50.

Lipiński, Edward. 2018. *Toponymes et Gentilices Bibliques Face à l'Histoire*. OLA 267. Leuven: Peeters.

Liwak, Rüdiger. 1992. "Sharuhen." Pages 1163–65 in Vol. 5 of *The Anchor Bible Dictionary*: Edited by David Noel Freedman et. al. New York: Doubleday.

Machinist, Peter. 2000. Biblical Traditions: The Philistines and Israelite History. Pages 53–69 in *The Sea People and Their World: A Reassessment*. Edited by Eliezer D. Oren. Philadelphia: University of Pennsylvania.

Maeir, Aren M. 2007. A Tale of Two Tells: A Comparative Perspective on Tel Miqne-Ekron and Tell eṣ-Ṣāfī/Gath in Light of Recent Archaeological Research. Pages 29–42 in *Up to the Gates of Ekron: Essays on the Archaeology and History of the Eastern Mediterranean in Honor of Seymour Gitin*. Edited by Sidnie White Crawford et al. Jerusalem: The W. F. Albright Institute of Archaeological Research.

Maeir, Aren M. 2012. Chapter 1: The Tell es-Safi/Gath Archaeological Project 1996–2010. Introduction, Overview and Synopsis of Results. Pages 1–88 in *Tell es-Safi/Gath I. The 1996–2005 Seasons. Vol. 1: Text*. ÄAT 69. Edited by Aren M. Maeir. Wiesbaden: Harrassowitz.

Mané, U. ²1970. "Temperature and Humidity." No. IV/1 in *Atlas of Israel: Cartography, Physical Geography, Human and Economic Geography, History*. Edited by David H. K. Amiran, et al. Jerusalem: Survey of Israel, Ministry of Labour.

McCarter, P. Kyle. 1980. *I Samuel: A New Translation with Introduction, Notes, and Commentary*. The Anchor Bible 8. Garden City, NY: Doubleday.

Münger, Stefan. 2018. References to the Pharaoh in the Local Glyptic Assemblage of the Southern Levant During the First Part of the 1st Millenium BCE. *Journal of Ancient Egyptian Interconnections* 18:40–62. Online: http://jaei.library.arizona.edu.

Münger, Stefan, and Thomas E. Levy. 2014. The Iron Age Egyptian Amulet Assemblage. Pages 741–64 in *New Insights into the Iron Age Archaeology of Edom, Southern Jordan: Surveys, Excavations and Research from the University of California, San Diego-Department of Antiquities of Jordan, Edom Lowlands Regional Archaeology Project (ELRAP)*. Monumenta Archaeologica 35. Edited by Thomas E. Levy, Mohammad Najjar and Erez Ben-Yosef. Los Angeles: Cotsen Institute of Archaeology Press.

Na'aman, Nadav. 1986. *Borders and Districts in Biblical Historiography: Seven Studies in Biblical Geographical Lists*. JBS 4. Jerusalem: Simor LTD.

Na'aman, Nadav. 1992. Israel, Edom and Egypt in the 10th Century B.C.E. *Tel Aviv* 19:71–93.

Na'aman, Nadav. 2005a. The Brook of Egypt and Assyrian Policy on the Border of Egypt. Pages 238–64 in *Ancient Israel and Its Neighbors: Interaction and Counteraction*. Collected Essays Vol. 1. Edited by Nadav Na'aman. Winona Lake, IN: Eisenbrauns.

Na'aman, Nadav. 2005b. The Shihor of Egypt and Shur That is Before Egypt. Pages 265–78 in *Ancient Israel and Its Neighbors: Interaction and Counteraction*. Collected Essays Vol. 1. Edited by Nadav Na'aman. Winona Lake, IN: Eisenbrauns.

Na'aman, Nadav. 2010a. David's Sojourn in Keilah in Light of the Amarna Letters. *VT* 60:87–97.

Na'aman, Nadav. 2010b. The Date of the List of Towns that Received the Spoil of Amalek: 1 Sam 30:26–31. *Tel Aviv* 38:175–87.

Naveh, Joseph. 1998. Achish-Ikausu in Light of Ekron Dedication. *BASOR* 310:35–37.

Niemann, Hermann Michael. 2002. Nachbarn und Gegner, Konkurrenten und Verwandte Judas: Die Philister zwischen Geographie und Ökonomie, Geschichte und Theologie. Pages 70–91 in *Kein Land für sich allein. Studien zum Kulturkontakt in Kanaan, Israel/ Palästina und Ebirnâri für Manfred Weippert zum 65*. Edited by Ulrich Hübner and Ernst Axel Knauf. OBO 186. Freiburg / Göttingen: Universitätsverlag Freiburg / Vandenhoeck & Ruprecht.

Niemann, Hermann Michael and Gunnar Lehmann. 2010. Zwischen Wüste und Mittelmeer: Qubur al-Walaydah und Seine Umgebung in Südwest-Palästina. *Die Welt des Orients* 40:216–43.

Niesiołowski-Spanò, Łukasz. 2016. *Goliath's Legacy: Philistines and Hebrews in Biblical Times*. Philippika Altertumswissenschaftliche Abhandlungen 83. Wiesbaden: Harrassowitz.

Noort, Ed. 1994. *Die Seevölker in Palästina*. Palaestina Antiqua 8. Kampen, The Netherlands: Kok Pharos Publishing House.

Noort, Ed. 1996. Text und Archäologie: die Küstenregion Palästinas in der Frühen Eisenzeit. *UF* 27:403–28.

Noort, Ed. 2003. "Philister. II. Archäologie und Ikonographie". Pages 1284–85 in Vol. 6 of *Religion in Geschichte und Gegenwart 4*. Edited by Hans Dieter Betz et al. Tübingen: Mohr Siebeck, 1998–2005.

Oren, Eliezer D. 1974. *Tell esh-Sheri'a (Tell Sera')*. Archaeological Division Ben-Gurion University of the Negev. Beersheva: Hanegev Press.

Oren, Eliezer D. 1982. Ziglag – A biblical city on the edge of the Negev. *BA* 45:155–66.

Oren, Eliezer D. 1993a. "Haror, Tel." Pages 580–84 in Vol. 2 of *The New Encyclopedia of Archaeological Excavation in the Holy Land*. Edited by Ephraim Stern, Ayelet Lewinson-Gilboa and Joseph Aviram. Jerusalem / Washington, DC: Israel Exploration Society / Biblical Archeology Society, 1993–2008.

Oren, Eliezer D. 1993b. "Sera', Tel." Pages 1329–35 in Vol. 4 of *The New Encyclopedia of Archaeological Excavation in the Holy Land*. Edited by Ephraim Stern, Ayelet Lewinson-Gilboa and Joseph Aviram. Jerusalem / Washington, DC: Israel Exploration Society / Biblical Archeology Society, 1993–2008.

Oren, Eliezer D. 1997a. "Sera', Tel." Pages 1–2 in Vol. 5 of *The Oxford Encyclopedia of Archaeology in the Near East*. Edited by Eric M Meyers. Oxford: Oxford University Press.

Oren, Eliezer D. 1997b. "Haror, Tel." Pages 474–76 in Vol. 2 of *The Oxford Encyclopedia of Archaeology in the Near East*. Edited by Eric M Meyers. 5 Oxford: Oxford University Press.

Orni, Efraim, and Elisha Efrat. 1980. *Geography of Israel.* Jerusalem: Israel Universities Press.

Picard, L., and L. Kadmon. ²1970. "Watercourse Gradients: Map B." No. V/2 in *Atlas of Israel. Cartography, Physical Geography, Human and Economic Geography, History.* Edited by David H. K. Amiran, et al. Jerusalem: Survey of Israel, Ministry of Labour.

Rainey, Anson F. 1984. Early Historical Geography in the Negeb. Pages 88–104 in *Beer-Sheba II: The Early Iron Age Settlements.* Publications of the Institute of Archaeology 7. Edited by Ze'ev Herzog. Tel Aviv: Tel Aviv University.

Ravikovitch, S. ²1970. "Soil Map." No. II/3 in *Atlas of Israel. Cartography, Physical Geography, Human and Economic Geography, History.* Edited by David H. K. Amiran, et al. Jerusalem: Survey of Israel, Ministry of Labour.

Reifenberg, A., and C. L. Whittles. ²1947. *The Soils of Palestine: Studies in Soil Formation and Land Utilisation in the Mediterranean.* London: Thomas Murby & Company.

Rendtorff, Rolf. 1971. Beobachtungen zur Altisraelitischen Geschichtsschreibung anhand der Geschichte vom Aufstieg Davids. Pages 428–39 in *Probleme biblischer Theologie.* Gerhard von Rad zum 70. Geburtstag. Edited by Hans Walter Wolff. München: Chr. Kaiser.

Roseman, N. ²1970. "Rainfall." No. IV/2 in *Atlas of Israel. Cartography, Physical Geography, Human and Economic Geography, History.* Edited by David H. K. Amiran, et al. Jerusalem: Survey of Israel, Ministry of Labour.

Seger, Joe D. 1984. The Location of Biblical Ziklag. *BA* 47:47–53.

Seger, Joe D. 1993. "Halif, Tel." Pages 553–59 in Vol. 2 of *The New Encyclopedia of Archaeological Excavation in the Holy Land.* Edited by Ephraim Stern, Ayelet Lewinson-Gilboa and Joseph Aviram. Jerusalem / Washington, DC: Israel Exploration Society / Biblical Archeology Society, 1993–2008.

Shavit, Alon. 2008. Settlement Patterns of Philistine City-States. Pages 135–64 in *Bene Israel. Studies in the Archaeology of Israel and the Levant During the Bronze and Iron Ages Offered in Honour of Israel Finkelstein.* Edited by Alexander Fantalkin and Assaf Yasur-Landau. Leiden: Brill.

Simons, Jan. 1937. *Handbook for the Study of Egyptian Topographical Lists Relating to Western Asia.* Leiden: E. J. Brill.

Singer, Arieh. 2007. *The Soils of Israel.* Berlin, Heidelberg: Springer Berlin.

Staubli, Thomas. 1991. *Das Image der Nomaden im alten Israel und in der Ikonographie seiner sesshaften Nachbarn.* OBO 107. Freiburg / Göttingen: Universitätsverlag Freiburg / Vandenhoeck & Ruprecht.

Stoebe, Hans Joachim. 1973. *Das Erste Buch Samuelis,* KAT 8,1. Gütersloh: Gütersloher Verlagshaus.

Stolz, Fritz. 1981. *Das Erste und Zweite Buch Samuel.* ZBK 9. Zürich: Theologischer Verlag Zürich.

Thiel, Winfried. 2005. Die David-Geschichten im Alten Testament. Pages 39–63 in *Gedeutete Geschichte: Studien zur Geschichte Israels und ihrer theologischen Interpretation im Alten Testament.* BThSt 71. Edited by Peter Mommer, Simone Portmann and Andreas Scherer. Neukirchen-Vluyn: Neukirchener Verlag.

Timm, Stefan. 1998. "Amalekiter." Page 386 in Vol. 1 of the *Religion in Geschichte und Gegenwart 4.* Edited by Hans Dieter Betz et al. Tübingen: Mohr Siebeck, 1998–2005.

Tsumura, David T. 2007. *The First Book of Samuel: The New International Commentary on the Old Testament.* Grand Rapids, MI: William B. Eerdmans.

Tufnell, Olga, and Aharon Kempinski. 1993. "Ajjul, Tell El-." Pages 49–53 in Vol. 1 *The New Encyclopedia of Archaeological Excavation in the Holy Land.* Edited by Ephraim Stern,

Ayelet Lewinson-Gilboa and Joseph Aviram. Jerusalem / Washington, DC: Israel Exploration Society / Biblical Archeology Society, 1993–2008.

Ulrich, Eugene. 2010. *The Biblical Qumran Scrolls: Transcriptions and Textual Variants*. VT.S 134. Leiden: Brill.

van Beek, Gus W. 1992. "Jemmeh, Tell." Pages 676–78 in Vol. 3 of *The Anchor Bible Dictionary*. Edited by Noel David Freedman et al. New York: Doubleday.

van Beek, Gus W. 1993. "Jemmeh, Tell." Pages 667–74 in Vol. 2 of *The New Encyclopedia of Archaeological Excavation in the Holy Land*. Edited by Ephraim Stern, Ayelet Lewinson-Gilboa and Joseph Aviram. Jerusalem / Washington, DC: Israel Exploration Society / Biblical Archeology Society, 1993–2008.

van Beek, Gus W. 1997. "Jemmeh, Tell." Pages 212–15 in Vol. 3 of *The Oxford Encyclopedia of Archaeology in the Near East*. Edited by Eric M. Meyers. Oxford: Oxford University Press.

Vette, Joachim. 2010. "Ziklag." In *Das Wissenschaftliche Bibellexikon*. Edited by Stefan Alkier, Michaela Bauks and Klaus Koenen. Online https://www.bibelwissenschaft.de/stichwort/15957/.

Weinstein, James D. 1997. "Far'ah, Tell el-." Pages 304–5 in Vol. 2 of *The Oxford Encyclopedia of Archaeology in the Near East*. Edited by Eric M. Meyers. Oxford: Oxford University Press.

Wirth, Raimund. 2016. *Die Septuaginta der Samuelbücher: Untersucht unter Einbeziehung ihrer Rezensionen*. De Septuaginta Investigationes 7. Göttingen: Vandenhoeck & Ruprecht.

Wüst, Manfried. 1975. *Untersuchungen zu den siedlungsgeographischen Texten des Alten Testaments*. BTAVO.B 9. Wiesbaden: Reichert.

Zwickel, Wolfgang. 2011. Die historischen Philister. Israels fremde Welt. Pages 146–57 in *Philister: Problemgeschichte einer Sozialfigur der Neueren Deutschen Literatur*. Edited by Remigius Bunia, Till Dembeck and Georg Stanitzek. Berlin: Akademia Verlag.

Zwickel, Wolfgang. 2012. The Change from Egyptian to Philistine Hegemony in South-Western Palestine during the Time of Ramessess III or IV. Pages 595–601 in *The Ancient Near East in the 12th–10th centuries BCE. Culture and History*. Proceedings of the International Conference held at the University of Haifa, 2–5 May, 2010. AOAT 392. Edited by Gershon Galil, Ayelet Gilboa, Aren M. Maeir and Dan'el Kahn. Münster: Ugarit-Verlag.

Zwickel, Wolfgang. 2015. Der Beitrag der Ḫabiru zur Entstehung des Königtums. Pages 61–76 in *Studien zur Geschichte Israels*. SBAB Altes Testament 59. Edited by Wolfgang Zwickel. Stuttgart: Verlag Katholisches Bibelwerk.

Mahri Leonard-Fleckman

All the גבול of Israel (1 Sam 27:1)

Israel's "Boundaries" in David's Wanderings

> *"This is probably all one can ask of history, and of the history of ideas in particular: not to resolve issues, but to raise the level of debate."* – Albert O. Hirschman[1]

Those of us who are diachronically-minded have a stake in dating texts, however relative this venture may be. We build our projects on two basic, foundational suppositions: 1) the Bible is comprised of textual layers that reveal earlier preserved material of historical value for understanding ancient Israel; and 2) as scholars, it is possible to peel back these layers and date them, at the very least relatively, based on textual evidence (inconsistencies, editorial explanations, repetitions, and so on). From the textual evidence we make decisions about what constitute "earlier" versus "later" textual strata based on certain operating theories, or we stand on the shoulders of others who have done so. Although all this may sound obvious to the reader, I think it necessary to state clearly the suppositions that underlie our work, and to reevaluate these suppositions periodically. And what better time than now, in the context of the great cloud of witnesses in this volume who have wagered their scholarship on the idea that the Bible preserves vestiges of the past that we can uncover, and for whom such an idea matters, however constructed or re-envisioned such vestiges may be.

In this paper I seek to undertake such a reevaluation through a particular case study; namely, the depiction of the social landscape of the Shephelah in the David-Gath story of 1 Sam 27. I am most interested in how the text utilizes geography and specific terminology, including "border/boundary" or "territory" (גבול) and the notion of "crossing over" (עבר), to construct a particular image of the social landscape in the relationship between David and the king of Gath, and how this image relates to other biblical tales in the Shephelah and to liter-

---

1 Hirschman 1977: 135.

Note: I wish to thank participants of the Jena colloquium for their comments on this paper, especially Sara Kipfer, as well as members of the Colloquium for Biblical and Near Eastern Studies, in particular Nathaniel (Ned) Greene, Dan Pioske, and Jonathan Wylie.

https://doi.org/10.1515/9783110606164-005

ary-historical questions.[2] While some biblical texts portray clearly-bordered and antagonistic relations between Israel and Gath (e.g. 1 Sam 17; 1 Sam 21:11–16), 1 Sam 27 describes a socially-ambiguous and un-bordered Shephelah in the cooperative relations between David and Gath's leader. Such a description blurs social lines and confuses the notion of antagonist interactions between Israel and the Philistines (these blurred lines also bleed into other parts of the David story; see 2 Sam 6:9–11 and 2 Sam 15:18–22). It is not new to call attention to this juxtaposition between bordered and porous social landscapes in 1–2 Sam, and scholars generally view 1 Sam 27 as containing some early "core," in part because of such blurred boundaries and cooperative, cross-cultural relations. My goal in this paper is to probe this perspective in order to unpack our assumptions about the relationship between writing, tradition and history. Does the depiction of cooperative relations between David and Gath in 1 Sam 27 necessarily reflect an earlier social and political landscape and, if so, does that automatically correlate to earlier writing and/or earlier traditions?

Therefore, this paper will reexamine the textual construction of the social landscape in 1 Sam 27 in relation to the history of diachronic scholarship, including other papers in this volume, and in conversation with the debatable archaeological portrait of the Shephelah in the tenth-seventh centuries BCE. Because biblical stories that take place in the Shephelah are uncommon, I will compare briefly 1 Sam 27 with other David-Gath material in 1–2 Sam and with one other Shephelah tale that depicts a similar permeable landscape, the Samson narrative in Judg 13–16. More broadly, my concern is whether, and to what extent, literary constructions of the social and political landscape have historical value. In other words, to what extent is it possible to distinguish between texts that construct landscape as idealizations, alternative realities or fabrications, and those that have older tentacles, that connect to or derive from older traditions or what was "remembered" in some sense, or that nonetheless reflect conceptions older than those of the finished text? What is the power of geography, including sites, terminology, and descriptions of geographical movement, for such constructions or "languaging"[3] of landscape and in our perceptions of a text's compositional history?

---

2 To define my terminology, I use the word "geography" as rooted in land and place, and "landscape" to reflect a broader, less tangible or imagined representation. See Adam T. SMITH (2003), who defines landscape as binding together geography or place; in this sense, landscape can be used more broadly than geography as the construction of less tangible representations, what Smith calls "imagined cartographies of possible worlds" (2003: 11). The key is that geography is not an objective, fixed backdrop for the social and political world; rather, it is created and shaped in relation to that world.
3 The term "languaging" comes from the field of secondary language acquisition and reflects the notion that the language we use, written or oral, externalizes or articulates the inner world

1 Gath and the Notion of Earlier Writing

1 Sam 27 depicts David seeking refuge in Gath, far enough away from the "territory" or limits (גבול) of Israel to halt Saul's pursuit. As Cynthia Edenburg describes in this volume, a series of disjointed encounters and circuitous stopovers in other locations in chs. 19–26 precede David's arrival in Gath, including the literary doublet of one prior, unsuccessful foray in the same location in 1 Sam 21:11–16.[4] As the scene opens in 1 Sam 27, we enter into David's inner world as he "speaks in his heart" to explain his impending actions; the best-case scenario for escaping Saul successfully, David says to himself, is to go to the "land of the Philistines," where Saul will give up hunting him through "all the גבול of Israel." He then "crosses over" (עבר) to King Achish of Gath (v. 2) with his retinue of wives, six hundred men and their families (v. 3), where he politely requests and is granted one of Gath's peripheral "country towns" (ערי השׂדה) in which to settle (v. 5).

Overwhelmingly, scholars have viewed and continue to view David's Gath adventure in 1 Sam 27 as containing a "core" of earlier David traditions subsequent to v. 1. This long-held view goes back at least as far as Julius Wellhausen, who argued that 1 Sam 27:2–6 contained earlier source material.[5] Aside from the more recent scholarship outlined in Kipfer's bibliography in this volume, see, for example, Jacob Wright, who includes 1 Sam 27:2–3a, [perhaps 5–6], and 7–11 as some of the earliest material about David, which he dates prior to the fall of Israel (ninth-eighth centuries BCE).[6] Edenburg carries the view further to

---

even as it internalizes or shapes ideas and perceptions (SWAIN 2006: 95–108; SWAIN 2009: 5–29). Swain builds upon the insights of psychologist Lev Vygotsky and his work involving language (written or oral) as a mediator between the internal and the external, between thoughts or ideas and a visible or audible product (see VYGOTSKY 1987: 243–85). For those of us dealing with ancient text that is highly literary (no matter how we understand the relationship between these ancient texts and "history"), Swain's research urges us to consider how texts and their audiences, including us, "language" or form a dialogical relationship in constructing ancient society; in other words, how texts externalize or construct a particular image of the social landscape that is internalized by and shapes the reader's or audience's perceptions, and how we do the same for the texts we study.

4 Cf. EDENBURG 2020. On "doublets," see HUTTON (2009: 231–45).

5 WELLHAUSEN 1899: 251. Wellhausen viewed vv. 7–12 a later addition to the text, demonstrated by David's deep inner difficulties and the assumption of Gath rather than Ziklag as the starting point of David's raids. In this volume, see Kipfer's genealogy of scholarship and support of this position.

6 Cf. WRIGHT 2014: 35–36.

propose that a much shorter, earlier account of David's flight from Saul would lead directly from Saul (1 Sam 19) to Gath (1 Sam 21:11 directly into 1 Sam 27:2).[7]

Underneath this well-trodden path lie three basic, often entangled arguments regarding the text's social and political landscape. Kipfer interweaves all three arguments in the first paragraph of her article in this collection, while elsewhere Walter Dietrich describes them more systematically.[8] The first of these arguments is that the depiction of David as a local leader or bandit (rather than a centralized leader of a larger polity) who circles the geography of ancient Israel with his ragtag group of followers is early writing, or at least reflects earlier traditions about David. As argued by such scholars as Israel Finkelstein and noted in Kipfer's discussion, such a depiction compares to that of local *hapiru* Canaanite bandits and soldiers from the Late Bronze Age Amarna correspondence and fits an early, pre-monarchic and early monarchic landscape. Such texts in 1 Sam, including ch. 27, must therefore contain material, or traditions, that date prior to the ninth century BCE.[9]

The second argument is that cooperative relations and the blurring of social and political boundaries between David and Gath must also resonate with this older reality. Conversely, antagonistic relations and clear boundaries between David and Gath, or between David and the Philistines, only develop over time. In other words, a more fluid landscape must be older; a more social "boundaried" landscape must be later. So, from the archaeological side, Aren Maeir cautions that a binary depiction of "the" Israelites versus "the" Philistines may reflect later Iron Age, or even post-Iron age "realities and ideologies" anachronistic to the "entangled" cultural reality of the early Iron Age.[10] He further calls attention to the lack of material evidence for hostility between Gath and highland communities in the early Iron Age, which, according to Daniel Pioske, suggests that texts such as 1 Sam 27 reflect older traditions.[11] From the text side,

7 Cf. EDENBURG 2020: 13 (also IDEM 2011: 34–38). Though she has yet to conduct a full independent analysis of 1 Sam 18–19, Edenburg suspects that 1 Sam 19:8–9 would belong to the earlier core directly preceding 1 Sam 21:11, followed by 1 Sam 27:2 (personal communication).
8 Cf. KIPFER 2020; DIETRICH 2012: 92–95.
9 Cf. FINKELSTEIN 2013: 131–50; see n. 8 for additional bibliography in Kipfer's article. In his recent dissertation, Nathaniel Greene makes a similar argument with a "base text" of 1 Sam 9:1–10:16 (see GREENE 2018: 173–265).
10 See MAEIR 2017: 133–54, esp. 135.
11 Cf. MAEIR 2017: 136. In a recent article focused on the ramifications of this evidence for biblical traditions about David and Gath, Daniel Pioske states that 1 Sam 27 is part of a "different, likely earlier collection of traditions" than those found in 1 Sam 21 (PIOSKE 2018b: 17–18). Elsewhere, he writes that such an account would not be invented, as it only "complicates" the story the biblical scribes are attempting to tell (PIOSKE 2018a: 143).

P. Kyle McCarter once explained the encounter with Gath as an *"embarrassing"* [italics his] and "ineradicable element of the [David] story," one that no later writer sympathetic to David would have invented.[12] More recently, Walter Dietrich argued that a "later, David-friendly tradition would never have implicated its hero in such escapades" with Gath, and proposed vv. 2–3, 6–7 as the oldest "dry account" of David's move to Gath.[13] Similarly, Jacques Vermeylen views 1 Sam 27 as "without a doubt" a "primitive" Saul-David story that reflects "historical circumstances," in contrast to the later 1 Sam 21:11–16, which has David feigning madness out of fear of the king of Gath.[14]

The third argument (which is linked with the second) comes from deeper engagement with the archaeological record from Gath, which confirms that the city was the dominant polity in the central and northern part of the western Shephelah until its destruction in the late ninth century BCE.[15] The specificity of the political geography in 1 Sam 27 and its focus on Gath as a viable safe haven for David, away from the territory of Israel, must therefore preserve material prior to or close to the time of Gath's destruction. Specifically, the notion that David would go to Gath, of all places, and to its "king" (which is unique biblical terminology for a Philistine leader) would be foreign to a later eighth century landscape or later. The same argument holds for references to Ziklag in the text, and the remembrance that Gath's control once extended this far south (1 Sam 27:5–6).[16] If the stories about David and Gath were later written inventions, as Dietrich explains, "then one would hardly have chosen Gath, of all places, as [David's] destination."[17] Rather, a writer would perhaps have chosen Ekron, a city that rises in importance subsequent to Gath's fall.

This particular argument gains traction with the juxtaposition of Gath's ongoing role as supporting actor throughout 1–2 Sam and its jarring disappearance

---

12 Cf. MCCARTER 1980: 416.

13 Cf. DIETRICH 2012: 89. Kipfer also cites this quote in this volume.

14 Cf. VERMEYLEN 2000: 162. See also Jeremy M. Hutton, who assigns this section to his "History of David's Rise" or HDR$_2$ and dates it to the tenth century (HUTTON 2009: 271–73).

15 Cf. MAEIR 2017: 139. On the archaeological evidence from Gath and the material evidence of Gath's destruction in the late ninth century BCE, see, MAEIR 2004: 319–34, esp. 327–38; and PIOSKE 2018a: 103–17.

16 Cf. PIOSKE 2018a: 141–54, esp. 147–53.

17 Cf. DIETRICH 2012: 93. See also NA'AMAN, 2002: 200–24; FINKELSTEIN 2013: 134–39; and EDENBURG 2011: 37. Na'aman writes (in reaction to those who date the "history" of the monarchy to the Persian period or later): "Inventing a historical environment that has nothing in common with the reality of the time of the author seems so unlikely that the assumption that the history of the United Monarchy was first composed in the Persian or Hellenistic periods must be considered untenable" (NA'AMAN 2002: 203).

from the Bible thereafter.[18] It gains further traction by examining the Neo-Assyrian sources, which attest to Gath only briefly in the western campaigns of Sargon II (721–705 BCE). In these annals, Gath appears not as an independent polity with its own leader, but in a short list of cities belonging to the larger polity of Ashdod and its king.[19] Sennacherib's third campaign against Jerusalem (c. 701 BCE) then includes Ashdod, Ashkelon, Ekron, Gaza and its kings in its lists of coastal and inland targets, while Gath is conspicuously absent. In other words, Gath is simply not a concern for the Neo-Assyrian kings in their western campaigns; from their perspective, it either exists in a greatly reduced, weak, and dependent fashion on other polities, or not at all.

So, to summarize: these three linked arguments just outlined view the David-Gath material as preserving "something" from the social-political landscape prior to Gath's fall in the eighth century BCE. And, indeed, it is entirely plausible that the landscape depicted in the story of David and Gath does bear the mark of some earlier reality. After all, 1 Sam 27 is not the only text to reveal a slightly mysterious (at least to the contemporary reader) comradery between David and Gath; see, for example, David's perplexing diversion of the ark to the house of a certain Obed-Edom ("servant of the [deity] Edom") in 2 Sam 6:9–11 for three months. After witnessing Yhwh's power to kill someone who unwittingly laid his hand on the ark in vv. 6–8, David fears the power of the ark and diverts it to this particular Gittite's home, evidently just outside of Jerusalem.[20] Though nothing is said about Obed-Edom's faithfulness to this god, one might infer from Yhwh's subsequent blessing of his household that the Gittite pays sufficient respect to the god of Israel. As McCarter notes, Chronicles then credits Obed-Edom with a Levitical genealogy and remembers him both as a musician and a gatekeeper (1 Chr 15:18,21,24; 16:5), perhaps, as McCarter suggests, be-

---

18 After 2 Kgs 2, we read that Gath is attacked by Aram-Damascus in 2 Kgs 12:18. Aside, then, from Chronicles and land lists in Joshua (11:22; 13:3), we find Gath only in two prophetic statements (Amos 6:2, where the reference is to Gath's destruction; and Mic 1:10). Gath is otherwise excluded from lists of Philistine cities in prophetic texts (e.g. Jer 25:20; 47:4–7; Amos 1:6–8; Zeph 2:4–7; 9:5–8). See also MAEIR 2004: 319–34.

19 "Azuri, king of Ashdod, planned in his heart not to pay (bring) (his) tribute, and sent (messages) to the kings round about him, (filled with) hatred of Assyria ... against Ashdod [as-du-du] ... Ashdod [as-du-di], Gath [gi-im-tu], Asdudimmu [as-du-di-im-mu], I besieged, I captured; his gods, his wife, his sons, his daughters, the property, goods (and) treasures of his palace, together with the people of his land, I counted as spoil." See the "Display Inscription" or *Prunkinschrift*, WINCKLER 1889: 115–16, esp. line 104; English translation in LUCKENBILL 1927: 32, par. 62.

20 Also, we do not know for certain that this Obed-Edom was from Gath of the Philistines.

cause later tradition was "troubled" by the fact that David left the ark in the care of a Gittite.[21]

Then, further into the David material, a certain Ittai and his crew of loyal Gittites march beside David as he leaves Jerusalem in the story of Absalom's revolt (2 Sam 15:18–22); Ittai later becomes a commander of David's troops (2 Sam 18:5). Reflecting care and concern for Ittai, David calls him a "foreigner" (נכרי) and one who has just consigned himself to "exile" (גלה), and who therefore should not commit to wander further with David. In language reminiscent of Naomi's words to Ruth, David calls to Ittai not to follow him but to "return" in "true faithfulness" (חסד ואמת) (vv. 19–20).[22] Finally, 1 Kgs 2:39–40 returns (arguably anachronistically) to the same Achish of Gath from 1 Sam; this time, Gath is the perceived safe haven for runaway slaves, at least until their Benjaminite owner travels to Gath and successfully reclaims them.[23] There is a certain ease in how the story depicts relations between Israel and Gath – ease of travel between Jerusalem and Gath, ease of communication between its ruler and Shimei, and ease of refuge for the runaway slaves – that implies a natural openness, geographically and socially, between Gath and Israel. To imagine this as a thoroughly-constructed relationship takes more effort than asserting the texts contain something of historical value for a tenth-ninth century relationship between David and Gath. As Pioske writes, "When reading between the lines of these stories it does not take a leap of the literary imagination to see a partnership between David and Achish, Jerusalem and Gath, that likely benefitted them both."[24]

The question, however, is to what extent this key geographical focus on Gath, in particular those texts that depict landscape as more fluid and socially malleable, do indeed correlate to "earlier" written material. A key distinction to be made here is between writing and tradition, complicated terms on their own that we tend to conflate when studying the Bible's compositional history. The notion of tradition as that which is preserved and handed down, whether "in-

---

21 Cf. McCarter 1984: 170. Daniel E. Fleming proposes that David's procession of the ark in 2 Sam 6 may belong to a "relatively early" and "pre-deuteronomistic" narrative that does not assume the prior ark narrative of 1 Sam 4:1–7:1 (Fleming 2013: 82).

22 On the comparison between Ruth and Naomi, David and Ittai, and the covenant language of "true faithfulness," see Sakenfeld 1978: 107–11; see also Leonard-Fleckman 2021: 211–24.

23 On the name "Achish" as derived from the historical ʾkyš, a seventh-century ruler from Ekron, and applied secondarily to Gath, see Edenburg 2011: 36–37.

24 Cf. Pioske 2018a: 100. For a careful overview of the various David-Gath texts, see ibid., 97–100. On the relationship between memory and writing, and the historical questions regarding the genesis of prose-writing in ancient Israel, see 1–84.

vented" or "genuine"[25] (and which, by strict definition outside of biblical studies, precludes writing), often links to current biblical studies of memory and a "remembered past" that may eventually be preserved in the writing process. Of course, biblical writing and oral traditions are hopelessly entangled, and scholars like David Carr have therefore adopted such terms as the "oral-written interface" in studies of transmission history.[26] Yet the issue comes when those of us involved in diachronic studies begin to collapse "tradition" and "writing" unconsciously or no longer examine our most essential terminology. Over time, this failure has, to my mind, only made the question of how text relates to ancient society more convoluted.[27]

As a clear example of this convolution, notice the tension in my own terminology throughout this article: "core" (quotes original on pp. 104 and 105); "tentacles" (p. 104); "traditions," "what was remembered" (p. 106); "material or traditions," "older reality" (p. 106); and "something real" or an "earlier reality" (p. 108). I have

---

25 On the terminology "invented" versus "genuine" tradition, see HOBSBAWM 1983: 1–14.
26 The term comes from CARR 2005: 4; see also PIOSKE 2018a: 8. Elsewhere, Carr uses the term "oral-written transmission" (CARR 2011: 13–26).
27 Philip R. Davies has an interesting discussion on the use of the word "tradition" in biblical studies within his broader argument on the entanglement of "tradition" with "history" (DAVIES 2009: 6–13). Though the notion of "traditions" within writing can be traced back at least as far as Wellhausen, Davies' genealogy begins with Hermann Gunkel's focus on oral traditions in transmission history. It seems to me, though, that Gunkel generally maintained a conscious separation between "writing" and a body of "oral traditions" in relation to the Pentateuch, distinguishing between "writing traditions" and "oral traditions" in conjunction with his discussion of "history" and "legends"; see, e.g., GUNKEL 1964: 4, 123–44. Davies blamed the conflation or confusion of "tradition" with "history" on Martin Noth (see, e.g., NOTH 1958); note also Noth's consistent references to "tradition," "old tradition," "traditional material" or "historical traditions" underlying the Deuteronomistic History (DtrH) (NOTH 1981: 1–2, 4, 8, 10, 26, 42, etc.). Noth's general interest was in writing, so it may seem that his definition of "tradition" generally meant pre-DtrH *written* tradition, though not always; for example, he stated that Dtr arranged and reinterpreted "existing traditional material, which was already in written form" (NOTH 1981: 77; also 83). Elsewhere, he wrote that Dtr's transmission of "traditional documents" makes his work an "invaluable historical source" and that Dtr wanted to present the history of Israel in an objective and unbiased manner, compiling rather than inventing earlier traditions (NOTH 1981: 78, 84, 88). Noth thus unwittingly conflated orality and textuality, traditions and history. One also wonders how he imagined such "traditions" were preserved over time, before the DtrH. According to Davies, Gerhard von Rad was the first to recognize this conflation as a problem (VON RAD 1960–61; idem, 1966 [from his 1938 article]). In his discussion of the complexes of traditions that are collected and built into literary units that lie behind the current literary forms of accounts, and the relationship between literature and historical evidence, von Rad ponders how in "attaining literary forms" the development of the traditions themselves becomes "ruthlessly cut off," and the original significance "abandoned" (VON RAD 1966: 49–50).

struggled with just how to present the question of whether and to what extent these literary texts articulate the "realities" (see?) of a pre- or early eighth-century landscape. And I am not alone in this. A cursory glance at my colleagues' articles in this volume demonstrates similar issues with language, particularly in their use of such terminology as "tradition," "core," "kernel," and "memory."[28] Of this terminology, the language of "core" or "kernel" exposes a separate though linked issue regarding the extent to which written evidence itself can be seen to preserve some unadulterated "kernel" or "core" of earlier, pre-written traditions. As von Rad once wrote in relation to the patriarchal narratives and the notion of how various "traditions" merged into a single "history": "Such a homogenous historical tradition would presuppose a corresponding historical bearer of the tradition. But where can we find the bearer of such a comprehensive and unified tradition?"[29] A similar discussion moves among the papers in this volume in relation to Samuel, particularly those who refute the notion of multiple, coexisting textual strands and envision an early "core narrative"[30] or a "base" or "basic layer"[31] elaborated over time. Of the voices in this discussion, and in light of that complex "oral-written interface," I find Jeremy Hutton's argument of various, interwoven strands to be more practical and persuasive.[32]

If we set aside the question of writing momentarily and settle on the laden term "tradition," Pioske argues in his recent study that the archaeological record, and the attention to particular places utilized within the Bible's stories, can provide fresh insight for the textual scholar. Writes Pioske, "it becomes necessary for the historian to consider how an ancient terrain, so often a repository of the physical ruins of previous eras, influenced the knowledge transmitted through memories recalled in response to this familiar environment."[33] This attention to Gath, of course, is not new to literary-historical arguments related

---

28 Edenburg, for example, writes that the Saul/David stories were "equally separate traditions" that were later combined (EDENBURG 2020). Kipfer states that texts about David as a mercenary or vassal of Gath contain "very old traditions and information" that only fits in the tenth or early ninth century (2020). Carl Ehrlich writes of the "biblical Achish tradition" and whether a "historical kernel" or "historical memory" lies behind that tradition (2020). Hannes BEZZEL examines the "sources" or "traditions" behind the History of David's Rise (HDR), and the HDR as literature that connects "traditions about Saul" with "traditions about David" (2020). Jeremy Hutton studies the various "traditions" underlying 1 Sam 21:2–10 and 22:6–23 (2020).

29 VON RAD 1960–61: 214; quoted in DAVIES 2009: 12. See also PIOSKE 2018a: 3–4.

30 EDENBURG 2020.

31 BEZZEL 2020.

32 HUTTON 2020.

33 PIOSKE 2018a: 167.

to 1 Sam 27 and other Gath texts in 1–2 Sam, as discussed above. Yet Pioske notes caution in subscribing the memory of these locations to earlier *writing*, particularly in light of the oral-written discussion and the arguably limited nature of textual production in the southern Levant prior to the ninth century BCE.[34] From the archaeological perspective, Elizabeth Bloch-Smith's current research examines specifically how ruins and physical remains, such as Jericho, Ai and Hazor, become the locus point for foundational myths and histories that cut across the fabric of time. Such sites become what she and others term "spatial narratives," narratives that are grounded in a specific time and place yet may be constructed, reframed or reinterpreted centuries later.[35]

The significance of the archaeological record for historical questions of ancient Israel is undeniable, especially given the impossibly-convoluted relationship between the Bible as a composite literary masterpiece and questions of ancient society. Of course, archaeology also continually engages with the Bible and relies on text for the simplest of things such as names and social/political categories. Both are interpretive disciplines. Yet archaeology and text are different bodies of material with entirely different methodological tools of engagement. As such, I find the use of material culture for demonstrating what must be an earlier "tradition" in textual evidence to be as helpful as it is ultimately unsatisfying. To go back to the questions of "tradition" versus writing, text is complicated, and the Bible is a composite literary masterpiece. Just because a text utilizes a place (Gath) and collapses social boundaries (David and Gath in 1 Sam 27) does not mean the text itself is older. An older tradition from before Gath was destroyed perhaps underlies the text, yet the *power* of the text and of ancient literature is how it constructs and shapes its own vision of society around whatever traditions it may have.

So, we might ask ourselves how a text utilizes not only geographical sites that are grounded in particular political spheres of influence at particular times, such as Gath and Ziklag in 1 Sam 27, but also specific *language* and literary descriptions related to such things as boundaries and territory, descriptions of geographical movement (such as going "up" or "down" or "crossing over"), and social identities (such as "Philistine"). How does place, connected with geographical descriptions, together construct, envision, or "language" a partic-

---

34 See the discussion and bibliography in Pioske 2018a: 30–38. Still, the potential role of writing in the Iron I and IIA is an area to be left open with caution, as demonstrated, for example, by Ron Tappy's dating of the abecedary from Tel Zayit to the tenth century (see Tappy et. al 2006: 5–46).

35 Cf. Bloch-Smith forthcoming; also 2015: 291–311.

ular social and political landscape?[36] To what extent does this construction of landscape aid in our historical questions and our studies of compositional history? This is not to privilege text over materiality (Pioske's caution),[37] but to allow text and materiality to communicate while doing what I do best as an ancient social historian and textual scholar. Therefore, it is to this exploration of landscape construction in 1 Sam 27 that I would like to turn now, beginning with the notion of borders, boundaries or territory (גבול), then turning to descriptions of geographical movement and social identities. As part of this exploration, I will compare the David material briefly with another key Shephelah story, Samson (Judg 13–16), and one of its central sites, Timnah.

2 Crossing to Gath from Israel's Territory

1 Sam 27 opens with a subtle yet unique description of the social landscape and the boundaries between Gath and Israel. First, David speaks of fleeing to the "land of the Philistines" as a safe haven away from the "territory of Israel" (גבול ישראל) (v. 1). He then "crosses over" (עבר) from Israel to Gath (v. 2). The text uses the expressions "land" (ארץ) (v. 1) and "countryside" (שדה) (vv. 7,11) to define Philistine territory as distinct from Israel. David then acquires Ziklag, one of the "country towns" (ערי השדה) within Gath's jurisdiction, as opposed to the "royal" (ממלכה) city of Gath (v. 5). Meanwhile, the leader of Gath is described more carefully than any other Philistine in the Bible. He is the only Philistine leader called a "king," and he is introduced by name and patrilineage rather than simply labeled "Philistine" (v. 2). The descriptive language throughout, and especially the notion of a landscape division between Israel and Gath's territory in the Shephelah (even vaguely depicted) is unique to the Bible's stories about Gath and worthy of discussion as it may apply to dating.[38]

To begin with the term גבול in the expression גבול ישראל (v. 1), the term has quite varied uses in the Bible, from a specific border that delineates a territory to an entire, sometimes indeterminate territory, as in the "territory of Israel" in 1 Sam 27:1.[39] Elsewhere, however, the term גבול represents a precisely-

---

36 On the verb "to language" see n. 3.
37 Cf. PIOSKE 2018a: 161–64.
38 Though we could attempt to divide the verses as "core" material versus later additions, as discussed above (in which case, v. 1, at least, is considered later), I think the text as a whole is worthy of discussion here in terms of the landscape construction.
39 Cf. WAZANA 2013: 12.

drawn boundary, particularly in those later texts where it appears with greatest frequency: Josh (84 ×), Ezek (43 ×) and Num (29 ×). In Josh and Num, these boundaries are often drawn along imagined political interfaces. As one example, Num 34 is particularly notable in how it creates a literary idealization of boundaries that does not correspond neatly to any other texts. According to Num 34, the southern גבול of Israel begins at the tip of the Dead Sea on the east, extends west with southern limits south of Kadesh-barnea toward the Wadi of Egypt to the Mediterranean (Num 34:2–5), then runs north along the Mediterranean without awareness that the coastal plain is inhabited by other people (Num 34:6). The northern border then extends to Lebo-Hamath at the source of the Orontes river south of Hamath, then moves inland to Zedad or Zadad east of the road from Damascus to Aleppo (34:7–9). The text therefore describes Israel's northern boundaries as extending beyond Byblos to include Phoenicia, and then far to the east. The command for the creation of these boundaries to the north and northeast (vv. 7–8, 10) is literally to "mark out" (תאה) or, arguably, to "draw lines" or even "desire" for yourself (from the root אוה in v. 10), before descending along the natural line of the Dead Sea.[40] As Baruch Levine and others have argued, the boundaries in this text mirror those of the Egyptian province of Canaan in the twelfth century BCE. In other words, in a relatively late period, writers of Num 34 use the term גבול to construct a vision of Israel's boundaries as the political landscape was "way back when," just before the beginning of the Iron Age.[41] Yet this "marked out" or "desired" construction does not correlate to Iron Age historical reality in Israel.

Elsewhere, the term גבול appears infrequently and often quite vaguely in texts that are often considered to include earlier source material. The Books of Samuel contain only eleven attestations.[42] In 1–2 Sam, the terms גבול and גבול

---

40 The root in vv. 7–8 is תאה, which is perhaps a by-form of תוה (cf. Ezek 9:4). Or, the root could be אוה as seen in v. 10, stemming from "to desire" (or v. 10 is a rare *hithpael* meaning "to sign, mark, describe with a mark"). Or, the verb is meant to be read from תאר "to mark" (see MILGROM 1990: 330).

41 Cf. LEVINE 2000: 540–41; see also the careful discussion in WAZANA 2013: 129–66. While Levine argues that the biblical scribes claim Israel as the legitimate successor to Egypt in Canaan, Wazana proposes that the boundaries rely on a well-known territorial division that lay beyond the borders of Israel, while not necessarily relying on known borders of the former Egyptian province.

42 Five of these references are to the more specific גבול ישׂראל, including 1 Sam 7:13; 11:3, 7; 27:1; and 2 Sam 21:5. This expression is uncommon throughout the Bible, and attested only nine times in the Former Prophets (aside from 1–2 Sam, these include: Judg 19:29 [mimicking 1 Sam 11:7]; 1 Kgs 1:3; 2 Kgs 10:32; 14:25). Only 2 Kgs 14:25 defines the precise limits for this "territory of Israel"; it extends from Lebo-Hamath to the sea of the Arabah in clear editorial language. Otherwise, the terminology in the Former Prophets gives little clear notion of what

ישׂראל generally delineate undefined swaths of territory rather than precise, carefully-constructed boundaries. For example, 1 Sam 11:3 and 7 use the גבול ישׂראל as a point of contrast to Ammon, though without further demarcating what, exactly, this "territory of Israel" includes. This story about Saul portrays the social or political landscape ambiguously: Ammon "goes up" (עלה) to threaten Jabesh-Gilead (v. 1), the elders of Jabesh stall Ammon by stating that they will send messengers through all the גבול ישׂראל for help (v. 3), the messengers from Jabesh then "go" (בוא) to inform Saul in Gibeah before "all the people" (v. 4), at which point Saul butchers and dispatches oxen pieces through all the גבול ישׂראל (v. 7), thus mustering "the people" (v. 7) for battle east of the Jordan river. Minus a potential editorial insertion that delineates precise, large numbers of warriors from Israel and Judah (v. 8), there is no clear sense of what Israel's "territory" is, how far it extends, or who it includes. The phrase גבול ישׂראל is therefore a defining element of a local, likely old tale of Saul that better suits the Judges stories than that of early kingship.[43]

Notably, the ark narrative contains five of the eleven total references to the term גבול in 1–2 Sam. All of these relate to the Shephelah and the Philistines. One of these denotes the "territory" of Ashdod (1 Sam 5:6), while the remainder refer to Israel's territory or boundaries. Twice the term גבול designates Beth-Shemesh as the specific boundary between Philistine territory and God's territory (1 Sam 6:9,12), and once Beth-Shemesh marks the indeterminate territory or גבול ישׂראל (1 Sam 7:13). 1 Sam 7:14 then describes Israel as regaining all its territory or גבול from the Philistines (one is to infer that this undefined territory refers to land in the Shephelah).

How does this study of terminology affect our understanding of 1 Sam 27:1? Even as a potential addition, the notion of David fleeing to Gath from the גבול ישׂראל provides a similar point of contrast to the land of the Philistines as in the ark narrative, though 1 Sam 27:1 lacks the precise Shephelah border of the ark narrative's Beth-Shemesh. The text is unconcerned with delineating Israel

---

Israel's "territory" is. Outside of the Former Prophets, references to the גבול ישׂראל are limited to Ezek 11:10–11; Mal 1:5; and 1 Chr 21:12.

43 See MILSTEIN 2016: 174–206. Milstein argues that an "old Saul complex" in Judg and 1 Sam dates to the pre-exilic period; this complex includes early versions of a Benjaminite war and its resolution (Judg 20–21), an old Saul birth story (1 Sam 1), and Saul's victory over the Ammonites (1 Sam 11). Nathaniel Greene questions this model in the following ways: first, it is difficult to know precisely when 1 Sam 1 was written; possibly, it was composed at a later date with both Saul and Samuel in view. Second, Judg 19 need not be definitely anti-Saulide; arguably, it could serve as a foil for Saul and 1 Sam 11. Finally, Greene would argue that 1 Sam 11 need not be about Saul at all, in an earlier form (personal communication).

or Gath's territories with precision, as we might find in texts such as Joshua in which גבול denotes a specific political boundary.[44] Notwithstanding its unde-fined sense of borders, however, David's flight to Gath contrasts with other tales of Gath in Samuel–Kings in a slightly sharper description of the social and po-litical landscape. This landscape comes alive most vividly in the notion of David "crossing over" (עבר) to Gath in v. 2. The verb עבר is a common biblical expres-sion for crossing lands, territorial and foreign, and the Jordan,[45] though it is rarely used in relation to Philistine territory and in stories about Gath.[46] Gener-ally, it is an expression reserved for Jordan and other regional, tribal, or nation crossings in and outside Israel, not for "crossing" from Israel or Judah into the Shephelah or Philistine territory. This makes the particular expression notewor-thy in 1 Sam 27:2.

Meanwhile, the remaining stories that demonstrate comradery between Da-vid (or Jerusalem) and Gath in Samuel–Kings lack any, even indefinite notion of geographical, social or political boundaries between Israel and the Philis-tines. As described above, in these texts movement between peoples is seam-less, cultural relations easy and un-bordered. In 2 Sam 6:9–11, David simply diverts the ark from Jerusalem and drops it off at the house of Obed-Edom the Gittite, wherever that may be; the only reference to geographical movement is that he "turns it aside" (נטה) from Jerusalem (v. 10) and then eventually brings the ark back "up" (עלה) (v. 12). Similarly, 1 Kgs 2:39–40 describes movement between Jerusalem and Gath as if describing a nearby town of refuge: Shimei's slaves simply run away to Gath, then Shimei goes to collect them. Though the notion of Gath as a place of refuge outside the political scope of Jerusalem has echoes in 1 Sam 27, there is no "crossing over" or discussion of where the boundaries lie between one political sphere of influence to the next. Other less-

---

44 Note that in the biblical corpus, the term גבול in conjunction with the Philistines (outside 1–2 Sam) can be found in Josh 13:3 (the "border" of Ekron and the five Philistine lords); Judg 1:18 (Judah captures the "territories" of Gaza, Ashkelon and Ekron); 2 Kgs 18:8 (the "borders" of Gaza); and Amos 6:2 (Gath's "territory").

45 For example, in Num–Deut the Israelites request to "cross over" various lands on their way to Israel, which culminates in the Jordan crossing (e.g. Num 20:17; 21:22; 32:5). Similarly, the Judges' narratives describe Jordan crossings (e.g. Judg 8:4), crossing through foreign lands (Judg 11:17) and crossing through the various clans and territories within Israel (e.g. Judg 11:29). Notably, in the land allotments of Joshua, the term עבר often connects to the often-used גבול to describe political geography; for example, the "boundary" or גבול extends or ascends from X place … and then "crosses over" to Y (see, e.g., Josh 15:4–7,10).

46 We find it only in Jonathan's "crossing" in 1 Sam 14, itself a complex of material, and in 1 Sam 29:2, which is likely a continuation of the plotline begun in 1 Sam 27.

than-positive portrayals of Gath in the David material shore up the image of clear social boundaries between Israel and Gath, though they are equally un-helpful in defining a clear sense of geographical borders (i.e. Goliath in 1 Sam 27; Achish in 1 Sam 21).

So, what does this construction of landscape in 1 Sam 27 reflect? Does the language of "territory" and "crossing over," the specificity with which the king of Gath is described, the geographical points of Gath and Ziklag, and the coop-erative relations between Gath and David necessarily point to earlier writing? Or is it possible that, no matter the memory of Gath's importance during the early monarchy, this text, like other Gath texts in Samuel–Kings, could be con-structed much later to point back to this wild and un-bordered landscape? Be-fore tackling these questions, I would like to extend the discussion further by turning briefly to a couple of other key Shephelah texts and their construction of landscape: Samson and Timnah in Judg 13–16.

3 Samson and Timnah

The Samson cycle is the only set of biblical stories to take place solely in the Shephelah. In addition, its descriptions of the social landscape are more de-tailed than any other texts pertaining to the Shephelah. For these reasons, the cycle provides a particularly fruitful comparison to the stories of David and Gath.[47] Unlike 1 Sam 27, the cycle lacks the term גבול altogether, which is some-what ironic given the propensity of scholars to call the cycle such things as a "border epic,"[48] "border fiction,"[49] and its characters a reflection of "border-crossing," "liminality,"[50] who are "ensnared in otherness."[51] Such terminology reflects the elusiveness and seeming "entanglement of identities" in the text,[52] as demonstrated primarily in Samson's core exploits and his relationships with women in Judg 14–16. Yet there are few clearly-defined "borders" in the narra-

---

47 As Sara Kipfer rightfully noted (personal communication), discussions of other "border towns" (e.g. the movement from Ekron to Gath to Beth-Shemesh in 1 Sam 5–7) would also have been fruitful, but for the constraints of space in this article.
48 STAGER 1991: 17–18. Stager credits Frank Moore Cross as the first to make this observation.
49 WEITZMAN 2002: 158–74.
50 MOBLEY 2006: 30.
51 GILLMAYR-BUCHER 2014: 33–51.
52 On the term "entanglement of identities," see MAEIR AND HITCHCOCK 2017: 150; also n. 10.

tive. Identity markers for Samson are limited and exist around the edges of the story to bind Samson into the book of Judges.[53]

Meanwhile, his core exploits disorganize identities and blur boundaries, using natural topography to describe movement "up" and "down" between the coast and the hill country. These tales are uninterested in clearly-defined social or geographical boundaries in the Shephelah. Samson himself does not fit clearly into Israelite, Danite or Philistine society, nor do the women with whom he consorts, who defy social constructs and norms. It is never clear whether Delilah is Philistine (Judg 16), while the nameless woman from Timnah in Judg 14–15 is first defined as "Philistine" (Judg 14:2–4), though her identity blurs in Judg 15. After Samson reacts to the news that she no longer belongs to him by destroying Philistines' crops in Timnah (15:4–5), the Philistines "go up" to Timnah and burn the woman and her father alive (15:6). The Philistines therefore punish the family for Samson's actions, thus treating Samson as one of them (or vice versa). Samson then disappears to a cave in an unknown location (15:8) and is eventually captured by the men of Judah and returned to the Philistines (15:11–13). These Judahites have nothing against Samson, yet from the geographical movement and the dialogues between various constituents, it is clear that he is an outsider, not quite one of them.

Attempts to date the Samson material range from the early Iron Age to the Persian Period. Those who would date the stories prior to Sennacherib's destruction of the area in 701 BCE note that the texts mirror the cultural ambiguity of the archaeological evidence from the Iron Age.[54] Pushing back against this notion that the cycle "mirrors" social reality, Steven Weitzman has described the Samson stories as a literary reflection of the geographic imagination, designed for and by a Judahite audience with the goals of "border maintenance" between Philistia and Judah.[55] In Weitzman's synchronic view of the cycle, the stories as a unified whole carefully construct a "stigma" of border crossing and warn of the dangers of social integration, in particular through Samson's use of riddles and the dysfunctional relationships between Samson and "the Philistines" as opposed to Samson and the Judahites.[56]

---

53 Cf. LEONARD-FLECKMAN (forthcoming). These identity markers that define Samson socially are found in 13:2,5,25; 14:1–4; 15:20 and 16:31. According to these descriptions, Samson is an Israelite, from the line of Dan, who grows up between Zorah and Eshtaol. He is a nazir of Yhwh before his birth. He will "begin to deliver" and "judge" Israel. In the bridge between Judg 13–14, the Samson's parents are then concerned with intermarriage with the "uncircumcised Philistines" of Timnah (14:3).
54 E.g. STAGER 1991: 17–18.
55 Cf. WEITZMAN 2016: 266–80.
56 IBID., 275.

Yet from a diachronic perspective, there is clear tension between border construction in parts of the Samson cycle, and a sort of border negation in the central stories of Judg 14–16. I propose that these core Shephelah stories reflect little interest in border maintenance. If we were to look for a literary idealization of borders based on Sennacherib's crushing defeat and reorganization of the Shephelah, we might look, rather, at the end of Josh 15, which contains three districts of the Judean Shephelah (15:33–44) followed by three Philistine cities: Ekron, Ashdod and Gaza (15:45–47). Ron Tappy has argued convincingly that these final verses are directly related to Sennacherib's campaign and the re-alignment of border towns between the Shephelah and the coastland.[57] This text reflects a clear literary construction of borders (including the term גְּבוּל) and an alternative reality; while in contrast, what we find in Samson's Shephelah wanderings is general up and down movement, yet a disinterest in identity or border classifications.

In terms of geographical sites, Gath is unattested in the cycle. This fact alone, some might argue, in conjunction with the cycle's clear Shephelah orientation, would suggest that the Samson cycle was composed after Gath's destruction, or that it reflects a post-Gath reality. Meanwhile, Timnah is of particular interest as the key Shephelah site at the core of the cycle, where it is depicted as a liminal place, a site of cultural ambiguity between the highlands and the coast. Such ambiguity can also be seen in the archaeological evidence from Tel Batash (Timnah) and other Shephelah sites whose material confusion make it difficult to define these areas culturally prior to Sennacherib's invasion in the seventh century BCE.[58] Elsewhere, the Bible attests to Timnah rarely: aside from the Samson cycle it appears only in the Tamar-Judah story of Gen 38 and in Joshua's land descriptions (where Timnah is part of Judah's allotments in Josh 15:10 and 57 and, reflecting awareness of Judg 18, Dan's allotments in 19:43). In both the stories of Samson and Tamar, questionable sexual or cross-cultural activity takes place in Timnah or on the road to Timnah (Gen 38:14), activity outside the appropriate contours and structures of society. In this sense, the

---

57 Cf. Tappy 2008a: 381–403.

58 The archaeological portrait is complex and distinct from site-to-site: places like Beth-Shemesh and Lachish appear to have thrived consistently through the tenth-eighth centuries as Judah's western border towns, while sites running ever-so-slightly west along the base of the Judean hills, including Tel Zayit and Timnah (Tel Batash), reflect an arguably changing degree of impact between Judah and Philistia prior to Sennacherib's campaign. Yet there is no clear consensus on the relationship between the material evidence and cultural reality. For a sampling of secondary sources on the material evidence and identities therein, see Bunimovitz / Lederman 2016: 40–62; articles in Lipschits / Maeir 2017; Tappy 2008b: 1–44; and Maeir / Hitchcock 2017.

Bible's Timnah is perhaps akin to what Foucault would describe as a heterotopia, an alternative construction of space incompatible with real society that inverts the known world as if looking through a mirror, a place reserved for moments of crisis or for deviant characters.[59]

Notably, outside the Bible, Timnah is also attested in the Neo-Assyrian sources for Sennacherib's third campaign (c. 701 BCE), where Timnah and another Shephelah town, Eltekeh, become the site of an important battle between Jerusalem and the Neo-Assyrians. These varied Neo-Assyrian witnesses depict Timnah similar to the Bible's depictions, which we would not expect given such disparate texts with disparate aims. In the campaign, after collecting tribute from various places and subduing Ashkelon on the coast, the text describes Sennacherib in battle against Ekron and Jerusalem in the Shephelah towns of Eltekeh and Timnah. All other cities in the third campaign are described in direct relation to a king or a larger polity, such as "Menahem of the city Samaria," "Mitinti of the city Ashdod," "Ṣidqâ king of the city Ashkelon," or "Bīt-Daganna, Joppa, Banayabarqa and Azuru, cities of Ṣidqâ."[60] Of all the sites listed in the campaign, however, only Eltekeh and Timnah appear without a clear affiliation. Some would say both are connected to Ekron from the textual description, while others would say Jerusalem.

According to the annals, the Neo-Assyrians first defeat Ekron, plunder Eltekeh, Timnah, and Ekron, then conquer numerous cities, fortresses, and other settlements of the land of Judah. (As an aside, it is as if the Neo-Assyrian witnesses and the land allotments of Josh 19 are communicating with each other in terms of geography, for the Bible's sole attestation to Eltekeh is found in the consecutive geographical list of Timnah, Ekron and Eltekeh as sites originally belonging to Dan in Josh 19:43–44.) At the very end of the campaign, Sennacherib "detaches" the cities he plundered from Hezekiah and gives them to the kings of Ashdod, Ekron and Gaza.[61] Would these cities have included Timnah and Eltekeh? It is unclear from the text. Yet according to traditional historical understanding, this is when the Shephelah, including Timnah, becomes conclusively Philistine.

To draw our discussion of Samson and Timnah to a close, in the Samson material, and in light of Timnah's import in the Neo-Assyrian campaigns of 701 BCE, it does seem that the depiction of Timnah reflects, in part, an imagined world from a post-701 perspective. Yet in my view, the cycle does not depict a uniform construction of border maintenance and of Judah versus the Philis-

59 Cf. FOUCAULT 1997: 330–36.
60 See Text 22, The Chicago/Taylor Prisms, col. ii, lines 50–72, GRAYSON / NOVOTNY 2012: 175.
61 Text 22, col. iii, lines 30–34 (RINAP 3/1:176).

tines; rather, the core exploits of Judg 14–16, in particular, contain a dynamic, internal complexity of perspectives. Imagined as they may be, the geography mimics *both* the material confusion of the ninth-eighth centuries *and* the later geography of Sennacherib's campaigns. It is as if the cycle remembers and mixes different periods, a process that Mark Smith has referred to as "shifting recollection."[62] The tension between these shifting texts and the eventual desire to organize and construct social borders around the edges of the cycle, reveal how these stories are sutured into the book of Judges, and into a broader framework that eventually connects with David. The Samson texts are therefore fascinating because of how they envision and construct society – boundaries, borders, and identities – in distinct ways as part of a complex literary history. How we view Samson depends on how we look through a kaleidoscope of options that the patchwork text gives us within its constructions of social geography.

4 Conclusion

How does this study of Timnah, and the literary construction of geography in these various texts, relate to 1 Sam 27, the broader Gath-Israel depictions, and to our discussion of text and tradition? The Gath-David material, it seems to me, also reflects this kaleidoscope of options or shifting recollections, what Pioske calls "entanglements of memory."[63] The site Gath, and the notion that Ziklag could belong to Gath, likely recalls a time when Gath was an important player in the social-political landscape. Yet this particular geographical recollection could be drawn into the heart of a much later story. In other words, the recollection itself need not have a direct correlation with earlier writing or with an earlier "core" of David material. I would also suggest caution in the correlation between David and the *hapiru* or *'apiru*, who are defined within a particular Egyptian framework in the Amarna correspondence as those outside Egyptian control. By the time of biblical writing, it seems a stretch to imagine this category as active in any real sense. In fact, one wonders whether this image of renegade, disaffected bandits could, in fact, fit a much later, more centralized monarchic landscape that depicts people outside of monarchic control through the same kind of prejudicial lens applied to the *'apiru* of the Amarna letters.[64]

---

62 SMITH 2002: 631–51.
63 PIOSKE 2018a: 167. Elsewhere, he refers to the "textured, multifaceted portrayal" of GATH 2018b: 26.
64 One question that would remain, however, would be what to make of potential *'apiru* references in 1 Sam 13:7a and 14:21.

From a literary-historical perspective, 1 Sam 27:1 may very well be "later" in part because of David's internal monologue,[65] though the vague, territorial use of the term גְּבוּל echoes in such old material as 1 Sam 11 and is quite distinct from the "borders" of such texts as Num 34. Meanwhile, vv. 2–3 (and perhaps 5–6a) could reflect something "older," as discussed earlier in this paper. Yet even in these potentially older verses, the name Achish may be tacked on,[66] and I would add that the notion of David "crossing over" to Gath constructs a more careful boundary to the social landscape than other David-Gath texts and is worthy of further discussion. It seems to me that attempting to separate out verses in this text to find that earlier core is ultimately ineffective.

Meanwhile, the argument that the positive, cooperative David-Gath stories are older also has its problems. First of all, other positive Gath-Israel or Gath-David stories in 1–2 Sam pay even less attention to social boundaries and explanations for *why* David relies on Gath than 1 Sam 27, including both 2 Sam 6:9–11 and 15:18–22. All it takes is one story, or one recollection, to then create literary echoes across the corpus.[67] If the Samson material in Judg 13–16 could create an un-bordered, socially ambiguous landscape from a post-701 perspective, so can the David material. The proposal that 1 Sam 27 represents earlier writing (or traditions?) because cooperative relationships between David and Gath would be embarrassing to a later audience gives pause. It is certainly plausible, and it is difficult to contradict a majority of scholarly opinion. Certainly, we do not find 1 Sam 27 and other such stories in Chronicles. Yet I also wonder to what extent this perspective comes from our own "languaging" of the text, our own perception of social boundaries and borders, including an overly-simplified perception that antagonistic relations between Israel or Judah and Gath must be both later and uniform.[68]

At the outset of this article, I quoted from economist Albert Hirschman, who concluded *The Passion and the Interests* with the statement, "This is probably all one can ask of history, and of the history of ideas in particular: not to resolve issues, but to raise the level of debate." Such was the aim of this essay, to enter into dialogue with previous diachronic studies, including studies in this vol-

---

65 Cf. Dietrich 2012: 85; also Kipfer 2020.

66 See n. 22.

67 In his study on oral traditions and the movement from oral traditions into writing, Vansina notes that when we find "converging evidence" to an event or situation across written expressions of a tradition, these are often interdependent or reflect some line of dependence. He cites the Synoptic Gospels as but one example of this phenomenon (Vansina 1985: 196).

68 Pioske has a similar observation, with a slightly different spin and perhaps a different conclusion, when he discusses scholarship that views a uniform hostility between Gath and the highlands (Pioske 2018b: 21–22).

ume, while raising a number of questions regarding our perceptions of the Da-vid-Gath material and our broader assumptions of the relationship between tra-dition, text and history. In the end, I propose that we step back and take greater care in how we work with the relationship between text and tradition. I also propose that we recognize the power of texts to utilize geography, geographical movement and social-political relations in order to construct a particular vision of the social and political landscape. Without knowing authors, it is impossible to know what worlds, understandings and motivations drove these textual con-structions at various times, or what old traditions might underlie these stories. Yet it also seems to me that we, as readers and as scholars, have the power to construct that landscape back, to make particular decisions regarding dating based on what we assume to have been true at a given time.

To close, perhaps these various biblical perspectives about borders, un-bor-ders, and Shephelah social geography tell us more about ourselves, about how *we* understand ancient literature than about whoever wrote these ancient texts. As Jonathan Z. Smith once stated, the colonist (or in our case, the western schol-ar) "imposes the 'shape' of his or her own culture" on the other, which helps organize and make that world recognizable.[69] If there is anything real about David, the king of Gath, the "territory of Israel" and the Iron Age Shephelah landscape before the eighth century, it is perhaps that at their core these charac-ters and these places defy our easy categorization and our ongoing wrestling to define their social relations at any given time, as perhaps many people and places did in the landscape of ancient Israel, even as they do today.

Bibliography

Bloch-Smith, Elizabeth. 2015. A Stratified Account of Jephthah's Negotiations and Battle: Judges 11:12–33 from an Archaeological Perspective. *JBL* 134:291–311.

Bloch-Smith, Elizabeth. Forthcoming: Building a Back-story: Archaeology and the Crafting of Israel's Conquest Narratives.

Bunimovitz, Shlomo, and Zvi Lederman. 2016. Archaeology of a Border Community. Pages 40–62 in *Tel Beth-Shemesh: A Border Community in Judah: Renewed Excavations 1990–2000: The Iron Age.* Vol. 1. Edited by Shlomo Bunimovitz and Zvi Lederman. SMNIA 34 Winona Lake, IN: Eisenbrauns.

Carr, David M. 2005. *Writing on the Tablet of the Heart: Origins of Scripture and Literature.* Oxford: Oxford University Press.

---

69 Cf. SMITH 1985: 46. I find Smith's discussion of the relative "other" relevant to the creation of biblical literature and the imposition of the narrator, who both creates and judges. In the case of David, the narrator lies outside the stories, as do the readers.

Carr, David M. 2011. *The Formation of the Hebrew Bible: A New Reconstruction*. Oxford: Oxford University Press.

Davies, Philip R. 2009. *The Origins of Biblical Israel*. LHBOTS 485. New York, NY et al.: T & T Clark.

Dietrich, Walter. 2012. David and the Philistines: Literature and History. Pages 79–98 in *The Ancient Near East in the 12th–10th Centuries BCE: Culture and History. Proceedings of the International Conference Held at the University of Haifa, 2–5 May 2010*. Edited by Gershon Galil et al. AOAT 392. Münster: Ugarit-Verlag.

Edenburg, Cynthia. 2011. Notes on the Origin of the Biblical Tradition Regarding Achish King of Gath. *VT* 61:34–38.

Finkelstein, Israel. 2013. Geographical and Historical Realities Behind the Earliest Layer in the David story. *SJOT* 27:131–50.

Fleming, Daniel E. 2013. David and the Ark: A Jerusalem Festival Reflected in Royal Narrative. Pages 75–96 in *Literature as Politics, Politics as Literature: Essays on the Ancient Near East in Honor of Peter Machinist*. Edited by David S. Vanderhooft et al. Winona Lake, IN: Eisenbrauns.

Foucault, Michel. 1997. Of Other Spaces: Utopias and Heterotopias. Pages 330–36 in *Rethinking Architecture: A Reader in Culture Theory*. Edited by Neil Leach. New York, NY: Routledge.

Gillmayr-Bucher, Susanne. 2014. A Hero Ensnared in Otherness? Literary Images of Samson." Pages 33–51 in *Samson: Hero or Fool? The Many Faces of Samson*. Edited by Erik Eynikel and Tobias Nicklas. *TBN* 17. Edited by Jacques van Ruiten et al. Leiden et al: Brill.

Grayson, Albert Kirk, and Jamie Novotny. 2012. *The Royal Inscriptions of Sennacherib, King of Assyria (704–681 BC), Part I*. RINAP 3/1. Winona Lake, IN: Eisenbrauns.

Greene, Nathaniel. 2018. Warlord and Scribe: The Nascent Israelite State beneath its Textual Veneers. PhD diss., The University of Madison-Wisconsin.

Gunkel, Hermann. 1964. *The Legends of Genesis: The Biblical Saga & History*. New York: Schocken Books.

Hirschman, Albert O. 1977. *The Passions and the Interests: Political Arguments for Capitalism before Its Triumph*. Princeton: Princeton University Press.

Hobsbawm, Eric. 1983. Introduction: Inventing Traditions. Pages 1–14 in *The Invention of Tradition*. Edited by Eric Hobsbawm and Terence Renger. Cambridge: Cambridge University Press.

Hutton, Jeremy. 2009. *The Transjordanian Palimpsest: The Overwritten Texts of Personal Exile and Transformation in the Deuteronomistic History*. BZAW 296. Berlin et al.: de Gruyter.

Leonard-Fleckman, Mahri. Forthcoming: Binding Samson to Yhwh: from Disorder to Order in the Samson Cycle. In *Divinity in the Deuteronomistic History*. Edited by Corrine Carvalho and John McLaughlin.

Leonard-Fleckman, Mahri. 2021. Ally or Enemy? Political Identity and Ambiguity in the Tales of David and Gath. Pages 211–24 in *The Book of Samuel and Its Response to Monarchy*. Edited by Sara Kipfer and Jeremy M. Hutton. BWANT 228. Stuttgart: Kolhammer.

Levine, Baruch. 2000. *Numbers 21–36: A New Translation with Introduction and Commentary*. AYBRL 4A. New Haven: Yale University Press.

Lipschits, Oded, and Aren M. Maeir, eds. 2017. *The Shephelah During the Iron Age: Recent Archaeological Studies*. Winona Lake: Eisenbrauns.

Luckenbill, Daniel D. 1927. *Ancient Records of Assyria and Babylonia*. Vol. 2 of *Historical Records of Assyria from Sargon to the End*. Chicago, IL: University of Chicago.

Maeir, Aren M. 2004. The Historical Background and Dating of Amos VI 2: An Archaeological Perspective from Tell Eṣ-Ṣâfî/Gath. *VT* 54:319–34.

Maeir, Aren M. 2017. Philistine Gath after 20 Years: Regional perspectives on the Iron Age at Tell eṣ-Ṣafi/Gath. Pages 133–54 in *The Shephelah during the Iron Age: Recent Archaeological Studies*. Edited by Oded Lipschits and Aren M. Maeir. Winona Lake, IN: Eisenbrauns.

Maeir, Aren M., and Louise A. Hitchcock. 2017. The Appearance, Formation and Transformation of Philistine Culture: New Perspective and New Finds. Pages 149–62 in *The Sea Peoples Up-To-Date: New Research on the Migration of Peoples in the 12th Century BCE*. Edited by Peter M Fischer and Teresa Bürge. Denkschrift der Gesamtakademie: Contributions to the Chronology of the Eastern Mediterranean 81. Vienna: Verlag der österreichischen Akademie der Wissenschaften.

McCarter, P. Kyle. 1980. *I Samuel: A New Translation with Introduction, Notes and Commentary*. AYBRL 8. New Haven, CT: Yale University Press.

McCarter, P. Kyle. 1984. *II Samuel: A New Translation with Introduction, Notes and Commentary*. AYBRL 9. New Haven, CT: Yale University Press.

Milgrom, Jacob. 1990. *The JPS Torah Commentary on Numbers: The Traditional Hebrew Text with the New JPS Translation*. Philadelphia, PA et al.: The Jewish Publication Society.

Milstein, Sara J. 2016. *Tracking the Master Scribe: Revision through Introduction in Biblical and Mesopotamian Literature*. New York, NY: Oxford.

Na'aman, Nadav. 2002. In Search of Reality Behind the Account of David's Wars with Israel's Neighbors. *IEJ* 52/2:200–24.

Mobley, Gregory. 2006. *Samson and the Liminal Hero in the Ancient Near East*. LHBOTS 453. New York, NY et al.: T & T Clark.

Noth, Martin. 1958. *The History of Israel*. London: A. & C. Black.

Noth, Martin. 1981. *The Deuteronomistic History*. Translated by Jane Doull. JSOTSup 15. Sheffield: Sheffield Academic Press.

Pioske, Daniel. 2018a. *Memory in a Time of Prose: Studies in Epistemology, Hebrew Scribalism, and the Biblical Past*. New York: Oxford University Press.

Pioske, Daniel. 2018b. Material Culture and Making Visible: On the Portrayal of Philistine Gath in the Book of Samuel. *JSOT* 43:3–27.

Sakenfeld, Katherine D. 1978. *The Meaning of Hesed in the Hebrew Bible: A New Inquiry*. HSM 17. Missoula: Scholars Press.

Smith, Adam T. 2003. *The Political Landscape: Constellations of Authority in Early Complex Polities*. Berkeley, CA: University of California Press.

Smith, Jonathan Z. 1985. What a Difference a Difference Makes. Pages 3–48 in *"To See Ourselves as Others See Us": Christians, Jews, "Others" in Late Antiquity*. Edited by Jacob Neusner and Ernest S. Frerichs. Chico, CA: Scholars Press.

Smith, Mark S. 2002. Remembering God: Collective Memory in Israelite Religion. *CBQ* 64:631–51.

Stager, Lawrence. 1991. *Ashkelon Discovered: From Canaanites and Israelites to Romans and Moslems*. Washington, DC: Biblical Archaeology Society.

Swain, Merill. 2006. Languaging, Agency and Collaboration in Advanced Second Language Proficiency. Pages 95–109 in *Advanced Language Learning: The Contribution of Halliday and Vygotsky*. Edited by Heidi Byrnes. London et al.: Continuum.

Swain, Merill, and Sharon Lapkin, Ibtissem Knouzi, Wataru Suzuki, Lindsay A. Brooks. 2009. Languaging: University Students Learn the Grammatical Concept of Voice in French. *The Modern Language Journal* 93:5–29.

Tappy, Ron E., and P. Kyle McCarter, Marilyn Lundberg, Bruce Zuckerman. 2006. An Abecedary of the Mid-Tenth Century from the Judaean Shephelah. *BASOR* 344:5–46.

Tappy, Ron E. 2008a. Historical and Geographical Notes on the 'Lowland Districts' of Judah in Joshua xv 33–47. *VT* 58:381–403.

Tappy, Ron E. 2008b. Tel Zayit and the Tel Zayit Abecedary in Their Regional Context. Pages 1–44 in *Literate Culture and Tenth-Century Canaan: The Tel Zayit Abecedary in Context*. Edited by Ron E. Tappy and P. Kyle McCarter. Winona Lake, IN: Eisenbrauns.

Vansina, Jan. 1985. *Oral Tradition as History*. Madison, WI: The University of Wisconsin Press.

Vermeylen, Jacques. 2000. *La loi du plus fort: Histoire de la rédaction des récits davidiques de 1 Samuel 8 à 1 Rois 2*. BEThL 154. Leuven: Leuven University Press.

von Rad, Gerhard. 1960–61. The History of the Patriarchs. *ET* 72:213–16.

von Rad, Gerhard. 1966. The Form-Critical Problem of the Hexateuch. Pages 1–78 in *The Problem of the Hexateuch and other essays*. Translated by E. W. Trueman Dicken. New York, NY: McGraw-Hill Book Company.

Vygotsky, Lev S. 1987. Thought and Word. Pages 243–95 in *The Collected Works of L. S. Vygotsky: Vol. 1, Problems of General Psychology*. Edited by Robert W. Rieber and Aaron S. Carton. New York, NY et al.: Plenum.

Wazana, Nili. 2013. *All the Boundaries of the Land: The Promised Land in Biblical Thought in Light of the Ancient Near East* Translated by Liat Qeren. Winona Lake, IN: Eisenbrauns.

Wellhausen, Julius. 1899. *Die Composition des Hexateuchs und der historischen Bücher des Alten Testaments*. Berlin: Georg Reimer.

Weitzman, Steven. 2002. The Samson Story as Border Fiction. *BibInt* 10:158–74.

Weitzman, Steven. 2016. Crossing the Border with Samson: Beth-Shemesh and the Bible's Geographical Imagination. Pages 266–80 in *Tel Beth-Shemesh, A Border Community in Judah: Renewed Excavations 1990–2000: The Iron Age*. Edited by Shlomo Bunimovitz and Zvi Lederman. Vol. 1. SMNIA 34. Winona Lake, IN: Eisenbrauns.

Winckler, Hugo. 1889. *Die Keilschrifttexte Sargons, Vol. 1: Nach den Papierabklatschen und Originalen*. Leipzig: Eduard Pfeiffer.

Wright, Jacob. 2014. *David King of Israel, and Caleb in Biblical Memory*. Cambridge: Cambridge University Press.

Walter Dietrich

Der Mann, mit dem Gott war. Kompositions- und quellenkritische Überlegungen zur Darstellung des Aufstiegs Davids in den Samuelbüchern

English Summary: The Man with whom God Was. The Description of David's Rise in the Books of Samuel: Considerations on Sources and Composition

The books of Samuel are not as old as was long supposed. The story of David's rise was part of a pre-Deuteronomistic narrative work written by a "Court Narrator" in Jerusalem after the fall of Northern Israel and containing the history of the early monarchy. This work was later inserted into the Deuteronomistic History. The Court Narrator made use of several older sources that were limited in extent and thematically focused. Also, he included some individual stories in his work. In the section on David's rise there are hints of the use of two larger narrative compositions. One of these sources deals with the "Rise and Decline of the Saulides." The second source is a "Collection about David the freebooter." This proposal is a kind of "Fragmentenhypothese" as opposed to forms of "Urkundenhypothese" defended by other scholars. In any case, neither the books of Samuel as a whole nor the integrated sources are to be considered an "apology" or "propaganda" for David.

1 Die Annahme einer sehr frühen Entstehung der Samuelbücher

Lange Zeit galt es als ausgemacht, dass die Geschichte Davids in den Samuelbüchern sich hauptsächlich aus zwei alten Quellen zusammensetzt: der «Aufstiegsgeschichte» und der «Thronnachfolgegeschichte Davids». Es war Leonhard Rost, der im Jahr 1926, also vor fast einem Jahrhundert, dieser Annahme zu fast kanonischer Geltung verhalf.[1] Nachdem er die Aufstiegsgeschichte nur eher kursorisch abgehandelt hatte, nahmen sich spätere andere – zuerst Artur Weiser in einem Aufsatz,[2] dann Jakob Grønbæk in einer Monographie[3] – ihrer

---

1 Rost 1926 = 1965.
2 Weiser 1966.
3 Grønbæk 1971.

https://doi.org/10.1515/9783110606164-006

intensiv an. Generell war man der Meinung, diese Aufstiegsgeschichte sei wegen ihres mosaikartigen Charakters eher älter als die stärker durchgestaltete Thronfolgegeschichte; und da Rost diese in die Salomozeit angesetzt hatte, musste die Aufstiegsgeschichte mindestens auch aus dieser, womöglich sogar aus der Davidzeit stammen.

Wäre das richtig, dann ginge der allergrößte Teil der Stoffmasse in 1Sam 16–2Sam 20 (und dazu 1Kön 1–2) auf das 10. Jahrhundert v. Chr. zurück – eine enorm frühe Ansetzung für einen so großen Textkomplex. Dem entsprach eine sehr zurückhaltende Einschätzung späterer Redaktionsarbeit. Martin Noth[4] hielt den dtr Textanteil in den Samuelbüchern insgesamt und erst recht in der Davidgeschichte für vergleichsweise gering, geradezu marginal. Gleichwohl war es seiner Meinung nach (erst) «der Deuteronomist», der in der Exilszeit, also fast ein halbes Jahrtausend nach ihrer Entstehung, die Aufstiegs- und die Thronfolgegeschichte zusammenführte und in seine große Geschichte Israels von der Landnahme bis zum Landverlust einsetzte.

2 Hauptthese 1: Der Aufstieg Davids bildete einen Teil eines vordeuteronomistischen Erzählwerks über die frühe Königszeit in Israel, das seinerseits wieder Teil des deuteronomistischen Geschichtswerks wurde

Im Fortgang der Forschung wurde die Annahme einer fast durchgehend sehr alten Davidüberlieferung und einer nur ganz schmalen dtr Bearbeitung von beiden Seiten her in Frage gestellt. Auf der einen Seite entdeckten Ernst Würthwein[5] und François Langlamet[6] namentlich im Textbereich der sog. Thronfolgegeschichte recht umfangreiche Bearbeitungen aus einer Zeit deutlich *nach* dem 10., aber auch *vor* dem 6. Jahrhundert. Auf der anderen Seite schrieb Timo Veijola[7] der dtr Redaktion (die er nicht mehr einstufig, sondern mehrstufig sah) ungefähr dreimal mehr Text zu als Noth, nämlich über 230 statt 75 Verse oder 15 statt 5 Prozent des Textbestands.[8] Ich selbst bin, was den Deuteronomismus in

4 Noth 1943 = 1957.
5 Würthwein 1974.
6 Langlamet 1976; 1978; 1979; 1980; 1981; 1982.
7 Veijola 1975.
8 Vgl. die Aufstellung bei Dietrich 2013: 51.

den Samuelbüchern anlangt, etwas moderater als Veijola, dafür meine ich eine breite vor-dtr Bearbeitungsschicht im Textbereich der sog. Aufstiegsgeschichte ausfindig gemacht zu haben, die mit den von Würthwein und Langlamet postulierten Bearbeitungen des Thronfolgestoffs zusammenhängt.

Diese Redaktionsschicht scheint mir derart grundlegend und umfassend, dass ich gar nicht mehr mit zwei voneinander separierbaren alten Geschichtswerken (über «Aufstieg» und «Thronfolge» Davids) rechne, sondern mit einem durchgehenden «Erzählwerk von den ersten Königen Israels», das über die Geschichte Davids hinaus auch diejenige Sauls und Salomos enthielt und von 1Sam 1 bis 1Kön 12 (abzüglich natürlich der späteren dtr und nach-dtr Einträge) reichte.[9] Viel spricht dafür, dass es in der mittleren Königszeit entstand, um die Wende vom 8. zum 7. Jahrhundert, in der Umgebung des Jerusalemer Hofes – jedoch nicht in völliger Abhängigkeit von diesem, als königliches Propaganda-Machwerk, sondern als hochrangiges Kunstwerk, das sich auszeichnet durch große geistige Freiheit und durch eine enorme Vielschichtigkeit, ja Ambiguität der geschilderten Charaktere wie der erzählten Handlungen.

Der Verfasser dieses Werkes – von mir mangels eines besseren, konkreteren Namens «Höfischer Erzähler» genannt – hat bei der Komposition des Davidstoffs seine Handschrift insbesondere in direkten Reden der handelnden Figuren hinterlassen: etwa in Dialogen zwischen Jonatan und David, zwischen David und Saul, zwischen Abigajil und David, zwischen David und den Mördern Sauls, Abners und Eschbaals. Dialoge sind sehr gut dazu geeignet, eine Erzählung, ohne ihren Ablauf zu stören, mit Deutungen zu versehen – und nun eben nicht eigenen, sondern denen von Erzählfiguren (die sich mit der Erzählermeinung decken können oder auch nicht). Hinzu kommen einige Geschichten, die der Höfische Erzähler als ganze selbst verfasst hat: etwa die von Sauls Verwerfung (die erste, in 1Sam 13,7b–15, während die zweite, in 1Sam 15, erst die dtr Redaktion eingebracht hat); dazu einige David-Geschichten, etwa die von seiner Salbung, die von seiner Flucht vor Saul zu Samuel oder von seiner Ausmusterung aus dem Philisterheer vor der Schlacht von Gilboa.

Der Klarheit halber lege ich hier eine Liste der dem Höfischen Erzähler von 1Sam 16 an zuzuschreibenden Textpassagen vor, wie sie sich mir im Verlauf der bisherigen Kommentararbeit ergeben hat:
1Sam 16,1–13; 17,10–14.19.23–39.41b.42.43b–46a.57b; 18,1.5.8–12.14–16.*17.21.25b.28–30; 19,1–8.18–24; 20,1a.8.12.13–17.23.32 f.40–42; 21,12b; 22,6a.14b; 23,7b.14b–18.21–23; 24,*5–8a.*10–22; 25,7b.8aα₁.10aβb.13bβ.15–17.21 f.24b.25a.28–31.32b–34a.*38b.39a; 26,1.*3.6.8–1.12bβγ.15b.16a.18–20a.21.22aα.23–25a; 27,1.3b.4 f.(8.)9–12; 28,1 f.6.15b. 16aβb.20b.23b; 29,*1–11; 30,1a.5.6–8.9b.10.18b.21–25.26b.29aββb; 31,1a;

9 Vgl. Dietrich 1997: 259–73; Dietrich 2016.

2Sam 1,1aβyb.2aα₁.3–5.8.10aβy.12aβb.13–16.17f; 2,1.2aβb.3.4b–7.17b. 26b.27.28aβ.30f; 3,1; 5,1f.10b–13.17; 6,1.14.16.20–23; 7,1a.2f.8*a.b.9.12ayb.15b; 11,[20.21a.23aβb.24.]27b; 12,1a.5–7a.9a.11–15a.*24f; 14,1–3.17–22.

Da es im Folgenden um vorredaktionelles Quellenmaterial gehen soll, ist es sinnvoll, an dieser Stelle auch gleich noch die Textanteile der dtr Redaktion zu benennen. Wie Veijola rechne ich mit drei dtr Bearbeitungsstufen. Im Bereich der (Saul- und) David-Geschichten massieren sich deren Textanteile in drei Kapiteln: dem von Sauls Amalekiterkrieg, dem von der Totenbeschwörung in En-Dor und dem von Natans Weissagung und Davids anschließendem Dankgebet. Hinzu kommt eine Reihe verstreuter kleinerer Bemerkungen und Ergänzungen.

Hier wieder eine Liste der einschlägigen Stellen:
DtrH: 1Sam 13,1; 23,1bβ.5b.*10.*11a.*13a; 2Sam 2,10aαb; 3,9–10.17–19; 4,2b.3; 5,4–5; 7,1b.11aβb.13.16.17a.18–21.25–29; 11,20.21a.23aβb.24 [?].
DtrP: 1Sam 14,48aβb; 15.1aβyb.10–12.16aβb.17–27a; 28,3.9–10.12b.17–19aα.21bβy; 12,7b. 8.9b10.
DtrN: 1Sam 13,13bα.14bβ; 15,2.6.*9.29; 2Sam 7,4–8aα.10.11aα.22–24.

Die Deuteronomisten haben, soweit ich sehe, in die David-Geschichte keine eigenen älteren Quellen mehr eingebracht, sondern sich ganz auf das ihnen vorliegende Höfische Erzählwerk gestützt.

3 Hauptthese 2: Im Höfischen Erzählwerk sind mehrere, umfangmäßig und thematisch begrenzte, ältere Quellen verarbeitet

Der Höfische Erzähler nun hat die David- (und die Saul- und die Salomo-) Geschichte nicht aus freien Stücken niedergeschrieben, also keinen selbsterdachten Roman verfasst, sondern in sein Werk eine beträchtliche Menge von Quellentexten eingearbeitet. Im Bereich der sog. Thronfolgegeschichte sind das nach meiner Ansicht zwei ehedem eigenständige Novellen: die eine über David, Batscheba und Salomo, den unter undurchsichtigen Umständen zur Welt und am Ende auf den Thron gekommenen Nachfolger Davids (in 2Sam 10–12 und 1Kön 1–2), die andere über Irrungen und Wirrungen im Hause Davids, zentriert um den Erst- und den Zweitgeborenen Davids, Amnon und Abschalom (in 2Sam 13–19).

Wie aber steht es im Umkreis der sog. Aufstiegsgeschichte, d. h. im Textbereich zwischen 1Sam 16 und 2Sam 5 (oder 8)? Hier hat man zu unterscheiden zwischen älteren, dem Höfischen Erzähler zugänglichen oder zugekommenen Einzeltexten und bereits vor ihm zusammengestellten Textkompositionen.

3.1 Unterthese 2.1: Der Höfische Erzähler hat eine Reihe von Einzelüberlieferungen aufgenommen

Die augenfälligsten Einzelstücke sind die Klagelieder Davids auf Saul und Jonatan (2Sam 1,19–27) sowie auf Abner (2Sam 3,33f). Zumindest für das erste ist eigens eine Quelle angegeben: «das Buch des Aufrechten», offenbar eine Sammlung von Liedern über (oder in diesem Fall: von) heroische(n) Gestalten aus der Frühzeit Israels. Ferner sind die beiden Listen von Söhnen Davids zu nennen: eine über die in Hebron geborenen Söhne, die auch die Namen ihrer Mütter angibt (2Sam 3,2–5), eine zweite über in Jerusalem geborene (2Sam 5,13–16). Diese Listen dürften in den Archiven des Jerusalemer Hofs aufbewahrt worden sein. Das Gleiche gilt wohl für drei weitere, sozusagen amtliche Listen: die erste mit den Namen judäischer Dörfer, die David aus der Beute eines Siegs über die Amalekiter beschenkt haben soll (1Sam 30,26–31), die zweite mit Kriegen und Siegen Davids gegen Nachbarvölker (2Sam *8,1–14), die dritte mit den Namen und Ressorts der führenden Beamten Davids (2Sam 8,16–23, und noch einmal, mit leichten Abweichungen, 2Sam 20,23–25). Schließlich kannte der Höfische Erzähler eine angeblich einst von Natan dem David übermittelte Dynastieweissagung, die anscheinend einen festen Platz im Jerusalemer Hofzeremoniell hatte (2Sam *7,11–16).

Eine Art Zwischending zwischen Einzeltext und Textkomposition ist das Kapitel 2Sam 6, das von der Überführung der heiligen Lade nach Jerusalem erzählt und das erst der Höfische Erzähler um eine Szene vom endgültigen Zerwürfnis zwischen David und der Saultochter Michal anreicherte (2Sam 6,16.20–23). Die Grunderzählung bildete einmal den Abschluss der sog. Ladegeschichte, deren erster Teil in 1Sam 4–6 steht.

3.2 Unterthese 2.2: Es gibt Hinweise auf zwei größere, im Bereich der Geschichte vom Aufstieg Davids verarbeitete Grundquellen

Sind die Textanteile der Redaktion sowie die quellenhaften Einzeltexte in Abzug gebracht, bleibt eine lange Reihe offensichtlich biografisch angeordneter Erzählungen: von Davids Auftauchen am Hof Sauls, seinem kometenhaften Aufstieg dort, seinem baldigen Absturz, d. h. der Vertreibung durch Saul, seinem Umherstreifen in der Wüste Juda, seiner Zeit als Philistervasall und Stadtkönig von Ziklag und schließlich seiner Einsetzung zum König zuerst Judas und dann Israels. Es ist dies eine veritable Vita, die in ihrem Detail- und Farbenreichtum in der antiken Literatur ihresgleichen sucht.

Freilich weist diese Vita eine Reihe auffälliger Dubletten (oder doppelter Linienführungen) auf:

- Die Erzählung von Davids Sieg über den Philisterrecken Goliat ist allem Anschein nach aus zwei verschiedenen Darstellungen des gleichen Ereignisses zusammengesetzt (ganz abgesehen davon, dass es noch eine dritte, vollkommen alternative Kurzversion in 2Sam 21,19 gibt).
- David findet, als ihm Saul mit zunehmender Missgunst begegnet, Unterstützung bei zwei Kindern Sauls: Jonatan und Michal. Beide erfüllen je auf ihre Weise die gleiche Funktion: die Königsmacht in einer legitimen, das heißt nicht-usurpatorischen, Weise von Saul auf David übergehen zu lassen.
- Michal hat noch ein weiteres, diesmal weibliches Gegenüber in Gestalt ihrer Schwester Merab, die allerdings einen viel schwächeren Part innehat.
- David schont das Leben seines ihm in die Hände gefallenen Verfolgers Saul zweimal: zuerst in einer Höhle bei En-Gedi (1Sam 24) und dann auf einer Anhöhe namens Hachila (1Sam 26).
- Saul stirbt im Kampf mit den Philistern auf zwei verschiedene Weisen: einmal vom Feind in die Enge getrieben von eigener Hand (1Sam 31), einmal schwer verwundet durch den Gnadenstoß eines Amalekiters (2Sam 1).
- David bestraft zweimal Menschen, die glauben, ihm durch die Beseitigung eines Widersachers einen Gefallen getan zu haben, mit dem Tod: den vorgeblichen Mörder Sauls (2Sam 1) und die tatsächlichen Mörder Eschbaals (2Sam 4).

Das sind, es sei betont, *stoffliche* Dubletten. Es gibt auch kleinere, gewissermaßen stilistische Wiederholungen: zum Beispiel das Frauenlied von Saul, der tausend, und David, der zehntausend erschlagen hat, das sogar dreimal vorkommt;[10] oder die zweimal erzählte Bedrohung des musizierenden David durch den Spieß Sauls;[11] oder die wie ein roter Faden sich durch die David-Erzählungen ziehende Mitseinsformel («Jhwh war mit David»);[12] oder die immer wieder stattfindenden Befragungen Jhwhs.[13] Solche Wiederholungen sind nicht quellenkritisch, sondern kompositionskritisch zu erklären: als Stil- und Gestaltungsmittel in der Hand des «Höfischen Erzählers».

Die aufgeführten Sach-Dubletten hingegen verdanken sich offensichtlich nicht der planenden Hand des Redaktors bzw. Verfassers, vielmehr hat dieser sie bereits vorgefunden und versucht, sie mehr oder minder überzeugend hin-

---

10 1Sam 18,7; 21,12; 29,5.
11 1Sam 18,10 f.; 19,10.
12 1Sam 16,18; 17,37; 18,14.28; 2Sam 8,6.14; 1Kön 1,37.
13 1Sam 23,6–13; 30,7 f.; 2Sam 2,1 f.; 5,19.23 f.

tereinander zu ordnen – wozu zu betonen ist, dass ihm solche Doppelungen ästhetisch und sachlich anscheinend weniger Mühe bereiteten als uns Modernen. Er findet es offenbar nicht nachteilhaft, wenn sich zwei Erzählfäden, etwa die von den Königskindern Jonatan und Michal, die sich mit dem Feind ihres Vaters verbünden, ineinander verschlingen und sich so die Aussage verdoppelt: Die Zukunft liegt bei David, nicht bei Saul.

Zu Zeiten der alten Pentateuch-Quellenkritik wurde gelegentlich die Ansicht vertreten, derartige Doppelungen seien der Beweis dafür, dass sich die Quellenfäden J(ahwist) und E(lohist) bis hinein in die Samuel- und womöglich noch in die Königsbücher fortsetzten.[14] Martin Noth hat solchen Theorien für die Bücher des dtr Geschichtswerks den Boden entzogen. Mittlerweile wird auch für den Pentateuch selbst die alte Urkundenhypothese kaum noch verfochten, stehen stattdessen diverse Formen von Fragmentenhypothesen im Vordergrund. Eine solche ist auch für die Samuelbücher, und gerade für die Erzählungen vom Aufstieg Davids, zu bevorzugen.

Der Höfische Erzähler hat sich hier, wenn ich es recht sehe, zweier größerer Quellen bedient und die diesen entnommenen Fragmente unter Beigabe eigener Verknüpfungen und Ergänzungen zu einem fortlaufenden Handlungszusammenhang verflochten. Allem Anschein nach lagen ihm diese Quellen schon in schriftlicher Form vor, doch zeigen sie noch deutlich ihren Entstehungsgrund in der mündlichen Erzähltradition. Ich spreche darum nicht von «Büchern», sondern von «Erzählkränzen», deren Schöpfer offenbar weniger als Autoren denn als Sammler anzusprechen sind. Diese haben in die ihnen überkommenen Geschichten nur selten spürbar eingegriffen, haben sie in der Hauptsache bloß aneinandergereiht, ohne ihnen ihr jeweiliges Kolorit zu nehmen. Die vorherrschende Textgattung in diesen Quellen ist somit die Einzelerzählung: mit in sich gerundetem Horizont, eigener Handlungs- und Personenführung, eigenem Erzählziel, eigenem Vokabular, oft auch eigener Topographie, auffallend häufig mit chiastischen Strukturen (welche vermutlich ästhetischen und mnemotechnischen Zwecken dienten).

3.3 Unterthese 2.3: Eine der beiden Hauptquellen zur Schilderung des Aufstiegs Davids war ein «Erzählkranz vom Aufstieg und Niedergang der Sauliden»

Durch die gesamten Samuelbücher, von 1Sam 9 an, ziehen sich Geschichten, in denen noch nicht oder nicht allein David die Hauptfigur ist, sondern Saul oder

---

14 So noch SCHULTE 1972.

ein Mitglied der Sauliden-Familie. Hierher gehören Geschichten wie die vom jungen Saul, der auszog, die Eselinnen seines Vaters zu suchen und die Königskrone fand, von Sauls und Jonatans Kampf mit den Philistern bei Gibea, von der «Entdeckung» Davids durch Saul anlässlich des Goliat-Sieges (die von mir so genannte Hirtenknaben-Version in 1Sam 17), die Erzählungen von der innigen und am Ende sich gegen Saul richtenden Freundschaft Jonatans mit David, vom Massaker Sauls an den Priestern von Nob, von der vergeblichen Jagd Sauls auf David in Keïla und bei der Höhe von Hachila, von Sauls Gang zur Totenbeschwörerin von En-Dor und von seinem Tod auf Gilboa, dann die Geschichten von Sauls Cousin Abner und seinem Sohn Eschbaal, von seinem Enkel (oder Sohn?) Meribaal, auch die von dem Sauliden Schimi und dem Benjaminiter Scheba, womöglich die vom Tod von sieben Sauliden in Gibeon. Ich denke, all diese Geschichten ergeben ein ebenso farbiges wie in sich stimmiges Bild vom Geschick der Sauliden-Familie und ihrem Verhältnis zu David.

> Zur raschen und klaren Verständigung seien hier die Texte im Einzelnen aufgelistet, die dieser Quelle m. E. zuzuweisen sind (wobei freilich spätere Zugaben seitens des Höfischen Erzählers, gelegentlich auch der dtr Redaktion, in Rechnung zu stellen wären):
> 1Sam 9,1 – 10,16; 13–14; 17,12–14.17 f.20–25.40 f.48–50.55–58; 18,2–4.6 f.13aßb.17a.18 f.; 20,2–7.9–11.18–23.25–31.34–39; 21,2–10; 22,6–18a.20–23; 23,1–13.14a.19.24a; 26; 28,4–25; 29,1b.2a.11b; 31;
> 2Sam 2,8 f.10aß.12–17a.18–32; 3; 4; 9; 16,1–13; 19,17–31; 20,1–22; 21,1–14(?).

Alle Erzählungen dieser Quelle haben ihren Wurzelgrund offenbar in Nordisrael, näherhin wohl in Benjamin, jedenfalls nicht in Juda. Sie vertreten damit gewissermaßen eine Gegenwelt zur judäisch-jerusalemer Welt des Höfischen Erzählers (und der anderen von ihm verwendeten Quellen im Bereich der David-Geschichte). Nicht zuletzt durch Aufnahme der Sauliden-Erzählungen gelang es ihm, eine virtuelle Welt des Miteinanders von Nord und Süd unter der Regentschaft Davids zu schaffen.[15]

Auch zur Zeit des Höfischen Erzählers, um 700 v. Chr., war diese Welt aus «Nord und Süd» keine rein theoretische, vergangenheitliche Größe, sondern durchaus konkret präsent: Das Nordreich war kurz zuvor untergegangen, eine große Zahl von Flüchtlingen war in das noch existierende Juda geströmt und hatte eine eigene Überlieferungswelt mitgebracht: etwa vom Erzvater Jakob und

---

15 Mit dieser Quellenzuweisung ist nicht der gerade im Schwange befindlichen Anzweiflung einer «United Monarchy» unter David und Salomo das Wort geredet; diese hat es gegeben – freilich in viel geringerem Umfang und mit wesentlich geringerem Glanz, als namentlich in der Salomo-Überlieferung dargestellt; vgl. dazu die Auslegung von 2Sam 5 und 2Sam 8 in Dietrich 2019.

dem aus seiner Familie hervorgehenden Israel oder vom Exodus Israels aus Ägypten oder von der Loslösung Israels vom davidischen Juda oder von den Königen Jerobeam oder Jehu oder von den Propheten Elija, Elischa und Hosea – und eben auch vom Gründerkönig Israels, Saul.

Der Saulidenerzählkranz ist nun aber nicht mehr rein nordisraelitisch geprägt. Vielmehr zeigt er das Schicksal dieser Königsfamilie im Zusammenhang mit David, der an ihr vorbei und über sie hinweg aufsteigt und eine Doppelmonarchie schafft, von der Saul nicht einmal hätte träumen können. Wohl führte dieser gelegentlich Kriegszüge in das Gebiet des späteren Juda (das es aber bis David nicht gab!), doch unterwarf er sich dieses Gebiet nicht dauerhaft. Auch seine anfänglichen Erfolge gegen die Philister wichen einer deutlichen Unterlegenheit, die ihn schließlich das Leben kostete. Die Sauliden spielen in diesem Erzählkranz die Rolle einer Initiations- und Übergangsgröße, die ihre Überbietung und ihr Ziel in der Herrschaft Davids findet. Anders gesagt: Diese Erzählsammlung ist bereits stark judäisch gefärbt – und insofern dem Höfischen Erzähler, zweifellos einem Judäer, nicht von Grund auf wesensfremd. Trotzdem liegt der nordisraelitische Entstehungshintergrund noch deutlich zutage.

Nehmen wir als Beispiel die Jonatan-Figur, die in den Sauliden-Überlieferungen eine auffällig starke Rolle spielt:

–   In 1Sam 13–14 läuft Jonatan seinem Vater Saul förmlich den Rang ab; letztlich ist er es, dem der erste große Sieg Israels über die Philister zu verdanken ist (und den sein cholerisch-sturer Vater um ein Haar liquidiert hätte). Diese Rollenverteilung scheint indes traditionsgeschichtlich auf einer zweiten Ebene zu liegen. Im ältesten Textstratum war *Saul* der Held, der die Philister aus dem Feld schlug. Offenbar gab es aber auch eine Heldengeschichte von Jonatan, die nachträglich über die von Saul gelegt wurde. Vielleicht war dafür erst der Höfische Erzähler verantwortlich,[16] möglicherweise aber auch schon der Autor des Sauliden-Erzählkranzes.

–   In 1Sam 18 verbündet sich Jonatan in engster Freundschaft (und/oder Liebe?)[17] mit David. Dass der Kronprinz dem jungen Goliat-Sieger seine königlichen Gewänder und seine Waffen übergibt, ist ein Akt von symbolhafter Bedeutung.

–   In 1Sam 19,1–7 warnt Jonatan seinen Freund vor dem Zorn seines Vaters – und schafft es, diesen fürs erste zu besänftigen, so dass David wie zuvor ungefährdet dem König dienen kann. Diese Episode beruht nach meiner Analyse nicht auf alter Überlieferung, sondern ist vom Höfischen Erzähler

---

16 So Dietrich 2015: 10–12.

17 Zur Frage der vermeintlichen oder wirklichen Homoerotik zwischen Jonatan und David vgl. Dietrich 2015: 414–17 und die dort angeführte Spezialliteratur.

frei ersonnen worden. Sie erhöht durch scheinbare Entspannung die Dramatik des dann Folgenden.

- In 1Sam 20 eröffnet David Jonatan seine Überzeugung, dass Saul ihm nach wie vor nach dem Leben trachte. Jonatan will das nicht glauben, stellt in Absprache mit David seinen Vater auf die Probe, erfährt, dass David recht hatte, wird selbst wegen seiner Freundschaft mit diesem beschimpft und sogar mit dem Tode bedroht und verhilft daraufhin David, nach tränenreichem Abschied, zur Flucht. So bewährt sich die Freundschaft im Augenblick der Gefahr, wird aber auch tragisch zerbrochen. Diese Erzählung stammt im Grundbestand aus dem Sauliden-Kranz, wurde aber vom Höfischen Erzähler durch einige Zusätze ideologisch und theologisch überhöht.[18]

- Die nächste Jonatan-David-Episode, 1Sam 23,14b–18, ist wieder reine Invention des Höfischen Erzählers: Jonatan schlägt sich zu dem von seinem Vater in die Wüste Juda vertriebenen David durch und dankt ausdrücklich zu dessen Gunsten ab: «Du bist es, der König über Israel sein wird, und ich werde der Zweite nach dir sein».

- In 1Sam 31 fällt Jonatan an der Seite seines Vaters: klar eine Geschichte aus dem Sauliden-Erzählkranz.

- Im zweiten Samuelbuch kommt anstelle Jonatans dessen überlebender, freilich körperbehinderter Sohn Meribaal in den Blick. Man erfährt (offenbar aus dem Sauliden-Erzählkranz), wie er zu Schaden gekommen war (2Sam 4,4), dass David ihm die – zuvor anscheinend konfiszierten – Ländereien Sauls zurückgibt (2Sam 9), dass Meribaal beim Abschalom-Aufstand, angeblich oder wirklich, Hoffnung schöpft, selbst an die Macht zu gelangen (2Sam 16,1–4), nach Davids Sieg aber froh sein darf, mit dem Leben (und dem halben bisherigen Besitz) davonzukommen (2Sam 19,25–31). All diesen Episoden liegen Informationen aus dem Sauliden-Erzählkranz zugrunde, doch hat offenbar der Höfische Erzähler sie untereinander zusätzlich vernetzt und die Gestalt Davids noch ein wenig positiver erscheinen lassen als in seiner Quelle.

Trotzdem ist nicht zu verkennen, dass allein durch die hartnäckige Präsenz von Sauliden in der Davidüberlieferung auf den Hauptprotagonisten ein Schatten fällt. Zwar werden schon der Sammler des Erzählkranzes und noch mehr der Höfische Erzähler nicht müde zu betonen, dass David keinem Saul-Nachkommen ein Haar gekrümmt habe. Trotzdem wird die Leserschaft dessen gewahr,

---

18 Vgl. die Analyse bei DIETRICH 2015: 522–26.

dass es in Nordisrael bzw. in Benjamin eine Familie gab, die *vor* David die Königswürde innehatte und die, solange David lebte, laut oder leise einen Anspruch auf die Rückgewinnung dieser Würde erhob. Und seltsam genug: Bis auf den behinderten Meribaal weiß die Überlieferung vom vorzeitigen Tod aller, aber auch *aller* Sauliden zu berichten – bzw. sie ist dazu gezwungen. Offenbar wusste man in Israel um die Verflochtenheit der Schicksale Sauls und Davids, und man vergaß nie, dass an David der Geruch der Usurpation haftete. Deutlich genug spricht der Saulide Schimi (wieder nach einer Überlieferung aus dem Sauliden-Kranz) von «all dem Blut des Hauses Sauls, an dessen Stelle du [David] König geworden bist» (2Sam 16,8).

Nicht zuletzt den Überlieferungen aus dem «Erzählkranz vom Aufstieg und Niedergang der Sauliden» (daneben aber auch einem Traditionsstück wie der David-Batscheba-Salomo-Novelle) ist es zu danken, dass das Bild Davids in den Samuelbüchern nicht in propagandistischer Manier rein positiv ausfällt, sondern gewissermaßen schattiert bleibt, mit ausgesprochen dunklen Flecken. David ist keine reine Licht-, sondern eine ambivalente Gestalt – und das macht nicht zum mindesten ihre Größe aus.

3.4 Unterthese 2.4: Die zweite Hauptquelle war der «Erzählkranz vom Freibeuter David»

Neben dieser einen Quelle verfügte der Höfische Erzähler noch über eine andere, die in einzelnen Episoden den Aufstieg Davids von seinem Auftauchen am Hof des israelitischen Königs Saul bis zu seiner eigenen Erhebung zum König Israels schilderte. Die ihr zuzurechnenden Stoffe finden sich zwischen 1Sam 16 und 2Sam 5. Ihr Hintergrund ist klar nicht israelitisch, sondern judäisch, und einzelne ihrer Bestandteile dürften zeitlich weit zurückreichen, womöglich bis in die Davidzeit.

Die Themen bzw. die Geschichten dieses Erzählkranzes sind überschaubar. Es handelt sich um die Erzählung von Davids Musiktherapie an Saul, von ihm als namenlosem Schleudersoldaten, der den Philisterhünen Goliat ausschaltet, von seiner Heirat mit Michal (sie ist hier, anstelle Jonatans, die Überträgerin der Königsmacht von Saul auf David), vom Spießwurf Sauls auf seinen Therapeuten und von dessen Flucht aus dem Haus Michals, von seinem ersten, misslungenen Versuch, beim Philisterkönig von Gat unterzukommen, vom Aufbau einer mehrhundertköpfigen Freibeutertruppe, von der Verfolgung durch Saul bei Keïla, Maon und En-Gedi, von dem Abenteuer mit Nabal und Abigajil in Karmel, von dem gelungenen Übertritt zu den Philistern und der Einsetzung zum Stadtkönig von Ziklag, von einer Razzia gegen die räuberischen Amalekiter, von der

Reaktion auf die Nachricht vom Tod Sauls und die Überbringung von dessen
Regalien, von der Einsetzung zum König von Juda in Hebron, der Einnahme
Jerusalems als neuer Hauptstadt und schließlich der Kür zum König von Israel.

> Wieder seien zur raschen Verständigung die betreffenden Stellen aufgelistet (wobei oft
> nur ein Grundbestand der jeweiligen Textpassagen gemeint ist):
> 1Sam 16,14–23; 17,1–9.48–54; 18,20–27; 19,9–17; 21,11–16; 22,1–5; 23,24b–28; 24; 25;
> 27,2.3a.6 f.; 30,1–25;
> 2Sam *1,2.6–12; 2,2aα.4a.11; 5,3.*6–10a.

In all diesen Geschichten ist eindeutig David die Hauptperson; um ihn dreht
sich jede einzelne Handlung wie auch die Gesamthandlung. In ihrer jetzigen
Abfolge bilden sie ein Itinerar ab mit den Stationen Gibea, Wüste Juda (mit
verschiedenen Unterpunkten), Ziklag, Hebron und Jerusalem – wobei ja zwischen dem Ausgangs- und dem Endpunkt geographisch nur wenige Kilometer
liegen, die der Held aber aufgrund der widrigen Umstände nicht direkt, sondern
nur über gewaltige Umwege zurücklegen kann. Hier zeichnet sich bereits das
Muster ab, das den Aufstieg Davids im großen Höfischen Geschichtswerk prä-
gen wird: *per aspera ad adstra*. Davids Weg nach oben ist nicht eben und gerade, sondern holprig und kurvenreich. Diesem Mann ist das Glück nicht in die
Wiege gelegt. Er ist ein Seiteneinsteiger am Hof des regierenden Königs, er wird
von diesem vertrieben und gejagt, schlägt sich mehr schlecht als recht als
Flüchtling und Milizenführer durch, muss sich gar zum Vasallendienst beim
Landesfeind herbeilassen. Und doch kann man sagen: Der David dieser Erzählungen ist auch ein Glückskind. So tief er fällt, er nimmt nie ernsthaft Schaden.
So sehr andere ihm übelwollen – vor allem Saul, aber auch der König von Gat,
natürlich Goliat von Gat, oder die Amalekiter –, er weiß auf jede Bedrohung
eine passende Antwort. Er ist Held und Antiheld zugleich, ein Underdog, der
doch unaufhaltsam nach oben strebt.

Der Sammler des Erzählkranzes hat, wenn ich recht sehe, in die ihm überkommenen Einzelgeschichten nur wenig eingegriffen. Mit das auffälligste Merk-
mal ist die Aufreihung von Fluchtgeschichten durch formelhafte Überleitungen
wie: «Und David floh und entrann» – von einem Ort zum andern, manchmal
vom Regen in die Traufe, aber nie ohne Ausweg, nie im Desaster endend. Ein
symptomatischer Fall ist das Entkommen vor Sauls überlegener Heeresmacht
am Fels Sela-Machlekot, wo nur die Meldung vom Einfall der Philister in Sauls
Stammgebiet David die Haut rettet (1Sam 23,24b–28). Wird da ein Zusammenspiel der Philister mit David sichtbar? Tatsächlich berichtet gerade dieser Erzählkranz von Davids Vasallendienst bei den Philistern (1Sam *27). Andererseits
aber weiß der Sammler auch davon, dass David sich bei einem ersten Versuch,
in Gat unterzukommen, nur um den Preis, als Verrückter zu gelten, dem Zugriff

der dortigen Sicherheitskräfte entziehen kann (1Sam 21,11–16). Gerade an dieser Episode ist zu sehen, wie sehr schon dem Sammler des Freibeuter-Kranzes die zuweilen doch recht unkonventionellen Karriereschritte Davids zu schaffen machten. Kann ein guter König sein, wer eine Zeitlang eine Freischärler-Truppe befehligte, wer die Frau eines wohlhabenden, auf ungeklärte Weise ums Leben gekommenen Schafzüchters ehelichte und sich sogar dem Landesfeind verdingte? Ja, ist die Antwort – aber all dies muss in größter Not und in lauterer Absicht geschehen sein: wie bei David.

Dass es Gott gewesen wäre, der David auf seinem komplizierten Weg führte und ihm aus schwierigen und demütigenden Situationen heraushalf, wird im Freibeuter-Erzählkranz nicht eigentlich betont. Es sind glückliche Zufälle, es ist vor allem die Gewitztheit Davids, die ihn immer wieder den Kopf aus der Schlinge ziehen und ihn immer weiter nach oben gelangen lassen. Dabei gebärdet er sich keineswegs als unbedachter Haudegen und rabiater Schlagetot. Selbst ausgemachten Gegnern wie Saul und Nabal schenkt er das Leben, und den Sauliden Abner und Eschbaal krümmt er kein Haar (obwohl diese alle umkommen!). Er erobert Jerusalem nicht mit brutaler Gewalt, sondern gewinnt die Stadt offenbar durch List, er zwingt die Judäer und Israeliten nicht unter seine Herrschaft, sondern lässt sich von ihnen die Krone reichen.

Der David dieses Erzählkranzes zeigt keine Berührungsangst mit dem Volk. Schon seine Freischärler-Truppe rekrutiert er aus den unteren Schichten der Gesellschaft, und seine Kämpfer gehen mit ihm durch dick und dünn. Unbestritten ist seine Führerschaft jedoch nicht. Nicht nur Könige wie Saul und Achisch fühlen sich als seine Herren. Auch Nabal kann es wagen, ihn schroff abzuweisen und übel zu beleidigen. Amalekitische Raubnomaden können seinen Wohnort Ziklag plündern und die Bewohner verschleppen, woraufhin seine eigenen Leute Anstalten machen, ihn zu steinigen. Hier liest man nicht Hofgeschichtsschreibung, hier hört man Volkes Stimme.

Wenn man so will, ist der David des Freibeuter-Erzählkranzes ein Vorabbild des Davids der Psalmen. Dieser hat überwiegend zu klagen und nur selten ein Siegeslied zu singen. Erstmals im Freibeuter-Erzählkranz – und in der Folge dann auch im Werk des Höfischen Erzählers – zeichnet sich ein Davidbild ab, das bei der Hörer- oder Leserschaft Mitgefühl weckt, sicher auch Achtung, nicht aber Furcht. Dieser David ist kein Übermensch, sondern ein aus kleinen Verhältnissen unglaublich hoch aufgestiegener Mensch, ein Regent, auf den die Untertanen stolz sein und bei dem sie sich geborgen fühlen können.

4 Exkurs: Ein alternatives Modell der Quellenkritik

Mit meiner Quellenscheidung in den Davidgeschichten sei jetzt ein Gegenmodell verglichen, das sich, in zwei Variationen, wieder der alten Urkundenhypothese nähert: Es rechnet mit zwei ursprünglich voneinander unabhängigen Großerzählungen über den Aufstieg Davids. Diese werden nicht mehr mit dem Pentateuch in Verbindung gebracht und heißen darum nicht «Jahwist» und «Elohist» o. ä., sondern neutral «Source A» und «Source B» oder, mehr stoffbezogen, «HDR$_1$» und «HDR$_2$« (von «History of David's Rise»).

> *Baruch Halpern*[19] schlägt folgende Aufteilung vor:
> «Source A»: 1Sam 9,1 – 10,13; 13–14; *17; 18,1–5.14–19; 19,8–10; 20–24; 28,3–25; 31.
> «Source B»: 1Sam 8; 10,14–27; 11–12; 15; 16; *17; 18,6–13; 18,20 – 19,7; 19,11–24; 25–27; 28,1–2; 29–30; 2Sam 1.
> *Jeremy Hutton*[20] teilt so auf:
> HDR$_1$: 1Sam 16,14–23; 17,1–11.32–40.42–48a.49.51–54;[21] 18,6aβb–8a.9.12a.13–16.20–21a.22–26a.27–29a; 19,11–17; 22,(6–8).9–23; 24,1–23; 28,3–25; 31; 2Sam *5–6.
> HDR$_2$: 1Sam *13–14; 17,12–14.17–31.41.48b.50.55–58;[22] 18,1–5.17a.18.30; 23,1–13; 27,1–28,2; 29–30; 2Sam *1; 2,1–4 (?)

Beide Vorschläge berühren sich in gewissen Punkten mit dem oben von mir vorgetragenen. Im Besonderen hat Halperns «Source A» eine gewisse Ähnlichkeit mit meinem «Sauliden-Erzählkranz». Seiner «Source B» hingegen lässt sich kaum ein deutliches Profil abgewinnen; in ihr mischen sich Texte, die m. E. der deuteronomistischen Redaktion (1Sam 8; 15), dem Höfischen Erzähler (1Sam 16,1–13; 19,1–7.18–24) sowie den beiden von mir postulierten Quellen zuzuweisen sind (z. B. 1Sam 25 dem Freibeuter- und 1Sam 26 dem Sauliden-Erzählkranz).

Beim Entwurf Huttons mischen sich in beiden Quellen Texte aus beiden Erzählkränzen, wobei jeweils der Freibeuter-Erzählkranz stärker vertreten ist: In HDR$_1$ wären ihm m. E. 1Sam 16,14–23; 22; 24; 2Sam 5, in HDR$_2$ 1Sam 23; 27;

---

19 HALPERN 2001: 277–79.
20 Hutton hat diese bei seinem Vortrag in Jena angedeutet und mir auf meine Bitte hin im September 2018 brieflich näher erläutert. Dabei machte er zuweilen ausdrücklich den Vorbehalt weiterer gründlicher Analyse. Dezidiert nicht festlegen wollte er sich für 1Sam 23,14 f.19–28. Doch vermisst man auch die Zuordnung des Jonatan-Textes 1Sam 20 und der Eschbaal-Abner-Geschichten 2Sam 2–4.
21 Das sind diejenigen Textabschnitte in der Goliat-Geschichte, die MT und LXX gemeinsam haben.
22 Also diejenigen Textabschnitte in 1Sam 17, die in MT über LXX überschießen.

30; 2Sam 1 zuzurechnen. Dem gegenüber stammen im einen Fall 1Sam 28, im anderen 1Sam 13–14 aus dem Sauliden-Erzählkranz.

Insgesamt zeigen die von diesen beiden Forschern postulierten Quellen kein inhaltlich klares Profil, erweisen sie sich vielmehr als *mixta composita*. Das ist insofern nicht verwunderlich, als die Grundannahme ja die zweier durchlaufender Erzählfäden ist, von denen jeder das Ganze des Aufstiegs Davids dargestellt haben soll. Doch wirkt keine der postulierten Quellen wirklich vollständig. Zudem heben sie sich nicht markant voneinander ab. Auch haben die beiden Forscher noch kaum Vorschläge hinsichtlich ihrer redaktionellen Verknüpfung vorgelegt.[23]

Ein Sonderproblem sei noch erwähnt: In beiden Entwürfen wird der Stoff von 1Sam 17,1–18,5 in Anlehnung an die unterschiedlichen Textversionen von MT und LXX auf die beiden Quellen verteilt: Der einen soll der Text angehören, den MT und LXX gemeinsam haben, der anderen der, den MT darüber hinaus bietet. Dem steht freilich entgegen, dass die MT-Überschüsse allein kaum eine geschlossene Erzählung ergeben. M. E. führt es weiter, die Differenzen zwischen MT und LXX wirklich nur als textkritisches Problem zu behandeln, literarkritisch bzw. literarhistorisch aber, wie oben schon angedeutet, im (größeren, dem MT-)Text *zwei* ineinander verflochtene Geschichten von Davids Sieg über Goliat zu unterscheiden, die sich wiederum den von mir postulierten Erzählkränzen gut zuweisen lassen.

5 Schlussbemerkung: Die Samuelbücher bieten keine «Apologie» Davids

In der gegenwärtigen Samuelforschung wird also auch wieder eine Art Urkundenhypothese vertreten, und die weitere Forschung wird zu ergründen haben, ob dies ein gangbarer Weg zur Erklärung des Textbefundes ist. Er scheint mir indes relativ anfällig für eine bestimmte, in neuerer Zeit recht populäre Fehldeutung der Davidgeschichte: dass sie eine «Apologie»[24] oder ein «königlicher

---

23 Immerhin weist Hutton im Bereich von 1Sam 17–18 folgende Passagen einer die Texte von HDR$_1$ und HDR$_2$ verbindenden Bearbeitung zu: 17,15.(16.)31; 18,6aα.8b.10aβ.*11(«zweimal»). 12b.17b.21b.26b.29b.

24 Siehe die Arbeiten von MᴄCᴀʀᴛᴇʀ 1980 und 1981, sowie die von Pᴀʏɴᴇ 1993. Doch schon nach Rᴏsᴛ (1952: 234) wurde die Thronfolgegeschichte «trotz allem ... *in majorem gloriam Salomonis*» geschrieben; in dem «trotz allem» steckt immerhin die Erkenntnis widerständiger Elemente im biblischen Text. Und Wᴇɪsᴇʀ nannte in seinem Aufsatz (von 1966) die Aufstiegsgeschichte sehr bewusst eine «Legitimation» Davids.

Propagandatext» sei,[25] so wie sie etwa hethitische oder auch babylonische Könige von sich verbreiten ließen.

Einer solchen Einschätzung der Samuelbücher käme zugute, wenn sie ganz oder zu großen Teilen schon in der frühen Königszeit entstanden wären. Denn ein schönfärberisches Bild Davids machte viel mehr Sinn zu seinen (oder allenfalls noch zu Salomos) Lebzeiten als Jahrhunderte *post festum*. Diejenigen, die die Samuelbücher und speziell die sog. Aufstiegsgeschichte Davids als Apologie lesen, rechnen denn auch recht unbefangen mit einem hohen Alter der Texte, und sie gehen zudem davon aus, dass sie in unmittelbarer Nähe des Königshofes entstanden seien.

All das ist bei meinem Vorschlag zur Literargeschichte der Samuelbücher anders. Den Geist einer «apology» trägt hier am ehesten noch der Freibeuter-Erzählkranz in sich, doch ist er stark geprägt von volkstümlicher Erzählweise und fast gar nicht von den Finessen und Konventionen höfischer Geschichtsdarstellung. Noch weniger passend erscheinen Kategorien wie «Apologie» oder «Propaganda» für den Sauliden-Erzählkranz, der dezidiert benjaminitisch-nordisraelitisches Traditionsgut überliefert, dies zwar in judäisch-davidischer Färbung, aber damit auch nicht mehr wirklich zeitgenössisch. Überhaupt nicht zutreffend sind jene Kategorien für den jetzt vorliegenden Endtext der Samuelbücher, der wesentlich im Zuge der Abfassung des «Höfischen Erzählwerks» und des «Deuteronomistischen Geschichtswerks» entstanden ist.

Die Deuteronomisten blickten, nach dem Untergang der Königreiche Israel und Juda, auf das Königtum – auch das Königtum Davids – ohnehin mit höchst gemischten Gefühlen zurück. Und der Höfische Erzähler, wiewohl im Königreich Juda lebend, verwandte außer dem Freibeuter- auch den Sauliden-Erzählkranz und dazu noch andere, teils recht widerborstige Quellen: etwa eine gänzlich undavidische Samuel-Saul-Geschichte oder, wie oben angedeutet, die sehr davidkritische Geschichte um Batscheba, Urija und Salomo oder die überaus düstere Amnon-Abschalom-Novelle. Offenbar legte er größten Wert darauf, mit seinem Werk hohen ästhetischen und moralischen Ansprüchen zu genügen. Wie es scheint, besaß er auch hinreichend Abstand zum Königshof, um in genügender Freiheit zu schaffen und zu gestalten. Gerade unter seinen Händen aber wurden die Samuelbücher zum unsterblichen Kunstwerk.

---

25 Als solche beschreibt MCKENZIE 2000: 25–46 die biblische Vita Davids.

Bibliographie

Dietrich, Walter. 1997. *Die Frühe Königszeit in Israel. Biblische Enzyklopädie 3.* Stuttgart: Kohlhammer.

Dietrich, Walter. 2011. *Samuel. 1Sam 1–12. BKAT* VIII.1. Neukirchen-Vluyn: Neukirchener.

Dietrich, Walter. 2013. The Layer-Model of the Deuteronomistic History and the Books of Samuel. Pages 39–65 in *Is Samuel among the Deuteronomists?: Current Views on the Place of Samuel in a Deuteronomistic History.* Edited by Cynthia Edenburg et al. Atlanta: SBL Press.

Dietrich, Walter. 2015. *Samuel: 1Sam 13–26. BKAT* VIII.2. Neukirchen-Vluyn: Neukirchener.

Dietrich, Walter. 2016. Stefan Heyms Ethan ben Hoshaja und der Erstverfasser der Samuelbücher. Pages 3–38 in *The Books of Samuel. Stories – History – Reception History. BETL* 284. Edited by Walter Dietrich et al. Leuven: Peeters.

Dietrich, Walter. 2019. *Samuel: 1Sam 27 – 2Sam 8. BKAT* VIII.3, Göttingen: Vandenhoeck & Ruprecht.

Grønbæk, Jakob H. 1971. *Die Geschichte vom Aufstieg Davids (1.Sam.15 – 2.Sam.5). AThD* 10. Copenhagen: Prostant apud Munksgaard.

Halpern, Baruch. 2001. *David's Secret Demons: Messiah, Murderer, Traitor, King.* Grand Rapids / Cambridge: Eerdmans.

Langlamet, François. 1976. Pour ou contre Salomon? La rédaction prosalomonienne de I Rois I-II. *RB* 83:321–79, 481–528.

Langlamet, François. 1978. Ahitofel et Houshaï: Rédaction prosalomonienne en 2 Sam 15–17? Pages 57–90 in *Studies in the Bibel and the Ancient Near East: FS Samuel Ephraim Loewenstamm.* Jerusalem.

Langlamet, François. 1979. David et la maison de Saül. Les épisodes 'benjaminites' de II Sam., IX; XVI, 1–14; XIX, 17–31; I Rois, II, 36–46. *RB* 86:194–213, 385–436, 481–513; 1980. *RB* 87:161–210; 1981. *RB* 88:321–32.

Langlamet, François. 1982. David, fils de Jessé. Une édition prédeutéronomiste de l'"histoire de la succession". *RB* 89:5–47.

McCarter, P. Kyle. 1980. The Apology of David. *JBL* 99:489–504.

McCarter, P. Kyle. 1981. 'Plots, True or False': The Succession Narrative as Court Apologetic. *Interp.* 35:355–67.

McKenzie, Steven L. 2000. *King David: A Biography.* Oxford: University Press.

Noth, Martin. [2]1957. *Überlieferungsgeschichtliche Studien: Die sammelnden und bearbeitenden Geschichtswerke im Alten Testament.* Tübingen: Mohr Siebeck.

Payne, David Frank. 1993. Apologetic Motifs in the Books of Samuel. *VoxEv* 23:57–66.

Rost, Leonhard. 1965. Die Überlieferung von der Thronnachfolge Davids (1926. *BWANT* 42 =). Pages 119–253 in *Das kleine Credo und andere Studien zum Alten Testament.* Heidelberg: Quelle.

Schulte, Hannelis. 1972. *Die Entstehung der Geschichtsschreibung im Alten Israel. BZAW* 128. Berlin: de Gruyter.

Veijola, Timo. 1975. *Die ewige Dynastie: David und die Entstehung seiner Dynastie nach der deuteronomistischen Darstellung. AASF.B* 193. Helsinki: Suomalainen Tiedeakatemia.

Weiser, Artur. 1966. Die Legitimation des Königs David. Zur Eigenart und Entstehung der sogen. Geschichte von Davids Aufstieg. *VT* 16:325–54.

Würthwein, Ernst. 1974. *Die Erzählung von der Thronfolge Davids – Theologische oder politische Geschichtsschreibung? ThSt* 115. Zürich: Theologischer Verlag.

A. Graeme Auld

David and his *Alter Ego* in the Desert

Summary: This paper signals a small shift from my previously published position about the Book of Two Houses (BoTH). It then sketches the questions arising from BoTH about the early David and identifies fresh resources within that older book for exploring these. The final section explores the altered David we find in the desert.

1 Text-criticism and the BoTH project

Developing proposals made in my Samuel commentary,[1] *Life in Kings*[2] defends three claims:
- BoTH (earlier BTH), the synoptic narrative common to Sam–Kgs and Chr, is a very distinctive sub-set of Sam–Kgs.
- BoTH is cohesive and artistically constructed: it could have existed independently.
- Many portions of non-synoptic Sam-Kgs can be explained as developments from BoTH, normally where two or more of its separate components have been thought together.

As much as 40 % of the text of 1–2 Samuel (1 Sam 16–31; 2 Sam 1–4; 9; 21:1–14[3]) concerns the relationship first between David and king Saul and then between David and Saul's house after that king's own death. And the story of Saul before David is told in 1 Sam 9–15. Saul and his house feature in more than half of the book. But in the source-material in BoTH there are only three mentions of Saul:
- the short chapter that tells of the death of the former king on Mt Gilboa (1 Sam 31 // 1 Chr 10)
- the note that when Saul was king David commanded the army (2 Sam 5:2 // 1 Chr 11:2)
- and the reference to Michal, identified as 'Saul's daughter', scorning David as he brought the ark into Jerusalem (2 Sam 6:16 // 1 Chr 15:29)

---

1 AULD 2011.
2 AULD 2017.
3 The route from BoTH to Samuel is sketched in AULD 2011 (especially 9–14) and AULD 2017 (esp. 103–15).

https://doi.org/10.1515/9783110606164-007

It is of course possible that the authors of Samuel had access beyond BoTH to other older sources about Saul. Yet such an assumption may not be necessary. The broad terms of the whole David / Saul conflict – and indeed of the earlier Saul story – could have been derived imaginatively from thinking together some details in synoptic 1 Sam 31 with others from 2 Sam 5–7 and 24.

My interest in Kings and Chronicles as divergent expansions from a shared source was sparked in part by working with Jeremiah (both MT in a big way and LXX in a small way are expansions from a shorter source-text), in part by noting similar prophetic language in Jeremiah and Kings, but not Chronicles.[4] Yet, despite this text-historical background, I made almost no reference to text-criticism in Life in Kings. I did not want to complicate things. I hoped to carry with me more conservative readers: readers who might more easily accept arguments if they saw that they were based on the traditional Hebrew texts of Kings and Chronicles, and not on what they could characterise as 'private scholarly reconstructions'. Then I knew from Samuel that there was a wide convergence between LXX readings and synoptic parallels in Chronicles. Where Samuel and Chronicles agreed in MT, there was little need to complicate matters with the LXX!

I should have known that matters were less simple with Solomon. I did feature the much shorter report in LXX of the ark being brought into the new temple, over against the longer version including Levites largely agreed between 1 Kgs 8:1–5 (MT) and 2 Chr 5:2–6.[5] And I mentioned – but know now I did not take seriously enough – the advice JULIO TREBOLLE offered in my own FS about a triple as well as double textual tradition in Solomon.[6] I hope my overall case is not too vulnerable.

ADRIAN SCHENKER has offered a careful demonstration that the shorter Jeroboam story preserved in Greek after 1[3] Kg[dm]s 12:24 is prior to the familiar version in 1 Kgs 11–14 (MT).[7] He accepts ZIPORA TALSHIR's demonstration that a Hebrew text underlies the Greek version, but not her literary-historical analysis.[8] She is among the majority in regarding this shorter (originally Hebrew) text as secondary to the familiar version. I agree with his comparative evaluation of the texts and differ from him only over the wider literary-historical assessment at the end of his essay.[9] I find that an older and shorter Jeroboam story fits

4 AULD 1984: 66–82; AULD 1983: 3–23 and 41–44; reprinted in AULD 2004: 29–43 and 45–61.
5 AULD 2017: 208–9.
6 TREBOLLE BARRERA 2006: 483–501.
7 SCHENKER 1996: 193–236.
8 TALSHIR 1993.
9 Auld 2020.

perfectly into BoTH. Equally, this shorter Jeroboam (without Bethel and Dan) cannot have formed part of a book of Kings, properly so called: FRANK MOORE CROSS was surely correct when he insisted that the sins of Jeroboam (completely absent from the older story) provided one of the two principal themes of that book.[10] The Jeroboam of the book of Kings, while not a dynastic founder, sets the religious trend for all his successors. This earlier Jeroboam was simply joint agent when David's family, in the person of unwise Rehoboam, lost most of Israel. BoTH had no interest in what Jeroboam went on to do in an Israel detached from Jerusalem – what the book of Kings calls 'the sins he made Israel to sin'. After my decision to follow the shorter LXX on bringing the ark into the new temple, I should have included this text in my reconstruction instead of 1 Kgs 12:1–19 and the very similar 2 Chr 10:1–19.

Near its start, BoTH had sketched two similar triangular relationships. One threesome was Saul-his sons-David, and the other Solomon-his son Rehoboam-Jeroboam. In each case – and uniquely so in all of BoTH – kingship passed not to the dead king's son but to someone who had previously been a leading servant of the king. In the first case, the former head of the army succeeded to all Israel – Saul's sons, after all, had died with him in battle. In the second case, the former corvée chief succeeded to most of Israel, while Solomon's son retained power in Jerusalem. Importantly, it is not just in *content* that the two triangles are similar: BoTH also *presents* the stories of Saul / David and Solomon / Jeroboam in similar fashion – neither David nor Jeroboam is mentioned until the old king's death has been reported. In each case a prior relationship had existed: David with Saul and Jeroboam with Solomon; but we learn this only in retrospect.

In BoTH, in the precursor narrative, the David flashback was stated much more briefly even if its implications were open-ended: Israel's leaders come to Hebron and say to him 'When Saul was king, it was you who led Israel out and in' (2 Sam 5:2 // 1 Chr 11:2). The Jeroboam flashback is also introduced immediately after the report in 3 Kgdms 12:24a of the old king's death but is much more extensive (12:24b–f). We are told about his origins, his service in Solomon's building projects, and his royal pretensions; that Solomon tried to kill him, but he escaped to Egypt where he fared well under the Pharaoh's protection; that sometime after Solomon's death, he returned to Ephraim. In this version it was only at the Shechem assembly – not before he ever went to Egypt – that Jeroboam received the acted oracle from the man of God about the cloak torn in twelve tatters.

---

10 CROSS 1973.

Religious or theological structuring is much less overt throughout BoTH than in Samuel and (even more so) in Kings. The author of this older history leaves much of its significance to be deduced by the reader from an intricate web of paired situations and descriptions. Many pairings clearly suggest comparison or contrast, though some resist easy analysis. Such quiet, unexplained, parallels as we have just noted in the introductions to David and Jeroboam are entirely typical of BoTH.

LXX^{B+L} are our best witnesses to BoTH on Jeroboam. While they tell a story much shorter than the familiar one, they do include some small +'s vis-à-vis that mostly longer version. One of these relates to the very issue that provided my title for *Life in Kings* and the content of its second chapter (pp. 29–38). In 1 Kgs 14:3, when Jeroboam dispatches his wife to Shiloh, he says that the prophet will tell her what will happen to their son. But in 3 Kgdms 12:24g, he tells her: 'Go, ask the deity about the lad, whether he will *live* (i.e. survive) from his illness.' By contrast, while Rehoboam in 3 Kgdms 12:24q, when confronted by the people's demands at Shechem, first consults 'the elders' (so described, without any elaboration), their introduction in 1 Kgs 12:6 continues '... who stood before Solomon his father when he was *alive*'. Each version is expansive: both include a quite different and unnecessary supplement containing the word 'live'. Each version exhibits – at a different place – one of the commonest characteristic differences between Sam–Kgs and its core. Any future attempt to reconstruct the text of BoTH must identify what is common not just to Sam–Kgs in Chr in MT but to a wider of range of witnesses.

Questions such as the following arise naturally out of synoptic David and the death of Saul:

1. Why was Saul followed as king by David, who was not of his family? For two reasons: (1) because all Saul's sons, or at least all his able-bodied sons, had died with him on the battlefield (1 Sam 31:6–7); and (2) because David had previously been Saul's commander-in-chief (2 Sam 5:2).
2. If David had previously been Saul's commander-in-chief, what was his relationship with Saul's sons? Jonathan had died with his father on Gilboa. Had David been friend or rival to Saul's son and heir?
3. We read in BoTH (2 Sam 6:16) that, as David brings the ark into Jerusalem, he is despised by Michal, termed significantly 'Saul's daughter'. How to explain this? Was there a previous relationship? Had the brave commander previously married the king's daughter, as in many good stories – and often in history too?
4. In BoTH, 'asking' (*š'l*) is associated only with David and Solomon: they alone 'ask Yahweh'; and only of them do others 'ask' (make requests). Their immediate predecessor bears the cognate name 'Asked' (*šā'ûl*). Did Shaul also ask Yahweh, even if this is not reported?

5. Why did Saul fail against the Philistines, but David succeed? Is this related to the previous question: David asked Yahweh (שאל ביהוה) before he engaged in battle (2 Sam 5:19,23), but Saul did not or could not?
6. Why, if David had been commander-in-chief, was he not at Gilboa?

These issues arise naturally out of synoptic David and the death of Saul. Such questions are just waiting for able story-tellers to provide the answers; and many of the answers are organic developments out of BoTH. The synoptic text supplies not only the questions, but also much of the material for the answers. Of course, the author[s] of Samuel may have had alternative sources available to help answer some of these questions. However, since we have at best internal evidence for such sources, it may be better to give credit to creative storytellers, when we can at least identify some of the problems they had wanted to solve.

2 David and Jeroboam in Samuel and Kings

I propose that the narrator[s] responsible for the latter chapters of 1 Samuel and for 1 Kgs 11–14 (and especially ch. 11) thought together the two triangular relationships identified above. For both David and Jeroboam, what BoTH had sketched in flashback is now told in real time – and more expansively. Jeroboam's origins, his early career, and his flight from Solomon to Egypt, are now narrated not after but *within* the Solomon story (1 Kgs 11:26–40). And the acted parable of the torn cloak is moved to an earlier position within the narrative, to help motivate Jeroboam's flight: he has received a word from the deity before he escapes from Solomon. The new narrator not only moves some of the pieces on the Solomon / Jeroboam chess-board but also adds two new pieces. One gives explicit recognition to what had been implicit in BoTH: the similar situations of David and Jeroboam. Using language from Nathan in BoTH (2 Sam 7:16) the torn-cloak prophet now promises Jeroboam a בית נאמן (1 Kgs 11:38): provided he is obedient, he will be a new David. The second piece helps explain why what was originally reported in flashback is now being retold in real time: it is not Rehoboam's kingdom that is being divided but Solomon's (11:31), and divided because of Solomon's religious mistakes (11:33) – only, not in Solomon's lifetime (11:34–35).

David makes these important contributions to the retelling of the early Jeroboam; but Jeroboam contributes much more to the retelling of the early David. Flight from the old king helps explain why the one-time commander-in-chief was not with his king for the decisive battle with Philistines. David enjoyed success in Philistine territory (1 Sam 27), like Jeroboam in Egypt. And David too had been addressed by a prophet about kingship while the old king was still alive (1 Sam 16). The authors of 1 Samuel used the Jeroboam framework as they explored the David and Saul questions identified above. Of course, David accumulating features from other characters in BoTH is no scholarly novelty: it has long been observed that El-Hanan killed Goliath (in 2 Sam 21:18–22 // 1 Chr 20:4–8) before David did (in 1 Sam 17)![11]

Moving more specifically to the theme of this volume, there has been much discussion of the narrative architecture of 1 Sam 24–26; and other participants have contributed to it. One debate that goes backward and forwards concerns the relative priority of the two very similar stories of David when he has Saul in his power: what should he do with his rival? In my commentary, I opted for 1 Sam 24 as prior. I do not want to argue that again here, but simply note in possible support that David cutting part of Saul's cloak in the cave (1 Sam 24:4–6) may carry an echo of Shemaiah's acted parable in front of Jeroboam with the robe torn in tatters (1 Kgs 12:24o). Schenker argues (226–27), I think successfully, that in the older shorter story of Jeroboam this acted parable meant threat rather than promise: 'Take these pieces if you like. They represent most of a robe, but it's in tatters and may not do you any good.'

When we read 1 Samuel from start to finish, 1 Sam 24 reminds us of Saul tearing Samuel's robe back in 1 Sam 15. Of course, 1 Sam 15 like 1 Sam 26 may be from a later stage in the growth of 1 Samuel than 1 Sam 24. Whatever the truth of that, if instead we see the scene in the cave from the perspective of Shemaiah and Jeroboam in BoTH, David may have realised (before it was too late) that cutting Saul's robe could presage dividing the kingdom he hoped to inherit. If 1 Sam 24 was older than 1 Sam 25–26, then it is more likely that it resonated with the older form of the Jeroboam story.

Several details of the David-Nabal-Abigail story use elements already part of the old Jeroboam tale in BoTH.

- Nabal rejects David (1 Sam 25:10) in a double question, with 'David' and 'son of Jesse' in unusual parallel ('Who is David, and who the son of Jesse?'), modelled on Israel rejecting Rehoboam (1 Kgs 12:24t).[12]
- David's retort is drawn from the same text: he tells his men he will leave Nabal with none to piss on a wall (1 Sam 25:22) and repeats the phrase as he assures Abigail of what he would have done had she not intervened (25:34). This expression occurs just once in BoTH, in Shemaiah's oracle to Jeroboam's wife (1 Kgs 12:24m).

---

11 AULD 2011: 13.
12 Sheba ben Bichri will do the same in 2 Sam 20:1.

However, both of these details are also part of the developed Jeroboam narrative; and we cannot be sure which stage of that story influenced David in the
desert. Other details clearly align the David-Nabal-Abigail story with the expanded account of Jeroboam.

– Abigail speaks to David rather like Shemaiah and Ahijah, the two men of
  God with oracles for Jeroboam (25:28,30). Like Ahijah addressing Jeroboam
  (1 Kgs 11:38; 14:7), she takes both נגיד and בית נאמן from Nathan's words
  to David in BoTH (2 Sam 7:9,16).[13]

Further links between 1 Sam 25 and 1 Kgs 11 are mediated by the Abner episode
in 2 Sam 3.

– When Abner comes to David with a group of men (2 Sam 3:20), David makes
  a feast for him – the only משתה in the books of Samuel apart from Nabal's,
  from which David and his men were excluded (1 Sam 25:36).
– At that party, Abner (2 Sam 3:21) makes the same promise to David as Ahijah
  will make to Jeroboam (1 Kgs 11:37): ומלכת בכל אשר־תאוה נפשך – 'you
  will be king in all that your *nephesh* desires'.
– David laments that Abner (2 Sam 3:33) has died like a fool / Nabal; and
  he regrets that Abner has fallen before בני עולה (3:34), scoundrels known
  elsewhere in the narrative books only in 2 Sam 7:10 (BoTH).[14]
– Delicious wordplay in 1 Sam 25:34,36 between *mšth* (feast) and *mštyn* (pissing) reinforces the 1 Sam 25 – 2 Sam 3 – 1 Kgs 11 link. David recalls to
  Abigail the threat against Nabal he had made to his men, 'there won't be
  left for Nabal till morning light anyone pissing on the wall' (עד אור הבקר
  משתין בקיר). She then goes back to her house and finds her husband: 'and
  he had a feast in his house like the king's feast' (והנה־לו משתה בביתו
  כמשתה המלך); but says not a word to him 'till morning light' (עד אור
  הבקר). When she does speak to him at morning-light, he is effectively finished too.

Similarities between the earlier accounts in BoTH of David succeeding Saul and
Jeroboam succeeding Solomon encouraged authors of the prequel in 1 Samuel
to BoTH to use the outline of Jeroboam in exile as they mapped David in flight
from Saul. Much of their detail was also drawn from the older royal narrative.

---

13 This theme is also anticipated in the threat to Eli in 1 Sam 2:35.
14 The fact that יסף hiphil is also used in both 2 Sam 3:34 and 7:10 makes it more likely that
3:34 has drawn on synoptic 7:10.

3 From BoTH to 1 Samuel

1 Samuel represents an extension – a projection – into earlier time of the David story told in BoTH. But it is also much more than a prequel to the familiar story: in important respects 1 Samuel takes us into a new story-world. Several minor elements of the synoptic David story play a much more prominent role in non-synoptic Samuel; and five of these will be briefly examined. All of them extend the narrative, but some clearly alter it as well. I would take 'asking of God / Yahweh' (שאל באלהים\ביהוה) as an example of simple extension, whereas prostration (השתחוה) before a human, concern with the king's 'life', and the category 'Yahweh's anointed' seem better examples of the second; and address-ing the king as 'my lord [king]' (אדני [המלך]) is harder to pronounce on. Each of these expressions is not only rare in BoTH but also rare elsewhere in HB.

1 Though at first sight 'to ask [of] Yahweh / God' is not a remarkable expression, its usage within HB is restricted to Judges and Samuel[15] – שאל ב is found 3 × elsewhere,[16] but never שאל ביהוה or שאל באלהים. We find the end of the Judg-es / Samuel series in 2 Sam 5:19,23 (//1 Chr 14:10,14), where David twice seeks divine clearance before attacking Philistines, and twice receives a positive re-sponse. These are the only synoptic instances; and, I suspect, far from marking the last of the series, they are the start of it all. What is reported twice about synoptic David is anticipated three times about non-synoptic David:

- In 1 Sam 23:2,4, before defending Keilah against Philistine attack, David also puts the question to the deity twice, just as in 2 Sam 5 – and Philistines are again the enemy.
- In 1 Sam 30:8, David asks before attacking Amalekites.
- In 2 Sam 2:1, the context is no longer explicitly military, but David's ques-tion is again in two parts: 'Shall I go up into any of the cities of Judah?' 'Yes.' 'To which shall I go up?' 'To Hebron.'

Where David always succeeds in his asking, Saul is never successful. The con-trast between the two kings is all the more obvious, because Philistines are the enemy putting pressure both on Saul in 1 Sam 14:37 and 28:6, and on David in 1 Sam 23:2,4 and 2 Sam 5:19,23.

The phrase is used in just two further contexts. Saul accuses the priest Ahi-melech of treason claiming that he had consulted the deity on behalf of Saul's rival David (1 Sam 22:10,13,15). And my last example is in fact the first that we

---

15 Apart from synoptic 1 Chr 14:10,14.

16 במשפט (Num 27:21) or בתרפים (Ezek 21:26) or בעצו (Hos 4:12).

meet in the book (1 Sam 10:21–22). שָׁאוּל בֶּן־קִישׁ is identified by lot as the divinely chosen king; but he cannot be found because he is hiding, and his location is discovered by 'asking of Yahweh'. This is not the first time that the verb שָׁאַל is used in the story of Saul;[17] but it is the first time that this verb is used so close to the name שָׁאוּל. Here Saul is not the subject of the enquiry, but its object. This asking by the people succeeds, just like each asking by David; but on each occasion when Saul initiates the asking, he fails. The whole series of 'askings' is part of a new narrative prologue that sets out to explain the opening stages of an older text (BoTH): Saul has faced the Philistines and been killed, and there has been no mention of Yahweh; David becomes king, consults Yahweh, and defeats the Philistines.[18]

2 The only instance of prostration within the synoptic David story comes at its end (2 Sam 24:20 // 1 Chr 21:21). When the Jebusite saw David and his men approaching, he went out and prostrated himself before the king. The verb הִשְׁתַּחֲוָה will occur in only three other contexts in BoTH: Solomon is warned against prostration before other gods (1 Kgs 9:6,9 // 2 Chr 7:19,22); Manasseh is blamed for prostration before the host of heaven (2 Kgs 21:3 // 2 Chr 33:3); and the Assyrian envoy tells Hezekiah's people that their king had instructed prostration before one particular altar in Jerusalem (2 Kgs 18:22 // 2 Chr 32:12). In all four cases in the BoTH narrative, a foreign element is present: there should be no prostration before 'other' gods; one non-Israelite prostrates before David; and another non-Israelite quotes – or misquotes – Hezekiah. You can't trust foreigners.

In non-synoptic Samuel, eight other characters prostrate before David: Abigail (1 Sam 25:23,41), the Amalekite who reports Saul's death (2 Sam 1:2), Mephibosheth (9:6,8), the wise woman from Tekoa (14:4), Joab (14:22), Absalom (14:33), Ziba (16:4), and Ahimaaz (18:28). Suitors also prostrate before Absalom (15:5), as does the Cushite messenger before Joab (18:21). And David himself prostrates before Jonathan (1 Sam 20:41) and Saul (24:9). David is involved in almost every scene, and even the two exceptions are very close to his person: Absalom his son and Joab his senior commander. The picture is similar in non-synoptic Kings. Bathsheba prostrates before David (1 Kgs 1:16,31), as does Nathan (1:23). Then both David (1:47) and Adonijah (1:53) prostrate before Solo-

---

17 It is not the first time we have met the verb שָׁאַל at all within the story of Saul. That comes in 1 Sam 10:4, where Samuel promises Saul a sign: three men will meet him and greet him – will wish him well (וְשָׁאֲלוּ לְךָ לְשָׁלוֹם).

18 Outer portions of the book of Judges (1:1; 18:5; 20:18,23,27) take up the theme of asking Yahweh; but that belongs to another topic.

mon, as does Solomon himself before his mother Bathsheba (2:19). Only two instances in Samuel–Kings are unrelated to David or to the Solomon of 1 Kgs 1–2: 'the sons of the prophets' prostrate before Elisha, recognizing him as *successor* to Elijah (2 Kgs 2:15), as does the Shunammite woman (4:37). And the very fact of a *succession* from Elijah to Elisha is suggestive of their quasi-regal – or alternatively regal – portrayal. Elsewhere in HB, we find prostration before a human mostly in parts of Genesis.[19]

3 There is a significant overlap between prostration before humans in Samuel–Kings and the use of the deferential 'my lord [king]' (אדני [המלך]).[20] The overlap is already noticeable in the synoptic tradition. Jebusite Araunah is the only character who prostrates before a human anywhere in BoTH. So too, the only synoptic instances of 'my lord king' are uttered by Joab and then the Jebusite in the same census narrative (2 Sam 24:3,22 // 1 Chr 21:3,23). Just as David is the only person to prostrate before Jonathan and Saul, so too only he addresses Saul as 'my lord king'; and he then addresses the Philistine Achish the same way.[21] David, prior to becoming king, expresses before current royal houses the deference that should become his due.[22] 'Lord' is paired with 'king' once each in relation to Solomon and Rehoboam, and three times in stories about Elisha.[23] Elsewhere in HB is it found only in 2 Kgs 18:23 // Isa 36:8; Jer 37:20; 38:9; and Dan 1:10.

4 BoTH reports only two anointings: of David and Joash, the only kings who did not immediately succeed to their fathers. The verb 'anointed' is plural in both 2 Sam 5:3 // 1 Chr 11:3 and 2 Kgs 11:12 // 2 Chr 23:11. In the case of David, 'the elders of Israel' are the subject. In the case of Joash, the subject of the verb 'anoint' is unstated (hence similarly general) in 2 Kgs 11:12, while the Chronicler supplies 'Jehoiada and his sons'. In neither case is there mention of divine initiative, such as we find in the narratives of Samuel anointing Saul and David (1 Sam 9:15–10:8; 16:1–13). The divine role in the anointing of Saul and David offers a narrative explanation of the title משיח יהוה ('Yahweh's anointed'). Be-

19 Gen 23:7; 27:29,29; 33:3,6,7,7; 37:10; 42:6; 43:26,28; 47:31; 48:12; 49:8; Exod 11:8; 18:7; Ruth 2:10; Esth 3:2,5.
20 [my] lord [king] from 2 Sam 24 + 1 Kgs 22 to 1 Sam 24:7,9,11; 25:10,14, 17,24,25,25,26, 26,27,27,28,28,29,30,31,31,31,41; 26:15,16,17,18,19. This is discussed in Kucová 2006: 248–49.
21 1 Sam 24:9; 26:15,17,19; 29:8.
22 2 Sam 3:21; 4:8; 9:11; 26 × in 2 Sam 13–19; and 12 × in 1 Kgs 1.
23 1 Kgs 2:38; 12:27; 2 Kgs 6:12,26; 8:5.

yond the 'prequel' narratives of Saul in David's power then mourned by him,[24] משיח יהוה is found in 8 psalms[25] and is rare elsewhere.[26]

5 I gave *Life in Kings* its title because חי \ חיה \ חיים (life / live / alive) are so much more prominent in Sam–Kgs than in BoTH. The proportions are no less striking for נפש: 4 × in BoTH and 78 ×[?] in non-synoptic Sam–Kgs.[27] Not only so: נפש and the חי-family never coincide in BoTH, though both are found (8 verses apart) in Solomon's long prayer.[28] However, their conjunction is another distinctive feature of our chapters. חי נפשך ("as your 'self' lives") occurs along-side the much commoner oath-formula חי יהוה ('as Yahweh lives') in 1 Sam 20:3 and 25:26 (and 8 × more in Sam–Kgs).[29] חי יהוה is used more frequently:

- once in BoTH (1 Kgs 22:14, and so not in its David story)
- 30 × in Sam–Kgs (more than half of these in the David story)
- And some 10 × elsewhere in HB[30]

נפש חיה ('living self') occurs 13 ×, mostly early in Genesis.[31] And נפש is obj. of חיה (in the sense of 'preserve life') some 10 ×.[32] Other usages are few (4 ×).[33]

About one-third of all instances of נפש and the חי-family combined are in Sam–Kgs, including every instance of חי נפשך – this oath-formula is unknown elsewhere in HB, and is in fact unique to stories involving David or Elisha. A few sentences after uttering it, Abigail demonstrates that her use of this unusual oath is far from simply formulaic by adding in explanation והיתה נפש אדני

---

24 1 Sam 24:7,7,11 and 26:9,11,16,23; 2 Sam 1:14,16,21.

25 Ps 2:2; 18:51; 20:7; 28:8; 84:10; 89:39,52; 105:15; 132:10,17. Ps 18 also appears as 2 Sam 22; and Ps 105:1–15 is included in 1 Chr 16:8–22 and Ps 132:8–10 in 2 Chr 6:41–42.

26 1 Sam 2:10, 35; 12:3,5; 16:6; 2 Sam 19:22; 23:1; Isa 45:1; Hab 3:13; Lam 4:20; Dan 9:25,26.

27 In non-synoptic Sam–Kgs it is used 74 × (32 × in 1 Sam, of which 4 × in the substantial MT + 1 Sam 17:55–18:5 – the others are 1 Sam 1:10,15,26; 2:16,33,35; 19:5,11; 20:1,3,4,17; 22:2,22,23; 23:15,20; 24:12; 25:26,29,29,29; 26:21,24,24; 28:9,21; 30:6).

28 נפש in 2 Sam 23:17 // 1 Chr 11:19; 1 Kgs 3:11 // 2 Chr 1:11; 1 Kgs 8:48 // 2 Chr 6:38; 2 Kgs 23:3 // 2 Chr 34:31; and חי etc indisputably in 1 Kgs 8:40 // 2 Chr 6:31; 1 Kgs 22:14 // 2 Chr 18:13; 2 Kgs 11:12 // 2 Chr 23:11; 2 Kgs 14:9,17 // 2 Chr 25:18,25 – in light of the earlier discussion of Jeroboam, 1 Kgs 12:6 // 2 Chr 10:6 has been removed from the list. It was argued in Life in Kings (29–30) that the plus in 1 Chr 11:8 about Joab 'letting live' or 'restoring to life' the remnant of Jerusalem should be taken seriously as witness to BTH; oddly, the plus in the parallel narrative (2 Sam 5:8) includes נפש דוד, although there is much textual variety over how that phrase relates to the verb 'hate' (AULD 2011: 394–95).

29 1 Sam 1:26; 17:55[M+]; 2 Sam 11:11; 14:19; 2 Kgs 2:2,4,6; 4:30.

30 AULD 2017: 33–34.

31 Gen 1:20,21,24,30; 2:7,19; 9:10,12,15,16; Lev 11:10,46; Ezek 47:9.

32 Gen 19:19; 1 Kgs 20:31; Isa 55:3; Jer 38:17,20; Ezek 13:18–19; 18:27; Ps 22:30; 119:175.

33 Ps 49:19; 66:9; Job 10:1; 12:10.

צְרוּרָה בִּצְרוֹר הַחַיִּים ('and my lord's self will be bound in the bundle of the living', 25:29).[34]

Persistent use of נפש starts with 1 Sam 19:5,11; of אדני in 20:38; and of השתחוה before a human with 20:41 – and the first instance of חי נפשך is in 20:3. Though both Saul and David were anointed at divine instigation in the first half of 1 Samuel, only in 1 Sam 24 and 26 are the implications explored of what it meant to be משיח יהוה. Each of these expressions may have its roots in BoTH; and their (minimal) role in synoptic David does warrant discussion elsewhere. As in BoTH, they play only a tiny part in the portrait of kingship in Israel and Judah that we find elsewhere in HB. By contrast, the role they play together in the books of Samuel (and to a lesser extent Kings) is quite novel and remarkable. Massed in the later chapters of 1 Samuel, they are elements of a narrated world that is *rooted* in BoTH yet *radically* different from it.

The later chapters of 1 Samuel develop relationships already implied in BoTH: David is compared with Jeroboam and is both contrasted and compared with Saul. But other pairings suggested in BoTH are also in play. I noted earlier that only stories relating to David and Solomon use שאל. In the account of Solomon's first vision, Yahweh promises him as a bonus what he had not asked for: ולא שאלת נפש איביך; and Abigail anticipates this promise to David.[35] Then, in BoTH, only David and Joash are anointed; a covenant is associated with both anointings; and Joash also reigns for 40 years. When Joash is anointed, the people also shout יחי המלך ('[long] live the king') – no empty formula: he was only seven, and all his siblings had been murdered. Abigail's והיתה נפש אדני צרורה בצרור החיים is an evocative elaboration of their shout. We could even propose יחי המלך as motto for the whole David-in-the-Desert story. Among her many qualities, Abigail was an intelligent reader of BoTH.

---

34 If I were determined to find a root in BoTH for as much as possible in Sam–Kgs, I would look to the poignant tale of David's heroes bringing him water from Bethlehem for the origin of בכל־אשר תאוה נפשך and related expressions. It is only there that BoTH uses any form of אוה; and one of only four instances of נפש is part of the same short episode.
35 1 Kgs 3:11 // 2 Chr 1:11 (though there the clause ends with שנאיך, 'your haters'); and 1 Sam 25:29.

Bibliography

Auld, A. Graeme. 1983. Prophets through the Looking Glass: Between Writings and Moses. *JSOT* 27:3–23.

Auld, A. Graeme. 1984. Prophets and Prophecy in Jeremiah and Kings. *ZAW* 96:66–82.

Auld, A. Graeme. 2004. Samuel at the Threshold: Selected Works of Graeme. SOTSM. Aldershot: Ashgate.

Auld, A. Graeme. 2011. I & II Samuel (OTL). Louisville KY: JKP.

Auld, A. Graeme. 2017. Life in Kings. Reshaping the Royal Story in the Hebrew Bible (AIL 30). Atlanta GA: SBL.

Auld, A. Graeme. 2020. Some Thoughts on the First Jeroboam. *BN* 185: 45-53.

Cross, Frank M.1973. Canaanite Myth and Hebrew Epic: Essays in the History of the Religion of Israel, Cambridge (MA): HUP.

Kucová, Lydie. 2006. Obeisance in the Biblical Stories of David. Pages 241–60 in *Reflection and Refraction: Studies in Biblical Historiography in Honour of A. Graeme Auld*. Edited by Robert Rezetko et al. VT.S 113. Leiden / Boston (MA): Brill.

Schenker, Adrian. 1996. 'Jéroboam et la division du royaume dans la Septante ancienne: LXX 1 R 12,24 a-z, TM 11–12; 14 et l'histoire deutéronomiste. Pages 193–236 in *Israël construit son histoire: L'historiographie deutéronomiste à la lumière des recherches récentes*. Edited by A. de Pury et al.MDB 34. Genève: Labor et Fides.

Talshir, Zipora. 1993. The Alternative Story, 3 Kingdoms 12:24A-Z. JBS 3. Jerusalem: Simor Ltd.

Trebolle Barrera, Julio. 2006. Kings (MT / LXX) and Chronicles: The Double and Triple Textual Tradition. Pages 483–501 in *Reflection and Refraction: Studies in Biblical Historiography in Honour of A. Graeme Auld*. Edited by Robert Rezetko et al. VT.S 113. Leiden / Boston (MA): Brill.

Hannes Bezzel

Saul and David – Stages of Their Literary Relationship

1 Point(s) of Departure

Within the so called "History of David's Rise", the relationship between Saul and David is the central theme along which the narrative unfolds. Like all inter-personal relationships, it undergoes some changes and developments. On a synchronic level, one may distinguish three phases: a) the young, handsome harpist, shepherd and warrior becomes more and more closely acquainted with the king (1 Sam 16–17); b) a relatively short honeymoon period in 1 Sam 18; and c) a long and nasty divorce of the two unequal partners in 1 Sam 19–27. This latter stage is full of jealousy and accusation, whether justified or not. Occasions of apparent reconciliation and remorse are not entirely absent (1 Sam 24; 26). Of course, all along there is more at stake than mere emotions, but it cannot be denied that love and fear are important factors in the advancement of the plot.

Viewed from a diachronic perspective, I think that all of the contributors to the current volume agree on the basic assumption that the literary relationship between Saul and David has undergone changes as well. In this article I attempt to trace some stages of this relationship.[1]

The presuppositions that shape this endeavour rest upon theories about or insights into the redaction history of the Books of Samuel in general and in detail. With these presuppositions, however, I am about to leave the domain of agreement common to all participants of our symposium. These four points of departure are:

1. There is a rather widespread theory that the "History of David's Rise" does not represent a once independent source or tradition,[2] as was Leonhard Rost's

---

[1] Within the last two decades, a large number of published monographs and articles has given witness to the current scholarly interest in the literature about the "Early Monarchic Period" and its protagonists, especially Saul and David. As a *pars pro toto* see DIETRICH 2004, and ADAM 2007.

[2] But note that, for example, Jacob Wright works with an independent David story (cf. WRIGHT 2014: 35–39), and Jeremy Hutton tries to find two independent sources which he labels HDR$_1$ and HDR$_2$ (cf. HUTTON 2009: 263).

Note: I would like to express my thanks to my friend and colleague Paul Keim, Goshen (IN), for correcting and improving my English. Of course, all remaining mistakes are my own.

https://doi.org/10.1515/9783110606164-008

idea,[3] but should be seen as a work of literature written for the purpose of connecting traditions about Saul on the one hand and David on the other.[4] Whether or not the authors of this integrated narrative made use of traditional material is another matter, and in my view, one of the main issues to be addressed in this symposium.

2. As Wellhausen and Budde have noted,[5] the bridgehead for this "History of David's Rise" can be seen in 1 Sam 14:52. This verse is an early addition to what I have called Saul's obituary, which originally rounded off the oldest Saul tradition in chapters 9–10*; 11*; 14*.[6] However, this does not mean that all the material between 1 Sam 14:52 and 2 Sam 5 should be regarded as belonging to this early redactional link between the traditions about Saul and David.

3. Based on observations about the different ways in which Saul's death is depicted after his obituary in chapter 14, in 1 Sam 31 and 2 Sam 1, I am led to conclude that 1 Sam 31:1–13* and 1 Sam 29:1, 11b should be understood as segments of an expanded Samuel-Saul-narrative which was still composed before it was connected with the material about David. This extended Samuel-Saul-Cycle is structured by references to the respective deployments of the Philistine army. These notations can be found similarly phrased in 1 Sam 4:1^{LXX}; 13:5; 17:1; 29:1[7] – and, on a secondary level, in 28:4 and 28:1.[8] In between we find the story of Saul and David's relationship.

Another observation is that 1 Sam 31 shows no interest in, or even knowledge of, a character named David. Taken by itself, it tells the story of a great king's heroic end.[9]

This last point looks quite different in 2 Sam 1. There the focus is no longer on Saul but on David. Generally following the analysis made by Alexander Fischer,[10] I have identified a basic layer of this chapter in 2 Sam 1:1aα. bα.2aα²·β.3.4.11.12a.bα¹β¹¹ and ascribed it to a first, or at least early, version of

---

3 Cf. Rost 1926: 132 f.
4 Cf. the independent studies by White 2000: 281 f., and Kratz 2000: 182–86. *Pace*, for example, Vermeylen, who has "[d]e 1 S 11 à 2 S 7 [...] un 'récit de base', cohérent, unifié par une logique narrative constante" (Vermeylen 2000: 484).
5 Cf. Wellhausen ⁴1963: 252; Budde 1902: 103.
6 Cf. Bezzel 2013: 340; Bezzel 2015: 143–47; 204–7.
7 Cf. Bezzel 2015: 229 f.
8 Cf. Veijola 2004: 264.
9 Cf. Bezzel 2015: 231.
10 Cf. Fischer 2004: 18–23, with 2 Sam 1:1aα.2aα2βγ, 3–4.11.12*, 17, 18aα (ויאמר), 19–27.
11 Cf. Bezzel 2015: 132.

a "History of David's Rise".[12] It may be understood, according to point 1 above, as a link between the once independent traditions about Saul and David. In what follows, this last result will have to be scrutinized once again.[13] For the time being, a slight modification of my statement will be in order: 1 Sam 31* does not *necessarily* know a "History of David's Rise" – but 2 Sam 1 *clearly* presupposes it – whatever its shape may have been. Taken together with 1 Sam 14:52, these episodes represent the two fixed points between which the net of the Saul-David relationship could be spread out.

4. Related to the question of how David originally found his way to Saul's court – whether as a player of the lyre, as related in chapter 16, as an armour bearer, as 16:21[14] has it, or as the one who killed the elite warrior of the Philistines, I think that Erik Aurelius has made a compelling case in favour of the latter option.[15] Whether a basic layer of chapter 16 once belonged to an independent source or rather should be explained in terms of a *Fortschreibung*, is not a crucial matter at this point in the discussion. However, I would tend to favour the second option, primarily based on the principle of Ockham's razor.[16] Second, the proposed original continuation of these supposed two independent versions of a Saul-David-story does not seem totally convincing to me.[17] Third, because 1 Sam 16:14–23 can be understood as an addition to 16:1–13. Again, I refer to Erik Aurelius who states, (*nota bene* using the subjunctive mood):

---

12 Cf. BEZZEL 2015: 236 f.

13 Cf. below, p. 174 f.

14 Cf. HEINRICH 2009: 125. The problem with Heinrich's idea of an isolated verse 16:21 as connecting link to 14:52 is that the reader is confronted with a certain "David" who has not been introduced before.

15 Cf. AURELIUS 2002: 64–66; see also Peter Porzig's contribution to this volume and his hint to Reinhard Kratz' change of mind in this question as it is displayed by the difference between the German and the English version of his "Komposition der erzählenden Bücher" (cf. PORZIG in this book).

16 Cf. AURELIUS 2002: 45.

17 *Pace* HUTTON 2009: 263. Hutton's HDR₁ begins with "1 Sam 16:14–23; 17:1–11,32–40,42–48a,49,51–54; 18:6aβb*–8a*,9,12a,13–16,20–21a,22–26a,27–29a" (ibid.), whereas his HDR₂ consists of "1 Sam 17:12* (with beginning emended to ויהי איש אפרתי...ושמו ישׁי, and with original ארבעה),13–14,16–18,20–23a,24–30,41,48b,(50),55–58; 18:1–2,(3),4–5,8b,(10–11a),12b,17–18*29b–30" (ibid.). To my mind, narrative problems in this independent HDR₂ appear in 17:16 (who is "the Philistine", הפלשתי, who suddenly appears on stage?) as well as in the transition between 17:30 and 17:41 with the Philistine approaching David all of a sudden and without reason.

"[D]ieses Stück [viz. 1 Sam 16:14–23] müßte aber nicht deshalb eine selbständige Überlieferung gewesen, sondern könnte eine Fortschreibung von 16,1–13 sein."[18]

2 Saul and David – An Amicable Relationship?

It is with these four presuppositions in mind that the literary-historical development of David and Saul's relationship between 1 Sam 17 and 2 Sam 1 shall be considered. My initial and leading question is simply whether or not the literary motif of Saul's change of attitude towards David was a constituent part of the "History of David's Rise" from the beginning, or whether the antagonism of the two players might represent a further elaborated form of the story.

Let me introduce two basic observations which might throw light on this question.

2.1 The flight-rescue-pattern

As stated above, that which I call the expanded narrative cycle of Samuel and Saul ("die erweiterte Saulüberlieferung") has been structured by means of references to the deployment of the Philistine army. Similarly – and different at the same time – there is a structuring element between 1 Sam 19 and 27 that binds the episodes of David's wanderings together. It consists of a formula like "and David fled to X" or "David escaped to Y" (using the roots ברח or מלט) – and, correspondingly, a phrase stating that Saul got wind of the refugee's whereabouts: "and Saul got to know that David was in Y" (with ידע). Accordingly, David flees or escapes in 1 Sam 19:18; 20:1; 21:11; 22:1; 27:1, and Saul comes to know where to find him in 19:19; 22:6; 23:7; 24:2; 26:1; 27:4. By means of this simple stylistic device, the respective chapters appear as one long "cat and mouse game"[19] that sends David on a tour from Benjamin through Judah with a side-trip to Gath.[20] Put differently, this flight and rescue pattern is the string on which the pearls of the separate episodes are strung.

---

18 "This piece [viz. 1 Sam 16:14–23] has not to be seen necessarily as an independent tradition but might as well have been a *Fortschreibung* of 16:1–13" (AURELIUS 2002: 65); cf. HEINRICH 2009: 123 f.

19 EDENBURG 2016: 479.

20 Cf. ADAM 2007: 97. For a more detailed analysis of this pattern, see also Cynthia Edenburg's contribution to this volume, EDENBURG in this book, speaking of a "flight and pursuit theme" (ibid.).

There are some irregularities in this pattern, though:

First, David flees from Najot in Rama in 20:1 but does not arrive at another place before 21:2, where we read that, he simply "comes" to Nob (ויבא דוד נבה). In between we find the touching and lengthy episode of Jonathan and David's covenant and farewell. It doesn't take a radical critic to doubt that the broadly extended material on the special friendship between Jonathan and David is part of the oldest material.[21]

Second, there is the exception of chapters 24–26. The episode about David and Abigail – or David, Nabal, and Abigail – (ch. 25) is self-explanatory in this context. Saul plays no part in this story whatsoever. The absence of any reference to David's flight at the end of chapter 24 is not surprising either, since both adversaries depart in peace. Likewise, no flight is necessary at the transition from chapter 23 to 24. Saul ceases his persecution of David due to a Philistine attack which he has to deal with urgently. The interruption comes just at the moment when a direct confrontation of the rivals seems imminent (1 Sam 23:27 f.). But even apart from these compositional aspects, fleeing would not be in the nature of David as he is depicted in chapters 24 and 26. This David acts in just the opposite way. When he receives intelligence that Saul and his men have approached his hiding place, he does not try to rescue himself but dares to perform a risky exploit. On the other hand, his final decision to avoid possible further confrontation with Saul in 27:1 does not fully fit this heroic and noble image of the king-to-be. Perhaps, in this case he displays more common sense instead.

For my present purpose, I would like to put chapters 24–26 into brackets, referring the reader to the papers by Natan Evron and Alexander Fischer in this volume[22] as well as to an earlier article by Cynthia Edenburg.[23] I will look instead at the third exception to the flight-rescue pattern.

This third exception can be found in the story about David in Keïla (ch. 23). At the beginning of this episode, the reader is not under the impression that David is fleeing. Instead, he is told of an emergency situation in Keïla and feels responsible to intervene on behalf of the residents of the town. It is not before v. 7 that Saul comes onto the scene, in a way that is not very well integrated into the rescue story, which already ends in v. 6.[24] Saul attempts to take advantage of the situation and capture David immediately. According to v. 7 he reasons that David has become trapped in a walled city. Accordingly, he starts to besiege

---

21 Cf. KRATZ 2000: 185.
22 Cf. EVRON in this book.
23 Cf. EDENBURG 1998.
24 Cf. VEIJOLA 1990: 29.

Keïla in 23:8. Nowhere in v. 1–6 is it mentioned that David has gone *into* the town, though. Rather, he simply travels *to* Keïla to defeat the Philistines. I will come back to a more detailed analysis of chapter 23 below.[25]

Bearing these primary observations in mind, I would like to draw a tentative conclusion. Whereas chapters 20 and 24–26 appear to be secondary to the flight-rescue-pattern – or at least might well be seen that way – in chapter 23 the situation is different. Here, matters are quite the reverse. It is the flight-persecution-pattern in verses 7–13 that is secondary to the story related in 23:1–6*.

With this in mind, we turn to David's affiliation with Achish of Gath[26] in chapter 27. According to Walter Dietrich, Jacob Wright and others, the framing of the story around the motif of David on the run is secondary here too.[27] It may be less obvious than in chapter 23, but it is at least possible to separate a beginning of this episode in 27:2 ("and David rose and went over [...] to Achish, Son of Maoch, king of Gath") from the notes about flight and persecution in 27:1,4.

With the suspicion that the flight-rescue-pattern might be secondary to a basic layer of the narrative in 1 Sam 17–2 Sam 1, one might naturally surmise that the entire motif of Saul persecuting David, and with it the enmity between both protagonists as a whole, could be secondary as well.

2.2 De mortuis nil nisi bene

The next observation is rather modest. The basic layer of 2 Sam 1 as proposed above, with David receiving the message of Saul's death on Mount Gilboa, does not tell the reader of any preceding confrontational history between the two. This does not necessarily mean much in light of the fact that the son of Jesse finds himself in a situation overshadowed by *de mortuis nil nisi bene*.

However, the *Fortschreibung*, which transforms the ragged messenger from the battlefield into "the young man who was reporting to him" (הנער המגיד לו),[28] signifies that the author of this literary layer was well aware of the enmity between David and Saul. Here the messenger's ill-fated attempt to please the

---

25 See below, p. 173–6, Veijola 1990, and Müller in this book.

26 During the conference, one main aspect of the discussion was the relation of 1 Sam 27* to a basic layer of the "History of David's Rise". I am thankful to all participants, and I have tried to integrate their questions and comments into this published version of the paper.

27 Cf. Dietrich 2019: 16 f., with 1 Sam 27:2,3a,6,7(8a); Wright 2014: 36, with 1 Sam 27:2–3a,[5–6],7–11; Heinrich 2009: 360, with 1 Sam 27:1–6*; see also Kipfer in this book, with 1 Sam 27:2,3a,5–12.

28 The identification of this unhappy person as an "Amalekite" in v. 8 happens on an even later stage of the literary development, cf. Bezzel 2015: 141.

king by handing over the royal insignia is recounted.[29] If the author of this stratum would not have known about some kind of conflict between the deceased and the future king, no doubt both characters would have acted differently in this scene. It is noteworthy that the "young man" is pictured as a counterpart to David himself. What the son of Jesse abstained from in chapters 24 and 26, this person is found guilty of, viz., laying a hand on the anointed one of YHWH (2 Sam 1:14, cf. 1 Sam 24:7,11; 26:9,11,23).

In contrast to this, on the level of the assumed basic layer in 2 Sam 1, things look differently. Here, when informed of the terrible defeat, David reacts with the appropriate mourning rites, as might be expected. Alexander Fischer has pointed out the parallels with 1 Sam 4.[30] So it is *de mortuis nil nisi bene* in both cases. The crucial difference is that the basic layer of 2 Sam 1 does not give any hint of a prior conflict between Saul and David. Yet such a conflict is clearly presupposed in the second layer. This observation does not constitute decisive proof, of course. But it is another piece of circumstantial evidence in favour of the hypothesis that a first version of the "History of David's Rise" was far less conflictual than its final form.

A third observation points back to chapter 18. This is the key passage for everything that follows when it comes to questioning the basic layer of the "History of David's Rise". Here we see the relationship between Saul and David at its height. At the same time we see the estrangement between them, or rather Saul's change of attitude. And we see this happen not once but several times. It has often been noted with surprise that the king offers his rival the chance to become his son-in-law while he was already "eyeing" him (18:9) and "fearing him" (18:5). If one does not want to attribute this incompatible behaviour to Saul's desolate mental constitution, a closer look at the literary stratification of 1 Sam 18 is necessary.

3 1 Sam 18

3.1 Long version and short version in 1 Sam 18

1 Sam 18 is the key chapter for analysing the "History of David's Rise" – and it is key for basic methodical discussions as well. The reason for the latter is the

---

29 This second layer of 2 Sam 1 would have comprised vv. 1aβ.bβ,2aα$_1$,b,5–7,9,10,13–16, cf. BEZZEL 2015: 140; see also FISCHER 2004: 32–36, and already BUDDE 1902: 193.
30 Cf. FISCHER 2004: 18–23.

fact that the well-known text-critical crux of 1 Sam 17 reaches over into chapter 18. There is a long version, represented by MT and the so-called Lucianic Greek text. There is also a short version (though containing notable pluses over the MT).[31] It is represented by the non-Lucianic Greek witnesses, for example, and most prominently, by Codex Vaticanus. As with the situation in chapter 17, there is reason to believe that a reconstruction of how these versions are related may never be a matter of scholarly consensus.

Three models are currently in circulation that attempt to explain the existence of both the long and the short version. 1) LXX[B] represents the *lectio brevior*, and should therefore be seen as the older version, whereas the pluses in the MT derive from later additions to the proto-Masoretic text.[32] 2) MT represents the *lectio difficilior* and should therefore be preferred over the short version, which is the result of deliberate elisions.[33] And finally, 3) there is the source-critical option, which regards the short version on the one hand and the pluses on the other as representatives of two independent traditions.[34] There used to be a fourth hypothesis suggesting that the differences between the long and the short version should be ascribed to either the translators of the Old Greek or to redactional alterations made in the course of the development of the Greek text. This option, however, may be ruled out due to studies in Septuagintal translation technique carried out over the past three decades,[35] beginning with Emanuel Tov's contribution to the important volume edited by Barthélemy, Gooding, Lust, and Tov.[36]

As for the remaining three hypotheses, it can be said that perhaps all arguments in favour or against each of them have been put on the table. The situation may be described best with the famous saying by the Bavarian artist Karl Valentin:

"Es ist schon alles gesagt, nur noch nicht von allen".[37]

Nevertheless, it is necessary to clarify my own point of view in this question. I will confine myself to highlighting the two points of contention which to me seem the most important:

---

31 These are to be found in 1 Sam 17:36,40,43.
32 Cf., for example, AULD 2004: 122 f., see also AULD and HO 1992: 19 f.; VERMEYLEN 2000: 101–6; ADAM 2007: 142; DRIESBACH 2016: 74 (with respect to 18:5 only).
33 Cf., for example, ROFÉ 2015: 69.
34 Cf., for example, HUTTON 2009: 263.
35 Cf. TOV 1986: 45; Wirth, in his 2016 monograph, does not even address the question but seems to take it for granted that the *Old Greek* would represent a Hebrew *Vorlage* par to par (cf. WIRTH 2016: 24, 233).
36 Cf. BARTHÉLEMY ET AL. 1986.
37 "Everything may already have been said, but not yet by everyone".

1. The differences between both textual versions are not coincidental but the result of deliberate redactional activity.[38]
2. In addition, the most crucial point seems to be that the short version, as represented by LXX[B], "in 20,8 und 18,6 f. die nur in MT vorhandenen Verse 18,3 bzw. 18,5 voraussetzt".[39]

Therefore, of the three options mentioned above I prefer option 2 *in general*: The long version, as represented by the MT, is prior to the short version as represented by LXX[B]. "In general" means that it is nevertheless possible that in the case of some of the minor pluses of the MT, it is LXX[B] which preserves the older text.

In chapter 18, the situation is as follows: The beginning in 18:1–5 (along with the end of chapter 17) is lacking in the short text. There is no reference to Jonathan's love for David, of David's being taken to Saul's house (18:2), nor any mention of David being appointed the king's general (18:5). Furthermore the short text contains no reference to an evil spirit descending upon Saul nor the attack with the spear in 18:10–11,12b; the king's first marriage scheme including Merab in 18:17–19, and the final reference to the Philistine leaders and David's continuing success in 18:30. There are, of course, other differences in detail as well.

In the case of 18:1–5, the situation is clearly in favour of an MT priority. According to the line of argument delineated above, the David-Jonathan motif in 18:1,3,4 and the closure of the Goliath story in 18:2,5 must be attributed to different hands.[40]

So along with Erik Aurelius and André Heinrich, I would maintain that the majority of the differences between the long and the short versions are due to deliberate shortening of the former by the *Vorlage* of the latter. This is especially the case when it comes to the end of the David and Goliath story. Here the missing pieces clearly extend over literary seams, in our case over the (secondary) first reference to the David-Jonathan-motif (18:1,3,4), and the closure of the Goliath story in 18:2,5. With the evil spirit, Saul's attack and the non-marriage of Merab, things might be different. Here, the MT pluses embrace coherent segments, each dealing with one specific topic respectively. Furthermore, they duplicate certain actions of Saul, e.g., his throwing of the spear and his plan to

---

38 Cf. AULD 2004: 125.

39 "That it presupposes in 20:8 and 18:6 f. the verses 18:3 and 18:5 respectively, which are extant only in MT" (AURELIUS 2002: 48; cf. BARTHÉLEMY 1986: 50). The case of 20:8 referring back to 18:3 seems to me to be more striking than the one of 18:6, *necessarily* referring to 18:3.

40 Cf. AURELIUS 2002: 60, n. 68; HEINRICH 2009: 178.

marry David to one of his daughters. In this respect, they bear a certain resemblance to 4Q51's version of 1 Sam 11, with the clearly secondary account of Nahash the Ammonite's eye gouging. In the case of Nahash, Alexander Rofé speaks of a "characteristic midrashic feature: the duplication of biblical events."[41] This means that "a single deed of one hero is multiplied, thus being transformed into a salient aspect of his character."[42] A similar motivation could explain the potentially secondary addition of 18:10,11,12b and 18:17–19,21b. As in 1 Sam 11, where Nahash becomes "an inveterate 'eye-gouger'",[43] so Saul appears to be a notorious spear thrower and schemer of pernicious marriages in the aforementioned pluses.

3.2 The basic layer of 1 Sam 18

For the following considerations of the stratification of chapter 18, however, I will start from the Masoretic text, while at the same time trying not to lose track of the short version.

In 1 Sam 18 there are some signals which point to the successive growth of the text. Besides several changes in Saul's attitude towards David, which could be explained by his evidently bipolar or multipolar character, there is the simple observation that David's promotion, his military success, and the people's response to his personality are recounted at least two, perhaps even three times, in 18:5; 18:13–16 and 18:28–30. Even the short version of LXX[B] has David's "going out and coming in" (ἐξεπορεύετο καὶ εἰσεπορεύετο) twice, in 18:13 and 18:16. If one accepts *Wiederaufnahme* as a typical marker of redactional activity, as can best be illustrated in 1Sam 1–3[44] – and all over 1 Samuel – one may wonder which of the passages under consideration may belong to the oldest version of the story. Things are a little more complicated here than in other instances, however, and one should avoid any mechanical application of the criterion.

In comparing these passages with each other, many significant differences are evident. Perhaps the most important of these is that 18:12–16 emphasises both Saul's fear of his new rival and YHWH's presence with David. More precisely, vv. 12,14 include YHWH's presence with David while vv. 13,15,16 lack this motif. Verses 18:28–29 imply both the motif of rivalry and also YHWH's presence

---

41 ROFÉ 1982: 130.
42 ROFÉ 1998: 66.
43 ROFÉ 1982: 132.
44 Cf. WONNEBERGER 1992: 227–40; PORZIG 2009: 104–21; BEZZEL 2015: 185–88.

with David. V. 30, however, does not do so. It simply states that David was more successful than Saul's servants. Read synchronically, the root of Saul's jealousy lies in David's success. From a diachronic perspective this also holds true. The motif of David's success is the root and kernel of the entire development of the enmity between both characters.

In 18:5, as in 18:30, both aspects which are highlighted in vv. 12–16 and 28 f., i.e., the rivalry and YHWH's presence with David, are completely absent. I would therefore opt for 18:5 as the oldest instance of the promotion motif. Furthermore, one may doubt whether the success motif had to be separated from David's promotion – at least in this case. The note about David's going out and successfully coming back in 18:5aα seems oddly placed before his promotion to general. In what capacity would the king have sent him? This is even more evident when verses 3 and 4 about Jonathan and David are identified as secondary. Finally, one *could* become suspicious about the change of verb forms from the narrative tense to the – iterative – *yiqtol* of the relative clause. In light of these factors I would make a case for omitting 18:5aα, or at least the relative clause, and identify the basic layer as 18:5aβ.b (perhaps with, rather than without, the preceding "and David went out"). This verse should be understood as the original continuation of 18:2:

ויצא דוד וישמהו שאול על אנשי המלחמה וייטב בעיני כל־העם וגם בעיני עבדי שאול

"And David went out, and Saul set him over the men of war, and it was good in the eyes of the entire people and also in the eyes of the servants of Saul."

But if the success motif is secondary in 18:5, where does it come from originally? It may be worthwhile to compare the respective references:

18:5: בכל אשר ישלחנו שאול ישכיל – "in everything Saul would send him he would succeed".

18:14: ויהי דוד לכל־דרכו משכיל ויהוה עמו – "and David was successful in all his way, and YHWH was with him".

18:15: וירא שאול אשר הוא־משכיל מאד – "and Saul saw that he was very successful".

18:30 מאד: ויהי מדי צאתם שכל דוד מכל עבדי שאול וייקר שמו מאד – "and whenever they [i.e. the Philistines] went out, David had success, more than all the servants of Saul, and his name became very precious".

In v. 14 David's success is combined with YHWH's presence with him, and in v. 15, it is combined with the motif of Saul's jealousy, both of which are absent from 18:30. If 5aα is indeed secondary, I would give 18:30 preference over the other instances – despite its absence in LXX[B]. This formulation also gives a different impression of David's success than 18:14 and 18:15. In 18:30 certain actions of the young hero against the Philistines are crowned with success

(שכל, *qatal*), whereas in v. 14 and 15 we read the participle מַשְׂכִּיל, related to "all his way" in the first instance. "Having success" or rather "being successful" has become a part of David's character in general.

Let us turn back to the connection between 18:2.5aβ.b and the continuation of the narrative thread. The reconstruction of the basic layer of v. 5 makes it possible to recognise the *Wiederaufnahme* in 18:16. Again, David's going out and coming back is recounted, together with the affection that accrues to him as a result. But now, the subject of this love is "all Israel and Judah" (כל־ישראל ויהודה). As Erik Aurelius states: "alles dazwischen dürfte daher Zusatz sein".[45]

One may well argue that 18:30 would be the next *Wiederaufnahme* at the end of the chapter, and thus indicate that all the remaining material would be secondary as well. This may be tempting, but if I were to do so, I am sure that I would be criticised for being hypercritical – and rightly so (in this case at least).[46] The reason is simple: With our reconstruction of v. 5, 18:30 does not appear to be a repetition of 18:5 at all. It is rather understood as a continuation. In v. 5 David wins the hearts of the "servants of Saul". In v. 30 he proves to be more valiant than they. In v. 5 it is David who "goes out". In v. 30, the initiative of "going out" is said to be on the side of the enemy.

Thus, I would be quite reluctant to remove the entire wedding story from the basic layer of the chapter. There is little doubt that the entire episode about Saul's elder daughter Merab in vv. 17–19 is a later addition,[47] and perhaps even LXX[B] represents an earlier textual version in this case.[48] But what can be questioned is the original purpose of the entire wedding plan in the section about *Michal*. Two noticeable doublings can be found. David is told twice about Saul's plan to marry him to Michal. The first time he is told directly in v. 21, and then a second time, in secret, by Saul's servants in v. 23. This second report is quite pointless, following the direct conversation between the king and his future son-in-law. The first dialogue is necessary, however, since it serves as a literary device to introduce the Merab episode and thus belongs with it.

---

45 "Everything in between ought to be additions". AURELIUS 2002: 67.

46 Cf., considering and dismissing the possibility of 18:30 as a Wiederaufnahme of 18:16, AURELIUS 2002: 67.

47 Cf., for example, MOMMER 2004: 199; WILLI-PLEIN 2004: 150. The case of the latter is a little bit difficult, though. On the one hand, she declares that only Michal would belong to the basic layer (cf. ibid.), on the other hand she suggests this basic layer to consist of 18:2,5–9,16–30 (cf. WILLI-PLEIN 2004: 166). This would include Merab.

48 See above, p. 167. Jeremy Hutton, however, interprets the duplications, in this case 18:17–18*, as witnesses for another source, HDR₂ (cf. HUTTON 2009: 239–43). But, as Mommer states, even with an exclamation mark: "Die Doppelungen reichen bis in Einzelzüge hinein!" ("The doublings reach even into detailed narrative traits", MOMMER 2004: 199). This point speaks rather against independent sources.

In the passage about Michal, the dialogue between the king's servants and David takes place twice in a similar fashion, and there is a small but instructive case of a *Wiederaufnahme* to be noted at the end. The phrase לְהִתְחַתֵּן בַּמֶּלֶךְ, "to become the king's son-in-law", is highlighted in v. 22, v. 23, v. 26, and v. 27aα. Of course this is what the entire passage is about. It should be noted, however, that in the latter case, it corresponds with David's action to adduce the bride price in the form of the required Philistine foreskins. It thus raises the suspicion that this motif is also secondary. The theme itself, in turn, is closely connected with the entire *first* dialogue between Saul's servants and David in v. 23–26 as well as with v. 21, Saul's evil intentions "that the hand of the Philistines be against him" (וּתְהִי־בּוֹ יַד־פְּלִשְׁתִּים).

Taking all of this into consideration, the core of the marriage scene would comprise the king's initiative in 18:22, David being told of the proposal by the king's servants (who have been in favour of the young man since v. 5αβb at the latest) in 18:26 – and the execution of the plan in 18:27b. Erik Aurelius includes v. 28 in the basic layer, with the remark about Michal's love for David: "Letztere Bemerkung ist zugegebenermaßen nicht notwendig für die Grundschicht (oder für spätere Schichten), aber sie ist erfreulich und insofern auch angebracht, als Michal bald bei Davids Flucht die Loyalität mit dem Vater brechen wird."[49] However, v. 28 has the motif of YHWH's presence with David[50] which, as noted above, was one reason to suspect v. 12,14 of being secondary compared with v. 5*. Furthermore, that the flight of David was already part of the basic layer of the "History of David's Rise" should not be taken for granted. Indeed, it is being questioned by this very study. Thus, I would opt for the theme of Michal's love to be part of the basic layer, as in the words of Aurelius, "not necessary but pleasant". But I would rather narrow it down to 18:28b. On the other hand, I would argue that 18:20 belongs to this stratum as well. V. 20 corresponds nicely with v. 5* and adds the affection of the princess to the favour of the people and the gentry. As the promotion of the young son of Jesse is "good in the eyes of all the people and also in the eyes of the servants of Saul" (וַיִּיטַב בְּעֵינֵי כָל־הָעָם וְגַם בְּעֵינֵי עַבְדֵי שָׁאוּל, v. 5), now Michal's love is "right in the eyes" of Saul (וַיִּשַׁר הַדָּבָר בְּעֵינָיו, v. 20).

As a result, all these observations and literary-critical operations leave us with a putative basic layer in 18:2.5αβ.b.20.22.26a.27b.28b.(30?). This proposal

---

[49] "Admittedly, this last remark is not necessary for the basic layer (nor for any later layer), but it is pleasant and also adequate insofar as Michal is going to break loyalties with her father soon, during David's flight" (AURELIUS 2002: 67).

[50] *Nota bene*: "In 1Sam dürfte 18,28 der älteste Beleg dieser Formel sein" ("in 1 Sam, 18:28 may be the oldest instance of this formula" (AURELIUS 2002: 68, n. 90).

comes very close to the conclusions reached by André Heinrich and Erik Aurelius.[51] In fact, the differences relate to a few verses or half-verses only and hardly affect the general gist of the story, which, admittedly, is rather short in any case. It describes David's rise at the Saulide court as a direct consequence of the former's military success in the Philistine wars. What is going on is good or right in everybody's eyes: the people's, Saul's servants' (v. 5), the king's (v. 20) – and David's (v. 26). And not to forget, Michal is said to love her husband (v. 20,28b). Having killed the dragon, so to speak, the hero wins the hand of the princess and, as a general, something like half of the kingdom. One is tempted to add: "And everybody lived happily ever after." However, the story has not yet come to an end. Therefore, it matters what one thinks about the original continuation of the story for understanding the entire "History of David's rise". Heinrich finds this continuation in 19:1a,11,12a; *22:1 f.,[52] Aurelius in 19:11,12; 21:2.[53] In both cases, Saul suddenly attempts to kill his newly appointed general and son-in-law. One might wonder about the reasons for this sudden change of mind. Of course, the proposed answers are: Because the king is jealous of the young hero's success, because he recognises him as a personal threat, or simply because he is mentally unstable. All these answers are reflected in the narrative itself. But according to our analysis, all these answers are given in secondary segments of the text. From the point of view of our basic layer, there may be more than enough reason to develop the literary motif of a rivalry between the king and the parvenu. But there is no narrative set-up in 1 Sam 18* for Saul's desire to kill David (19:1a or 19:11) – and thus no reason for the latter to flee from the court (19:12).

This fits well with the macro-structural observation made above about the flight-rescue-pattern in the following chapters. The framework appeared to be secondary to some stories, while other stories were well-integrated into it – and a third group seemed to be more recent than the pattern. Taken together with our hypothesis about the basic layer in chapter 18, we will next have to consider the passages which can be read independently of this framework. But if Saul's change of attitude and his schemes seeking David's life are absent from the basic layer of chapter 18, most of the following chapters are ill-suited to be its continuation. This affects 22:1 f. most prominently, perhaps, depicting David's flight to the cave of Adullam and his gathering of a band of desperados. In

---

51 Heinrich finds a basic layer in 18:5a,20,22–25a,26a,27,28a* (cf. HEINRICH 2009: 243), Aurelius defines it in 18:2a,5,27b,28.
52 Cf. HEINRICH 2009: 360.
53 Cf. AURELIUS 2002: 68.

general, this note is seen as a pivotal part of the old or oldest traditions.[54] These two verses are the basis for the literary reconstruction of an ancient "Erzählkranz vom Freibeuter David"[55] as well as for a historical reconstruction of David as an 'Apiru leader.[56] Verse 22:1, however, is part of the flight-rescue-pattern, as is 22:3. Both begin with וַיֵּלֶךְ דָּוִד מִשָּׁם ("and David went from there"). What *might* be possible, though, is to directly continue with 22:2 after 18:30. David's name came to be revered because of his military success, and as a consequence, another 400 volunteers join his forces. Whether the 2nd millennium 'Apiru model is the best analogy to describe this process is another question altogether.

With the case of 22:2 left pending, the next story, David in Keïla (ch. 23), is clearly independent from the flight-rescue-pattern. This is where we have to look next.

4 The Continuation: 1 Sam 23; 27

Regarding 1 Sam 23 I will be very brief. The classical analysis was made by Timo Veijola in 1984 (reprinted in 1990). Reinhard Müller's revision of it is to be found in the current volume.[57] Veijola clearly delineates the division of the chapter. One section involves David alone (vv. 1–5 + 6) and a second part brings Saul to the stage (vv. 7–13).[58] According to Veijola, the second section is derived from the author of the "History of David's Rise", integrating elements of an ancient tradition.[59] However, I think it is better understood as a *Fortschreibung*. Further, Veijola identifies the phrases that evoke the saviour formula in verses 2bβ and 5b and the threshing floors in v. 1bβ[60] as secondary additions. One might also ask whether the hesitation of David's men and the second act of divination in vv. 3–4 might be secondary as well. Note, for example, the use of a more elabo-

---

54 Cf., as a *pars pro toto*, FINKELSTEIN 2013: 134.

55 "narrative cycle about David the privateer" (DIETRICH 1997: 248; and cf. Dietrich's contribution to this volume, DIETRICH, in this book). "Die Nachricht in 1f, wonach David eine Miliz um sich sammelte, ist unentbehrlich für den Freibeuter-Erzählkranz" ("The note in v. 1f., according to which David gathered a militia, is indispensable for the privateer narrative cycle", DIETRICH 2015: 611).

56 Cf. FINKELSTEIN 2013: 149.

57 Cf. also, without making literary-critical differentiations in the chapter, NAʾAMAN 2010.

58 Cf. VEIJOLA 1990: 29.

59 Cf. VEIJOLA 1990: 34 f.

60 Cf. VEIJOLA 1990: 27 f.

rate *Übergabeformel* כִּי־אֲנִי נֹתֵן אֶת־פְּלִשְׁתִּים בְּיָדְךָ ("for I am giving the Philistines into your hand").[61]

Notwithstanding these analytical details, 23:1–5* provide us with an excellent continuation of chapter 18* as well as of 22:2. Here David is presented in the role of Saul's general, leading a counterstrike in Keïla. *Nota bene*: Read from this perspective, "his men" first and foremost designates those אַנְשֵׁי הַמִּלְחָמָה ("men of war") over whom David is made leader in 18:5. This contingent may possibly, but not necessarily, be supplemented with the outlaws of chapter 22:2. That David becomes a freelance leader of a gang of "Merry Men" only becomes necessary when he is no longer the commander of Saul's troops – because he had to flee. Thus, the figure of "David the privateer" entirely depends on the flight-rescue-pattern. Historically, the difference between a general of a Levantine Early Iron Age king and a Bronze Age ʿApiru leader may well have been rather small in substance – but this is another question.

The similarity of David's act of divination in chapter 23:2abα with the one in 2 Sam 2:2 (and 1 Sam 30:8, 2 Sam 5:19)[62] has long been noted. This connection should not be underestimated, especially with regard to the first instance. Here, in 2 Sam 2 (or, to be more precise, in 2 Sam 2:1.2aα.3a^{LXX}.4a [without עַל־בֵּית יְהוּדָה], followed directly by 2 Sam 5:6),[63] we are dealing with the basic level of a "History of David's Rise". In 2 Sam 2, after the death of Saul, David asks YHWH whether he shall go up – and gets the approving answer that he is to go to Hebron. The phrase "to go up" means, according to 2 Sam 1:1bα,[64] from Ziklag to Hebron.

David's presence in Ziklag, however, depends on his relation with Achish of Gath, as noted in chapter 27. In the version of this paper presented in Jena during the symposium, I expressed the opinion that 1 Sam 27 should be understood in terms of the flight-rescue-pattern. This would have meant to proceed directly from Keïla to Gilboa, with the note about the Philistine deployment in 29:1 located in between. This decision caused considerable difficulty with the posited basic layer of 2 Sam 1, and led to a major discussion among the participants of the symposium. Upon further reflection, I allowed myself to be convinced that indeed at least a kernel of 1 Sam 27:2–6* (such as vv. 2*,3a,5,6) should not be excluded from the basic narrative. The plausible historical back-

---

61 This is quite exactly the same result as Müller's, who ends up with "vv. 1abα, 2abα, 5a*(without וַאֲנָשָׁיו), and 13a* (ohne כְּאַרְבַּע מֵאוֹת אִישׁ)" (MÜLLER in this book). However, I would keep "and his men" in the basic layer in v. 5a just as in v. 13a.

62 Cf. VEIJOLA 1990: 10–13.

63 Cf. BEZZEL 2021: 176–9.

64 Cf. FISCHER 2004: 14.

ground for an Early Iron Age setting of this story has been pointed out more than once.[65] This is especially so regarding the role of Gath, which would mirror a pre-Hasaël situation. What holds true archaeologically and historically may hold true redaction-critically as well: "One cannot simply sweep the major polity in the region under the carpet."[66]

Here I would add the less consequential observation that in the undisputed basic stratum of 27: 2*,3a,5,6, reference is made to "Achish of Gath". But the identity marker "Philistine" is not applied to him. It is only found in the secondary framework of vv. 1 and 7, which states that, with this move, David entered the "land of the Philistines". Without overemphasizing the point, it seems that for the first "History of David's Rise" the Philistines are the enemy against whom David fights. Therefore, when David operates within the sphere of influence of Achish, he is not collaborating with an enemy leader. In other words, a collective Philistine identity is construed first and foremost as an enemy identity.[67]

This implies that David's operations in the precincts of Gath do not necessarily presuppose a breach of his relations with Saul. Omer Sergi states that: "David is quite independent (as a leader of a warrior band) whenever he acts in the Judean hill country and its foothills (1 Sam 23–26 and 2 Sam 5). But he is at the service of the king of Gath whenever he crosses to the west or the south (cf. 1 Sam 27; 29–30)."[68] With respect to the analysis of 1 Sam 18 and 23 put forward in this article, I would modify the first part of this statement to clarify that even "as a leader of a warrior band" in the hill country, David may well remain at the service of king Saul – in quite the same way as he is at the service of *king*[69] Achish in chapter 27.

From a redaction-critical point of view it may be worth noting that, once again, it is "David and his men" who appear as subject of the plot (27:3; cf. 23:5,13a; 2 Sam 2:2aα,3a; 2 Sam 5:6*[LXX]). These verse numbers in brackets may give the outline of a first "History of David's Rise". It is another question, if anything about David's actions in chapter 30 could be ascribed to it, too.[70] But

---

65 Cf. Naʾaman 2006: 39 f.; Dietrich 2012: 93; Maeir 2012: 44–49; Finkelstein 2013: 138 f.; Sergi 2015: 72 f.; Sergi 2019: 228; Maeir 2017: 139–41; on Achish see Edenburg 2011: 36 f.

66 Maeir 2017: 141.

67 On the question of a Philistine identity cf. Maeir 2017: 137; Maeir 2019: 155, speaking of a "city-oriented identity".

68 Sergi 2019: 228.

69 "Scholars have long observed that Achish, ruler of Gath in the David stories, is called *mlk*, king, in contrast to *srn*, the more common title for a high-ranking Philistine in the Books of Joshua–Samuel" (Sergi, Lipschits and Koch 2019: 188).

70 Kratz and Heinrich both regard 1 Sam 30 as secondary (cf. Kratz 2000: 186; Heinrich 2009: 84 f.), whereas Wright includes its basic stratum into his HDR (Wright 2014: 44 f.).

this question is not of great relevance for this paper, since in ch. 30 the relationship between Saul and David is affected only indirectly. However, the intention of ch. 30 obviously is to make clear that a) while Saul was fighting the Philistines at Gilboa, David was as far away as possible from the events there; and b) David is forced to clean up after Saul because of the latter's disobedience in 1 Sam 15. Note furthermore that the reference back to 1 Sam 30 in 2 Sam 1aβ is secondary.[71] This provides another point of argument for the Amalekite thread not belonging to a basic layer of the "History of David's Rise".

What this HDR integrates by redactionally linking traditions about Saul with those about David, are the already existing segments of an enhanced Saul cycle, found in 1 Sam 29:1,11b; 31:1,2*(without the names of the sons),3–5,6[LXX],8,9a[LXX],10b–13.[72]

In the end there is the story of how a young Ephratite guy from Bethlehem builds an astonishing career at the court of the king of Israel. He not only becomes this king's son-in-law, but proves himself to be a warrior-leader in the service of this king, as well as a liege of Achish of Gath. Not surprisingly, after the death of Saul and his sons he is the natural successor to the throne and is made king himself by the "men of Judah" (אנשי יהודה, 2 Sam 2:4).[73]

All in all, this story does not relate anything about a rift between Saul and David, but rather gives the impression of a continuing, amicable relationship.

5 Stages

The literary relationship between Saul and David underwent considerable development. My starting point was the synchronic observation of a development from harmony to estrangement with phases of remorse and reconciliation. *Cum grano salis*, the diachronic analysis of the "History of David's Rise" gives a similar picture. Its first layer appears to present a "harmonic" narrative. Saul discovers David's military talent and fosters him as his mentor. David gets access to the kinship system of the Saulide clan by marriage and thus appears to be the king's natural successor when Saul and his three sons die on Mount Gilboa. He is made king by the "men of Judah" and together with "his men" goes up to Jerusalem. From the connecting verse in 1 Sam 14:52 on, this story continues through 17*;[74] 18:2,5aβ.b,20,22,26a,27b,28b,(30?); (22:2?); 23:1abα,2abα,5a; 27:2*,

---

71 Cf. FISCHER 2004: 18–23.
72 Cf. BEZZEL 2015: 248.
73 Cf. BEZZEL 2021: 176 f.
74 For the basic layer of 1 Sam 17 cf. AURELIUS 2002.

3a,5,6; 29:1,11b; 31:1–13*; 2 Sam 1:1aα.bα,2aα².β,3,4,11,12a.bα¹β; 2:1. 2aα.3aᴸˣˣ.4a (without יהוה עַל־בֵּית); 5:6. Thus, what I propose to be understood as the oldest continuing narrative thread comes close in some respects to what Walter Dietrich regarded in 2012 as the oldest – independent – traditions about David and the Philistines in this part of the books of Samuel (with some differences in detail).[75]

This relationship is then problematized secondarily. Looking back into chapter 18, we can see the beginning of this tendency in 18:6–9,13; 19:1. The atmosphere is marred by jealousy – and with it, by Saul's fear of losing control. Initially he demotes his general (if this is indeed a demotion) to a שַׂר אֶלֶף ("captain of a thousand", 18:13), then he plans to kill him (in 19:1).[76] Afterwards, with 19:11–14* (agreeing with André Heinrich),[77] we see David on the run. This is the prime example for all the following flight episodes in their corresponding contexts, which are not always so easy to identify. (21:11–16*; 22:1–4; 23:7–8,13; 27:1,4).

What can be learned from chapter 18 is that matters tend to escalate further when another character becomes involved in this already complicated web of love, hate and jealousy among Saul, David, Michal, and the people of Judah and Israel. This character is God. When Saul realises that YHWH is "with David" – and no longer "with him", the conflict between both is raised to another level. This is the case with 18:(10–12),14–16,28a,29, and with the preceding episode about the Philistine foreskins, which is dependent upon these last two verses (18:28a,29). This motif of YHWH's presence with David is closely connected with chapter 16 – and it can also be found in 28:15, in the core of – or, according to Alexander Fischer, in a first reworking of[78] – the story about Saul's necromantic session at En Dor.

Accordingly, with this motif the stage is set for Saul's (and Jonathan's) insight into this reality and the third phase, remorse. Remorse takes place in the touching scenes of chapter 24 and 26 as well as in 23:16–18. David's behaviour becomes more and more saint-like,[79] and even a character like Saul – in his enlightened moments – is able or compelled to realise this.

---

75 Cf. DIETRICH 2012: 87–90, with 1 Sam 17–18*; 23*; 27*; 29:1.2a,11b; 2 Sam 1 (the lament in vv. 19–27); 2 Sam 5 (the battles against the Philistines in vv. 17–21, 22–25) – but cf. differently, DIETRICH in this volume.

76 18:21,23–25,27a may be a later development of this motif. In substance, they belong to the same "stage".

77 Cf. HEINRICH 2009: 360. Heinrich, however, locates this connection on the level of the basic layer.

78 Cf. FISCHER 2005: 115–22.

79 For the drift towards a sanctification of David, see KRATZ 2000: 187.

Bibliography

Adam, Klaus-Peter. 2007. *Saul und David in der judäischen Geschichtsschreibung: Studien zu 1 Samuel 16–2 Samuel 5*. FAT 51. Tübingen: Mohr Siebeck.

Auld, A. Graeme / Ho, Craig Y. S. 1992. The Making of David and Goliath. *JSOT* 56:19–39.

Auld, A. Graeme. 2004. The Story of David and Goliath: A Test Case for Synchrony *plus* Diachrony. Pages 118–28 in: *David und Saul im Widerstreit – Diachronie und Synchronie im Wettstreit: Beiträge zur Auslegung des ersten Samuelbuches*. Edited by Walter Dietrich. OBO 206. Fribourg / Göttingen: Vandenhoeck & Ruprecht.

Aurelius, Erik. 2002. Wie David ursprünglich zu Saul kam (1 Sam 17). Pages 44–68 in *Vergegenwärtigung des Alten Testaments: Beiträge zur biblischen Hermeneutik. Festschrift für Rudolf Smend zum 70. Geburtstag*. Edited by Christoph Bultmann, Walter Dietrich, and Christoph Levin. Göttingen: Vandenhoeck & Ruprecht.

Barthélemy, Dominique. 1986. Trois niveaux d'analyse (a propos de David et Goliath). Pages 47–54 in: (Eds.). 1986. *The Story of David and Goliath: Textual and Literary Criticism: Papers of a Joint Research Venture*. Edited by Dominique Barthélemy et. al. OBO 73. Fribourg / Göttingen: Éditions Universitaires / Vandenhoeck & Ruprecht.

Barthélemy, Dominique et. al., eds. 1986. *The Story of David and Goliath: Textual and Literary Criticism. Papers of a Joint Research Venture*. OBO 73. Fribourg / Göttingen: Éditions Universitaires / Vandenhoeck & Ruprecht.

Bezzel, Hannes. 2013. The Numerous Deaths of King Saul. Pages 325–47 in *Is Samuel Among the Deuteronomists? Current Views on the Place of Samuel in a Deuteronomistic History*. Edited by Cynthia Edenburg and Juha Pakkala. Ancient Israel and Its Literature 16. Atlanta (GA): Society of Biblical Literature.

Bezzel, Hannes. 2015. *Saul: Israels König in Tradition, Redaktion und früher Rezeption*. FAT 97. Tübingen: Mohr Siebeck.

Bezzel, Hannes. 2021. Der „Saulidische Erbfolgekrieg" – Responses to Which Kind of Monarchy? Pages 165–81, in *The Book of Samuel and Its Response to Monarchy*. Edited by Sara Kipfer. BWANT 228. Stuttgart: Kohlhammer.

Budde, Karl. 1902. *Die Bücher Samuel*. KHC 8. Freiburg im Breisgau: Mohr.

Dietrich, Walter. 1997. *Die frühe Königszeit in Israel: 10. Jahrhundert v. Chr.* BE 3. Stuttgart: Kohlhammer.

Dietrich, Walter. ed. 2004. *David und Saul im Widerstreit – Diachronie und Synchronie im Wettstreit: Beiträge zur Auslegung des ersten Samuelbuches*. OBO 206. Fribourg / Göttingen: Vandenhoeck & Ruprecht.

Dietrich, Walter. 2012. David and the Philistines: Literature and History. Pages 79–98 in *The Ancient Near East in the 12th–10th Century BCE: Culture and History. Proceedings of the International Conference held at the University of Haifa 2–5 May, 2010*. Edited by Gershon Galil et al. Münster: Ugarit Verlag.

Dietrich, Walter. 2015. *Samuel: Teilband 2. 1Sam 13–26*. BK 8/2, Neukirchen-Vluyn: Neukirchener.

Dietrich, Walter. 2019. *Samuel: Teilband 3. 1Sam 27–2Sam 8*. BK 8/3, Göttingen: Vandenhoeck & Ruprecht.

Driesbach, Jason K. 2016. *4QSamuel^a and the Text of Samuel*. VT.S 171. Leiden / Boston: Brill.

Edenburg, Cynthia. 1998. How (Not) to Murder a King: Variations on a Theme in 1 Sam 24; 26. *SJOT* 12:64–85.

Edenburg, Cynthia. 2011. Notes on the Origin of the Biblical Tradition Regarding Achish King of Gath. *VT* 61:34–38.

Edenburg, Cynthia. 2016. "David Reproached Himself": Revisiting 1Sam 24 and 26 in light of 2Sam 21–24. Pages 469–80 in *The Books of Samuel: Stories – History – Reception History*. Edited by Walter Dietrich. *BEThL* 284, Leuven: Peeters.

Finkelstein, Israel. 2013. Geographical and Historical Realities behind the Earliest Layer in the David Story. *SJOT* 27:131–50.

Fischer, Alexander A. 2004. *Von Hebron nach Jerusalem: Eine redaktionsgeschichtliche Studie zur Erzählung von König David in 2Sam 1–5*. BZAW 335. Berlin / New York: de Gruyter.

Fischer, Alexander A. 2005. *Tod und Jenseits im Alten Orient und Alten Testament*. Neukirchen-Vluyn: Neukirchener.

Heinrich, André. 2009. *David und Klio: Historiographische Elemente in der Aufstiegsgeschichte Davids und im Alten Testament*. BZAW 401. Berlin / New York: de Gruyter.

Hutton, Jeremy M. 2009. *The Transjordanian Palimpsest: The Overwritten Texts of Personal Exile and Transformation in the Deuteronomistic History*. BZAW 396. Berlin / New York: de Gruyter.

Kratz, Reinhard G. 2000. *Die Komposition der erzählenden Bücher des Alten Testaments: Grundwissen der Bibelkritik*. UTB 2157. Göttingen: Vandenhoeck & Ruprecht.

Maeir, Aren M. 2012. The Tell eṣ-Ṣafi/Gath Archaeological Project 1996–2010: Introduction, Overview and Synopsis of Results. Pages 26–43 in *Tell eṣ-Ṣafi/Gath I: The 1996–2005 Seasons. Part 1. Text*. Edited by Aren M. Maeir. Ägypten und Altes Testament 69. Wiesbaden: Harrassowitz.

Maeir, Aren M. 2017. Philistine Gath after 20 Years: Regional Perspectives on the Iron Age at Tell eṣ Ṣafi/Gath. Pages 133–54 in: *The Shephelah during the Iron Age: Recent Archaeological Studies*. Edited by Oded Lipschits and Aren M. Maeir. Winona Lake (IN): Eisenbrauns.

Maeir, Aren M. 2019. Philistine and Israelite Identities: Some Comparative Thoughts. *WdO* 49:151–60.

Mommer, Peter. 2004. David und Merab – eine historische oder eine literarische Beziehung? Pages 196–204 in *David und Saul im Widerstreit – Diachronie und Synchronie im Wettstreit: Beiträge zur Auslegung des ersten Samuelbuches*. Edited by Walter Dietrich. OBO 206. Fribourg / Göttingen: Vandenhoeck & Ruprecht.

Na'aman, Nadav. 2006. In Search of Reality behind the Account of David's Wars with Israel's Neighbors [2002]. Pages 38–61 in *Ancient Israel's History and Historiography: The First Temple Period*. Collected Essays Volume 3. Winona Lake (IN): Eisenbrauns.

Na'aman, Nadav. 2010. David's Sojourn in Keilah in Light of the Amarna Letters. *VT* 60:87–97.

Porzig, Peter. 2009. *Die Lade im Alten Testament und in den Texten vom Toten Meer*. BZAW 397. Berlin / New York: de Gruyter.

Rofé, Alexander. 1982. The Acts of Nahash According to 4QSam[a]. *IEJ* 32: 129–33.

Rofé, Alexander. 1998. 4QMidrash Samuel? – Observations Concerning the Character of 4QSam[a]. *Textus* 19: 63–74.

Rofé, Alexander. 2015. David Overcomes Goliath (1 Samuel 17): Genre, Text, Origin and Message of a Story. *Hen* 37:66–100.

Rost, Leonhard. 1926. *Die Überlieferung von der Thronnachfolge Davids*. BWANT 42. Stuttgart: Kohlhammer.

Tov, Emanuel. 1986. The Nature of the Differences Between MT and the LXX in 1 Sam. 17–18. Pages 19–46 in *The Story of David and Goliath: Textual and Literary Criticism. Papers of a Joint Research Venture*. OBO 73. Fribourg / Göttingen: Éditions Universitaires / Vandenhoeck & Ruprecht.

Sergi, Omer. 2015. State Formation, Religion and "Collective Identity" in the Southern Levant. *HeBAI* 4:56–77.

Sergi, Omer. 2019. Israelite Identity and the Formation of the Israelite Polities in the Iron I–IIA Central Canaanite Highlands. *WdO* 49:206–35.

Sergi Omer, Oded Lipschits, and Ido Koch. 2019. Memories of the Early Israelite Monarchy in the Books of Samuel and Kings. Pages 173–94 in *Writing, Rewriting, and Overwriting in the Books of Deuteronomy and the Former Prophets: Essays in Honour of Cynthia Edenburg*. Edited by Ido Koch, Thomas Römer and Omer Sergi. BETL 304. Leuven: Peeters.

Veijola, Timo. 1990. David in Keïla: Tradition und Interpretation in 1Sam 23,1–13* [1984]. Pages 5–42 in: *David: Gesammelte Studien zu den Davidüberlieferungen des Alten Testaments*. Schriften der Finnischen Exegetischen Gesellschaft 52. Helsinki: Finnische Exegetische Gesellschaft / Göttingen: Vandenhoeck & Ruprecht.

Veijola, Timo. 2004. Geographie im Dienst der Literatur in ISam 28,4. Pages 256–71 in *David und Saul im Widerstreit – Diachronie und Synchronie im Wettstreit: Beiträge zur Auslegung des ersten Samuelbuches*. Edited by Walter Dietrich. OBO 206. Fribourg / Göttingen: Vandenhoeck & Ruprecht.

Vermeylen, Jacques. 2000. *La Loi du Plus Fort: Histoire de la rédaction des récit davidiques de 1 Samuel 8 à 1 Rois 2*. BETL 154. Leuven: Peeters.

Wellhausen, Julius. ⁴1963. *Die Composition des Hexateuchs und der Historischen Bücher des Alten Testaments: Vierte unveränderte Auflage*. Berlin: de Gruyter.

White, Marsha C. 2000. "The History of Saul's Rise": Saulide State Propaganda in 1 Samuel 1–14. Pages 271–92 in *"A Wise and Discerning Mind": Essays in Honor of Burke O. Long*. Edited by Saul M. Olyan and Robert C. Culley. BJSt 325. Providence (RI): Brown University Press.

Willi-Plein, Ina. 2004. ISam 18–19 und die Davidshausgeschichte. Pages 138–71 in *David und Saul im Widerstreit – Diachronie und Synchronie im Wettstreit: Beiträge zur Auslegung des ersten Samuelbuches*. Edited by Walter Dietrich. OBO 206. Fribourg / Göttingen: Vandenhoeck & Ruprecht.

Wirth, Raimund. 2016. *Die Septuaginta der Samuelbücher: Untersucht unter Einbeziehung ihrer Rezensionen*. De Septuaginta Investigationes 7. Göttingen: Vandenhoeck & Ruprecht.

Wonneberger, Reinhard, 1992. *Redaktion: Studien zur Textfortschreibung im Alten Testament, entwickelt am Beispiel der Samuel-Überlieferung*. FRLANT 156. Göttingen: Vandenhoeck & Ruprecht.

Wright, Jacob. 2014. *David, King of Israel, and Caleb in Biblical Memory*. New York: Cambridge University Press.

Ronnie Goldstein
On a Redaction Technique in 1 Sam 19:18–21:1

The long and complicated episode in 1 Sam 20 ends with the final encounter between David and Jonathan, followed by their emotional farewell:

וַיִּפֹּל לְאַפָּיו אַרְצָה וַיִּשְׁתַּחוּ שָׁלֹשׁ פְּעָמִים וַיִּשְּׁקוּ אִישׁ אֶת רֵעֵהוּ וַיִּבְכּוּ אִישׁ אֶת רֵעֵהוּ עַד ...
דָּוִד הִגְדִּיל וַיֹּאמֶר יְהוֹנָתָן לְדָוִד לֵךְ לְשָׁלוֹם אֲשֶׁר נִשְׁבַּעְנוּ שְׁנֵינוּ אֲנַחְנוּ בְּשֵׁם ה' לֵאמֹר ה' יִהְיֶה
בֵּינִי וּבֵינֶךָ וּבֵין זַרְעִי וּבֵין זַרְעֲךָ עַד עוֹלָם וַיָּקָם וַיֵּלַךְ וִיהוֹנָתָן בָּא הָעִיר

"… He flung himself face down on the ground and bowed low three times. They kissed each other and wept over each other; David wept the longer. Jonathan said to David, 'Go in peace! For we two have sworn to each other in the name of the Lord: 'May the Lord be [witness] between you and me, and between your offspring and mine, forever! David then went his way, and Jonathan returned to the town" (1 Sam 20:40–21:1).[1]

In a previous study, I focused on the difficult ending of v. 41 in the Masoretic text (MT): וַיִּשְּׁקוּ אִישׁ אֶת רֵעֵהוּ וַיִּבְכּוּ אִישׁ אֶת רֵעֵהוּ **עַד דָּוִד הִגְדִּיל**, rendered normally as "They kissed each other and wept over each other; *David wept the longer*.", and proposed that the original version of those words was: **עַד *בּוֹר** ***הַגָּדוֹל**.[2] The following summarizes my claims:

The MT of these last words, meaning 'David increasingly crying,' or 'David wept the longer', is odd, with some deeming the phrase "incomprehensible".[3] These particular issues have led some scholars to omit a translation of these words and to assert that the text here is defective, without further qualification.[4]

---

1 The English translation of biblical passages generally follows the NJPS translation, with some adaptations.
2 See GOLDSTEIN 2021.
3 See esp.: SMITH 1904: 196. For suggestions regarding the Hebrew *Vorlage* of the LXX, most of which are untenable guesses, see the summary of STOEBE 1973: 380. JULIUS WELLHAUSEN set the tone for understanding this verse among modern scholars. Following him, many tend to explain the Septuagint as developing from a supposed text that read עד הגדל, which they accept as original. See WELLHAUSEN 1871: 121. This presumed text has also been justifiably rejected: see esp. AULD 2011: 283, 245. One should reject additional suggestions to emend the Hebrew text based on the LXX. For a summary of the main suggestions, see esp. STOEBE 1973: 380; GOLDSTEIN (2021).
4 See for example SMITH 1904: 196; MCCARTER 1980: 334.

Note: My thanks go to the organizers of the "David in the Desert" conference, Prof. Reinhard Kratz and Prof. Hannes Bezzel for creating the best environment to study the book of Samuel. I thank also Prof. David Vanderhooft and Prof. Avi Winizter for reading and commenting on a draft of this article.

https://doi.org/10.1515/9783110606164-009

However, it is possible to reconstruct the original version of this verse on the basis of a different *Vorlage*, partly preserved by the rendering of the Septuagint (LXX) of the last words of the verse, ἕως συντελείας μεγάλης. LXX μεγάλης probably reflects הגדול, 'the great', instead of the Hebrew verb הגדיל in the MT. Furthermore, LXX does not render the word 'David,' but in its place has συντελείας, which normally renders various Hebrew words, including 'end' and forms of כלה. These factors hint that the Greek translator encountered in his Hebrew *Vorlage* the syntactical form 'until the great X'. To restore the original text of 1 Sam 20:41, I called attention to the previous episode in the David and Saul narratives, which mentions a specific geographic location that takes the form of עד בור הגדול 'until the Great Cistern': "So he [Saul] himself went to Ramah, and he came *to the Great Cistern* at Secu (**עַד בּוֹר הַגָּדוֹל** אֲשֶׁר בַּשֶּׂכוּ), and he asked, 'Where are Samuel and David?' (someone) said 'Behold, in Naioth at Ramah'" (1 Sam 19:22, according to the MT). The graphic similarity between עד בור הגדול of 1 Sam 19:22 and עד דוד הגדיל of 1 Sam 20:41 suggests that the former expression was the original Hebrew form also prensent in the latter passage:

וַיִּשְּׁקוּ אִישׁ אֶת רֵעֵהוּ וַיִּבְכּוּ אִישׁ אֶת רֵעֵהוּ **עַד *בּוֹר הַגָּדוֹל***

"They kissed each other and wept over each other *as far as the Great Cistern*"

Following this suggestion, the original reading of the verse named the place (for other place names in these narratives collocated with "cistern," see 1 Sam 30:30: בור עשׁן, and 2 Sam 3:26: בור הסירה) that David and Jonathan reached before they parted ways. The reconstructed phrase "They wept together until the Great Cistern" is understood to mean that they walked along crying until reaching the Great Cistern, where they took leave of one another. Both in the MT and in the LXX *Vorlage*, graphic errors led to the present corrupt versions. It is possible that the original sequence was וישקו איש את רעהו ויבכו *וילכו* איש את רעהו עד *בור הגדול*, "They kissed each other and wept, and *walked* together *as far as the Great Cistern*", and that the verb וילכו has been left out on account of its graphical similarity to ויבכו. Whatever the case, the present suggestion offers a better solution than do previous proposals in terms of both the text and context.

This small textual emendation has other implications for our understanding of the composition's history of the relevant episodes in the book of Samuel. As I will try to show, there is reason to suspect that the mention of 'the great cistern' in the two episodes in the Book of Samuel was added secondarily into already existing sources, as a redaction technique applied to 1 Sam 19:18–21:1. This presents an opportunity to illumine the evolution of those passages and the editorial effort to bring them together in the present sequence.

The story of Saul prophesying in Ramah in 19:18–24 is shaped according to the 'three and four' pattern.[5] According to this pattern, it seems that the original tradition mentioned three messengers who failed to bring David and Samuel to Saul, ending with Saul coming himself and failing. One might expect the climax of the story to be simple: after the failure of his messengers, Saul himself now goes to Ramah and prophesies as did they: "Then he too stripped off his clothes and he too spoke in ecstasy before Samuel" (v. 24).

The mention of 'the Great Cistern' as a midpoint along Saul's route in the MT of 1 Sam 19:22 creates difficulties in the sequence of this episode's events, and there are reasons to suspect that this break was not part of the original tradition.[6] According to verse 19, Saul already knew the exact location of David and Samuel, which is also clear from verses 20–21, according to which the messengers went directly to Ramah. This is similarly the case for the beginning of v. 22, according to which Saul himself is headed to Ramah. The whole scene in v. 22 seems redundant, and the need to stop and ask again about the whereabouts of David and Samuel requires further explanation. Furthermore, the description of Saul in v. 23, "and he walked on, prophesying" until arriving in Naioth in Ramah is discordant and repetitious in relation to v. 24, according to which Saul started prophesying only when he reached David's and Samuel's location at Ramah. To this incoherence, we may also add the threefold repetition of Saul coming to Ramah in verses 22–23:

22 וַיֵּלֶךְ גַּם הוּא הָרָמָתָה
23 וַיֵּלֶךְ [מ]ʾשָׁם אֶל נויות [נָיוֹת] בָּרָמָה
23 וַיֵּלֶךְ ... עַד בֹּאוֹ בנויות [בְּנָיוֹת] בָּרָמָה

Many readers of the passage have explained the present sequence, including the stop at the great pit in v. 22, as an integral part of the story about Saul prophesying in Ramah.[7] It seems, however, that the original sequence was in-

---

5 ZAKOVITCH 1977: 279–82. See also: ALTER 1999: 122.

6 Although some scholars have suggested that the narrative is composite, the passage 19:18–24 is generally taken as a coherent composition. See the survey in: NIHAN 2006: 88–118, and especially 102–3. Only a few scholars noted the problematic sequence in v. 22. NOWACK 1902: 101, noted some of the problems created by the present sequence, but dealt with them differently; TUR SINAI 1967: 167, is among the few scholars who partly noted the redundancy created by the mention of the בור הגדול in the present sequence. According to him: "the whole fact that an extra place was inserted here, as the place in which Saul asked about David ... is entirely strange." TUR SINAI tried to solve this in a different way, which cannot be accepted.

7 It is possible to explain these verses as intended to create some suspense in the story. FOK-KELMAN 1986: 279, e.g., called this a 'surprising retardation'. Other possible factors could affect the shaping of this scene, where Saul stops and asks for the whereabouts of David and Samuel. FOKKELMAN 1986: 281, pointed to the similarity between it and 1 Sam 9:6–19, where Saul seeks

deed designed as a simple three-four pattern-based story, in which after the
messengers fail three times, the king himself fails in the same way. This original
sequence was expanded by verses 22–23 in one or more stages. Taking out the
scene about the great pit creates a relatively smoother sequence. Accordingly,
the original sequence probably ran:

וַיִּשְׁלַח שָׁאוּל מַלְאָכִים לָקַחַת אֶת דָּוִד וַיַּרְא אֶת לַהֲקַת הַנְּבִיאִים נִבְּאִים וּשְׁמוּאֵל עֹמֵד נִצָּב עֲלֵיהֶם
וַתְּהִי עַל מַלְאֲכֵי שָׁאוּל רוּחַ אֱלֹהִים וַיִּתְנַבְּאוּ גַּם הֵמָּה. וַיַּגִּדוּ לְשָׁאוּל וַיִּשְׁלַח מַלְאָכִים אֲחֵרִים
וַיִּתְנַבְּאוּ גַּם הֵמָּה וַיֹּסֶף שָׁאוּל וַיִּשְׁלַח מַלְאָכִים שְׁלִשִׁים וַיִּתְנַבְּאוּ גַּם הֵמָּה. **וַיֵּלֶךְ גַּם הוּא הָרָמָתָה**
[ ] **וַתְּהִי עָלָיו גַּם הוּא** רוּחַ אֱלֹהִים] **וַיִּפְשַׁט גַּם הוּא** בְּגָדָיו **וַיִּתְנַבֵּא גַּם הוּא** לִפְנֵי שְׁמוּאֵל
וַיִּפֹּל עָרֹם כָּל הַיּוֹם הַהוּא וְכָל הַלָּיְלָה עַל כֵּן יֹאמְרוּ הֲגַם שָׁאוּל בַּנְּבִיאִם.

… and Saul sent messengers to seize David. They saw a band of prophets speaking in
ecstasy, with Samuel standing by as their leader; and the spirit of God came upon Saul's
messengers and they too began to speak in ecstasy. When Saul was told about this, he
sent other messengers; but they too spoke in ecstasy. Saul sent a third group of messengers; and they also spoke in ecstasy. So he himself went to Ramah. [ ] and the spirit of
God came upon him too [ ] and he too stripped off his clothes and he too spoke in ecstasy
before Samuel; and he lay naked all that day and all night. That is why people say, "Is
Saul too among the prophets?"

According to this reading, Saul's deed was close in content and style to that of
the three groups of messengers before him (and in accordance with the 'three
and four' pattern, was slightly longer):

20 **וַתְּהִי עַל מַלְאֲכֵי שָׁאוּל רוּחַ אֱלֹהִים וַיִּתְנַבְּאוּ גַּם הֵמָּה**
21 **וַיַּגִּדוּ לְשָׁאוּל וַיִּשְׁלַח מַלְאָכִים אֲחֵרִים וַיִּתְנַבְּאוּ גַּם הֵמָּה**
21 **וַיֹּסֶף שָׁאוּל וַיִּשְׁלַח מַלְאָכִים שְׁלִשִׁים וַיִּתְנַבְּאוּ גַּם הֵמָּה**
*24–22 **וַיֵּלֶךְ גַּם הוּא הָרָמָתָה וַתְּהִי עָלָיו גַּם הוּא רוּחַ אֱלֹהִים וַיִּפְשַׁט גַּם הוּא בְּגָדָיו וַיִּתְנַבֵּא גַּם
הוּא** *

This fits nicely with the main goal of the story, if only as an explanation to the
saying הֲגַם שָׁאוּל בַּנְּבִיאִם, by stating that וַיִּתְנַבֵּא גַּם הוּא. To this sequence two
short passages were added:

וַיִּשְׁלַח שָׁאוּל מַלְאָכִים לָקַחַת אֶת דָּוִד וַיַּרְא אֶת לַהֲקַת הַנְּבִיאִים נִבְּאִים וּשְׁמוּאֵל עֹמֵד נִצָּב עֲלֵיהֶם
וַתְּהִי עַל מַלְאֲכֵי שָׁאוּל רוּחַ אֱלֹהִים וַיִּתְנַבְּאוּ גַּם הֵמָּה וַיַּגִּדוּ לְשָׁאוּל וַיִּשְׁלַח מַלְאָכִים אֲחֵרִים
וַיִּתְנַבְּאוּ גַּם הֵמָּה וַיֹּסֶף שָׁאוּל וַיִּשְׁלַח מַלְאָכִים שְׁלִשִׁים וַיִּתְנַבְּאוּ גַּם הֵמָּה וַיֵּלֶךְ גַּם הוּא הָרָמָתָה
[וַיָּבֹא עַד בּוֹר הַגָּדוֹל אֲשֶׁר בַּשֶּׂכוּ וַיִּשְׁאַל וַיֹּאמֶר אֵיפֹה שְׁמוּאֵל וְדָוִד וַיֹּאמֶר הִנֵּה בְנָיֹת
(בְּנָיוֹת) בָּרָמָה וַיֵּלֶךְ שָׁם אֶל נָוִית (נָיוֹת) בָּרָמָה] וַתְּהִי עָלָיו גַּם הוּא רוּחַ אֱלֹהִים [וַיֵּלֶךְ הָלוֹךְ
וַיִּתְנַבֵּא עַד בֹּאוֹ בְנָיֹת (בְּנָיוֹת) בָּרָמָה] וַיִּפְשַׁט גַּם הוּא בְּגָדָיו וַיִּתְנַבֵּא גַם הוּא לִפְנֵי שְׁמוּאֵל
וַיִּפֹּל עָרֹם כָּל הַיּוֹם הַהוּא וְכָל הַלָּיְלָה עַל כֵּן יֹאמְרוּ הֲגַם שָׁאוּל בַּנְּבִיאִם.

Samuel. It is possible also to think that there is a play on words here with Saul's name שָׁאוּל
and וַיִּשְׁאַל, "he asked" (so, ALTER 1999: 122). However, the discrepancies in this passage require a different explanation, as offered here.

... and Saul sent messengers to seize David. They saw a band of prophets speaking in ecstasy, with Samuel standing by as their leader; and the spirit of God came upon Saul's messengers and they too began to speak in ecstasy. When Saul was told about this, he sent other messengers; but they too spoke in ecstasy. Saul sent a third group of messengers; and they also spoke in ecstasy. So he himself went to Ramah. **When he came to the great cistern at Secu, he asked, "Where are Samuel and David?" and was told that they were at Naioth in Ramah. And He went from there to Naioth in Ramah**, and the spirit of God came upon him too; **and he walked on, speaking in ecstasy, until he reached Naioth in Ramah,** and he too stripped off his clothes and he too spoke in ecstasy before Samuel; and he lay naked all that day and all night. That is why people say, "Is Saul too among the prophets?"

The repetition of the words וַיֵּלֶךְ *מ*שָׁם אֶל נוית (22) and וַיֵּלֶךְ גַּם הוּא הָרָמָתָה [נָיוֹת] בָּרָמָה (23) in the present sequence is best explained in my view as a *Wiederaufnahme*, created after the insertion of the stop in v. 22.[8] According to the ending of v. 23: וַיֵּלֶךְ הָלוֹךְ וַיִּתְנַבֵּא עַד בֹּאוֹ בנוית [בְּנָיוֹת] בָּרָמָה, Saul's prophetic experience started on his way to Ramah, which, as mentioned, contradicts v. 24 (according to which Saul started prophesying only when he reached Ramah). These words probably reflect a further expansion of the text based on v. 22 or part of the same expansion to the original sequence.[9] Here again, the expansion included a *Wiederaufnahme* to the main sequence עַד בֹּאוֹ בנוית [בְּנָיוֹת] בָּרָמָה. This process explains the threefold repetition of: וַיֵּלֶךְ גַּם ... עַד בֹּאוֹ וַיֵּלֶךְ ... הוּא הָרָמָתָה (v. 22), וַיֵּלֶךְ [מ]שָׁם אֶל נוית [נָיוֹת] בָּרָמָה (v. 22) and בנוית [בְּנָיוֹת] בָּרָמָה (v. 23).

One may suggest, therefore, that the main tradition regarding Saul's prophesying in Naioth in Ramah did not originally include the stop at the 'Great Cistern', but rather that this was added secondarily, by a scribe or redactor that wanted to connect this story to that location by adding another stop to the king's itinerary.[10]

---

8 At the beginning of v. 22 a small emendation is needed (with the Septuagint): וַיֵּלֶךְ *מ*שָׁם אֶל נוית [נָיוֹת] בָּרָמָה. See e.g.: Driver 1913: 159.

9 One may wonder whether in the case of the words in v. 23 וַיִּתְנַבֵּא הָלוֹךְ וַיֵּלֶךְ בנוית עַד בֹּאוֹ [בְּנָיוֹת] בָּרָמָה we have a more complex case. It is possible that the words עַד בֹּאוֹ בנוית [בְּנָיוֹת] בָּרָמָה were based on a misinterpretation of the words וַיֵּלֶךְ הָלוֹךְ וַיִּתְנַבֵּא, which originally could express the duration and intensity of Saul's prophesying in Ramah (see: BDB, s. v. הלך, 233; HALOT, s. v. הלך, 246). A possible original sequence: וַיֵּלֶךְ גַּם הוּא הָרָמָתָה וַתְּהִי עָלָיו גַּם הוּא רוּחַ אֱלֹהִים וַיֵּלֶךְ הָלוֹךְ וַיִּתְנַבֵּא meaning: "So he himself went to Ramah and the spirit of God came upon him too, **and he constantly prophesied**", was later interpreted as meaning literally 'he walked prophesying', and consequently the words עַד בֹּאוֹ בנוית [בְּנָיוֹת] בָּרָמָה were added, according to which Saul started prophesying already on his way to Ramah. But, compare 1 Sam 10:5, which implies a procession of prophets, similarly to Saul walking and prophesying in 19:23.

10 The geography of this passage is problematic. Besides the totally unknown שכו, if a place name is intended, the meaning of ניות and the exact relationship between it and רמה is still a

LXX represents in 1 Sam 19:22 a reading different than the MT. Instead of *'until the Great Cistern'* that is in Secu', it translates: ἕως τοῦ φρέα-τος τοῦ ἅλω τοῦ ἐν τῷ Σεφ, possibly reflecting a Hebrew *Vorlage* עד בור הגורן אשר בשפי "until the cistern of the threshing floor, which is on the bare height".[11] There is no advantage to the assumed reading "cistern of the threshing floor" over the MT's 'Great Cistern', and it seems that in this case the MT reading was corrupted in LXX.[12] It is possible that this corruption occurred in the Hebrew *Vorlage* of LXX; yet this seems to reflect an exegetical difficulty of the translator, who could not identify the place name בור הגדול.[13]

In a manner similar to the case of 1 Sam 19:18–24, the place of David and Jonathan's parting at the 'Great Cistern,' in 1 Sam 20:41, according to the reconstruction suggested here, is likely secondary to the main original sequence of that episode. The suggested original sequence וַיִּשְּׁקוּ אִישׁ אֶת רֵעֵהוּ וַיִּבְכּוּ אִישׁ **אֶת רֵעֵהוּ עַד *בּוֹר הַגָּדוֹל*** "They kissed each other and wept with each other until the Great Cistern," means that David and Jonathan walked, while crying, until they reached the 'Great Cistern'. This is, as mentioned, still somewhat problematic, and one expects the necessary (and perhaps original) reading to be: וישקו איש את רעהו ויבכו *וילכו* איש את רעהו עד *בור הגדול*. This difficulty is partly explained if we assume that the phrase עַד *בּוֹר הַגָּדוֹל* was added to the existing story at a secondary stage. It seems here again that the original episode lacked mention of a specific place, and ended only with the mention of the friends weeping and then parting ways. The original sequence in verses 41–42 thus probably ran:

וַיִּפֹּל לְאַפָּיו אַרְצָה וַיִּשְׁתַּחוּ שָׁלֹשׁ פְּעָמִים **וַיִּשְּׁקוּ אִישׁ אֶת רֵעֵהוּ וַיִּבְכּוּ** [ ] וַיֹּאמֶר יְהוֹנָתָן לְדָוִד לֵךְ לְשָׁלוֹם אֲשֶׁר נִשְׁבַּעְנוּ שְׁנֵינוּ אֲנַחְנוּ בְּשֵׁם ה' לֵאמֹר ה' יִהְיֶה בֵּינִי וּבֵינֶךָ וּבֵין זַרְעִי וּבֵין זַרְעֲךָ עַד עוֹלָם

He flung himself face down on the ground and bowed low three times. **They kissed each other and wept**, and Jonathan said to David, 'Go in peace! For we two have sworn to each other in the name of the Lord: "May the Lord be [witness] between you and me, and between your offspring and mine, forever!"

---

puzzle. See for example: DRIVER 1913: 158–59; SMITH 1904: 181–83; in any case, the stop at the בור הגדול on his way to Ramah is redundant, and creates difficulties in the present sequence.
11 See: BUDDE 1894: 18, 67; DRIVER 1913: 159, and many others after them.
12 See STOEBE 1973: 366; HERTZBERG 1964: 167. The decision between the MT's בשכו and the LXX's בשפי is not critical for our discussion.
13 See e.g. ROFÉ 2018: 429–30; I tend, in this case, towards the suggestion of TUR SINAI 1964: 167, according to which ἅλω is just an internal Greek error and the original version was μεγάλου. See also, BROCK 1996: 139–40.

This sequence was then expanded (by using similar language as וַיִּשְׁקוּ אִישׁ
אֶת רֵעֵהוּ), forming a new sequence: *וַיִּבְכּוּ אִישׁ אֶת רֵעֵהוּ עַד בּוֹר הַגָּדוֹל* (or
וַיִּבְכּוּ וַיֵּלְכוּ אִישׁ אֶת רֵעֵהוּ עַד בּוֹר הַגדוֹל), thus creating a geographical stop
in בּוֹר הַגדוֹל. This suggestion can serve as a partial explanation to the oddity
of the phrase וַיִּבְכּוּ אִישׁ אֶת רֵעֵהוּ: an original וַיִּבְכּוּ, 'and they wept', better
fits than weeping "each other," which is unparalleled in the Hebrew Bible (the
reciprocal meaning of אִישׁ אֶת רֵעֵהוּ befits kissing and hugging, but not weeping).

If indeed the 'Great Cistern' was added to both 1 Sam 19:22 (MT) and 20:41
(emended text), as suggested here, this intervention can serve as an example
of an editorial technique that relates two stories to the same geographical location with the intent to strengthen the relationship between them. The additions
in the stories sketch a kind of geographic continuity of David's movements,
which included 'the Great Cistern', both as the place where Saul prophesied
and the place from which David and Jonathan parted ways.[14]

As in other parts of the Book of Samuel and more specifically in the David
and Saul narratives, the sequence of stories about David running away from
Saul comprises different episodes from different origins that do not always form
one continuous sequence. Even without analyzing the composition of each unit,
we can point out that the episode of Saul's prophesying in Naioth in Ramah in
1 Sam 19:18–24 does not follow naturally what came beforehand, and it is not
at all connected to the following story of Jonathan and David, in which David
is (again?) near the court of Saul, who expects him to join the royal meal.[15]
Furthermore, the story that includes Samuel in 19:18–24 and the story in chapter
20 clearly stem from different origins.[16] The episode in 19:18–24 could have
found its place later in the narrative, somewhere after the episode in ch. 21
about David and Ahimelech, and probably was not intended by its author to
enter this present place. Similarly, the episode regarding Jonathan and David
meeting in ch. 20 is awkward after 19:18–24, since David has already left Saul's
court, running for his life. It is also weakly connected to the following episode

---

14 This technique is implemented in biblical texts in different ways, and demands further
exploration. See N. Evron's article in the present collection: EVRON 2021: 274 n. 25. For another
similar case, see, for example, Jer 37:15–16. The accumulation of places in these verses, and
especially the mention of the house of Jonathan the scribe, are explained partly by the need
of the redactor of the present sequence to create a connection between the different originally
unrelated episodes. See: GOLDSTEIN 2013: 52–54.
15 See e.g. McCARTER 1980: 330.
16 The different origin of 19:18–24 was recognized by WELLHAUSEN 1885: 267–68, and followed
by many scholars since; see e.g. McCARTER 1980: 330.

of David at Nob, the city of priests. One of the prominent gaps between the different episodes in the current sequence is the apparent illogical geographical order witnessed in David's escape from Geba (Saul's place) to Ramah (19:18), followed by his return (20:1) to a place close to Saul's court (in Geba?), and culminating in his flight to Nob, the city of priests (21:2).[17]

Furthermore, there is clear tension between the scene of David and Jonathan's meeting in 1 Sam 20:40–42 and the main story in 1 Sam 20. According to the main story, we might expect that following the secret warning signs of Jonathan, David would run away from the place, and that the story would then end, leaving the short episode of their meeting in 20:40–42 unnecessarily redundant.[18] Accordingly, the whole scene becomes suspect as secondary to the main story, and it possibly entered the sequence of the story of David, Jonathan, and the arrows at a later stage.[19] This tension adds to the many gaps between the different episodes of David's flight from Saul, which reinforce the complex nature of the sequence before us.

It seems, therefore, that the text in 1 Sam 19:22 (MT) and 1 Sam 20:41 (according to the suggested emendation) attempted to bridge the gaps between the originally unrelated stories by connecting them by way of a geographic thread. In this way, we can explain both the connection between the story of Saul and David at Naioth in Ramah to the 'Great Cistern' and the connection of the following story of David and Jonathan to that same 'Great Cistern' as secondary. Whether or not the mention of the 'Great Cistern' is secondary in the two episodes as is claimed here, it seems that we have found a redactor's hand trying to tighten the connection between the stories by linking these to the same geographical location. We cannot know for certain how the redactor made sense of the geographical sequence in these stories. Either way, the addition of 'the Great Cistern' strengthened their inner relationship.

The endings of the two stories about Saul in Naioth and – according to the reconstructed text – about David and Jonathan's meeting connect those two

---

17 This problematic itinerary was noted by many scholars. See e.g.: KLEIN 2008: 195.

18 WELLHAUSEN 1885: 266, and many others after him in a different fashion; see: NOWACK 1902: 108–9; GRESSMANN 1910: 85; and the summary by HERTZBERG 1964: 176. According to this, 21:1 was probably the original ending of the story. For concluding stories with the parting of both sides, see: SEELIGMANN 1962 / 2004: 120–23.

19 The decision regarding the exact essence of this passage (20:40–42) is not critical for my suggestion here. It is possible that vv. 40–42 are a fragment of a parallel tradition about the meeting between David and Jonathan inserted here, but the possibility that those are an editorial addition to the main tradition cannot be ruled out. See e.g. SMITH 1904: 183, 196, who sees in them "an editorial expansion, pure and simple". So too KENNEDY 1905: 146 ff. Others see in these verses a Deuteronomistic redaction, without a justifiable basis in my view; see e.g. McCARTER 1980: 343–44; KLEIN 2008: 209–10.

episodes. Although the main goal of this connection was probably simply to reinforce the inner coherence of the present sequence, it is possible that the redactor intended more than just that. It makes sense that, by connecting these two episodes to 'the Great Cistern' in the land of Benjamin, the redactor reinforced the contrast between Saul, who goes from Geba to the Great Cistern in order to chase David, and his son, who saves David from his father – this by relating their final farewell in tears to the same geographical spot. In other words, the placement of the passage 19:18–24 near 20:1–21:1 creates a contrast between the king and his son, and the connection of both passages to the Great Cistern reinforces this contrast. It is suggestive that the connection of the passages to the Great Cistern was the work of the redactor who first created the sequence in 1 Sam 19:18–21:1, based on passages that originally were unrelated.

In light of what has been discussed here, there is good reason to re-examine the history of the traditions regarding the place known as 'the Great Cistern'. The site "the Great Cistern" was misconstrued on another occasion in the Hebrew Bible. In Jer 41:9, which in the MT mentions בְּיַד גְּדַלְיָהוּ, the original Hebrew must be restored based on the LXX: φρέαρ μέγα τοῦτό, reflecting the Hebrew *Vorlage* בּוֹר גָּדוֹל, or, perhaps better, בּוֹר הגדול.[20] According to Jer 41, this place is connected to two traumatic events: (1) the murder of Gedaliah and the people from the cities of Ephraim and Benjamin by the hands of Ishmael son of Nethaniah from the royal line and (2) the struggle between Asa, King of Judah, and Baasha, King of Israel. There is room to suggest that the geographical location of the Great Cistern, probably adjacent to the border between Judah and the North, attracted traditions regarding the tension between Israel and Judah. Therefore it is not surprising that this place was connected in the Book of Samuel to the traditions regarding Saul and David and the tension between them, and specifically to two scenes that are critical for David's eventual move-

---

20 See the survey by MCKANE 1996: 1021, and see now GOLDSTEIN 2021. According to the Jeremiah passage, this place is "the one that King Asa had constructed on account of King Baasha of Israel". The tradition in 1 Kgs 15:22, mentions Ramah, Geba, and Mizpah, and this last place is mentioned in the story of Gedaliah. For an attempt to reconstruct the geographical and historical background of this passage, see FINKELSTEIN 2012: 14–28. We can assume that the Great Cistern mentioned in Jer 41:9 is the Great Cistern of MT 1 Sam 19:22, which is close to Ramah, and it is the same Great Cistern referred to in the reconstructed text of 1 Sam 20:41, also in the region of the land of Benjamin. Such a water installation was undoubtedly a major public work, whatever the period of its construction, and known as a definite feature of the landscape. The exact location of this place is unknown, but from the sources reflecting it, there is good reason to believe that it was a Benjaminite place, not very far from Ramah and Mizpah, and close to the border between Judea and Israel. Compare: FINKELSTEIN 2012: esp. n. 72.

ment beyond the reach of the house of Saul. These scenes (and especially the one in 1 Sam 20:41 connecting the 'Great Cistern' to David and Jonathan's final farewell) fit well to a place located on the border between the south and the north (between Saulide Benjamin and Davidic Judah).[21] At some other point in history, the place and its connections to those traditions were forgotten, and the biblical passages about it were corrupted.

In summary, based on an emendation to 1 Sam 20:41, the present study offers a new connection between this passage and the previous story in the Book of Samuel relating Saul's prophesying in Naioth in Ramah. It is claimed here that the mention of the 'Great Cistern' is secondary in both passages, and was added to the stories to reinforce the present sequence of events in 1 Sam 19:18–21:1 by narrowing the geographical gaps between the various traditions regarding David and Saul. If so, this hypothesis opens a small window into the redactional processes that these stories underwent. Although it is possible that the mention of the place in both passages is part of a late redaction, those are better explained as a technique applied by the author/redactor who created the present sequence in the book of Samuel.

Bibliography

Alter, Robert. 1999. *The David Story: A Translation with Commentary of 1 and 2 Samuel*. New York: W. W. Norton.

Auld, A. Graeme. 2011. *1 & 2 Samuel*. OTL. Louisville. KY: Westminster John Knox Press.

Brock, Sebastian P. 1996. *The Recensions of the Septuagint Version of I Samuel*. Turin: Zamorani.

Budde, Karl. 1894. *The Books of Samuel*. Leipzig: Hinrichs.

Driver, Samuel R. 1913. *Notes on The Hebrew Text and The Topography of The Books of Samuel*. Oxford: Clarendon Press.

Evron, Nathan. 2021. *'David is Hiding among Us': The Stories about David, Saul, and the Ziphites (1 Sam 23:19–24; 26:1)*. In *David in the Desert*. Edited by Hannes Bezzel and Reinhard G. Kratz. Berlin: de Gruyter.

Finkelstein, Israel. 2012. The Great Wall of Tell En-Nasbeh (Mizpah), the First Fortifications in Judah, and 1 Kings 15:16–22. *VT* 62:14–28.

---

21 There is room to ponder whether the strange story about Ishmael leaving Mizpah to meet the people coming from the north הֹלֵךְ הָלֹךְ וּבֹכֶה "weeping as he walked," (Jer 41:6), killing them, and then piling their bodies into the cistern (Jer 41:7), is somehow connected to the stories dealt with here from the Book of Samuel, i.e., the crying of David and Jonathan at the Great Cistern and the walking of Saul וַיֵּלֶךְ הָלוֹךְ וַיִּתְנַבֵּא "he walked on prophesying" in this exact place.

Fokkelman, Jan P. 1986. *The Crossing Fates (1 Samuel 13–31 and 2 Samuel 1)*. Vol. 2 of *Narrative Art and Poetry in the Books of Samuel: A Full Interpretation Based on Stylistic and Structural Analyses*. Assen: van Gorcum.

Goldstein, Ronnie. 2021. עַד בּוֹר הַגָּדוֹל (1 Sam 19:22) – עַד הַגָּדוֹל (1 Sam 20:41) עַד דּוֹד הַגָּדִיל. *VT* (2021) 1–13.

Goldstein, Ronnie. 2013. *The Life of Jeremiah*. Jerusalem: The Bialik Institute (Hebrew).

Gressmann, Hugo. 1910. *Die Schriften des Alten Testaments 2/1*. Göttingen: Vandenhoeck & Ruprecht.

Hertzberg, Hans Wilhelm. 1964. *I & II Samuel: A Commentary*. Translated by John S. Bowden. OTL. London: SCM Press.

Kennedy, Archibald Robert Stirling. 1905. *Samuel*. Century Bible. Edinburgh: T. C. & E. C. Jack.

Klein, Ralph W. 2008. *I Samuel*. WBC. Nashville: Thomas Nelson.

McCarter, P. Kyle. 1980. *I Samuel: A New Translation with Introduction, Notes & Commentary*. AB. Garden City, NY: Doubleday.

McKane, William. 1996. *Jeremiah*. Vol. 2. ICC. Edinburgh: T. & T. Clark.

Nihan, Christophe. 2006. *Saul among the Prophets*. Pages 88–118 in *Saul in Story and Tradition*. Edited by C. S. Ehrlich and M. C. White. FAT I/47. Tübingen: Mohr Siebeck.

Nowack, Wilhelm. 1902. *Die Bücher Samuelis*. HKAT. Göttingen: Vandenhoeck & Ruprecht.

Rofé, Alexander. 2018. *The Religion of Israel and the Text of the Hebrew Bible*. Jerusalem: Carmel (Hebrew).

Seeligmann, Isac Leo. 1962. Hebräische Erzählung und biblische Geschichtsschreibung. *Theologische Zeitschrift* 18:305–25. Repr. 2004. Pages 119–36 in *Gesammelte Studien zur Hebräischen Bibel*. Edited by Erhard Blum. FAT 41. Tübingen: Mohr Siebeck.

Smith, Henry Preserved. 1904. *Samuel*. ICC. Edinburgh: T. & T. Clark.

Stoebe, Hans Joachim. 1973. *Das erste Buch Samuelis*. KAT. Gütersloh: Mohn.

Tur Sinai, Naftali Herz. 1964. *Peshuto shel Miqra*. Vol. 2. Jerusalem: Kiryat Sepher (Hebrew).

Wellhausen, Julius. 1871. *Der Text der Bücher Samuelis untersucht*. Göttingen: Vandenhoeck.

Wellhausen, Julius. 1885. *Prolegomena to the History of Ancient Israel*. Translated by J. Sutherland Black and Allan Menzies. Edinburgh: Adam and Charles Black.

Zakovitch, Yair. 1977. *The Pattern of The Numerical Sequence Three-Four in The Bible*, Jerusalem: Makor (Hebrew).

Jeremy M. Hutton
David and the Priests of Nob: Collusion or Illusion?

1 1 Sam 21:2–10* + 22:6–23*: Collusion?

The biblical narratives regarding the young David's sojourn in the wilderness
(spanning 1 Sam 19–2 Sam 1), have long been recognized as forming an important literary stage in his accession to the throne of Israel. These chapters are
often included in the slightly larger complex of episodes typically called the
"History of David's Rise" (roughly, 1 Sam 16–2 Sam 5).[1] Focusing primarily on
the period of David's flight from his one-time liege, these episodes offer an inti-
mate portrait of Israel's future king as he transitioned from the lowly status of
a small town shepherd boy to serving as a courtier and military commander of
a troubled king, then to his status as a fugitive on the run, and finally the inher-
itor of the Israelite kingdom. The narratives contained here recount his first
marriage to Michal, daughter of Saul (18:20–27), and his friendship and covenant with Saul's son Jonathan (19:1–7; 20:1–42, esp. vv. 16–17,23,41–42; and
23:16–18). They provide an account of David's subsequent "courtship" of and
marriage to Abigail, wife of Nabal the Carmelite (25:2–42), and a notice of his
further marriage to Ahinoam the Jezreelite (v. 43). They relate his flight to the
Philistine lands to escape Saul's pursuit (21:11–16; 27:1–6), along with episodes
of David's derring-do while delivering the Judahite town of Qeilah (1 Sam 23:1–
13), sparing Saul's life on two separate occasions (1 Sam 24; 26), and a counter-
raid on an Amalekite raiding party (1 Sam 30).

   The present study attempts to reconstruct the composition history of a small
portion of the so-called History of David's Rise, spanning 1 Sam 21:2–22:23*. It
attempts to do so by employing both source- and redaction-critical approaches.
It is therefore primarily a literary-critical study. I do not claim to evaluate here

---

1 E.g., NÜBEL 1959; WEISER 1966; GRØNBAEK 1971; METTINGER 1976: 33–47; McCARTER 1980b;
KAISER 1990; HEINRICH 2009; HUTTON 2009: 228–88; KNAPP 2015: 161–248.

Note: It is a pleasure to thank here H. BEZZEL and R. G. KRATZ for their kind invitation to
contribute to this volume and to the seminar in which it was first presented. I thank also the
seminar's other attendees, many of whom offered insightful comments and critique that
helped to sharpen some of the argumentation. The joys of scholarship rest in friendly, but
serious, argumentation followed by a common meal and laughter. Finally, I owe gratitude to
both J. WYLIE and N. E. GREENE; both saved me from some textual embarrassment and asked
pointed questions, further refining my analysis.

https://doi.org/10.1515/9783110606164-010

the historical claims made by the text: with Heinrich, I recognize that the "rolling tradition" – the process of *Komposition* and *Fortschreibung* – necessarily complicates any evaluation of the text's historical claims.[2] Nonetheless, I follow in the tradition inaugurated by Albrecht Alt and represented in the Anglophone world by Kyle McCarter, Steven McKenzie, Baruch Halpern, and, most recently, Andrew Knapp, in arguing that the historical *assumptions* of the text's oldest isolatable stratum point to its origins in a milieu in which it served as the legitimation of the Davidic dynasty in Judah, and perhaps even more broadly.[3] Yet, far from drawing any historical conclusions from the text, I will argue that the *political* and *historical collusion* of which Saul has accused the Nobite priests is likely a *literary illusion* skillfully created by the juxtaposition of two originally independent episodes.

Despite recognizing narrative disjunctures and literary gaps, commentators have almost ubiquitously treated the chapters under investigation here, 1 Sam 21:2–10* and 22:6–23*, as a cohesive unit.[4] Accordingly, this literary unit details David's none-too-stealthy visit to Nob for provisions and military supplies, and, once Saul learns of the Nobite priests' treachery, his ensuing slaughter of the priests. In most readings of this putative narrative unit, David obfuscates his real status as a fugitive, instead claiming to Ahimelech, chief priest of the Nobite sanctuary, that he is on an urgent mission of the king. As such, Saul's punishment of the Nobite priesthood, while horrific in its overzealous thoroughness, is at least understandable from the point of view of a monarch who suspected collusion between the aspiring usurper David and the priesthood that purportedly aided and abetted his escape from Gibeah. In the present form of the text, the accusation of "collusion" that Saul levels against the priests of Nob has some substance to it.

Regardless of whether the priest Ahimelech harbors rebellious sympathies for David from the beginning of the account, or is merely hoodwinked into aiding and abetting the fugitive Bethlehemite, his failure to inform his liege of David's departure qualifies as sedition (שֶׁקֶר) in ancient Near Eastern Law. As a roughly contemporaneous example, we might consider one of the treaty texts from Sefire.[5] In these three long treaty texts from ancient Arpad, a suzerain

2 See esp. HEINRICH 2009: 40.
3 ALT 1953; MCCARTER 1980b; MCKENZIE 2000; HALPERN 2001; KNAPP 2015: 161–248.
4 E.g., SMITH 1904: 205; DHORME 1910: 193, 202, 206 (attributing both episodes to E); HERTZBERG 1964: 179; ACKROYD 1971: 170; MCCARTER 1980a: 351–58; PAYNE 1982: 110–11, 114–16; KLEIN 1983: 212; CAMPBELL 2003: 222; TSUMURA 2007: 527–34, 541–49; BODNER 2009: 224–28, 233–39; FIRTH 2009: 232–40; HUTTON 2009: 275–76; AULD 2011: 265.
5 On this text, see already GREENFIELD 1965: 5; WEINFELD 1972: 99 n. 4; 1976: 387–89. I am grateful to Cynthia EDENBURG for pointing me to WEINFELD's studies.

imposes stipulations on his vassal.[6] One of these stipulations in stele Sf III de-mands that the vassal should neither feed nor support any fugitive. Instead, he should extradite the fugitive, or detain him long enough for the suzerain to do so himself:

‫4... והן יקרק מני קרק חד פקדי או חד אחי או חד 5סרסי או חד עמא זי בידי ויהכן חלב‬
‫לתס[ך ל]הם לחם ולתאמר להם שלו על אשרכם ולתהרם נ6בשהם מני רקה תרקהם‬
‫ותהשבהם לי והן לי[שב]ן בארקך רקו שם עד אהך אנה וארקהם והן תהרם נבשה7ם מני‬
‫ותסך להם לחם ותאמר להם שבו לתחתכ[ם] ואל תפנו באשרה שקרתם בעדיא אלין ...‬

Now if a fugitive flees from me, one of my officials, or one of my brothers, or one of my courtiers, or one of the people who are under my control, and they go to Aleppo, you must not gi[ve th]em food (לתסך להם לחם) or say to them, "Stay quietly in your place"; and you must not incite them against me. You must *placate* (√רקה) them and return them to me. And if they [do] not [dwell] in your land, *placate* (them) there, until I come and *placate* them. But if you incite them against me and give them food and say to them, "Stay where [yo]u are and do not (re)turn to his region," you shall have been unfaithful (שְׁקַרְתֶּם) to this treaty. (Sf III:4–7)[7]

The accusation that the negligent vassal will have been unfaithful, Aram. √שקר, is cognate to the Hebrew verb denoting "sedition" or "rebellion" (שֶׁקֶר; e.g., 1 Kgs 22:22,23), or, more broadly, "breaking of a covenant bond" (1 Sam 25:21 [David, asserting a relationship with Nabal]; and 1 Sam 15:29 [where it is YHWH who does *not* perform this action]).

Two other ancient Near Eastern texts have been adduced as parallels, simi-larly justifying the slaughter of the priests in legal terms. Jim Roberts points to a loyalty oath sworn by oracular specialists at Mari under the direction of Zimri-Lim (ARM XXVI, no. 1 = M.13091).[8] According to this oath, diviners were re-quired to reveal each and every oracle to the king, but to withhold information from the general public and to report any inkling they had of sedition. Roberts argues on the basis of this oath that Saul's slaughter of the Nobite priests was

---

6 The relationship between these three stelae remains difficult to discern. Sefire stele I fea-tures the as yet unidentified king of KTK, who goes by the moniker Bar-Ga'yah (Sf I A:1, 3; B:1–4; etc.; cf. Sf II, where only KTK is mentioned [C:5], but not Bar-Ga'yah), and Mati'-'el, king of Arpad (Sf I A:1, 3–4; B:1–4; Sf II C:14–15). Sefire stele III (Sf III = KAI 224) does not retain the personal names (although ברגאיה is perhaps to be reconstructed in line 25) and makes refer-ence only to Arpad (lines 1, 3, 16, 27). We should perhaps not conflate the three stelae, as do most interpreters (see further discussion in CROUCH / HUTTON 2019: 258–63).
7 FITZMYER 1995: 136 (text), 137 (translation; italics original). FITZMYER uses the English word "placate" to render Aram. √רקה (cf. Heb. √רצה), but it has the sense in this passage of actually detaining the individual.
8 The "Protocol of the Diviner," first published by DURAND (1988: 11–13, no. 1 = M. 13091); for an earlier application of this text to 1 Sam 3, see HUROWITZ 1994.

legally justified, even if morally reprehensible. As an oracular specialist, Ahimelech would have been bound by oath to relate any suspicions concerning David's plot directly to Saul; his failure to do so made him culpable in David's sedition.[9] And the story itself relates two points at which Ahimelech *must* have become suspicious, according to Roberts: First, the priest's "trembling" (וַיֶּחֱרַד) at David's approach indicates that the priest knows something is amiss (see also 1 Sam 16:4). Second, pointing to the specific questions posed in 1 Sam 23, Roberts asserts that David would necessarily have asked questions of the oracle in such a way that Ahimelech's suspicions *must* have been aroused.[10] It goes almost without saying that Roberts takes Doeg's testimony in 1 Sam 22:9b–10 as instructive of the narrator's intentions for what the reader should draw from the earlier episode (1 Sam 21:2–10), despite the fact that no oracular inquiry is mentioned there explicitly.

Ada Taggar-Cohen points to ancient Near Eastern comparanda in support of reading 1 Sam 21:2–10 + 22:6–23 as an integrated unit. She gestures to a Hittite text stipulating loyalty between a sovereign and his vassal (Bo 86/299; the "Bronze Tablet," containing a treaty between Tudḫaliya IV and his cousin and vassal, Kurunta).[11] In this text, the suzerain Tudḫaliya swears to his vassal, "I will be loyal to you" (§ 13, line 42) recognizing that Kurunta has also sworn his support and loyalty solely for Tudḫaliya (§ 13, lines 38–41). Taggar-Cohen thereby argues (a) that David and Jonathan had similarly sworn fealty to one another, with David taking on the role of the subordinate (1 Sam 20:8; see also vv. 13–16,42);[12] and (b) that Saul had misinterpreted the nature of that oath (citing 22:7–8).[13] As in Roberts's argument, the priests were bound by their own loyalty oaths sworn to Saul, making them culpable for any collusion with potential usurpers.[14] Accordingly, David does not seem to view the slaughter of the priests as illegal. In Taggar-Cohen's view, David's assessment is given in 1 Sam 22:22 (esp. v. 22b), where he pronounces his own culpability for the slaughter.[15] Further, Taggar-Cohen grounds the legality of the slaughter in the מִשְׁפַּט הַמְּלֻכָה

9 ROBERTS 1999: 21–29. ROBERTS also points to the so-called "Vassal Treaty of Esarhaddon," published in PARPOLA / WATANABE 1988: 33, no. 6.108–22; see already FRANKENA 1965: 143.
10 ROBERTS 1999: 24–25.
11 TAGGAR-COHEN 2005, citing OTTEN 1988; see more recently, HOFFNER 2002: 100–6.
12 TAGGAR-COHEN 2005: 253–54.
13 TAGGAR-COHEN (2005: 260) quotes 1 Sam 22:7–8, but mistakenly cites 1 Sam 20:7–8.
14 TAGGAR-COHEN 2005: 263, citing the Hittite "Instructions for Temple Officials" (CTH 264). For the text, see STURTEVANT 1934; and STURTEVANT – BECHTEL 1935: 127–74.
15 TAGGAR-COHEN 2005: 266. This interpretation is in line with that of scholars who point to this passage as indicating David's acceptance of the legality of Saul's punishment (e.g., ROBERTS 1999).

of 1 Sam 10:25. Yet, Taggar-Cohen remains somewhat ambivalent as to whether the reader is supposed to understand Saul's actions as illegal: she admits that "the biblical author views the fulfillment of the punishment as illegal, by using the term לִשְׁלוֹחַ יָד [sic]."[16] As in the case of Roberts's interpretation, Taggar-Cohen imports terminology and concepts from other passages into her interpretation of 1 Sam 21:2–10 + 22:6–23. In particular, she conjoins these passages with David's oath to Jonathan in 1 Sam 20:4–5.

In this synchronic reading, the servants' refusal to kill the priests forces us to wrestle with the inherent ambiguity of the account: Is the audience supposed to view Saul's slaughter of the priests as problematic? If so, do we do so by reading against the grain of the biblical text, viewing it as an improper vengeance-killing because Ahimelech was conned by the seditious young David? Do we view it as troublesome, along with Taggar-Cohen, because Saul was incorrect in his assessment of David's motives to begin with? Alternatively, are we supposed to recognize the legitimacy of Saul's actions on the legal basis of ancient Near Eastern law? Finally, should we even read 1 Sam 21 and 22 together, as part of the same account, such that the ancient Near Eastern comparanda are only fully comparable when the two are read together?

Pamela Tamarkin Reis has offered a creative – if somewhat fanciful – reading of these episodes in an effort to alleviate this ambiguity. Reis views Ahimelech as eminently aware of Doeg's presence at the very beginning of the passage. "How could he not know?" she asks. "He has obviously come to the sanctuary for a religious reason, and he has been there for some time."[17] Trembling – and fearful that David is on the lam from Saul – Ahimelech runs to meet him. He seeks to warn the young fugitive that there is a Saulide spy at the sanctuary, "lest, by his first words, David incriminates them both."[18] Anticipating David's purposes for coming, "Ahimelech's interrogative first words ... are ingenious. They inform David that Ahimelech is not alone and yet appear completely innocuous and perfectly consistent with the priest's feigned assumption that David is still Saul's officer."[19] Because of the redundancy in Ahimelech's question, David immediately catches on to the priest's deception.[20] Together the two seamlessly formulate a series of questions and answers so as to conceal David's real purposes, while at the same time obtaining what he had come to

---

16 TAGGAR-COHEN (2005: 265) has provided here a slight transformation of the MT's לשלח אֶת־יָדָם (v. 17b).
17 REIS 1994: 61.
18 REIS 1994: 62.
19 REIS 1994: 64.
20 REIS 1994: 65.

Nob to acquire: provisions. According to Reis, the sword of Goliath is merely an afterthought, in case Doeg follows David out of town.[21] (Reis's reading thus explains the fact that David's request for the sword in vv. 9–10 follows immediately upon the narrator's mention of Doeg's presence in Nob, related in v. 8.) Doeg is taken in by Ahimelech's ruse, and David is soon able to ditch the sword: it "is of no further use to him."[22] It is only later, when Saul berates his attendants, that Doeg realizes he has had the wool pulled over his eyes. He vindictively reports David's appearance at the city in such a way as to make Ahimelech appear all the more guilty of collusion: Doeg fabricates the report of an oracle, leading Saul to impose the death penalty upon Ahimelech, his father's house, and the entire city of Nob.[23]

2 1 Sam 21:2–10* + 22:6–23*: Illusion?

Despite Reis's clever attention to detail, she fails to make a compelling case for her reading. As a result, few commentators have followed her example.[24] Georg Hentschel has identified the salient difficulties with Reis's reading:

> Allerdings ergeben sich auch hier Fragen: Wer konnte der Doppelfrage in 1 Sam 21,2 entnehmen, dass sich der Edomiter Doëg ebenfalls am Heiligtum von Nob aufgehalten hat? Da sich Doëg in Nob kaum versteckt hat, kann David von der Anwesenheit Doëgs auch so erfahren haben. Wenn aber die Doppelfrage Ahimelechs nicht die Einleitung eines Täuschungsmanövers ist, mit dem Doëg hinters Licht geführt werden soll, dann wird auch die These fragwürdig, dass Ahimelech ein Komplize Davids gewesen sein soll. Wir sind zudem ganz und gar auf das angewiesen, was der Erzähler vorträgt. Wir können nicht ohne weiteres ein historisches Ereignis hinter der erzählten Welt postulieren, das such durch scharfsinnige Beobachtungen exakter erkunden ließe.[25]

Besides this concern not to move beyond what the text gives us, Hentschel draws attention to the literary disjunctures between the two stories: "Es ist schon lange bekannt, dass diese Erzählungen nicht nahtlos aufeinander folgen."[26]

---

21 Reis 1994: 65–68.
22 Reis 1994: 68.
23 Reis 1994: 69–70.
24 Bodner (2009) is one of very few exceptions to this generalization; in part, his decision rests on the literary-synchronic nature of his commentary on 1 Samuel.
25 Hentschel 2010: 189–90.
26 Hentschel 2010: 195.

Hentschel is representative of a sizeable minority of commentators that has viewed these episodes as originally separate from one another. Many of these scholars have viewed one or the other of the two episodes dealing with Nob as redactionally dependent on the other. For example, Jacques Vermeylen views the connection between the two episodes as minimal. He argues that an original storyline could be found in 21:2a,9–10, which led directly into 22:6–23*.[27] This *texte ancien* narrates, maximally, David's arrival at Nob and request for a sword, before the narrator's viewpoint moves to Saul's encampment at Gibeah. But Vermeylen considers all the passages concerning Doeg to be secondary (vv. 9–10,17–18,21–23), since the Edomite connection evinces a late context of composition.[28] Accordingly, Saul becomes a cipher for the northern kingdom / Samaria and its opposition to Jerusalem.[29] Vermeylen also considers vv. 13b and 15 to have been added secondarily, but he does not seem to offer much guidance concerning *when* they were added.[30]

Similarly, Jürg Hutzli has argued that the entirety of 1 Sam 22:6–23 was inserted secondarily: this passage was authored by the same redactor who inserted 1 Sam 2:27–36 (esp. v. 33, which predicts the violent deaths of Eli's household) and 14:3 (which will be discussed briefly below).[31] This passage thus belonged to "a comprehensive redactional layer covering the Books of Samuel."[32] Accordingly, Hutzli locates these passages in "the conflict between Zadokites and Levites which was virulent probably in Babylonian and in Persian period [sic] and also later."[33] Although I disagree with Hutzli's dating of the additions, as well as his estimation of the relationship between the two passages, he has skillfully summed up the literary disjunctures of the two passages. Although a thorough enumeration of these disjunctures would extend beyond the confines of the allotted space, I describe a few of them below (Section IV).

Hentschel has similarly suggested that the two episodes have been produced by two different hands. In his 1994 commentary, Hentschel argued that the connection between 21:2–10 and 22:6–23 had been crafted redactionally: an originally independent narrative comprising 1 Sam 22:9–18bα,20–23 was secondarily added into the History of David's Rise, and overlaid with redactional

---

27 VERMEYLEN 2000: 131–33, 137–39. Although VERMEYLEN nowhere in the relevant section explicitly accounts the exact contours of his "texte ancien," it would seem to consist maximally of vv. (6?), 11–12,13b,14,16, and 19–20.
28 VERMEYLEN 2000: 138.
29 VERMEYLEN 2000: 138.
30 VERMEYLEN 2000: 139.
31 HUTZLI 2014: esp. 148, 151, 152, 155. See also HEINRICH 2009: 346, 350–51.
32 HUTZLI 2014: 152.
33 HUTZLI, 2014: 150.

materials (vv. 6–8).[34] In a more recent study, Hentschel has elaborated on the model only hinted at in his commentary. Indeed, he explicitly states that "Die Unterschiede zwischen 1 Sam 21,2–10 und 22,6–23 erklären sich leichter, wenn nicht eine der beiden Erzählungen von der anderen abhängig ist."[35]

Hentschel participates in the minority report, represented by Vermeylen and Hutzli, by regarding these two episodes as deriving from different hands. Yet, in viewing them as wholly independent from one another, he pushes into somewhat unfamiliar territory. Few recent interpreters have made the argument that the two constituent episodes dealing with the Nob priesthood actually constitute separate, independent traditions. One notable exception to this generalization is Joachim Stoebe, whose discussion of the relevant passages in his 1973 commentary handled the topic in a similarly oblique manner.[36] Stoebe rejected the idea of separating Samuel into two long-running parallel strands continuing on from the Pentateuchal sources, but he did suggest that, "Vermutlich handelt es sich also um eine Komposition aus verschiedenen Überlieferungsstücken und Ausformungen, die zuerst auf ihre besondere Absicht hin gehört werden müssen."[37]

We may ask whether it is necessary to be so atomistic with respect to the text as is Stoebe. Many earlier scholars approached the History of David's Rise – even the Book of Samuel as a whole – through the *Quellenmodell*, heavily influenced by the incipient Documentary Hypothesis of the late-19th century.[38] Although each of these scholars saw at least two long parallel passages extending through Samuel, their respective approaches to the problem of the passages under study here differed.[39] The inability of source-critics to reconcile their respective models fueled the fires of dissatisfaction with the model predicated on other grounds. By the 1950's, then, the *Quellenmodell* was largely ripe for rejec-

---

34 HENTSCHEL 1994: 124, 127. HENTSCHEL also considers the phrase נצב על עבדי שאול (22:9) to be a secondary addition (p. 128). Verse 18bβ is a younger "Präzisierung" of v. 18bα; the fact that it now forms a doublet suggests we should find the break here (p. 129). Verse 19 can be eliminated from the earliest storyline, since the destruction of the city makes it "überflüssig" that Saul called all the priests from Nob.

35 HENTSCHEL 2010: 196.

36 STOEBE 1973: esp. 390–91.

37 STOEBE 1973: 391.

38 BUDDE 1902; SMITH 1904; DHORME 1910.

39 Unfortunately, a full accounting of the various related proposals is impractical here. CORNHILL (1887: 30–31), for example, attributed several sections of the HDR to E, but dismissed the several disjunctures between 21:2–10 and 22:7–23 that WELLHAUSEN (1871) and STADE (1887) had pointed to. BUDDE (1902: 147) considered 21:2–10 to belong to E, following directly upon 19:17 or the first words of v. 18. In contrast, he considered the bulk of 22:6–23* to belong to J. Accordingly, 21:8 was inserted by R$_{JE}$ (1902: 149), and although the lexemes of 22:7 resemble

tion with the publication of Albrecht Alt's "Die Staatenbildung der Israeliten in Palästina."[40] Subsequently, scholars have tended to work with a unilineal model of textual development, in which a single "History of David's Rise" has been repeatedly reworked by successive *Bearbeitern.*

Stoebe's oblique reference to the present configuration of 1 Sam 21–22 as "eine Komposition aus verschiedenen Überlieferungsstücken" thus represents a feeling of unease with the model that is otherwise assumed to be the status quo; at the same time, it seems to try to avoid a model positing two or more intertwined sources. Yet, there is much to recommend the older view, held by Cornill, Budde, and Dhorme, with some modifications. In the following sections, I argue that an emended version of the *Quellenmodell,* designated here as the Parallel-Source model, provides a suitable explanation of the disjunctures between 1 Sam 21:2–10* and 22:6–23*.

3 Global Observations on the History of David's Rise

A short survey of the narrative disjunctures between 1 Sam 21:2–10* and 22:6–23* raises further suspicions that *Fortschreibung* may not be a fully compelling explanation of the observed phenomena – regardless of whether we consider 21:2–10* the proleptic *Fortschreibung* of 22:6–23* (with Vermeylen), or 22:6–23* to be the *Fortschreibung* of 21:2–10* (along with Hutzli and Heinrich). In my view, this assessment still leaves unanswered too many questions: Wouldn't a *Bearbeiter* intent on reshaping a tradition merely by *adding text* work harder to make sure that the narrative disjunctures between these two texts have been smoothed out, beyond simply the recurrence of significant characters, such as Doeg the Edomite (21:8; 22:9, 18 [*bis*]) or Ahimelech[41] the priest of Nob (21:2,3 [MT],7 [LXX[BL]],9; 22:9,12,14 [MT],16,20)?

E, from v. 8 onward, the source is clearly J, given that Jonathan is a hallmark of the Jahwist (1902: 153). Only v. 19, which BUDDE claimed uses the language of E, can be isolated as the continuation of 21:10 (1902: 154). Conversely, DHORME attributed both passages to E (1910: 193, 202, 206). See also the source-critical reflections of SMITH 1904: xv–xxix.

40 ALT 1953:1–65, cited by HEINRICH 2009: 43, along with another important essay by WEISER (1966).

41 In these chapters, the LXX[OG] normally reads Ἀβειμέλεχ. The phonological variation from the Hebrew has been frequently discussed in the literature, and I leave this point to the side for now.

Stoebe's phrase, "verschiedenen Überlieferungsstücken," explicitly assumes only short, disconnected fragments of traditions. Yet, the very assumption that these are in fact *fragments* gestures at the earlier discourse regarding longer, more replete strands of traditions that could be disarticulated and woven together in new patterns to form a "History of David's Rise." Working from this preliminary hypothesis, I have elsewhere suggested that we have both thematic and textual evidence for two parallel sources.[42] Each of these sources was itself a composite cycle of short episodes that was compiled with the purpose of legitimating David's accession to the throne.[43] These cycles were overlaid with connective (redactional) material – perhaps while still independent, and definitely once they had been brought together. The earlier of these independent Histories of David's Rise (HDR$_1$) was ambivalent in its representation of David. In my opinion, it incorporated two of the three Narratives of Saul's Rise (the NSR$_A$ [1 Sam 11:1–11*,15*] and NSR$_B$ [9:1–10:16*; 14:6–16*]), both of which were extant by the time of its composition. It left ambiguous David's role in Saul's death (1 Sam 31*), and likely culminated in his accession to the throne.[44] But most important for the present study, the HDR$_1$ used Michal, daughter of Saul, as the "bridge-figure": David was qualified for the throne by virtue of his marriage to Michal.[45] In contrast, the latter of these Histories (HDR$_2$) presented David in a significantly more sympathetic light. It made explicit claims that David had an alibi exonerating him from Saul's death on Gilboa (1 Sam 29–30*; 2 Sam 1*). This apologetic text was incorporated into an early form of the Court History (or the Solomonic Succession Narrative) *before* the complex was later combined with the HDR$_1$ and its various components.[46] Again, one of Saul's children played the role of the "bridge-figure" who conveyed legitimacy to David's acceptance of the throne, but in this case, it was Jonathan, son of Saul, who fulfilled this role.[47]

In that earlier study, I predicated the use of Michal and Jonathan as diagnostic criteria for the separation of two Davidic Histories on the work of Otto Kaiser and Ina Willi-Plein. Whereas Kaiser had viewed Jonathan as the foundational figure, over whom the Michal passages were laid, Willi-Plein viewed Michal as the earlier figure. Accordingly, in her model the passages involving

---

42 HUTTON 2009: 228–88.

43 HUTTON 2009: 365, 366: "a loose collection of stories," or a "loose collection of pro-Davidic material."

44 HUTTON 2009: 366.

45 HUTTON 2009: 274–79.

46 HUTTON 2009: 284–88.

47 HUTTON 2009: 235–65 (esp. 260–63), 287, 366.

Jonathan were added later.[48] Although both Kaiser and Willi-Plein adduced copious evidence in support of their respective arguments, Willi-Plein's model was undergirded by an additional thematic observation. She argued that the passages involving Michal "focused on the theme 'Monarchy over Israel' and ... knew of a nascent Israelite state in which Israel and Judah were not separate political entities but rather geographic ones."[49] Furthermore, "The monarchy was assumed as the paradigmatic form of political leadership, but it was not taken for granted that the institution was hereditary."[50] In contrast, in the Jonathan-based passages, "the hereditary monarchy is taken to be the norm, and it is this conception that the redactor who added these passages had to address."[51] This recognition undergirded and dovetailed with the model I laid out in *The Transjordanian Palimpsest*, wherein the HDR$_1$ *culminated* in David's accession to the throne of Israel and *justified* the fact of his rule, but made explicit no further claims regarding the future of Davidic rule. The HDR$_2$, however, was quickly used as the foundational document that justified not only David's rule but that of his successor Solomon as well.[52]

Textual evidence bolsters this model: the well-known case in 1 Sam 17–18 involving textual discrepancies between MT and OG (= LXX^B) offers an objective witness to the source division. These two textual traditions overlap in a single story-arc comprising 17:1–11,32–40,42–48a,49,51–54; 18:6aβb*–8a*,9,12a,13–16,20–21a,22–26a,27–29a. But a second story can be made out in the verses missing from the much shorter recension in the Old Greek (as represented by LXX^B, which is missing 17:12*,13–14,16–18,20–23a,24–30,41,48b,[50],55–58; 18:1–2,[3],4,[5],8b,[10–11a],12b,17–18*, 29b–30[53]). Each set of verses traces out its own storyline; each introduces one of Saul's children who will serve as David's conduit to the throne. Michal figures into those passages that are common to both MT and LXX^B [esp. 18:20]); Jonathan is found only in those passages that are limited to MT (18:1, [3, possibly DtrH], 4). Furthermore, each involves David's marriage to a daughter of Saul (the unfortunate Merab of the HDR$_2$ [18:17] having been redactionally married off to Adriel in v. 19 in order to make way for the "second" [cf. בשתים, v. 21] daughter of Saul in vv. 20–21).[54] While I remain

---

48 KAISER 1990; WILLI-PLEIN 2005. See also the summary and discussion in HUTTON 2009: 235–45.
49 HUTTON 2009: 238, summarizing WILLI-PLEIN 2005.
50 HUTTON 2009: 238, summarizing WILLI-PLEIN 2005.
51 HUTTON 2009: 239, summarizing WILLI-PLEIN 2005.
52 HUTTON 2009: 223–27.
53 In this list, those verse numbers in [brackets] are secondary harmonizations designed to link the two narrative threads.
54 For a much fuller accounting, see the discussions in HUTTON 2009: 257–65; and CHAVEL and DeGRADO 2020. The problem has also been attended to by POE HAYS 2017; and SEPPÄNEN 2014.

unable to account fully for the odd textual distribution of 1 Sam 17–18 in the comparatively late manuscript data provided by Vaticanus (LXX[B]), the objective testimony provided by the textual tradition permits the foundational assumption of a Parallel-Source model. I posit this model in the remaining sections.

4 Literary Discontinuities between 1 Sam 21:2–10* and 22:6–23*

In *The Transjordanian Palimpsest*, I allotted to the HDR$_1$ both 1 Sam 21:2–10 (indeed, vv. 11–16 as well) and 22:9–23 (with the possibility of including vv. 6–8, despite the fact that Jonathan makes an appearance there). More focused study of these passages, occasioned by the "David in the Desert" colloquium, has occasioned my rethinking of their relationship to one another. There are several points of narrative disjuncture that we may point to as not only ruling out composition by the same hand, but also as making a relationship of (dependent) redactional intervention on an earlier text unlikely. I organize the following discussion around three principals: narrative continuity, narrative integrity, and narrative consistency. I hope to demonstrate under the first two headings that each of the constituent units both (a) shows a basic narrative continuity with *other* passages, and (b) stands stylistically independent of the other episode. The third heading collects several thematic disjunctures between the two episodes.

4.1 Narrative Continuity

Many previous interpreters have noted the apparent narrative continuity between David's successful, if rushed, flight from Saul in the dead of night – thanks to Michal's stalling tactic (ending in ca. 1 Sam 19:17) – and his arrival at Nob, hungry and without a weapon. Over a century ago, Smith concluded that

> The condition in which [David] appears before the priest is the natural sequel of only one preceding section, and that is the one where David is hastily let down through the window of his house at a time when guards were already posted, when there might be danger in the gleam or clash of weapons, and when in sudden terror, bread would not be thought of. These reasons seem to justify the connexion immediately with 19:17.[55]

---

55 SMITH 1904: 196–97.

Moreover, Smith posited that David's escape happened on his wedding night to Michal.[56] Although never explicitly stated, this supposition creates several satisfying textual and literary features.

First, the materials duplicated between MT and LXX[B] in 1 Sam 17–18 mention only that David had secured double the quoted bride-price for Michal, and that Saul gave Michal to David in marriage (18:20–21a,22–26a,27). Immediately afterwards, the summary material in 18:28–29a recognizes that Saul views David as a threat and fears him because David is loved by both God and Michal. The notice of Saul's fear in v. 29a fits very smoothly with the beginning of the next episode in which Michal appears (19:11–17):

> (18:29a*) And Saul still feared[57] David, (19:11) so Saul sent messengers to the house of David to watch him …

According to Smith's reconstruction, the episode in 19:11–17 ends with David escaping through the window, thanks to Michal's diversion, and slipping away to Nob in the dead of night. Nob's geographic location, easily reachable from Gibeah first thing in the morning on the way south to Judah, thus comprises a commonsense stopping point on the way to David's hometown of Bethlehem, or further south to the Judean Wilderness.[58]

If the arrangement of 21:2–10* immediately following 19:17 (or a similar notice of David's flight [וימלט]) is correct, then a number of compositional and redactional observations follow. Positing a connection between these passages not only explains David's hunger and defenselessness as authentic to the story's *Grundschrift*, but also reveals a sly wittiness in his conversation with the priest. If Smith is correct that the episode in 19:11–17 occurs on the night that David and Michal were married, then they presumably have not yet officially consummated their marriage. Although he has been lying to the priest about meeting a contingent of men, David is perhaps more justified than interpreters have traditionally realized, when he responds ironically, "In fact,[59] women have al-

---

56 SMITH 1904: 197.
57 I omit ויוסף as a redactional suture that subsequently underwent corruption to ויאסף. I reread לרא as a defective form of לירא, with DE BOER (BHS note).
58 SMITH 1904: 197; HERTZBERG 1964: 178; FIRTH 2009: 233. Contrast the opinion of DHORME (1910: 193), whose conviction that David was initially headed toward Gath led him to locate Nob elsewhere; CAMPBELL (2003: 222–23) expresses ambivalence over whether 21:2 follows more immediately on 19:17 or 21:1.
59 ARNOLD / CHOI (2003: 153) count this usage of כי אם under the asseverative function, describing it as "highlight[ing] a negative oath." A few manuscripts omit אם.

ways[60] been withheld from us, when I went out"[61] (כִּי אִם־אִשָּׁה עֲצֻרָה־לָנוּ
כִּתְמוֹל שִׁלְשֹׁם בְּצֵאתִי; 21:6aα[2]). The infinitive construct בְּצֵאתִי is even more tem-
porally ambiguous in the Hebrew than in the English translation given here,
referring potentially to a regular event ("whenever I would go out") or to the
single departure from his own house that he has just made ("when I left").
This observation might offset Carmichael's indignant accusation that "David
claiming a consecrated status abuses the showbread offering by lying about
his state of ritual purity."[62] If our supposition concerning the timing of David's
departure on his wedding night is correct, then he was *not* lying: Michal, whom
David conceived to be his rightfully-betrothed-and-espoused wife, had effectively been withheld from him by his jealous and paranoid father-in-law. In
this light, we should also observe the oft-recognized corporeal overtones of the
following protestation: "the 'equipment'[63] of the young men has been holy!"
(וַיִּהְיוּ כְלֵי הַנְּעָרִים קֹדֶשׁ; v. 6aβ).[64] Even if Smith may have overread the newness
of David and Michal's nuptial bond, his supposition of a close relationship between these passages provides a literarily satisfying *double entendre*, the pious
protestation masking a sexually frustrated lament. If this reading is correct,
then 1 Sam 21:2–10* would logically be assigned to the complex of episodes
featuring Michal that we might schematically label as HDR$_1$.

---

60 For MT כְּתְמוֹל, CROSS ET AL. (2005: 231) reconstruct מֵאֶתְמֹל. The LXX tradition here has
ἀπὸ γυναικός ἀπεσχήμεθα, "we have kept our distance from women," and affiliated readings.
MCCARTER (1980a: 347) emends to כִּי מֵאִשָּׁה עֲצֻרֵנוּ; his emendation of כְּתְמוֹל to תְּמוֹל (because
the former purportedly means "*as in the past*") is probably unnecessary. WALTKE / O'CONNOR
list several uses of כ in various temporal constructions, including approximations (*IBHS*
§11.2.9b: Ruth 1:4, "about [ten years]"); comparison (§11.2.9c: Isa 9:3, "as on [the day ...]");
and temporal (§11.2.9e: 1 Sam 9:16, "about [this time...]"). Of these, comparison seems to be
the most likely idiomatic usage in this case, as was already recognized by DHORME (1910: 194):
"comme toujours lorsque je me mets en route." The construction כְּתְמוֹל also appears in
Gen 31:2,5 (defective); Exod 5:7,14; Josh 4:18; and 2 Kgs 13:5.
61 CROSS ET AL. (2005: 231) reconstruct [בְּצֵאתִי בַדֶּרֶךְ] הָיוּ. LXX^B adds εἰς ὁδόν, but this is
probably a clarifying addition, as implied by MCCARTER (1980a: 347).
62 CARMICHAEL 2010: 202–3.
63 4QSam^b reads כֹל instead of MT כְלִי; compare LXX^{OG} πάντα (τὰ παιδάρια). DRIVER (1890:
139) and THENIUS (1898: 96) read "vessels" literally rather than figuratively, but cf. TSUMURA
(2007: 533): "why would David bring up literal 'weapons'? That is not what Ahimelech is concerned about." The euphemistic usage is cited also by BUDDE 1902: 149; and HERTZBERG 1964:
177 n. b. See the significant list of prior interpreters in DHORME 1910: 195. One wonders also
whether "the king's matter (lit. 'word') was urgent" (21:9) is also another *double entendre*.
64 We expect קֹדֶשׁים to match number with כְלִי. Interpreters have handled this in a variety of
ways. MCCARTER (1980a: 346–47) and KLEIN (1983: 211), for example, correct to "each of [my]
servants" (כֹל הַנְּעָרִים), following LXX^B. This would solve the problem of the grammatical number of קֹדֶשׁים, but would remove the euphemistic reading (see the previous note).

In contrast, the first verses of chapter 22 relate Saul's continued residence in Gibeah, and his paranoid accusation of his retainers, culminating in v. 8:

> You all have conspired against me (כִּי קְשַׁרְתֶּם כֻּלְּכֶם עָלַי),[65] and no one has informed me (וְאֵין־גֹּלֶה אֶת־אָזְנִי) when my son cut [a covenant] with the son of Jesse (בִּכְרָת־בְּנִי עִם־בֶּן־יִשַׁי)![66] And none of you has grown sick[67] concerning me and informed me (וְאֵין־חֹלֶה מִכֶּם עָלַי וְגֹלֶה אֶת־אָזְנִי) that my son has supported my servant against me (כִּי הֵקִים בְּנִי אֶת־עַבְדִּי עָלַי) to ambush [me] today! (22:8)

Two observations are merited here. First, although many interpreters recognize that vv. 6–8 may be redactional additions in order to bring these two episodes into connection with one another,[68] few observe explicitly the signs of redactional development within v. 8 itself. The central part of the accusation, that "no one has informed me" (וְאֵין־גֹּלֶה אֶת־אָזְנִי; v. 8aα²) is doubled in v. 8αβ (וְאֵין־חֹלֶה מִכֶּם עָלַי וְגֹלֶה אֶת־אָזְנִי). So too is the basic accusation that Jonathan has supported David in his attempt to ambush (לָאֹרֵב) or in his enmity with (לְאֹיֵב) Saul.[69] But a significant lexical difference emerges here: in the second accusation, Jonathan has "supported" (הֵקִים) David's sedition (v. 8b), but in the first, he has "cut" – presumably a covenant (בְּרִית) – with the son of Jesse (v. 8aα²). This difference in locution points to editorial intervention of some sort.

---

65 LXX[B] translates σύγκειμαι … ἐπ᾽ ἐμέ, 'reclined … together with me.' This is the only place in B other than Sir 43:26 where σύγκειμαι is used to render Heb. קשר.
66 LXX[OG] makes explicit that the "cutting" here has to do with a "covenant" (διαθήκην); see the assumption of TAGGAR-COHEN (2005: 261), TSUMURA (2007: 543), FIRTH (2009: 239), and especially BODNER (2009: 235): "when my son cuts a deal with the son of Jesse!" DHORME (1910: 202) supposes that we should reconstruct בְּרִית. But, as McCARTER (1980a: 364) points out, the reading of MT is stated "in a general way – the formal covenant-making described in 18:3 (cf. 20:8) is not mentioned except in the late supplements to the text which are missing from LXX[B]." It may be possible, then, that no emendation is necessary.
67 Cf. LXX[B] πονῶν, "working, undergoing trouble"; THENIUS (1898: 99) suggests that חֹמֵל may have been intended here (citing DRIVER 1890: 142; see also BUDDE 1902: 153; SMITH 1904: 206; DHORME 1910: 202; McCARTER 1980a: 362, citing the correspondence חֲמַלְתֶּם ~ ἐπονέσατε in 23:21). TAGGAR-COHEN (2005: 260 n. 32) derives the form from הלה, which in the *piel* means, in her words "to appear in front of someone who can help, for a request, for help." Accordingly, in the *qal* stem here, Saul was asking, "Is there no one to approach me and inform me about the conspiracy?" but this seems to posit an *ad hoc* and imprecise meaning for the word. FIRTH (2009: 240) defends MT on literary grounds.
68 E.g., GRØNBAEK 1971: 127; HENTSCHEL 1994: 124, 127; VERMEYLEN 2000: 137–38.
69 The text-critical data is ambivalent here. MT uses לָאֹרֵב, but cf. CROSS et al. (2005: 240), who reconstruct לְאֹיֵב in 4QSam[b]. This comports with the observation of DE BOER that LXX reads εἰς ἐχθρόν (see already DRIVER 1890: 142–43; SMITH 1904: 206; DHORME 1910: 202). Contrast McCARTER (1980a: 362), who opts for MT's לָאֹרֵב as the *lectio difficilior* (similarly BUDDE 1902: 153). Compare the similar reading in v. 13. Regardless of which reading is judged to be the primary one, the effective difference is minimal.

Second, Heinrich has pointed to the lexical similarities between 22:6–23*
and chapter 20.[70] Previous interpreters have observed concerning 1 Sam 20 that
many of the verses explicitly describing the pact between David and Jonathan
seem to be later insertions anticipating the entry of Mephibosheth into David's
entourage in 2 Sam 9 (see esp. 1 Sam 20:11–17,23,40–42; compare the explicit
use of ברית in 18:3; 20:8; and 23:16–18 [esp. v. 18]; and notice in particular the
locution of "cutting," כרת, without a collocated use of ברית in both 20:16 and
22:8aα²*). McCarter, for example, excises 20:11–17 with the observation that "The
answer to David's question in v 10 is found in Jonathan's long speech that begins in v 18."[71] He jettisons v. 23 on the basis of its reference to the Saulide
family (cf. 20:15, to which it seems to refer). Regardless of the relative antiquity
or youth of these passages, they all fall into what I consider to be the HDR$_2$ or
its redactions.[72] Although interpreters have produced various proposals to account for the origins of these particular additions, it seems advisable to suggest
that 22:8aα²* (בָּכְרָת בְּנִי אֶת־בֶּן־יִשַׁי) is a late addition on the basis of the other
covenant-passages. A later *Bearbeiter* added this short reference to the covenant, along with one member of the *Wiederaufnahme* (וְאֵין־גֹּלֶה אֶת־אָזְנִי; cf.
20:12) on either side of it. This excision retains reference to Saul's son in 22:8b,
allowing preliminary assignment of this passage to the HDR$_2$. Because Jonathan
plays a minimal role, however, more evidence will have to be adduced to support the source-critical separation I am proposing here.

4.2 Narrative Integrity (and Style of Narration)

Despite frequent claims to the contrary, the narrative arc of each unit is sufficient to account each as self-contained. Hutzli and Heinrich, both of whom view
the *Grundschrift* of 21:2–10,(11)* as the primary account, clearly recognize the
independence of that account. This assessment has been made especially force-
fully by Heinrich.[73] Commentators tend to be less convinced of the independence of the *Grundschrift* of ch. 22, however. Even Vermeylen, who viewed the

---

70 HEINRICH 2009: 350.
71 MCCARTER 1980: 342, see further discussion on pp. 343–44.
72 Accordingly, it is difficult to isolate whether these additions were made before the combination of the HDR$_2$ with the HDR$_1$, or afterwards. MCCARTER (1980: 344) accounts them to the
Deuteronomistic Historian ("the Josianic historian himself"), which in my view would introduce them long after the combination of the two narrative strands. This point is relatively
unimportant here.
73 HEINRICH 2009: 335–42, 346–51.

primary account as lodged *mostly* in a limited portion of 22:6–23*, argued that some of the material from 1 Sam 21:2–10* was necessary to provide the background for the account.[74] This is a common assumption, both for Vermeylen and for those who view the two accounts as authentically connected at a more fundamental level. But is the assumption absolutely necessary?

Comparison may be drawn to the individual narratives recounting the death of Saul on Gilboa. Although we do not have empirical manuscript evidence for the source-critical separation of these two accounts, we might extrapolate the premise laid out earlier that Michal and Jonathan act as "bridge-figures" in their respective sources. The narrator of the HDR₁ relates Saul's demise on Gilboa from the relatively omniscient perspective (1 Sam 31*). In this account, the narrator knows Saul's last actions before his death, something no survivor who was physically present at the battle was likely to have known. The account is fabricated and fictionalized. Moreover, the narrator's focus stays securely on Saul: Although the reader is informed that Saul and his three sons (Jonathan, Ishvi, and Malkishua) died together in battle (vv. 2,6,8), Jonathan is mentioned here only as one of three of Saul's offspring old enough to bear arms. The narrator's focus is on Saul alone, as indicated by the narrator's use of 3.m.sg. morphemes: the Philistines cut off "his head" (רֹאשׁוֹ, v. 9), despoil "his weapons" (כֵּלָיו, vv. 9,10), hang "his body" from the walls of Beth-Shean (גְּוִיָּתוֹ, v. 10).[75] Even when the sons are mentioned, it is all three together as a single group: the inhabitants of Beth-Shean take down "the body of Saul and the bodies of his sons" (אֶת־גְּוִיַּת שָׁאוּל וְאֵת־גְּוִיֹּת בָּנָיו, v. 12). In contrast, the narrator of the HDR₂ account (comprising the *Grundschrift* of 1 Sam 27; 29–30; and 2 Sam 1) relates the battle from a much more limited perspective, knowing only David's second-hand receipt of the information from the Israelite survivor.[76] Strikingly,

---

74 Overall, VERMEYLEN assigns 21:2b–7 to a late redactor on account of the motif of the bread, the opposition of the holy and the profane, and the refraining from sex (2000: 132). He identifies three points of tangency with 1 Sam 16, which he similarly considers late: the verb וַיֶּחֱרַד (16:4); the נְעָרִים (v. 11); the five loaves of bread (v. 20); and the importance of Bethlehem (16:1,4,8; p. 132), although many of these correspondences strike me as vacuous. Furthermore, he claims, the author presents David as a quasi-priest, and the five loaves of bread correspond to the five books of the Torah (2000: 132). All this adds up to a view much like that of the Chronicler, in his view. He also argues that v. 8 is secondary, but he chalks it up to the same redactor that added vv. 2–8. He considers the Persian-era provenance of the text to be established by the role played by Doeg as a "renegade" (2000: 133).

75 HUTTON 2009: 284–88.

76 Subsequent to the publication of *Transjordanian Palimpsest*, I have had opportunity to engage with A. A. FISCHER's analysis of 2 Samuel 1, wherein he demonstrates compellingly the secondarity of the Amalekite messenger (FISCHER 2004: 14–23). For my appreciation of the analysis there, see my review (HUTTON 2011).

Jonathan is present, but Ishvi and Malkishua are not. The report of the Israelite soldier serves to highlight Jonathan to the detriment (indeed, the silence) of his brothers (וגם שאול ויונתן בנו מתו, v. 4). David's eulogy, in turn, lauds only Saul and Jonathan (2 Sam 2:17,22,23,25,26). Regardless of whether David's lament comprises part of the *Grundschrift* or is a secondary interpolation, it draws attention to the heightened role played by Jonathan in this narrative strand.

The most important point to highlight here is the complete difference in narrative style achieved by the two separate accounts. Clearly, a foundational tradition of Saul's death on Gilboa informed both reports. But neither is strictly necessary as an anticipation or a foundation for the other: in the HDR₁, the narrator simply follows the action as it unfolds; since David is nowhere around – or, at least, nowhere that the storyteller wants to admit – Saul becomes the focus of the narrator's attention. The HDR₂, on the other hand, is less direct. In that strand, the narrator allows the report to unfold naturally, from the limited perspective of David, who, we learn explicitly, was at the far end of Judah, in Ziklag, when Saul died on Gilboa. Gilmour has summarized the effects of this juxtaposition in a synchronic reading:

> Two points of view, the first given authoritatively by the narrator and the second by the self-interested Amalekite, drive forward the plot. David acts on the second report to establish his loyalty to Saul, but the existence of the first report creates ambiguity in David's character as the reader questions David's ready acceptance of the story. Thus a clash of viewpoints gives the reader privileged access to this conflict and conveys significance in the second account.[77]

The same tendencies may be seen in the passages at hand, where another "clash of viewpoints" has confounded both synchronic readers and redaction-critical specialists. In 1 Sam 21:2–10* (HDR₁), the narrator follows the action. In this case, David has narrowly escaped from the trap laid around his own house, and readers wait anxiously to find out what he will do, where he will go, how he will survive. The narrator of 1 Sam 22:6–23* (which we may now confidently attribute to the HDR₂), however, relates the story from a detached distance: Saul, along with the reader, only learns of David's visit to Nob through the intervention of an eye-witness, Doeg, who merely happened to be in the right place at the right time and saw David enter Nob and receive bread, a weapon, and an oracle. Although this tradition, like its parallel, clearly assumes that David stopped by Nob for supplies, the author does not seem to have felt the need to provide an omniscient account of David's arrival at the priestly city.

---

77 GILMOUR 2011: 160.

4.3 Narrative Consistency

In addition to these two large thematic points, I quickly enumerate several more circumscribed textual points that have become nearly ubiquitous in the literature. A longer accounting is therefore unwarranted. All of these deal with consistency in the details shared between the two episodes.

4.3.1 Vocabulary

Different vocabulary pervades the two accounts. For example, David claims that he will be meeting "the young men" (הנערים) at a pre-arranged place (21:3).[78] Clearly, this is part of his prevarication, so we should not put too much weight on it as a diagnostic feature of continuity or discontinuity with the following episode. David's evasiveness towards the priest's question resonates with the reader (who knows that David escaped alone from Gibeah and has come straight to Nob). But it does seem odd that the text of 22:6 mentions "David and the men (אנשים) who were with him." This reference is, of course, predicated on the intervening material (22:1–5, esp. vv. 1–2). As Grønbaek pointed out, it may be secondary material incorporated to link these verses with an earlier stage of 22:9–23*.[79] At the very least, it demonstrates a startling lack of reference to 1 Sam 21:2–10*. So, too, does the informant, Doeg, who never mentions the cleverness of David's ruse. While synchronic approaches might justify this silence in different ways, the failure of 1 Sam 22:7–23* to point back to 21:2–10* on this point is startling.

---

78 On the basis of LXX[OG] διαμεμαρτύρημαι, DRIVER (1890: 137; see also BUDDE 1902: 147 [for a variety of options]; THENIUS 1898: 95; COOK 1994: 450) suggested emending to a form of יעד. This suggestion has been borne out by 4QSam[b] יעדתי (for other Greek evidence, see also BHS [DE BOER], citing Symm. συνεταξάμην, Vulg. *condixi*; cf. Jer 49:19 [par. 50:44]; Job 9:19). See CROSS ET AL. (2005: 235) for extensive notes. SMITH (1904: 199) considered the form to point to an underlying העדתי, "which was read as if from עוד," corrupted from an original יעדתי (see also DHORME 1910: 193). But this seems unnecessary, since יעדתי will suffice. In defense of MT, see TSUMURA (2007: 530, citing BARR 1968: 21–22). While rendering MT's פלני אלמוני, LXX[OG] adds "the place called 'Faith of God' (τῷ τόπῳ τῷ λεγομένῳ Θεοῦ πίστις)," and seems to consider Φελλανει Μαελμωνει a toponym; see also DHORME 1910: 194 (reconstructing אל־אמנים following KLOSTERMANN 1887: 93); MCCARTER 1980a 347; and AULD (2011: 246).

79 GRØNBAEK 1971: 127.

4.3.2 View of the Priesthood and Identities of the Priests

The respective pictures of the priesthood presented by these chapters is not incommensurate; it has typically been massaged together with adaptive reading strategies. Yet, close attention to detail uncovers a few salient variations.

The first datum to be mustered here is the reconstructed *Urtext*, insofar as it may reasonably be reconstructed from MT, LXX[B], and 4QSam[b]. Although the priest is named in both 21:2a (אֲחִימֶלֶךְ ~ Αβιμελεχ) and v. 2b (Αβειμελεχ; this form persists in LXX[B] through the rest of the text),[80] the text-critical situation seems to indicate that its appearances on a few of the later occasions within 21:2–10* comprise clarifying additions. Whereas MT includes the name in v. 3 (= LXX v. 2; לַאֲחִימֶלֶךְ הַכֹּהֵן), LXX[B] and 4QSam[b] assume only לַכֹּהֵן.[81] Both MT and LXX[B] retain only הַכֹּהֵן in vv. 5 and 6 (= LXX vv. 4 and 5), and whereas MT preserves only הַכֹּהֵן in v. 7 (= LXX v. 6), LXX[B] and LXX[L] have added the name (Ἀβειμέλεχ / Ἀχειμέλεχ ὁ ἱερεύς). Both traditions again preserve the name in v. 9 (= LXX v. 8), and both omit it again in v. 10 (= LXX v. 9). Heinrich attempts to use this alternation and ambivalent evidence for redaction-critical purposes,[82] but it is not entirely clear to me that the evidence can support some of the conclusions he draws. In my opinion, the ambivalence gives the impression that the priest was not named in the earliest version of the story. At the very least, he is never listed by his patronymic until ch. 22, where the patronymic "son of Ahitub" occurs four times in quick succession (vv. 9,11,12,20). Some commentators have attempted a literary explanation,[83] but redaction-critical scholars have reasonably seen this sudden assertion of the patronymic as an attempt to connect the genealogy of Abiathar (the son of Ahimelech, son of Ahitub; 22:20) to the Shilonite clan of Elides.[84]

A related question is whether Ahimelek should be considered to be the same person as the Ahijah of 1 Sam 14:18, who is the oracular specialist accom-

---

80 The variant forms of the Hebrew and Greek are frequently picked up in the literature. While there is textual data in LXX[B] in support of the MT reading (see HEINRICH 2009: 336), this discrepancy is of minimal concern here.

81 COOK (1994: 450), for example, prefers the shorter form.

82 HEINRICH 2009: 336–41.

83 E.g., BODNER 2009: 224, 237.

84 E.g., HUTZLI 2014: 150–51. Indeed, many commentators have trusted the historical veracity of the priestly genealogies given, assuming the Shilonite derivation of the priestly family at Nob and sometimes citing the curses of 2:27–36 and 3:11–14. See, e.g., PAYNE 1982: 111–12; KLEIN 1983: 222; VERMEYLEN 2000: 131; CARMICHAEL 2010: 202. MCCARTER (1980: 349) is somewhat more reserved, stating only that Nob "inherited at least some of the authority of Shiloh after the fall of the latter."

panying Saul into battle. Many commentators argue that the equation posed by the simple alternation in theophoric element (*mɛlɛk ~ yāh*) signals that Saul had in his employ a single priest in the battle of Michmash (1 Sam 14*), who then was all the more reviled by the king for assisting David in his flight from the royal court (1 Sam 21–22*).[85] But several recent commentators have dismissed the identification of these two priests altogether, sometimes on the assumption that they were brothers,[86] and sometimes on the grounds that redaction could have produced the neatly ordered genealogy.[87]

This question regarding the identity of Ahimelek and Ahijah strikes me as the wrong one to be asking. It too easily presumes a history behind the text, while at the same time seeking to assimilate the constituent traditions into one another, sanding down the discrepancies in order to produce a single coherent whole. The priest in 1 Sam 14:18 is Ahijah ben-Ahitub; the priest in 1 Sam 21:2–10* is Ahimelek; and the priest featured in 1 Sam 22:6–18* is Ahimelek ben-Ahitub. At the most, we might say that a redactor sought secondarily to connect Ahimelek to the Elide dynasty through a textual intervention in 1 Sam 14:3– perhaps solely through the addition of "brother of Ichabod"[88] – and that this was likely done in order to explain the demise of the Nobite priesthood as a fulfillment of the prophecy of the man of God (1 Sam 2:27–36). I therefore agree with Hutzli that these passages are redactional, and that this redaction already has the slaughter in 22:18 in view.[89]

4.3.3 Doeg's Status in Saul's Troop

The status of Doeg in the two chapters differs considerably. Doeg is essential to the earliest layer of ch. 22, despite Vermeylen's attempts to jettison him completely: Doeg provides the sole testimony both condemning David and implicat-

---

85 See, for example, BUDDE 1902: 147; DHORME 1910: 193, 205; HERTZBERG 1964: 112, 179; GRØNBAEK 1971: 132; STOEBE 1973: 258; VERMEYLEN 2000: 131 n. 2; and MÜLLER 2009: 653.

86 E.g., McCARTER 1980a: 239, 349; KLEIN 1983: 212, 214; TSUMURA 2007: 529.

87 HUTZLI 2014: 148.

88 Compare VEIJOLA (1975: 38–42, esp. 41), who excises all of 14:3a as Deuteronomistic addition; see HUTZLI (2014: 148–49) for further discussion.

89 Notice, though, that HUTZLI's (2014) reconstruction is not the only way to make sense of the episodes. He attributes 1 Sam 2:27–36 and 14:3a to the same *Bearbeiter* who composed 22:6–23*, but neglects the possibility that 1 Sam 2:27–36 and 14:3a were composed precisely to incorporate an already extant story of Saul's slaughter of the Nobite priests (who were originally no relation to the priestly family of Shiloh) and, perhaps even more importantly, to reframe the Ark Narrative (I am grateful to J. WYLIE for stressing the latter point to me).

ing Ahimelech (vv. 9–10). Further, he performs the execution of Saul's wrath on the priests (v. 18).[90] By virtue of his presence in v. 9, Doeg motivates the main action of the chapter. In contrast, Doeg's appearance in 21:8 sits uncomfortably in the rest of that chapter. He has no grammatical ties outside v. 8, and the reader is forced to intuit the logical relationships between v. 8 and the remainder of the context.[91] Without the benefit of a reading strategy that permits the audience to go well beyond what is on the page, the reader can only conclude that Doeg is completely inessential to 21:2–10*. He has no effective purpose in 21:2–10* other than to point ahead to 22:6–23*. One would have to rely on other data to make a compelling case for the foundational unity of 21:2–10* + 22:6–23*.

Even the consonantal orthography in the Hebrew text is grounds for identifying Doeg's role in these passages as problematic. The name appears in 21:8 and 22:9[92] in a form some interpreters have identified as "Hebrew" (דֹּאֵג), but as the putatively "Aramaic" form דּוֹיֵג in 22:18 (bis), 22.[93] There is no obvious pattern to the distribution of these spellings (other than that, perhaps 1 Sam 21:8 originally exhibited דאג, which occasioned the change in 22:9 from an original דויג. The latter form, however, was preserved in the three subsequent usages in 1 Sam 22. Thus, the textual situation gives no unanimous testimony, but points only to a history of textual fluidity with respect to Doeg's name. At best, the most sensical rationale must posit that the name's orthography originally diverged between these two chapters and that 22:9 was brought into alignment with 21:8 during the transmission process.

Not only is the spelling of Doeg's name ambivalent, but also the descriptors by which he is called defy easy analysis. Much ink has been spilled concerning the professional office that Doeg occupies in MT 1 Sam 21:8: "a mighty one of the shepherds belonging to Saul" (אביר הרעים אשר לשאול). Some modern interpreters have tried to emend the text to achieve a clearer reading. McCarter, for example, follows earlier commentators in emending to "the mighty one of the runners that Saul had" (אביר הרצים אשר לשאול), but admits that this

---

90 It is unclear who the agent of the verb in v. 19 is intended to be. Although some have argued that Doeg himself slaughtered the entire city of Nob, since he is the nearest antecedent, it seems more likely that Saul should be understood as the one who commanded the depredations.

91 In fact, many redaction-critics have seen the disjuncture posed by v. 8 as license to omit vv. 9–10 from the *Grundschrift* as well; see, e.g., HEINRICH 2009: 347–48.

92 DHORME (1910: 202) argues that we should read דויג here, with the orthography from later in this chapter; the spelling דאג he considers to be due to 21:8 (although, given that he assigns both passages to E, it is not clear how this emendation alleviates the problem).

93 E.g., HEINRICH 2009: 340.

solution does not rest on any textual evidence.[94] Others use interpretive processes to bring this passage into alignment with 22:9, where Doeg is described
as one "who was stationed[95] over the servants of Saul."[96] Accordingly, these
commentators interpret Doeg as an important figure in Saul's retinue in both
passages. This tactic has a long history: most recensions of LXX deliberately
heightened the parallel. For example, LXX[B] seems to conflate 21:8 with 1 Sam
9:1, reading "a tender of the mules of Saul" (νέμων τὰς ἡμιόνους Σαούλ).[97] And
at 22:9, LXX[B] reads ὁ καθεστηκὼς ἐπὶ τὰς ἡμιόνους Σαούλ ("who was stationed
over the donkeys of Saul"), harmonizing with 21:8.[98]

We can probably leave the assumed high-rank of Doeg untouched in 21:8
(even if I would consider that verse clearly secondary). Shawn Zelig Aster has
offered a spirited and sophisticated defense of MT in light of Hittite and other
ANE livestock-herding titles belying military affiliations. If Zelig Aster is correct,
אביר הרעים may indicate that Doeg was an official in Saul's nascent *military*,
rather than some sort of expert in animal husbandry.[99] Yet, this approach, too,
runs the risk of flattening the text, since Zelig Aster does not demonstrate any
concern with teasing apart the text's compositional units, preferring instead to
treat it as a unity.

In contrast, we should question the locution in MT 22:9, along with several
earlier commentators: should this simply be understood as a notice that Doeg
was "standing among (נצב על) the servants of Saul"?[100] This movement away

---

94 McCarter 1980a: 348, citing Graetz (see 1873: 209), Budde (see 1902: 149), and Smith
(see 1904: 200; see also Driver 1890: 140). For further discussion, see Dhorme (1910: 197).
95 MT: והוא נצב; cf. Cross et al. (2005: 240), who reconstruct הנצב in 4QSam[b]. This comes
after a posited *vacat*, so the Hebrew reading seems somewhat speculative.
96 Ackroyd (1971: 178) suggests that ...נצב על is, in fact, a harmonizing addition to connect
this episode with the one in vv. 6–8. Overall, Ackroyd seems to view 21:2–10 + 22:9–23 as a
single unit (= my HDR¹?), with 22:6–8 somewhat distinct (= my HDR²?). For MT והוא נצב על
עבדי שאול, LXX[B] reads ὁ καθεστηκὼς ἐπὶ τὰς ἡμιόνους Σαούλ, "who was stationed over the
donkeys of Saul," harmonizing with 21:9 (see, e.g., Smith 1904: 206–7; Dhorme 1910: 203;
McCarter 1980a: 362). Thenius (1898: 99), conversely suggests that the phrase indicates that
Doeg "stood to the fore." Budde (1902: 153) argues that Doeg was not intentionally among
Saul's servants, "sondern nur zufällig dazu gefunden hat." Dhorme (1910: 203) is careful to
remark that the author of 22:6–23 knows 21:8 (but does not consider the possibility of an alternate ordering).
97 See also Josephus, *Ant.* 6.244; b′ reads similarly ονους, "donkeys".
98 See, e.g., Smith 1904: 206–7; Dhorme 1910: 203; McCarter 1980a: 362.
99 Zelig Aster 2003: 353–61.
100 Dhorme 1910: 203; Klein 1983: 224; Tsumura 2007: 543. See esp. Thenius (1898: 99),
who suggests that the phrase indicates that Doeg "stood to the fore." Dhorme (1910: 203) is
careful to remark that the author of 22:6–23 knows 21:8 (but does not consider the possibility
of an alternate ordering).

from any indication of Doeg's station among Saul's soldiers does not necessarily present an inescapable contradiction. But in light of the conclusions regarding the lack of continuity between 21:8 and the rest of 21:2–10*, we certainly cannot take any putative continuity in Doeg's title to create a thematic linkage between these passages. In no instances does Doeg himself provide evidence that would support an assessment of unity between 21:8 and 22:6–23 at the level of the *Grundschrift* of either unit. Any literary continuity provided by the presence of Doeg is minimal, and has likely been cultivated as part of a secondary redaction (21:8).

4.3.4 Doeg's Testimony

Even more problematic than Doeg's disconnected presence in Nob (21:8), or his descriptions (21:8; 22:9) is the testimony that he gives. Commentators have ubiquitously noted that Doeg's testimony does not line up with the events as they are recounted in 21:2–10*. This is especially the case with respect to the oracle that he claims David received through the intermediation of Ahimelek.[101] This datum has been a point of constant speculation for interpreters. Many have tried to make sense of the passage by assuming that the reader has simply not been told about an oracle in the preceding episode,[102] or that Doeg has fabricated his report of an oracle in order to impugn David and Ahimelek.[103]

David Firth, for example, has argued that Doeg used the fact that the sword was "wrapped in a garment, behind the ephod" (21:10) as an opportunity to deliberately misconstrue the nature of David's request from Ahimelek.[104] Most modern commentators have recognized that the ephod was typically conceptualized as a cultic object first–probably a divine image of some sort–and only later transitioned into a garment.[105] Firth's interpretation thus introduces a clever play into the story: it would not be surprising to find the Philistine's sword delivered before a physical image of the deity. But it also introduces difficulties in narration. First, precisely because the ephod seems to have been an

---

101 As merely one example, see Hentschel 2010: 195.
102 This seems to be the assumption of Roberts (1999: 24), who notes also that other oracles will be mentioned in 1 Sam 23.
103 E.g., Reis 1994: 70; Bodner 2009: 234–35.
104 Firth 2009: 242.
105 Budde 1902: 148, 150; Klein 1983: 214; Tsumura 2007: 546. See also Smith (1904: 199), who points to the item's omission from LXX^OG as indicating that the author disliked it, since it was not a garment or accoutrement.

image (as in Judg 8:27), we are confronted with the description of the slaughtered priests in 22:18 as "each carrying a linen ephod" (אִישׁ נֹשֵׂא אֵפוֹד בָּד). Commentators frequently point out that (a) normally, people are not said to "carry"
(נשׂא) clothing in Biblical Hebrew but instead to "wear" it (לבשׁ)[106]; and (b) that
text-critical investigation casts suspicion on the word "linen" (בד) here: Most
manuscripts of LXX read πάντας αἴροντας ἐφούδ (i.e., reflecting Heb. כל, but
not בד, "linen").[107] Just as problematic is the text-critical status of the ephod in
1 Sam 21:10. LXX[B] does not represent the phrase אַחַר הָאֵפוֹד, despite the fact
that 4QSam[b], which frequently patterns with LXX[B],[108] does contain the phrase
(or, at least, a similar one, אַחֵר אפד). That this is not a text-critical corruption
peculiar to LXX[B], but is endemic to OG as a whole, is probably represented by
the fact that Sinaiticus (LXX[A]) and the Lucianic manuscripts (boc₂e₂ = LXX[L])
use the term επωμιδος. This is the usual replacement for אֵפוֹד in the Pentateuch, but not in Samuel.[109] All this points to a complicated text-critical situation that does not permit us even to read with the veneer of a fully synchronic
reading, in which the Philistine's sword is stored in a garment closet, behind
the priest's linen ephod.

A diachronic reading is necessary here: Assuming the ephod was original
to 1 Sam 21, it would be far better to understand the sword as spoil from the
battle of the Valley of Elah, placed before a cultic image, and carried by the
priests as a sort of battle palladium or cultic emblem (cf. 1 Sam 4:4–9).[110] The
"linen ephod" of 22:18 is accordingly an ahistorical entity that was probably
invented textually so as not to have a prominent priestly lineage carrying
around a cult image of YHWH.

But this conclusion still does nothing to confirm the hypothesis that Ahimelek granted David an oracular consultation: Ahimelek's stipulation of the

---

106 E.g., Budde 1902: 154; Dhorme 1910: 204; Veijola 1975: 40; Klein 1983: 220; McCarter
1980a: 362–63; I thank my student Jesse Kisman for confirming this point in a paper written
for the class "1 Samuel" at the University of Wisconsin–Madison (fall, 2018). Cf. Tsumura
(2007: 546) and Imes 2017: 87, who take "linen ephod" in 22:18 at face value.
107 McCarter (1980a: 362–63) considers the omission of בד to be due to haplography, with
the insertion of כל "a simple expansion." But this may be problematic in light of the fact that
the ephod seems to have been an oracular device as well – would it have been made out of
linen at such an early date?
108 E.g., Brock 1996: 303; Cross et al. 2005: 221–24.
109 Auld 2011: 257.
110 See, e.g., Miller / Roberts 1977. Observe in 17:54 (also HDR₁) that David is said to have
"put [the giant's] equipment (את־כליו) in his tent." One would have to conclude that from
David's tent, the sword was eventually transferred to Nob; see, e.g., McCarter 1980a: 294–
95, 350.

sword's location is merely an offhand, casual remark noting where it had been stored, nothing more. Other interpreters, however, have explained the lack of an oracular report in 1 Sam 21:2–10* as the result of editorial intervention. Hertzberg, for example, explains the mismatch between chs. 21 and 22 as an effect of a deletion:

> the narrative [in ch. 21] does not really have a conclusion, but ends before David receives or takes the sword. Might a missing part have contained David's request to the priest to inquire of the Lord for him – while they were standing right in front of the Ephod! – and the granting of the request?[111]

Both Mowinckel and Nübel argued that an oracular inquiry was *assumed* in 21:2–10. But after considering their respective arguments, Jakob Grønbaek concluded, "Doch kann Kap. 21,2 ff. unmöglich diese Einleitung [i.e., to ch. 22] gewesen sein."[112] He therefore concludes that 21:2–10 *replaced* an original introduction, "in der wirklich von einer Gottesbefragung die Rede war."[113] Similarly, Vermeylen found reason to believe that the *Grundschrift* of ch. 21, which he recognizes in vv. 2a,9–10, originally culminated in an oracular inquiry. Although he excised all the verses involving the bread (vv. 2b–7) as late innovation, Vermeylen believed that the sword of Goliath fit naturally into the storyline: It introduces the ephod into the narrative, thus causing the crucial problem motivating the story's continuation in 1 Sam 22:9–13.[114]

Despite the cleverness with which interpreters have sought to reconcile Doeg's testimony with the earlier episode's narrative form, the simplest explanation is that the oracular consultation in Doeg's testimony in 22:9–11 was original to that account, but not to the account in 21:2–10. The juxtaposition of these two sources then *creates the illusion* of an oracular consultation in 21:2–10*. This is the case regardless of whether we attribute the juxtaposition to a process of *Fortschreibung*, or to the combination of extant sources. In my opinion, it is more likely that a redactor combined two extant narrative threads (as we saw to be the case in the narratives of David's defeat of Goliath and of Saul's death on Gilboa). In each of these three cases, we see an example of what might be termed *authorial creation through juxtaposition*.[115]

---

111 HERTZBERG 1964: 178.
112 GRØNBAEK 1971: 140.
113 GRØNBAEK 1971: 140.
114 VERMEYLEN 2000: 132.
115 See e.g., HUTZLI 2014: 152.

5 Conclusion

The goal of this paper has been to question whether the composition history of the Nob episodes (1 Sam 21:2–10 + 22:6–23) in fact lends credence to Doeg's charge of Nobite *collusion* with David. Clearly, the charge as levelled in 22:9–11 constitutes co-conspiracy, at least from the standpoint of ancient Near Eastern law. Poor Ahimelech was doomed from the very moment David walked through the gate of Nob; this fate was sealed when the priest failed to inform Saul of his interaction with David. But does this charge of treason credibly represent what the original composer(s) of 22:6–23* assumed to precede the events of his pre-served account? I have argued it does not. The discrepancies that interpreters have traditionally and repeatedly adduced between chapters 21 and 22 can, no doubt, be massaged together. I would liken the process of composition-criticism to an act of refurbishing an antique dresser: We can sand down the rough edges through text-critical observations, redactional hypotheses (including sometimes even large-scale omissions), and creative interpretations. But when we analyze the text in light of all this sanding and polishing, we can see that a significantly greater amount of wood-working has been done here than merely the finishing work. We see the grain of the wood misaligned in enough places to know that there are joints. The question remains: are those joints the result of working together large pieces of nice hardwood? Or are we working with sheets of ply-wood or pressboard, composed of hundreds of small fragments? My impression is that the former is indeed the case.

Departing somewhat from the constrained title of this paper, I have ad-dressed several passages from 1 and 2 Sam in the course of this discussion: 1 Sam 17–20; 1 Sam 31–2 Sam 1; and especially 1 Sam 21–22. I have given here only a modestly detailed account of chapters 21–22; a full accounting of the entire History of David's Rise would require a monograph-length treatment. Nonetheless, I can state the main points of my analysis somewhat more briefly: the testimony given by 1 Sam 21:2–10* and 22:6–23* conforms to a single, wide-spread pattern spanning from at least 1 Sam 16:13 to 2 Sam 1:16.[116] Throughout the *Aufstiegsgeschichte*, we repeatedly see the editorial juxtaposition of two long-running and intertwined narratives, neither of which can properly be con-strued as the *Grundschrift* for the other. Instead, each likely comprises the *Grundschrift* upon which various other redactional elaborations have been made. These elaborations often sought to address small issues within the tradi-

---

[116] When redactional elaborations are added, the textual span extends further back, at least to 1 Sam 16:1.

tions separately, but could also be used to harmonize the discrepant traditions, crafting a single entity out of the constituent parts.

In light of the larger textual swaths examined here, I would conclude the following: the slaughter of the priests of Nob – regardless of whether it was enacted on only eighty-five priests (as narrated by MT 1 Sam 22:18) or on the city as a whole (according to what appears to be a Deuteronomistic addition of v. 19, following Veijola[117]) – is clearly the punishment for the accusation lodged by Doeg in 22:9–11. But from a redaction-critical vantage, the execution of the priests in 1 Sam 22 cannot properly be viewed as a punishment for any putative collusion that occurred in chapter 21. These two accounts are so wholly disconsonant with one another that we cannot understand their differences merely as features of textual growth designed to bend an extant text to the interpretive wishes of a later *Bearbeiter*. Instead, I propose, the evidence suggests that we should return to a modified and scaled-back version of the Parallel-Sources model. The respective *Grundschriften* of 21:2–10* and 22:6–23* comprise constituent units of two divergent traditions. These traditions were brought together by a redactor intent on crafting a single historiographical account of David's rise and reign.

Bibliography

Ackroyd, Peter R. 1971. *The First Book of Samuel*. CBC. Cambridge: Cambridge University Press.
Alt, Albrecht. 1953. Die Staatenbildung der Israeliten in Palästina. Pages 1–65 in vol. 2 of *Kleine Schriften zur Geschichte des Volkes Israel*. 3 vols. Munich: Beck'sche Verlag.
Arnold, Bill T., and John H. Choi. 2003. *A Guide to Biblical Hebrew Syntax*. Cambridge: Cambridge University Press.
Auld, A. Graeme. 2011. *I & II Samuel*. OTL. Louisville, KY: WJKP.
Barr, James. 1968. *Comparative Philology and the Text of the Old Testament*. Oxford: Oxford University Press. Repr. 1987. Winona Lake, IN: Eisenbrauns.
Bodner, Keith. 2009. *1 Samuel: A Narrative Commentary*. HBM 19. Sheffield: Sheffield Phoenix Press.
Brock, Sebastian P. *The Recensions of the Septuagint Version of I Samuel*. Quaderni di Henoch 9. Turin: Silvio Zamorani.
Budde, Karl. 1902. *Die Bücher Samuel*. KHAT 8. Tübingen: Mohr Siebeck.
Campbell, Antony F. 2003. *1 Samuel*. FOTL. Grand Rapids: Eerdmans.
Carmichael, Calum. 2010. David at the Nob Sanctuary. Pages 201–12 in *For and Against David: Story and History in the Books of Samuel*. BETL 232. Leuven: Peeters.

---

117 Veijola 1975: 40–41.

Chavel, Simeon, and Jessie DeGrado. 2020. Text- and Source-Criticism of 1 Samuel 17–18: A Complete Account. *VT* 70: 553–80.

Cook, Edward M. 1994. 1 Samuel xx 26–xxi 5 According to 4QSam[b]. *VT* 44:442–54.

Cornill, Carl. 1887. Zur Quellenkritik der Bücher Samuelis. Pages 23–59 in vol. 1 of *Königsberger Studien: Historisch-Philologische Untersuchungen.* Königsberg: Hübner & Matz.

Cross, Frank M., and Donald W. Parry, Richard J. Saley, Eugene Ulrich. 2005. *Qumran Cave 4,* vol. XII: *1–2 Samuel.* DJD XVII. Oxford: Clarendon Press.

Crouch, C. L., and Jeremy M. Hutton. 2019. *Translating Empire: Tell Fekheriyeh, Deuteronomy, and the Akkadian Treaty Tradition.* FAT 135. Tübingen: Mohr Siebeck.

Dhorme, Paul. 1910. *Les livres de Samuel.* Études Bibliques. Paris: Gabalda.

Driver, S. R. 1890. *Notes on the Hebrew Text of the Books of Samuel.* Oxford: Clarendon Press.

Durand, Jean-Marie. 1988. *Archives épistolaires de Mari* I/1. ARM XXVI. Paris: Editions Recherche sur les Civilisations.

Firth, David G. 2009. *1 & 2 Samuel.* Apollos Old Testament Commentary. Downers Grove, IL: InterVarsity.

Fischer, Alexander Achilles. 2004. *Von Hebron nach Jerusalem: Eine redaktionsgeschichtliche Studie zur Erzählung von König David in II Sam 1–5.* BZAW 335. Berlin: de Gruyter.

Fitzmyer, Joseph A. 1995. *The Aramaic Inscriptions of Sefire.* Rev. ed. BiOr 19/A. Rome: Pontifical Biblical Institute.

Frankena, Rintje. 1965. The Vassal-Treaties of Esarhaddon and the Dating of Deuteronomy. *OtSt* 14:122–54.

Gilmour, Rachelle. 2011. *Representing the Past: A Literary Analysis of Narrative Historiography in the Book of Samuel.* VTSup 143. Leiden: Brill.

Graetz, Heinrich. 1873. *Geschichte der Israeliten von ihren Uranfängen (um 1500) bis zum Tode des Salomos (um 977 vorchr. Zeit).* Vol. 1 of *Geschichte der Juden von den ältesten Zeiten bis auf die Gegenwart.* Leipzig: Oskar Leiner.

Greenfield, Jonas C. 1965. Stylistic Aspects of the Sefire Treaty Inscriptions. *Acta Orientalia* 29:1–18.

Grønbaek, Jakob H. 1971. *Die Geschichte vom Aufstieg Davids (1. Sam. 15– 2. Sam. 5): Tradition und Komposition.* Copenhagen: Munksgaard.

Halpern, Baruch. 2001. *David's Secret Demons: Messiah, Murderer, Traitor, King.* Grand Rapids, MI: Eerdmans.

Heinrich, André. 2009. *David und Klio: Historiographische Elemente in der Aufstiegsgeschichte Davids und im Alten Testament.* BZAW 401. Berlin: de Gruyter.

Hentschel, Georg. 1994. *1 Samuel.* Neue Echter Bibel. Würzburg: Echter Verlag.

Hentschel, Georg. 2010. Die Verantwortung für den Mord an den Priestern von Nob. Pages 185–99 in *For and Against David: Story and History in the Books of Samuel.* Edited by A. Graeme Auld and Erik Eynikel. BETL 232. Leuven: Peeters.

Hertzberg, Hans Wilhelm. 1964. *I & II Samuel.* OTL. Translated by J. S. Bowden. Philadelphia, PA: Westminster.

Hoffner, Harry. 2002. The Treaty of Tudḫaliya IV with Kurunta of Tarḫuntašša on the Bronze Tablet Found in Ḫattuša. *CoS* 2:100–6, no. 2.16.

Hurowitz, Victor. 1994. Eli's Adjuration of Samuel (1 Sam. iii 17–18) in the Light of a 'Diviner's Protocol' from Mari (*AEM* I/1, 1). *VT* 44:483–97.

Hutton, Jeremy M. 2009. *The Transjordanian Palimpsest: The Overwritten Texts of Personal Exile and Transformation in the Deuteronomistic History.* BZAW 396. Berlin: de Gruyter.

Hutton, Jeremy M. 2011. Of David's Actions and Davidic Redaction: A Review of Alexander Achilles Fischer, *Von Hebron nach Jerusalem: Eine redaktionsgeschichtliche Studie zur Erzählung von König David in II Sam 1–5* (BZAW 335; Berlin: de Gruyter, 2004). *JHebS* 11. Accessed online at: http://www.arts.ualberta.ca/JHS/reviews/reviews_new/review571.htm.

Hutzli, Jürg. 2014. Elaborated Literary Violence: Genre and Ideology of the Two Stories I Sam 22,6–23 and II Sam 21, 1–14. Pages 147–65 in *Rereading the* relecture? Edited by Uwe Becker and Hannes Bezzel. FAT II/66. Tübingen: Mohr Siebeck.

Imes, Carmen Joy. 2017. Bearing YHWH's Name at Sinai: A Reexamination of the Name Command of the Decalogue. BBRSup19. Winona Lake, IN: Eisenbrauns.

Kaiser, Otto. 1990. David und Jonathan. Tradition, Redaktion und Geschichte in I Sam 16–20: Ein Versuch. *ETL* 66 281–96.

Klein, Ralph W. 1983. *1 Samuel*. WBC. Waco: Word Books.

Klostermann, August. 1887. Die Bücher Samuelis und der Könige. Vol. 3 of *Kurzgefasster Kommentar zu den heiligen Schriften Alten und Neuen Testaments sowie zu den Apokryphen: Altes Testament*. Edited by Hermann L. Strack and Otto Zöckler. Nördlingen: Beck.

Knapp, Andrew. 2015. *Royal Apologetic in the Ancient Near East*. WAWSupp 4. Atlanta: SBL Press.

McCarter, P. Kyle. 1980a. *I Samuel: A New Translation with Introduction, Notes, and Commentary*. AB 8. New York: Doubleday.

McCarter, P. Kyle McCarter, P. Kyle. 1980b. The Apology of David. *JBL* 99:489–504.

McKenzie, Steven L. 2000. *King David: A Biography*. Oxford: Oxford University Press.

Mettinger, Tryggve N. D. 1976. *King and Messiah: The Civil and Sacral Legitimation of the Israelite Kings*. ConBibOTS 8. Gleerup: CWK.

Miller, Patrick D., and Jimmy J. M. Roberts. 1977. *The Hand of the Lord: A Reassessment of the "Ark Narrative" of 1 Samuel*. Baltimore: Johns Hopkins University Press. Repr. 2008. Atlanta: Society of Biblical Literature.

Müller, M. C. 2009. Ahimelech. Pages 652–56 in vol. 1 of *Encyclopedia of the Bible and Its Reception*.

Nübel, Hans U. 1959. *Davids Aufstieg in der frühe israelitischer Geschichtsschreibung*. Bonn: Diss. Rheinische-Friedrich-Wilhelms Universität.

Otten, Heinrich. 1988. *Die Bronzetafel aus Boğazköy: Ein Staatsvertrag Tuthalijas IV*. StBoT 1. Wiesbaden: Harrassowitz.

Parpola, Simo, and Kazuko Watanabe, eds. 1988. *Neo-Assyrian Treaties and Loyalty Oaths*. SAA 2. Helsinki: Helsinki University Press.

Payne, David F. 1982. *I & II Samuel*. Daily Study Bible. Philadelphia: Westminster.

Poe Hays, Rebecca. 2017. A Problematic Spouse: A Text-Critical Examination of Merab's Place in 1 Samuel 18:17–19 and 2 Samuel 21:8. *ZAW* 129:220–33.

Reis, Pamela T. 1994. Collusion at Nob: A New Reading of 1 Samuel 21–22. *JSOT* 61:59–73.

Roberts, Jim. 1999. The Legal Basis for Saul's Slaughter of the Priests of Nob (1 Samuel 21–22). *JNSL* 25/1:21–29.

Seppänen, Christian. 2014. David and Saul's Daughters. Pages 353–64 in *In the Footsteps of Sherlock Holmes: Studies in the Biblical Text in Honour of Anneli Aejmelaeus*. Edited by Kristin De Troyer, T. Michael Law, and Marketta Liljeström. CBET 72. Leuven: Peeters.

Smith, Henry P. 1904. *A Critical and Exegetical Commentary on the Books of Samuel*. ICC 9. Edinburgh: T&T Clark.

Stade, Bernhard. 1887. *Geschichte des Volkes Israel*. Vol. 1 of Allgemeine Geschichte in
    Einzeldarstellungen. Edited by Wilhelm Oncken. Berlin: G. Grote'sche
    Verlagsbuchhandlung.
Stoebe, Hans J. 1973. *Das Erste Buch Samuelis*. KAT VIII/1. Gütersloh: Gütersloher
    Verlagshaus Gerd Mohn.
Sturtevant, Edgar H. 1934. A Hittite Text on the Duties of Priests and Temple Servants. *JAOS*
    54:363–406.
Sturtevant, Edgar H., and George Bechtel. 1935. *A Hittite Chrestomathy*. Philadelphia:
    Linguistic Society of America.
Taggar-Cohen, Ada. 2005. Political Loyalty in the Biblical Account of 1 Samuel xx–xxii in the
    Light of Hittite Texts. *VT* 55:251–68.
Thenius, Otto. 1898. *Die Bücher Samuelis*. Leipzig: Hirzel.
Tsumura, David T. 2007. *The First Book of Samuel*. NICOT. Grand Rapids, MI: Eerdmans.
Veijola, Timo. 1975. *Die ewige Dynastie: David und die Entstehung seiner Dynastie nach der
    deuteronomistischen Darstellung*. AASF B193. Helsinki: Suomalainen Tiedeakatemia.
Vermeylen, Jacques. 2000. *La loi du plus fort: Histoire de la redaction des récits davidiques
    de 1 Samuel 8 à 1 Rois 2*. BETL 154. Leuven: Peeters.
Waltke, Bruce K., and Michael P. O'Connor. 1990. *An Introduction to Biblical Hebrew Syntax*.
    Winona Lake, IN: Eisenbrauns.
Weinfeld, Moshe. 1972. *Deuteronomy and the Deuteronomistic School*. Oxford: Clarendon.
Weinfeld, Moshe. 1976. The Loyalty Oath in the Ancient Near East. *UF* 8:379–414.
Weiser, Artur. 1966. Die Legitimation des Königs David: Zur Eigenart und Entstehung der
    sogen. Geschichte von Davids Aufstieg. *VT* 16:325–54.
Wellhausen, Julius. 1871. *Der Text der Bücher Samuelis*. Göttingen: Vandenhoeck & Ruprecht.
Willi-Plein, Ina. 2005. 1Sam18–19 und die Davidshausgeschichte. Pages 138–71 in *David und
    Saul im Widerstreit–Diachronie und Synchronie im Wettstreit: Beiträge zur Auslegung
    des ersten Samuelbuches*. Edited by Walter Dietrich. OBO 206. Fribourg / Göttingen:
    University Press / Vandenhoeck & Ruprecht.
Zelig Aster, Shawn. 2003. What Was Doeg the Edomite's Title? Textual Emendation Versus a
    Comparative Approach to 1 Samuel 21:8. *JBL* 122/2:353–61.

Georg Hentschel
David's Flight to the King of Gath

There are two rather different stories about David's flight to the king Achish of Gath (1 Sam 21:11–16 and 27:1–28:2 including 29:1–11). At first shall we analyse and compare their literary form. Then we have to ask whether there are traditions about David's relationship to the city of Gath which are earlier than the late monarchy.

1 One moment at Gath (21:11–16)

The first of both stories has only a loose connection to the context. Why did David ask for Goliath's sword (21:10) when he immediately fled to Gath, Goliath's hometown? It would be not clever, if David comes to Gath with the sword of this Philistine in his hand.[1] Goliath's sword would arouse suspicion.[2] Fortunately, he lightly could leave Gath and hide himself in the cave of Adullam (22:1). There could the sword be very useful. Obviously is the judgement justified: This episode is exceptionally isolated in its present position. It is "unconnected to anything before or after."[3]

The story is very short, but the role behavior is clearly recognizable. The servants of the king Achish find out straightaway who is the stranger (21:12). David becomes very much afraid of king Achish.[4] He quickly alters his behavior and acts like a mad man (21:4). The king says to his servants: "Why did you bring him to me? Am I short of madmen that you bring this one to plague me?" (21:15bβ,16) Who told such a story had the laugh on his side.[5] And the people did not take offence that David fled to Gath. An awkward rumor has been covered up. The story is a popular anecdote.[6]

---

[1] For DIETRICH 2015: 567, it is "wenig klug von David …, mit dem Schwert Goliats ausgerechnet in dessen Heimatstadt Gat zu laufen."

[2] Cf. STOEBE 1973: 400, and GASS 2009: 212. EDENBURG 2011: 34 is convinced, however, that the servants recognized David, "because he carried Goliath's sword."

[3] BRUEGGEMANN 1990: 156. Cf. already CRÜSEMANN 1980: 218.

[4] Cf. DIETRICH: 2015: 586: "Notabene ist dies das einzige Mal in den gesamten David-Geschichten, dass David Angst zeigt."

[5] Cf. HENTSCHEL 1994: 126: "Das musste die israelitischen Hörer natürlich aufs höchste erfreuen und belustigen." Similar CRÜSEMANN 1980: 221: "Man kann sich das befreite Auflachen der Zuhörer schon vorstellen."

[6] Cf. STOLZ 1981: 168.

https://doi.org/10.1515/9783110606164-011

2 David's place in Ziklag (27:1–28:2 and 29:1–11)

How established is the second flight David's to Gath in the *context*? One does not expect after Saul's conciliatory words (26:25) that David flees again to king Achish. But David voices in his monologue (27:1) that he can only escape[7] if he flees to the territory of the Philistines. These words are trustworthy: „David is speaking only to himself, and he cannot be playing a deceptive game with *himself*."[8] David's deliberation has been confirmed: Saul ended the persecution when he heard that David escaped to Gath (27:4). Since Achish granted refuge and David got the town Ziklag, the story culminates with the question whether David shall participate in the war against Israel (28:1–2; 29:1–11). After David's returning to Ziklag there is only an aftermath (30:1–29): The Amalekites captured Ziklag and burned it down, but David defeated them, delivered the captives and allotted the spoil. The Philistines, however, play no part in this chapter.

While David fears Achish and immediately escapes in the first story (21:11–16), is his *part* in the second story another one. Now he comes to the king of Gath not as an individual, but as a leader of 600 men. And there is no question at all whether he will be accepted or not. David remains with Achish as though it would be quite natural. Perhaps that was the case. Leaders of mercenary soldiers hire, now here now there.[9] David asked for a place in one of the towns which Achish had at command. David received Ziklag. The roles of both men have been clarified. David accepted his part as vassal of a Philistine suzerain.

But the relationship between David and Achish was complicated. David lived on raiding the Geshurites, the Gizrites and the Amalekites (27:8). He took flocks and herds, asses and camels, and clothes too. But when Achish put the question, where David's last raid was, he did not tell him the truth (27:10). He said that they had been raiding the Negev of Judah and related tribes. Therefore he left no witnesses, neither man nor woman (27:9,11). Achish should believe that David broke with his past. While David did not reveal his purposes, Achish trusted his vassal and proved to be gullible.[10]

But there came a day, when the Philistines mustered their army for an attack on Israel. Achish as suzerain said to his vassal that he must fight with him against Israel. David's answer is very short (28:2): "You will learn what your

---

7 The verb מלט has been repeted three times in this verse.
8 JOBLING 2004: 83.
9 DIETRICH 2016: 20: David takes refuge with Achisch – "so als wäre dies ganz selbstverständlich. Vielleicht war es das auch: Söldnerführer heuern bald hier, bald dort an".
10 Cf. ADAM 2007: 75.

servant will do." David did not precisely express himself.[11] And Achish did not sense that David's answer was not very clear. He made David his bodyguard for life. Because the suspense was already very high, a redactor put the story about Saul's visit of the wise woman on this place (28:3–25). That is very skillful.

After the break (28:3–25) the Philistines went already to Aphek (29:1). The princes discovered the „Hebrews" (29:3) Achish warranted their presence in view of David: He did not find a fault in David, since he came to him. The indignant commanders demanded David's return to Ziklag. He should not fight with them, side by side. He could become an adversary in the battle and regain the favor of Saul with heads of Philistines (29:4).[12] The commanders quoted the song of Israel's women about Saul and David (29:5; cf. 21:12). They did not pay attention to the rivalry between David and Saul, but picked out the close brotherhood in arms.[13]

While the unwitting Achish let escape David in the first story (21:15–16), he had now the task to send back David (29:6–10). He underlined once again that he did not find anything wrong in David's behavior. But the Philistine princes did not agree with him (29:6). Achish urged David to return and to do nothing wrong in the eyes of the princes (29:7). David underlined his innocence and inquired why he could not fight "against the enemies of my lord the king" (29:8). How sincere was that? Who was his lord and king, Saul or Achish? Did David disguise his attitude? Should Achish not guess that he was very glad, if he need not fight against Israel?

These questions already occupied the Jewish scholars of the Middle Ages. Gersonides (1288–1344) thought that "David was compelled to do what Achish ordered". But David wanted to change the front during the battle, "and this would be easier if they trusted him."[14] Abravanel is also convinced "that David was loyal to Saul", but David did not oppose Achish: "Far be it from so honorable a man as David to repay Achish ... evil for good. That would have been a conspiracy and most unseemly."[15] Some present scholars judge in a similar way. D. Jobling explains David's aims like this: „He has made his fate depend entirely on decisions to be made by the Philistine leaders."[16] David "submitted

---

11 David's answer is obviously ambiguous – so HERTZBERG 1968: 175, and STOEBE 1973: 482. BAR-EFRAT 2007: 350, comments: David avoided to say what he will do and left it Achish to interpret his words.

12 Cf. HEINRICH 2009: 343.

13 Cf. DIETRICH, 2016: 111.

14 Cf. the translation of Gersonides' commentary by SHEMESH 2007: 75.

15 Cf. again the translation of Abravanel by SHEMESH 2007: 75 f.

16 JOBLING 2004: 82.

his destiny to them."[17] K. W. Whitelam's judgment is similar: "David, as vassal of Achish, was more than willing to take part in the campaign against Saul".[18] These scholars could refer to David who took care not to contradict the commanders of the Philistines. He had already concealed the sparing of the Judeans and their kindred tribes from Achish.

But did David readily follow the Philistines? Y. Shemesh is convinced, "that for the biblical narrator the possibility that David might fight against his own people is absurd."[19] The Philistines fortunately delivered David out of a situation "that would strike a mortal blow at his plans and hopes of ruling Israel."[20] David's hazardous flight did not lead to the result that he willingly support them.

Is the second story also an apology in favor of David? There is a clear contrast against 21:11–16. The longer story follows its own path, but achieves a similar goal. After Saul's numerous persecutions it is completely understandable that David fled to Gath for a limited time. He did not damage his people. The story pursues a clear apologetic intention.

3 Observations to the development of the stories

3.1 The revision of the anecdote (21:11–16)

The short scene quickly reveals that it is not so old, as it seems to be. Achish's designation as "king" corresponds with Israel's understanding.[21] But one would not estimate the story older, if the narrator had used סרן (cf. 29:2,6,7).[22] David is at a later time "the king of that country", but not yet now. The song about Saul and David has been taken from 18:7 or 29:5.[23] F. Crüsemann has every right to say that nobody wants to defend the historicity of the story in 21:11–16.[24]

---

17 JOBLING 2004: 83.
18 WHITELAM 1979: 105.
19 SHEMESH 2007: 74.
20 SHEMESH 2007: 79.
21 DIETRICH 2015: 565, ascribes the title to the "höfischer Erzähler".
22 If סרן has something to do with the Greek τύραννος, then we have to bear in mind that τύραννος did not appear before the 7th century BCE. Cf. FINKELSTEIN 2002: 137.
23 DIETRICH 2015: 565.
24 CRÜSEMANN: 1980: 218.

Does there anything remain, if we take the younger elements out of the story? Without parallel is the statement that David was afraid of Achish (13b). It attracts also our attention that Achish put the question: "Why do you bring him to me?" Did not David come immediately to Achish? Existed once a something other story? Achish' confession was indispensable in each case: "Am I so in need of madmen?" It elicited a laugh of the listeners. A little strange is that the anecdote does not mention Philistines.

3.2 The late formation of the second story (27:1–28:2 and 29:1–11)

Achish is also in the longer story a "king" (27:2,6 and 29:3,8). The song about Saul and David is also here quoted (29:5). E. Gass has explained in a very detailed article, why both stories cannot go back to the early monarchy in Israel: The Philistines as main enemy and most dangerous adversary are only a literary retrojection and not a historically reliable description of the conditions in Iron Age I.[25] That corresponds to a judgement of I. Finkelstein: "Philistia reached its peak power and prosperity only with the Assyrian conquest and the transformation of its cities into agents of Assyrian economic and political interests. Then, and only then, do the Philistines of archaeology become the Philistines of the Bible."[26] Philistia appears as own political might not until 8th century BCE.[27]

There is a second argument. The name Achish "represents the only attested instance of a non-Semitic personal name for a ruler of one of the five city states in Philistia."[28] But "Achish" is not only the name of a king of Gath in the Bible,[29] but also of a king of Ekron in a dedicatory inscription which dates back to the 7th century BCE.[30] Achish was probably as king of Ekron the most important political figure in the northern Shephelah during the first half of the 7th century BCE.[31] He could expand his territory to the Judean region. And he was able to use the Judeans as cheap human capital, because they knew the cultivation and

---

25 GASS 2009: 229: "Die Stilisierung der Philister als Hauptfeind und gefährlichster Gegner des frühen Israel ist jedoch nur eine literarische Rückprojektion und darf nicht als historisch zuverlässige Beschreibung der Zustände in der Eisenzeit I missverstanden werden."
26 FINKELSTEIN 2007: 522.
27 GASS 2009: 238.
28 EDENBURG 2011: 36.
29 1 Sam 21:11,15; 27:2,3,5,6,9,10,12; 28:1,2; 29:2,3,6,8,9; 1 Kgs 2:39,40.
30 Cf. SASSON 1997: 627–39.
31 GASS 2009: 237. The Assyrian kings Esarhaddon and Ashurbanipal called him "Ikausu". Cf. ANET 291 and 294.

treatment of olives. Therefore he earned a wrong image in the eyes of the Judean people. Following E. Gass it was possible that the Judeans made fun of the literary fiction of king Achish of Gath, whom they identified with the king of Ekron who had the same name.[32] The story about Achish of Gath in 1 Sam 21:11–16 is presumably only a creation which has been made not earlier than in the 7th century BCE.[33] That would apply, of course, also to the longer text in 1 Sam 27:1–28:2 and 29:1–11.

C. Edenburg added a variant thesis to these considerations. She believes it possible that the name of the Philistine ruler of Gath got lost. An editor in the 7th century could identify the unknown ruler with king 'kyš of Ekron. Perhaps he wanted to underline that the older "king" of Gath had a Philistine identity. But he could also wish to make the story more current.[34]

3.3 Critical questions

3.3.1 The name "Achish"

Some scholars are convinced that there is only one rare name Achish. Is it impossible that such a name existed a second time? V. Sasson points to an Egyptian name '(A)kasht in a list of 'Keftiu (Cret) names and concludes – perhaps a little hastily: "Achish was a prevalent name."[35] We can ask, of course, whether Achish of the dedicatory inscription could be the same as Achish of the Bible, since the father of the king of Ekron is called Padi, whereas the father of the king of Gath has the name Maoch (1 Sam 29:2) or Maacha (1 Kgs 2:39).[36]

3.3.2 Ekron or Gath?

If the storyteller had Achish of Ekron in his sight, then the question arises which I. Finkelstein formulates: "Why not say that David cooperated with a previous

---

32 GASS 2009: 237: "Insofern wäre es gut möglich, dass man sich mit der literarischen Fiktion eines Achisch von Gat über den gleichnamigen König von Ekron lustig gemacht hat."
33 GASS 2009: 238.
34 EDENBURG 2011: 232.
35 SASSON 1997: 632.
36 Cf. STOLZ 1981: 169: The differences between the two names witness that both names of Achish's father are independent.

Achish of Ekron?"[37] If we want to give a persuasive answer, we should outline the history of both cities.

Gath has been located on the Tell es-Safi. This city was already in the late Bronze Age the second largest city after Hazor.[38] About 1200 it has been destroyed by fire, perhaps by the so-called see-peoples. Gath reached its largest extent in the Iron Age IIA. But it has been destroyed again at the end of 9th or the beginning of the 8th century BCE. The trench which has been made during the siege contained neither Assyrian nor Egyptian pottery, but pieces from Northern Syria. Therefore it is probable that this destruction has to do something with the notice in 2 Kgs 12:18: "Then Hazael, king of Aram, attacked and fought against Gath and captured it." This news can go back to a historical memory, as E. Gass explains.[39] On top of this the Assyrian king Sargon II. destroyed Gath again in the year 712 BCE. After this campaign of Sargon II Gath is never mentioned in biblical or in other sources.[40] "The prominent place of Gath in the history of David is in marked contrast to the city's political position in the eighth-seventh century BCE."[41] Biblical texts of the late monarchy or the exile mention only four cities of the Philistines.[42] The older pentapolis became a tetrapolis (Ashkelon, Gaza, Ekron and Ashdod).[43]

Ekron was in the Iron I more or less on par with Gat. But it had been destroyed in the first quarter of the 10th century and greatly reduced.[44] Ekron became again a "fortified city", as an Assyrian relief from Sargon II's palace at Khorsabad shows.[45] Sanherib successfully conquered Ekron 701 BCE. That leads, however, not to the collapse, but to prosperity, as E. Gass has already explained. "Ekron thus became an integral part of the new Assyrian international economic system." Ekron has been "the largest ancient industrial center for the production of olive oil excavated to date."[46]

This short outline of the history of both cities shows that Gath did not play an important part in the 7th century. Therefore I. Finkelstein explains that "there may have been a memory that in the past distance, before the emergence of

---

37 FINKELSTEIN 2002: 134.
38 Cf. GASS 2009: 238.
39 GASS 2009: 233. Cf. Am 6:2.
40 GASS 2009: 234.
41 NA'AMAN 2002: 202.
42 Cf. Jer 25:20; Am 1:6–8; Zeph 2:4; Zech 9:5–6.
43 Cf. EHRLICH 2002: 58.
44 Cf. GITIN 2009: 340.
45 GITIN 2009: 355 Fig. 6.
46 GITIN 2009: 341.

Ekron to prominence, Ziklag was ruled by Gath."[47] But it is still more urgent to ask: "Why not say that David cooperated with a previous Achish of Ekron?"[48] W. Dietrich formulates: Why does the narrator not tell that David fled to Ekron and not to Gath which was irrelevant since more than 150 years?[49] W. Dietrich put further questions: Why should they tell in Judah that Achish, the king of Gath, has far more might than David, if it would not be the case?[50] And why should stories originate first in the 7th century and not in the 10th or 9th century, as Gath was still mighty?[51] Why should we give up biblical information in favor of non-biblical sources ...?[52]

3.3.3 David as leader of an Apiru band

I. Finkelstein has meanwhile pointed at an "early layer in the David Rise in 1 Samuel", which "seems to shed light on the territorio-political situation in the south in the 10th and early 9th centuries BCE."[53] The „geographical information embedded in the early David story" reveals "the existence of three territorial units" in the 10th and 9th centuries "in any event, before ca. 840 BCE."[54] These three territorial units are: "an early north Israelite polity that ruled as far south as the area of Bethlehem-Hebron, with a possible extension to the northeastern Shephelah; the kingdom of Gath, which ruled over much of the Shephelah as far south as the boundary of the Beersheba Valley; and the desert formation of Tel Masos in the Beer-sheba Valley and further to the south."[55]

I. Finkelstein detects similarities between the Apiru of the Late Bronze and David's band. "Despite of the centuries-long chronological distance, the reality of the late Bronze is constructive for understanding the situation described in

---

47 FINKELSTEIN 2002: 136.
48 FINKELSTEIN 2002: 135. His answer is interesting, but ambiguous (ibd. 135 f.): "The obvious answers are that there might have been an ancient folk tale which connected David with Gath or that the biblical authors used the name Achish as a symbol for Philistine rulers."
49 Cf. DIETRICH 2015: 572: "Warum hätte man David ... nicht gleich nach Ekron, sondern in das seit über 150 Jahren praktisch bedeutungslose Gat fliehen lassen."
50 DIETRICH 2015: 572: "Warum hätte man sich in Juda erzählen sollen, dass der König von Gat David an Macht weit überlegen war, wenn es nicht wirklich so gewesen wäre?"
51 DIETRICH 2015: 572: "Und warum sollten die Geschichten darüber erst im 7. und nicht schon im 10. oder 9. Jh. entstanden sein, als Gat noch mächtig war?"
52 DIETRICH 2015: 572: "Warum sind Angaben aus biblischen Quellen zugunsten solcher aus außerbiblischen Quellen sofort aufzugeben ...?"
53 FINKELSTEIN 2013: 144.
54 FINKELSTEIN 2013: 149.
55 FINKELSTEIN 2013: 149.

the biblical text ..."[56] The "early layer contains stories about David as leader of an Apiru band that was active on the southern fringe of the highlands of Judah."[57] David and his people played "their cards between the kingdoms of Saul and Gath."[58] "Thus a story about the ploy of an unruly Apiru band in the Hebron highlands must depict a reality earlier than the late 9th century BCE." Because "scribal activity gained prominence only in the late 8th century and more so in the 7th[...] pre-late 8thcentury materials must have been transmitted orally."[59]

Summary

Two different stories assume that David fled from Saul to king Achish of Gath for a short moment (21:11–16) or for a year and four months (27:1–28:2 and 29:1–11). There is – especially in the second story – presupposed that Gath was yet a mighty city at that time. That is only true until the end of the 9th century, when Hazael conquered and destroyed Gath (2 Kgs 12:18). An early layer in the Rise of David in 1 Samuel contains stories about David as leader of an Apiru band. David and his men could play cards between Saul and Gath. In contrast to the anecdote (21:11–16) had David no problem in the second story to find refuge with Achish. He became Achish's vassal and obtained the small town Ziklag. – The narrator describes David as a leader who did not tell the truth about his raiding foreign tribes (27:8–11), whereas Achish seems to be gullible (27:12). The suspicion of the other Philistine commanders protected David to fight against Saul and his own people (29:4). David pretends that he wants to fight "against the enemies of my lord, the king" (29:8). But he does not more precisely say who is his king. And Achish lets deceive himself as in the anecdote (21:15,16).

Bibliography

Adam, Klaus-Peter. 2007. *Saul und David in der judäischen Geschichtsschreibung: Studien zu 1 Samuel – 2 Samuel 5*. FAT 51. Tübingen: Mohr Siebeck.
Bar-Efrat, Shimon. 2007. *Das Erste Buch Samuel. Ein narratologisch-philologischer Kommentar*. BWANT 176. Stuttgart: Kohlhammer.

---

56 FINKELSTEIN 2013: 134.
57 FINKELSTEIN 2013: 133.
58 FINKELSTEIN 2013: 135.
59 FINKELSTEIN 2013: 135.

Brueggemann, Walter. 1990. *First and Second Samuel.* Interpretation: A Bible Commentary for Teaching and Preaching. Louisville, KY: John Knox Press.

Crüsemann, Frank. 1980. Zwei alttestamentliche Witze: I Sam. 21,11–15 und II Sam. 6,20–23 als Beispiele einer biblischen Gattung. *ZAW* 91:215–27.

Dietrich, Walter. 2015. *Samuel: 1 Sam 13–26.* BKAT VIII/2. Göttingen: Vandenhoeck & Ruprecht.

Dietrich, Walter. 2019. *Samuel: 1Sam 27–2Sam 8.* BKAT VIII/3. Göttingen: Vandenhoeck & Ruprecht.

Edenburg, Cynthia. 2011. Notes on the Origin of the Biblical Tradition regarding Achish of Gath. *VT* 61:34–38.

Ehrlich, Carl S. 2002. Die Suche nach Gat und die neuen Ausgrabungen auf Tell es-Safi. Pages 56–69 in *Kein Land für sich allein: Studien zum Kulturkontakt in Kanaan, Israel/ Palästina und Ebirnâri: FS Manfred Weippert.* Edited by Ulrich Hübner et al. OBO 186. Freiburg, Schweiz / Göttingen: Universitätsverlag / Vandenhoeck & Ruprecht.

Finkelstein, Israel. 2002. The Philistines in the Bible. A Late Monarchic Perspective. *JSOT* 27.2:131–67.

Finkelstein, Israel. 2007. Is the Philistine Paradigma Still Viable? Pages 517–23 in *The Synchronization of Civilizations in the Eastern Mediterranean in the Second Millennium B.C. III: Proceedings of the SCIEM 2000.* Edited by Manfred Bietak and Ernst Czerny. VÖAW 37. Wien: Verlag der österreichischen Akademie der Wissenschaften.

Finkelstein, Israel. 2013. Geographical and Historical Realities behind the Earliest Layer in the David Story. *SJOT* 27/2:131–50.

Gass, Erasmus. 2009. Achisch von Gat als politische Witzfigur. *ThQ* 189:210–42.

Gitin, Seymour. 2010. Philistines in the Book of Kings. Pages 301–64 in *The Book of Kings. Sources, Composition, Hitsoriography and Reception.* Edited by Baruch Halpern and André Lemaire. VT.S 129. Leiden et al.: Brill.

Heinrich, André. 2009. *David und Klio: Historiographische Elemente in der Aufstiegsgeschichte Davids und im Alten Testament.* BZAW 401. Berlin et al.: de Gruyter.

Hentschel, Georg. 1994. *1 Samuel.* NEB 33. Würzburg: Echter-Verlag.

Hertzberg, Hans Wilhelm. ⁴1968. *Die Samuelbücher.* ATD 10. Göttingen: Vandenhoeck & Ruprecht.

Jobling, David. 2004. David and the Philistines. With Methological Reflections. Pages 74–85 in *David und Saul im Widerstreit – Diachronie und Synchronie im Wettstreit: Beiträge zur Auslegung des ersten Samuelbuches.* Edited by Walter Dietrich. OBO 206. Fribourg / Göttingen: Academic Press / Vandenhoeck & Ruprecht.

Na'aman, Nadav. 2002. In Search of Reality Behind the Accounts of David's War with Israel's Neighbors. *IEJ* 52:200–24.

Sasson, Victor. 1997. The Inscription of Achish, Governor of Eqron and Philistine Dailect, Cult and Culture. *UF* 29:627–39.

Shemesh, Yael. 2007. David in the Service of King Achish of Gath: Renegade to His People or a Fifth Column in the Philistine Army? *VT* 57:73–90.

Stoebe, Hans-Joachim. 1973. *Das erste Buch Samuelis.* KAT VIII/1. Gütersloh: Gütersloher Verlagshaus.

Stolz, Fritz. 1981. Das erste und zweite Buch Samuel. ZBK.AT 9. Zürich: Theologischer Verlag.

Whitelam, Keith. 1979. *The Just King: Monarchical Judicial Authority in Ancient Israel.* JSOTS 12. Sheffield: Sheffield Academic Press.

Carl S. Ehrlich
David and Achish: Remembrance of Things Past, Present, or Future?

When I entered graduate school in the late 1970s, the history of ancient Israel was still thought to begin with a historically attested Patriarchal Period, as was reflected for instance in John Bright's at-that-time standard *History of Israel*.[1] However, at about the same time important historical and literary studies particularly by Thomas Thompson[2] and John Van Seters[3] called that consensus into question. Ironically, the final nail in the coffin of a historically localizable Patriarchal Period was provided by David Noel Freedman, when he infamously attempted to argue for such an era on the basis of Genesis 14 and what turned out to be a misreading of the texts from Ebla.[4]

This re-evaluation of the putative Patriarchal Period had a domino effect. In the ensuing years, a more critical and nuanced approach to reading the biblical text as literature occasioned a calling-into-question of many additional long-held historical assumptions. The casualties quickly mounted: the descent to, sojourn in, and exodus from Egypt, the desert wanderings, the conquest of the Promised Land, and the period of the judges.[5]

Indeed, part of the reason that the find of a fragment of an Aramaic victory stela,[6] obliquely mentioning King David as the founder of a dynasty, at Tel Dan in 1993 made such a splash is that by then the very notion of a Davidic empire or indeed of a historical personage named David, whoever he may or may not have been and whatever he may or may not have done, was teetering on the brink of the historical abyss.[7]

Somewhat cynically, it could be claimed that the field of biblical studies has not advanced much in the quarter century since then. We are still engaged in marshalling our respective troops on the battlefield of the united Israelite monarchy, whether we are inclined more to side with the recently-departed Phi-

---

1 Bright 2000.
2 Thompson 1974.
3 Seters 1975.
4 Freedman 1978.
5 See the discussion of the history of scholarship on these periods in Moore / Kelle 2011: 77–144.
6 See, e.g., Ehrlich 2001, Athas 2005, Hagelia 2009.
7 Moore / Kelle 2011: 232–44.

https://doi.org/10.1515/9783110606164-012

lip Davies, who viewed ancient Israel as an ex post facto invention,[8] or with Eilat Mazar, who has claimed to have found archaeological evidence of David's palace in Jerusalem.[9] I suspect that most of us fall somewhere on the very broad continuum between these two extremes.

While I am neither an expert on the book of Samuel nor on the study of David, I have had occasion to dip my toes quite gingerly into this storm-tossed sea,[10] particularly as it intersects with my own sporadic studies on Philistine history and culture. In both my doctoral dissertation and its slightly revised and published form,[11] I have had the opportunity to examine the relationship between Israel and Philistine Gath, incorporated mainly and respectively by their rulers, David and Achish. Looking at my own earlier words from the remove of over two decades, I am somewhat shocked at my youthful naïveté regarding the literary artifice of the biblical text. If I were to write my work anew, it would be quite different. Hence, I am grateful to the organizers of this symposium and its subsequent volume for affording me the opportunity to revisit my earlier work on David and Achish from what I hope will be a somewhat more nuanced and contemporary perspective. In place of my earlier confidence in the essential historicity of the biblical text, I will probably be raising more questions than I answer and entertaining more doubts than coming to conclusions. Since I am coming to my topic from the perspective of Philistine studies, my focus will be on Achish rather than on David, the latter of whom will enter my remarks mainly in the context of his literary interactions with the Philistines.

Achish, the king of Gath, appears in only a handful of biblical texts; in all, his name is mentioned a total of twenty-one times in 1 Sam 21; 27; 28; and 29, as well as in 1 Kgs 2. In addition, there appears to be an oblique reference to him in the superscription of Ps 34 (v. 1), where, however, the king before whom David feigns madness is termed Abimelech, in this manner presumably confusing Achish the king of Gath in 1 Samuel with Abimelech the Philistine king of Gerar in Gen 20 and 26, the two of whom are the only Philistine rulers referred to as king (מלך *melek*) in the biblical text.

The two narratives of unequal length about Achish in 1 Sam 21 and 1 Sam 27–29 frame the larger collection of stories about "David in the desert" on the run from Saul,[12] whose centre is the account of how David was able to acquire the wealthy widow Abigail as his wife (1 Sam 25).[13] When David flees from

---

8 See, e.g., Davies 1992.
9 Mazar 2006.
10 E.g., Ehrlich 2016.
11 Ehrlich 1996.
12 Dietrich 2006: 135–39; Halpern 2001: 284–87; McKenzie 2000: 89–110.
13 Peetz 2008.

Saul's court at the urging of his friend and Saul's son Jonathan, he first goes to Ahimelech the priest of Nob, who gives him the sword of Goliath that had been deposited in his sanctuary (1 Sam 21:1–10).[14] From there he continues on to Achish, the king of Gath, whose courtiers recognize David as "king of the land" (מֶלֶךְ הָאָרֶץ) and repeat the song that had so angered King Saul following David's victory over Goliath: "Saul has slain his thousands, and David his ten-thousands" (1 Sam 21:12).[15] Fearing Achish on account of his now revealed association with Saul (and, hence, with killing Philistines), David feigns madness by clawing at the door and drooling, whereupon Achish sends the madman on his way (1 Sam 21:11–16). The proleptic reference to David as "king of the land" (1 Sam 21:12) establishes this text as a literary creation meant to prepare the reader for David's future role in the narrative, not only as the ruler of Judah and Israel, but of an allegedly large empire.[16] The courtiers, therefore, express the perspective of the narrator; while Achish's remark referring to David as mad and his sending him away establish David as one rejected by all and beholden to none.

Achish enters the David narrative again in the lead-up to Saul's fatal defeat at Mount Gilboa (1 Sam 31). Still fearing Saul's wrath, which is ironically presented as uncontrollable insanity in distinction to David's previous intentionally-feigned and controlled madness, David flees once again to Achish son of Ma'okh, the king of Gath (1 Sam 27:2). Since he arrives in Gath this time as an established enemy of Saul and as a mercenary warrior at the head of a troop of six hundred men and their families, David is welcomed with open arms and becomes a Philistine vassal.[17] As a reward for David's entering his service, Achish presents him with the town of Ziklag (1 Sam 27:6), far from the Philistine heartland, which protected the southeastern Philistine flank. For the following sixteen months David would use Ziklag as his base of operations while raiding and plundering the various tribal and ethnic groups living in the Negev desert.

The biblical text has a fine line to walk in narrating the David story from now until the time of Saul's demise (1 Sam 31), which presents us readers with a somewhat oxymoronic portrayal of David's sojourn among the Philistines. On the one hand, he is loyal to his suzerain Achish and seemingly does nothing to betray Achish's confidence in him. Indeed, Achish eventually even appoints

---

14 ISSER 2003: 34–37.

15 A quotation from 1 Sam 18:7. Compare the differing interpretations of this latter passage in McCARTER 1980: 311–12 and ALTER 1999: 113.

16 For a differing interpretation of the reference to the "king of the land," see ALTER 1999: 133.

17 On David as Philistine vassal, see, e.g., DIETRICH 2006: 140–44.

David his bodyguard (1 Sam 28:2). On the other hand, the biblical text conveys the impression that David actually uses his base on the Philistine periphery to act in Israel's interest, covering up his actions by slaughtering all those who could bear witness against him in a Philistine court of law (to use a presumably anachronistic expression). Many commentators have drawn attention to David's playing of Achish for a fool by pulling the wool over his eyes, both in the case of his feigning madness the first time he fled to Gath and in the case of his acting on behalf of Israel once he had become a Gittite vassal.[18] Additionally, as modern readers, we may be disturbed by David's duplicity, not to mention by the murderous covering up of his tracks. However, the biblical text presents this course of action as praiseworthy, since it serves a higher purpose, namely establishing David's right to rule over all of Israel. Just as he had killed the lions and bears that had threatened his flocks (1 Sam 17:34–36), so too would David, the shepherd of Israel, kill all those who threatened his people ... or his own person and security.

The ambiguity of David's actions comes to the fore in chapter 28:2, when he answers Achish's call to him to march against Israel with the Philistines, "You certainly know what your servant (i.e. David) will do." Achish understands this as assent, but the narrator puts these words into David's mouth in order to allow David the wriggle room to continue acting clandestinely against his suzerain's interests.

Chapter 29 goes to great lengths to ensure David's absence from the battlefield on the day of Saul's demise. In an interesting doublet of chapter 21, in which David had first feigned madness before Achish, this time David is marching to battle with Achish at the rear of the Philistine forces. Upon the other Philistine lords' questioning of the identity of David and his men, Achish identifies David as "the servant of Saul, the king of Israel" (1 Sam 29:3) yet adds that he has been his loyal vassal for over a year. Nonetheless, the other Philistine lords demur and urge Achish to send David packing, once again noting that "Saul has slain his thousands, and David his ten-thousands" (1 Sam 29:5), the victims in both cases being Philistines.

When David protests his loyalty, Achish assures him that he has always known him to be an honest man. Nonetheless, David must go on account of the other lords' suspicions. When reading this text, it is obvious that it is not Achish, the Philistine king, who is being quoted. Rather, Achish serves here as the mouthpiece of the narrator. The paean to David's character, the invocation of YHWH (v. 6), and the comparison of David to "an angel of God" (v. 9) are all

---

18 On David's deceiving Achish, see, e.g., MCKENZIE 2000: 101–2.

couched in the ideological and religious terminology of the Judean author. Thus, it happens that David, the Philistine vassal, avoids bearing any responsibility for the death of Saul on Mount Gilboa, which occurrence is related in 1 Sam 31.

This account of Saul's death is framed by two chapters that serve to underline David's supposed lack of responsibility. The first one of these, 1 Sam 30, relates how David and his men were in the extreme south of Canaan rescuing their womenfolk and possessions from the evil Amalekites. And the second one of these, 2 Sam 1, relates how an Amalekite brought news of Saul's death to David expecting a reward, only to be rewarded with a death sentence for participating in the demise of Saul, YHWH's anointed. In this manner, the biblical narrator has managed (1) to have David sent far away from the battle and (2) to have David engaged in another campaign in the Negev, while (3) placing Saul's final battle in the north, far away from both the Philistine and the Saulide heartland, thus making it impossible for David to have participated, in any way, shape, or form, in Saul's defeat on both the narrative and the geographic levels. Indeed, these manifold hoops, through which the biblical narrator jumps, make the opposite conclusion very tempting.[19]

The picture that emerges of Achish in the narrative being discussed is of a trusting yet naïve ruler, more in line with Shakespeare's King Lear than with President Ronald Reagan, the latter of whom had an apparent affinity for the Russian proverb "Trust, but verify,"[20] something that neither King Lear nor King Achish did. Ostensibly a Philistine, Achish nonetheless sounds – but doesn't act – more like an Israelite. With the exception of the anachronistic Abimelech, king of Gerar, in Genesis, Achish is not only the only Philistine ruler referred to as a king (מלך *melek*) rather than as a lord (**seren* סרן or *śar* שׂר), but is also the only one who is named and plays a singular role in the Deuteronomistic History – if one is still allowed to refer to it as such.

The question is how to interpret that role. Was Achish as king of Gath the *primus inter pares* among the Philistine rulers? Or did his status as king indicate a subservient position vis-à-vis the Philistine *s^erānîm* (סרנים)? Was his position bringing up the rear in the Philistine march to battle indicative of his position in the Philistine hierarchy? Or was he positioned last in the column because of his superior hierarchical position, similar to that of Agamemnon at Troy (*Iliad* Book 2)? And if he was the *primus inter pares* among the Philistine lords, then why did he have to bow so quickly to the will of his inferiors in the matter of David? I am not, of course, suggesting that the biblical text is in this case an

---

19 In a similar vein, see HALPERN 2001: 78–81.
20 SWAIM 2016.

accurate reflection of a historical reality. I am merely attempting to understand it and the logic of its "reality" on its own terms.

Achish is mentioned once more in the biblical narrative near the inception of Solomon's reign in 1 Kgs 2:39–40, when the escape of two of Shimei's slaves to "Achish, son of Ma'akhah, the king of Gath" gives Solomon the pretext to have another one of his enemies and potential rivals executed (or murdered) in order to establish "the kingdom ... in Solomon's hand" (1 Kgs 2:46b). After all, Shimei had accused David of Saul's murder when David was fleeing Jerusalem before his son Absalom (2 Sam 16:7–8), an accusation that the narrator of 1 Samuel's Achish stories was implicitly arguing against. While I have dealt with the legal implications of the flight and extradition of slaves in the Shimei and Solomon narrative in other contexts,[21] what is of interest to me today is what – if anything – this passage has to add to the Hebrew Bible's sketchy portrait of Achish.

There are two major issues that prove problematic in this passage. The first one concerns Achish's patronymic. Is the patronymic of Achish in this passage, namely Ma'akhah (מעכה), simply a biform of or even a scribal mistake for Ma'okh (מעוך), his patronymic in 1 Sam 27:2? Or are these the names of two different people? How one answers this question depends on how one deals with the second issue: the length of Achish's reign. There is an over forty-year gap in time according to the biblical chronology between the Achish who interacts with David in the period leading up to the battle of Mount Gilboa and the Achish to whom Shimei's slaves escape a few years into the reign of Solomon. Were these the same Achish? Writing in *WiBiLex* (*Das wissenschaftliche Bibellexikon im Internet*), Matthias Ederer is convinced that they were: "... doch lässt die Charakterisierung des Achisch in 1 Kön 2,39–40 als Sohn des Maacha und König von Gat keinen Zweifel daran, dass die hier erwähnte Person mit dem König aus der Davidserzählung zu identifizieren ist."[22] This is certainly also the position taken by Mordechai Cogan in his commentary on the passage.[23] Albeit, the late general editor of the Anchor Bible series, David Noel Freedman, could not resist adding a parenthetical comment to Cogan's volume that "Probably papponomy is at work here, and this Achish is the grandson of David's patron."[24] While Freedman's proposal certainly would cut the Gordian knot of an extremely long – but not impossibly so – reign and of the possible conflict between Achish's patronymics, my guess is that the perspective of the biblical

---

21 Ehrlich 1994; 1996: 41–50.
22 Ederer 2008.
23 Cogan 2001: 179.
24 Cogan 2001: 179.

narrator is that these two uniquely named kings of Gath were one and the same person.

Until the nineteenth century, the name Achish was only known from the biblical tradition. However, another king whose name is equated with Achish is now known from at least two additional linguistic spheres.[25] The first mention is of a king or ruler of Ekron (*Amqar[r]una*) named Ikausu or Ikayus (Ikayuš), who is known from lists of tributaries dating to the reigns of the neo-Assyrian kings Esarhaddon[26] and Ashurbanipal,[27] which would place this ruler roughly in the period of 680–665 BCE according to Lawson Younger, Jr.[28]

The second is in the so-called Ekron Dedicatory Inscription, found in Temple 650 at Tel Miqne-Ekron in 1997, during the excavation's last season in the field.[29] This inscription, the longest Philistine inscription thus far uncovered, was commissioned by the ruler (שׂר *śar*) of Ekron in honour of his patron goddess, whose controversial name has been transcribed along the lines of Patgaya, Pythogaia, or Potnia. The inscription itself presents us with a genealogical sequence of five generations of (possible) rulers of Ekron, two of whom were previously known from Assyrian inscriptions, namely the one who commissioned the inscription, and his father Padi, who is mentioned in the context of Sennacherib's famous third campaign of 701 BCE.[30]

The name of the ruler who commissioned the inscription is orthographically identical to that of the biblical Achish (אכישׁ), ruler of Gath. While the most popular theory regarding the derivation of this name had been that it was derived from the Greek Anchises, as in the father of Aeneas, who famously fled burning Troy with his father on his back, it is now clear that the Masoretes mispointed the name, whose correct vocalization Achayush is indicated by the Ekronite ruler's appearance in the aforementioned Assyrian inscriptions as Ikausu. Hence, the name is most probably to be derived from the Greek word *Achaios* and means Achaean.[31] In its import, it may be compared with the name

---

25 Younger (in HALLO 2003: 164 n. 1 = *COS* 2.42 n. 1) cites a 1997 article by Jack Sasson in *UF* 29: 627–39 that mentions an occurrence of the name Achish in a 16th century Egyptian text from Crete (Caphtor).

26 WEIPPERT 2010: 340 and n. 15 (text #188 – a building inscription from Nineveh).

27 WEIPPERT 2010: 345 (text #191 – in a list of western vassals from Ashurbanipal's first campaign).

28 In HALLO 2003: 164 = *COS* 2.42.

29 See the translations in HALLO 2003: 164 = *COS* 2.42; and WEIPPERT 2010: 346–47 (text #192). For a selection of the many studies on this inscription and its enigmatic divine name *Ptgyh* or *Ptnyh*, see GITIN, DOTHAN, and NAVEH 1997; DEMSKY 1997; SCHÄFER-LICHTENBERGER 2000; PRESS 2012; SCHÄFER-LICHTENBERGER 2015.

30 HALLO 2003: 303–03 = *COS* 2.119B; WEIPPERT 2010: 329–33 (text #181).

31 GITIN, DOTHAN, and NAVEH 1997:11.

Iamani, meaning "the Greek" (compare the Hebrew יְוָנִי *yᵉwānî*), the usurper
king of Ashdod during the reign of Sargon II in the late eighth century BCE.[32] It
is unclear whether the names Achayush/Achayus and Iamani were truly personal names or nicknames. Whichever they were, the use of these names indicates an identification with the Aegean world, although it is unclear whether
this represents a short-lived Philistine ethnic revival, employing names from
the distant past, or the absorption of Greek mercenaries and/or recent arrivals
into the local population. Be that as it may, Achayush's father Padi is well-
known from Sennacherib's inscriptions, in which he functions as one of the
Levantine rulers who remained loyal to Assyria at the time of the anti-Assyrian
revolt instigated by Hezekiah of Judah.[33] After he was deposed by Hezekiah,
Sennacherib reinstalled Padi as king of Ekron following his victory over the
anti-Assyrian coalition in 701 BCE. Like Padi, the three generations preceding
him (consisting of Yasad, Ada, and Ya'ir) all bear names that appear Semitic
and not Aegean in origin.

We are thus left with two – or possibly three – different Achishes in first
millennium Canaan/Israel/Philistia: First, there is the king of Gath near the end
of Saul's reign. Possibly second is the king of Gath at the beginning of Solomon's reign, who may or may not be identical to the first, although my guess
is that it is the former from the perspective of the biblical narrator. And third,
there is the king of Ekron in the early seventh century BCE.[34] Assuming for the
sake of argument two Achishes, namely the king of Gath around 1000 BCE and
the ruler of Ekron around 670 BCE, we are faced with a historical conundrum.
We seem to know much more about the earlier Achish, who figures quite prominently in the Davidic narrative; and yet, we can be more comfortable in assuming the historical reality of the later Achish, who is attested in incontrovertibly
contemporaneous sources.

In my above remarks, I attempted to demonstrate the deliberate literary
construct of the biblical figure of Achish; after all, David's interactions with him
form the framework of the "David in the desert" motif. Although a Philistine,
he is depicted sounding like a YHWH-worshipper. Indeed, in his evaluation of
David, he becomes the narrator's mouthpiece. He attests to both David's nobil-
ity and his loyalty. Finally, and most importantly, Achish serves to demonstrate
why David could not possibly have been involved in Saul's defeat and death at

---

32 See HALLO 2003: 294 (= *COS* 2.118A where Yamani is mistakenly spelled Yadna) as well as
HALLO 2003: 296–97 (= *COS* 2.218E–F), and WEIPPERT 2010: 300, 306–9 (texts #160–63).
33 See HALLO 2003: 302–3 (= *COS* 2.119B) and WEIPPERT 2010: 326–34 (text #181).
34 Leaving aside the mention of Achish in the 16th century Egyptian text from Crete (see above
n. 25).

Mount Gilboa. In this case, as in so many others, Shakespeare probably said it best: "The lady doth protest too much, methinks" (*Hamlet* Act 3 Scene 2). The very fact that the biblical text presents the reader with so many proofs of David's absence from the battlefield serves as a sign that things were probably not as the narrator would have us believe.

And here I finally come to the question I posed in the title of this presentation: "David and Achish: Remembrance of Things Past, Present, or Future?"[35] The issue in the present case has to do both with the dating of the biblical Achish tradition and with the question of the historical kernel – if any – of that tradition. Or, formulated in another manner, does the biblical Achish tradition reflect a historical memory of a past event, is it a metaphor for events contemporaneous with its narrator, or is it a prescriptive text attempting to establish a future reality based upon a reworking, rewriting, or reinvention of the past? Unfortunately, there are strong arguments to be made for each of these positions.

Those who would defend the essential historicity of the biblical David and Achish tradition make a number of points in their defense. Among these, the strongest are: First, the sheer preponderance of the biblical evidence; second, the very fact of David being a Philistine vassal would be so embarrassing that, were it not true, it would not appear in the Deuteronomistic History.[36] As Walter Dietrich has written, "Wenn David nicht wirklich bei den Philistern gewesen wäre, hätte die prodavidische biblische Geschichtsschreibung es sich niemals angetan, ihn dorthin zu versetzen."[37] Nonetheless, Dietrich leaves open the question of whether David participated in the Philistine battle against Saul. Not surprisingly, the sanitized version of the David story in 1 Chronicles dispenses with Achish completely. Hence, depending on when one dates Chronicles, one would have a rather lengthy *terminus ante quem* for the development of the Deuteronomistic Achish tradition.

In addition, there is a theme running throughout the David cycle of stories that indicates close ties and interactions between David and the city of Gath apart from our present focus on Achish.

Among these one may mention the following: On its way to its permanent home in Jerusalem, the ark of the covenant lodges for about three months in the home of a certain Obed-Edom the Gittite (2 Sam 6:10–12; 1 Chr 13:12–14;

---

35 For those not familiar with English translations of French literature, this title is an allusion to Marcel Proust's *À la recherche du temps perdu*, which is most commonly known in English as *Remembrance of Things Past*.
36 If one still is allowed to use this term.
37 DIETRICH 2006: 142.

15:25). Although later tradition in the book of Chronicles makes of Obed-Edom a Levite, his designation as a Gittite makes his presumed geographic origin clear. Taking this tradition at face value, it is within the realm of the possible that he entered David's service during the latter's time as a Gittite vassal.[38]

Another case of Gittites entering David's service may be found in the touching account of Ittai and his Gittite troops at the time of David's flight from Absalom (2 Sam 15:18–22; 18:2,5,12). During David's flight from Jerusalem, the only one who remains loyal to him and wishes to follow his suzerain into exile is Ittai the Gittite, presumably a mercenary who entered David's service along with his troops at the time that David served as a Philistine vassal. The irony of having the only ones loyal to David at the time of his distress be foreign mercenaries should not be lost on the attentive reader. In addition, David's attracting of Philistine mercenaries may also be hinted at in his acquiring the services of the Cherethites and Pelethites,[39] whose exact origins are unknown, but who appear to have been located at some point in the southern reaches of Canaan, since the biblical text includes a reference to the Negev of the Cherethites.

To these accounts, ostensibly dated to David's time, we may add the aforementioned episode of the escape of Shimei's slaves to Gath during the reign of Solomon.[40] Unlikely to date to the period in question nor to refer to Philistine Gath, is the reference to Solomon's son Rehoboam's fortification of Gath mentioned in 2 Chronicles (11:5–12).[41] Once again, the sheer preponderance of narrated ties between David and Gath serves to bolster the argument that there is a historical kernel of some sort – or if you will, a remembrance of things past – here.[42]

While the archaeological evidence does not directly support this line of reasoning. It too has been adduced in this context, particularly in light of the ongoing excavations of Tell eṣ-Ṣafi / Gath.[43] These have provided evidence for the importance of Gath during the period associated with the events under consideration here, when Gath appears to have been the most important Philistine city – which may be echoed in Achish's status in the biblical narrative as the *primus inter pares* of the Philistine lords, up until the time of the Aramean destruction of the city during the campaign of Hazael in the late ninth century BCE.

---

38 Ehrlich 1996: 36–37.
39 See EHRLICH 1996: 37–41.
40 EHRLICH 1996: 41–50.
41 EHRLICH 1996: 58–63.
42 In the present context, I am leaving out of consideration those narratives that imply enmity between David and Gath, such as the Goliath story (1 Sam 17) and the legends associated with David's heroes (2 Sam 21:15–22; 23:9–17; 1 Chr 11:12–19; 20:4–8).
43 E.g., MAEIR 2012; 2017; 2018.

The possible usages of the Achish traditions as remembrances of things present and future are frequently linked. Ultimately, they base themselves on a literary analysis of the texts and their dating. Quite often, scholars date the relevant texts to the seventh century. As an example of one who does so, one may cite Reinhard Gregor Kratz, who has argued that the purpose of 1 Sam 1–2 Kgs 2 is to allow Judah through the development of these legends to lay claim to Israel's territory and history following the fall of the northern kingdom in circa 722 BCE.[44] This certainly would not conflict with the late Frank Moore Cross, Jr.'s dating of his proposed initial redaction of the Deuteronomistic History to the reign of Josiah (639–609 BCE) in support of the latter's expansionist foreign policy,[45] which encroached upon formerly Israelite territory that had been part of the Assyrian province of Samaria or Samarina. If one were to accept this date for the initial compilation of DtrH, the only question is whether these texts were meant to justify Josiah's expansionist *fait accompli* (i.e., a remembrance of things present) or to offer a blueprint for a policy that he was hoping to pursue (in other words, a remembrance of things future).

In his contribution to this symposium, Jacob Wright provided us with dates that I think are relevant also for the formation of the biblical Achish and David tradition, namely the time period between the fall of Israel in 722 BCE and that of Judah in 586.[46] During this timeframe, there are three major candidates during whose reigns it is possible that these traditions, which serve to lay claim to Israel on behalf of Judah, developed: Hezekiah (2 Kgs 18–20; 2 Chr 29–32), Manasseh (2 Kgs 21:1–18; 2 Chr 33:1–20), and Josiah (2 Kgs 22:1–23:30; 2 Chr 34–35). Hezekiah's reign comes into consideration, since he moved against some of the Philistine cities – but was allied with others – in the course of his larger revolt against Assyrian domination. Manasseh's long and peaceful rule during the *pax assyriaca* does not provide fertile ground for the development of the David and Achish tradition, since Manasseh appears not to have been able to pursue an expansionist foreign policy. Josiah's rule, however, does come into consideration. It meets the criteria that are also met by Hezekiah's reign and adds to them a time after the rule of the one historically attested Achish over Ekron. In addition, it comes at a time when the Assyrian Empire found itself in a steep and rapid decline. And finally, the biblical account bears witness to Josiah's expansion into Benjaminite and, hence, Israelite territory. Thus, Josi-

---

44 See KRATZ 2015: 112, where the author argues that 1 Sam 16–2 Sam 5 (8–10) are "an interlude."

45 CROSS 1973: 287–89.

46 With all due respect to Omer Sergi in this volume, this dating does not preclude the incorporation of earlier traditions into this later composition.

ah's reign would be my preferred timeframe for the development of the David and Achish tradition.

The fact that the name Achish is not attested extra-biblically in Palestine until the early seventh century BCE would lend support to those who would argue (1) that it was at this time, namely during the late seventh century, that this name was retrojected into the newly compiled David narrative, and (2) that therefore the Achish tradition could only have developed after Achish of Ekron's time. This is admittedly slim evidence, even when taken together with the somewhat similar and roughly contemporaneous name of Yamani and with the historical circumstances outlined above.

Were I a betting person, I would put my money on the biblical Achish traditions incorporating remembrances of both past and what we may term future-present. The association of David with the Philistines in general and with Gath specifically is strong enough to indicate that there was in the seventh century a remembrance of a past in which David was a Philistine vassal. The name of Achish, however, lies in the narrative's future and enters the text anachronistically centuries later, based on the name of a ruler of Ekron, which lies just eleven kilometers north of Gath, which latter city had been reduced by the seventh century to an insignificant satellite of Ashdod. His function in the David cycle is more reflective of the narrator's present needs than of any historical reality. Achish is one of quite a number of central narrative figures in 1 Samuel who play the role the narrator assigns them of artificially linking David with the house of Saul and justifying his – and therefore Judah's – claim to Israelite territory centuries later. Among these figures, one may mention Samuel, Jonathan, Ahimelech, and others.

Even the motif of David's marriage to Saul's daughter Michal may be construed as part of this attempt to link David secondarily with the house of Saul. If the marriage never took place, then there could have been no progeny. This would explain the biblical author's need to invent a story about why it happened that David and Michal had no children, in spite of being married in the narrator's probably invented reality.

In conclusion, while I am comfortable assuming the essential historicity of David's relationship with one or more of the Philistine city-states, and specifically Gath, I am much less sanguine about the details of that relationship as conveyed in the later biblical text. In addition, contrary to what I thought as I began writing this essay, I am now inclined to agree with the conclusion reached by Cynthia Edenburg in a 2011 *Vetus Testamentum* article[47] and answer

47 Edenburg 2011.

the question of whether there was a ruler of Gath named Achish who lived around the year 1000 BCE in the negative. If David interacted with a Gittite ruler – and it appears quite likely that he did, this ruler's original name has most probably been lost to history.

Bibliography

Alter, Robert. 1999. *The David Story: A Translation with Commentary of 1 and 2 Samuel*. New York / London: W. W. Norton & Company.

Athas, George. 2005. *The Tel Dan Inscription: A Reappraisal and a New Introduction*. London: T&T Clark.

Bright, John. 2000. *A History of Israel*. 4th ed. Louisville, KY: Westminster John Knox Press.

Cogan, Mordechai. 2001. *I Kings*. AB 10. New York et al.: Doubleday.

Cross, Frank Moore, Jr. 1973. *Canaanite Myth and Hebrew Epic: Essays in the History of the Religion of Israel*. Cambridge, MA / London, UK: Harvard University Press.

Davies, Philip R. 1992. *In Search of 'Ancient Israel'*. JSOTSup 148. Sheffield: Sheffield Academic Press.

Demsky, Aaron. 1997. The Name of the Goddess of Ekron: A New Reading. *JANES* 25:1–5.

Dietrich, Walter. 2006. *David: Der Herrscher mit der Harfe*. Biblische Gestalten 14. Leipzig: Evangelische Verlagsanstalt.

Edenburg, Cynthia. 2011. Notes on the Origin of the Biblical Tradition Regarding Achish King of Gath. *VT* 61:34–38.

Ederer, Matthias. 2008. Achisch. *WiBiLex* (*Das wissenschaftliche Bibellexikon im Internet*). Retrieved from https://www.bibelwissenschaft.de/stichwort/12396/.

Ehrlich, Carl S. 1994. Sklavenauslieferung in der Bibel und im alten Orient. *Trumah* 4:111–18.

Ehrlich, Carl S. 1996. *The Philistines in Transition: A History from ca. 1000–730 B.C.E.* SHANE 10. Leiden / New York / Köln: E. J. Brill.

Ehrlich, Carl S. 2001. The *bytdwd*-Inscription and Israelite Historiography: Taking Stock after Half a Decade of Research. Pages 57–71 in *The World of the Arameans II: Studies in History and Archaeology in Honour of Paul-Eugène Dion*. Edited by P. M. Michèle Daviau, John W. Wevers, and Michael Weigl. JSOTSup 325. Sheffield: Sheffield Academic Press.

Ehrlich, Carl S. 2016. Biblical Gentilics and Israelite Ethnicity. Pages 413–21 in *The Books of Samuel: Stories – History – Reception History*. Edited by Walter Dietrich. BETL 284. Leuven / Paris / Bristol, CT: Peeters.

Freedman, David Noel. 1978. The Real Story of the Ebla Tablets: Ebla and the Cities of the Plain. *BA* 41:143–64.

Gitin, Seymour, Trude Dothan, and Joseph Naveh. 1997. A Royal Dedicatory Inscription from Ekron. *IEJ* 47:1–16.

Hagelia, Hallvard. 2009. *The Dan Debate: The Tel Dan Inscription in Recent Research*. Recent Research in Biblical Studies 4. Sheffield: Sheffield Phoenix Press.

Hallo, William W. 2003. *The Context of Scripture, Volume II: Monumental Inscriptions from the Biblical World* (= *COS* 2). Leiden / Boston: Brill.

Halpern, Baruch. 2001. *David's Secret Demons: Messiah, Murderer, Traitor, King*. The Bible in Its World. Grand Rapids, MI / Cambridge, UK: William B. Eerdmans Publishing Company.

Isser, Stanley. 2003. *The Sword of Goliath: David in Heroic Literature*. SBL 6. Atlanta: Society of Biblical Literature.

Kratz, Reinhard Gregor. 2015. *Historical and Biblical Israel: The History, Tradition, and Archives of Israel and Judah*. Translated by Paul Michael Kurtz. Oxford: Oxford University Press.

Mazar, Eilat. 2006. Did I Find King David's Palace? *BAR* 32/1:16–27, 70.

McCarter, P. Kyle. 1980. *I Samuel*. AB 8. Garden City, NY: Doubleday & Company.

McKenzie, Steven L. 2000. *King David: A Biography*. Oxford / New York: Oxford University Press.

Maeir, Aren M., ed. 2012. *Tell Es-Safi/Gath I: The 1996–2005 Seasons*. 2 volumes. Ägypten und Altes Testament 69. Wiesbaden: Harrassowitz.

Maeir, Aren M, ed. 2017. *Special Issue: The Tell eş-Şâfi/Gath Archaeological Project. Near Eastern Archaeology* 80/4.

Maeir, Aren M, ed. 2018. *Special Issue: The Tell eş-Şâfi/Gath Archaeological Project. Near Eastern Archaeology* 81/1.

Moore, Megan Bishop and Brad E. Kelle. 2011. *Biblical History and Israel's Past: The Changing Study of the Bible and History*. Grand Rapids, MI / Cambridge, UK: William B. Eerdmans Publishing Company.

Peetz, Melanie. 2008. *Abigajil, die Prophetin: Mit Klugheit und Schönheit für Gewaltverzicht*. FB 116. Würzburg: Echter Verlag.

Press, Michael D. 2012. (Pytho)Gaia in Myth and Legend: The Goddess of the Ekron Inscription Revisited. *BASOR* 365:1–25.

Schäfer-Lichtenberger, Christa. 2000. The Goddess of Ekron and the Religious-Cultural Background of the Philistines. *IEJ* 50:82–91.

Schäfer-Lichtenberger, Christa. 2015. PTGYH–Divine Anonyma? The Goddess of the Ekron Inscription. *UF* 46:341–72.

Seters, John Van. 1975. *Abraham in History and Tradition*. New Haven / London: Yale University Press.

Swaim, Barton. 2016. 'Trust, but verify': An Untrustworthy Political Phrase." *The Washington Post* (March 11, 2016). Retrieved from https://www.washingtonpost.com/opinions/trust-but-verify-an-untrustworthy-political-phrase/2016/03/11/da32fb08-db3b-11e5-891a-4ed04f4213e8_story.html.

Thompson, Thomas L. 1974. *The Historicity of the Patriarchal Narratives: The Quest for the Historical Abraham*. BZAW 133. Berlin: De Gruyter.

Weippert, Manfred. 2010. *Historisches Textbuch zum Alten Testament*. GAT/ATD Ergänzungsreihe 10. Göttingen: Vandenhoeck & Ruprecht.

Reinhard Müller

David in Keïla

Zur Literargeschichte von 1Sam 23,1–13

Einführung

Die Episode 1Sam 23,1–13, die von Davids Aufenthalt in der am Rande der Schefela gelegenen Stadt Keïla handelt, gibt wichtige Einblicke in die literargeschichtliche Entwicklung der Davidüberlieferung. Der Text weist umfangreiche
Bearbeitungsspuren auf, scheint aber einen verhältnismäßig alten Kern zu enthalten; darin sind vielleicht sogar Erinnerungen an den historischen David zu
greifen.

Trotz der Kürze des Abschnitts erweisen sich die literargeschichtlichen
Verhältnisse als kompliziert. Im Folgenden soll – beginnend mit den jüngsten
Zusätzen, die teils durch die ihrerseits recht komplexe Textüberlieferung do-
kumentiert sind – analytisch zurückgefragt werden, um Schritt für Schritt die
wahrscheinlich jüngeren Textelemente von den älteren und ältesten Stufen
abzuheben. Zu betonen ist, dass die Rekonstruktion umso hypothetischer wird,
je weiter zurück sich die Analyse wagt.

1 Späte Nachträge und Glossen

Kleinere Nachträge, die als Randglossen in den Text gelangt sein könnten, sind
in V. 2.5.9.13 zu erkennen. In V. 5 fällt die Wendung ואנשיו (gelesen mit dem
Qerê) „und seine Männer" auf, die auf die Eingangsworte וילך דוד „Und David
ging" folgt. Zwar ist eine solche Verbindung zweier Subjekte mit einer singulari-
schen Narrativform für sich genommen syntaktisch möglich.[1] Timo Veijola wies
jedoch darauf hin, dass weitere Narrativformen dann im Plural stehen müssten.
So ist es etwa in V. 13 belegt: ויצאו ... ויקם דוד ואנשיו „Und David stand auf
mit seinen Männern ..., und *sie zogen hinaus*".[2] Das lässt darauf schließen, dass
ואנשיו „und seine Männer" nachträglich eingefügt wurde.[3] Der Zweck der Glosse dürfte darin bestanden haben, V. 5 stärker mit der vorausgehenden Szene in

---

1 Vgl. GKC § 146 f.
2 Veijola 1990: 27, unter Verweis auf GKC § 146 h.
3 Veijola 1990: 27.

https://doi.org/10.1515/9783110606164-013

V. 3–4 zu verknüpfen, wo Davids Männer ihm ihre Furcht vor den Philistern gestehen, was zur Folge hat, dass David ein zweites Mal das Jahweorakel befragt (V. 4). Ohne die offenbar nachträglich hinzugesetzte Erwähnung der Männer Davids spricht V. 5 dagegen allein von David, was natürlich die Vorstellung einer mit David kämpfenden Truppe einschließt. Auch in V. 1–2 ist allein David das handelnde Subjekt, was an manche altorientalische Königsinschrift erinnert; zu vergleichen ist etwa die Meschastele, wo der König allein von *seinem* Kämpfen spricht, ohne die ihn begleitenden Truppen zu erwähnen.[4] Die Glosse in V. 5 verknüpft also die Szene von V. 3–4 enger mit den rahmenden Versen. Dieses Phänomen muss bei einem späteren Schritt der Analyse noch einmal bedacht werden.[5]

Im Masoretischen Text von V. 9 wird Abjatar ausdrücklich als הכהן „der Priester" bezeichnet. Das fällt zunächst insofern auf, als in V. 6, wo Abjatar in dieser Episode zum ersten Mal erwähnt wird, zwar Abjatars Vatersname Ahimelech genannt wird, die Berufsbezeichnung Priester aber fehlt. Die Erwähnung von Abjatars Priestertum ist in V. 9 sachlich durchaus berechtigt, da die Handhabung des Efodorakels offenbar eine priesterliche Tätigkeit ist. Allerdings wird Abjatar bei seiner ersten erzählerischen Erwähnung in 1Sam 22,20 lediglich als Sohn des Ahimelech eingeführt, der dem Massaker an den Priestern von Nob entrinnt. Natürlich impliziert das, dass auch Ahimelechs Sohn Abjatar Priester war. In einem Teil der Textüberlieferung zu 1Sam 23,9, wozu v. a. einige griechische Minuskeln zählen, fehlt jedoch die Wendung „der Priester",[6] ebenso in einigen verstreuten und marginalen hebräischen Textzeugen.[7] Es lässt sich von vornherein kaum ausschließen, dass diese Überlieferungen eine ältere lectio brevior bezeugen. Allerdings ist der Wert dieser Textzeugen schwer zu beurteilen, und es erscheint als genauso möglich, dass die nach 1Sam 22,20 vielleicht als überraschend oder unnötig empfundene Bezeichnung „der Priester" in einem Teil der Textüberlieferung nachträglich ausgelassen wurde. In diesem Fall könnte das auffällige Stichwort „der Priester" vielmehr einen Hinweis auf die literargeschichtliche Stellung des Verses bieten.[8]

Deutlicher ist der wahrscheinlich sekundäre Charakter der Wendung כשש מאות איש „etwa 600 Mann" – oder nach der Septuaginta כארבע מאות איש „etwa 400 Mann" in V. 13. Die Angabe sieht wie eine nachträgliche Präzisierung aus, die ad vocem ואנשיו „und seine Männer" hinzugefügt wurde.[9] Die Zahl

---

4 *KAI* 181:14, 22, 30 etc.; vgl. WEIPPERT 2010: 244–48.
5 S.u. 2.
6 Scil. die Minuskeln efmswa₂ (BROOKE, MCLEAN und THACKERAY 1927: 78).
7 S. *BHS*.
8 S.u. 3. und vgl. 1Sam 30,7; 1Kön 1,7 etc.
9 VEIJOLA 1990: 28.

600 scheint in 1Sam 27,2 und 30,9 verankert zu sein; 400 entspricht dagegen der ersten Erwähnung der Männer Davids in 1Sam 22,2. Welche der beiden Zahlen ursprünglicher ist, lässt sich schwer entscheiden, zumal auch an anderen Stellen die Zahl der Männer Davids in der Textüberlieferung zwischen 400 und 600 schwankt.[10] Meist nimmt man an, dass sich die 400 der Septuaginta einer nachträglichen Angleichung an 1Sam 22,2 verdankt.[11] Allerdings könnte auch die 400 in 600 verändert worden sein, um Davids Gefolgschaft etwa im Blick auf 1Sam 25,13 zu vergrößern. Wenn es hier ursprünglich „etwa 400 Mann" hieß, diente die Wendung zur stärkeren Verknüpfung mit 1Sam 22,2, wo berichtet wird, wie David die Männer um sich scharte und ihr Anführer wurde; wenn dagegen von „etwa 600 Mann" die Rede ist, weist das auf 1Sam 25,13 und 27,2 sowie vor allem 1Sam 30 (V. 10 ff) voraus.

Ein weiterer kleiner Zusatz ist wahrscheinlich im Masoretischen Text von V. 2 zu greifen, und zwar in der Einleitung zu Jahwes Orakelanwort; diese lautet im MT ויאמר יהוה אל דוד „Und Jahwe sprach zu David". In Teilen der Septuaginta ist die Wendung „zu David" dagegen nicht bezeugt,[12] was wohl als ursprünglichere lectio brevior zu erklären ist, da sich umgekehrt kaum verstehen ließe, weshalb das „zu David" in der Vorlage der Old Greek oder durch den griechischen Übersetzer ausgelassen worden sein sollte. Zwar wird auch andernorts mitunter durch eine kurze Präpositionalphrase benannt, an wen die Antwort des Jahweorakels erging;[13] die ursprüngliche Form scheint aber schlicht in der knappen Redeeinleitung ויאמר יהוה „Und Jahwe sprach" bestanden zu haben, wie sie auch in V. 11b und V. 12b belegt ist.[14]

Neben diesen glossenartigen Wendungen sind zwei etwas längere Passagen zu betrachten, die ebenfalls des Nachtrags verdächtig sind. Im Masoretischen Text von V. 11 fällt die eröffnende Frage היסגרני בעלי קעילה בידו „Werden die Herren von Keïla mich in seine Hand ausliefern?" auf. Sie nimmt den Gegenstand der zweiten Orakelanfrage in V. 12 vorweg: Da die Frage dort fast wörtlich wiederholt wird, lässt sich vermuten, dass V. 11aα₁ nachgetragen wurde, um die beiden Orakelanfragen enger zu verknüpfen. Allerdings bietet die Textüberlieferung nicht unerhebliche Probleme:

10 Vgl. 1Sam 27,2 und 30,9.
11 Im Gefolge von WELLHAUSEN 1871: 128; vgl. z. B. BUDDE 1902: 157.
12 V.a. in B (BROOKE, McLEAN und THACKERAY 1927: 78).
13 Vgl. 1Sam 30,8; 2Sam 2,1; 5,19.
14 Vgl. Ri 1,2; 20,18.23.28; 1Sam 10,22; 2Sam 5,23.

	MT	*LXX*
V. 11	היסגרני בעלי קעילה בידו	εἰ ἀποκλεισθήσεται;
	הירד שאול	καὶ νῦν εἰ καταβήσεται Σαουλ,
	כאשר שמע עבדך	καθὼς ἤκουσεν ὁ δοῦλός σου;
	יהוה אלהי ישראל הגד נא לעבדך	κύριε ὁ θεὸς Ισραηλ, ἀπάγγειλον τῷ δούλῳ σου.
	ויאמר יהוה	καὶ εἶπεν κύριος
	ירד	Ἀποκλεισθήσεται.
V. 12	ויאמר דוד	
	היסגרו בעלי קעילה אתי ואת אנשי ביד שאול	
	ויאמר יהוה	
	יסגירו	

V. 11	„Werden die Herren von Keïla mich in seine Hand ausliefern?	„Wird sie eingeschlossen werden?
	Wird Saul herabsteigen,	Und nun – wird Saul herabsteigen,
	wie dein Knecht gehört hat?	wie dein Knecht gehört hat?
	Jahwe, Gott Israels, tu es doch deinem Knecht kund!"	Herr, Gott Israels, tu es doch deinem Knecht kund!"
	Und Jahwe sprach:	Und der Herr sprach:
	„Er wird herabsteigen."	„Sie wird eingeschlossen werden."
V. 12	Und David sprach:	
	„Werden die Herren von Keïla mich und meine Männer ausliefern in die Hand Sauls?"	
	Und Jahwe sprach:	
	„Sie werden ausliefern."	

Die Septuaginta liest die erste Frage Davids in V. 11 als εἰ ἀποκλεισθήσεται; „Wird sie eingeschlossen werden?", worauf als Überleitung zur nächsten Frage ein καὶ νῦν „und nun" folgt; die zweite Frage entspricht wiederum dem MT. Die Antwort Jahwes am Ende von V. 11 lautet in der Septuaginta jedoch wiederum Ἀποκλεισθήσεται „Sie wird eingeschlossen werden", während der gesamte V. 12 fehlt. Wahrscheinlich lautete schon die Vorlage der Old Greek anders als der Masoretische Text.[15] Es ließe sich erwägen, dass der kürzere Text der ursprünglichere war, womit die zweite Orakelbefragung in V. 12 eine sekundäre Auffüllung im MT darstellen würde. Da jedoch hinter dem griechischen Ἀποκλεισθήσεται eine Form von סגר zu stehen scheint – wohl das Nifʻal תסגר, legt sich eher nahe, dass die Vorlage der Septuaginta durch einen Textausfall wegen Haplographie entstanden ist: So vermutete Julius Wellhausen, dass die Haplo-

---

15 Die bei BROOKE / MCLEAN / THACKERAY 1927: 79 verzeichneten Varianten zu B bezeugen z. T. nachträgliche Angleichungen an MT, v. a. zu Beginn von V. 12. In 4QSamᵇ ist der Passus nicht erhalten; laut Rekonstruktion scheint die Frage aber zu fehlen, während vor הירד ein ועתה gestanden haben könnte (ULRICH 2010: 282).

graphie durch das zweifache ויאמר יהוה in V. 11b und V. 12aα ausgelöst wurde, was am Ende von V. 12 wiederum die Änderung der Form יסגירו „Sie werden ausliefern" in תסגר „Sie wird eingeschlossen werden" nach sich zog; denn ohne vorherige Nennung der Herren von Keïla ist die Aussage „Sie werden ausliefern" sinnlos.[16] Als nun יסגירו „Sie werden ausliefern" in תסגר „Sie wird eingeschlossen werden" geändert wurde, muss auch zu Beginn von V. 11 die entsprechende Frage התסגר „Wird sie eingeschlossen werden?" ergänzt worden sein, da diese Frage zum Verständnis von Jahwes Antwort in V. 12b nötig ist. Die als nachgetragen vermutete erste Frage im Masoretischen Text von V. 11 (V. 11aα₁) wird also auch textgeschichtlich als sekundär ausgewiesen, freilich nur indirekt, da der Zusatz offenbar unabhängig von der durch die Septuaginta bezeugten Textüberlieferung in die proto-masoretische Texttradition gelangt ist.[17] Die Vorlage der Septuaginta und der proto-masoretische Text haben sich offenbar ab einem bestimmten Punkt unabhängig voneinander entwickelt.

Ausgangsfassung:

11 הירד שאול כאשר שמע עבדך
יהוה אלהי ישראל הגד נא לעבדך
ויאמר יהוה ירד
12 ויאמר דוד
היסגרו בעלי קעילה אתי ואת אנשי ביד שאול
ויאמר יהוה יסגרו

11 „Wird Saul herabsteigen, wie dein Knecht gehört hat?
Jahwe, Gott Israels, tu es doch deinem Knecht kund!"
Und Jahwe sprach: „Er wird herabsteigen."
12 Und David sprach: „Werden die Herren von Keïla mich und meine Männer in die Hand Sauls ausliefern?"
Und Jahwe sprach: „Sie werden ausliefern."

Durch LXX bezeugte Texttradition	*Proto-MT*
Textausfall durch Haplographie:	*Ergänzung von V. 11aα₁:*

Die rechte Spalte (Proto-MT):

11 היסגרני בעלי קעילה בידו
הירד שאול כאשר שמע עבדך
יהוה אלהי ישראל הגד נא לעבדך
ויאמר יהוה ירד
12 ויאמר דוד
היסגרו בעלי קעילה אתי ואת אנשי ביד שאול
ויאמר יהוה יסגרו

Die linke Spalte:

11 הירד שאול כאשר שמע עבדך
יהוה אלהי ישראל הגד נא לעבדך
ויאמר יהוה יסגרו

11 „Wird Saul herabsteigen, wie dein Knecht gehört hat?
Jahwe, Gott Israels, tu es doch deinem Knecht kund!"
Und Jahwe sprach: „Sie werden ausliefern."

11 „Werden die Herren von Keïla mich in seine Hand ausliefern?

16 Wellhausen 1871: 128.
17 Vgl. Dhorme 1910: 210, Anm. 11: „Le texte du TM est dù à une anticipation du v. 12."

Sinnbedingte Änderung von יסגרו in תסגר und Ergänzung der entsprechenden Frage samt überleitendem ועתה:

התסגר 11

ועתה הירד שאול כאשר שמע עבדך

11 יהוה אלהי ישראל הגד נא לעבדך

ויאמר יהוה תסגר

„Wird sie eingeschlossen werden?
Und nun: Wird Saul herabsteigen, wie dein Knecht gehört hat?
Jahwe, Gott Israels, tu es doch deinem Knecht kund!"
Und Jahwe sprach: „Sie wird eingeschlossen werden."

LXX^B:

εἰ ἀποκλεισθήσεται;
καὶ νῦν εἰ καταβήσεται Σαουλ, καθὼς ἤκουσεν ὁ δοῦλός σου; κύριε ὁ θεὸς Ισραηλ, ἀπάγγειλον τῷ δούλῳ σου.
καὶ εἶπεν κύριος Ἀποκλεισθήσεται.

Wird Saul herabsteigen, wie dein Knecht gehört hat?
Jahwe, Gott Israels, tu es doch deinem Knecht kund!"
Und Jahwe sprach: „Er wird herabsteigen."

12 Und David sprach: „Werden die Herren von Keïla mich und meine Männer in die Hand Sauls ausliefern?"
Und Jahwe sprach: „Sie werden ausliefern."

Ein weiterer Nachtrag ist nach Veijola in V. 6 zu greifen.[18] Auch hier geht die Textüberlieferung auseinander:

	MT	LXX
V. 6	ויהי בברח אביתר בן אחימלך אל דוד קעילה	Καὶ ἐγένετο ἐν τῷ φυγεῖν Αβιαθαρ υἱὸν Αβιμελεχ πρὸς Δαυιδ
	אפוד ירד בידו	καὶ αὐτὸς μετὰ Δαυιδ εἰς Κεϊλα κατέβη ἔχων εφουδ ἐν τῇ χειρὶ αὐτοῦ.
	Und es geschah, als Abjatar ben Ahimelech zu David nach Keïla floh, stieg der Efod hinab in seiner Hand.	Und es geschah, als Abjatar, der Sohn des Abimelech, zu David floh, stieg er selbst mit David nach Keïla hinab, wobei er den Efod in seiner Hand hielt.

Die masoretische Fassung von V. 6b wirkt syntaktisch und inhaltlich merkwürdig: אפוד ירד בידו „da stieg der Efod hinab in seiner Hand" ist zwar nicht völlig unverständlich, jedoch ist nirgends sonst der Efod auf vergleichbare Weise personifiziert und Subjekt eines Verbs der Bewegung. Die Septuaginta liest dagegen καὶ αὐτὸς μετὰ Δαυιδ εἰς Κεϊλα κατέβη ἔχων εφουδ ἐν τῇ χειρὶ αὐτοῦ „da stieg er selbst (scil. Abjatar) mit David nach Keïla hinab, wobei er den Efod in

---

18 Veijola 1990: 23–27.

seiner Hand hielt". Im Vergleich der beiden Lesarten ließe sich der Masoretische Text als ursprünglichere lectio difficilior deuten.[19] Die Personifikation des Efod scheint auf die göttliche Kraft verweisen, die in ihm wohnt.[20] Die Lesart der Septuaginta wäre als lectio facilior zu erklären, die den ungewöhnlichen Ausdruck geglättet und die Personifikation vielleicht sogar bewusst vermieden hätte. Freilich wäre zu prüfen, ob dem griechischen Übersetzer des Samuelbuches ein solcher interpretierender Eingriff in den Text zuzutrauen ist – was in diesem Zusammenhang nicht geschehen kann. Auch wäre zu fragen, weshalb die Bildung einer lectio facilior dazu geführt hat, den Text auf diese Weise zu erweitern; die inhaltlich schwierige Aussage, dass der Efod „hinabstieg in seiner Hand", hätte sich einfacher schlicht durch die Übersetzung „da hielt er den Efod in seiner Hand" lösen lassen. Hinzu kommt, dass die Aussage des MT, Abjatar sei zum genannten Zeitpunkt zu David nach Keïla geflohen – sozusagen auf direktem Wege von Nob nach Keïla – im Zusammenhang schwer vorstellbar ist: Laut 1Sam 22,20 floh Abjatar bereits deutlich vor der Keïla-Episode zu David und befand sich seither in Davids Gefolge. Die mechanische Annahme einer lectio difficilior könnte den Blick auf die textliche Entwicklung verstellen. Als Vorlage des griechischen Textes ließe sich nämlich etwa והוא עם דוד ירד קעילה אפוד בידו „und er war mit David nach Keïla hinabgestiegen, den Efod in seiner Hand" denken;[21] die Worte והוא עם דוד könnten durch aberratio oculi vom ersten דוד zum zweiten ausgefallen sein, was im proto-masoretischen Text die Umstellung der Worte ירד und קעילה nach sich zog:

Rekonstruierte Ausgangsfassung:

ויהי בברח אביתר בן אחימלך אל דוד
והוא עם דוד ירד קעילה
אפוד בידו

Und als Abjatar ben Ahimelech zu David floh
– er aber war mit David nach Keïla hinabgestiegen –,
da war der Efod in seiner Hand.

LXX^B:

Καὶ ἐγένετο ἐν τῷ φυγεῖν Αβιαθαρ υἱὸν Αβιμελεχ πρὸς Δαυιδ
καὶ αὐτὸς μετὰ Δαυιδ εἰς Κεϊλα κατέβη
ἔχων εφουδ ἐν τῇ χειρὶ αὐτοῦ.

Proto-MT
Textausfall durch Haplographie:

ויהי בברח אביתר בן אחימלך אל דוד
ירד קעילה
אפוד בידו

---

19 So namentlich DIETRICH 2014: 657.
20 DIETRICH 2014: 676.
21 So z. B. BUDDE 1902: 156; DRIVER 1913: 184; ähnlich VEIJOLA 1990: 24 (in Abstimmung mit Anneli Aejmelaeus, s. Anm. 58, der lediglich statt והוא „und er" גם הוא „auch er" annimmt).

Und als Abjatar ben Ahimelech zu David floh,
stieg er hinab nach Keïla,
den Efod in seiner Hand.
Sinnbedingte Umstellung von ירד *und* קעילה
(= MT):

ויהי בברח אביתר בן אחימלך אל דוד קעילה
ירד אפוד בידו

Und als Abjatar ben Ahimelech zu David
nach Keïla floh,
stieg der Efod hinab in seiner Hand.

So oder so fällt V. 6 im Kontext auf: Der Verweis auf Abjatars Flucht zu David und – wenn man den Septuagintatext voraussetzt – seine Begleitung Davids nach Keïla ist nachholender Erzählstil – was als solches nicht ungewöhnlich ist, jedoch an dieser Stelle überraschend wirkt, da man die Erwähnung Abjatars und des Efod ja schon im Zusammenhang von V. 2–4 erwarten könnte. Außerdem liest sich die Formulierung von V. 6 – namentlich in Gestalt der hypothetischen Septuaginta-Vorlage – stilistisch auffallend holprig; sie will offenbar betonen, dass Abjatar, als er David nach Keïla begleitete, auch den Efod dorthin brachte. Veijola hat in diesem Zusammenhang auf die eigentümliche Artikellosigkeit des Wortes אפוד verwiesen, die sich etwa von V. 9 unterscheidet; das Wort „Efod" wirkt hier geradezu wie ein Eigenname.[22] Im Samuelbuch begegnen drei weitere Stellen, wo אפוד ebenfalls ohne Artikel verwendet ist und wo sich ein spezifisches Interesse an der kontinuierlichen Weitergabe des Efod durch die Hand von Priestern zeigt (1Sam 2,28; 14,3; 22,18). Veijola schrieb diese Stellen dem deuteronomistischen Erstredaktor DtrH zu.[23] Damit dürfte das redaktionelle Gewicht der insgesamt vier Stellen überschätzt sein: Eher lassen sich die Erwähnungen des priesterlichen Tragens des Efod in 1Sam 14,3; 22,18 und 23,6 einem Bearbeiter zuweisen, der sich an die Erwähnung des Efod in der priesterlichen Strafrede an Eli in 1Sam 2,28 angelehnt und das Motiv dementsprechend in der folgenden Erzählung hervorgehoben hat. Ein größerer redaktioneller Zusammenhang dieser Stellen muss nicht angenommen werden.

2 Ergänzungen im Zusammenhang des Jahwekriegs

Für die weitere Analyse der Keïla-Episode hat erneut Veijola den Weg gewiesen, indem er in 1Sam 23,1–13 ein ganzes Bündel weiterer Zusätze entdeckte, die

---

22 Veijola 1990: 26–27.
23 Veijola 1990: 27.

viel stärker als alles bisher Genannte die Substanz der Erzählung erweitert und
verändert haben; Veijola schrieb auch diese Erweiterungen dem deuteronomistischen Geschichtsschreiber DtrH zu.[24] Walter Dietrich hat diese literar- und re-
daktionskritischen Vorschläge zum größeren Teil übernommen, teils auch mo-
difiziert.[25] Die folgende Rekonstruktion geht teilweise über Veijola hinaus und
bietet für die redaktionsgeschichtliche Kontextualisierung der Zusätze einen
neuen Vorschlag.

Veijolas Ausgangspunkt war die sehr auffällige Erweiterung der dritten Orakelanfrage in V. 10–11. Während Jahwes Antwort nach V. 11b lapidar ירד „Er
wird herabsteigen" lautet, was nichts anderes ist als ein schlichtes „Ja", ist die
entsprechende Orakelanfrage Davids in ein recht ausführliches Gebet eingebettet (V. 10–11a*):

> „Jahwe, Gott Israels, dein Knecht hat gewiss gehört, dass Saul sucht, nach Keïla hereinzu-
> gelangen, dass er die Stadt um meinetwillen verheere! Wird Saul herabsteigen, wie dein
> Knecht gehört hat? Jahwe, Gott Israels, tu es doch deinem Knecht kund!"

Der Kontrast zwischen dieser langen Gebetsanfrage und der lapidaren Antwort
fällt v. a. im Vergleich mit der vierten Orakelanfrage auf, von der in V. 12 erzählt
wird:

> Und David sprach:
> „Werden die Herren von Keïla mich und meine Männer ausliefern in die Hand Sauls?"
>
> Und Jahwe sprach:
> „Sie werden ausliefern."

Ähnlich knappe Frage-Antwort-Schemata finden sich in V. 2 sowie außerhalb
der Episode in Ri 1,2; 1Sam 30,10 und 2Sam 2,1. Angesichts dessen machte Veijola den sehr plausiblen literarkritischen Vorschlag, dass das eigentliche Gebet
Davids in V. 10–11a* nachgetragen wurde, während die ursprüngliche Anfrage
nur die Worte הירד שאול „Wird Saul herabsteigen?" enthielt. Diese literarkritische Hypothese lässt sich kaum mit dem Argument entkräften, dass altorientalische Orakelanfragen, wie sie v. a. aus mesopotamischen Ritualtexten bekannt
sind, in umfangreiche Rituale einschließlich langer Gebete eingebettet waren:[26]
Vergleichbares mag man auch für das Jahweorakel annehmen, entscheidend ist
aber, dass in den narrativen Texten, die vom Jahweorakel sprechen, ein Stan-
dardformular belegt ist, das die Orakelanfrage in größter Knappheit wiedergibt.

24 VEIJOLA 1990: 6–23; vgl. idem 2000: 176–81.
25 DIETRICH 2014: 669–70.
26 So NA'AMAN 2010: 90 mit Anm. 9.

Die offenbar geprägte Weise, in der solche Orakelfragen in erzählenden Texten dargestellt wurden, muss von der tatsächlichen Ritualpraxis unterschieden werden. Davids Gebet hat außerdem Ähnlichkeiten mit Klagegebeten der sogenannten Exilszeit; vergleichbare Nachträge, die ein kurzes, aber theologisch gewichtiges Klagegebet enthalten, begegnen namentlich in der Erzählung von Achans Diebstahl (Jos 7,7–8) und bei Gideons Berufung (Ri 6,13).[27]

Eine weitere Beobachtung Veijolas betrifft das Ende von V. 1 (V. 1bβ). Die Wendung והמה שסים את הגרנות „und sie sind (gerade) dabei, die Tennen zu plündern" ist syntaktisch und stilistisch nach dem einleitenden הנה פלשתים נלחמים בקעילה „Siehe, Philister kämpfen gegen Keïla" auffällig, da das Pronomen המה „sie" das Subjekt unnötig wiederaufnimmt; man hätte auch schlicht הנה פלשתים נלחמים בקעילה ושסים את הגרנות sagen können. Die Plünderung der Tennen erinnert an den Motivzusammenhang der Plünderung Israels durch seine Feinde, der mit dem Verb שסה in Ri 2,16; 1Sam 14,48 und 2Kön 17,20 formuliert wird. Letztgenannte Stellen erweisen sich als redaktionell und im Fall von Ri 2 und 2Kön 17 eindeutig deuteronomistisch,[28] wobei es auf die genauere redaktionsgeschichtliche Einordnung hier nicht ankommt. Im Licht dieser Vergleichstexte soll die Plünderung der Tennen wahrscheinlich andeuten, dass Keïla, dessen Bewohner zum Gottesvolk gezählt werden, von Israels Feinden heimgesucht wird – was wiederum David veranlasst, Keïla zu retten.

In diesem Zusammenhang erhält eine weitere Beobachtung Veijolas Gewicht, die das Motiv der Rettung Keïlas in V. 2 und V. 5 betrifft: In V. 2 schießt die Wendung והושעת את קעילה „und rette Keïla!" über die entsprechende Orakelanfrage Davids hinaus, was erneut das geprägte Schema sprengt, in dem Frage und Antwort einander genau entsprechen (vgl. V. 12). Zwar ließe sich das vielleicht noch als narrative Ausgestaltung der Orakelszene erklären. Nimmt man jedoch V. 5b hinzu, erhärtet sich der Verdacht, dass der Auftrag zur Errettung Keïlas hinzugesetzt wurde; hier fällt auf, dass das Subjekt דוד nach der voranstehenden Narrativkette, die ebenfalls David zum Subjekt hat, wiederholt wird, was syntaktisch eigentlich unnötig wäre, aber einen gewissen Neueinsatz bedeutet, der auf eine zweite Hand schließen lässt:

וילך דוד קעילה וילחם בפלשתים וינהג את מקניהם ויך בהם מכה גדולה

וישע דוד את ישבי קעילה

Und David ging nach Keïla, kämpfte mit den Philistern, trieb ihr Vieh davon und fügte ihnen einen großen Schlag zu.
Und David rettete die Bewohner von Keïla.

---

27 Veijola 2000.
28 Vgl. Noth 1967: 6; zu 1Sam 14,48 Müller 2004: 156; Bezzel 2015: 146–47.

Nimmt man diese Beobachtungen zusammen, zeichnet sich in V. 1bβ.2bβ.5b eine Bearbeitung ab, die David als göttlich beauftragten Retter vor den Plünderungen Israels durch seine Feinde stilisiert hat. Eine sachlich präzise Vorlage findet dies im Proömium zur Richterzeit in Ri 2,16: ויקם יהוה שפטים ויושעיום מיד שסיהם „Und Jahwe ließ ihnen Richter aufstehen, die retteten sie aus der Hand ihrer Plünderer." Im Licht dieser Aussage erscheint der David von 1Sam 23,1–5 geradezu als von Jahwe erweckter Richter.[29]

Über Veijolas Beobachtungen hinaus ist zu erwägen, dass auch die gesamte zweite Orakelanfrage Davids samt der einleitenden Szene (V. 3–4) nachgetragen wurde und in denselben oder einen ähnlichen literarischen Zusammenhang gehört.[30] Die Glosse, die in V. 5 die Erwähnung von Davids Männern nachgetragen hat, zeigt, dass die Szene mit Davids Männern in V. 3 in einer gewissen Spannung zu V. 1–2.5 steht, wo David allein als Subjekt des Handelns genannt ist. Auch inhaltlich fällt auf, dass V. 3 von der Furcht der Männer Davids spricht:

הנה אנחנו פה ביהודה יראים ואף כי נלך קעלה אל מערכות פלשתים

„Siehe, wir fürchten uns hier in Juda, und wieviel mehr, wenn wir nach Keïla gehen zu den Schlachtreihen der Philister!"

Die Wendung מערכות פלשתים „Schlachtreihen der Philister" hat lediglich eine, dafür aber aussagekräftige Parallele, nämlich in 1Sam 17,23 in der Goliaterzählung, die ab ovo von der Theologie des Jahwekrieges geprägt ist. Auch dort sind die Israeliten von Furcht vor dem philistäischen Feind erfüllt (vgl. 1Sam 17,11.24 etc.). Weil sich seine Männer vor den Philistern fürchten, befragt David hier das Orakel ein zweites Mal, wobei besonders die Antwort Jahwes auffällt: Die Einleitung ויענהו יהוה „Und Jahwe antwortete ihm" ist bei Orakelanfragen singulär, und Jahwes tatsächliche Antwort קום רד קעילה כי אני נתן את פלשתים בידך „Auf, geh hinab nach Keïla, denn ich gebe die Philister in deine Hand!" geht vor allem mit der sogenannten Übergabeformel deutlich über das übliche Schema hinaus. Traditionsgeschichtlich ist diese Formel tatsächlich im Orakelwesen verwurzelt; sie begegnet unter anderem bereits in den prophetischen Orakeln aus Mari.[31] In den historischen Büchern erweist sie sich literargeschichtlich aber sehr häufig als Nachtrag; namentlich in den Büchern Josua und Richter findet sich eine große Zahl von Belegen, wo der sekundäre Charakter klar zu erkennen ist – der theologische Zusammenhang ist das heilsgeschichtliche Konzept des Jahwekriegs, das nachträglich in die älteren Kriegserzählungen

---

29 KLEIN 1983: 230.
30 Vgl. WRIGHT 2014: 52.
31 Vgl. ARM 26 214:12–14 = NISSINEN 2003: 48.

eingearbeitet wurde.[32] In 1Sam 23,4 erweist sich wiederum die Differenz zum üblichen Schema der Orakelanfragen als entscheidend, was bereits der Vergleich mit der rekonstruierten Urform der dritten Orakelanfrage (V. 10–11*) sowie der vierten Anfrage in V. 12 zeigt. Die Vermutung, dass V. 3–4 nachgetragen wurden, wird dadurch bestätigt, dass V. 5 glatt an die rekonstruierte Fassung von V. 2 anschließt:

2 ... ויאמר יהוה לך והכית בפלשתים

5 וילך דוד קעילה וילחם בפלשתים וינהג את מקניהם ויך בהם מכה גדולה

2... Und Jahwe sprach: „Geh und schlage die Philister!"
Da ging David nach Keïla, kämpfte mit den Philistern, trieb ihr Vieh davon und fügte ihnen einen großen Schlag zu.

Ein letztes Element, das möglicherweise dieser Bearbeitung zuzuweisen ist, bietet V. 7b:

ויאמר שאול מכר אתו אלהים בידי כי נסגר לבוא בעיר דלתים ובריח

Da sprach Saul:
„Gott hat ihn in meine Hand <verkauft>,[33] denn er hat sich eingeschlossen, indem er in eine Stadt mit Torflügeln und Riegeln hineingegangen ist."

Die Rede Sauls ist wohl als Selbstgespräch zu deuten. Dietrich, der den Halbvers literargeschichtlich vom Kontext abhebt, schreibt ihn dem „Verfasser des Höfischen Erzählwerks" zu, der einen „Sauliden-Erzählkranz", aus dem die Keïla-Episode stamme, mit einem „Freibeuter-Erzählkranz" „verflochten" habe. Die vergleichbaren Selbstgespräche Sauls in 1Sam 18,17b und 18,21a seien ebenfalls dem Höfischen Erzähler zuzuschreiben.[34] Allerdings ist zu beachten, dass Sauls fälschliche Annahme, Gott habe David in seine Hand verkauft, eine Art Gegenstück zu Jahwes Unterstützung Davids nach V. 4 bietet: Vom Zusammenhang her ist klar, dass Saul sich täuscht. Sauls Rede über אלהים „Gott" deutet dabei eine Distanz zum Gott Israels an – womit er sich von David unterscheidet, der in V. 10 vertrauensvoll zu Jahwe als אלהי ישראל „Gott Israels" betet. Diese implizite Theologie von V. 7b liegt auf einer ähnlichen Ebene wie die Zusätze in V. 1bβ.2bβ.5b und V. 10*(ab יהוה).11aα₃βγ, die David als von Jahwe beauftragten

---

32 Vgl. MÜLLER 2009.
33 So die Versionen. Das נָכַר des MT wird herkömmlich als „Breviloquenz" erklärt: „Gott hat ihn verleugnet (u. gegeben) i. meine Hand" (GESENIUS 2010: 819; dort jedoch als unsicher gekennzeichnet); vgl. WELLHAUSEN 1871: 127: „נכר scheint aus מכר (LXX) und נתן zusammengeflossen."
34 DIETRICH 2014: 668.

Retter Israels charakterisieren. Allerdings bietet der Text von V. 7–8 keine eindeutigen Indizien dafür, dass V. 7b nachgetragen wurde; zwar lässt sich V. 8 gut an V. 7a anschließen, und Sauls Selbstgespräch unterbricht auf eine gewisse Weise den Handlungsfaden, jedoch steht V. 7b nicht in deutlicher Spannung zu seinem unmittelbaren Kontext.

Die Stilisierung Davids als eines göttlich beauftragten Retters Israels, die sich nach Veijola in V. 1*.2*.5*.10–11* greifen lässt, nach der vorliegenden Analyse auch V. 3–4 und vielleicht V. 7b umfasst, wurde von Veijola dem deuteronomistischen Erstredaktor DtrH zugeschrieben.[35] Dagegen spricht, dass die genannten Elemente in 1Sam 23,1–13 keine im engeren Sinne redaktionelle Funktion haben. Die Zusätze unterstreichen vielmehr Davids heilsgeschichtliche Bedeutung, wobei das höchste Gewicht dem Titel „Knecht Jahwes" zukommt, den David in seinem Gebet an den Gott Israels in V. 10–11 für sich in Anspruch nimmt. Obwohl seine Männer voller Furcht sind, rettet David im Auftrag Jahwes Keïla und besiegt die dem Gottesvolk feindlichen Philister; Jahwe wiederum rettet ihn vor den Nachstellungen Sauls. Dieser umfassende theologische Zusammenhang dürfte deutlich jünger sein als die ältesten deuteronomistischen Elemente in den Büchern Richter, Samuel und Könige.[36]

3 Ein Stück einer annalistischen Quelle im Saul-David-Zyklus

Abgesehen von den genannten Zusätzen ist der Text der Perikope klar in zwei Teilszenen gegliedert: V. 1–5* berichten von Davids Sieg über die Philister in Keïla, während V. 6/7–13* davon handeln, wie David von dort dem Saul entkam.

Es ist möglich, diese gestaffelte Erzählung als im Wesentlichen literarisch einheitlich zu betrachten. Dietrich etwa schreibt die Episode dem „Erzählkranz vom ‚Aufstieg und Niedergang der Sauliden'" zu, worin sie auf die beiden Episoden um die Priester von Nob (1Sam 21,2–10 und 22,6–19) einschließlich Abjatars Flucht zu David (1Sam 22,20–23) gefolgt sei; der Sammler dieses Erzählkranzes, auf den unter anderem V. 13 zurückgehe, habe sie mit der nachfolgenden Sifiter-Episode verknüpft.[37] „Das Motiv für Davids Handeln" sei in diesem Erzählkranz „die Verfolgung durch Saul": „Womöglich ist sie auch als Grund dafür zu denken, dass David sich nach Keïla wagt, jedenfalls bewirkt

35 Veijola 1990: 6–23; vgl. Dietrich 2014: 669–70.
36 Vgl. dazu Levin 2013; Müller 2019.
37 Dietrich 2014: 666–68.

sie, dass er von dort wieder abzieht."[38] Tatsächlich ist der zweite Teil der Episode (V. 6/7–13) ausdrücklich auf die Verfolgung Davids durch Saul bezogen.

Umso mehr fällt auf, dass in V. 1–5 mit keiner Silbe von Saul geredet wird: Hängt Davids Weg nach Keïla wirklich mit der Verfolgung durch Saul zusammen? In V. 1–5 wirkt David nicht wie ein Verfolgter. Als er von dem philistäischen Angriff auf Keïla erfährt, sieht er vielmehr die Gelegenheit, „diese Philister" zu schlagen, was durch das Jahweorakel bestätigt wird; der offenbar überraschende Angriff gelingt. Inwiefern dieser Angriff dadurch ausgelöst ist, dass Saul David zu stellen sucht, bleibt unklar. Auch fällt auf, dass bei der Orakelbefragung im zweiten Abschnitt der Episode in V. 9 – anders als beim ersten Mal – ausdrücklich Abjatar und der Efod genannt werden. Das schlägt den Bogen zurück zu 1Sam 22,20, wo Abjatar eingeführt wird als derjenige, der dem Blutbad an den Priestern von Nob entkam und zu David flüchtete. Es ist aber merkwürdig, dass Abjatar nicht schon im Zusammenhang von V. 2 genannt wird: Die erste Orakelbefragung müsste ja genauso von Abjatar durch den von ihm mitgebrachten Efod vorgenommen worden sein. Mit anderen Worten: Die Bemerkung von V. 9 „und er sprach zu Abjatar: ,Bring den Efod herbei!'" wäre eher vor V. 2 zu erwarten. Das spricht dafür, dass die Episode, die sich im Grundbestand von V. 1–5 findet, nicht im Zusammenhang mit dem Saul-David-Zyklus entstanden ist.[39] Stützen lässt sich dies mit der Gestalt von V. 13: V. 13b ist zwar ausdrücklich auf Sauls Verfolgung Davids bezogen. Bei V. 13a legt sich das aber nicht zwingend nahe: ויקם דוד ואנשיו ויצאו מקעילה „Und David stand auf mit seinen Männern, und sie zogen hinaus aus Keïla" muss nicht als Flucht verstanden werden, wie V. 13b suggeriert, wo es heißt, David habe sich „aus Keïla in Sicherheit gebracht" (נמלט דוד מקעילה). Auch die eigentümlich pleonastische Wendung ויתהלכו באשר יתהלכו ist nicht eindeutig auf die Fluchtmotivik bezogen; der Ausdruck lässt sich als „und sie streiften umher, wo sie umherstreifen wollten" verstehen,[40] was gut zu dem ḫapiru-Charakter von Davids Bande nach 1Sam 22,2 passt, aber nicht zwingend mit der Verfolgung durch Saul verbunden ist. V. 13a lässt sich zudem als Fortsetzung zu V. 5a lesen:[41]

> 1* Und sie taten David kund: „Siehe, Philister kämpfen gegen Keïla." 2* Und David befragte Jahwe: „Soll ich gehen und diese Philister schlagen?" Und Jahwe sprach <>:[42]

---

38 DIETRICH 2014: 666.

39 Vgl. bereits MCCARTER 1980: 372: „Verses 1–5 seem to represent a complete unit by themselves." Dass die Episode ursprünglich noch nicht mit dem Saul-Zyklus verknüpft war, wird namentlich von WRIGHT 2014: 51–54, klar erkannt.

40 Vgl. etwa die bei DRIVER 1913: 185–86, angeführten idiomatischen Wendungen aus anderen semitischen Sprachen.

41 WRIGHT 2014: 52.

42 Mit LXX; s. o. 1.

„Geh und schlage die Philister!" 5* Da ging David nach Keïla, kämpfte mit den Philistern, trieb ihr Vieh davon und fügte ihnen einen grossen Schlag zu.

13* Und David stand auf mit seinen Männern, und sie zogen hinaus aus Keïla und streiften umher, wo sie umherstreifen wollten.

Hier handelt es sich offenbar um einen eigenen Quellenfaden. Er könnte mit der Nachricht in 1Sam 22,2 verbunden gewesen sein, wo berichtet wird, wie David eine Freibeuterbande um sich gesammelt hat. Als die Philister Keïla attackieren, wohl um den wohlhabenden Ort zu plündern, greift David sie überraschend an: Er kann die Philister schlagen und ihr Vieh erbeuten – sein erster Coup. Sozialgeschichtlich lässt sich das durchaus als historische Erinnerung vorstellen. Na'aman hat die Szene zu Recht mit den Umtrieben von ḫapiru-Banden in und um Keïla im 14. Jahrhundert verglichen, wovon in der Amarna-Korrespondenz berichtet wird (EA 279; 280; 289).[43] Allerdings fällt auf, dass der Warlord und Bandenführer David durch die Befragung des Orakels zugleich mit dem späteren Jerusalemer Dynastiegott Jahwe verbunden ist: Religionsgeschichtlich dürfte sich darin das längst etablierte Jerusalemer Königtum spiegeln, was wohl auf eine Zeit verweist, die bereits weit nach den Tagen Davids lag. In der Erwähnung des „großen Schlags" (מכה גדולה), den David den Philistern zugefügt haben soll (V. 5*), klingt zugleich eine herrschaftslegitimierende Dimension an, da dieses Motiv die militärische Macht des Ahnherrn der Jerusalemer Könige unterstreicht.[44] Stilistisch ist das kurze Quellenstück auffallend knapp und berichtend gehalten – was durch die Erweiterungen kaum verändert wird. Das Ganze wirkt annalistisch, was eine gewisse Stilisierung nicht ausschließt. Ähnliche Stücke sind namentlich in 1Sam 27 sowie in 2Sam 2 zu greifen.

Der Abschnitt über Sauls Verfolgung Davids, der den Kern von V. 7–12 und V. 13b bildet, liest sich demgegenüber als Fortschreibung:[45]

... 5* Da ging David nach Keïla, kämpfte mit den Philistern, trieb ihr Vieh davon und fügte ihnen einen großen Schlag zu.

7* *Da wurde Saul mitgeteilt, dass David nach Keïla hineingegangen war. 8 Und Saul bot das ganze Volk zur Schlacht auf, um nach Keïla hinabzusteigen, um David und seine Männer zu belagern. 9 David aber erfuhr, dass Saul gegen ihn Böses schmiedete, und sprach zu Abjatar, dem Priester: „Bring den Efod herbei!" 10* Und David sprach: 11* „Wird Saul herabsteigen? Und Jahwe sprach: „Er wird herabsteigen." 12 Und David sprach: „Werden die Herren von Keïla mich und meine Männer ausliefern in die Hand Sauls?" Und Jahwe sprach: „Sie werden ausliefern."*

---

43 NA'AMAN 2010: 92–97; vgl. WRIGHT 2014: 54–55.
44 Vgl. dazu MÜLLER 2017: 207–12.
45 So auch WRIGHT 2014: 53–54.

13* Und David stand auf mit seinen Männern, und sie zogen hinaus aus Keïla und streiften umher, wo sie umherstreifen wollten.
*Saul aber wurde mitgeteilt, dass David sich aus Keïla in Sicherheit gebracht hatte,
und er hörte auf, auszuziehen.*

Der annalistische Stil des ersten Abschnitts wird weitergeführt; die Orakelbefragung wird um eine weitere, gleich zweifache Orakelanfrage ergänzt. Die Fortschreibung erfüllt offenbar einen redaktionellen Zweck: Der Abschnitt über
Sauls vergeblichen Versuch, David in Keïla einzuschließen, verknüpft die Keïla-
Episode mit dem größeren Erzählzyklus über Davids Flucht vor Saul und seine
Verfolgung durch ihn.[46] Das gewichtigste Motiv des hinzugefügten Abschnitts
ist sicherlich die Aussage in V. 9, „dass Saul Böses gegen David schmiedete"
(כי עליו שאול מחריש הרעה), die einen klaren Kontrast zwischen den beiden
Hauptfiguren impliziert; der metaphorische Gebrauch von חרש (eigtl. „pflü-
gen") ist ansonsten aus weisheitlicher Tradition bekannt,[47] was eine Verbindung des Saul-David-Zyklus mit höfischer Weisheit anzeigen könnte. Wie dieser
Erzählzyklus in seiner ältesten Gestalt ausgesehen hat, lässt sich allein aufgrund von 1Sam 23 nicht entscheiden. Ebensowenig lässt sich von hier aus er-
schließen, zu welchem Zeitpunkt der Saul-David-Zyklus mit der annalistischen
David-Quelle verbunden wurde.

Zugegeben sei, dass die rein literarkritischen Erwägungen auf dieser frühen
Ebene hypothetischer bleiben als auf den jüngeren Ebenen der Literargeschichte, namentlich im Zusammenhang mit der Textüberlieferung. Hinzu kommt,
dass immer auch mit Textausfällen und nicht mehr rekonstruierbaren älteren
Vorstufen zu rechnen ist.[48] Gleichwohl lassen sich der Kern der Keïla-Episode
und die Grundzüge ihrer Entwicklung verhältnismäßig gut greifen. 1Sam 23,1–
13 könnte sich insgesamt als ein Schlüssel für die Literargeschichte der Davidüberlieferung erweisen.

Summary

The episode of David's sojourn in Keïla in 1 Sam 23:1–13 contains various traces
of a surprisingly complex literary historical development. According to the proposed analysis, late glosses of various origin can probably be detected in

46 Vgl. die grundlegenden Beobachtungen, die auf eine sekundäre Verzahnung von Saul- und
Davidüberlieferung deuten, bei Kratz 2000: 179–87.
47 Vgl. Prov 3,29; 6,14.18; 12,20; 14,22; Hi 4,8; Sir 7,12; 8,2.
48 Vgl. Müller, Pakkala, and ter Haar Romeny 2014: 220–25.

vv. 2,5,6 (txt. emd.), 11 (indirectly corroborated by the LXX), and 13. A comprehensive edition that interpreted the events according to the concept of *Jahwekrieg* can be found in vv. 1bβ, 2bβ, 3–4, 5b, 7b, 10*(beginning with יהוה), and 11aα₃βγ. The original episode comprised only vv. 1abα, 2abα, 5a*(without ואנשו), and 13a*(without כארבע מאות איש). Written in annalistic style, it depicts David as the leader of a *ḥapiru*-like band, who led a surprise attack against the Philistines during their battle against Keïla. This short report seems to have been secondarily embedded in the story about David's flight from Saul by the added vv. 7a, 8–9, 10aα*(without יהוה אלהי ישראל), 11aα₂b, 12, and 13b. Notwithstanding the hypothetical character of the proposed literary critical reconstruction, the episode is a potential key for the literary history of the stories about David's rise.

Bibliography

Bezzel, Hannes. 2015. *Saul: Israels König in Tradition, Redaktion und früher Rezeption.* FAT 97. Tübingen: Mohr Siebeck.

Brooke, Alan E., and Norman McLean, Henry St. John Thackeray, eds. 1927. *I and II Samuel.* Vol. 2.1 of *The Old Testament in Greek: According to the Text of Codex Vaticanus, Supplemented from Other Uncial Manuscripts, with a Critical Apparatus Containing the Chief Ancient Authorities for the Text of the Septuagint.* London: Cambridge University Press.

Budde, Karl. 1902. *Die Bücher Samuel.* Tübingen: Mohr (Siebeck).

Dhorme, Paul. 1910. *Les livres de Samuel.* Paris: Gabalda.

Dietrich, Walter. 2014. *Samuel (1 Sam 13–26).* BKAT VIII/2 (9. Lfg.). Göttingen: Vandenhoeck & Ruprecht.

Driver, Samuel R. ²1913. *Notes on the Hebrew Text and the Topography of the Books of Samuel.* Oxford: Clarendon.

Klein, Ralph. 1983. *1 Samuel.* WBC 10. Waco, TX: Word Books.

Kratz, Reinhard G. 2000. *Die Komposition der erzählenden Bücher des Alten Testaments: Grundwissen der Bibelkritik.* Göttingen: Vandenhoeck & Ruprecht.

Gesenius, Wilhelm. 1995. *Hebräische Grammatik: Völlig umgearbeitet von E. Kautzsch.* 7. Nachdruckauflage der 28. Aufl. Hildesheim: Olms.

Gesenius, Wilhelm. ¹⁸2010. *Hebräisches und Aramäisches Handwörterbuch über das Alte Testament.* Edited by Herbert Donner. Heidelberg: Springer.

Levin, Christoph. 2013. Die Frömmigkeit der Könige von Israel und Juda. Pages 144–77 in *Verheißung und Rechtfertigung: Gesammelte Studien zum Alten Testament II.* BZAW 431. Berlin: de Gruyter.

McCarter, P. Kyle, Jr. 1980. *I Samuel.* AB 8. New York: Doubleday.

Müller, Reinhard. 2004. *Königtum und Gottesherrschaft: Untersuchungen zur alttestamentlichen Monarchiekritik.* FAT 2.3. Tübingen: Mohr Siebeck.

Müller, Reinhard. 2009. Jahwekrieg und Heilsgeschichte. *ZThK* 106:265–83.

Müller, Reinhard. 2017. Herrschaftslegitimation in den Königtümern Israel und Juda: Eine Spurensuche im Alten Testament. Pages 189–230 in *Herrschaftslegitimation in vorderorientalischen Reichen der Eisenzeit.* Edited by Christoph Levin and Reinhard Müller. ORA 21. Tübingen: Mohr Siebeck.

Müller, Reinhard. 2019. The Redactional Framework of Judges. Pages 121–35 in *Writing, Rewriting, and Overwriting in the Books of Deuteronomy and the Former Prophets.* FS Cynthia Edenburg. Edited by Ido Koch, Thomas Römer and Omer Sergi. BETL 304. Leuven: Peeters.

Müller, Reinhard, and Juha Pakkala, Bas ter Haar Romeny. 2014. *Evidence of Editing: Growth and Change of Texts in the Hebrew Bible.* SBLRBS 75. Atlanta: Society of Biblical Literature.

Na'aman, Nadav. 2010. David's Sojourn in Keilah in Light of the Amarna Letters. *VT* 60:87–97.

Nissinen, Martti. 2003. *Prophets and Prophecy in the Ancient Near East.* SBLWAW 12. Atlanta: Society of Biblical Literature.

Noth, Martin. [3]1967. *Überlieferungsgeschichtliche Studien: Die sammelnden und bearbeitenden Geschichtswerke im Alten Testament.* Tübingen: Niemeyer.

Ulrich, Eugene, eds. 2010. *The Biblical Qumran Scrolls: Transcriptions and Textual Variants.* Leiden: Brill.

Veijola, Timo. 1990. David in Keïla: Tradition und Interpretation in 1Sam 23,1–13*. Pages 5–42 in *David: Gesammelte Studien zu den Davidüberlieferungen des Alten Testaments.* SESJ 52. Helsinki / Göttingen: Finnische Exegetische Gesellschaft / Vandenhoeck & Ruprecht.

Veijola, Timo. 2000. „Das Klagegebet in Literatur und Leben der Exilsgeneration am Beispiel einiger Prosatexte." Pages 176–91 in *Moses Erben: Studien zum Dekalog, zum Deuteronomismus und zum Schriftgelehrtentum.* BWANT 149. Stuttgart: Kohlhammer.

Weippert, Manfred. 2010. *Historisches Textbuch zum Alten Testament.* GAT 10. Göttingen: Vandenhoeck & Ruprecht.

Wellhausen, Julius. 1871. *Der Text der Bücher Samuelis.* Göttingen: Vandenhoeck & Ruprecht.

Wright, Jacob L. 2014. *David, King of Israel, and Caleb in Biblical Memory.* New York: Cambridge University Press.

Natan Evron
"David is Hiding among Us"

The Stories about David, Saul, and the Ziphites (1 Sam 23:19–24; 26:1)

Introduction

> "I should be at pains enough if I were to try and harmonize all the narratives contained in this first book of Samuel so that they should seem to be all written and arranged by a single historian."[1]

These words, written by Spinoza in 1670, can be considered the first steps of the modern critical study of the book of Samuel. In the centuries that have passed since, scholars have often pointed to double stories as a tool necessary to reconstructing the sources of the book. This phenomenon, though not unique to the book of Samuel, appears there particularly often, especially in the section dealing with David's rise to the monarchy.[2] One prominent example is the pair of stories about the Ziphites who come to Saul with a report about David's hiding place (1 Sam 23:19–24; 26:1). This article will examine the relationship between these two scenes.

The unit that deals with Saul's pursuit of David contains two episodes concerning the people of Ziph, a city in the territory of Judah,[3] who came to Saul to provide him with information about David's hiding place. The first (1 Sam

---

1 SPINOZA 1670: 138.
2 Examples of double stories in the history of David include those recounting David's arrival at the courtyard of Saul, once as a harp player (1 Sam 16:14–23) and once after his war against Goliath (1 Sam 17); the casting of Saul's spear at David (1 Sam 18:10–11; 19:9–10); David's marriage to Saul's daughter, once to Merab (1 Sam 18:17–19) and again to Michal (1 Sam 18:20–27); the three covenants between David and Jonathan (1 Sam 18:3–4; 20:12–17; 23:16–18); David's escape to the court of Achish in Gath (1 Sam 21:11–16; 27); and the description of Saul's death (1 Sam 31; 2 Sam 1:6–10).
3 Outside of the stories of David and Saul, Ziph is mentioned in the Hebrew Bible in the list of cities of Judah in the book of Joshua, near the towns of Maon, Carmel, and Juttah (Josh 15:55), and in Chronicles in the list of cities in Judah that Rehoboam fortified (2 Chr 11:8). According to the genealogical list in Chronicles, Ziph is a member of Caleb's family (1 Chr 2:42). Most scholars identify the biblical Ziph with modern Tel Zif, about seven kilometers south of Hebron (LANCE 1992). In addition, *Zip* is among the names, together with *śwkh*, *ḥbrn* and *mmšt*, which appear on the *LMLK* seals found in archaeological excavations in Judea; see NA'AMAN 1986.

https://doi.org/10.1515/9783110606164-014

23:19–24) describes the event in detail: Some Ziphites visit Saul at Gibeah and volunteer information about David's hiding places along with a proposal to turn him over (vv. 19–20). Saul greets them, thanks them, and requests that they return to Ziph to verify their information and relay it back to him, promising that he will then join them and go to look for David (vv. 21–23). The Ziphites return, and we are immediately informed that Saul pursues David to the wilderness of Maon (vv. 24–25). The second scene concerning the Ziphites (26:1) is more concise. They are described as coming to Saul and telling him that David is hiding "at the hill of Hachilah facing Jeshimon" (26:1).[4] After Saul receives the report, he sets out quickly, along with three thousand of his men, "to search for David in the wilderness of Ziph" (v. 2).

The resemblance between the scenes' opening verses is immediately clear to the reader:

> 23:19 Some **Ziphites** went up **to Saul at Gibeah and said: "David is hiding** among us in the strongholds at Horsha, **at the hill of Hachilah** south of **Jeshimon"**
>
> 26:1 The **Ziphites** came **to Saul at Gibeah and said: "David is hiding at the hill of Hachilah** facing **Jeshimon"**.

While this linguistic parallel alone is sufficient to indicate a connection between the texts, the similarity becomes stronger when one examines the context in which they are presented. Both episodes are reported soon before a story of how David spared Saul's life. In chapter 23, one scene (vv. 25–28) intervenes between the Ziphites' report and the story of the encounter between David and Saul in the cave at En Gedi in chapter 24. In chapter 26, the Ziphites' report appears to be part of the exposition of the story of David's nighttime infiltration of Saul's camp.

1 The Ziphites' reports in their context

Until the early 1970s, many scholars accepted the identification of the first account of the Ziphites' report (1 Sam 23:19–24$_a$) as a natural prelude to the stories that follow it (23:24$_b$–24:23).[5] This idea is expressed in critical analyses of the

---

[4] Translation of the biblical text is taken from the modern JPS edition (1985) with minor emendations.

[5] Among the first to propose such a delineation was DE WETTE (1833: 228 §179 and n. c), who included the episode of the Ziphites from 23:19 onwards as part of the story of David and Saul's encounter in the cave.

book of Samuel in general, and of the stories about David's ascension to the monarchy in particular. Biblical scholars who believed that the book of Samuel was created by combining two or three parallel sources generally attributed 23:19–24:23 to the same source, considering these verses to be an indivisible unit.[6]

Others, who reconstructed the historical formation of David's stories differently, generally referred to the first scene concerning the Ziphites ($23:19-24_a$) as an introduction to the events immediately following. For example, Wellhausen suggested that the story of David's ascension to the monarchy was originally one continuous source, but the final composition as it exists today was yielded by the addition of subsequent layers;[7] he attributed the entire unit (1 Sam 23:19–24:23) to one such layer.[8] Thus, while the above scholars disagreed on many details, almost all shared the view that the first scene dealing with the visit of the Ziphites to Saul properly belongs to the plot sequence in which it is located.[9]

Notwithstanding, an examination of this first scene betrays several difficulties that undermine the possibility that it is situated in its original context. The first and central difficulty relates to the inconsistency between Saul's instructions to the Ziphites and the events that follow their meeting. After the Ziphites report on David's whereabouts, the king asks them to gather more information and return to him with an answer: "Go, make yet more sure. Look around and learn what places he sets foot on [and] who has seen him there ... and return to me of a certainty" (23:22–23). At this point the reader expects the Ziphites to go to Ziph and return to the king to report to him exactly where David and his men are hiding. However, as some scholars have noted, such a report does not appear.[10] The Ziphites indeed leave in v. 24, but they do not return to Saul, who decides on his own to pursue David in v. 25. In fact, the Ziphites are no longer

---

6 See for example: THENIUS 1864: xiv–xvi, 110, 114, 120; BUDDE 1894: 22–24; EISSFELDT 1931: 18–19, 58; EISSFELDT 1965: 271–80; SMITH 1899: xx–xxvi; HALPERN 1981: 149–74.

7 WELLHAUSEN 1883: 262–63.

8 WELLHAUSEN 1883: 264–65; see also: SEGAL 1964: 22; MCCARTER 1980a: 375; MCCARTER 1980b: 492–93.

9 Among the scholars who divided the book of Samuel into parallel sources, STEUERNAGEL'S approach is unique in that it separated the stories about the Ziphites and the pursuit in the wilderness of Maon (1 Sam 23:19–28) from the story of Saul and David's encounter in the cave at Ein Gedi (24:1–23). In his view, the former episodes belong to the source that he called S^a while chapter 24 is part of S^b. He also attributed ch. 26 to the S^a source, thus grouping the two accounts of the Ziphites' report together as parts of a single narrative describing two different events. He characterized a situation in which the Ziphites provided David's location to Saul several times as "*durchaus nicht unwahrscheinlich*" (STEUERNAGEL 1912: 320).

10 E.g., GRØNBÆK 1971: 160.

mentioned and play no further role until the end of ch. 24.[11] Another difficulty arises in the transition from v. 24 to 25. While in v. 24 David is found in the wilderness of Maon ("David and his men were then in the wilderness of Maon, in the Arabah, to the south of Jeshimon"), it is only in verse 25 that he flees there ("and he went down to the rock and abode in the wilderness of Maon").[12] These challenges have forced scholars to question the consensus described above and entertain the possibility that the passage was not originally associated with the stories that have become its context.

The second scene that describes the Ziphites' report to Saul (26:1), and which serves as an introduction to the story of David's infiltration of Saul's camp, presents its own difficulties. Shorter than the first account, it seems at first glance more naturally situated. Immediately after the Ziphites inform Saul of David's location "in the hill of Hachilah facing Jeshimon," Saul goes with his men to the wilderness of Ziph and encamps there (26:2). However, several scholars note that the Ziphites' role in the overarching plot is unclear – they cease to be mentioned later in the chapter, and their appearance in the opening verse does not advance the story beyond guiding Saul to the wilderness of Ziph.[13] Both accounts, therefore, seem to require a solution that can explain the mutual relations between them, as well as between each of them and its own context.

2 Scholarly solutions

Several scholars have offered such solutions. Among the first voices calling to separate the first scene from its aftermath was J. H. Grønbæk, whose study discusses the main challenges presented above regarding the context of the first

---

11 This fact has led some commentators to argue that there originally was a continuation of the story that described the Ziphites' return to Saul (e.g., WELLHAUSEN 1871: 129; HERTZBERG 1964: 194).

12 The LXX version of the verse deals with this tension by a slight change in the wording of v. 25: καὶ κατέβη εἰς τὴν πέτραν **τὴν** ἐν τῇ ἐρήμῳ Μααν (= "and he went down to the rock *that is* in the wilderness of Maan"). In other words, David was already in the wilderness of Maon before he went down to the rock, and the second verse only indicates that the rock was also in the wilderness of Maon. However, it is impossible to prove that the Greek translator possessed a different Hebrew version, and it is reasonable to assume that the translation was itself intended to solve the contradiction between the verses.

13 E.g., GRØNBÆK 1971: 159; WRIGHT 2014: 60. Even if the author of the story or the editor of the unit wanted to create a linking sentence that would transfer the plot to the wilderness of Ziph, this could have been done by means of a general statement that Saul received information about the presence of David there, as was done elsewhere (e.g. 1 Sam. 23:7,25; 24:2).

scene: the absence of a description of the expected second encounter between Saul and the Ziphites,[14] the absence of additional intelligence reports, and the disappearance of the Ziphites from v. 24$_b$ onward. Grønbæk claimed that the story about the Ziphites was interrupted after v. 23, and that it previously included a continuation describing the return of the Ziphites to Saul and the king's departure with them. In Grønbæk's view, the local etiological tradition of "Rock of Separation" (*slʿ hmḥlqwt*; 23:25–28) was incorporated in the text to replace the original conclusion of the story about the Ziphites.[15] Grønbæk, however, failed to explain why it was necessary to erase the end of the story rather than simply including the tradition of the "Rock of Separation" alongside it.

Other scholars have suggested that the two reports of the Ziphites' betrayal both belong to a later phase of redaction that situated them in their present locations within the text. Thus, for example, J. Van Seters suggested identifying in Samuel an original account A to which a later stratum (account B) has been added. According to him, source A belongs to the Deuteronomistic school (Dtr) whereas B had no independent existence, but was rather added by a late author-editor, the final author of the saga of King David.[16] Van Seters identified the first account as an independent literary unit detached from what precedes and follows it and belonging to the additional material comprising source B. He also attributed the second account of the Ziphites' report to the secondary layer. In his view, the two stories, like the story of Keilah (23:6–13), illustrate that there

---

14 GRØNBÆK understood the difficult phrase אל נכון (23:23) as meaning "to an unspecified place" (1971: 160). As a result, he expected a second meeting between Saul and the Ziphites in a place other than Gibeah. For a different interpretation of this phrase, see below.

15 GRØNBÆK (1971: 160) proposed identifying two parts of verses as fragments from the missing sections of the ancient story. In the words "They left at once for Ziph, ahead of Saul" (23:24$_a$), GRØNBÆK saw a fragment of the story of Saul's walk with the Ziphites, after they had returned to him once again. In addition, he saw in the text about David: "and (he) understood that Saul was come of a certainty" (26:4$_b$) another fragment from the original story, that was mistakenly incorporated into the story in ch. 26. It should be noted that according to GRØNBÆK, the additional report of the Ziphites at the beginning of ch. 26 is a later rewriting of the material from ch. 23, which is an artificial exposition of the story in Saul's camp (1971: 158). The separation suggested by GRØNBÆK between the episodes about the Ziphites and the stories about the David and Saul's encounters was accepted by number of scholars, who dealt with the comparison between the stories and focused on chapters 24 and 26 only (e.g. EDENBURG 1998: 74–75 and n. 30; MCKENZIE 2010).

16 VAN SETERS 2009: 196. According to VAN SETERS's view, the original account A supported David, while layer B contains an anti-monarchist ideology that also opposes David's dynasty. In his book he demonstrates how each of the additions works to establish the new ideology (2009: 196–97).

are groups that opposed David.[17] However, this approach does not solve the main difficulty, since removing the first account from its present context still leaves the episode unfinished. Still Saul arranges another meeting with the Ziphites which never materializes.

Another suggestion is that of A. F. Campbell,[18] who considered 1 Sam 23–26 to be a unified text written on the basis of oral traditions.[19] Campbell contested the claim that there is no second meeting between Saul and the Ziphites subsequent the first account, arguing that the return of the Ziphites is indeed reported – in the second account, at the beginning of ch. 26. He thus sought to solve the difficulty by connecting the two episodes: the Ziphites' visit to Saul in the second is itself the anticipated return absent from the first.[20]

However, Campbell himself pointed out that the second report of the Ziphites (26:1) does not add any information that does not appear in the first (23:19). He therefore argued that although the story of the Ziphites is based on an ancient tradition, the form it takes in the book of Samuel is not an accurate rendition thereof, but a free application employed only to frame the literary unit (chs. 23–26).[21] In his commentary to chapter 26, Campbell also assumes that the story of David and Abishai's infiltration of Saul's camp (26:2–25) was previously independent, before it was integrated into the literary unit in chs. 23–26.[22] In other words, while the second episode (26:1) is a continuation of the first (23:19–24$_a$), it was originally divorced from its own context in ch. 26.

---

17 VAN SETERS 2009: 175, 200, 202; J. WRIGHT (2014: 61–62) also identifies the episodes concerning the Ziphites as late additions of common origin. Recognizing the resemblance between the stories of the Ziphites and the story of Keilah, he suggests that all three were authored by the same pen. In his view, both accounts of the Ziphites' report are later additions intended to paint the Ziphites as traitors. The hypothesized background for these additions is the struggle between Caleb's family and the House of David over hegemony within the tribe of Judah. Ziph, a city in Caleb's territory (and Caleb's son in 1 Chr 2:42; see n. 3 above) symbolizes the competing family, which the Jerusalemite writer sought to denounce as traitorous.
18 CAMPBELL 2003.
19 According to CAMPBELL (2003: 242), the stories about the cave (ch. 24), Nabal (ch. 25) and David's infiltration of Saul's camp (ch. 26) are organized as a unit whose purpose is to present David as one who does not shed innocent blood, an idea expressed stated twice in the text, once by Saul and once by Abigail. The sequence, as it is before us, presents Saul's hostility as exaggerated and prepares the reader for David's decision not to kill Saul in ch. 26.
20 CAMPBELL (2003: 246) saw this as proof of his claim about the literary unity of chs. 23–26, for which the Zipites' reports serve as an *inclusio*.
21 In his commentary to chapter 23 CAMPBELL writes: "Whatever may have happened to the original traditions in organizing the present composition, the Ziphite offer is now made in ch. 23 and acted on in ch. 26" (2003: 247 see also p. 264).
22 CAMPBELL 2003: 264.

Campbell's approach is unique in that it seeks to explain the duplication of story of the Ziphites' by uniting the duplicates. However, it does not offer a convincing solution to the difficulties Campbell himself raises, especially the absence of significant new information in the second report. What's more, Campbell himself views the Ziphites' story as incomplete, divorcing it from the story of the infiltration of Saul's camp (26:2–25).

In conclusion, several solutions have been proposed attempting to address the discrepancy between the accounts of the Ziphites' meetings with Saul and the stories surrounding them. Contrary to popular opinion, these scholars do not regard the Ziphites' report as part of the story of the Rock of Separation, or the story of Saul and David meeting in the cave. Ultimately, however, these theories have struggled to provide answers to all questions arising from the dissonance between the scenes and their context.

3 A different resolution

Pursuant to the above, a new explanation can be proposed as to the connection between the two scenes. The argument for separating the first episode from what follows is convincing. As noted, the comment in v. 24$_b$ interrupts the story before it. Afterward, the Ziphites are no longer mentioned, nor do we find any fulfillment of the mission with which Saul charges them in vv. 22–23. We must therefore conclude that the story of the Ziphites in ch. 23 is incomplete. As we have seen however, the various proposed solutions to this problem are unsatisfying and sometimes raise additional difficulties.

It seems that the natural continuation of the first story can be found in the description of the second visit to Saul (26:1). In this view, the second story, which most scholars consider to be a duplicate of the first one, is actually the missing continuation of it. The reconstructed story tells us that after Saul sent the Ziphites to gather more intelligence (23:22–23), they did so (23:24$_a$) and returned with the necessary information (26:1). Only then did Saul and his men set out to capture David (26:2). The last words in the first scene: "They left at once for Ziph, ahead of Saul" (23:24$_a$) should be understood as a description of the Ziphites traveling back to the area where David is hiding for the purpose of collecting new information, and not, as some commentators have claimed, traveling with Saul after they had already given him another (unreported) report.[23] In addition, this reconstruction of the sequence provides a context to the

---

23 E.g., WELLHAUSEN 1871: 129; HERTZBERG 1964: 194; GRØNBÆK 1971: 160. It is true that the phrase "to go ahead" (הלך לפני) appears in the Hebrew Bible primarily in the sense of gui-

mention of the Ziphites at the beginning of ch. 26 and explains their narrative role. If so, there appears to be no reason to claim discontinuity between 26:1 and the following narrative. This approach solves the difficulties we have pointed out regarding the two accounts of the Ziphites' report, resolving the interruption of the first scene and the second's lack of context simultaneously.

Still, if we are to claim that the second account is in fact a continuation of the first, we would assume that the Ziphites' second report should contain some new information beyond what is given in the initial one. But as noted above, this is not the case – the main information of the second report, David's presence in the Hill of Hachilah (26:1), appears already in the first.[24] Therefore, we should consider the possibility that in its original form the Ziphites' first report was shorter and did not contain the information regarding the "Hill of Hachilah." Several scholars have already suggested that the great detail in the first report of the Ziphites – "David is hiding among us in the strongholds at Horsha, at the hill of Hachilah south of Jeshimon" – is the result of later additions and expansions of the original report.[25] In their view, the words "the Hill of Hachilah" are the result of a late assimilation between the Ziphites' reports.[26] It can

---

dance (e.g. Exod 13:21; 14:19; 23:23; 32:1,23,34; Deut 1:30,33), but in the context of espionage this combination may have a broader meaning of pre-examination. While there are no cases in which the phrase is employed in this sense unmistakably, usage in Deut 1:22 may be indirect evidence to this effect: "Then all of you came to me and said, 'Let us send men *ahead* (לפנינו) to reconnoiter the land for us and *bring back* word on the route we shall follow and the cities we shall come to." In this case it is clear that the spies are sent ahead of the people with the goal of gathering information and relaying it back to them.

24 As noted above, this fact led CAMPBELL (2003: 47) to speculate that 26:1 in its present form does not reflect the original tradition that continued 23:19–24$_a$.

25 WELLHAUSEN, SMITH, and DRIVER regarded the words "at Horsha, at the hill of Hachilah south of Jeshimon" as a secondary addition but left "in the strongholds" in place (WELLHAUSEN 1871: 128; SMITH 1899: 213–14; DRIVER 1913: 188). STEUERNAGEL argued that only the words "at Horsha, at the hill of Hachilah" should be considered an addition (STEUERNAGEL 1912: 320). In my opinion, the original report of the Ziphites contained only the words "David is hiding among us." The rest of the toponyms brought into the report from the episodes near the Ziphites' scene – 23:14: "strongholds"; 23:15,16,18: "Horsha"; 23:24: "south of Jeshimon". It is reasonable to assume that this is an artificial combination of toponyms, whose function is to link the places in which David was located in the various episodes in the chapter, that originally were separate from each other. In the current textual situation, when the Ziphites reported that David was hiding among them (in Ziph) and in the strongholds and at Horsha and at the hill of Hachilah and south of Jeshimon, a geographical connection was created between all these places, which appear in the different parts of ch. 23, and thus a chronological closeness was created between the events that took place there. By the combination of the toponyms, the unit's editor reinforced the artificial chronological order he had created.

26 See also GRØNBÆK 1971: 157–58.

be assumed that this process occurred at a time when the two scenes had already been separated and placed in different contexts in the Book of Samuel and therefore were perceived as two different stories. In fact, Saul's request to the Ziphites (23:22–23) to return to him with a detailed report on David's position reinforces the hypothesis that the report in v. 19 was shorter in the past, since the version before us is rich in details and it is difficult to understand why Saul needed further clarification.

Among scholarly opinions, Campbell's approach is thus the closest to the solution proposed here, but it is fundamentally different in some points. Campbell believed that the reports of the Ziphites was not originally joined to the scene in Saul's camp (26:2–25). However, this claim appears to have no textual justification. As will be shown below, the story in ch. 26 actually displays thematic and linguistic affinity with the first scene of the Ziphites. In addition, Campbell argues that the relationship between the two accounts depends primarily on the desire to establish an envelope structure for the chs. 23–26 and does not rely on the continuity of events between the episodes.[27] However, the narrative continuity between the passages is the strongest proof of the connection between them. Reconstruction of the original literary sequence of these stories should not be based on presumed literary superstructures but should rather arise out of a concrete narrative need, i.e., the expectation of the return of the Ziphites to Saul, which is satisfied only by the unification of the episodes.

4 The Ziphites' report and the scene in Saul's camp

The connection between the first report of the Ziphites and the story of David's infiltration of Saul's camp (26:1–25) is strengthened by the common theme of spies sent to confirm and verify information received. Generally, espionage missions in the Hebrew Bible are simple: Those who need information send their men to obtain it; the spies return and report back; based on the information received the senders plan their resultant actions.[28] The account of the Ziphites'

---

27 CAMPBELL 2003: 264.

28 Incidents of espionage can be found in the Hebrew Bible in the following places: Num 13; 21:32; Deut 1:22–25; Josh 2; 7:2; 14:7; Judg 1:22–26; 7:9–15; 18:2–10; 2 Sam 15:27–28. Alongside these examples, there are cases in which people are wrongfully suspected of being spies: Gen 42:9–14 (in which the suspicion was pretended); 2 Sam 10:1–5; 2 Kgs 6:11. It is possible that the envoys of Merodach-baladan to Hezekiah should also be added to this list (2 Kgs 20:12–19 = Isa 39:1–8).

report and the scene in Saul's camp are the only cases in which a demand for further examination and information is described. In the first scene, Saul sends the Ziphites to obtain more specific intelligence,[29] while in ch. 26, after David learns that Saul has come to look for him, he too sends spies to corroborate this information (26:3–4). Furthermore, in both cases a rare phrase is used. At the end of his instructions to the Ziphites, the king says: "and return to me when you are certain (אל נכון)" (23:23); after David's spies returned to him, he "made certain (אל נכון) that Saul had come" (26:4). In both cases, certainty is expressed by the same Hebrew phrase, which appears nowhere else in the Hebrew Bible.

Most scholars correctly understand the syntactic role of this phrase as an adverb with a similar sense to the English "certainly."[30] However, the phrase requires further clarification. When the word "נכון" is used in biblical Hebrew to describe information, it usually refers to facts that are examined and verified. For example: "you shall investigate and inquire and interrogate thoroughly. If it is true, and the thing certain (נכון) ..." (Deut 13:15; also 17:4).[31] This meaning is sometimes found in other words from the root כון in biblical Hebrew[32] and other Semitic languages.[33]

This holds the key to understanding the beginning of Saul's instructions to the Ziphites: הכינו עוד (23:22). Stemming from the same root, this command

---

29 Although in this case the initiative for the original report was not Saul's; still his request for verification goes beyond what is found elsewhere in the Hebrew Bible.

30 E.g., BUDDE 1902: 159; MCCARTER 1980a: 378; KLEIN 1983: 228. Nowhere else does Biblical Hebrew use a conjunction of the preposition אל with any noun or an adjective to create an adverb, which makes it difficult to understand the phrase אל נכון as such. However, a similar structure with the word על is sometimes used as an adverb (DRIVER 1913: 189; SEGAL 1964: 187; MCCARTER 1980a: 378). Cf. the phrase על שקר (Lev 5:22) which is contrary to the supposed meaning of אל נכון. See also: על נקלה (Jer 6:14), על רצון (Isa 60:7). In the Targum, too, the role of אל נכון as an adverb is reflected as בקשוט, i.e., truly.

31 This is probably also the meaning in the words of Joseph to Pharaoh: "As for Pharaoh having had the same dream twice, it means that the matter has been determined (נכון) by God, and that God will soon carry it out" (Gen. 41:32). The fact that Pharaoh's dream was repeated twice corroborates and verifies its content.

32 For example: "Ask the generation past, study (וכונן) what their fathers have searched out" (Job 8:8).

33 The Akkadian verb *kânu* is sometimes used in the sense of proof or presentation of evidence in court. This is the case in several times in the Code of Hammurabi and in other law collections, for example: "If a man comes forward to give false testimony in a case but cannot bring evidence (*lā uktīn*) for his accusation, if that case involves a capital offence, the man shall be killed." (Code of Hammurabi §3, trans. Roth 1995: 81). In other cases, *kânu* is used in the sense of confirming information, sometimes contrary to the verb *nakāru* which means "to deny" (CAD K: 168–70). See more below.

must be understood as "ascertain and corroborate further." Thus, Saul's speech, which begins with this imperative, concludes with the expectation that they will return to him with a verified and proven report (אל נכון).[34]

This proposed definition of the phrase אל נכון suits its second occurrence well (26:4). At first glance it would seem that after it became known to David that Saul was following him in v. 3, the apprehension of that same fact in v. 4 adds no new information.[35] However, if the phrase אל נכון indicates merely the *verification* of information, then v. 4 is not redundant. First David learned that "Saul came after him into the wilderness" (v. 3), but only after he sent spies he knew for certain – "אל נכון" – that Saul had arrived (v. 4). Some scholars who did not understand the exact meaning of the phrase sought to correct the Masoretic text based on the Greek, seeing the word "נכון" as a corrupted version of the name of the place to which Saul arrived.[36] However, in clarifying the meaning of the phrase we can see that there is in fact no redundancy between the two verses and therefore no need for emendation.[37] The phrase אל נכון fits its context in both instances, and there is no reason to claim that in one of them was added secondarily. The uniqueness of this phrase reinforces the conclusion that both stories were written by the same hand.[38]

---

34 It should be noted that in LXX B, a section in v. 23, from מכל to אל נכון, is missing. Although some scholars preferred the LXX B version (e.g., WELLHAUSEN 1871: 129; McCARTER 1980a: 378), the MT appears to be better. The LXX omits the words "and return to me when you are certain," thus solving the main difficulty in the narrative – the absence of the return of the Ziphites to Saul. According to the LXX the Ziphites were never asked to return. On the other hand, it is difficult to understand why a copyist of the MT will add this difficulty to the text. See also: BUDDE 1902: 159.

35 DRIVER 1913: 205.

36 E.g., ibid.; WELLHAUSEN 1871: 136; BUDDE 1902: 169; SEGAL 1964: 203; HERTZBERG 1964: 192. SMITH (1899: 231) suggested emending the text to read: אל נכחו, i.e., "to the point just in front of him". Most versions of LXX render the text: ἐκ Κεϊλα (from Keilah), while the Lucianic version has εις σεχελαγ (to Ziklag). Thornhill (1964) shows that both versions were the result of an error in the Greek, and that the original translation was εις εχελα (to Hachilah). These details have led many modern commentators to prefer Thornhill's revised version (see McCARTER 1980a: 405; KLEIN 1983: 255). LXX reflects also the word נכון (ἕτοιμο – a regular translation of the word נכון in the sense of "ready," e.g., in Exod 34:2) that appears in MT. But it seems that this is a double version (WELLHAUSEN, 1871: 136).

37 It seems that in any case, the Greek version reconstructed by THORNHILL (see note above) should not be seen as original, since the name "Hachilah" never appears alone in the Hebrew Bible, but always as part of the combination "the hill of Hachilah (גבעת החכילה)." Although THORNHILL (1964: 466) comments on this, he does not consider this sufficient reason to prefer the text of MT.

38 Another direction chosen by commentators and scholars in interpreting the phrase אל נכון has been to understand the word נכון as a place name (IBN ĞANÂḤ 1896: 214; VILNAY 1941: 114–15; cf. 2 Sam 6:6). Thus, Saul's words to the Ziphites (1 Sam 23:23) could be translated:

While the demand to verify intelligence can found in the Hebrew Bible only in the story of the Ziphites, there are several examples of this phenomenon documented in intelligence letters from the ancient Near East, both in the second and the first millennia BCE.[39] An examination of these reports may indicate that they share background with the story of the Ziphites. For example, in a letter sent to Tiglath-Pileser III, the author mentions a request by the king to clarify information sent to him in the past:

> [ina] ⸢muḫḫi x x x⸣ [x x] ⸢ša⸣ šarru bēlī iš⸢pur⸣[anni] ⸢ma⸣ mīnu ša ṭēn⸢šūni⸣ ḫurṣa šupra ina mātišu šū ⸢dul⸣lušu eppaš
> [As t]o [..., about wh]om the king, my lord, wro[te to me]: "Clarify (ḫurṣa[40]) what is the news about him and write it to me." He is in his country and does his work.
> (SAA 19 78:r 1'–5')

From the letter it can be understood that, as in the case of Saul and the Ziphites, the king had previously received a report about a certain person, but the information did not satisfy him. The king therefore asked the author of the inscription to clarify the information, with which request he complied.[41]

Another example, is a letter sent by Išmē-Dagan, King of Mari, to one of his vassal kings, Kuwari, ruler of Šamšāra, regarding intelligence previously sent by Kuwari to Išmē-Dagan:

> inanna ṭēmam šâti kinnamma annītam lā annītam šupram
> Now, confirm (kinnam) this report and write to me whether (the situation is) this or that!
> (SH 865:r 15–18)[42]

"and return to me to [the place named] Nākôn," and likewise in 26:4. Other scholars have suggested that the word נכון should be attributed the general meaning of "an unspecified place" (GRØNBÆK 1971: 160; HERTZBERG 1964: 192). Both suggestions compound more difficulties to the text than they solve. First, the agreement of Saul and the Ziphites to reach the place called נכון, where to give and receive the name of the new report is not carried out. In fact, there is no meeting between the parties in a place other than Gibeah. In addition, the identification of נכון as the name of a place creates a contradiction in ch. 26 between v. 3 and 4 – in v. 3 Saul is located at "the hill of Hachilah" while in v. 4 he is in "Nākôn."

39 For a review of the subject of intelligence mechanisms in the ancient Near East, see, e.g., DUBOVSKÝ 2006; COHEN 2000; SHELDON 1989; HONGGENG 2004.

40 The Akkadian verb ḫarāṣu, whose basic meaning is "to cut," can also be used in the sense of "clarify" or "determine" (CAD Ḫ: 94). Cf. also the meaning of the root חרץ in Biblical Hebrew (HALOT I:356).

41 For another example, see the letter sent to Sargon II about the war between the Urarṭians and the Cimmerians: "Up till now we have not clarified (lā niḫarraṣa) the information. When we clarify (niḫtarṣa), we will send you [what] the report will be" (SAA 1 30:b.e. 9'–r 2).

42 For a translated and annotated version of the text, see LÆSSØE 1959: 51–55.

Like Saul, Išmē-Dagan received an intelligence report and asks to confirm it. Furthermore, Išmē-Dagan uses the Akkadian verb *kânu* (*kinnam*), the etymological equivalent to the Hebrew root כון, to express this demand, similar to Saul's command "הכינו."[43]

A similar report in terms of content and language can be found in a letter sent from Amurru Kingdom to Egypt during the Amarna period. According to, the addressee of the letter was not the Egyptian king but Aziru, king of Amurru, who was in Egypt at that time.[44] The report contains information regarding the deployment of a large Hittite force in the Beqa'a Valley in Lebanon, but this intelligence needs to be confirmed:

> *u amata la nutarriṣ šumma ina kitti ibaššûnim*
>
> …
>
> *kīmê panîšunu niṣabbat u* ^LÚ*mār šipriya arḫiš ana muḫḫika ašappar kīmê amatam uttêrka šumma ibašši ū šumma yānu*
> But that word, we have not confirmed, whether in truth (*ina kitti*) they really are.
>
> …
>
> When we establish contact with them, then I will send my envoy immediately to you, so that he may give a reply to you whether it really is or whether it isn't.
> (EA 170:r 24–25, 30–35)

In terms of content, there is a similarity between this and the Ziphites' report. Both initially contain general and unverified information about the presence of people of interest to the king in a particular geographical area. In both cases, the information must be confirmed and verified. On the linguistic side, a more specific similarity can be discerned. In their report, the Amorites note that the initial information was not certain: "But that word, we have not confirmed, whether in truth (*ina kitti*) they really are." The Akkadian phrase *ina kitti* is used as an adverb of the verb *ibaššū* (they are) and concerns the reliability of the report. Here again, the noun *kittu* is derived from the Akkadian root *k'n*, the etymological equivalent of the Hebrew כון. As mentioned above, the Hebrew phrase אל נכון functions similarly, and the word נכון derives from the same root. This is to say that Saul's instructions to the Ziphites and the Amarna letter,

---

43 There are other examples of the use of *kânu* in the sense of confirmation or verification of information in many inscriptions. For example, in the text of ARM 2 73, Yarem-Addu reports on Elamite messengers that Hammurabi, king of Babylon, sent back to Elam unaccompanied. It was not clear to the writer of the report whether the messengers had already departed, and so he wrote: "Until now the matter of sending or not sending them I have not verified (*ul ukīnma*) and to my lord I did not send. When these people are sent, I will verify (*ukannamma*) the report about them, and the full report regarding them to my master I will send." (ARM 2 73:18–26). See also: ARM 2 27:r 3'–5'.

44 MORAN 1992: 257n1.

which are typologically close to one another, use similar phrases to refer to the credibility of intelligence.

Thus, the resemblance between the espionage scenes, as well as their unique use of the phrase אֶל נָכוֹן, serves as further evidence of the affinity between the first account of the Ziphites' report and the scene in Saul's camp. In addition, it can be assumed that the author of the story had a degree of familiarity with intelligence activity that normally took place in royal courts. He knew the process and terminology of sending a request for clarification of information – a phenomenon not repeated in the Bible but well documented in other materials from the ancient Near East.

5 Dynamics of the reconstructed story

A comparison between the actions of the Ziphites and those of David's spies shows that the first account of the Ziphites' report, which we now establish as the reconstructed prelude to the larger story of the infiltration of Saul's camp, suits its contextual dynamics well. According to the reconstructed story, at first the Ziphites come to Saul and offer to turn David over to him, but Saul delays the offer and sends them to gather better information about David's location (23:19–24$_a$). After the Ziphites return with an improved report (26:1), Saul follows them and encamps at the hill of Hachilah (26:2–3$_a$). David, who has heard that the king has come to look for him, verifies the information using his own spies (26:3$_b$–4). David and Abishai then steal into Saul's camp at night, and instead of killing the king, take his belongings, which later served as proof of their actions (26:5–12). David's dialogs with Abner and Saul take place at the end of the story, where David reprimands Abner for not keeping the king safe and insists upon his own righteousness in not having killing Saul (26:13–25).

A central motif of this story is the inversion of the characters' roles. In the words of W. Brueggemann:

> For a long stretch of the narrative, Saul is the stalker seeking out David; David is the one stalked, who must always seek escape ... As this narrative begins, however, their roles are reversed. Abruptly and unexpectedly, Saul is the hunted one and David is the hunter.[45]

The addition of the first report of the Ziphites as the opening scene of the story preserves and even enhances this dynamic between the characters. Now David's commission of spies (26:3–4) stands in contrast to the Ziphites' mission by Saul.

---

45 BRUEGGEMANN 1990: 182.

After David hears that Saul has come after him to the wilderness (26:3) he sends spies who confirm the information – אל נכון (v. 4). This concise description is a mirror image of Saul's instructions to the Ziphites. In both cases, the characters receive information about the enemy's location, and both ask the spies to confirm and refine the report. Ultimately, David's efforts succeed, underscoring Saul's parallel failure. It should be noted that in ch. 26 as it stands today it is difficult to explain what literary value is added by the account of David's spies. However, when viewed in light of the reconstruction proposed here, the two contrasting scenes of espionage are shown develop the internal dynamics of the story as a whole.

Comparison and contrast between David and Saul are also expressed through the vocabulary of the story. In Saul's instructions to the Ziphites, he repeats twice the imperative "know and see (דעו וראו)" (23:22–23).[46] The same verbs appear when David discovers Saul's arrival: "And he saw (וירא) that Saul came after him... and made certain (וידע...אל נכון) that Saul had come" (26:3–4). Another instance where these verbs are used in the story is David and Abishai's departure from Saul's camp: "No one saw (ראה) or knew (יודע) or woke up; all remained asleep" (26:12). This is an ironic note: Saul, who twice asked the Ziphites to "know and see," is exposed to the attack of his enemy while none of his men sees or knows – a clear failure of intelligence.

It is possible to detect the inversion motif in David's words to Saul as well, concerning the possible causes of the king's hostility toward him: "If the LORD has incited you against me, let him be appeased by an offering: but if is men, may they be accursed of the LORD" (26:19). It is reasonable to assume that this curse is not directed toward specific people but is rather suggested hypothetically. However, the narrator may intend that these words hint at the Ziphites.[47] While the Ziphites did not actually incite the king against David but only helped to locate him, they nonetheless represent people who shared Saul's hostility. If the curse is intended for the Ziphites, then the first part of the story in ch. 23 emphasizes the inversion in this sense as well. Saul's response to the report on

---

46 A double imperative with the verbs ידע and ראה is common in the Hebrew Bible (1 Sam 12:17; 14:38; 24:12; 25:17; 2 Sam 24:13; 1 Kgs 20:7,22; 2 Kgs 5:7; Jer 2:19,23; 5:1). SEELIGMANN (1977: 428–29) suggests that in such cases, the root of ידע loses the semantic charge of "cognitive perception, to know," and its meaning is similar to that of the root ראה ("to see"). However, it seems that this combination may have a meaning that is more closely related to that of the root ידע itself. Compare, for example, the sentence: "So know and consider (דעי וראי) what you should do" (1 Sam 25:17) to others such as: "now you know (דעו) what you have to do" (Judg 18:14; also 1 Kgs 2:9). It therefore appears that the combination of ידע and ראה has a broader semantic range than SEELIGMANN suggests.
47 VAN SETERS 2011: 102 and n. 15.

David's location opens with a blessing to the Ziphites: "May you be blessed of the LORD for the compassion you have shown me" (23:21). Poetically, those hinted at in David's curse are none other than those who, at the beginning of the story, are blessed.[48]

Conclusions

The identification of the two accounts of the Ziphites (1 Sam 23:19–24$_a$; 26:1–25) as two parts of the same story, rather than parallel stories, resolves the literary difficulties that these passages pose separately, especially the incompleteness of the first scene. In addition, the thematic and linguistic continuity of the reconstructed story reinforces the narrative sequence of the two parts, deepening and enriching the inversion motif. The delegation of the spies by David (26:4) makes a neat comparison to Saul's commission of the Ziphites: While both men spy on one another, it is David who ultimately succeeds in locating Saul, and not vice versa. The language of the passages also indicates a connection between them, with the rare phrase אֶל נָכוֹן, which appears in both parts of the story, pointing to a commonality of authorship. The phenomenon of confirmation and verification of intelligence information, shared by both parts of the reconstructed story, is also unique within the Hebrew Bible. The presence of this phenomenon in external texts from the ancient Near East, as well as the use therein of language close to that of the reconstructed story, may serve as some indication of the author's background.

The reconstruction of the original narrative sequence proposed here redefines the boundaries of the story. In light of this hypothesis, it is imperative to revisit the question of the relation between the stories in which David spares Saul's life. In addition, it is necessary to explain why the story was split in two and what editorial motivations argued in favor of placing the first scene in its current context. These issues should be examined in future research.

---

48 It should be noted that the phrase "accursed of the LORD" (אָרוּר לִפְנֵי יהוה) is rare in the Hebrew Bible and appears in one more place (Josh 6:26). Outside the Bible, the phrase אָרֻר לַיהוה is found in two inscriptions from caves near Khirbet el-Qom (AḤITUV 2012: 223–24).

Abbreviations

ARM 2   Jean, Charles F. *Lettres Diverses*. Archives Royales De Mari 2. Paris: Imprime-
             rie Nationale, 1950
CAD   *The Assyrian Dictionary of the Oriental Institute of the University of Chicago*.
             Chicago: The Oriental Institute of the University of Chicago, 1956–2006
EA   El-Amarna tablets. According to the edition of Anson F. Rainey and William M.
             Schniedewind. *The El-Amarna Correspondence: A New Edition of the Cunei-
             form Letters from the Site of El-Amarna Based on Collations of All Extant Tab-
             lets*. Leiden: Brill, 2015
HALOT   *The Hebrew and Aramaic Lexicon of the Old Testament*. Ludwig Koehler, Wal-
             ter Baumgartner, and Johann J. Stamm. Translated and edited under the su-
             pervision of Mervyn E. J. Richardson. 4 vols. Leiden: Brill, 1994–1999
SAA 1   Parpola, S. *The Correspondence of Sargon II, Part I: Letters from Assyria and
             the West*. State Archives of Assyria 1. Helsinki: Helsinki University Press, 1987
SAA 19   Luukko, M. *The Correspondence of Tiglath-pileser III and Sargon II from Ca-
             lah/Nimrud*. State Archives of Assyria 19. Helsinki: The Neo-Assyrian Text Cor-
             pus Project, 2012
SH   Field Registration of Tell Shemshāra Excavations Discoveries, 1957

Bibliography

Aḥituv, Shmuel. ²2012. *HaKetav VeHamiḵtav: Handbook of Ancient Inscriptions from the Land
    of Israel and the Trans-Jordanian Kingdoms from the First Commonwealth Period*. The
    Biblical Encyclopaedia Library 21. Jerusalem: Bialik Institute.
Budde, Karl. 1894. *The Books of Samuel*. SBOT 8. Leipzig: J. C. Hinrichs.
Budde, Karl. 1902. *Die Bücher Samuel*. KHC 8. Tübingen: J. C. B. Mohr.
Brueggemann, Walter. 1990. *First and Second Samuel*. Louisville, KY: John Knox Press.
Campbell, Antony F. 2003. *1 Samuel*. FOTL 7. Grand Rapids, MI: Eerdmans.
Cohen, Raymond. 2000. "Intelligence in the Amarna Letters." Pages 85–98 in *Amarna
    Diplomacy: The Beginnings of International Relations*. Edited by Raymond Cohen and
    Raymond Westbrook. Baltimore, MD: Johns Hopkins University Press.
De Wette, Wilhelm M. L. ⁴1833. *Die Einleitung in das Alte Testament enthaltend*. Vol 1 of
    Lehrbuch der historisch-kritischen Einleitung in die Bibel Alten und Neuen Testamentes.
    Berlin: G. Reimer.
Driver, Samuel R. 1913. *Notes on the Hebrew Text and the Topography of the Books of
    Samuel*. Oxford: Clarendon Press.
Dubovský, Peter. 2006. *Hezekiah and the Assyrian Spies: Reconstruction of the Neo-Assyrian
    Intelligence Services and its Significance for 2 Kings 18–19*. BibOr 49. Roma: Pontificio
    Istituto Biblico.
Edenburg, Cynthia. 1998. How (Not) to Murder a King: Variations on a Theme in 1 Sam 24;
    26. *SJOT* 12:64–85.
Eissfeldt, Otto. 1931. *Die Komposition der Samuelisbücher*. Leipzig: J. C. Hinrichs.
Eissfeldt, Otto. 1965. *The Old Testament: An Introduction*. Translated by Peter R. Ackroyd.
    New York: Harper and Row.

Grønbæk, Jakob H. 1971. *Die Geschichte vom Aufstieg Davids (1. Sam. 15 – 2. Sam. 5): Tradition und Komposition*. ATDan 10. Copenhagen: Prostant Apud Munksgaard.

Halpern, Baruch. 1981. *The Constitution of the Monarchy in Israel*. HSM 25. Chico, CA: Scholars Press.

Hertzberg, Hans Wilhelm. 1964. *I and II Samuel: A Commentary*. OTL. London: SCM Press.

Honggeng, GUO. 2004. The Assyrian Intelligence Activities during the Assyrian Empire. *JAAS* 18:59–71.

Ibn Ǧanâḥ, Abulwalîd Merwân (R. Jona). 1896. *Sepher Haschoraschim*. Edited by Wilhelm Bacher. Translated by Jehuda Ibn Tibbon. Berlin: H. Itzkowski.

Klein, Ralph W. 1983. *1 Samuel*. WBC 10. Waco, TX: Word Books.

Læssøe, Jørgen. 1959. *The Shemshāra Tablets: A Preliminary Report*. Kopenhagen: Munksgaard.

Lance, H. Darrell. 1992. "Ziph (PLACE)." Page 1104 in vol. 6 of *The Anchor Bible Dictionary*. Edited by David N. Freedman. 6 vols. Yale: Yale University Press.

McCarter, P. Kyle. 1980a. *I Samuel: A New Translation with Introduction, Notes, and Commentary*. AB 8. Garden City, N. Y.: Doubleday & Co.

McCarter, P. Kyle. 1980b. The Apology of David. *JBL* 99:489–504.

McKenzie, Steven L. 2010. Elaborated Evidence for the Priority of 1 Samuel 26. *JBL* 129:437–44.

Moran, William L. 1992. *The Amarna Letters*. Baltimore, MD: Johns Hopkins University Press.

Na'aman, Nadav. 1986. Hezekiah's Fortified Cities and the "LMLK" Stamps. *BASOR* 261:5–21.

Roth, Martha T. 1995. *Law Collections from Mesopotemia and Asia Minor*. WAW 6. Atlanta, GA: Scholars Press.

Segal, M. H. 1964. *The Books of Samuel*. Jerusalem: Kiryat Sefer.

Seeligmann, Isaac L. 1977. Erkenntnis Gottes und historisches Bewusstsein im alten Israel. Pages 414–15 in *Beiträge zur alttestamentlichen Theologie: Festschrift für Walther Zimmerli zum 70 Geburtstag*. Edited by Herbert Donner et al. Göttingen: Vandenhoeck & Ruprecht.

Sheldon, Rose M. 1989. "Spying in Mesopotamia." *Studies in Intelligence* 33:7–12.

Smith, Henry P. 1899. *A Critical and Exegetical Commentary on the Books of Samuel*. ICC 9. Edinburgh: T. & T. Clark.

Spinoza, Benedictus de. 1670. Theologico-Political Treatise. Pages 1–266 in *The Chief Works of Benedict de Spinoza*. 2nd ed. vol. 1. Translated by R. H. M. Elwes. London: G. Bell, 1887. Translation of *Tractatus Theologico-Politicus*.

Steuernagel, Carl. 1912. *Lehrbuch der Einleitung in das alte Testament mit einem Anhang über die Apokryphen und Pseudepigraphen*. Tübingen: J. C. B. Mohr.

Thenius, Otto. ²1864. *Die Bücher Samuels*. EHAT 4. Leipzig: S. Hirzel.

Thornhill, Raymond. 1964. A Note on אֶל-נָכוֹן, 1 Sam. XXVI 4. *VT* 14:462–66.

Van Seters, John. 2009. *The Biblical Saga of King David*. Winona Lake, IN: Eisenbrauns.

Van Seters, John. 2011. Two Stories of David Sparing Saul's Life in 1 Samuel 24 and 26: A Question of Priority. *SJOT* 25:93–104.

Vilnay, Zev. 1941. Names of places in Eretz-Israel as words and expressions in Hebrew. *Lěšonénu: A Journal for the Study of the Hebrew Language and Cognate Subjects* 11:109–22. (Hebrew)

Wellhausen, Julius. 1871. *Der Text der Bücher Samuelis*. Gottingen: Vandenhoeck & Ruprecht.

Wellhausen, Julius. ²1883. *Prolegomena to the History of Ancient Israel*. Translated by J. Sutherland Black and A. Enzies. New York: Meridian Books, 1957. Translation of *Prolegomena zur Geschichte Israels*. Berlin: Reimer.

Wright, Jacob L. 2014. *David, King of Israel, and Caleb in Biblical Memory*. New York: Cambridge University Press.

Cynthia Edenburg
Wilderness, Liminality and David's Rite of Passage

The portion of the Book of Samuel known as "the History of David's Rise" re-
volves around the issue of legitimizing the Davidic dynasty, particularly since
David was not Saul's natural successor, and would be considered a "son of
nobody" in Neo-Assyrian terms.[1] While the Tel Dan inscription provides external evidence that David was considered the founder of the ruling dynasty of the
kingdom of Judah ("the House of David," בית דוד), the historical setting for Saul
continues to elude us.[2] What does seem clear to a growing number of scholars
is that the story of Saul and the story of David were originally separate traditions that were later combined.[3]

According to the basic tenet of royal ideology throughout the Ancient Near
East, a legitimate king is the son of a preceding king, therefore, royal inscriptions usually carefully detail the king's lineage and thereby establish his legitimacy. Although Ancient Near Eastern royal inscriptions were composed with an
eye to demonstrating that the king enjoys the favor of the gods, they do not
always explicitly claim that a specific king was called, named or otherwise designated for kingship by his god. In the first millenium BCE such claims are
particularly forwarded by those whose kingship was *not* self-evident, whether
they established a new dynasty (e.g. Zakkur and Nabonidus), or were appointed
by their fathers as heir apparent to the detriment of older brothers (e.g., Esarhaddon and Ashurbanipal), or whether their rule was troubled by other rivals
(e.g., Panammu).[4] Since both Saul and David are cast as founders of new dynas-

---

1 E.g., "Ashur-Dugul, son of a nobody (who) never sat on the throne," in the Assyrian King
List, GRAYSON 1972: 31 and "Hazael, son of a nobody, took the throne" in Shalmaneser III's
Assur Basalt statue inscription, YAMADA 2000: 188–89.
2 See, e.g., NA'AMAN 2006: 168–70. Although Andre Lemaire's proposal to read "House of David" (בתדוד) in line 31 of the Mesha inscription has had many adherents, the reading has
recently been contested, and see FINKELSTEIN, et al. 2019; LANGLOIS 2019.
3 See, e.g., WEISER 1966: 333–34; KRATZ 2005: 177; RÖMER 2005: 96; DIETRICH 2007: 274; FIN-
KELSTEIN 2006: 173–78; VAN SETERS 2009: 3, 82–83, 122–23; BRETTLER 2010: 48.
4 See ISHIDA 1977: 6–14; KNAPP 2015: 47–48. Ishida points out instances of Assyrian kings who
relate their authority to both lineage and to divine election. However, it is telling that whereas
Panammu relates that he received the scepter of authority from the gods (KAI 214.2–3), Barrak-
ab his son admits to being seated on his throne by virtue of the combined support of his god
and of his suzerain Tiglath-Pilesar (KAI 216.4–7). By contrast, Kilamua, who belongs to the
fourth generation of the previous royal dynasty of Yaudi, makes no allusion to divine designation.

https://doi.org/10.1515/9783110606164-015

ties – even though Saul's dynasty is not realized – the motif of divine designation was most likely integral to the earliest literary form of Saul's and David's rise.[5] Even if the earliest account of David's kingship did not presume that he succeeded Saul, the eventual combination of David's narrative with that of Saul necessitated vindicating David from the theoretic charge of ousting the previous divinely sanctioned dynasty. In the case of Saul and David, the facile resolution took the form of delegitimizing Saul, thus justifying the replacement of his ruling house by David's.[6] Hence, it is highly doubtful whether it is possible to retrieve an early compositional layer from the so-called History of David's Rise by means of excising its apologetic tendency.[7]

Furthermore, the genre of the extended third person narrative of royal origins is uncommon in the Ancient Near East. Thus, any account of the origins of the so-called History of David's Rise needs to consider the historiographic perspective implied by the extended third person narrative, which differs considerably from that of both first person narrative in royal inscriptions as well as of fictional autobiography.[8] This implies that the apology embedded in the narrative of David's rise does not presume an audience contemporaneous with the first three generations or so of Davidic kings, but is the product of later reflection.[9] The fall of the kingdom of Israel could well have provided the impetus for viewing David as the successor of Saul, which then in turn raised the problem how to delegitimize a previous divinely sanctioned dynasty.[10] These observations provide a starting point for the rest of my discussion: already the earliest version of the third person narrative of David's rise to kingship presumed that David was preceded by a king who sought to found a dynasty, but failed, and accordingly, the narrative always was apologetic in tendency. Furthermore, although oral folktales might have circulated about David, the extended third person account of David's rise represents a new literary genre, which is the product of long-term developments in scribal erudition and literary craft. This genre is (as yet) unparalleled in the Iron Age Levant, and most likely

---

5 WEISER 1966: 326–38, 352–54.

6 Compare Sargon II's attempt to defame Shalmeneser V in the Assur Charter, and see VERA CHAMAZA 1992: 21–33. See also KNAPP 2015: 52–54.

7 See VAN SETERS 1983: 267–68.

8 The question of the genesis of the extended third person prose narrative genre has mostly been ignored, and see brief comments by GREENSTEIN 1988: 347–54, here 349; KAWASHIMA 2004: 9; PIOSKE 2018.

9 Cf. NA'AMAN 2009: 342–45; Na'aman, however, holds that the early story of Saul and David was inspired by a genuine antiquarian interest (345).

10 Cf. FINKELSTEIN 2013: 47–49.

emerged later than the crafting of extended first person royal inscriptions in the mid-ninth century in Phoenicia, Moab and the Neo-Hittite kingdoms.

In the following, I will address the problem of the purpose of the "David in the Desert" theme, and my approach will integrate different methods. First, the boundaries of the text need to be established by means of literary and redaction criticism. The structure of the text will be evaluated by analysis of patterns, key words, geographic plotting and comparative study. Finally, I will engage the function of the "David in the Desert" theme by examining the values and spacial attributes of the Hebrew מדבר in light of motif and anthropological studies. In my conclusions I will distinguish between different stages in the growth of the main section of the so-called History of David's Rise, and suggest that the association of the wilderness with liminal space in the collective consciousness of Judean scribes prompted the structuring of David's flight from Saul so that it would reflect a rite of passage from royal retainer to king in the making.

1 David in Flight within Benjamin: an Editorial Deviation

By far the most extensive section of the final form account of David's rise to kingship is that which details his flight from Saul. This section is marked off in the present form of the text by the words "and David fled and escaped that night" (1 Sam 19:10 ודוד נס וימלט בלילה הוא) and extends for more than six chapters until David finds refuge with Achish king of Gath (1 Sam 27:4 "Saul was told that David escaped to Gath and therefore he pursued him no longer"). In word count, this section is twice as long as any other discrete section in 1 Sam 16:1–2 Sam 4:12, as well as the core account of David's reign in 2 Sam 5:1–8:18.[11] This alone gives a strong indication of the significance scribes attributed to the flight and pursuit theme within the evolving David tradition.

At the same time, the sheer length of the section, along with its many doublets and inconsistencies hints that the account of David's flight from Saul has

---

11 The count is based upon the MT of four discrete sections, prior to literary and redaction analysis. All figures are approximate and based upon copying the text from the MGKeter program into a Word document.

1 Sam 16:1–19:17	David at Saul's court	1730 words
1 Sam 19:18–26:25	David in flight	3060 words
1 Sam 27:1–31:13	David in Ziklag and Saul's demise	1300 words
2 Sam 1:1–4:12	David king of Judah	1500 words
Cf. 2 Sam 5:1–8:18	David king of Judah and Israel	1240 words

a long and complex compositional history. After the initial escape notice in 1 Sam 19:10 follows a series of episodes in which David is abetted by those closely connected to Saul: Michal his daughter (1 Sam 19:11–17) and Jonathan his son (20:1–42), Samuel his prophet (19:18–24) and Ahimelek[12] son of Ahitub his oracle priest (21:1–10; 22:9–10). The openings to these episodes share a similar pattern: *verb of flight* (e.g. ברח, מלט) followed by *came to* (ויבא, 1 Sam 19:18; 20:1; cf. 21:1–2).[13] The formulations are varied, but they are linked by a noticeable graduated chain pattern (e.g. abc, bcd, cde). Such associative linkage is typical of editorial efforts to create continuity between disjunctive materials.[14]

	D	C	B	A
19:10	**בלילה הוא**	וימלט		ודוד נס
19:12		וימלט	ויברח	וילך
19:18	**ויבא** אל שמואל הרמה	וימלט	ברח	ודוד
20:1	**ויבא** ויאמר לפני יהונתן		ויברח דוד	
21:1–2	**ויבא** דוד נבה			ויקם וילך
21:11	**ויבא** אל אכיש מלך גת		ויברח **ביום ההוא**	ויקם דוד

The disjunctive nature of this material becomes apparent after any attempt to map David's movements.[15] In the sequence of the final form of the narrative, David flees *the very night* after he escaped from Saul's manic attempt to kill David with his spear (1 Sam 19:9–10), but immediately afterwards he is in his home – presumably in Gibeah – with his wife Michal and eludes Saul's ambush by escaping through the window (19:11–17). The next episode opens with David's flight to Samuel's home in Ramah, *north* of Gibeah (19:18–24); we might think that David's purpose was to consult Samuel, but although the narrative clearly states that David told him all that Saul had done to him, nothing is related about Samuel's reaction or instructions.[16] After Saul *is told* (ויגד ל-) that David is with Samuel in Ramah, David again flees, this time *back* to the vicinity of Gibeah where he waits for several days for Jonathan to bring him news regarding Saul's disposition (20:1–42).[17] From there David continued south-east to

---

12 Apparently identified with Ahijah son of Ahitub, 1 Sam 14:3,18–19.
13 Cf. Grønbaek 1971: 114, 264.
14 See, e.g., Grønbaek 1971: 114, 121; Edenburg 2018: 360.
15 Cf. Wellhausen 1899: 250–51.
16 19:18–24 is frequently thought to be a secondary insertion, and see, e.g., Wellhausen 1899: 250–51; Grønbaek 1971: 117–20; McCarter 1980: 330–31; Van Seters 2009: 171–72.
17 Grønbaek 1971: 120–33.

Nob, just a few kilometers away from Saul in Gibeah, and only after his visit with Ahimelek does he truly distance himself from the vicinity of Saul by fleeing south-west to Gath (21:11–16), and then to Adullam in the Judean heartland (22:1; cf. Josh 15:35; 2 Sam 23:13–14; Neh 11:30; 2 Chr 11:7).

Despite the repeated statements that David fled (1 Sam 19:10,12,18; 20:1; 21:1–2), the itinerary detailed in the sequence of the material in 1 Sam 19:10–21:1–2 has David wandering almost in circles in dangerous proximity to Saul.[18] Even if one were to ignore the several instances of apparent doublets,[19] these geographic details in themselves call into question the narrative coherence and credibility of the section dealing with David's flight from Gibeah in 1 Sam 19–21. All this raises the question whether this section of David's flight might be an editorial deviation.

2 David's Reception in Gath: a *Wiederaufnahme*?

Various attempts have been made to sort out the text into two separate strands, but these have not succeeded in eliminating all the inconsistencies and doublets.[20] Therefore, it is more likely that a limited core narrative was elaborated with new materials over many generations of transmission as new copies of the composition in written form were prepared. As previously mentioned, chaining variation of unit openings is one of the editorial devices that hints at the process of growth (ברח וימלט ויבוא וימלט, נס וימלט, ברח וימלט). So too, framing repetition can bracket off blocks of accretions and hint at an original continuity. I suggest that this is the case with the large block of narratives and notices about David's wanderings after he absconded from Saul's service and until he received refuge under the patronage of Achish in Gath.

---

18 Van Seters 2009: 171–72; cf. Büdde 1890: 223.

19 Saul's murderous spear throwing (1 Sam 18:10–11; 19:9–10; 20:33); his charismatic ravings that gave rise to a popular saying (1 Sam 10:10–12; 19:23–24); Jonathan's pact with David (1 Sam 18:3; 20:8,13–16; 23:18); and Jonathan's attempt to uncover Saul's disposition towards David (1 Sam 19:1–7; 20:1–31). Some of these doublets occur in MT pluses (1 Sam 18:1–5,10–11), but others are also attested by the LXX, thus the LXX *Vorlage* was not free from discrepancies and doublets, and see Tov 1985: 98–130.

20 E.g., Büdde 1902: xvii–xxi; Grønbæk 1971: 129–31; Van Seters 2009: 195–206; and compare Hutton's survey and his own proposal in Hutton 2009: 235–88. Quite telling is Smith's admission: "In claiming that the book is made up of two fairly continuous histories, I do not mean to assert that these are not themselves composite. There is every probablility in favour of this being the case," Smith 1898: xxvi.

A number of details accent the end to David's flight and wanderings in
1 Sam 27:1–4. Verbs denoting David's flight are particularly concentrated in
1 Sam 19:10–22:1,[21] and then reappear in concentration in 27:1,4 ending with
Saul's desisting from the chase: "David said to himself: There is nothing better
for me than to escape (המלט אמלט) to the land of the Philistines; then Saul will
give up [...] and I will escape (ומלטתי) him. [...] When Saul was told that David
had fled (ברח) to Gath, he did not pursue him anymore."[22] At the same time,
the end of David's flight is marked by the note that he took up residence (ישב)
with Achish in Gath (27:3). The short section in 1 Sam 27:1–4 is clearly familiar
with details such as Saul's persistent pursuit of David, David's acquisition of a
sizable band of loyal followers, as well as two new wives; in other words, 27:1–
4 presumes some form of the narrative block in 22:1–26:25. However, David's
flight to Gath is *already* anticipated in 21:11, before David begins his undeter-
mined period of random wanderings in the wilderness. This suggests that one
or more of the notices regarding David's flight might stem from employing the
editorial device of "sewing" a newly composed or conceived section into a pre-
existing context by means of an introductory or concluding repetition that picks
up the wording or idea of the seam in the source text.

Here it is necessary to distinguish between true repetitive resumption
(*Wiederaufnahme*) that picks up the continuity after a digression, and framing
devices that bracket or enclose a text and mark it as a discrete compositional
unit (inclusio). In the case of inclusio, the initial bracket might be introduced
in order to set off the section – which is a different literary strategy from that
of repetitive resumption. Not every *Wiederaufnahme* or inclusio is by necessity
an editorial tool for masking seams when late material is added since they can
also be a stylistic device employed at the compositional level.[23] Hence it is critical to consider the degree of consistency of style, content, thought and ideology.
Only if the repetition is *also* inconsistent with the context, or if the material it
frames is inconsistent with the context, then the repetition might provide
grounds for redactional analysis.

On this basis, I find that in the final form of the David and Saul narrative,
the notice in 21:11 anticipates David's residence in Gath (*David got up and fled*

---

21 ברח occurs four times with David as subject in narrative report (1 Sam 19:12,18; 20:1; 21:11),
once in direct speech (22:17) and once in reported speech (27:4). מלט also occurs four times
with David as subject in narrative report (19:10,12,18; 22:1), and an additional four times in
direct speech (19:11,17; 20:29; 27:1) and once in reported speech (23:13).
22 Cf. KIPFER 2016: 287.
23 On Wiederaufnahme, see, e.g., TALMON 1993: 118–22; SEELIGMANN 2004: 128–29, 135; LONG
1987: 385–99; ANBAR 1988: 385–98. On the repetition and reiteration within speech, negotia-
tion and oral performance, see, e.g., POLAK 2010: 167–98; PERSON 2016: 142–79.

that day and came to Achish the king of Gath), which is reported in 27:2–3 (*David got up and crossed over to [...]to Achish son of Maoch king of Gath, and David settled with Achish in Gath*). At the same time, 19:10 (*David escaped **that night** and fled* וימלט) anticipates 21:11 (*David got up and fled* ויברח ***that day***). These three notices regarding David's initial escape and flight to Gath are also shaped in a progressive chain, in which each subsequent note takes up an element of the one that precedes. Thus, David's flight "on that night" (19:10) is echoed by his flight "on that day" (21:11), while David's "getting up" to go "to Achish the king of Gath" is combined with different elements in 21:11 and 27:2–3.

19:10		וימלט **בלילה הוא**	נס	ודוד
	Block A			
21:11	**אל אכיש מלך גת**	ויבא	ויברח **ביום ההוא**	ויקם דוד
	Block B			
27:2–3	**אל אכיש בן מעוך מלך גת**	ויעבר		ויקם דוד
	<u>ויֵשב</u> דוד עם אכיש בגת			

These reiterative notices frame two blocks, both of which lack narrative and geographic coherence, and each of which is composite in itself: Block A (19:10–21:11) details David's flight from his home with Michal in Gibeah, via Ramah, then back to Gibeah, down to Nob and finally to Gath; while Block B (22:1–26:25) relates David's rather random wanderings through a large area south of Benjamin. If the reiterative notices are evidence for editorial activity, then two scenarios present themselves for the growth of the narrative of David's flight from Saul. On the one hand, 21:11 could be viewed as a secondary formulation, which combines elements from both 19:10 and 27:2–3; in this case, the narrative of David's rise originally related that David escaped directly from Gibeah to Gath, with 27:2–3 directly following 19:10 (19:10 *David escaped that night and fled*, 27:2–3 *and verily crossed over to Achish and settled with Achish in Gath*). This option is the most "economic" although its implications are far reaching, since one of the main themes usually attributed to the History of David's Rise – that of David's flight and Saul's pursuit – would now be relegated to a series of revisional accretions.[24] On the other hand, the notices in 19:10 and 27:2–3 could have been drafted in imitation of 21:11. In this case, 19:10 was conceived as the opening frame

---

24 MCCARTER 1980: 358–59, sidesteps the problem by viewing 21:11b–16; 22:3–5 as "narrative scraps" that "were included at this point for want of a better occasion." Thus he is able to maintain the basic integrity of the flight and pursuit section, with the exception of limited additions, such as 19:18–24; 21:11b–16; 22:3–5; 23:14–24:23.

for the preliminary flight section, in which David is successively aided by figures close to Saul (Michal, Samuel, Jonathan and Ahimelek), while 27:2 would have been formulated as an editorial *Wiederaufnahme* to bridge over the lengthy series of David's wilderness wanderings. The matter at stake is the extent of the flight narratives within the context of the original David and Saul story.

3 David in the Wilderness: Motifs, Editing and Purpose

The series of David's wanderings outside the region of Benjamin lacks any noticeable progression, narrative cohesion or geographic logic, and is aptly summed up by the statement in 1 Sam 23:13 that "David and his men wandered about as they will." Between 22:1 and 26:25 David changes location at least fourteen times, visiting ten properly named places, some of which recur in different parts of the section: Adullam (22:1), Mizpeh Moab (22:3), Hereth forest (22:5), Keilah (23:5), Ziph wilderness (23:14; 23:15; 26:2), Horesh (23:15,16,18–19), Hachilah hill (23:19; 26:1,3), Maon wilderness (23:24–25), Ein Gedi (24:1–2), Paran wilderness (25:1).[25] Albeit, the material in this block is loosely held together by the motif of the growth of David's following,[26] and particularly by the theme of Saul's pursuit and persecution of David.

This pursuit and persecution theme is brought to the fore not only by general content, but also by the repeated key words: *to pursue* רדף (1 Sam 23:25,28; 24:15; 25:29; 26:18,20) and *to seek to kill or harm* בקש נפש / רעה (23:14–15,25; 24:3,10; 25:26,29; 26:2,20).[27] In fact, all instances of רדף in connection to Saul's

---

25 Some of the verses describing David's movements are so overloaded with general geographic designations that they probably reflect alternate readings or glossings: e.g., 23:14 "David stayed in the wilderness (במדבר), in fortresses (במצדות) and stayed in the hill country (בהר), in the wilderness of Ziph," and cf. 23:19, 24. Recurring general geographic designations include: the wilderness (במדבר, 23:14; 26:3), fortress(es) (מצודה, 23:14,19; 24:23), the steppe (ערבה 23:24), and possibly the desert if Jeshimon is not taken as a toponym (הישימון 23:19,24; 26:1,3).

26 The MT has a gradual increase in David's followers: his clansmen (22:1), four hundred more malcontents (22:2–3), and finally six hundred in all (23:13; 25:13; 27:2). By contrast, the LXX reads 400 for 600 in 23:13 and 27:2, but elsewhere in 25:13 and 30:9–10 it does reflect the total 600 (400+200).

27 The verb בקש with regard to seeking to kill or harm David is found throughout 1 Sam 19–27, but still the greatest concentration occurs in 1 Sam 23–26 (1 Sam 19:2,10; 20:1,16; 22:23; 23:14–15,25; 24:2,9; 25:26,29; 26:2,20; 27:1,4). Cf. KIPFER 2016: 285.

pursuit of David occur in 1 Sam 23–26. Surprisingly, the narration of David's wanderings in 1 Sam 22:1–26:25 contains but a single instance of verbs denoting David's flight – מלט in 1 Sam 22:1 – and two more instances in direct or reported speech,[28] whereas these verbs (including one instance of נוס in 19:10) are repeated eleven times in the much shorter section of 19:12–21:11.[29] Instead of depicting David *fleeing* from Saul, the wilderness section in 22:1–26:25 details David's itinerary by means of periodic wanderings alternating with sojourns. Four reports are set in the pattern of *David went* הלך *(from there to) [place name]* (22:1,3,5), followed by six reports that David *stayed* (ישב) at different locations (23:14,16,25; 24:1; 26:3), and twice relating how *he went up* עלה or *went down* ירד from one place to *stay* at another (23:25; 24:1).

Thus, the final compilation and editing of the account of David's wilderness wanderings marks a contrast between Saul's relentless pursuit of David and David's seemingly unhurried "going" from one place to "stay" for a while in another. Once again, the editorial phenomenon of "chaining" is discernible at the seams of the different sections. The beginning of David's wanderings in 22:1 is cast in the pattern of "he went from there to X place", but it is combined with the last instance of a flight verb (מלט), which recurs only when the flight motif is resumed as David expresses his intent to escape (המלט) to Gath in 27:1, followed by Saul's hearing that he had fled (ברח 27:4). So also the account of David's favorable reception in Gath in 27:3 picks up the pattern of the previous section recounting David's wilderness sojourn by reiterating the verb ישב to denote staying at a place.[30]

Particularly striking is the high concentration of the term מדבר, which recurs *fifteen* times within 1 Sam 23–26,[31] compared to *twenty-four* times in all of the Book of Samuel. Only twice more is the term found in the so-called History of David's Rise (1 Sam 17:28; 2 Sam 2:24), five times in the story of Absalom's rebellion (2 Sam 15:23,28; 16:2; 17:16,29) and twice more before David appears on the stage (1 Sam 4:8; 13:18). Such frequency in the narrative books of the Bible is only superseded by the Pentateuchal accounts of the sojourn in the wilderness.[32] The pattern of the concentration of the term in the Book of Samuel in comparison to the other narrative books speaks against the possibility that the depiction of David sojourning in the מדבר stems solely from narrative necessity.

---

28 ברח 22:17; מלט 23:13; cf. 22:20 on Abiathar's escape.
29 נס 19:10; ברח 19:12,18; 20:1; 21:11; מלט 19:10–12 (3 ×),17–18; 20:29.
30 Cf. KIPFER 2016: 287.
31 1 Sam 23:14–15 (3 ×),24–25 (3 ×); 24:2; 25:1,4,14,21; 26:2–3 (4 ×).
32 Num 48 times, Exod 27 times, Deut 19 times, but only four times in Lev, three of which deal with the Azazel goat in Lev 16:10,21–22.

As Shemaryahu Talmon demonstrated מדבר does not regularly denote desert, but more frequently represents uncultivated open space, which might be on the outskirts of a settled area, or might be an expanse of wilderness or steppe.[33] Only when accompanied by descriptions of aridness and desolation does the term acquires the connotation of desert. Hence, David's wanderings in the מדבר are not a desert sojourn, but rather transpired on fringe of civilization. David's sojourn in the wilderness is conceptually parallel to Robin Hood's Sherwood Forest – an uninhabited expanse providing refuge, but fitting to the relatively unwooded topography of central Israel.

4 Wilderness and the Fugitive Hero Pattern

Even so, it is not self-evident that a narrative about David as fugitive or outlaw should require a wilderness sojourn. Edward Greenstein recently undertook an analysis of the narrative elements common to a specific type of Ancient Near Eastern hero tale that recurs in different periods and cultures, a type he calls "the fugitive hero narrative pattern."[34] Previous scholars already noticed various similarities between the story of David's rise and some of these Ancient Near Eastern compositions, but as Greenstein states, none previously "proposed a full narrative pattern."[35] The Ancient Near Eastern tales he analyzed include the story of Sinuhe, the Idrimi inscription, the Apology of Hattushili III, the Apology of Esarhaddon, and the story of Nabonidus (Harran inscriptions), while the Biblical narratives considered included those of Jacob, Moses and David. Greenstein's comparison yielded 14 common narrative elements nearly all of which are also found in the story of David's rise. According to this pattern, the hero is a younger brother, who flees home or is exiled due to a political or personal crisis. In exile he is aided by a female protector and assumes a position of responsibility in his host's household. He has a divine encounter through direct revelation or divination. He repels attacks and takes plunder, returns home and is restored to a position of honor and/or leadership.

When faced with the general similarity in narrative pattern, it is all the more striking that most of the exiled or fugitive heroes in the Ancient Near Eastern narratives do not actually pass their period of exile in the wilderness. Idrimi flees Aleppo and finds refuge with his mother's kin in Emar, which is hardly

---

33 Talmon 1966: 40–42; 1997: 97–114.
34 Greenstein 2015: 17–53.
35 Greenstein 2015: 21.

beyond the pale of settlement.[36] Esarhaddon's apology merely states that when his brothers plotted against him the great gods let him dwell in a "secret place" where they could safeguard him for royalty.[37] While an oracle delivered to his mother Naqia quotes her complaint that Esarhaddon had been "expelled to roam the steppe,"[38] one might expect this type of hyperbole from the queen mother. As for Sinuhe, he spends a lengthy period of self-imposed exile in Upper Retenu (Canaan), which in Egyptian eyes might be a distant "uncivilized" land, but still the figure of Sinuhe describes it as a fertile settled land under the rule of a chieftain.[39] Hattushili III does not describe himself as a fugitive in the wilderness, but more as an exiled member of the royal family who was given "desolate countries" to govern. However the mode of first person report in this text casts doubt on the question how "desolate" the land of Hattushili's exile really was, particularly since does he does term Ḫapkiš and Ištaḫara as cities.[40]

Finally, Nabonidus does leave Babylon for an extended period, but it is a *self-imposed* exile, which he undertakes *after* he ascends to kingship and begins his cultic activities. The reasons for Nabonidus's lengthy stay in Tema are subject to much speculation, but there is no actual evidence that his rule in Babylon was disputed or that he was a fugitive. Whether the reasons were religious, or whether his interest was tightening Babylonian control of trade routes, the historical Nabonidus does not appear to have been on the run.[41] Nevertheless, the figure of Nabonidus depicted by the first person report on the Harran stele is travelling back and forth between the cities of north-west Arabia (Tayma, Dadanu, Padakku, Hibra, Yadihu, "as far as Yatribu"), and in the style of Neo-Assyrian royal inscriptions he claims to have surmounted immense topographical difficulties on his way, which took him through "distant mountain regions and inaccessible paths."[42] This theme of prevailing over the landscape properly belongs to sphere of Ancient Near Eastern *royal* heroic narrative, and is not paralleled in the other fugitive hero stories Greenstein considers.

This brief survey not only shows that the sojourn in the wilderness motif is not a basic element of Ancient Near Eastern fugitive hero narratives, but it also suggests that a fugitive hero who is destined for greatness – as opposed to a

---

36 COS 1.148 lines 10–16.
37 Leichty 2011: 1.23–44.
38 Parpola 1997: 1.8 lines v 12–25.
39 COS 1.38 lines 80–90.
40 COS 1.77 § 8.
41 For religious causes see, e.g., Gadd 1958: 88 and Livingstone 2005: 29–30; for trade and political motivations see, e.g. Dandamaev 1989: 40–41; Albertz 2004: 67.
42 Gadd 1958: 57–61.

common outlaw – is more likely to seek refuge with potential allies than to hide out in the wilderness. Indeed, the narrative pattern of the fugitive hero stories reinforces my literary analysis of the flight section of the account of David's rise (1 Sam 19:10–27:4). Thus, there are good grounds to conclude that the lengthy description of David's flight from Saul and wilderness wanderings is an elaboration of a much shorter story in which David left Saul's court after the first signs of hostility from the king, and immediately sought and found refuge in Gath. Nonetheless, the question remains, why and when would a series of scribes be motivated to add such a lengthy elaboration, and thereby radically change the outline of the early story of David's rise?

5 Wilderness as Liminal Space

For the moment, I will set aside diachronic and contextual analysis in favor of a synchronic approach that considers how modern anthropologic theory regarding liminal space and rites of passage might cast light on the depiction of David's lengthy sojourn in the wilderness.

In 1909, the Francophone anthropologist, Arnold van Gennep coined the term "rites of passage" to indicate rituals that accompany stages of transition, whether spacial (e.g., entrance new dwelling or sanctuary, passing into or through foreign territory, etc.), temporal (e.g., new moon, new year), life cycle (birth, puberty, marriage, death), or social (e.g., induction into professional guild).[43] Van Gennep examined a wealth of material from diverse cultures from antiquity to modernity, and found that rites of passage or transition follow a general common pattern consisting of three stages: separation, transition (spacial or temporal), and finally incorporation.[44] The middle stage, that of transition was characterized by van Gennep as one of liminal (or threshold) rites.[45] Van Gennep held that rites of passage mark "entry from one domain or situation into another," and hence do not necessarily require repetition once the subject has passed into the new state.[46] As an anthropologist, van Gennep was dealing with true rituals as practiced or as directly described in literature. However, concrete ritual patterns also are cognitively processed by members of society and reapplied in various ways that are totally divorced from the sphere of sacral

---

43 GENNEP 1960: 2–3.
44 GENNEP 1960: 10–11.
45 GENNEP 1960: 21.
46 GENNEP 1960: 177.

rites. Hence, if a certain ritual pattern indeed has universal relevance and application, then it should not be surprising to find it transposed into literary patterns and narrative emplotments.

In elucidating the role of liminality in territorial passage van Gennep pointed to the part of buffer zones or neutral zones, which historically separated territories. Such neutral zones comprise deserts, swamplands, mountain ranges, rivers and virgin forests. In symbolic terms, the passage between territorial zones involves "wavering between two worlds" for a certain period of time.[47] Finally, van Gennep noted that "passage from one social position to another is identified with a *territorial passage*."[48] Although he had a change of residence in mind, or any such passage through built space, this observation also can be applied to journeys whether or not they lead to a return home.

One can easily critique various details of van Gennep's analyses of rituals. After all, his study was first published at the beginning of the twentieth century and was based on what *then* was current encyclopediac knowledge or hearsay (which is especially evident in his discussion of Jewish practice). Nevertheless, there is much to be said for his structural view of social transitions in the life of the individual and the community, and particularly for his introduction of the concept of liminality into the discussion of space and territorial passage. Although his work was neglected for decades, it was "rediscovered" in the mid-twentieth century and provided the springboard for new sociological and spacial models.[49] In short, van Gennep's analysis of transitional phases and states provides a productive conceptual framework for examining the story of David's rise, his frequent change of place and the emplotment of David's period in the wilderness.

In a synchronic reading of David's Rise we see David physically passing several thresholds: for example, through the window of his home with Michal in Gibeah, in and out of the caves at Adullam and Ein Gedi, in and out of various strongholds (1 Sam 22:4–5; 23:14,19; 24:1,23). David is frequently in transition from place to place, until he arrives at Gath and is granted Ziklag. Particularly significant in my eyes is that much of these passages transpire in the liminal area of the wilderness, beyond the pale of settlement, where David sojourns while he is between periods of service to two different patrons: Saul on the one side and Achish on the other. During this period David seems to be tested so he may prove to his audience within and without the story that he is worthy of his destiny, as particularly comes to the fore in 1 Sam 24–26. Despite the spoiler

---

47 GENNEP 1960: 18.
48 GENNEP 1960: 192.
49 See, e.g., ROTHEM 2018; THOMASSEN 2018.

presented by 1 Sam 15–16, the wilderness period also marks a transition that fleshes out the growth of David's character and prepares the reader for his new role as king.[50]

Admittedly, I think the wilderness section, and indeed all of David's flight from Gibeah, to be a conglomeration of material that accrued to the David story over several stages (each stage representing a new copy of what became the Samuel scroll). And of course, there is a large degree of incongruence, if not anachronism, in proposing that an ancient literary text reflects a modern anthropological theory of ritual. Instead, I think that "David's rite of passage in the wilderness" reflects cognitive categories of space and transition, which are present in collective consciousness *regardless* whether they find expression in specific ritual or not. If, as I suggest, the early narrative had David seek refuge with Achish shortly after Saul's enmity was first manifest, then a subsequent reader would likely try to replot the story so that a period of transition would serve as a buffer between David's leaving Saul to his switching sides. This transitional period then took on a literary life of its own in order to enhance the picture of David being "betwixt and between", proving himself again and again as he is repeatedly tested. David's sojourn in the wilderness was not dictated by narrative necessity, but rather as a means to enhance the liminality of his passage from Gibeah to Ziklag.

The emplotment of David's flight from Saul as a sojourn in the wilderness seems to have had an afterlife, since we find David in the wilderness once again in the account of Absalom's rebellion (2 Sam 15:23,28; 16:2; 17:16,29). There, David's being "in the wilderness" is emphasized five times within the three chapters in 2 Sam 15–17. However, there the wilderness appears to be an incremental motif that may well have been patterned upon the final form of David's Rise. The resulting effect is one of framing David's reign with two periods of exile in the wilderness.

6 Relative Dating the Wilderness Elaboration

Although the development of the "David in the wilderness" section cannot be traced in a definitive fashion, it is worthwhile to outline some preliminary suggestions to be tested, rejected or refined by further discussion.

---

50 Compare other studies of Biblical representations of the wilderness as a liminal landscape connected with testing, e.g. Talmon 1966: 37, 54; Cohn 1981: 12–15; Feldt 2012. On liminal space, see Thomassen 2012: 21–26.

The first block might have comprised 1 Sam 23:14,19; 26:2–25, since it is marked by a frame that opens with David seeking refuge in the wilderness of Ziph and Saul seeking him out, and it closes with the parting of ways after David's and Saul's final encounter. At this stage, 1 Sam 23:14 could have followed straight upon 1 Sam 21:1a ("David got up and went … to stay in the wilderness;" ויקם וילך ... וישב דוד במדבר).

I suggest that the latest set of additions comprised 1 Sam 21:11b–16; 23:19–25:44. The narratives included in this set share a similar dark and ominous character, and some of them offer alternate, satiric versions of traditions included in the earlier narrative sequence, like the cave story in 1 Sam 24 and the account of David's first encounter with Achish in 1 Sam 21:12–16.[51] This does not imply that this set of additions is of one piece, or that its constituent materials were brought together in a single process. It is possible that the two episodes dealing with Nob were also included at this time (1 Sam 21:2–10; 22:6–23), since here we find an equivocal portrayal of both David and Saul. In 1 Sam 21 David deliberately deceives Ahimelek with disastrous consequences for the innocent community of Nob, and in 1 Sam 22 the person who incites Saul against Nob and who carries out the massacre is an Edomite, suggesting that the narrative was composed as a late anti-Edomite polemic.[52] The only link between the Nob material and the other narratives is the lineage of Abiathar in 1 Sam 22:20; 23:6; 30:7, but this lineage has been devised in order to integrate the Nob chapters into the larger narrative and to demonstrate how the anonymous man of God's oracle of doom was realized in subsequent history. However, this oracle also has been shown to be of late composition.[53]

In conclusion, it seems that the section of the story of David's rise that describes his flight from Saul achieved its present shape though a complex process of revision by accretion. I do not believe it possible (or desirable) to ascribe all the accretions to distinct redactional layers that can be characterized and labeled. The early version of David's rise might have originated in the late seventh century as part of a program to advance Josiah's claim to Benjamin and to the territories of southern Samaria,[54] but the disjointed nature of the section and the amount of doubled narratives and alternate versions suggests that it was considerably shorter than it is now. The elaboration of David's flight from Gibeah and his random wanderings in the wilderness might have part of a Babylonian period revision of the Samuel scroll. The story how David spared Saul's

---

51 See EDENBURG 2011: 34–35; 2016: 475–76.
52 Cf. VAN SETERS 2009: 172–73, 199.
53 See BRETTLER 1997: 601–12.
54 See, e.g., RÖMER 2005: 95–97.

life during a night raid on Saul's camp in Chap 26 is part of the material that belongs to this layer. This story ends with David and Saul parting ways and is immediately followed by David finding refuge in Gath in Chap 27. While there is nothing specifically Deuteronomistic in this version, various elements of its language suggest that it was composed in the Babylonian period or later.

The flight from Saul section subsequently grew with the addition of materials that did not share the ideal view of the Davidic dynasty. In this stage the satiric version how David spares Saul in a cave in Chap 24 was composed and inserted in order to reshape the attitude of readers towards a more critical stance *vis à vis* David. This stage of revision included also the account of David's first attempt to receive refuge in Gath (1 Sam 21:11–16),[55] and probably also the story of Nob (1 Sam 21:2–10; 22:6–23).

As a final note, historical geography might provide an additional indication of the provenance of the material in this section. The toponyms in David's wilderness itinerary, which are also mentioned in other Biblical books, happen to be significant sites also in the Persian period. According to Neh 3:17–18, Keilah was a half-district capital, and Neh 11:30 included families from Adullam among those resettling Jerusalem. Adullam, Ziph and Ein Gedi are also mentioned in Chronicles *Sondergut* in sections that clearly reflect the Chronicler's interests and historical context (2 Chr 11:7–8; 20:2). In addition, there is material evidence for Persian period settlement at Keilah, Ein Gedi and Ziph.[56] Hence, the stations in David's wilderness itinerary were not necessarily selected from a district list of Iron Age Judah (Josh 15), but might reflect later conditions of the Persian period. This fits well with the literary archaeology of 1 Sam 19:10–26:25.

Bibliography

Albertz, Rainer. 2004. *Israel in Exile: the History and Literature of the Sixth Century B.C.E.*
    Leiden: Brill.
Anbar, Moshe. 1988. La 'reprise'. *VT* 38:385–98.
Brettler, Marc Zvi. 1997. The Composition of 1 Samuel 1–2. *JBL* 116:601–12.

---

55 Cf. BÜDDE 1890: 225; EDENBURG 2011: 34–35.
56 Stratum IV at En Gedi is attributed to the Persian period, and yielded Attic pottery dating to mid-fifth and early fourth centuries BCE as well as local Persian period pottery, in addition to Yehud seals, lion seals and Aramaic ostraca. The settled area of stratum IV stretched over all the summit of the tel and beyond. Surveys conducted in 1968 by Kochavi identified Persian period pottery at both Tel Zif and Khirbet Kilah, and see STERN 2001: 438–39, 442–43, 453–54.

Brettler, Marc Zvi. 2010. The David Tradition. Pages 25–53 in *Israel in Transition; from Late Bronze II to Iron IIa (c. 1250–850 B.C.E.)*. Vol. 2 *The Texts*. Edited by Lester L. Grabbe. New York: T & T Clark.

Budde, Karl. 1890. *Die Bücher Richter und Samuel: ihre Quellen und ihr Aufbau*. Giessen: Ricker.

Budde, Karl. 1902. *Die Bücher Samuel*. KHAT. Tübingen: Mohr Siebeck.

Cohn, Robert L. 1981. *The Shape of Sacred Space: Four Biblical Studies*. Chico, CA: Scholars Press.

Dandamaev, Mukhammed Abdulkagyrovich. 1989. *A Political History of the Achaemenid Empire*. Leiden: Brill.

Dietrich, Walter. 2007. *The Early Monarchy in Israel: The Tenth Century B.C.E.* Atlanta: SBL Press.

Edenburg, Cynthia. 2011. Notes on the Origin of the Biblical Tradition Regarding Achish King of Gath. *VT* 61:34–38.

Edenburg, Cynthia. 2016. 'David Reproached Himself': Revisiting 1 Sam 24 and 26 in Light of 2 Sam 21–24. Pages 469–80 in *The Books of Samuel: Stories – History – Reception History*. Edited by Walter Dietrich et al. BETL 284. Leuven: Peeters.

Edenburg, Cynthia. 2018. Envelopes and Seams: How Judges Fits (or not) within the Deuteronomistic History. Pages 353–69 in *Book-Seams in the Hexateuch I: The Literary Transitions between the Books of Genesis/Exodus and Joshua/Judges*. Edited by Christoph Berner et al. FAT 120. Tübingen: Mohr Siebeck.

Feldt, Laura. 2012. Wilderness and Hebrew Bible Religion – Fertility, Apostasy and Religious Transformation in the Pentateuch. Pages 55–94 in *Wilderness in Mythology and Religion, Approaching Religious Spatialities, Cosmologies, and Ideas of Wild Nature*. Edited by Laura Feldt. Religion and Society 55. Boston and Berlin: De Gruyter.

Finkelstein, Israel. 2006. The Last Labayu: King Saul and the Expansion of the First North Israelite Territorial Entity. Pages 171–87 in *Essays on Ancient Israel in its Near Eastern Context; a Tribute to Nadav Naaman*. Edited by Yairah Amit et al. Winona Lake, Ind.: Eisenbrauns.

Finkelstein, Israel. 2013. *The Forgotten Kingdom: The Archaeology and History of Northern Israel*. Atlanta: SBL Press.

Finkelstein, Israel, Nadav Na'aman and Thomas Römer. 2019. Restoring Line 31 in the Mesha Stele: The 'House of David' or Biblical Balak? *Tel Aviv* 46:3–11.

Gadd, Cyril John. 1958. The Harran Inscriptions of Nabonidus. *Anatolian Studies* 8:35–92.

Gennep, Arnold van. 1960. *The Rites of Passage*. Chicago: University of Chicago Press.

Grayson, Albert Kirk. 1972. *Assyrian Royal Inscriptions, Volume I: From the Beginning to Ashur-resha-ishi I*. Wiesbaden: Harrassowitz.

Greenstein, Edward L. 1988. On the Genesis of Biblical Prose Narrative. *Prooftexts* 8:347–54.

Greenstein, Edward L. 2015. "The Fugitive Hero Narrative Pattern in Mesopotamia." Pages 17–35 in *Worship, Women, and War; Essays in Honor of Susan Niditch*. Edited by John J. Collins, et al. BJS 357. Providence, RI: Brown University.

Grønbæk, Jakob H. 1971. *Die Geschichte vom Aufstieg Davids (1. Sam. 15 – 2. Sam. 5); Tradition und Komposition*. ATDan 10. Copenhagen: Prostant Apud Munksgaard.

Hutton, Jeremy M. 2009. *The Transjordanian Palimpsest. The Overwritten Texts of Personal Exile and Transformation in the Deuteronomistic History*. BZAW 396. Berlin and New York: de Gruyter.

Ishida, Tomoo. 1977. *The Royal Dynasties in Ancient Israel: a Study on the Formation and Development of Royal-Dynastic Ideology*. BZAW 142. Berlin: de Gruyter.

Kawashima, Robert S. 2004. *Biblical Narrative and the Death of the Rhapsode*. Bloomington: Indiana University Press.

Kipfer, Sara. 2016. "David Under Threat: an Exegetical and Reception Historical Analysis of 1 Samuel 16 – 1 Kings 2. Pages 293–302 in *The Books of Samuel: Stories – History – Reception History*. Edited by Walter Dietrich et al. BETL 284. Leuven: Peeters.

Knapp, Andrew. 2015. *Royal Apologetic in the Ancient Near East*. WAWSup 4. Atlanta: SBL Press.

Kratz, Reinhard Gregor. 2005. *The Composition of the Narrative Books of the Old Testament*. Translated by John Bowden. London: T & T Clark.

Langlois, Michael. 2019. "The Kings, the City and the House of David on the Mesha Stele in Light of New Imaging Techniques." *Sem* 61:23–47.

Leichty, Erle. 2011. *The Royal Inscriptions of Esarhaddon, King of Assyria (680–669 BC)*. RINAP 4. Winona Lake, Ind: Eisenbrauns.

Livingstone, Alasdair. 2005. "Taimā' and Nabonidus: It's a Small World." Pages 29–39 in *Writing and Ancient Near Eastern Society; Papers in Honour of Alan R. Millard*. New York: T & T Clark.

Long, Burke O. 1987. Framing Repetitions in Biblical Historiography. *JBL* 106:385–99.

McCarter, Peter Kyle. 1980. *I Samuel*. Anchor Bible. New York: Doubleday.

Na'aman, Nadav. 2006. Beth-David in the Aramaic Stela from Tel Dan. Pages 166–72 in *Ancient Israel's History and Historiography: The First Temple Period*. Winona Lake: Eisenbrauns.

Na'aman, Nadav. 2009. Saul, Benjamin and the Emergence of 'Biblical Israel' (part 2). *ZAW* 121:335–49.

Parpola, Simo. 1997. *Assyrian Prophecies*. SAA 9. Helsinki: Helsinki University Press.

Person, Raymond F. 2016. *From Conversation to Oral Tradition: A Simplest Systematics for Oral Traditions*. Routledge Studies in Rhetoric and Stylistics 10. New York: Routledge.

Pioske, Daniel. 2018. *Memory in a Time of Prose: Studies in Epistemology, Hebrew Scribalism, and the Biblical Past*. Oxford: Oxford University Press.

Polak, Frank H. 2010. Forms of Talk in Hebrew Biblical Narrative: Negotiations, Interaction, and Sociocultural Context. Pages 167–98 in *Literary Construction of Identity in the Ancient World: Proceedings of a Conference, Literary Fiction and the Construction of Identity in Ancient Literatures*. Edited by Hanna Liss et al. Winona Lake: Eisenbrauns.

Römer, Thomas. 2005. *The So-called Deuteronomistic History: a Sociological, Historical, and Literary Introduction*. London and New York: T & T Clark.

Rothem, Nitzan, and Shlomo Fischer. 2018. Reclaiming Arnold Van Gennep's Les rites de passage (1909): The Structure of Openness and the Openness of Structure. *Journal of Classical Sociology* 18:255–65.

Seeligmann, Isac Leo. 2004. Hebräische Erzählung und biblische Geschichtsschreibung. Pages 119–38 in *Gesammelte Studien zur Hebräischen Bibel*. Edited by Erhard Blum. FAT 41. Tübingen: Mohr Siebeck.

Smith, Henry Preserved. 1898. *The Books of Samuel*. ICC. Edinburgh: T & T Clark.

Stern, Ephraim. 2001. *Archaeology of the Land of the Bible. Volume II. The Assyrian, Babylonian and Persian Periods 732–332 BCE*. ABRL. New York, Doubleday.

Talmon, Shemaryahu. 1966. The 'Desert Motif' in the Bible and in Qumran Literature. Pages 31–63 in *Biblical Motifs; Origins and Transformations*. Edited by Alexander Altmann. Cambridge, MA: Harvard University Press.

Talmon, Shemaryahu. 1993. The Presentation of Synchroneity and Simultaneity in Biblical Narrative. Pages 112–33 in *Literary Studies in the Hebrew Bible – Form and Content; Collected Studies*. Jerusalem: Magnes Press, and Leiden: Brill.

Talmon, Shemaryahu. 1997. "מדבר *midbār*." TDOT 8:87–118.

Thomassen, Bjørn. 2012. Revisiting Liminality: the Danger of Empty Spaces. Pages 21–35 in *Liminal Landscapes: Travel, Experience and Spaces In-between*. Edited by Hazel Andrews. London and New York: Routledge.

Thomassen, Bjørn. 2018. Thinking with Liminality; To the Boundaries of an Anthropological Concept. Pages 39–58 in *Breaking Boundaries: Varieties of Liminality*. Edited by Agnes Horvath, et al. New York and Oxford: Berghahn Books.

Tov, Emmanuel. 1985. The Composition of 1 Samuel 16–18 in Light of the Septuagint Version. Pages 98–130 in *Empirical Models for Biblical Criticism*. Edited by Jeffrey H. Tigay. Philadelphia: University of Pennsylvania Press.

Van Seters, John. 1983. *In Search of History*. New Haven: Yale University Press.

Van Seters, John. John. 2009. *The Biblical Saga of King David*. Winona Lake, Ind.: Eisenbrauns.

Vera Chamaza, Galo W. 1992. Sargon II's Ascent to the Throne: the Political Situation. *State Archives of Assyria Bulletin* 6:21–33.

Weiser, Artur. 1966. Die Legitimation des Königs David. VT 16:325–54.

Wellhausen, Julius. 1899. *Die Composition des Hexateuchs und der historischen Bücher des Alten Testaments*. 3rd ed. Berlin: G. Reimer.

Yamada, Shigeo. 2000. *The Construction of the Assyrian Empire: A Historical Study of the Inscriptions of Shalmanesar III (859–824 B.C.) Relating to His Campaigns to the West*. CHANE 3. Leiden: Brill.

Alexander A. Fischer
Der Spieß wird umgedreht

Saul und David in 1 Samuel 26

„Noch am gleichen Tag ergriff David die Flucht vor Saul und kam zu Achisch, dem König von Gat." So beginnt in 1 Sam 21,11 die kurze Erzählung von Davids fehlgeschlagenem Versuch, sich in das Gebiet der Philister abzusetzen und sich so vor Saul in Sicherheit zu bringen. Ihre Stellung im Kontext ist kompositionell begründet.[1] Sie spannt einen Bogen bis zu der Erzählung in 1 Sam 27,1 ff, in der David seinen Übertritt zu den Philistern letztendlich vollzieht, und öffnet so einen narrativen Raum für die dazwischengeschalteten Verfolgungsgeschichten.[2] David muss in das judäische Land zurückkehren. Saul versucht wiederholt, ihn aufzuspüren und zu töten. Die Geographie der Fluchtbewegungen im judäischen Gebirge ist verwirrend.[3] Es scheint so, dass hier verschiedene Einzelüberlieferungen aneinandergereiht worden sind. Die dadurch entstandenen Fluchtwege lassen sich kaum anders als redaktionsgeschichtlich erklären, die bestimmten und unbestimmten Ortsangaben sind teilweise vorgegeben, teilweise ergänzt. Darüber hinaus gewinnt man den Eindruck, dass die als literarische Quellen vorliegenden Einzelüberlieferungen ohne besondere Rücksicht auf ihren Inhalt und Zusammenhang aufgenommen und nach den eigenen Belangen des Gesamterzählers umgestaltet worden sind. Weder Davids Rettung der Stadt Keila noch sein Zusammentreffen mit Saul in der Höhle von En-Gedi noch seine Konfrontation mit Nabal in der Gegend von Maon setzen einen Fluchtkontext zwingend voraus. Vielmehr scheint das ständige Hin und Her Sauls auf der Suche nach David erst durch den Gesamterzähler geschaffen, der nach dem endgültigen Bruch zwischen Saul und David am Königshof ein Versteckspiel inszeniert, durch das er die weitere Entwicklung ihres Verhältnisses zur Darstellung bringen will.[4] Ob diese Annahmen zutreffen, soll an dem Kapitel überprüft werden, das den Fluchtkontext abschließt, nämlich an der Erzählung in 1 Sam 26, in der David in das feindliche Heerlager eindringt, Sauls Leben verschont und stattdessen (nur) seinen Spieß und seine Wasserflasche entwendet.

---

1 Vgl. STOEBE 1973: 401.
2 Vgl. EDENBURG 1998: 79 f. Zur Sache vgl. KLEIN 2005: 176–84.
3 Vgl. STEIN 1997: 64 Anm. 158, mit Hinweis auf die Karte „David's Flight From Saul" bei MCCARTER 1980: 352–53.
4 Vgl. dazu auch EDENBURG 2016: 479: „On the literary level, the meta-narrative creates the effect of a cat and mouse game, but on the compositional level the loose joining of materials suggest a process of incremental growth."

https://doi.org/10.1515/9783110606164-016

Meine Ausführungen konzentrieren sich zunächst auf die literarkritische und redaktionsgeschichtliche Analyse des Kapitels. In einem ersten Schritt möchte ich Umfang, Inhalt und Absicht des Traditionsstücks resp. der literarischen Quelle bestimmen, die den Kern der Erzählung ausmacht. Dabei wird sich zeigen, dass die Einzelüberlieferung deutlich kürzer ist, als bislang in der Forschung angenommen wird. In einem zweiten Schritt betrachte ich die Aus- und Umgestaltung der literarischen Quelle durch den Gesamterzähler, der Davids Heldentat in eine Verschonungsgeschichte Sauls uminterpretiert. Das in dieser Fassung geschilderte Verhalten Davids hat eine Reihe weiterer Bewertungen und theologischer Nachinterpretationen angeregt, die in einem dritten Schritt in den Blick genommen werden. Dabei lässt sich nicht übersehen, dass sich auf dieser Stufe des literarischen Wachstums die meisten Entsprechungen zwischen 1 Sam 24 und 26 ergeben. Offenbar verdanken sich eine Reihe solcher Entsprechungen dem Vorgang eines bewussten Aufeinander-Zuschreibens, einer gewollten Parallelisierung der beiden Kapitel.[5] Dieser Hinweis von Walter Dietrich mahnt zur Vorsicht, die in der gegenwärtigen Forschung verhandelte Frage nach der literarischen Abhängigkeit zu schnell anzugehen. Denn die Auswertung von Einzelbeobachtungen, die für die Priorität des einen oder anderen Kapitels in Anspruch genommen werden,[6] kann zu Fehlschlüssen führen, wenn nicht zuvor die redaktionsgeschichtliche Frage für beide Parallelerzählungen beantwortet ist, sei es im Entwurf einer Schichtung der beiden Kapitel oder in der Begründung ihrer Einheitlichkeit. In diesem Sinne sind die folgenden Ausführungen auch als ein Beitrag zur Problemlösung der gegenwärtig verhandelten Frage zu verstehen.

1 David vollbringt eine heldenhafte Tat

Es ist nicht von der Hand zu weisen, dass in 1 Sam 26 eine Reihe von Doppelungen, Spannungen und Unstimmigkeiten sowie Brüche in Wortwahl, Syntax und Stil zu beobachten sind. Dabei ist immer auch mit der Möglichkeit zu rechnen, dass sich das eine oder andere Textphänomen narratologisch erklären und damit auf eine bestimmte Erzählstrategie zurückführen lässt. Doch die bloße Möglichkeit kann und darf eine redaktionsgeschichtliche Analyse nicht ersetzen.

---

5 Vgl. DIETRICH 2004: 236 f. (2012: 175). Vgl. dazu schon CASPARI 1926: 341: „I 24 und 26 haben gelegentlich ihren Wortlaut gegenseitig bereichert."
6 Aus der jüngsten Debatte seien zwei Beiträge genannt: Für die Priorität von 1 Sam 26 votiert McKENZIE 2010: 437–44. Dagegen wendet sich VAN SETERS 2011: 93–104, der 1 Sam 26 als Parodie der Parallelerzählung beurteilt und 1 Sam 24 die Priorität einräumt.

Ich beginne mit einem Detail, dem kaum größere Aufmerksamkeit geschenkt wird. In V. 12 heißt es: „David nahm den Spieß und die Wasserflasche vom Kopfende Sauls." An anderen Stellen ist dagegen nur von seinem Spieß die Rede. Warum wird die Wasserflasche nur gelegentlich erwähnt? Ist sie ein überflüssiges Detail, das für die Erzählung keine tragende Bedeutung hat?[7] Oder eine jüngere Ausschmückung, die durch Doppelung die Dramatik des Geschehens zu steigern versucht?[8] Oder ein Gegenstand, den David erst sehen konnte, als er bereits neben dem schlafenden Saul stand und nach seinem Spieß griff?[9] Erklärungen wie diese überzeugen nicht wirklich. Doch gibt es zu der Frage nach Herkunft und Funktion der Wasserflasche aus redaktionsgeschichtlicher Sicht eine recht einleuchtende Lösung: In dem Traditionsstück, das in die Erzählung aufgenommen worden ist, geht es durchgängig um Spieß und Wasserflasche (V. 12 und 16), in den redaktionellen Passagen ist dagegen allein vom Spieß die Rede (V. 7, 8 und 22). Nur die Erwähnung der Wasserflasche in V. 11, der den eingeschobenen Dialog zwischen David und Abischai beschließt, scheint eine Ausnahme zu bilden. Doch ist schon an dem grammatischen Nachklapp der Wasserflasche leicht zu erkennen, dass sie hier – offenbar zur Glättung der redaktionellen Fuge – nachgetragen worden ist. Mit diesem Ergebnis ist zugleich ein grundlegender Unterschied zwischen Tradition und Redaktion berührt. In der Textvorlage – der Heldengeschichte Davids – stehen Spieß und Wasserflasche symbolisch für die Kampfkraft Sauls in der Schlacht.[10] Indem David beide Gegenstände am helllichten Tag (sic!) mitten aus dem Kriegslager entwendet, beraubt er Saul nicht nur augenfällig seiner Kampfkraft, sondern gibt ihn – den von seiner Streitmacht umringten König – auch noch der Lächerlichkeit preis.[11] In der Gesamterzählung wandelt sich dagegen der Spieß vom symbolischen Gegenstand zu einer realen Mordwaffe, wobei der weitere Kontext der Geschichte von Davids Aufstieg in die Darstellung eingeholt wird. Es handelt sich um eben jenen Spieß, den Saul in Tötungsabsicht schon zweimal nach David geworfen hat (18,11; 19,10) und der nun gegen ihn selbst gerichtet wird.

Das in die Gesamterzählung aufgenommene und ausgestaltete Traditionsstück lässt sich tatsächlich fast lückenlos rekonstruieren (s. Anhang): Seine Exposition scheint in V. 3aαbα vorzuliegen, hier werden beide Protagonisten ein-

7 Vgl. STOEBE 1973: 467.
8 Vgl. KOCH 1981: 173.
9 Vgl. DIETRICH 2015: 822.
10 Vgl. dazu noch die Bemerkung von CASPARI 1926: 337, dass die Lanze des Feldherrn das Zeichen zum Beginn und Ende der Schlacht gibt. Mit ihrer Wegnahme sei Saul auch seiner Kommandogewalt beraubt worden.
11 Vgl. STOLZ 1981: 164.

geführt. Saul errichtet sein Lager in Gibea-Hachila, während sich David in der Wüste aufhält.[12] Was zuvor in V. 1–2 mitgeteilt wird, stammt vom Gesamterzähler, der das Traditionsstück in den bereits ausgeführten Fluchtkontext stellt, vgl. auch V. 3bβ. Die Verse sind aus 23,19 und 24,3 kompiliert. Ihre fast wörtliche Übernahme signalisiert, dass nun eine weitere Verfolgungsgeschichte Sauls erzählt werden soll.[13] Auf die ursprüngliche Exposition der literarischen Quelle folgt unmittelbar eine Aktion Davids in V. 5aα. Er macht sich auf den Weg und erreicht den Lagerplatz Sauls.[14] Die beiden Umstandssätze in V. 5b skizzieren die Situation, die David hier vorfindet: Saul schläft in der Mitte, während sich seine Truppen in einem Ring um ihn herum lagern.[15] Es wird nicht gesagt, dass das Kriegsvolk schläft (vgl. aber V. 7b!), und auch nicht, dass es Nacht gewesen sei, als David sich in das Lager schlich (vgl. aber V. 7a!). Im Traditionsstück erscheint damit die Aktion fast unmöglich: Kein Mensch kann am helllichten Tag in ein solches Kriegslager eindringen und bis zu Saul vordringen, es sei denn ein Held so tollkühn wie David. V. 5aβγ wurde hingegen vom Gesamterzähler resp. der Redaktion eingefügt, erkennbar zu dem Zweck, Abner als Heerführer Sauls in die Erzählung einzuführen, dessen Anwesenheit ja in V. 7 und 14–16aα vorausgesetzt wird.[16] Nur Saul und Abner (ebenfalls schlafend?) werden in dem Einschub erwähnt, die Lagerordnung des Kriegsvolks ist der Redaktion bereits durch die Tradition in V. 5b vorgegeben. Im Blick auf die Fortsetzung in V. 6a ist schon immer gerätselt worden, warum hier der Hetiter Ahimelech als Begleiter Davids eingeführt und angesprochen wird, obwohl er dann keine Rolle mehr spielt, ja nicht einmal mehr erwähnt wird. Auch dafür gibt es eine einleuchtende redaktionsgeschichtliche Erklärung: Ahimelech ist

---

12 V. 3bα ist ein für Erzähleinleitungen typischer Umstandssatz.

13 Die Determination bei den Sifitern in 26,1 setzt ihre Einführung in 23,19 voraus, vgl. Tsumura 2007: 596. Dass ihre Mitwirkung im Blick auf die folgende Erzählung eigentlich unerheblich ist, bemerkt Hertzberg 1956: 165.

14 Es ist darauf hinzuweisen, dass hier nicht das Verb הלך, sondern das Verb בוא steht; vgl. Tsumura 2007: 596. David ist nicht auf dem Weg zu dem Platz, an dem Saul sein Lager errichtet hatte, sondern dort angekommen.

15 Zum Part. plur. masc. nach kollektivem Subjekt vgl. Meyer 1992: § 94, 4b). Das Lager ist kreisförmig angelegt (במעגל), so dass Saul von allen Seiten durch seine Soldaten geschützt ist, vgl. Bar-Efrat 2007: 338.

16 Zuvor wird Abner erwähnt in 1 Sam 14,50.51; 17,55; 17,57; 20,25. Ausführlich erzählt wird von ihm in 2 Sam 2–4.

als (einziger) Begleiter und Gesprächspartner im Traditionsstück verankert.[17]
Deshalb wird er auch in V. 6aα an erster Stelle genannt. Abischai wird dagegen
vom Gesamterzähler an zweiter Stelle eingeführt, ersetzt Ahimelech als Gesprächspartner und beherrscht die folgende von der Redaktion ausgeführte Dialogszene. Diese Annahme wird durch eine weitere Beobachtung gestützt. Die
Worte Davids, die er an Ahimelech richtet, werden mit dem Verb עָנָה eingeführt,
das allgemein mit „antworten" übersetzt wird, in erster Linie aber „reagieren"
bedeutet. Da Ahimelech zuvor nicht genannt ist, „reagiert" David offenbar nicht
auf eine Frage Ahimelechs, sondern auf die unmittelbar von ihm wahrgenom-
mene und in V. 5b beschriebene Situation.[18] Man erwartet nun, dass David seinem Begleiter eröffnet, was er zu tun beabsichtigt und wie er vorgehen will.
Doch diese mutmaßlich in der Heldengeschichte ausgeführte direkte Rede ist
nicht mehr erhalten, sondern durch den eingefügten Dialog zwischen David
und Abischai verdrängt. Dass in V. 6aα eine redaktionelle Fuge vorliegt, bestätigt sich auch von anderer Seite. Davids Frage nämlich, die der Gesamterzähler
in V. 6aβ folgen lässt („Wer steigt mit mir hinunter zu Saul in das Lager?"),
entspricht nicht der Situation. Vielmehr wird der Punkt, den die Erzählung von
der Heldentat Davids bereits erreicht hat, noch einmal zurückgesetzt. David ist
offenbar – im Sinne der Redaktion – noch gar nicht bis zum Lagerplatz Sauls
gekommen (V. 5aα), sondern äußert erst seine Absicht, mit einem Begleiter dorthin hinabzusteigen (V. 6aβ).[19] Dieser geschickte und bereits durch V. 5aβγ vor-
bereitete Rückgang in der Geschehensfolge[20] hat eine zweifache Funktion: Erstens eröffnet dieser Rückgang einen Raum für die ausgeführte Dialogszene
(V. 6b–11), zweitens gestattet er der Redaktion, das für den König durchaus
peinliche Husarenstück Davids etwas zu entschärfen. Saul wird nun nicht mehr
am helllichten Tag übertölpelt. Vielmehr dringt David im Schutz der Nacht in

---

17 Dass dem Helden ein Begleiter zur Seite gestellt wird, ist nicht ungewöhnlich, sondern ein
in Heldenerzählungen gerne verwendetes Motiv; vgl. Ri 7,9 ff (Gideon und Pura) oder 1 Sam
14,6 ff (Jonatan und sein Waffenträger). Ob der Ausländer (?) Ahimelech zu Davids Bande gehört hat (1 Sam 22,2) und ob sein Name in einer uns nicht erhaltenen Überlieferung genannt
wurde, darüber kann man nur spekulieren; vgl. ISSER 2003: 130.
18 Vgl. LABUSCHAGNE 1984: 339, mit Hinweis auf Ri 18,14; 1 Sam 14,28; 2 Sam 13,32. Dementsprechend ist zu übersetzen: „*Daraufhin* wandte sich David an Ahimelech, den Hetiter, ...".
19 Vgl. KLEIN 2002: 172.
20 Die Formulierung „David konnte sogar den Ort sehen, an dem Saul sich schlafen gelegt
hatte ..." lässt offen, wie weit David noch davon entfernt war, und bezieht den in der Heldengeschichte folgenden Umstandssatz in V. 5b nunmehr in die Inspektion Davids ein. Der Leser
kann sich die Verhältnisse nun so zurechtlegen, dass David zunächst aus sicherer Entfernung
das gegnerische Lager ausgespäht habe – vielleicht von dem Berg aus, auf den er sich nach
vollbrachter Tat zurückziehen wird, vgl. DIETRICH 2015: 818.

das Lager ein, als Abner und seine Soldaten schon schlafen (V. 7). An dieser Stelle sei noch angemerkt, dass der später (zusammen mit V. 10) eingefügte V. 12bβ der ursprünglichen Aktion Davids schließlich jeden Anstrich einer Heldentat nimmt. Denn allein Jahwe[21] hat sie ermöglicht, indem er Saul und seine gesamte Mannschaft in einen tiefen und besinnungslosen Schlaf fallen ließ.[22]

Nachdem David seinen Gefährten, den Hetiter Ahimelech, in seinen Plan eingeweiht hat, – ich folge weiter dem vorliegenden Traditionsstück – schreitet er sofort zur Tat: David entwendet Spieß und Wasserflasche, dann stehlen sich beide davon, niemand merkt etwas. Der folgende Gedanke „niemand wachte auf, denn sie schliefen alle" ist erkennbar eine Ergänzung des Gesamterzählers und setzt die von ihm eingefügte Abischai-Szene voraus. Das folgende כי in V. 12bβ, das einen weiteren Begründungssatz einleitet,[23] markiert eine zusätzliche Nachinterpretation, nämlich dass Gott selbst einen Tiefschlaf herbeigeführt hat (s. o.). Nach dem gelungenen Heldenstück begibt sich David in V. 13a sogleich auf die andere, dem Lagerplatz gegenüberliegende Seite und stellt sich dort oben auf den Berg. Die hier asyndetisch angeschlossene Erläuterung in V. 13b[24] nämlich dass David sich in einiger Entfernung postiert habe, „so dass der räumliche Abstand zwischen ihnen groß war",[25] unterbricht erkennbar die Narrativkette der Heldengeschichte[26] und ist vom Gesamterzähler zu dem Zweck eingefügt, noch einmal den Fluchtkontext einzuspielen. Das Aufstellen auf dem Berggipfel, das ursprünglich die Rede Davids auf erhöhtem Podium inszeniert, soll nunmehr zeigen, dass es für den Verfolger und seine Kriegsleute unmöglich war, David zu erreichen.[27] Durch die Unterbrechung der Narrativkette („David ging auf die andere Seite hinüber, stellte sich auf einen Berggipfel und rief zu dem Kriegsvolk") musste der Bearbeiter allerdings zu Beginn von V. 14 „David" nochmals ausdrücklich als Subjekt nennen. In der folgenden Rede sind auffälligerweise an erster Stelle die Kriegsleute angesprochen, an zweiter Stelle der

---

21 Jahwe wird durch den Gen. auctoris als Verursacher des Tiefschlafs ausgewiesen, vgl. HAL 1645a und Gen 2,21; 15,12; vgl. Jes 29,10. Anders ADAM 2009: 18–21, der das Nomen rectum offenbar als Gen. qualitatis deuten möchte und dementsprechend ausführt, dass Jahwe gerade nicht das logische Subjekt der Aussage sei.

22 Damit ist aber auch Davids Vorwurf an Abner in V. 15 passé. Denn Gott hatte es ja so gefügt, dass Abner gar nicht über seinen Herrn und König wachen konnte.

23 Das erste כי fehlt in G und 4Q51. Diese Lesart ist als *lectio facilior* anzusehen, sie glättet den Text und verdeckt damit die redaktionelle Fuge.

24 Vgl. KÖNIG 1897: § 402k.

25 Vgl. GAMBERONI 1984: 1116.

26 Vgl. dazu Ri 9,7; 2 Sam 2,25 f.

27 Vgl. BAR-EFRAT 2007: 341. Der Bezug des Suffixes 3. plur. masc. am Ende von V. 13 bleibt unbestimmt und lässt sich nur aus dem Kontext bestimmen.

Heerführer Abner. Wir stoßen hier auf eine V. 6a entsprechende redaktionelle Fuge: Die von David angerufenen Kriegsleute sind im Traditionsstück verankert. Abner dagegen wird vom Gesamterzähler eingefügt, um so den folgenden, ausschließlich zwischen David und Abner geführten Dialog in die Erzählung zu integrieren (V. 14aβb–16aα).[28] Das V. 6a entsprechende Redaktionsverfahren, das hier wie dort zur Einbindung einer Dialogszene dient, hat aber im vorliegenden Fall die ursprüngliche Rede Davids an das Kriegsvolk nicht gänzlich verdrängt, sondern nur an den Schluss verschoben.[29] Der abrupte Numeruswechsel vom Sing. zum Plur. in V. 16aβ zeigt an, dass jetzt die ursprüngliche Rede an die Kriegsleute folgt und damit die Heldengeschichte fortgesetzt wird. Davids Worte, die sich auch als eine Schmährede charakterisieren lassen,[30] beginnen feierlich mit einer Schwurformel: „So wahr Jahwe lebt, ihr alle habt den Tod verdient!"[31] Der Vorwurf an die Wachsoldaten, den der Gesamterzähler auch in seinem Einschub an Abner gerichtet und damit gedoppelt hat (V. 15aβ), lautet: Ihr habt euch verfehlt, weil ihr nicht einmal eure einfachste Pflicht erfüllt und euren Herrn beschützt habt. Das am Ende von V. 16a asyndetisch an „euren Herrn" angeschlossene und nachklappende „den Gesalbten Jahwes" stammt wiederum vom Gesamterzähler, der den Vorwurf militärischer Pflichtvernachlässigung durch Bezug auf den von Gott eingesetzten König noch einmal anders ins Licht setzt (s. u.). Dieser Zug ist der Heldenerzählung jedoch fremd und im Zusammenhang überhaupt nur vor dem Hintergrund des eingeschobenen Dialogs zwischen David und Abischai verständlich (vgl. V. 9 und 11). Nunmehr ist mit V. 16b die Schlusspointe des Traditionsstücks erreicht, nämlich die Aufforderung an die Wachsoldaten, jetzt nachzuschauen,[32] wo Sauls Spieß und Wasserflasche geblieben sind, die sich an seinem Kopfende befanden.[33]

---

28 Die Lesart von G in V. 14aα „und David rief das Kriegsvolk und zu Abner sprach er" lässt sich daher auch als eine bewusste Glättung der redaktionellen Fuge interpretieren, vgl. BUDDE 1902: 171; sowie den Hinweis bei STOEBE 1973: 463. Dass David, als auf seinen ersten Zuruf niemand reagiert habe, nunmehr den Heerführer namentlich anrief, wird nicht gesagt; vgl. aber DIETRICH 2015: 827, u. a.
29 Dadurch erklärt sich auch, warum Abner eine Antwort schuldig bleibt. Sie käme hinter der aus dem Traditionsstück stammenden Rede Davids in V. 16 zu spät. Ganz im Sinne der Redaktion lässt sich das dann auch narratologisch so erklären, als habe es Abner die Sprache verschlagen.
30 Vgl. STOLZ 1981: 166.
31 So der Sinn der hebräischen Idiomatik: „Söhne des Todes seid ihr!", vgl. dazu 1 Sam 20,31; 2 Sam 19,29; 1 Kön 2,26.
32 Der Imp. sing. masc. spricht nicht gegen die hier vertretene Auslegung, dass die Aufforderung auf eine Allgemeinheit resp. die Kriegsleute Sauls zu beziehen ist. רְאֵה siehe! kann auch gegenüber mehreren gesagt werden, vgl. Dtn 1,8; 4,5; etc., und dazu HAL 1081a.
33 Zumeist wird angezweifelt, dass der Text in M korrekt überliefert sei, und vorgeschlagen, die Nota accusativi vor der Wasserflasche in das Fragepronomen zu ändern. Vielleicht liegt in

Davids Frage erzielt ihre Wirkung am helllichten Tag und nicht in der Nacht. Sie genügt voll und ganz als Beweis, dass er unbemerkt in das Lager eingedrungen und bis zu Saul vorgedrungen ist, zumal das Publikum ja schon weiß, dass die übereilte Suche nach den beiden Gegenständen vergeblich sein wird. Man muss sich nur einmal die verdutzten Gesichter der Kriegsleute vorstellen, als sie erkennen müssen, dass Spieß und Wasserflasche ihres Herrn verschwunden sind. Dann wird man zugeben, dass die Tradition ihre Geschichte von Davids Heldentat nicht ohne einen gewissen Humor erzählt.

Ich fasse zusammen: Kern des Kapitels bildet eine kurze Heldengeschichte, die der Gesamterzähler als literarische Quelle vorgefunden, aufgenommen, aus- und umgestaltet hat. Das Traditionsstück lässt sich fast lückenlos rekonstruieren:[34] Es erzählt von einer tollkühnen Tat Davids, der am helllichten Tag mit seinem Gefährten Ahimelech in das Lager Sauls eindringt, sich durch den um Saul gebildeten Ring von Wachsoldaten schleicht und ihm seinen Spieß und seine Wasserflasche stiehlt. Anschließend konfrontiert er die gegnerischen Kriegsleute mit ihrem Versagen und öffnet ihnen die Augen. Sie haben die Gefahr nicht erkannt, ja sie haben nicht einmal das Fehlen von Sauls Spieß und Wasserkrug bemerkt. Die erzählte Anekdote zeigt, wie schon der junge David durch Heldenmut und Geschicklichkeit seinem übermächtigen Gegner Saul zu begegnen und ihn sogar zu übertölpeln weiß. David ist hellwach und lässt durch seine Heldentat das Publikum schmunzeln, Saul schläft die ganze Zeit und trägt den Spott davon. Das Traditionsstück steht für sich. Auf dieser frühen literarischen Stufe hat 1 Sam 26 bis auf den ähnlichen Plot einer Heldengeschichte (noch) nichts mit seiner Parallelgeschichte in 1 Sam 24 gemein. Erst durch den Gesamterzähler wird das vorliegende Traditionsstück in den Kontext der Fluchtgeschichten Davids eingeschrieben und zu einer weiteren Verschonungsgeschichte Sauls ausgeschrieben.

2 David beschützt den Gesalbten Jahwes

Die Rekonstruktion der literarischen Vorlage ist insofern weiterführend, als sich das Darstellungsinteresse des Gesamterzählers davon deutlich abheben lässt.

M aber auch eine Kontamination zweier Lesarten vor, vgl. G (Vaticanus) mit V. Ob der Text überhaupt zu korrigieren ist, wird von BUDDE 1902: 171, in Zweifel gezogen, der die vorliegende grammatische Konstruktion im Hebräischen für möglich hält (vgl. auch KÖNIG 1897: § 270b). Wie man sich auch immer in dieser Frage positioniert, rechtfertigt der textkritische Befund keine literarkritische Ausscheidung der Wasserflasche.
34 Das Traditionsstück umfasst: V. 3aαbα.5aαb.6aα₁(Lücke).12abα(bis יוד).13a.14aα₁.16aβγ (ohne על־משיח יהוה).16b.

Die hier vorgenommene Kennzeichnung des Bearbeiters als „Gesamterzähler"
lässt offen, ob er hier mit dem von Walter Dietrich vertretenen Höfischen Erzähler,[35] mit der von mir in 2 Sam 1–5 ermittelten David-Redaktion[36] oder mit einer
noch späteren Kompositionsschicht zu identifizieren ist. Außer Frage steht jedoch, dass der Gesamterzähler bereits eine Reihe von Davidserzählungen, insbesondere auch Erzählungen aus dem Bereich der sogenannten Thronfolgegeschichte vor Augen hat und auf sie zurückgreift (s. u.). Darüber hinaus legt sich
die Annahme nahe, dass der Gesamterzähler in den beiden Kapiteln 1 Sam 24
und 26 ähnlich vorgegangen ist, hier wie dort eine literarische Quelle (Anekdote, Heldengeschichte) aufgenommen, bearbeitet und nach eigenen Belangen
umgestaltet hat.[37] Wenn es so wäre, müsste sich in beiden Texten ein gemeinsames Aussageinteresse ermitteln lassen. Für 1 Sam 26 rücken damit die vom Gesamterzähler gestalteten Dialogszenen in den Blickpunkt, zum einen die Abischai-Szene (V. 6*–9.11) und zum anderen die Abner-Szene (V. 14*–16aα).

In der ersten Dialogszene wird offensichtlich die Frage verhandelt, ob David
seinen Verfolger Saul resp. den König Israels hätte töten können und dürfen,
als sich ihm die Gelegenheit dazu bot. Allein zu diesem Zweck wird Abischai
in die Erzählung eingeführt, sein Charakter wird nicht entwickelt, sondern als
bekannt vorausgesetzt.[38] Abischai gehört zu den Helden Davids. Nach 2 Sam
21,17 tötete er einmal einen Philister im Kampf, als dieser sich damit brüstete,
er werde David erschlagen. Offenbar ist Abischai ein Mann der Tat, ebenso wie
sein Bruder Joab, der nach 2 Sam 20,10 seinen Widersacher Amasa mit einem
einzigen Stoß in den Bauch tötete, einen zweiten brauchte er nicht – so die fast
wörtliche Entsprechung zu der von Abischai in 1 Sam 26,8 geäußerten Tötungsabsicht. Vor diesem Hintergrund duldet es keinen Zweifel, dass Abischai sein
Ansinnen auch ausgeführt, den Spieß Sauls umgedreht und den auf dem Boden
schlafenden König mit einem einzigen Stoß durchbohrt hätte.[39] Dass Abischai
tatsächlich die Gelegenheit dazu hatte, wird vom Gesamterzähler entsprechend
inszeniert. Im Gegensatz zum Traditionsstück dringen David und Abischai im
Schutz der Nacht in das feindliche Lager ein, diesmal schläft nicht nur Saul,
Abner und die Soldaten schlafen auch (V. 7b). Trotz dieser günstigen Gelegen-

---

35 Vgl. Dietrich 1997: 259–73; speziell zu 1 Sam 24–26 vgl. Dietrich 2004: 247–51 (2012: 185–89).
36 Vgl. Fischer 2004: 269–91.
37 Für 1 Sam 24 vgl. grundlegend die Analyse von Conrad 2005: 23–42.
38 Vgl. McKenzie 2011: 300: „Abischai functions for a strict narrative purpose ... his character is not developed here." Vgl. dazu auch Klein 2002: 172 Anm. 345.
39 Eine Entfremdung zwischen David und Abischai resp. den Söhnen der Zeruja, wie sie sich in den (narrativ wie literarhistorisch) späteren Texten 2 Sam 3,38f; 16,9f; 19,22f; widerspiegelt, ist hier noch nicht gegeben; vgl. Fischer 2004: 110.

heit gelingt es David, Abischai von einem Königsmord zurückzuhalten, allerdings mit einem kaum situationsgerechten, sondern eher theoretischen Argument (V. 9): „Vernichte ihn nicht! Denn wer könnte seine Hand gegen den Gesalbten Jahwes ausstrecken und käme ungestraft davon?" Die rhetorische Frage lässt sich wohl kaum anders als vor dem Hintergrund von 2 Sam 1,13–16 sachgerecht beantworten. Denn dort wird der amalekitische Königsmörder resp. der Mörder Sauls von David unverzüglich mit dem Tod bestraft. Der Amalekiter hatte sich nämlich nicht gescheut, seine Hand auszustrecken, um den Gesalbten Jahwes zu vernichten. Das Verb שחת „vernichten" stammt offenkundig aus diesem Kontext, wird vom Gesamterzähler in V. 9 aufgenommen und dann noch einmal im Gespräch mit Abner in V. 15 verwendet. Es liegt darum nahe, dass es sich bei dem Gedanken von der Unantastbarkeit des Gesalbten Jahwes nicht um eine alte sakrale Vorstellung, sondern um ein literarisches Motiv handelt, das aus 2 Sam 1,13–16 herausentwickelt worden ist.[40] Dafür spricht insbesondere der Befund, dass der Ausdruck „Gesalbter Jahwes"[41] in Verbindung mit der Formulierung „die Hand gegen jmdn. ausstrecken" im Alten Testament überhaupt nur in den Samuelbüchern vorkommt, nämlich in 2 Sam 1,14 sowie (davon abhängig) in 1 Sam 24,7.11 und 26,9.11.23. Es ist darüber hinaus bezeichnend, dass der Gesamterzähler diese Redewendung noch einmal in 26,11a aufgreift und nun David ausdrücklich beteuern lässt, er selbst werde seine Hand gewiss nicht gegen den Gesalbten Jahwes ausstrecken. Damit nimmt der Gesamterzähler von David allen Verdacht einer Mordabsicht. Ja, er entlastet ihn sogar davon, dass er seine Hand nach Sauls Spieß (und Wasserflasche) ausgestreckt habe, indem er David dieses Unterfangen an seinen Gefährten Abischai delegieren lässt (V. 11b). Offenbar nimmt der Gesamterzähler dadurch die Spannung bewusst in Kauf,[42] dass in der Heldengeschichte nicht Abischai, sondern vielmehr David die Gegenstände entwendet hat (V. 12a). Die redaktionelle Fuge tritt somit noch deutlicher hervor.[43]

Innerhalb der Dialogszene ist bezeichnend, dass Abischai von Saul als dem Feind Davids spricht (V. 8).[44] Offenbar hat er hier im Blick, dass Saul in der Absicht gekommen sei, David aufzugreifen und zu töten.[45] David spricht dage-

---

40 Vgl. ähnlich BEZZEL 2015: 136.

41 11mal im Alten Testament belegt, vgl. 1 Sam 24,7(2mal).11; 26,9.11.16.23; 2 Sam 1,14.16; 19,22 sowie Thr 4,20.

42 Es handelt sich also durchaus nicht um „eine kleine Ungenauigkeit des Schriftstellers, die nicht viel zu bedeuten hat", so aber der Erklärungsversuch von SCHULZ 1919: 372f.

43 Zur Einbeziehung von V. 11b in die Ergänzungsschicht vgl. auch DIETRICH 2004: 238 Anm. 27 (2012: 177 Anm. 27).

44 Vgl. dazu 1 Sam 18,29.

45 Vgl. 1 Sam 20,1; 22,23; 23,15; 25,29; 2 Sam 4,8.

gen von Saul als dem Gesalbten Jahwes und bringt seine Überzeugung zum Ausdruck, dass man in keinem Fall gegen Saul als den von Gott eingesetzten König gewaltsam vorgehen darf. Damit aber weist David resp. der Gesamterzähler über die gegebene Situation hinaus und nimmt die kommenden Geschehnisse in den Blick, durch die David dem Verdacht ausgesetzt ist, er habe Saul und die Sauliden gewaltsam ausgeschaltet und sich so ihr Königtum angeeignet. Mehrfach muss sich David in den folgenden Erzählungen gegen diesen Verdacht zur Wehr setzen und bekräftigen, dass er am Tod Sauls unschuldig ist (2 Sam 1,16) und dass er auch mit den Morden an Sauls Heerführer Abner (2 Sam 3,31–37) und Sauls Sohn Ischboschet (2 Sam 4,9–12) nichts zu tun habe.[46] Es bleiben allerdings Zweifel. Es ist daher vollkommen verständlich, dass der Gesamterzähler die Gelegenheit genutzt hat, durch die Abischai-Szene in 1 Sam 26 zu demonstrieren, dass bereits der junge David der Versuchung zur Usurpation widerstand.[47] Seine Heldentat besteht nunmehr darin, dass er Abischai den Königsmord verwehrt und für sich selbst jedes gewaltsame Vorgehen gegen den von Gott eingesetzten König ausgeschlossen hat. Offenbar geht es in der Abischai-Szene nicht nur darum, das Leben Sauls zu verschonen. Es soll auch gezeigt werden, dass David nicht dazu bereit gewesen ist, durch einen Königsmord die saulidische Herrschaft zu vernichten. Dem entspricht, dass in V. 9 und 15 das Verb שחת „vernichten" verwendet wird (s. o.).

Wie verhält sich zu dieser Aussageabsicht nun der zweite vom Gesamterzähler ausgeführte Dialog mit Abner, der in V. 14*–16aα in die ursprüngliche Rede Davids eingeschoben ist? Es fällt zunächst auf, dass David dem Heerführer Sauls durchaus mit Respekt begegnet und ihn als einen Mann anerkennt, dem kein anderer in Israel gleichkommt (V. 15). Diese Hochschätzung Abners liegt wohl auf einer Linie mit 2 Sam 3,31ff und es gibt keinen Anhaltspunkt im Text, dass sich David in dieser Weise über Abner habe lustig machen wollen.[48] Wenn dies richtig gesehen und die Hochachtung Abners ernst gemeint ist, dann lässt sich die folgende Frage weniger als Anklage denn als Ausdruck der Verwunderung lesen, warum dieser so hochgeschätzte und fähige Mann nicht (besser) auf seinen Herrn und König achtgegeben hat.[49] David klärt Abner sogleich über sein Versagen auf und teilt ihm mit, dass einer aus dem Volk gekommen ist,[50]

---

46 Die in diesem Zusammenhang zitierten Texte gehören zur David-Redaktion, vgl. FISCHER 2004: 35–40, 162–65, 182–88.

47 Vgl. dazu auch CONRAD 2005: 40.

48 Vgl. aber SCHULZ 1919: 373; u. a. DIETRICH 2015: 827, spricht von Komplimenten an Abner, die jedoch vergiftet seien.

49 Der in der Frage enthaltene Vorwurf ist eine Dublette zu V. 16aγ.

50 Vgl. die Wiederaufnahme von בוא aus V. 5 und V. 7 (sic!).

um den König zu vernichten (V. 15b). Vor dem Hintergrund der ebenfalls vom Gesamterzähler gestalteten Abischai-Szene ist völlig klar, dass mit dem „einen aus dem Volk" nur Abischai gemeint sein kann (vgl. das Stichwort שׁחת „vernichten").[51] Der hätte Saul töten können. Abner hätte das nicht verhindert, David aber hat es verhindert! Offenbar soll der Leser eben diesen Schluss ziehen: Nicht einmal Abner, der Gefolgsmann Sauls, konnte den König beschützen. David dagegen erweist sich – im Hintergrund der Szene – als der eigentliche Beschützer Sauls und seines Königtums.[52] Im Weiteren fällt auf, dass die anschließende Kritik an Abner in V. 16aα ausgesprochen milde ausfällt, wenn David ihm vorhält, dass diese (eine) Sache, nämlich die unzureichende Bewachung des Königs, nicht gut gewesen sei. Und dies fällt um so mehr auf, wenn man damit die ursprüngliche Reaktion Davids in der Heldengeschichte vergleicht, der dort in V. 16aβγ mit einem feierlichen Schwur die Wachsoldaten mit dem Tod bedroht, weil sie ihre Pflicht zum Schutz des Königs vernachlässigt haben. Die Funktion des Sätzchens („Diese Sache war nicht gut, die du getan hast!") lässt sich näherhin so bestimmen, dass es den hochangesehenen Feldherrn Sauls von den übrigen Kriegsleuten absetzen will und die vom Gesamterzähler eingeschobene Abner-Szene abrunden soll. Der folgende asyndetische Anschluss der Schwurformel „So wahr Jahwe lebt!" verrät hier wiederum die redaktionelle Fuge. Denn innerhalb der Rede wäre zumindest ein כי oder ein ועתה zu ihrer Einführung zu erwarten gewesen.[53] Wahrscheinlicher ist deshalb, dass die Schwurformel einmal unmittelbar auf die Redeeinleitung in V. 14aα folgte („Und er rief zu dem Kriegsvolk, indem er sagte: So wahr Jahwe lebt, …!").[54]

Im Rückblick lassen sich nun die Gemeinsamkeiten mit 1 Sam 24 bestimmen, die in der Verantwortung des Gesamterzählers liegen und sich auf seiner Bearbeitungsstufe ergeben: Erstens verwenden die Männer Davids in 1 Sam 24 das gleiche, wenn auch etwas anders formulierte Argument wie Abischai, als er David gegenüber erklärt: „Heute hat Gott deinen Feind in deine Hand ausgeliefert" (vgl. 26,8 mit 24,5).[55] In 24,5 lässt der Gesamterzähler allerdings offen, ob die Männer dadurch David zum Mord an Saul drängen wollten. Dagegen begründet Abischai in 26,8 damit ausdrücklich seine Tötungsabsicht. Zweitens

51 Anders CRYER 1985: 387.
52 Vgl. STOEBE 1973: 469; DIETRICH 2015: 828.
53 Vgl. 1 Sam 14,39 bzw. 1 Sam 25,26; 1 Kön 2,24.
54 Mit קרא und אמר vgl. 1 Sam 29,6; mit שׁבע und / oder אמר vgl. Ri 8,19; 1 Sam 19,6; 26,10; 28,10; 2 Sam 4,9; 12,5; 14,11; 15,21; 1 Kön 1,29; 17,1.12; 18,15; 2 Kön 2,2.6; 3,14; 4,30; 5,16.
55 Dass die Übergabeformel in 26,8 mit dem Verb סגר „(in die Hand) liefern" (vgl. 1 Sam 17,46; 24,19; 2 Sam 18,28), in 24,5 dagegen mit נתן „(in die Hand) geben" formuliert ist, fällt so sehr nicht ins Gewicht. Die Textpassagen unterscheiden sich auch sonst in ihrem Wortlaut.

findet sich in beiden Kapiteln eine feierliche Beteuerung Davids, dass er nicht gegen Saul vorgehen werde (vgl. 26,11 mit 24,7). Die Formulierung חלילה לי מיהוה („Das sei mir fern um Jahwes willen!") ist identisch und im Alten Testament sonst nur noch in 1 Kön 21,3 belegt. Drittens beinhaltet die Beteuerung in beiden Kapiteln die gleiche, wenn auch etwas anders formulierte Aussage, dass David seine Hand nicht gegen den Gesalbten Jahwes ausstrecken werde (vgl. 26,11 mit 24,7). Obwohl man zugeben muss, dass 24,7 deutlich überfüllt wirkt,[56] entsprechen sich beide Verse in ihrem Aussageinteresse. Bei den benannten Gemeinsamkeiten lässt sich freilich kaum entscheiden, ob der einen oder anderen Fassung die Priorität zukommt. Es ist deshalb in Betracht zu ziehen, dass beide Textpassagen auf ein und dieselbe Hand resp. auf den hier skizzierten Gesamterzähler zurückzuführen sind.[57] Zu der von ihm in 1 Sam 26,14*–16aα eingefügten Abner-Szene gibt es in 1 Sam 24 allerdings keine Entsprechung.

3 Und Saul?

Und Saul? Der schläft! Das ist seine ihm in der Heldengeschichte und seiner Bearbeitung zugewiesene Rolle. Oder schläft er doch nicht?[58] Es scheint so, dass Saul zuerst durch ein redaktionelles Interesse an seiner Person aus dem Schlaf aufgeweckt wurde. Vom Publikum fast schon vergessen, betritt er ganz unvermittelt und plötzlich die Bühne und wendet sich an David mit der Frage: „Ist das nicht deine Stimme, mein Sohn David?" Man kann zwar zugeben, dass dieser Anschluss irgendwie versucht, die gegebene Situation aufzugreifen. Es ist ja Nacht (vgl. V. 7), sodass der Sprecher nicht gesehen, sondern nur an seiner Stimme erkannt werden kann, zumal auch seine Identität noch nicht abschließend geklärt worden ist (vgl. V. 14bβ).[59] Doch das folgende Gespräch zwischen David und Saul hat doch sehr den Charakter eines Vier-Augen-Gesprächs, als

---

56 Vgl. STOEBE 1973: 435 und 440.
57 Vgl. dazu die Analyse von CONRAD 2005: 41, der 24,5a und 24,7 seiner Redaktionsschicht C (zweite Bearbeitung) zuweist. Sie konvergiert mit der Bearbeitungsschicht des Gesamterzählers.
58 SCHULZ 1919: 374, kommentiert V. 14 wie folgt: „Unterdessen ist Saul aufgewacht und erkennt David an seiner Stimme."
59 Häufig wird diese Beobachtung dafür in Anspruch genommen, dass sich die Frage „Ist das nicht deine Stimme?" nur hier kontextuell einfügen und deshalb 1 Sam 26 die Priorität gegenüber 1 Sam 24 zukommen würde. Dann aber müsste man sofort hinzufügen, dass die Anrede mit „mein Sohn David" umgekehrt für die Priorität von 1 Sam 24,17 spräche. Denn nur hier ist sie kontextuell vermittelt und wird durch die Anrede Sauls mit „mein Vater" in 24,12 vorbereitet.

dass es bei Nacht und dazu noch über eine weite Entfernung hinweg geführt würde.[60] Auch die Anrede mit „mein Sohn David"[61] bringt einen ganz anderen Ton in das Gespräch und steht im Widerspruch zu der soeben geschilderten Konfrontation zwischen Saul und David. Darüber hinaus ist festzustellen, dass der Dialog keinerlei Bezug mehr zu der vorhergehenden Situation hat:[62] Saul reagiert weder auf den Diebstahl noch auf den damit verbundenen Affront noch auf die gegen seine Soldaten ausgesprochene Todesdrohung. Und man kann das wohl kaum so erklären, dass Saul von all dem nichts mitbekommen oder dass er inzwischen eine innere Wandlung vollzogen habe. Schließlich hat sich auch das Thema grundlegend verschoben. Es geht nicht mehr um die Verschonung Sauls, sondern nur noch um die Frage, wen eigentlich die Schuld an dem Konflikt trifft, David oder Saul.[63]

Was also haben wir hier eigentlich vor uns? Das ist eine spannende und reizvolle Frage. Denn der ausgeführte Dialog, in dem fast nur David redet, wirkt überfüllt und reflektiert die Frage nach der Schuld an dem Zerwürfnis aus unterschiedlichen Perspektiven. Das Gespräch ist aber auch ein schillerndes Gebilde (ebenso wie 1 Sam 24,9–25),[64] zeigt es doch einerseits einen selbstbewussten David, der Saul vorhält, dass er ihn zu Unrecht verfolgt (V. 18), andererseits einen seinem Herrn und König treu ergebenen Diener, der Saul von Schuld freispricht und sie anderen anlastet (V. 19).[65] Der Eindruck, dass hier verschiedene Stimmen zu Wort kommen, kann man nicht ganz von der Hand weisen, besonders vor dem Hintergrund, dass man mit einem bewussten Aufeinander-Zuschreiben, einer wechselweisen Parallelisierung der beiden Kapitel 1 Sam 24 und 26 zu rechnen hat (s. o.). Lassen sich aber in der Rede Davids vor der Höhle von En-Gedi eine Reihe von Zuwächsen feststellen,[66] dürfte das auch bei seinen

---

60 Vollkommen zu Recht erklärt VAN SETERS 2011: 99: „This form of dialogue is entirely appropriate for the scene between David and Saul in chap 24, but totally inappropriate here. To imagine such an exchange at such a great distance in the middle of the night is quite ludicrous."
61 Vgl. noch 1 Sam 24,17; 26,21.25. Da Saul sonst nirgends David als seinen Sohn bezeichnet oder anredet, können die beiden Verse 24,17 und 26,17 nicht unabhängig voneinander entstanden sein.
62 Vgl. STEIN 1997: 51. Auch die beteiligten Personen wie Abischai und Abner sind ganz aus dem Blickfeld verschwunden.
63 Vgl. HENTSCHEL 2003: 172.
64 Vgl. CONRAD 2005: 27–29.
65 Zutreffend bemerkt dazu STOEBE 1973: 469, dass David hier fast wieder wie ein Höfling (vgl. 1 Sam 16) erscheint und in die Rolle eines in Ungnade gefallenen und ungerecht behandelten Dieners schlüpft.
66 Vgl. z. B. CONRAD 2005: 35–41. Angestoßen wurde die Diskussion bereits durch VEIJOLA 1975: 90–93. Er beurteilte 24,18–19.20b–23a als Ergänzung durch DtrH.

auf dem Berggipfel gesprochenen Worten der Fall sein, zumal David und Saul hier in 1 Sam 26 ein letztes Mal miteinander reden und damit – narrativ gesprochen – die letzte Gelegenheit für Nachinterpretationen gegeben ist. Deshalb soll auch hier der Frage nachgegangen werden, ob sich in dem Gespräch 1 Sam 26,17–25 eine Grundschicht ermitteln lässt.

Ich beginne wiederum mit einem Detail, das nur am Rand in den Blick tritt: mit dem Floh und dem Rebhuhn, mit denen sich David in V. 20 vergleicht. In der Regel wird das Verhältnis beider Tiere resp. Tiervergleiche zunächst als ein textkritisches Problem verhandelt. Denn es ist schon immer gesehen worden, dass im Masoretentext die Nota accusativi mit dem unbestimmten Objektakkusativ „ein einziger Floh" (אֶת־פַּרְעֹשׁ אֶחָד) zusammensteht, was grammatisch sehr ungewöhnlich, wenn auch nicht unmöglich ist.[67] Dagegen bietet die griechische Überlieferung anstelle von „einen einzigen Floh zu suchen" die Lesart „meine Seele zu suchen" (אֶת־נַפְשִׁי),[68] was im Sinn von „mir nach dem Leben zu trachten" eine gängige Formulierung darstellt. Deshalb wird für gewöhnlich M als *lectio difficilior* beurteilt und G als eine die grammatische Konstruktion glättende und durch den weiteren Kontext motivierte[69] Textänderung gedeutet. Das ist im Rahmen der textkritischen Methode durchaus plausibel. Das textkritische Argument der *lectio difficilior* scheidet jedoch aus, wenn die unterschiedlichen Versionen nicht durch einen Prozess des Abschreibens, sondern durch einen redaktionsgeschichtlichen Vorgang entstanden sind. Denn der Floh kommt ja auch in 24,15 vor und könnte – zur Angleichung beider Kapitel (s. o.) – in 26,20 eingetragen worden sein, ohne dass sich diese Angleichung in der griechischen Überlieferung niedergeschlagen hat. Diese Annahme setzt allerdings voraus, dass der Floh ursprünglich in 1 Sam 24 beheimatet war und von dort nach 1 Sam 26 herübergesprungen ist.[70] Und genau dies ist der Fall, wie die folgenden Beobachtungen zeigen: In 24,15 stehen die beiden Tiermetaphern „ein toter Hund" und „ein einziger Floh" (beide indeterminiert) nebeneinander und liegen in ihrer Aussageabsicht auf einer Linie. David redet von sich als einem toten Hund, was als Selbstbezeichnung im höfischen Stil die völlige Bedeutungslosigkeit gegenüber dem König zum Ausdruck bringen will.[71] Ähnlich verhält es sich auch mit dem Floh. Denn schon der Größenvergleich führt vor Augen, dass dieses

---

67 Vgl. König 1897: § 288 f.

68 Die lukianische Version folgt dagegen M, in 4Q51 ist die Textstelle nicht erhalten.

69 Zu der auf Saul als Subjekt bezogenen Wendung „(David) nach dem Leben trachten" vgl. 1 Sam 20,1; 22,13; 23,15; (25,29); 2 Sam 4,8.

70 Vgl. Caspari 1926: 346 f. (Fußnote 3 zu 26,20).

71 Vgl. 2 Sam 9,8 und dazu Bar-Efrat 2009: 98.

winzige Tier doch keinerlei Beachtung durch den König wert ist.[72] Beide Tiervergleiche bringen mithin – als Doppelargument – zum Ausdruck, dass die Verfolgung eines so unbedeutenden und ungefährlichen Menschen wie David ein
völlig unsinniges Unternehmen darstellt.[73] Im Gegensatz dazu liegen die Ver-
gleichungen in 26,20 gerade nicht auf einer Linie. Vielmehr wird die Rede vom
Suchen eines einzigen Flohs durch einen anschließenden weiteren Tierver-
gleich erläutert, was schon an sich sehr ungewöhnlich ist.[74] Allerdings – und
das ist nicht zu übersehen – hat die Suche nach einem Floh mit der Jagd auf
ein Rebhuhn so gut wie nichts gemeinsam. Denn bei der Jagd eines Rebhuhns
hat man es schon „vor Augen", man verfolgt es und scheucht es so lange auf,
bis es völlig erschöpft ist. Dann kann es nicht mehr wegfliegen, läuft nur noch
auf dem Boden hin und her, sodass man es mit einem Stock totschlagen kann.[75]
Der Vergleich mit dem Rebhuhn läuft darum ins Leere, wenn man ihn an den
Floh anschließt und nicht direkt an die Aussage der Septuagintaversion, dass
der König Israels ausgezogen sei, um David zur Strecke zu bringen. Denn die
Rebhuhnjagd entspricht ja sehr genau der Situation Davids am Ende (!) der
Fluchtgeschichten in 1 Sam 26 und ist damit ein angemessener Vergleich. David
blickt zurück auf seine andauernde Verfolgung durch Saul, bei der dieser immer
wieder versucht, ihn in die Enge zu treiben und totzuschlagen.[76] Eben dieser
Fluchtkontext ist im Blick und bekommt noch dadurch eine besondere Pointe,
dass David, der auf dem Gipfel des Berges (רֹאשׁ־הָהָר V. 13) steht und ruft (קרא
V. 14), sozusagen auf den hinunterschaut, der in den Bergen (בֶּהָרִים V. 20) das
Rebhuhn (הַקֹּרֵא) jagt.[77] Es ist also durchaus denkbar und recht wahrscheinlich,
dass die offenkundige und auch anderswo erklärte Tötungsabsicht Sauls[78] –
vielleicht angeregt durch die zugunsten Sauls vorgetragenen Entlastungsargu-

---

72 STOEBE 1973: 436, bemerkt hinzu, dass hier im Gegenüber zum König nicht auf die Schnel-
ligkeit des Flohs, sondern auf seine Bedeutungslosigkeit angespielt wird.

73 Dagegen meint DIETRICH 2004: 241 (2012: 179), dass der Flohvergleich besser in 1 Sam
26,20 als 1 Sam 24,15 verankert wäre, obwohl er nachfolgend erklärt, dass ja die Suche nach
einem Floh ebenso sinnlos sei wie die Jagd auf einem toten Hund.

74 Dass eine Vergleichung wieder mit etwas Anderem verglichen wird, ist aber, weil unnatür-
lich, auch beispiellos; so bereits THENIUS 1842: 111.

75 Vgl. RIEDE 1995: 89.

76 Daran schließt sich dann auch die Begründung in 1 Sam 27,1 nahtlos an, in der David
seinen Übertritt zu den Philistern rechtfertigt: „Eines Tages werde ich ja doch von der Hand
Sauls weggerafft werden."

77 Für den Zusammenhang kann man auch auf das Wortspiel verweisen zwischen David, der
„ruft" (V. 14), und dem Rebhuhn, das im Hebräischen „Rufer" genannt wird (V. 20); vgl. dazu
BAR-EFRAT 2007: 343; TSUMURA 2007: 605 f.

78 Vgl. 1 Sam 18,11; 19,1.10.15; 20,1.7.31; 23,15; 24,12; vgl. ferner 18,17.21.25.

mente (V. 19) – durch den Flohvergleich nachträglich verdeckt werden sollte.[79] Jedenfalls lässt sich der Rebhuhnvergleich als tatsächlichen Zielpunkt der ersten Rede Davids bestimmen (s. o.).

Vor diesem Hintergrund skizziere ich nun die Grundschicht des Gesprächs: Es beginnt in V. 18 mit der Frage Davids an Saul, warum er ihn verfolge, wobei diese durch das dem Fragewort zugesetzte Demonstrativpronomen זֶה einen vorwurfsvollen Ton bekommt.[80] Zwei weitere Fragen, die auf die Unschuld Davids zielen, verschärfen den Ton.[81] Der Verfasser scheint hier auf 20,1 zurückzugreifen, wo David schon einmal gegenüber Jonatan den Vorwurf äußerte, dass Saul ihm grundlos nach dem Leben trachte. Wie in 20,1bβ lassen die Fragen fast zwingend einen mit כִּי eingeleiteten Folgesatz erwarten.[82] Dieser liegt in 26,20b auch vor und schließt sich grammatisch und inhaltlich nahtlos an V. 18 an („Er sagte: Warum nur jagt mein Herr hinter seinem Knecht her? Ja, was habe ich denn getan, was habe ich Böses verbrochen, ... dass der König Israels ausgezogen ist, um mir nach dem Leben zu trachten, wie man ein Rebhuhn in den Bergen jagt?"). Die Satzkonstruktion wird jedoch durch den Einschub V. 19.20a unterbrochen. Mit der auch in deuteronomistischen Texten gebrauchten rhetorischen Partikel וְעַתָּה „und jetzt"[83] wird ein neuer Gedanke in die Rede eingeführt. David geht es nun nicht mehr darum, eine mögliche Schuld seinerseits entschieden von sich zu weisen, sondern darum, eine offensichtliche Schuld Sauls (!) in Frage zu stellen. Dazu werden zwei Möglichkeiten erörtert: Entweder steht Gott selbst dahinter[84] oder es waren gewisse Leute, die Saul gegen ihn aufgehetzt haben. Die zweite Möglichkeit wird weiter ausgeführt und diesen Leuten vorgeworfen, dass sie David heute aus der Gemeinschaft[85] mit dem Gottesvolk[86] vertrieben haben (Perfekt!), verbunden mit der Aufforderung an ihn: „Geh und diene anderen Göttern!"[87] Hier ist ganz offenbar eine Exilssituation

---

79 Vgl. auch NOWACK 1902: 132: „eine aus 24,15 geflossene Glosse, die den ursprüngl. Text verdrängt hat."

80 Vgl. HAL 254a und z. B. Gen 18,13.

81 Die Fragen lassen sich hier im Sinne eines negativen Aussagesatzes verstehen: „Ich habe gar nichts getan!"

82 Vgl. GK § 166b und z. B. Gen 20,9; 1 Sam 29,8.

83 Vgl. dazu WEINFELD 1972: 175.

84 Vgl. 2 Sam 24,1 (סוּת) mit 24,25bα „und Jahwe ließ sich für das Land gnädig stimmen". In diesem Kapitel lassen sich V. 1.3.4a.10.17.25bα auf DtrP zurückführen, vgl. DIETRICH 1992: 36 mit Anm. 24.

85 HAL 721b „zugehörig sein (zu einer Gemeinschaft)", vgl. das Qal in 1 Sam 2,36 (DtrS).

86 Der nominale Ausdruck נַחֲלַת יְהוָה begegnet sonst nur noch 2 Sam 20,19; 21,3; vgl. 14,16. Er meint in 1 Sam 26,19 „the worshipping community", vgl. TSUMURA 2007: 605.

87 Die Formulierung setzt erkennbar dtr Sprachgebrauch voraus, vgl. Dtn 28,14.36.64; Jos 23,16; 24,2.16; Ri 2,12.19; 10,13; 1 Sam 8,8; 1 Kön 9,6; 11,4.10; Jer 7,6.9; u. ö. Damit ist nicht

im Blick. Doch die Versuche, eine solche Exilssituation mit Davids Aufenthalt im Philisterland in Verbindung zu bringen, sind mehr als gezwungen. Erstens wurde David im hier vorliegenden Erzählzusammenhang nicht aus Israel vertrieben, sondern hat sich selbst für den Übertritt ins Philisterland entschieden (vgl. 27,1). Zweitens wird sein Aufenthalt in Ziklag nicht wirklich als ein Exil verstanden (vgl. 27,6). Und drittens legt sein Dienst beim Philisterfürsten Achisch in keiner Weise nahe, dass damit die Verehrung anderer Götter verbunden gewesen wäre (vgl. 29,6; 30,8; 30,23). Der Schluss ist daher unumgänglich, dass es sich bei V. 19 um eine aus großem zeitlichen Abstand formulierte Reflexion handelt.[88] Offenbar wird hier eine nachexilische Frage verhandelt und eine Gruppe von Gegnern ausgemacht, denen nicht nur die Schuld am Exilsgeschick angelastet, sondern auch noch unterstellt wird, dass sie damit den Abfall der Davididen vom Gott Israels betrieben haben. Ähnlich verhält es sich auch mit der in V. 20a wiederum mit וְעַתָּה eingeleiteten und an Gott (nicht an Saul!)[89] gerichteten Bitte Davids, sein Blut möge nicht fern vom Angesicht Jahwes zu Boden rinnen.[90] Dabei lässt sich schwer entscheiden, wie diese im biblischen Hebräisch singulär formulierte Bitte zu interpretieren ist: Soll Gott dafür sorgen, dass David nicht in einem fremden Land sterben muss, oder soll er dafür sorgen, dass sein Tod nicht ungesühnt bleibt?[91] In beiden Fällen aber verweist der folgende Kausalsatz in V. 20b nur allgemein auf eine Gefahr, die für das Leben Davids besteht,[92] nennt aber keine Umstände, die Davids Bitte tatsächlich konkretisieren und begründen würden. Die Beobachtung schließlich, dass hier der Folgesatz der Grundschicht (V. 18.20b) durch den Einschub (V. 19.20a) nunmehr in die Funktion eines Kausalsatzes einrückt, lässt wiederum die redaktionelle Fuge deutlich hervortreten.

Auf Davids Rede in V. 18.20b folgt in der Grundschicht das Schuldeingeständnis Sauls,[93] und sein Rückkehrangebot an David in V. 21aα. Das Rückkehr-

---

gesagt, dass für 1 Sam 26,19 eine dtr Herkunft anzunehmen ist, sondern nur, dass hier auf eine dtr Formulierung zurückgegriffen wird.

88 Vgl. EDENBURG 2016: 476 mit Anm. 25.

89 Anders BAR-EFRAT 2007: 343. Doch das hieße, Saul könne und möge David auf der Stelle töten, damit er nicht fern von Gott in einem fremden Land sterben müsse.

90 Bereits THENIUS 1842: 111, kommentierte die Stelle wie folgt: „Auch die dieser und der Aeusserung im vorigen V. zum Grunde liegende *Sehnsucht nach dem Nationalheiligthume* weist auf eine spätere Abfassung dieses Abschnittes hin."

91 Für gewöhnlich wird auf Gen 4,10; Hi 16,18; verwiesen, vgl. BUDDE 1902: 171, u. a.

92 Es ist offensichtlich, dass der Ergänzer von V. 20a die Lesart der Septuaginta in V. 20b voraussetzt. Denn die Bitte, dass Davids Blut nicht ... zu Boden rinnen solle, folgt aus der Absicht Sauls, David das Leben zu nehmen.

93 Synchron gelesen macht Saul also keinen Gebrauch von den ihm in V. 19 durch David angebotenen Antwortmöglichkeiten, seine Schuld einzuschränken und anderen anzulasten.

angebot begründet Saul mit der Erklärung, dass er David in Zukunft nichts Böses mehr antun will.[94] An diese erste, durch כִּי eingeleitete Begründung wird in V. 21aβ eine weitere Begründung angeschlossen. Ihr Anschluss erfolgt durch die präpositionale Verbindung תַּחַת אֲשֶׁר „dafür, dass", die sonst nur in deuteronomistischen und späten Texten vorkommt.[95] Diese zweite Begründung, die nur vordergründig das Rückkehrangebot als Gegenleistung für die Verschonung Sauls in den Blick rückt, bereitet vielmehr die Einfügung von V. 24 vor und steht mit ihr in einem Zusammenhang. Eine weitere Nachinterpretation dürfte in V. 21b vorliegen, die auf Samuels Kritik an Saul in 13,13 (dtr) zurückgreift (סכל)[96] zugleich aber Saul dadurch in Schutz nimmt, dass er seinen schweren Fehler irrtümlich (vgl. שָׁגָה)[97] gemacht habe. Diese Ergänzung relativiert freilich das Schuldeingeständnis Sauls in V. 21aα und liegt insofern auf einer Linie mit V. 19, als beide Einfügungen in unterschiedlicher Weise versuchen, das Verhalten Sauls zu entschuldigen.

In der Grundschicht antwortet David auf Sauls Schuldeingeständnis und Rückkehrangebot kurz und bündig: „Siehe, hier ist der Spieß des Königs![98] Einer von den jungen Leuten soll herüberkommen und ihn abholen!" Es entspricht dem Geschick des Erzählers, dass er David hier gar nicht auf die Rede Sauls eingehen lässt und somit die Deutung seiner Geste sowie die mit der Rückgabe von Sauls Spieß verbundene Symbolik offenlässt. Nur der die Grundschicht abschließende Satz in V. 25b („Danach ging David seiner Wege und Saul kehrte an seinen Ort zurück")[99] gibt indirekt zu erkennen, dass David das Rückkehrangebot Sauls nicht angenommen hat – offenbar, weil er ihm nicht mehr vertraute.[100] Mithin bilden Davids Heldentat und sein Auftritt auf dem Gipfel

Vielmehr nimmt Saul die volle Schuld auf sich und „drückt damit die Meinung des Verfassers und des Lesers aus", so HERTZBERG 1956: 167.

94 Man beachte den modalistischen Gebrauch des Imperfekts: Saul erklärt seine Absicht, gibt aber keine feste Zusage (z. B. durch einen Schwursatz).

95 Vgl. Num 25,13; Dtn 28,47 (dtr); 28,62 (dtr); 2 Kön 22,17 (dtr); 2 Chr 21,12; 34,25; Jes 53,12; Jer 29,19 (dtr); 50,7 (dtr); Ez 36,34; ferner 2mal in Rechtssätzen vgl. Dtn 22,14; 22,29.

96 Das Verb begegnet sonst nur noch in 2 Sam 15,31 (spät) und 24,10 (DtrP), vgl. DIETRICH 1992: 68 Anm. 26.

97 Sonst nicht in geschichtlichen Texten belegt, vgl. BUDDE 1902: 172.

98 Die Wiederaufnahme von V. 16 widerrät, dem Ketib von M zu folgen und einen Vokativ anzunehmen. Das Ketib, das bereits durch das Qere verbessert wurde, erklärt sich durch Doppelschreibung des He, vgl. DELITZSCH 1920: § 98a. Das Qere bestätigen 4Q51 sowie die Versionen.

99 Konventioneller Erzählschluss. Man beachte dabei die Reihenfolge „David – Saul", die dafür spricht, dass sich V. 25b ursprünglich an die Antwort Davids in V. 22 anschloss und nicht an die Rede Sauls in V. 25a. Vgl. beispielsweise Num 24,25.

100 Vgl. BAR-EFRAT 2007: 344.

des Berges den Höhepunkt und Abschluss der Fluchtgeschichten. Der Übertritt zu den Philistern in 27,1 schließt sich folgerichtig an.

Zwischen den ursprünglichen Zusammenhang von V. 22 und 25b[101] treten noch zwei Nachinterpretationen, in V. 24.25a eine ältere und in V. 23 eine jüngere.[102] In der älteren Ergänzung scheinen die Worte Davids, dass sein Leben (נֶפֶשׁ) bei Jahwe so viel zähle, dass er ihn aus aller Gefahr erretten wird (נצל), auf sein künftiges Königtum hinzuweisen. Dafür spricht jedenfalls, dass sich David in den beiden Schwursätzen 2 Sam 4,9 und 1 Kön 1,29 darauf bezieht und feststellt, es sei Jahwe gewesen, der sein Leben (נֶפֶשׁ) aus aller Gefahr erlöst hat (פדה). Noch deutlicher scheint das in der Antwort Sauls in V. 25a der Fall zu sein. Sein Segen und Zuspruch, dass alles, was David anpacke, auch Erfolg haben wird,[103] öffnet einen weiten Horizont und schließt wohl die Anerkennung Davids als des künftigen Königs von Israel ein, auch wenn dies nicht direkt ausgesprochen wird.[104] Für diesen Einschub mag sich eine deuteronomistische Herkunft nahelegen, doch lässt sich dafür kein Sprachbeweis führen. Die jüngere Ergänzung in V. 23 setzt wiederum einen anderen Akzent. Ihr geht es um Davids Gerechtigkeit. Dazu greift sie auf V. 8–11 zurück und stellt heraus, dass die Verschonung Sauls resp. des Gesalbten Jahwes eine wahrhaft gerechte Tat Davids gewesen sei, die ihm Jahwe deshalb zur Gerechtigkeit anrechnen wird.[105] Dass der Ergänzer diesen Gedanken David selbst in den Mund gelegt hat, darf aber nicht dahingehend verstanden werden, dass David hier sein eigenes Lob verkündet und sich selbst Gutes verheißt.[106] Vielmehr möchte der Ergänzer, wahrscheinlich durch 24,18–20 angeregt, nochmals gegenüber Saul betonen, dass sich David beispielhaft gerecht und in Einklang mit Gott verhalten hat, bevor er ihn seiner Wege gehen lässt.

4 Fazit

Die redaktionsgeschichtliche Analyse von 1 Sam 26 hat ergeben, dass der Erzählung eine Einzelüberlieferung zugrunde liegt, die von einer Heldentat Davids

---

101 Vgl. bereits die Bemerkung von STOEBE 1973: 471. Ähnliche Lösungen in Bezug auf die Grundschicht vertreten HENTSCHEL 2005: 171; DIETRICH 2004: 241 (2012: 180).
102 Vgl. dazu auch KOCH 1981: 181.
103 Der Gesamterzähler formuliert diese Gedanken für gewöhnlich mit dem Verb שׂכל, vgl. 1 Sam 18,5.14.15.30.
104 So STOEBE 1973: 471 f.; vgl. dazu auch DIETRICH 2015: 835: „Von Davids Königtum spricht er nicht mehr (wie in 1 Sam 24,21), aber er meint es vielleicht."
105 Die Wendung שׁוב + צדקה ist sonst nur noch belegt in 2 Sam 22,25 (vgl. Ps 18,25) und Hi 33,26! Zum Gebrauch von אמונה vgl. JEPSEN 1973: 341–43.
106 So THENIUS 1842: 112.

handelt. Dass es solche Einzelüberlieferungen gegeben hat, bestätigen auch und zumal die in 2 Sam 23 zusammengestellten Heldengeschichten.[107] Das vorgefundene Traditionsstück von Davids Heldentat wurde von einem Gesamterzähler aufgenommen, der mit seinem Thema von der Verfolgung Davids durch Saul einen ersten durchgängigen, Kap. 21 mit 27 verbindenden Erzählfaden geschaffen hat. Die Verwendung von älteren Traditionsstücken und ihr Einbau in einen neuen Erzählzusammenhang ist im Übrigen nichts Ungewöhnliches. Nicht zuletzt lässt sich ein solches redaktionelles Verfahren in 1 Sam 21–26 beobachten. Der Gesamterzähler hat hier nicht nur die Anekdote von Davids Vortäuschen seines Verrücktseins in 1 Sam 21* aufgegriffen, sondern auch die Tradition von Davids Rettung der Stadt Keila, die den Kern der Erzählung in 1 Sam 23* bildet[108] und mit den Nachstellungen Sauls ursprünglich nichts zu tun hat. Komposition und Gestaltung liegen mithin bei dem Gesamterzähler, der ähnlich wie in 1 Sam 24 auch in 1 Sam 26 ein ihm schriftlich vorliegendes Traditionsstück aufgenommen und zu einer Verschonungsgeschichte Sauls umgearbeitet hat. Auf dieser Redaktionsstufe, dem Darstellungszusammenhang des Gesamterzählers, liegen die Gemeinsamkeiten zwischen 1 Sam 24 und 26 erstens in einem ähnlichen Plot der beiden aufgenommenen und umgestalteten Traditionsstücke, zweitens in einer Parallelisierung der Erzählexpositionen und damit der Einbindung beider Einzelüberlieferungen in einen Fluchtkontext sowie drittens in dem Erzählinteresse, dass David bereits in jungen Jahren der Versuchung widerstanden hat, durch Usurpation die Herrschaft des saulidischen Königtums an sich zu reißen. Der Gesamterzähler hat diese Entsprechungen selbst geschaffen, so dass sich auf dieser Redaktionsstufe die Frage der Priorität gar nicht stellt. Anders jedoch liegen die Dinge bei der späteren Ausgestaltung, insbesondere bei den Gesprächspassagen zwischen David und Saul. Hier ist mit einem gewachsenen Komplex von literarischen Abhängigkeiten und wechselweisen Beeinflussungen zu rechnen, die einer gesonderten Untersuchung bedürfen.

Abschließend sollen noch ein paar Fragen gestellt und Schlussfolgerungen gezogen werden, die auf eine Einordnung des redaktionsgeschichtlichen Befundes hinzielen:

1) Lässt sich für 1 Sam 26 ein historischer Hintergrund feststellen? Oder: Ist die erzählte Heldengeschichte – um eine Formulierung von Walter Dietrich aufzugreifen – „leise angelehnt an die geschichtliche Realität"?[109] Ich vermag das nicht zu sagen und kann dazu nur feststellen: Zum Zeitpunkt der Traditi-

---

107 Vgl. beispielsweise 2 Sam 23,13–17.
108 Vgl. dazu den Beitrag von Reinhard Müller in diesem Sammelband.
109 DIETRICH 2015: 815.

onsbildung von Davids Heldenstück bestand offenbar eine Gegnerschaft zwischen dem Norden und dem Süden. Den „point of view" bildet jedenfalls das judäische resp. davidische Königtum. Trotz der militärischen Übermacht des Nordens resp. Sauls erweist sich der Süden resp. David als seinem Widersacher überlegen. Saul ist unfähig und schläft, David ist hellwach und jederzeit in der Lage, seinen Gegner zu übertölpeln. So kann man sich auch die Verhältnisse zwischen Israel und Juda der mittleren Königszeit zurechtrücken. Ist das nun geschichtliche Realität oder judäisches Wunschdenken? Folgt man Stanley Isser, dann basiert das Heldenstück in 1 Sam 24 auf einem „bathroom joke" und in 1 Sam 26 auf einem „act of bravado".[110] Damit ist wohl alles gesagt.

2) Warum bewegt sich Saul mit seinem Heer so tief im Süden, sei es als benjaminitischer Herrscher oder als König von Israel? Für 1 Sam 21–26 lässt sich das literarhistorisch so beantworten, dass die hier aufgenommenen Einzelüberlieferungen zur Davidgeschichte gehören und im Bereich seines frühen und eigentlichen Machtzentrums rund um Hebron angesiedelt sind. Durch die Einbindung in die Verfolgungsgeschichten werden sie zu einem Teil der Saulgeschichte. Die Saulüberlieferung selbst bezeugt jedoch in ihrem Grundbestand keine militärischen Aktionen im Süden. Insbesondere der Feldzug Sauls gegen die Amalekiter in 1 Sam 15 lässt sich dafür nicht anführen. Denn dieser ist sehr wahrscheinlich durch die Erzählung 1 Sam 30 inspiriert, in der David wegen der Zerstörung seines Stützpunktes Ziklag gegen die Amalekiter vorgeht.[111]

3) Bei dem die Traditionsstücke verbindenden Darstellungszusammenhang in 1 Sam 21–26 handelt es sich um eine konstruierte Erzählung. Dabei ist bemerkenswert, dass die verschiedenen Geschichten von einer fortgesetzten Verfolgung Davids durch Saul nirgendwo auf eine tödliche Konfrontation hinauslaufen. Vielmehr stellt sich das vom Gesamterzähler konzipierte Versteckspiel in der judäischen Wüste als eine Reihe verpasster Gelegenheiten (seitens Sauls) und verhinderter Gelegenheiten (seitens Davids) dar: In 23,6–13 verpasst Saul den Zeitpunkt, David in Keila festzusetzen, in 23,24–28 laufen Saul und David auf der einen und anderen Seite des Berges aneinander vorbei; in 24,1 ff. trifft David in der Höhle von En-Gedi auf Saul, ohne ihm etwas anzutun; in 25,1 ff. verhindert Abigajil eine Konfrontation Davids mit Nabal (dem *alter ego* Sauls); in 26,1 ff. verschläft Saul sein Zusammentreffen mit David, als dieser ihm Spieß und Wasserflasche stiehlt. Mithin führen die Feindseligkeiten Sauls gegenüber David zu keinem Ergebnis, zeigen aber, dass sich David gegenüber Saul fair und wohlwollend verhält. Mit welcher Zeitsituation lässt sich dieses Darstellungsinteresse verbinden? Aus meiner Sicht kommt dafür das späte 8. Jh. bzw.

---

110 Vgl. Isser 2003: 130.
111 Vgl. Heinrich 2009: 83–85.

das 7. Jh. v. Chr. in Frage, weil sich in dieser Zeitsituation die davidische Dynastie resp. das judäische Königtum um die ehemaligen Bewohnern Israels und jetzigen Bewohnern der assyrischen Provinz Samarina bemüht und sich ihnen freundschaftlich verbunden zeigt. Dazu passt nicht zuletzt der den Erzählfaden abschließende Auftritt Davids in 1 Sam 26, so er den saulidischen Herrscher als den von Gott eingesetzten König anerkennt (V. 9.11) und ihn schützt (V. 9.15.16).

4) Ich neige dazu, auch das in 26,17 folgende Gespräch zwischen David und Saul in seiner Grundschicht V. 18.20b.21aα.22 dem Gesamterzähler zuzuweisen.[112] Es würde einen guten Abschluss der Fluchtgeschichten bilden und durch die Rückgabe des Spießes zeigen, dass David seinem Verfolger Saul das Königtum belässt. Es könnte aber auch sein, dass in beiden Kapiteln – 1 Sam 24 und 26 – das sich zwischen David und Saul entwickelnde Gespräch später hinzugekommen ist.[113] Wie dem auch sei, lässt sich kaum bestreiten, dass in beiden Kapiteln das Gespräch durch deuteronomistische und spätere Erweiterungen theologisch aufgeladen worden ist. Im Wesentlichen geht es jetzt um die Frage, wie es sich mit der Schuld am Zerwürfnis zwischen Saul und David und wie es sich mit der Gerechtigkeit verhält. Dabei wäre genauer zu untersuchen, wie sich die verschiedenen Fortschreibungen des Gesprächs in 1 Sam 24 und 26 zeitlich zueinander verhalten. Dann ließe sich wahrscheinlich zeigen, dass sich die Frage nach der Priorität des einen oder anderen Kapitels in einen redaktionellen Prozess auflöst.

5) Die Redensart „der Spieß wird umgedreht" kann im Deutschen bedeuten, dass der Jäger zum Gejagten wird, oder auch, dass der Unterlegene mit dem Überlegenen die Rollen tauscht. Ist das bei Saul und David der Fall? In historischer Hinsicht wohl nicht. Dafür lässt sich weder das Traditionsstück noch die Gesamterzählung in Anspruch nehmen. In moralischer Hinsicht dagegen schon. Hier wird der Spieß tatsächlich umgedreht, indem sich David seinem Widersacher als überlegen erweist: Saul will David töten, verpasst aber die Gelegenheit. David hat die Gelegenheit dazu, verhindert aber, dass Saul getötet wird. Der künftige König vergreift sich nicht an dem, der ihn ums Leben bringen will.

---

112 Dazu ließe sich dann das von Hügel zu Hügel inszenierte Gespräch zwischen Abner und Joab in 2 Sam 2,25–29 vergleichen, das in ähnlicher Weise auf eine Verständigung zielt und den gegebenen Kriegszustand zwischen Israel und Juda missbilligt. Für die Zuweisung dieses Textes zur David-Redaktion vgl. FISCHER 2004: 94–98 und 273.

113 Ungewöhnlich wäre das nicht, vgl. beispielsweise die Nabot-Novelle in 1 Kön 21,1–16 und das sich daran anschließende Gespräch zwischen Elia und Ahab in 21,17–29. Zur Auslegung vgl. WÜRTHWEIN 1984: 247–53.

Anhang: Das Traditionsstück in 1 Sam 26,1–16

[3] Saul errichtete sein Lager in Gibea-Hachila, ... während David sich in der Wüste aufhielt ...[5] David machte sich auf und kam zu dem Platz, an dem Saul sein Lager errichtet hatte ... Saul lag schlafend im Lagerring, während das Kriegsvolk um ihn herum lagerte.[6] Da wandte sich David an Ahimelech, den Hetiter: (...)[12] Und David nahm den Spieß und die Wasserflasche, die sich an Sauls Kopfende befanden. Dann gingen sie schnell davon. Niemand sah etwas und niemand merkte etwas ...[13] David ging hinüber auf die andere Seite, stellte sich auf den Gipfel des Berges ...[14] und rief zu dem Kriegsvolk hinüber ...[16] ...: „So wahr Jahwe lebt, ihr alle habt den Tod verdient! Denn ihr habt nicht auf euren Herrn aufgepasst! ... Und jetzt, schaut nach: Wo sind der Spieß des Königs und die Wasserflasche, die sich an seinem Kopfende befanden?"

Bibliographie

Adam, Klaus-Peter. 2009. Nocturnal Intrusion and Divine Interventions on Behalf of Judah: David's Wisdom and Saul's Tragedy in 1 Samuel 26. *VT* 59:1–33.

Bar-Efrat, Shimon. 2007. *Das Erste Buch Samuel: Ein narratologisch-philologischer Kommentar*. BWANT 176. Stuttgart: Kohlhammer.

Bar-Efrat, Shimon. 2009. *Das Zweite Buch Samuel: Ein narratologischer-philologischer Kommentar*. BWANT 181. Stuttgart: Kohlhammer.

Bezzel, Hannes. 2015. *Saul. Israels König in Tradition. Redaktion und früher Rezeption*. FAT 97. Tübingen: Mohr Siebeck.

Budde, Karl. 1902. *Die Bücher Samuel*. KHC VIII. Tübingen / Leipzig: Mohr.

Caspari, Wilhelm. 1926. *Die Samuelbücher*. KAT VII. Leipzig: A. Deichertsche Verlagsbuchhandlung.

Conrad, Joachim. 2005. *Die Unschuld des Tollkühnen: Überlegungen zu 1 Sam 24*. Pages 23–42 in *Ideales Königtum. Studien zu David und Salomo*. Edited by Rüdiger Lux. *ABG* 16. Leipzig: Evangelische Verlagsanstalt.

Cryer, Frederick H. 1985. David's Rise to Power and the Death of Abner: An Analysis of 1 Samuel xxvi 14–16 and its Redactional-Critical Implications. *VT* 35:385–94.

Delitzsch, Friedrich. 1920. *Die Lese- und Schreibfehler im Alten Testament*. Berlin / Leipzig: Vereinigung wissenschaftlicher Verleger.

Dietrich, Walter. [2]1992. *David, Saul und die Propheten: Das Verhältnis von Religion und Politik nach den prophetischen Überlieferungen vom frühesten Königtum in Israel*. BWANT 122. Stuttgart: Kohlhammer.

Dietrich, Walter. 1997. *Die frühe Königszeit in Israel: 10. Jahrhundert v. Chr*. BE 3. Stuttgart: Kohlhammer.

Dietrich, Walter. 2004. *Die zweifache Verschonung Sauls (1Sam 24 und 26): Zur „diachronen Synchronisierung" zweier Erzählungen*. Pages 232–53 in *David und Saul im Widerstreit – Diachronie und Synchronie im Wettstreit*. Edited by Walter Dietrich. OBO 206, Fribourg / Göttingen: Academic Press / Vandenhoeck & Ruprecht (reprinted

2012. Pages 171–90 in *Die Samuelbücher im deuteronomistischen Geschichtswerk: Studien zu den Geschichtsüberlieferungen des Alten Testaments II*. Edited by Walter Dietrich. BWANT 201. Stuttgart: Kohlhammer).

Dietrich, Walter. 2015. *Samuel (1 Sam 13–26)*. BK VIII/2. Neukirchen-Vluyn: Neukirchener Theologie.

Edenburg, Cynthia. 1998. How (Not) to Murder a King: Variations on a Theme in 1 Sam 24; 26. *SJOT* 12:64–85.

Edenburg, Cynthia. 2016. *"David Reproached Himself": Revisiting 1Sam 24 and 26 in light of 2Sam 21–24*. Pages 469–80 in *The Books of Samuel: Stories – History – Reception History*. Edited by Walter Dietrich. BEThL 284, Leuven: Peeters.

Fischer, Alexander A. 2004. *Von Hebron nach Jerusalem: Eine redaktionsgeschichtliche Studie zur Erzählung von König David in II Sam 1–5*. BZAW 335. Berlin / New York: de Gruyter.

Gamberoni, Johann. 1984. "מקום." Pages 1113–24 in *ThWAT* IV. Stuttgart: Kohlhammer.

Heinrich, André. 2009. *David und Klio: Historiographische Elemente in der Aufstiegsgeschichte Davids und im Alten Testament*. BZAW 401. Berlin / New York: de Gruyter.

Hentschel, Georg. 2003. *Saul. Schuld, Reue und Tragik eines "Gesalbten"*. Biblische Gestalten 7. Leipzig: Evangelische Verlagsanstalt.

Hertzberg, Hans Wilhelm. 1956. *Die Samuelbücher*. ATD 10. Göttingen: Vandenhoeck & Ruprecht.

Isser, Stanley. 2003. *The Sword of Goliath: David in Heroic Literature*. SBL 6. Atlanta: Brill.

Jepsen, Alfred. 1973. "אמן." Pages 313–48 in *ThWAT* I. Stuttgart: Kohlhammer.

Klein, Johannes. 2002. *David versus Saul. Ein Beitrag zum Erzählsystem der Samuelbücher*. BWANT 158. Stuttgart: Kohlhammer.

Klein, Johannes. 2005. Davids Flucht zu den Philistern (1 Sam. XXI 11 ff; XXVII–XXIX). *VT* 55:176–84.

Koch, Klaus. ⁴1981. *Was ist Formgeschichte? Methoden der Bibelexegese*. Neukirchen-Vluyn: Neukirchener Verlag.

König, Eduard. 1897. *Historisch-comparative Syntax der Hebräischen Sprache. Schlusstheil des historisch-kritischen Lehrgebäudes des Hebräischen*. Leipzig: Hinrichs.

Labuschagne, Casper J. ³1984. "ענה I." Pages 335–41 in *THAT* II. München / Zürich: Kaiser / Theologischer Verlag.

McCarter, Peter Kyle. 1980: *I Samuel: A New Translation with Introduction and Commentary*. AncB 8. Garden City, N.Y.: Doubleday.

McKenzie, Steven L. 2010. Elaborated Evidence for the Priority of 1 Samuel 26. *JBL* 129:437–44.

McKenzie, Steven L. 2011. *The Sons of Zeruiah*. Pages 293–313 in *Seitenblicke: Literarische und historische Studien zu Nebenfiguren im zweiten Samuelbuch*. Edited by Walter Dietrich. OBO 249. Fribourg / Göttingen: Academic Press / Vandenhoeck & Ruprecht.

Meyer, Rudolf. 1992. *Hebräische Grammatik*. Vol. I–IV. Berlin / New York: de Gruyter.

Nowack, Wilhelm. 1902. *Die Bücher Samuelis*. HK I/4. Göttingen: Vandenhoeck & Ruprecht.

Riede, Peter. 1995. David und der Floh. Tier und Tiervergleiche in den Samuelbüchern. *BN* 77:86–117.

Schulz, Alfons. 1919. *Die Bücher Samuel*. EHAT 8/1, Münster: Aschendorff.

Stein, Peter. 1997. "Und man berichtete Saul ...": Text- und literarkritische Untersuchungen zu 1. Samuelis 24 und 26. *BN* 90:46–66.

Stoebe, Hans Joachim. 1973. *Das erste Buch Samuelis*. KAT² VIII/1. Gütersloh: Gütersloher Verlagshaus.

Stolz, Fritz. 1981. *Das erste und zweite Buch Samuel*. ZBKAT 9. Zürich: Theologischer Verlag Zürich.

Thenius, Otto. 1842. *Die Bücher Samuels*. KEH IV. Leipzig: Weidmann'sche Buchhandlung.

Tsumura, David Toshio. 2007. *The First Book of Samuel*. NICOT. Grand Rapids, MI / Cambridge: Eerdmans.

Van Seters, John. 2011. Two Stories of David Sparing Saul's Life in 1 Samuel 24 and 26: A Question of Priority. *SJOT* 25:93–104.

Weinfeld, Moshe. 1972. *Deuteronomy and the Deuteronomic School*. Oxford: Oxford University Press (Reprinted 1992.Winona Lake, IN: Eisenbrauns).

Würthwein, Ernst. 1984. *Die Bücher der Könige: 1. Kön 17 – 2. Kön 25*. ATD 11/2. Göttingen: Vandenhoeck & Ruprecht.

General Index

https://doi.org/10.1515/9783110606164-017

Index of Selected Text Passages

Non-Biblical Ancient Near Eastern Texts

Hebrew Bible

https://doi.org/10.1515/9783110606164-018

21:12	*20*
30:31	*20*
33:7	*27*
33:26	*324*
40:28	*72*

Proverbs

3:29	*264*
6:14	*264*
6:18	*264*
12:20	*264*

Ruth

1:4	*206*
2:10	*154*

Lamentations

4:20	*155*

Esther

3:2	*154*
3:5	*154*
7:6	*27*

Daniel

1:10	154
8:17	*27*
9:25	*155*
9:26	*155*

Nehemiah

3:17–18	300
11:28	77
11:30	289; 300
12:27	*20*

1 Chronicles

2:42	*267*; *272*
2:55	91
4:39	*78*
4:30	77
7:8	*73*
10	145
10:9	73
10:12	46
11:2	145; 147
11:3	154
11:8	*155*

11:12–19	244
11:19	*155*
13:5	*87*
13:8	*20*
13:12–14	243
14:10	152
14:14	152
15:16	*20*
15:18	108
15:20	*20*
15:21	108
15:24	108
15:28	*20*
15:29	145
16:5	*20*; 108
16:8–22	*155*
20:4–8	150; *244*
21:3	154
21:12	*115*
21:21	153
21:23	154
21:30	*27*
23:6–24	17
25:1	*20*
25:3	*20*
25:6	*20*
27:32	17

2 Chronicles

1:11	*155–156*
2:9	91
2:23–27	91
2:33	91
2:42	91
5:2–6	146
5:12	*20*
6:31	*155*
6:38	*155*
6:41–42	*155*
6:42	*14*
7:19	153
7:22	153
9:11	*20*
9:26	73
10:1–19	147
10:6	*155*
11:7–8	300
11:7	289

Josephus